D1521356

Studies in
Medieval Jewish History
and Literature

EDITED BY

Isadore Twersky

HARVARD UNIVERSITY PRESS

*Cambridge, Massachusetts
and London, England*
1979

Library of Congress Cataloging in Publication Data
Main entry under title:

Studies in Medieval Jewish history and literature.

(Harvard Judaic monographs)
Includes index.
1. Judaism—History—Medieval and early modern
period, 425-1789—Addresses, essays, lectures.
2. Philosophy, Jewish—Addresses, essays, lectures.
3. Philosophy, Medieval—Addresses, essays, lectures.
I. Twersky, Isadore. II. Series.
BM180.S78   296'.09'02   79-11588
ISBN 0-674-85192-7

In memoriam

Harry Austryn Wolfson

1887-1974

Contents

Foreword

This volume, wide ranging in its specific inquiries and textual analyses, focuses on the intellectual history of the Middle Ages. Students of Jewish history, literature, religion, and philosophy will find here new interpretations, novel insights or theses, critical revisions, unpublished material, and unperceived associations.

We have gathered here the work of scholars who have taught or studied at Harvard. The participation of a number of younger scholars is especially noteworthy. It is appropriate that income from the bequest of Professor Harry A. Wolfson, late Littauer Professor of Hebrew Literature and Philosophy at Harvard University, was used to defray the expenses of publication.

It was considered desirable not to impose any thematic or methodological restrictions. The reader will quickly realize, furthermore, that no attempt was made to achieve complete uniformity of style and format. In the interests of economy, diacritical marks have been omitted.

I wish to thank Carol Cross of Harvard's Department of Near Eastern Languages for her steady and gracious assistance in many different ways.

Isadore Twersky

ABBREVIATIONS

AJS	*Association for Jewish Studies Review*
HUCA	*Hebrew Union College Annual*
IL	*Isrealietische Letterbode*
JJS	*Journal of Jewish Studies*
JQR	*Jewish Quarterly Review*
KS	*Kiryat Sefer*
REJ	*Revue des Études Juives*
RHC	*Recueil des Histoires des Croisades*

1

Creation and Emanation in Isaac Israeli: A Reappraisal

Alexander Altmann

In my account of Isaac Israeli's Neoplatonic doctrine I suggested that his cosmological scheme knew of three kinds of causality by which the world came into being.[1] Interpreting the pseudo-Aristotelian source[2] on which he drew, I distinguished between (1) creation, by which first matter and first form (wisdom), the first two simple substances, are produced "from (by) the power and the will," thereby giving rise to the hypostasis of intellect as the combination of the two; (2) emanation, which denotes the process of the coming into being of the lower hypostases (the three souls and nature, i.e., the spheric power); and (3) natural causality, the production of the corporeal substances through the operation of the sphere. It is the purpose of this paper to reexamine the validity of this differentiation, which has been challenged so far as the distinction between creation and emanation is concerned.[3] The procedure I shall follow amounts to a rewriting of the chapter on "Creation, Emanation, and Natural Causality" in the light of the critical points raised and with due regard to the progress made in Neoplatonic research during the intervening period of twenty years.[4]

Israeli draws a clear line between the way in which intellect comes into being from first matter and first form (wisdom), and the manner in which the subsequent hypostases originate. The difference is, in brief, one between creation "by the power and the will," on the one hand, and emanation on the other. Wherein the difference lies is explained by him in the *Book of Substances* (III, 3r-v)[5] in a passage of considerable weight. Refuting an imaginary opponent, Israeli tries to account for the way in which he had outlined the series of hypostases from intellect down to nature. Each higher hypostasis, he said, produces by its emanation (by its "ray and shade")[6] the specific nature ("specificity" or "substantiality") of the next lower. Intellect is "the specificity of all substances, and the form which establishes their essence, since its ray and light, which emanate from its shade, are the fountain of their substantiality and the root of their forms and specificity."[7] Having thus placed intellect as the *summum genus* at the very top of the series of emanations and having left out of account the still higher two simple substances (first matter and first form or wisdom), which originate from the power and will, Israeli rightly anticipates this objection: "Why do you not add that the power and the will are the fountain of the specificity of all substances, since it is the power and the will that bring into being wisdom, which is the form and specificity of the intellect and that which perfects its essence?" In other words, why do you differentiate between the function of intellect as an emanative source and the function of power and will?

Israeli's answer is: "You have made an absurd objection, because you have compared an influencing and acting thing (*shay' atharī fi 'lī*) to one essential (*dhātī*). The light of wisdom is brought into being from the power and the will (*min al-qudra wa-l-irāda*) by way of influence and action ('*alā sabīl al-ta' thīr wa-l-fi 'l*), while the light which emanates (*al-munbi'a*) from intellect is essential and substantial (*dhātī jauharī*), like the light and shining of the sun, which emanate from its essence and substantiality. Specific form is not brought into being from an influencing and acting thing, but from an essential one—like reason which establishes the essence of man, and which does not come from the soul in the way of influence and action, but is essential." The salient point of this distinction must be seen in the difference between essential causality and causality by action. As an illustration of what is meant by essential causality the "causes" of a definition, and more especially, the specific difference, for example, rationality (reason) in the definition of man (rational animal), are quoted.[8] This would seem to indicate that Israeli regards the procession of the simple substances from intellect as constituting a logically necessary order in contrast to the coming into being of intellect which is due to an act of power and will. As for causality by way of influence and action, it can denote only creation out of nothing. In his *Book of Definitions* (#42-44)[9] Israeli distinguishes between two kinds of action (causation; creation): (1) innovation and making-anew (*al-ibdā' wa-l-ikhtirā'*), which is defined as "making existent existences from the non-existent" (*ta'yīs al-aysāt min lays*); and (2) the action of "bringing into being existences from the existing." The first kind of action belongs to none except the Creator. The second is performed by the spheric power which is "appointed" by the Creator "for the action of coming-to-be and passing-away, for example, the causing-to-be of animals and plants." Occasionally, Israeli calls the action of the spheric power also one of "influencing" coming-to-be and passing-away,[10] which clearly shows that the two terms "acting" and "influencing" are synonymous. The same is true of "innovation" and "making-anew." Since the emanation of the substances from intellect is said to represent essential causality and not the causality of action and influencing, it is obvious that Israeli wishes to differentiate between *creatio ex nihilo* and emanation as two distinct stages in the genesis of the spiritual world.

He had, we believe, good reasons for combining an emanationist metaphysic with the concept of creation out of nothing. In so doing he followed a precedent set in certain circles of early Islamic Neoplatonism. Ammonius' book *On the Opinions of the Philosophers*, which was discovered by Stern, attributes Neoplatonic doctrines to the ancient Greek philosophers.[11] It opens with a discussion of the problem of creation: did the Creator create (*abda'a*) this world and the form contained in it from something or from nothing (*min shay'in am min lā shay'*). The two alternatives are explained in these terms: if from something, then that thing is co-eternal with the Creator, which is not permissible; if from nothing, the question arises whether the form of the thing was with Him, or whether He created things without having their forms with Him in essence. We may interpret the two options posed as *creatio ex nihilo* in the sense of an emanation of forms out of God's essence and as *creatio ex nihilo* in the more orthodox sense of a divine fiat. Using Israeli's terminology, we might describe the two meanings of creation out of nothing as essential causation and causation by way of influence and action from power and will. Ammonius states in the name of Thales: "As He is the one who brings the existents into being, and 'bringing into existence' means from no preexistent thing and from nothing, yet bringing it into existence, it follows that He who brings the existent into existence need not have the form of the existents with Him in order to bring them into existence . . . As the first Creator has the utmost excellence, He cannot have forms with Him." This view clearly corresponds to the orthodox doctrine of *creatio ex nihilo*. Ammonius rejects Plutarch's opinion to the contrary: the Creator had infinite forms present with Him in His foreknowledge. He finally records in Xenophanes' name the view which is similar to Thales': the Creator created what He desired and as He willed; He was He, and nothing existed together with Him. This view, it is explained, denies the eternity of form and matter, and of everything else besides God.[12] Israeli could well have followed this trend in Islamic Neoplatonism.

What probably clinched his adoption of the concept of *creatio ex nihilo* and his interpretation of it as "action" rather than emanative and "essential" was the very text of his pseudo-Aristotelian source which called for an exegesis along the lines followed by him. The text[13] commences its account of the coming-into-being of the spiritual substances with a description of the first stage which contains no reference whatsoever to emanation: "The first of created things (*awwal al-mukhtar'āt*) are two simple substances, the first matter . . . and the form which precedes that which is found with it, i.e., the perfect wisdom, by the conjunction of which with matter the nature of intellect came into being with the result that intellect, being composed of it and matter, is a species of it."[14] The first mention of emanation occurs only after intellect has appeared: "After the nature of intellect had been established,[15] a flame went forth from it and a light like the flame which goes forth from the sun and falls upon glass in a dark house. From this flame arose the rational soul." It seems, therefore, that emanation plays no part in the genesis of first matter and first form. Hence the need for assuming an act of creation *ex nihilo* from the power and the will.

One further consideration could have motivated Israeli's positing of creation *ex nihilo* prior to the series of emanations. In all Neoplatonic systems the principle prevails that from the One only one substance can proceed. As Aenesidemus put it, two cannot arise out of the One.[16] In Plotinus' *Enneads* and the Arabic texts based on it (the vulgate version of the *Theology of Aristotle*; the *Epistle on Divine Knowledge*; the *Dicta of the Greek Sage*)[17] it is intellect that immediately follows the One. In the pseudo-Empedoclean *Five Substances* matter alone is interposed between God and the intellect: "When the Creator, blessed be He, created the world, He created the world of matter, alive with eternal intellectual life. Matter draws this life from the Creator . . . and in that matter are all forms of that world in the most subtle, simple, glorious, and beautiful manner possible . . . After He had created this matter, He created intellect."[18] The description of matter as containing "all forms" does not indicate a dual hypostasis of matter and form, let alone two distinct substances such as we meet in the Israeli source. It merely characterizes the nature of matter as the matrix of all forms.[19] There is a clear distinction between the positing of two simple substances (first matter and first form or wisdom) in the Israeli source and the positing of matter in Pseudo-Empedocles. Here the unitary character of the first emanation is upheld, irrespective of whether or not the presence of "all forms" in matter is consistent with the principle that from the One only one substance can emanate. The fact that Israeli's Neoplatonic source places two simple substances at the very top of the series of emanations must have presented a problem to Israeli. This fact obviously precluded the assumption that the two first substances owed their existence to a process of emanation. Creation *ex nihilo* as an act by power and will must have suggested itself as the only sensible interpretation. The adoption of such a theory was not altogether a novelty in a Neoplatonic context, as we have seen. It is doubtful, however, whether the combination of a creationist and an emanationist doctrine within one system had any precedent.

Israeli's positing of two simple substances as "the first of created things" may be considered as the most potent argument against any attempt of interpreting his use of the term creation *ex nihilo* in an emanationist sense. A valiant attempt of this kind was made by the late Harry A. Wolfson.[20] The identification of creation *ex nihilo* with emanation, he pointed out, was not unknown in the history of philosophy. Examples cited by him are John Scotus Erigena in Christianity, al-Farabi and Ibn Miskawaih in Islam, and *Sefer Yesirah*, Ibn Gabirol, and Crescas in Judaism.[21] He could have added the long Arabic recension of the *Theology of Aristotle* which describes the Word (*kalima*) as *nihil* (*laysa*) on account of its being neither at rest nor moving, and which designates the Word as the "Cause of Causes" and as the "First Creator."[22] Creation *ex nihilo* here undoubtedly means creation out of the Word, emanation. In Wolfson's view Israeli should be counted among those who identified *ex nihilo* with emanation. There was no need of attributing to Israeli "an unheard-of hybrid theory—creation *ex nihilo* of the two first substances constituting the intellect and emanation of the spiritual substances below the intellect." The contrast drawn by Israeli between the causality of action and essential causality was not necessarily a contrast between creation *ex nihilo* and emanation. "It may be a contrast between two kinds of emanation, one an emanation immediately from God, which follows directly from the will and power, and the other an emanation from intermediaries, which on the part of those intermediaries is an unconscious act, like the shining of the sun."[23] Wolfson further outlines his view of Israeli's position:[24] "What we have here in Israeli is a theory of a volitional and presumably also noneternal process of emanation in which the first emanated being is described as having been created *ex nihilo* on the ground that it was not created from a pre-existent eternal matter or in the likeness of a pre-existent eternal ideal pattern." We may sum up Wolfson's interpretation of Israeli as a two-stage theory of emanation: at the first stage the "emanated being"—Wolfson ignores the two first substances—arises directly from the power and the will, without any pre-existent matter or form being involved; hence the designation "creation ex nihilo"; at the second stage emanation proceeds as an unconscious act, unlike the "volitional" character of the first stage. Both emanations are a noneternal process, that is, they occur in time. What is not explained here is how by way of emanation two simple substances could have arisen simultaneously.

Ibn Gabirol, who followed Israeli in positing universal matter and universal form at the top of the series of spiritual substances, was confronted with the same problem. He did identify creation *ex nihilo* with emanation, as Wolfson pointed out,[25] and he had therefore to account for the duality of the two uppermost principles in the hierarchy of emanations. He solved the problem by deriving form from the will and matter from the essence of God, a solution bristling with difficulties.[26] There are no grounds for assuming that Israeli linked form with the will and matter with the power of God in order to resolve the problem presented by the emanation of these two first substances. Such a problem simply did not exist for him. He eliminated it by drawing a line between creation *ex nihilo* and emanation.

The deliberate manner in which Israeli explains this distinction can leave no doubt as to the seriousness with which he viewed it. It is important to bear this in mind so as not to be misled by occasional lapses in his terminology which may be due to his familiarity with the usual type of purely emanationist Neoplatonic sources. Thus, when discussing the reasons for the difference in the degree of light between the various substances, he says:[27] "Regarding the quality of the emanation of the light from the power and the will (*inbi'āth al-nūr min al-qudra wa-l-irāda*), we have already made it clear that its beginning is different from its end, and the middle from both extremes, and this for the following reason: when its beginning emanated from the power and the will, it met no shade or darkness to make it dim and coarse—while its end met various imperfections and obscurities which made it dim and coarse; the middle partook of both extremes." In this passage the "beginning" of the series can only mean what is referred to earlier in the same context as "the first of created things [which] are two simple substances," and yet this "beginning" is said to have "emanated" from the power and the will. In another sentence prior to the one quoted Israeli speaks of "the quality of the emanation of the light which is created from the power and the will." He obviously applies here the terms "created" and "emanated" indiscriminately.

Israeli's distinction between creation and emanation calls for some closer analysis of the meaning of these two terms. The remaining part of this chapter will be devoted to such an analysis.

The creation of first matter and first form which constitute the intellect is described as an action "by power and will." This phrase presents a combination of terms that is at variance with what we find in the Arabic Plotinus texts, with the sole exception of the Long Recension of the *Theology* where, however, power and will, like "commandment" (*amr*) are but synonyms of the Word (*kalima*).[28] In the other texts power is opposed rather than allied to will. It is associated with utter repose, motionlessness, and necessity. "The First Agent must be in repose (*sākin*) and motionless (*ghair mutaharrik*), if it is necessary that some thing is secondary to Him. His action must be without reflection (*rawīya*), motion (*haraka*), and volition (*irāda*) which would be inclined toward the action product. The first action product—the intellect—emanated (*inbajasa*) from the high-degree potency of the repose of the agent (*min shiddati sukūn al-fā'il wa-quwatihi*).[29] The element of necessity is expressed by the simile of heat emanating from fire and of cold emanating from snow. The "high-degree potency" of the First Agent is said to operate in a similar fashion.[30] A parallel to this text from the *Dicta of the Greek Sage* is found in the *Epistle on Divine Knowledge*:[31] "The First Agent acts while in repose and in stability . . . From His perfection an act is produced . . . out of a very mighty power. The First Agent . . . is the power of all things." The simile of fire-heat, which comes from Plotinus, is reproduced here in greater detail. "Fire is a heat which completes the essence of fire; then from that heat there is born in some object another heat, resembling the heat which completes the essence of fire." The first heat is produced by an act which is the very substance of fire, whereas the second heat is by an act *from* the substance, a distinction which exemplifies the twofold nature of the act of the First Agent. As Plotinus explained it: "There is in everything the act of the essence and the act going out from the essence: the first act is the thing itself in its realized identity, the second act is an *inevitably* following outgo from the first, an emanation distinct from the thing itself."[32]

Here necessity relates to the second phase of the creative process rather than to the first which is seen as the very substance of the agent. Only insofar as a distinct being emerges is there any necessity. This kind of distinction opens up a possibility of interpreting Plotinus as by no means excluding will from the creative act. The nature of the One itself might be regarded as its will, and ultimately even necessity could be identified with the One's own will, as has been suggested by J. M. Rist.[33] Yet any such view was obviously far removed from the way Plotinus was understood by those who compiled the Arabic texts with which we are dealing. Thus, another passage in the *Epistle* clearly states that precisely because the First Agent "acts solely by the fact of His being," His action cannot be attributed to volition.[34] The Plotinian simile of the sun's radiation suggested a supreme Being in utter repose and acting without an exercise of will: "It is not that He wished to originate intellect, and then intellect came into being, after the volition . . . He makes and originates things all at one go, being fixed and stable in one state . . . without motion of any kind . . . The first action of the First Agent is intellect. Intellect is light flowing from the noble substance as sunlight flows over things from the sun."[35] The absence of will in creation is also implied in the negation of all attributes in the One, who, in a passage of the *Theology*, is referred to as "the first light":[36] the first light is not a light in anything but is light alone, self-existing. Therefore that light comes to illumine the soul by means of intellect, without attributes like the attributes of fire or anything else of active things. All active things perform their activities by virtue of attributes within them, not by their own self, but the First Agent makes things not by any attribute, for in Him there is no attribute at all, but He makes them by His own self." The corollary of this view is the exclusion of will. Power is the only term admissible to denote the activity of God.

Israeli's phrase "by power and will" has an almost polemical ring when held against the background just described. It asserts that creation, as distinct from emanation, is not a necessary process following from the very essence of God and being expressive of his power alone but declares it to derive from both power and will. As he puts it in the passage answering an imaginary opponent,[37] "The light of wisdom is brought into being from the power and the will by way of influence and action, while the light which emanates from the intellect is essential and substantial, like the light and shining of the sun, which emanate from its essence and substantiality." In the Arabic Plotinus passage quoted above the shining of the sun is the simile characteristic of necessary, essential emanation. It is highly significant that Israeli applies it to the emanative activity of the intellect and contrasts it with the action by the power and the will. It should also be noted that the term for power (potency) found in the Arabic sources, *qūwa*, which reflects the Greek *dynamis*, is no longer used by Israeli with respect to God. He substitutes for it the term *qudra* which, in Kalam, denotes the power to act and in the long recension of the *Theology* signifies the Divine power. Israeli retains *qūwa* when speaking of the "light and powers" of the hypostases below God.[38] His change of terminology indicates his deviation from a purely emanationist form of Neoplatonism.

The creation of the two first substances by power and will is described by Israeli as an act performed "without mediation" (*bi-lā wāsita*) or "without the mediation of another substance" (*min ghair tawassut jauhar ākhar*). The meaning of this phrase requires some elucidation. One is tempted to suggest that this formula implies the rejection of a school of thought which interposes a mediating power between God and the two first substances. Thus the Logos doctrine of al-Nasafī and the Ismā'īlī sect postulates the Word

(*amr*) as such an intermediary, and the long version of the *Theology*, probably reflecting the Ismāʿīlī doctrine, as Pines suggested,[39] describes the first
intellect as "united with the word of the Creator." Israeli's repeated emphasis on the unmediated character of the creation of first matter and first form
could therefore be said to carry a polemical significance. Yet it can easily be
shown that this interpretation is not correct. The simple meaning of the
phrase is that the first substances are more perfect than the subsequent ones
because nothing stands between them and the Creator. Intellect, too, is said
to "receive the light from the power and will without mediation" because it
"receives the light of wisdom without the mediation of any other substance
between itself and wisdom,"[40] whereas the rational soul receives it through
the intermediacy of intellect, the animal soul through the intermediacy of
intellect and rational souls, and so on. The term "mediation" is therefore
equivalent to "intervening stage," and the phrase "without mediation" simply means without intervening, light-obscuring stages. Only occasionally
does it signify the sole agency of God, as in the statement that "the sphere
and the substances above . . . are generated by the power and will without
the mediation of any agent except the Creator, while the compound and
sensible bodies under the sphere are made by nature."[41]

The vulgate version of the *Theology* uses the phrase in exactly the same
sense in which it is generally employed by Israeli. We quote a few passages
which will show this clearly. "Although all the things gush forth from It [the
One], the first being, by which I mean the being of intellect, gushes forth
from It first, without intermediary. Thereafter there gush forth from It all
the beings of the things that are in the upper world and the lower world,
through the medium of the being of the intellect and the intelligible world."
The passage goes on to explain that everything mediated and remote from
the source is deficient, and that only the unmediated is perfect.[42] Only intellect is unmediated in an absolute sense. In a relative sense, compared with
the lower world, the entire spiritual world may be called unmediated. "You
must understand that intellect and soul and the other intelligible things are
from the first originator, not passing away or disappearing, on account of
their originating from the first cause without intermediary, whereas nature
and sense perception and the other natural things perish and fall under corruption because they are effects of causes that are caused, that is, of intellect
through the medium of the soul."[43] As we have seen, Israeli too applies the
term "without mediation" in its relative sense to all spiritual substances. In
the Hebrew fragments of the pseudo-Empedoclean *Five Substances*[44] the
term "without mediation" (*belī ʾemsaʾuth*) is used in the same sense.

In discussing Israeli's concept of creation we have already noted some
contrasting features of his view of emanation. Israeli defines emanation as
an "essential" causality distinct from "influence and action," and that he regards the spiritual substances as each emanating from the light or "essence
and substantiality" of the preceding one. Essential causality implies necessity and is illustrated by the similes of fire-heat and the sun's radiation. The

metaphor of "radiance" and the comparison with the sun are frequently employed by Israeli.[45] The view of emanation underlying this imagery (which is not consistently maintained) accords with the account of the series of emanations in the pseudo-Aristotelian source quoted in the Mantua Text,[46] where emanation is described in terms of a "radiance and splendor" going forth in turn from intellect and the three souls. At each successive stage the radiance becomes "less and dimmer" because of the growing distance from the source.

We meet with an entirely different conception of emanation in writings of Israeli other than the Mantua text. Its keynote is the assumption that each successive hypostasis acquires not only light but also "shadow" (*zill*) and "darkness" (*zalām*) from the preceding one, and that the shadow and darkness grow more dense at each stage, thus accounting for the progressive lessening of the spiritual force. The *Book of Definitions* uses the formula describing the lower substance as coming into being "in the horizon (*ufq*) and shadow" or "in the horizon and out of the shadow" of the higher one.[47] The use of the term "horizon" in this connection is familiar from the vulgate version of the *Theology*, which describes the soul as placed "within the horizon" of the intelligible world,[48] and from the *Liber de Causis* (#2).[49] The motifs of "shadow" and "darkness" as concomitants of emanation may have been known to Israeli from the pseudo-Aristotelian source, although the text quoted in the Mantua Text omits all reference to them. They occur, however, in Abraham ibn Hasday's parallel passage[50] and in the Long Version of the *Theology*,[51] both of which are based on pseudo-Aristotle,[52] and also in Israeli's own quotation from the pseudo-Aristotelian source in his *Book on Spirit and Soul* (#9),[53] where the terms used are shadow and exhaustion, that is, darkness. The metaphor of shadow is found also in the *al-Mudkhal al-Saghīr* (attributed to al-Rāzī the physician), where it is stated that intellect projected a shadow, from which God created the rational soul; that the latter projected a shadow from which God created the animal soul, and so on.[54] The frequent use he made of it was noted by Albert the Great, who describes it as an "elegant" saying and quotes it in many places.[55]

In the *Book of Substances* Israeli makes an interesting attempt at combining the two metaphors of light and shadow by introducing the formula "ray and shade": the form of nature is brought into being "from the shade of the vegetative soul and its ray" (*min fai' al-nafs al-nabātiya wa-shu'ā'hā*); the latter "from the shade of the animal soul and its ray," and so on. "Thus it is evident that the ray and shade of the intellect are the specificity of the rational soul; the ray and shade of the rational soul are the specificity of the animal soul."[56]

How does Israeli conceive the nature of emanation under the aspects of "shadow" and "ray and shade" respectively? The only text offering something like a conceptual analysis of the imagery used is a passage in the *Book of Definitions* (#6) where the difference between the higher and the lower substances is discussed. The passage explains why the former remain unaffected by what issues from them, that is, by the emanant substance, while the latter, the elements and composite bodies, are changed by what derives from them. The answer given is that "the lights . . . of the higher substances, the three souls, are not increased or decreased by the issue of what is derived from them, as these come from the shadow of their light, not from their light itself in its essence and substantiality."[57] The elements and bodies, on the other hand, are themselves changed, increased, and decreased. The point which interests us here is Israeli's theory that emanation is not really an efflux of the very light or substance of the source but the casting of a shadow by the light, and the coming-to-be of a new substance out of the shadow. More precisely, the shadow *is* the new substance. In a less radical sense, the lower substance is said to originate from both the light and the shadow, or "in the horizon and shadow," or "from the ray and shade" of the higher one. The radical interpretation, is, however, borne out by Israeli's statement, "It is clear that in every brilliant thing the light in its essence and substantiality is brighter and has a greater splendor than the light of its shadow; thus it is clear that the brilliance of the vegetative soul is greater and stronger than that of the sphere which is derived from its shadow."[58] This view might seem to imply that emanation is no longer viewed as an "essential" causality "like the light and shining of the sun, which emanates from its essence and substantiality." For it distinctly affirms that emanation is but the casting of a shadow and that the emanant substance originates in the shadow cast, not in the substance or essence of the source. Yet Israeli does not appear to have noticed any contradiction, since in the same treatise in which he describes emanation as "essential" causality he also speaks of emanation in terms of "light which issues from the shadow of a substance."[59] In fact, the two metaphors of light and shade or "ray and shade," as Israeli's formula has it, designate two aspects of the emanative process, and both derive ultimately from Plotinus.

As noted before,[60] Plotinus distinguishes between two kinds of essential act, one of the essence and one resulting, as a by-product as it were, from the essence. The analogy adduced by him is heat as the very act of fire, and heat produced in something else by the first heat.[61] The very same distinction is repeated in *Enneads* II.6.3, where the heat produced from the essence is said to be a mere quality and likened to "a trace, a shadow, an image" (*ichnos, skia, eikōn*). In *Enneads* V.1.7 intellect is called an "image" (*eidōlon*) of the Originator, which in turn produces a "light and trace" (*phōs kai ichnos*). Since elsewhere Plotinus equates trace and shadow, the formula "light and trace" might also be read as "light and shade," which would give Israeli's phrase a very respectable ancestry. Plotinus uses the term shadow in yet another passage (IV.3.9) where he speaks of the "shadow" projected by the soul. In *Enneads* V.2.1 intellect is said to have produced a "form" (*eidos*) of itself, that is, the soul, and soul to have made an "image" (*eidōlon*) of itself. *Enneads* V.4.2 speaks of the product of intellect as something resembling it and as an "imitation" (*mimēma*) and "image" (*eidōlon*). Thus it is obvious that in Plotinus the terms image, imitation, trace, and shadow are synonyms expressive of what is considered to be the second phase of emanation, the act resulting from the essence. In a less specific and more general sense these terms simply denote the inferior status of the copy or "imprint" (*typos*) compared with the "original" (*archetypos*),[62] a contrast that has Philonic overtones.[63] Israeli seems to have caught the more sophisticated Plotinian nuances of these terms and to have used the simile of "shadow" accordingly.

Israeli's insistence that emanation does not imply any change, decrease or increase in the source likewise reflects the Plotinian doctrine.[64] In Plotinus it is one of the functions of the simile of radiation (*perilampsis*) to illustrate the fact that emanation leaves the source unaffected.[65] It also entails a more or less pantheistic metaphysics.[66] Israeli obviates any such interpretation by introducing the idea of an act of creation *ex nihilo* prior to the stage of emanation.

The progressive reduction of the light in the course of emanation is made the subject of a special discussion in the *Book of Substances*.[67] The question posed concerns "the reasons for the difference of the substances, and the precedence of one substance to another." Israeli suggests three reasons. (1) The light—in this instance the reference is not to intellect but to the light created by power and will, that is, wisdom, also described here as "caused to emanate from the power and will"[68]—met no shadow at the beginning, while its end met various imperfections and obscurities. This represents a certain variation of the motif of "shadow," since it is no longer maintained that the light is unaffected by the issue of what derives from it. Instead, it is suggested that the light is vitiated by what it meets on its way, that is, by being mixed with darkness. (2) The reception of the light by one substance from the other varies according to the degree of "mediation," that is, the intervening stages. Only intellect receives the light without the mediation of another substance; the others receive it through one, two, three, or more intermediaries.[69] This adds yet another motif in explaining the progressive lessening of the light. In the *Book on Spirit and Soul* (#9)[70] it appears jointly with that of "shadow and exhaustion": the splendor and brilliance of the rational soul "are less than the splendor and brilliance of intellect; the reason being that the degree of intellect is intermediate between the soul and its Creator, so that the soul acquired shadow and exhaustion, that is, darkness, as the intellect intervened between it and the light of the Creator." The two motifs of "shadow" and "mediation" are joined also in the *Book of Definitions* (#5),[71] where it is said that "the animal soul . . . comes into being from the shadow of the rational soul, on account of which it is removed from the light of the intellect and acquires shadow." (3) A third reason is "the difference between that which bestows and that which is bestowed, the bestowing and the reception of the bestowal." This reason is not further explained, however, in the text, as our fragment breaks off before the discussion of this point is reached.

One of the most significant traits of Plotinus' concept of emanation is the doctrine of the two moments of the generative process in its completeness. Unlike the two phases discussed earlier, those designated as act of the essence and act from the essence, the two moments refer (1) to the emergence of the emanant and (2) to its stabilization and completion. Even though brought into being from the essence as a separate entity, the emanant attains to permanency and creative power only after it has turned its gaze back to its source and beheld it in an act of contemplation. In A. H. Armstrong's appraisal:[72] "Here we meet another of the great principles of the philosophy of Plotinus: that all derived beings depend for their existence, their activity, and their power to produce in their turn, on their contemplation of their source." This doctrine has been preserved, however fragmentarily, in the Arabic Plotinus. It appears in the *Dicta of the Greek Sage* ("After its emanation from the First Agent, it turned to its cause and looked at it according to its potency; it thus became intellect and substance"),[73] in the vulgate version of the *Theology*,[74] and in the Hebrew fragments of the *Book of the Five Substances* attributed to Empedocles.[75] No trace of this doctrine can be found in Israeli. It may well be that his interposition of a divine creative act between the Creator and the process of emanation thwarted the employment of this motif.

NOTES

1. A. Altmann and S. M. Stern, *Isaac Israeli: A Neoplatonic Philosopher of the Early Tenth Century* (Oxford, 1958, reprint edition, Greenwood Press, 1979), pt. 2, pp. 147-217. See esp. chapter 4, pp. 171-180. The work is subsequently referred to as Altmann-Stern.

2. The distinctive features of what I called "the Israeli source" and its difference from other known types of Neoplatonism, including the Long Version of the *Theology of Aristotle*, were pointed out by me in my article "Isaac Israeli's 'Chapter on the Elements' (MS. Mantua)," *JJS*, VII (1956), 31-57. S. M. Stern elaborated the subject in his article "Ibn Hasdāy's Neoplatonist: A Neoplatonic Treatise and Its Influence on Isaac Israeli and the Longer Version of the Theology of Aristotle," *Oriens*, XIII-XIV (1961), 58-120. This article will be referred to as Stern, "Ibn Hasdāy's Neoplatonist."

3. See Harry A. Wolfson, "The Meaning of *Ex Nihilo* in Isaac Israeli," *JQR*, N.S., L (1959), 1-12; reprinted in: Harry Austryn Wolfson, *Studies in the History of Philosophy and Religion*, ed. Isadore Twersky and George H. Williams, I (Cambridge, Mass., 1973), 222-233; see pp. 229-233 (to be referred to as Wolfson, "The Meaning").

4. See Josef van Ess, "Jüngere orientalistische Literatur zur neuplatonischen Überlieferung im Bereich des Islam," in Kurt Flasch, ed., *Parusia . . . Festgabe für Johannes Hirschberger* (Frankfurt a.M., 1965), pp. 333-350.

5. Arabic text: S. M. Stern, "The Fragments of Isaac Israeli's 'Book of Substances'," *JJS*, VII (1956), 20-21; English translation by Stern: Altmann-Stern, p. 84.

6. For the meaning of these terms, see below.

7. *Book of Substances*, III, 3r; Stern, *JJS*, VII, 20; Altmann-Stern, pp. 83 f.

8. On the Aristotelian "causes" of a definition see Harry A. Wolfson, *The Philosophy of Spinoza* (New York, 1969), I, 321 f.

9. Altmann-Stern, pp. 66 f. The distinction offered here is indebted to al-Kindī's *Book of Definitions*; see pp. 68 ff. and S. M. Stern, "Notes on al-Kindī's Treatise on Definitions," *Journal of the Royal Asiatic Society* (April 1959), 33, 42. On al-Kindī's concept of "innovation" (*ibdāʿ*) see also Alfred L. Ivry, *Al-Kindī's Metaphysics* (Albany, N.Y., 1975), p. 166.

10. *Book of Substances*, III, 2v; Stern, *JJS*, VII, 20; Altmann-Stern, p. 83.

11. Altmann-Stern, pp. 70 f.

12. Ibid.

13. See the reconstructed text in Stern, "Ibn Hasdāy's Neoplatonist," pp. 104 f.

14. It should be noted that despite his disavowal of power and will as the *summum genus* Israeli admits that intellect is a species of the genus "wisdom." Yet he does not admit an emanation of intellect from wisdom. It is the conjunction of first matter and wisdom that brings about intellect.

15. According to Plotinus the hypostases attain to creative power only after they are fully established by virtue of their contemplation of the source. This aspect of the Plotinian doctrine is absent in Israeli (see below). The phrase "established" (*qāmat*) in the text quoted may, nevertheless, be a faint remnant of the Plotinian concept.

16. See Simon van den Bergh, *Averroes' Tahafut Al-Tahafut* (London, 1954), I, 63.

17. All these texts are assembled in Paul Henry and Hans-Rudolf Schwyzer, *Plotini Opera*, II (Paris & Brussels, 1959). For the literature on these texts see Josef van Ess, "Zur neuplatonischen Überlieferung."

18. Hebrew text in David Kaufmann, *Studien über Salomon Ibn Gabirol* (Budapest, 1899), p. 19; quoted by me in English in Altmann-Stern, p. 162.

19. The position is somewhat confused in the *Ghayāt al-Hakīm* passage quoted by me (Altmann-Stern, pp. 162 f.), which seems to reflect the Israeli source. In his review of the book (*KS*, XXXV [1960], 457-459), the late Martin Plessner suggested that ps.-Empedocles' matter containing all forms was identical with the two first substances of the Israeli source, a view which does not seem tenable to me. In Abenmasarra's system, which follows ps.-Empedocles, prime matter as symbolized by the divine throne is prior to intellect, as we know from Ibn ʿArabī's report. See Miguel Asín Palacios, *Abenmasarra y su Escuela* (Madrid, 1914), p. 75. The late Samuel M. Stern and I planned a joint annotated re-edition of the pseudo-Empedoclean fragments published by Kaufmann. The project came to grief owing to the death of Dr. Stern.

20. See note 3.

21. Wolfson, "The Meaning," pp. 231 f.

22. See S. Pines, "La Longue Recension de la Théologie d'Aristote dans ses Rapports avec la Doctrine Ismaélienne," *Revue des Etudes Islamiques* (1954), p. 10; also Gershom Scholem, "Schöpfung aus Nichts und Selbstverschränkung Gottes," *Eranos-Jahrbuch*, XXV (1957), 101 ff.

23. Wolfson, "The Meaning," p. 230.

24. Ibid., p. 233.

25. Wolfson (p. 232) quotes *Fons Vitae*, V.41, ed. Clemens Baeumker, p. 330,

11.17-20: "The creation of things by the Creator, that is, the going out (*exitus*) of forms from the prime source, that is, from the will (*voluntate*) . . . is like the going out (*exitus*) of water emanating (*emanantis*) from its source."

26. See Julius Guttmann, *Philosophies of Judaism*, trans. David W. Silverman (New York, 1964), pp. 101 f.; Jacques Schlanger, *La Philosophie de Salomon Ibn Gabirol* (Leiden, 1968), pp. 288 ff.

27. *Book of Substances*, IV, 8v; Stern, *JJS*, VII, 24; Altmann-Stern, p. 88.

28. See Pines, "La Longue Recension," p. 10.

29. Franz Rosenthal, "Ash-Shaykh al-Yūnānī and the Arabic Plotinus Source," *Orientalia* (Rome), XXI (1952), 476-477; reproduced in Henry and Schwyzer, *Plotini Opera*, II, 275; *Enneads* V.1.6.25-37.

30. Ibid.

31. See Henry and Schwyzer, *Plotini Opera*, II, 337; *Enneads*, V.4.2.26-38.

32. Quoted from *Enneads*, V.4.2 in MacKenna's translation and discussed by J. M. Rist, *Plotinus: The Road to Reality* (Cambridge, 1967), p. 70.

33. Rist, *The Road to Reality*, pp. 81 ff. See also Klaus Kremer, "Das 'Warum' der Schöpfung: 'quia bonus' vel/et 'quia voluit' . . . ," in Kurt Flasch, ed., *Parusia* (see note 4), pp. 241-264.

34. *Plotini Opera*, II, 321.

35. Ibid; *Enneads*, V.3.12.40. For the simile of the sun in Plotinus, see also V.1.6; V.3.16.

36. *Plotini Opera*, II, 383. Ibn Sīnā, commenting on this passage, identified the first light with God. See G. Vajda, "Les Notes d'Avicenne sur la Théologie d'Aristote," *Revue Thomiste* (1951), 379 ff. This interpretation must be considered correct. The objection ventured by me in Altmann-Stern, p. 173 cannot be upheld.

37. See note 7.

38. *Book of Substances*, III, 2r; *JJS*, VII, 20; Altmann-Stern, p. 83.

39. Pines, "La Longue Recension," p. 156, n. 1.

40. *Book of Substances*, IV, 9v; *JJS*, VII, 25; Altmann-Stern, p. 89.

41. *Book of Substances*, V, 12v; *JJS*, VII, 27; Altmann-Stern, p. 91.

42. *Plotini Opera*, II, 291; see also 441.

43. *Plotini Opera*, II, 297; see also 245.

44. David Kaufmann, *Studien*, p. 19.

45. See Altmann-Stern, pp. 40 f. (lines 36-42); 110 f.; 119.

46. See Altmann-Stern, p. 119; Stern, "Ibn Hasdāy's Neoplatonist," pp. 104-5.

47. Altmann-Stern, p. 41 (line 49); 45 (lines 6-7).

48. *Plotini Opera*, II, 67.

49. See Jacob Guttmann, *Die philosophischen Lehren des Isaak b. Salomon Israeli* (Münster, 1911), p. 18.

50. Abraham ben Hasday, *Ben ha-Melek ve-ha-Nazir*, ed. A. M. Haberman (Tel-Aviv, 1951), p. 202; Stern, "Ibn Hasdāy's Neoplatonist," p. 67.

51. See Stern, "Ibn Hāsday's Neoplatonist," pp. 84, 88.

52. Ibid., pp. 64, 79-81.

53. Altmann-Stern, p. 111.

54. Quoted by Vajda, *REJ*, N.S., XII (1935), 30, note 1, from a manuscript in the Bibliothèque Nationale.

55. See Jacob Guttmann, *Die Scholastik des dreizehnten Jahrhunderts* (Breslau, 1902), p. 57, and *Israeli*, p. 42.

56. *Book of Substances*, III, 3r; *JJS*, VII, 20; Altmann-Stern, pp. 83 f.

57. Altmann-Stern, pp. 45 f. Ibn Gabirol (*Fons Vitae*, III.52) makes the point that what emanates from the source is not the essences (*essentiae*) but powers (*virtutes*) and rays (*radii*) or qualities (*qualitates*).

58. *Book of Definitions*, #6; Altmann-Stern, p. 46, lines 28-33.

59. *Book of Substances*, IV, 9r; *JJS*, VII, 25; Altmann-Stern, p. 88.

60. See n. 32.

61. Cf. *Enneads*, V.4.2.28 ff.; *Epistola de Scientia Divina*, nos. 169-179 in *Plotini Opera*, II, 337.

62. *Enneads*, V.9.5; *Epistola*, #22 in *Plotini Opera*, II, 419.

63. See Philo, *Legum Allegoria*, III, 33.99-104, where the world is said to be but the "shadow" of the "archetype," and Besal'el (lit., "in the shadow of God") is described as an artificer working from mere "images" (miméta) of the archetypes. Cf. Harry A. Wolfson, *Philo* (Cambridge, Mass., 1962), II, 85 f.

64. *Enneads*, VI.9.9. For further references see Kremer, "Das Warum," pp. 246 f. (notes 24-25). See *Dicta Sapientis Graeci*, II, 10 in *Plotini Opera*, II, 267.

65. See A. H. Armstong, *The Architecture of the Intelligible Universe in the Philosophy of Plotinus* (Cambridge, 1940), p. 52.

66. Ibid., p. 62.

67. IV, 8r ff.; *JJS*, VII, 23-26; Altmann-Stern, pp. 88-90.

68. Concerning this inconsistency see above.

69. See note 40.

70. Altmann-Stern, p. 111.

71. Altmann-Stern, p. 41, lines 55-58.

72. A. H. Armstrong, *Plotinus* (London, 1953), p. 34.

73. *Plotini Opera*, II, 275; *Enneads*, V.1.7.5-6.

74. *Plotini Opera*, II, 291 f.; *Enneads*, V.2.1.9-11.

75. David Kaufmann, *Studien*, pp. 20 f.

2

Maimonides' Secret Position on Creation

Herbert Davidson

1. The problem of Maimonides' esoteric doctrines may well be of a kind that is not susceptible to a definitive resolution. On the one hand, traditionalists who would think no doctrinal ill of Maimonides will always contrive harmonizations for untoward passages; as Maimonides once put it, "the gates of interpretation" are never closed.[1] On the other hand, those who absolutely insist on discovering a nontraditional philosophic system concealed below the surface of Maimonides' professed system will be able to withstand any evidence to the contrary. Such evidence will merely illustrate to them Maimonides' skill in hiding his genuine views. An analogy from our day is ready to hand. Those who insist on discovering a conspiracy underlying this or that contemporary event easily withstand the contrary evidence. Such evidence merely reveals to them how deep the conspiracy is, to what extent even the most trusted authorities are implicated.

The present chapter does not attempt to deal with every aspect of the problem of Maimonides' esoteric doctrines nor to resolve the issue once for all. I shall examine only a small number of passages, and the conclusion I shall draw will be of an *ad hominem* character. My conclusion will be that the thoroughgoing esotericists, as I shall call them, are refuted by the logic of their own approach.

Maimonides, in effect, invited esotericist interpretations of his philosophy by statements appearing in the introduction to the *Guide for the Perplexed*. He there lists seven separate reasons for the occurrence of contradictions in books of various types and he confesses that sometimes he too contradicted himself in the *Guide*. Now whereas contradictions occurring in books other than the *Guide* may be inadvertent and due to the authors' carelessness, none of the contradictions appearing in the *Guide* are, Maimonides stresses, to be so regarded. Only mediocre writers contradict themselves unwittingly, through carelessness or bad reasoning. And Maimonides assures us, without the slightest hint of false modesty, that he was a fully competent philosopher and like every self-respecting, competent philosopher, above carelessness.

Two reasons,[2] he explains, account for competent philosophers' contradicting themselves and for his contradicting himself in the *Guide*. One reason—the fifth in the complete list of seven—is pedagogical. When an author is developing a topic, the early stages of the discussion may require an over-simplified statement. Then at a later stage of the discussion, the author is able to make a more accurate statement. And the two statements, the over-simplified one and the accurate one, will contradict each other.[3] Maimonides informs us that he sometimes found himself in that predicament during the composition of the *Guide*. He sometimes had to make a simplified statement at an early stage of a particular discussion, and subsequently made a more accurate statement, the result being that the two statements, taken as they stand, contradict each other.[4] It may be noted that the commentators are hard put to discover a single contradiction in Maimonides which is in fact attributable to the reason just given, that is to say, a contradiction with a pedagogical end.[5]

The other reason given by Maimonides for the occurrence of contradictions in the works of competent philosophers and in his own work is the last in the list of seven. Maimonides explains: when an author is discussing a difficult and profound subject, he may find that the truth would be dangerous to the common folk and consequently must remain partly concealed. In the course of hiding part of the truth, the author is forced to make a statement that contradicts what he says elsewhere, the inaccurate statement serving to conceal what cannot be publicized. If ever such occurs, if an author ever does have to make an inaccurate statement in order to conceal dangerous truths, the uninitiated reader must, Maimonides warns, be kept completely in the dark. Not only must the esoteric doctrine be concealed; the contradiction must be concealed as well, to forestall embarrassing questions from the common folk. They must not even be allowed to suspect that a contradiction has occurred.

Maimonides informs us that he found himself in predicaments of this sort too during the writing of the *Guide for the Perplexed*. Sometimes he had to hide part of the truth and was thereby forced to make inaccurate statements that contradict correct statements appearing elsewhere. The contradictions were made consciously and were part of a deliberate plan. Maimonides goes as far as to declare that the very wording of his book reflects a deliberate plan. To quote him, the entire *Guide* is written with "great exactitude and exceeding precision." Inasmuch as the contradictions in the *Guide* serve a function, Maimonides adjures intelligent readers who do sniff contradictions to remain silent about whatever they might unearth.[6]

Maimonides' declarations could of course be regarded irreverently and cynically. His claiming to be above carelessness does not guarantee his being so; not everyone who claims infallibility is recognized by the rest of us to possess the attribute. As far as I know, however, Maimonides' declarations concerning the contradictions in the *Guide* have not ever been read in a cynical light. Apparent instances of poor organization and, what is more important, any instances of contradictions in the *Guide* have been viewed as intentional and have been assumed to be integral to the plan of the book.

If Maimonides is taken at his word and the contradictions in the *Guide* are assumed to be deliberate, a narrow, and a comprehensive approach are possible to the question of the doctrines Maimonides was hiding. On the narrow approach, Maimonides' overall system in the *Guide* would be accepted as it stands, and here and there, on individual issues, Maimonides would be understood to have embraced doctrines that, he thought, should be concealed from the common folk; these would be the esoteric doctrines to which he refers.[7] On the comprehensive approach, the entire philosophic system put forward by Maimonides in the *Guide* would be pure simulation, and Maimonides would be understood to have secretly subscribed to a completely different system. The comprehensive approach to Maimonides' esotericism is pursued by those whom I call the throughgoing esotericists. It is obviously the more provocative approach, positing, as it does, a clandestine untraditional Maimonides lurking behind the respectable public figure of the same name. It is not a new approach, having already been pursued by medieval commentators.[8] In part, perhaps, just because of its very provocativeness it was revived by modern students of Maimonides' philosophy, most notably by Leo Strauss.[9]

The thoroughgoing esotericist approach to Maimonides depicts the following situation: Maimonides publicly represented himself as believing in a deity who is possessed of free will; who created the world and can intervene in it; who has knowledge of His creatures; and who exercises providence over them. What Maimonides genuinely believed, however, was quite different. He genuinely believed, according to the thoroughgoing esotericists, in an Aristotelian style deity who has no free will; who is, indeed, the cause of the universe, but eternally so and not as a creator; who cannot interfere in the universe; and who has no knowledge of anything outside Himself. The contrast might strike us as one between a personal and an impersonal deity, but that is not language Maimonides would use. From Maimonides' standpoint, the critical factor is will, and the thesis of the thoroughgoing esotericists may be summarized by saying that Maimonides professed a belief in a God who is possessed of free will, while secretly believing in a God who has no free will.[10]

The esotericist thesis affects virtually all parts of Maimonides' philosophy, but the touchstone for the thesis is Maimonides' discussion of creation. As Maimonides explained, the position any philosopher takes on creation determines—as well as being determined by—the philosopher's concept of God. The creation of the world implies a God who is possessed of will, who has some sort of knowledge of what He created, and who is in principle capable of intervening in the universe.[11] The eternity of the world—taken together with the assumption that the world has a cause—has opposite implications. An Aristotelian rule had affirmed that eternity and necessity are mutually implicative.[12] Consequently, the eternity of the world and of God's relation to it imply a deity who is bereft of free will and bound by necessity, who cannot possibly intervene in the world, and who can have no knowledge of the changing events outside Himself.[13] The doctrine of creation thus implies the system of beliefs ostensibly espoused by Maimonides in the *Guide*; and the doctrine of eternity implies the system that the thoroughgoing esotercists wish to discover hidden below the surface. If Maimonides did secretly believe in the eternity of the world, the thesis of the thoroughgoing esotericists would, then, be correct, whereas if Maimonides' genuine belief was creation, the thesis is wrong.

The only guidance for discovering what Maimonides' esoteric beliefs might have been is provided by his remarks concerning contradictions. When difficult subjects are treated—Maimonides writes in connection with the seventh reason for contradiction—it may be necessary "to hide some things while disclosing others, with the result that . . . the discussion must proceed in one passage on the basis of a given proposition and . . . in another passage . . . on the basis of a proposition contradicting the first."[14] In other words, each pair of contradictory propositions comprises an inaccurate proposition designed to hide what must be hidden, and an accurate proposition designed to disclose, with caution, what may be disclosed to the chosen few. Strauss, in particular, emphasized the importance of contradictions for interpreting Maimonides. He even drew up a calculus for determining, in every instance, which of two contradictory statements in the *Guide* would reflect Maimonides' exoteric position and which would reflect his esoteric position.[15] When we turn to Maimonides' treatment of the issue of creation and eternity, significant contradictions do appear. They ought to furnish the key to Maimonides' genuine beliefs. If the esotericist thesis is correct, the accurate proposition in each pair of contradictory propositions should disclose a secret belief in eternity and in a deity bereft of free will.

2. *Maimonides' evaluation of the Platonic position on creation.* Maimonides opens his discussion of creation by setting forth the positions that might be taken on the issue. Earlier he had advanced a set of proofs for the existence of God and he was confident that the existence of a first cause of the universe—the existence of God—had been established conclusively.[16] Once a first cause is granted, Maimonides writes, three positions are possible on the issue of creation and eternity. For convenience I shall call them the *scriptural*, the *Aristotelian*, and the *Platonic* positions.[17]

The first of the three positions is, to be exact, designated by Maimonides as the position of "all who believe in the Law of Moses," and again as the position of "everyone who follows the Law of Moses and our father Abraham." Maimonides formulates it thus: during a period extending back through eternity, nothing but God existed. Then, in the finitely distant past, God exercised "His will," and by an act of will "brought the universe . . . into existence."[18] The scriptural position is, in short, the doctrine of creation *ex nihilo*, the creation of the world from absolutely nothing through a supreme primordial miracle. As will be noted, the scriptural position is closely tied by Maimonides to its theological implication: Creation *ex nihilo* goes hand in hand with God's possessing free will.

A second position, that of "Aristotle, his followers, and the commentators on his works," is the contrary of the first. Whereas the scriptural position affirms that God created the world through an act of will, the Aristotelian position affirms that the causal nexus between the world and the first cause, or God, is eternal, necessary, and unchanging.[19] Again the theological implication is carefully brought out by Maimonides: the eternity of the world and of God's relation to it go hand in hand with God's being bound by necessity and not possessing free will. The first and second positions therefore give rise to a clear-cut confrontation of two conceptions of God, a deity possessed of will as against a deity bereft of free will.

The third position, which is attributed by Maimonides to Plato and additional, unnamed philosophers, falls between the previous two. It affirms that the world is created in one respect, in respect to form, and eternal in another respect, in respect to matter. According to the Platonic position, the coming into existence of something from absolutely nothing is inconceivable, and the underlying matter of the world must consequently be eternal. But the present state of the world was, according to the Platonic position, created: God created, or formed, the universe out of preexistent matter that had existed from all eternity.[20]

Maimonides certainly expected his readers to understand that the position he espoused was the first, the doctrine of creation *ex nihilo*. He characterizes creation *ex nihilo* as the position of "all who believe in the Law of Moses"[21] and as "our position."[22] And he scrupulously refutes every argument against creation *ex nihilo* which was known to him.[23] Yet the thoroughgoing esotericists maintain that Maimonides secretly believed in eternity. They have, for their part, given weight to Maimonides' use of the expression *our position*. By describing creation *ex nihilo* as "our" position rather than explicitly calling it "my" position, Maimonides could be intimating that his personal position is different.[24] Likewise, it has been claimed that Maimonides' defense of the scriptural position, though ostensibly both exhaustive and minute, is in actuality unconvincing and hence a mere smoke screen which clever readers should be able to penetrate.[25]

We have still not met any contradictions, however, and they alone can furnish convincing evidence of Maimonides' esoteric beliefs. As it happens, Maimonides' presentation of the possible positions on creation and eternity does contain a contradiction.

Maimonides' object in setting forth the three possible positions was to prepare the ground for an examination of arguments that might be adduced for and against each position.[26] But once having spelled out the three possible positions, Maimonides restricts his attention to two. "No benefit," he writes, is to be derived from giving separate attention to the Platonic position. For it, like the Aristotelian position, "affirms eternity; and from our standpoint there is no difference between the [Platonic] belief that the heavens must come into existence from something [already existent and eternal] . . . and Aristotle's belief . . . that the heavens are [in their form as well as their matter] ungenerated."[27] The Platonic position is lumped together by Maimonides with the Aristotelian, and the issue is drawn between the Aristotelian position and the scriptural position.

Now the stand taken here by Maimonides is very strange. The Platonic position is, as we have seen, hardly identical with the Aristotelian position. It lies between the Aristotelian and scriptural positions, affirming the creation of the present state of the world although not creation *ex nihilo*. The various theoretical considerations that Maimonides will offer for preferring the scriptural position to the Aristotelian need not, therefore, constitute grounds for preferring the scriptural position to the Platonic.[28] And, what is more important, the theological implications of the Platonic position are by no means identical with the theological implications of the Aristotelian position. If God created the world, even from a preexistent matter, He would be possessed of will and not bound by necessity. He would in principle be capable of intervening in the universe, inasmuch as He effected the greatest imaginable intervention through His act of creation; He would be capable of a grand revelation such as occurred at Sinai; and so on. Instead of declaring that "there is no difference" between the Platonic and Aristotelian positions, Maimonides should have said that the Platonic position lies between the scriptural and Aristotelian positions; and from a theological point of view, there is little difference between the Platonic and scriptural positions. The sole theological difference between the Platonic and scriptural positions is that the former rejects, while the latter recognizes, one specific type of miracle, the bringing of matter into existence out of nothing.

And, behold, Maimonides later changes his stand. After completing his entire discussion of creation, after weighing the divers arguments for and against the scriptural and Aristotelian positions, and after determining that the scriptural position is philosophically more plausible, Maimonides adds a sort of epilogue. There he acknowledges that in its theological implications the Platonic position is fully as acceptable as the scriptural position. The Platonic position, unlike the Aristotelian, does not destroy "the foundations of the Law"; it is wholly compatible with revelation, miracles, and providence. Maimonides goes so far as to concede that the Platonic position can easily be harmonized with the text of the Bible, and that many passages in the Bible and in other authoritative branches of Jewish literature tend to support it. Why then did Maimonides reject the Platonic position? In the epilogue Maimonides explains in a subdued voice that he rejected the Platonic position because creation *ex nihilo* seems more in harmony with the obvious sense of Scripture.[29]

Thus at the beginning of his discussion Maimonides dismisses the Platonic position as equivalent to the Aristotelian position, whereas at the end of his discussion he acknowledges that the Platonic position is, from a theological point of view, virtually equivalent to the scriptural position. That is a serious contradiction.

If contradictions are indeed the key to Maimonides' genuine views—I am not completely sure that they are—a single conclusion is indicated. The logic of the contradictions in the *Guide* requires that in each pair of contradictory propositions, one proposition be deemed correct and the other, incorrect.[30] Since the eternity of the world is nowise involved in the contradiction under consideration, the conclusion to be drawn cannot be that Maimonides secretly embraced the eternity of the world. The contradiction concerns the doctrine of creation from a preexistent matter, one proposition branding the doctrine as theologically unacceptable, the other acknowledging its acceptability. Maimonides would have no motive for hiding the former proposition. Therefore the contradiction, if deliberate, could only indicate that Maimonides secretly subscribed to, or secretly countenanced, creation from a preexistent matter; and in order not to shock sensitive readers, he publicly embraced the doctrine of creation *ex nihilo*. The outcome is far from sensational; it is even anticlimactic.

3. *The relationship of the possible positions on prophecy to the possible positions on creation*. Maimonides opens his discussion of prophecy, as he opened his discussion of creation, by setting forth the possible positions on the issue; he set forth, to be exact, the positions that might be taken regarding the process whereby men become prophets. He finds again that once the existence of God is granted, three positions are possible. The proponents, however, are now different. The first position on the issue of prophecy is attributed by Maimonides to "ignoramuses" (*jāhilīya*)[31] among Jews as well as non-Jews; the second position is that of the "philosophers"; the third position is that of "our Law."[32]

The first position, the position of "ignoramuses," affirms that nothing prepares a person for prophecy, although moral rectitude is a precondition, since God would not appoint an evil or licentious person as His prophet. Persons who are, apart from moral rectitude, in no way more qualified for the distinction than anyone else are transformed by God into prophets and are sent on prophetic missions.[33]

The second position on prophecy, that of the "philosophers," is the contrary of the first. Here prophecy is construed as a purely natural phenomenon that excludes any direct role for God—though God, as the ultimate cause of the universe may be considered the ultimate cause of prophecy. According to the philosophers' position, a number of qualifications have to be met, and when they are met, the qualified candidate automatically becomes a prophet. Maimonides discusses the qualifications at length but the details are not important for our purpose. Stated generally, the theory is that the candidate for prophecy has to be born with certain psychological and intellectual gifts. If he successfully develops his native gifts, he reaches a stage where he is vouchsafed an emanation from the supernal realm—from the active intellect[34]—which renders him a prophet. What is significant for us is that the prophet is not in any sense chosen to receive the emanation. The emanation rendering him a prophet is at all times available in the universe, like a radio transmission that is broadcast constantly and unvaringly. Anyone who develops the requisite faculties tunes himself in, as it were, to the ever available transmission, or emanation, and immediately is endowed with prophecy.[35] The first and second positions form a clear-cut confrontation: the doctrine that prophecy is a sheer miracle is confronted by the doctrine that prophecy is a purely natural phenomenon, the automatic accompaniment of a specific state of individual human development.

The third position on prophecy, the position of the Jewish "Law," is, as formulated by Maimonides, a restatement of the philosophic position with the addition of a single critical proviso. In the position of the Jewish Law, prophecy is construed once more as a natural phenomenon. To attain prophecy, a person must be born with certain psychological and intellectual gifts, develop his gifts, and reach the stage where he can receive the emanation of the active intellect. But—and this is the added proviso—the person who reaches the stage in question does not necessarily prophesy. If God should so wish, He can intervene and prevent the man who is completely qualified and prepared for prophecy from becoming a prophet in actuality; God has the power of veto over prophecy. Maimonides emphasizes that the intervention preventing a qualified person from prophesying would be an act of "divine will" and a "miracle." It would be a miracle inasmuch as it would be an interruption of the natural course of events. According to the third position, then, prophecy is not a sheer miracle, as in the first position, nor exclusively a natural phenomenon, as in the second. Prophecy is an interaction of nature and miracle.[36]

At the very beginning of his discussion of prophecy, before setting forth the three possible positions, Maimonides makes a seemingly casual remark. He observes that the possible positions on prophecy are "like the positions" on creation; and he continues: "Just as those who are convinced of the existence of God have three positions on the issue of eternity and creation, . . . so too the positions on prophecy are three."[37] If Maimonides is merely pointing out that the number happens to be the same, if he has in mind no inner correspondence between the positions on prophecy and the positions on creation, his observation is most insignificant and insipid. He could, as Abravanel comments, equally have observed that the number of positions is the same as the number of the Patriarchs—Abraham, Isaac, and Jacob— or the same as the number of the divisions of Scripture—Pentateuch, Prophets, Hagiographa.[38] Presumably, Maimonides does have in mind some intrinsic similarity between the possible positions on prophecy and the possible positions on creation.

And an intrinsic similarity is readily detected. In the first place, creation *ex nihilo* corresponds to the doctrine that prophecy requires no prior preparation. The parallelism is perfect: both the existence of the world and the appearance of a prophet are construed as sheer miracles, the coming into existence of something from nothing. In the second place, the doctrine that the world is eternal, necessary, and unchanging, corresponds to the doctrine that prophecy is a purely natural phenomenon, occurring automatically whenever the requisite conditions are satisfied. Again the parallelism is perfect: the existence of the world and the circumstances bringing about the emergence of a prophet are necessary, and unchanging. In the third place, there stands on the side of creation the doctrine of creation from a preexistent matter, and on the side of prophecy the doctrine that prophecy is a natural phenomenon which is subject to divine veto. Here also the parallelism is evident, though not as complete as in the previous two instances. In both the doctrine of creation from a preexistent matter and the doctrine that prophecy is a natural phenomenon subject to divine veto, God's power is limited by the law that something cannot come into existence from nothing. In both doctrines God can, however, intervene miraculously when conditions are ripe: given a preexistent matter, God can create a world; given a person qualified for prophecy, God can decide whether or not an actual prophet will emerge. The reason the parallelism is incomplete is that the doctrine of creation from a preexistent matter has God acting miraculously in a positive manner, whereas the corresponding doctrine on prophecy has God acting miraculously solely in a negative manner, by preventing the natural process from bearing fruit.

The overall parallelism is nonetheless striking. The doctrine of the creation of the world *ex nihilo* corresponds perfectly to the doctrine that God transforms men who have no prior preparation into prophets, creating prophets, in a sense, *ex nihilo*. The doctrine of the eternity of the world corresponds perfectly to the doctrine that prophecy is a purely natural phenomenon. The doctrine of creation from a preexistent matter corresponds closely, although not completely, to the doctrine that prophecy is a natural phenomenon over which God can exercise a veto. Maimonides' observation that the positions on prophecy are "like the positions" on creation turns out to be highly apt.

Yet something is wrong; for the designations of the proponents of the several positions do not in every instance match. In one instance the designations do match. The doctrine of the eternity of the world corresponds to the doctrine that prophecy is a purely natural phenomenon. The former is designated as the Aristotelian position on the issue of creation and eternity, and the latter is designated as the philosophers' position on prophecy. In the Middle Ages, "philosopher" is often a synonym for "Aristotle" and therefore here the corresponding positions have received corresponding designations. The discrepancies appear in connection with the remaining positions.

The doctrine of creation *ex nihilo* corresponds to the doctrine that prophecy is a sheer miracle. But creation *ex nihilo* is designated as the position of the Law, whereas its counterpart, the doctrine that prophecy is a sheer miracle, is designated as the position of ignoramuses. The discrepancy is nothing less than scandalous: a scriptural position is matched with a position attributed to ignoramuses. Then creation from a preexistent matter corresponds to the doctrine that prophecy is a natural phenomenon subject to divine veto. But the former is the Platonic position whereas the latter is designated as the position of the Law; the Platonic position on creation, originally dismissed by Maimonides as unworthy of attention,[39] corresponds in prophecy to the position of the Law, which is the approved position.

The following table may be helpful:

Creation and eternity	*Prophecy*
The Law—creation *ex nihilo*	Ignoramuses—sheer miracle
Aristotle—eternity	Philosophers—natural phenomenon
Plato—creation from a preexistent matter	The Law—natural phenomenon subject to divine veto

Maimonides has apparently contradicted himself. He has stated that the positions on prophecy are "like the positions" on creation; that is to say, the positions correspond. And while they do indeed correspond, the proponents do not. Conceivably, of course, Maimonides may merely have intended to point out the trivial fact that the number of positions on prophecy happens to be the same as the number of positions on creation. Conceivably too he may have been referring to the inner correspondence between the positions while failing to notice the discrepancies in his designations of the proponents. But if Maimonides is to be taken at his word, he wrote the *Guide for the Perplexed* with, as he puts it, "great exactitude and exceeding precision";[40] he was not guilty of trivial observations or careless remarks that could throw perspicacious readers into a quandary. On such a reading of Maimonides—and it is the reading that the thoroughgoing esotericists bid us adopt—Maimonides has contradicted himself, the contradiction is deliberate, and the object was to hide Maimonides' secret beliefs.

On that reading of Maimonides, a single conclusion is indicated. The logic of the contradictions in the *Guide* requires that in a pair of contradictory propositions, one proposition be deemed correct and the other, incorrect.[41] The pair of contradictory propositions we are faced with comprises the affirmation that the positions on prophecy correspond to the positions on creation; and the assigning of designations for the proponents of the several positions which do not match. Aristotle's position on eternity and the "philosophers' " position on prophecy are nowise involved in the contradiction. There, not only the positions but also Maimonides' designations of them correspond perfectly. The contradiction affects the remaining positions alone. The contradictory propositions are, to be precise, the affirmation, on the one hand, that the positions correspond; and, on the other hand, the assigning of disparate designations specifically to the non-Aristotelian positions. Of the two contradictory propositions, the inaccurate one, which is designed to conceal Maimonides' esoteric belief, clearly cannot be the affirmation that the positions correspond. If the positions on prophecy do not correspond to the positions on creation, nothing imaginable could be concealed by Maimonides' affirming that they do. The inaccurate proposition, which is designed to conceal an esoteric belief, could only be the assigning of discrepant designations to the non-Aristotelian positions. To uncover Maimonides' esoteric belief, the designations of those positions would have to be adjusted in such a fashion that the discrepancies are removed and the positions correspond not merely in content but also in the designations of their proponents.

Surely no corrections are called for in the designations of the positions on prophecy. The doctrine of prophecy as a sheer miracle would never have been attributed by Maimonides to ignoramuses had he secretly believed it to be the scriptural position and embraced it himself. Nor would Maimonides have attributed to Scripture a restatement of the philosophic position on prophecy with just a single saving proviso,[42] had he secretly believed prophecy to be a sheer miracle. Prophecy as a sheer miracle is no one's esoteric position; and no one would endeavor to conceal an esoteric position through an exoteric position that is more sophisticated and more philosophical.

On the assumption that Maimonides deliberately designated the non-Aristotelian positions inaccurately, the inaccuracy must then lie on the side of creation. The designation of creation *ex nihilo* as the scriptural position and the designation of creation from a preexistent matter as the unacceptable, Platonic position must, in other words, be incorrect. And if they are incorrect, while the designations of the positions on prophecy are correct, the genuine scriptural position on creation as well as Maimonides' own esoteric belief would have to be the position that corresponds to the scriptural position on prophecy. The genuine scriptural position on creation as well as Maimonides' own esoteric belief would have to be the doctrine of creation from a preexistent matter.

In fine, if the positions on prophecy are truly "like the positions" on creation and if the discrepancies in Maimonides' designations of the proponents are deliberate, the logic of the contradiction leads to a result that does not touch the Aristotelian positions. The result must be this: Maimonides secretly understood that creation *ex nihilo*, the counterpart of the position held by ignoramuses on prophecy, is not after all the scriptural position; it like its counterpart is an unenlightened[43] position. And Maimonides secretly believed that the genuine scriptural position on creation is the position corresponding to the scriptural position on prophecy, to wit, creation from a preexistent matter. The positions on prophecy will now fully correspond to the positions on creation: The creation of the world from nothing and the transformation of unqualified persons into prophets will be parallel unenlightened positions. The creation of the world from a preexistent matter and the doctrine of prophecy as a natural phenomenon subject to divine veto will be parallel scriptural positions—and also, presumably, Platonic positions, although that is no longer of importance. The eternity of the world and the doctrine of prophecy as a purely natural phenomenon will be parallel positions of the Aristotelian school.

As for the problem of Maimonides' esotericism, the result will be similar to the unsensational result reached earlier:[44] Maimonides secretly believed in creation from a preexistent matter, but publicly professed creation *ex nihilo* in order to avoid shocking sensitive readers.

4. *Maimonides' arguments for creation.* The issue of creation and eternity, Maimonides writes, is not amenable to "demonstration" (*burhān, apodeixis*).[45] A demonstration in the technical sense takes its departure from true and certain premises, and proceeds by syllogistic or equally valid reasoning to a conclusion that is as indisputable as the premises.[46] Alternatively, a demonstration may be effected in an indirect manner: if all the possible positions on an issue can be isolated and if all but one of them can be eliminated through valid reasoning based on true and certain premises, then the one remaining will have been demonstrated. In characterizing the issue of creation and eternity as not amenable to demonstration, Maimonides means that the requisite premises are not available for either a direct or indirect demonstration of any of the positions.

Demonstrations being ruled out, the several positions on the issue of creation and eternity may at most, Maimonides further explains, be supported through nondemonstrative "arguments" (*dalīl, hujja*). One or another of the positions may, in other words, be supported through reasoning that, although not based on true and certain premises, reveals the plausibility of the given position or the implausibility of all of the rest.[47] Because the authority of Aristotle was so weighty, Maimonides also takes pains to determine how Aristotle had assessed the probative force of his proofs of eternity. Maimonides analyzes four separate passages[48] where Aristotle had referred to his proofs of eternity and through careful exegesis shows that Aristotle had recognized the limits of his proofs, that he too had not presumed to offer demonstrations.[49]

Maimonides, for his part, advances three arguments in support of his own position on the issue. He introduces them, writing: "I shall undertake to tip the scales . . . in favor of our position (*da'wā*) . . . through a theoretical argument . . . That is to say, [I shall undertake] to tip the scales in favor of the thesis of creation over the thesis of eternity."[50] In a summary of the first of his arguments, he remarks, in the same vein, that he had proved "our position (*ra'y*), [that is to say, the position of] the advocates of the creation of the world."[51] By describing the "position" of the Jewish religion as the "creation of the world," Maimonides, it is to be observed, has contradicted himself once again or has at least fallen short of the exactitude and precision that he promised his readers.[52] For when he set forth the possible positions on the issue, he defined the position of the Jewish Law as creation *ex nihilo*; and he represented the doctrine of creation without the qualification that creation took place from nothing as wholly unacceptable.[53] Yet now in presenting his arguments in favor of the position of the Jewish Law, he describes that position merely as "creation," omitting the supposed indispensable qualification. As it happens, the first two arguments offered by Maimonides in support of what he calls "our position" are, indeed, designed to establish only creation, not creation *ex nihilo*.

The argument from the structure of the heavens. Maimonides' first argument for creation—which is a rethinking of an earlier Kalam argument for creation as well as of a passage in Ghazali's *Tahāfut*[54]—focuses on two general aspects of the structure of the heavens: the directions and velocities of the motions of the celestial spheres; and the location of the stars and planets within the spheres.

The total number of spheres—primary spheres as well as subspheres— which had to be assumed by ancient and medieval astronomers exceeded fifty in some versions.[55] The function of the theory of the celestial spheres was to account for the motions of the stars and planets. Each sphere was assumed to rotate with a constant velocity. In order, however, to account for all the apparent motions of the stars and planets, some spheres had to be assumed to rotate with a greater, and some with a lesser, velocity than others; some had to be assumed to rotate westward, and others, eastward. Maimonides' contention is that these diversities in the motions of the spheres cannot be subsumed under any law.

Since the spheres were assumed to be constituted of a common material substance,[56] the diversity in their motions cannot, he reasons, be explained through a diversity of substance; the diversity of motion must be due to something apart from the material substance of the spheres. Now if a regular pattern could be discerned in the diverse directions and velocities of the several spheres, a uniform, natural explanation would be feasible in which each sphere is taken to be responsible for the motion of the succeeding one. The outermost sphere would be understood to communicate a proportion of its motion to the next sphere, the latter to communicate an analogous proportion of its motion to the next, and so forth.[57] But in actuality, according to Maimonides, no pattern is discernible which would permit such a hypothesis; for in the assumed sequence of the spheres, westward and eastward movements, rapid and slow movements, succeed each other at random. Inasmuch as the directions and velocities of the motions of the celestial spheres fail to disclose any regular pattern they can, Maimonides maintains, be subsumed under no conceivable law. Consequently, the sole plausible explanation is that a voluntary agent[58] must have assigned the spheres "whatever direction and velocity of motion it wished."[59]

The other general aspect of the structure of the heavens considered by Maimonides is the location of the stars and planets in the spheres. The spheres, according to the enlightened medieval consensus, rotate constantly, whereas the stars and planets, which are carried by the spheres, do not undergo any motion of their own. Maimonides deduces herefrom that the substance of the spheres must be radically different from the substance of the stars and planets. In addition, the supposed fact that the spheres are transparent whereas the stars are luminous furnished him with further evidence of the radical difference between the substance of the spheres and the substance of the stars and planets.[60] Now, Maimonides reasons, no law of nature and no principle of regularity can explain how stars of one substance come to be conjoined with spheres of a completely different substance. Nor, moreover, can any law of nature or principle of regularity explain the distribution of stars in the so-called sphere of the *fixed* stars, the sphere that was assumed to contain all the *fixed* or true stars, in contradistinction to the *wandering* stars, or planets. In some areas of the sphere of the fixed stars, stars of different magnitudes were seen to be clustered in constellations; in other areas, stars were seen to be scattered at random; and still other areas were devoid of stars. Inasmuch as the presence and distribution of the stars within the spheres—like the motion of the spheres—reveal no regular pattern and can be subsumed under no law of nature, that phenomenon too, Maimonides maintains, must be attributed to an act of choice by a voluntary agent.[61]

Having reached this stage, Maimonides cites the rule that eternity implies necessity and is incompatible with the exercise of free choice.[62] His conclusion is that the agent who, through free choice, introduced irregularities into the structure of the heavens cannot have acted from eternity. The voluntary agent must have brought the world into existence after it had not existed.[63]

Maimonides' argument is a peculiar inversion of the teleological line of thinking. Instead of evincing phenomena that are so well designed that a human observer cannot fail to see the plan, Maimonides evinces phenomena that are too irregular to be subsumed by a human observer under any imaginable law of nature.[64] The argument is cogent because it can presuppose a prior demonstration of the existence of God. Given the existence of a first cause of the universe, free choice and hence the creation of the world can be inferred from the very absence of observable order in the structure of the world. Maimonides, as should be noted, has offered exactly what he proposed, namely an argument, not a demonstration. His argument is not demonstrative, since it does not take its departure from true and certain premises and proceed therefrom to an indisputable conclusion. It operates instead in the realm of plausibilities, showing the thesis of creation to be far more plausible than the thesis of eternity. Inasmuch as no regular pattern and no unitary set of physical laws could be discovered to explain fundamental aspects of the structure of the world, the thesis of necessity and eternity lacks, while the thesis of creation wins, plausibility. Maimonides recognized, though, that a future philosopher or scientist might yet detect an underlying regularity in the structure of the heavens; and the argument would then collapse. Fanciful though the possibility might seem to Maimonides and other medieval astronomers, a set of astronomical laws might even be developed which would dispense with celestial spheres altogether.

Maimonides' argument clearly endeavors to establish that the ultimate cause of the world, God, is possessed of free will. The argument endeavors to establish the creation of the structure of the heavens and—since the sublunar region is subordinate to, and dependent on the celestial region—the creation, as well, of the structure of the entire world. But the argument has nothing to say about the creation or eternity of the matter from which the world is constituted.

The argument from the union of matter and form in the celestial spheres. It was an explicitly articulated and prominent Aristotelian thesis that celestial objects are constituted of a different material substratum from that of sublunar objects. Evidence therefor was drawn from the supposed fact that the natural motion of sublunar objects is rectilinear whereas the natural motion of the celestial spheres is circular.[65] According to Maimonides' reading of Aristotle and according to what he understood to be the best scientific description of the universe, the world contains no less than three distinct types of matter: sublunar objects have their common matter, as is indicated by the fact that their natural motion is rectilinear; the celestial spheres have a different matter, as indicated by the fact that their natural motion is circular; and the stars have still a third matter, as indicated by the fact that they differ from both the celestial spheres and sublunar objects in undergoing no natural motion of their own.[66] Celestial objects, Maimonides further understood, do resemble sublunar objects in one respect, insofar as they do contain the distinction of matter and form.[67] The celestial spheres are thus understood by him to have a matter common to them and different from the matter of the other objects in the universe; and each individual sphere consists in the union of the common matter of the spheres with the unique form of the particular sphere. The stars similarly have a matter common to them and different from the matter of both spheres and sublunar objects; and each star consists in the union of the common matter with the unique form of the particular star.

Against the background of the foregoing theory, Maimonides formulates a second argument for creation, which is related to his first argument.[68] The central thought goes back to John Philoponus[69] and seems to have been suggested to Maimonides by Ghazali.[70]

The essence of matter, Maimonides reasons, is to receive, spontaneously, whatever form is appropriate to it. If the spheres are all constituted of a common matter, the material substratum of each given sphere is as adapted to receive the form of any other sphere as it is to possess the form of its own sphere. By the same token, if the stars too are all constituted of a common matter, the material substratum of each given star is as adapted to receive the form of any other star as it is to possess the form of its own star. Should events take their natural course, the matter of the spheres and of the stars would behave as the matter of the sublunar region does, repeatedly shedding one form and taking on another. The matter of each sphere would shed its form and successively adopt the forms of the other spheres, with the changes manifesting themselves through repeated changes in the direction and velocity of the sphere's motion. The matter of each star would likewise shed its form and successively adopt the forms of the other stars, the changes here manifesting themselves by changes in the quality of the light radiated by the star. But events plainly do not take their natural course. Neither the matter of the spheres nor the matter of the stars behaves as matter should behave, successively taking on all the forms it is adapted to receive.

The situation perceived by Maimonides is, then, as follows: the spheres have the common characteristic of moving circularly, and that, by the laws of nature, should betoken a common matter. The stars have the common characteristic of not undergoing any motion of their own, and that should also betoken a common matter. Yet neither the common matter of the spheres nor the common matter of the stars behaves as, by the laws of nature, a common matter should behave. In neither case does the common matter receive all the forms that it is adapted to receive. Since the situation does not lend itself to a natural explanation, Maimonides once more submits a nonnatural explanation. A conscious voluntary agent must permanently assign each individual sphere and star its peculiar character—in the case of the spheres, the character of constantly undergoing a given particular circular motion, and in the case of the stars, the character of constantly radiating a given particular light.[71]

Having come this far, Maimonides concludes as before: eternity implies necessity and is incompatible with the action of a voluntary agent. The agent who, through an act of will, determined the particular fixed character of each sphere and star cannot therefore act from eternity; and the heavens together with everything subordinate to them must have been created.[72]

Maimonides has again offered an argument, not a demonstration; he does not proceed from true and certain premises to his conclusion, but operates in the realm of plausibilities, exposing the implausibility of the hypothesis of eternity and the attendant plausibility of creation. Maimonides' argument clearly is designed to establish that the ultimate cause of the world is possessed of free will and that the structure of the heavens, hence the structure of the entire world, is created. The argument does not in any way address the question whether the matter of the world is created.

Recapitulation. In the present section we have met a contradiction at two levels. In advancing his arguments for what he calls "our position," that is to say, his position and the position of the Law, Maimonides describes the same not as creation *ex nihilo*, but merely as creation.[73] Earlier, by contrast, he insisted on defining the position of the Jewish Law specifically as creation *ex nihilo*, the qualification that creation took place from nothing being indispensable.[74] That is one contradiction. Should it be dismissed, despite Maimonides' promise of "great exactitude and exceeding precision," as simply due to careless wording, there remains an additional contradiction superimposed upon it. The arguments we have examined purport to "tip the scales" in favor of what Maimonides calls "our position"; and in summarizing the first argument Maimonides asserts that the argument did prove his position. But in fact the two arguments establish only creation, not creation *ex nihilo*. If Maimonides' position can be proved by arguments that establish only creation, then his position must be just creation and not creation *ex nihilo*. And yet he earlier defined his position and the position of the Jewish Law specifically as creation *ex nihilo*. He has therefore contradicted himself here also.

Once again, the Aristotelian position, the doctrine of eternity, is nowise involved in the contradictions. The contradictions concern the doctrine of creation *ex nihilo* and the doctrine of creation without the *ex nihilo* qualification. One pair of contradictory propositions comprises Maimonides' earlier affirmation that creation *ex nihilo* is the position of the Law as well as his position; and his present description of his position and the position of the Law merely as creation. The other pair consists in the earlier affirmation that creation *ex nihilo* is the position of the Law as well as his position; and his advancing, as proof of his position, arguments that turn out to prove creation alone, not creation *ex nihilo*. On the assumption that the contradictions are deliberate, each pair of contradictions must contain an accurate and an inaccurate proposition, the latter intended to conceal Maimonides' esoteric belief. It would be paradoxical to suppose that the accurate proposition and Maimonides' genuine belief is creation *ex nihilo*, while the deliberately inaccurate proposition and his feigned belief is creation without the qualification that creation took place from nothing—to suppose, in other words, that Maimonides secretly believed in creation *ex nihilo* but tried to conceal the belief by publicly espousing creation without the *ex nihilo* qualification. Accordingly, if Maimonides has indeed deliberately contradicted himself, the only reasonable conclusion would have to be that his secret, genuine belief was creation without the qualification that it took place from nothing, while his public espousal of creation *ex nihilo* was feigned. The result is similar to the result reached in earlier sections.

The argument from the theory of emanation. To cap the construction that has been evolving so consistently, Maimonides' third argument should also prove creation alone, not creation *ex nihilo*. Unfortunately, that is not what we find.

The third argument relates to a theory of emanation supposedly propounded by Aristotle. Aristotle, as most medieval Arabic philosophers read him,[75] bore a Neoplatonic guise. He was understood, that is, to have recognized a first cause not merely of the motion of the universe but of the existence of the universe as well; and he was understood to have maintained that the first cause emanates the universe continually and eternally. Aristotelian philosophy in its Neoplatonic guise had, accordingly, to face a perennial Neoplatonic problem. It had to explain how a highly complex universe can flow out of an absolutely simple first cause, considering that, as the formula went, "from one, only one can proceed."[76]

Al-Farabi and Avicenna presented a solution to the problem, a solution that, we may conjecture, was rooted in late Greek Neoplatonism. They explained: the first cause, which consists in pure thought,[77] emanates its effect by the mere act of thinking. Since it has a single object of thought, namely itself, what it emanates is a single being; and the latter, flowing from an incorporeal being that consists in pure thought, is likewise incorporeal and consists in pure thought.[78] There is nevertheless a respect in which the incorporeal being that is emanated differs from the incorporeal first cause that emanates it. Whereas the first cause has one object of thought, the emanated being has two, namely itself and its cause.[79] And inasmuch as the second being has two objects of thought, it, through the mere act of thinking, emanates two things. It eternally emanates a celestial sphere and an additional incorporeal being consisting, once again, in pure thought. The additional incorporeal being also has two objects of thought—itself and the first cause; hence it also emanates two things, a second celestial sphere and yet another incorporeal being consisting in pure thought. The process is repeated over and over until the emanation of the active intellect, which is the last of the beings consisting in pure thought, and the sublunar corporeal region, which is the last stage of corporeal existence.[80]

Such is the scheme of emanation presented in the name of true Aristotelianism by al-Farabi and Avicenna. The scheme was subjected to a harsh critique by Ghazali[81] and, following him, by Judah ha-Levi,[82] their intent being to expose the depths of absurdity into which philosophy had fallen. Maimonides now puts forward a critique that is unmistakably dependent on Ghazali's.[83] His aim is not, however, wholly negative and destructive as was the aim of Ghazali and ha-Levi. Maimonides develops his critique into an argument for creation.

The principle at the heart of the question is ascribed by Maimonides to "Aristotle and everyone who has philosophized," and the pregnant formulation Maimonides gives the principle reads: "From a simple thing only one simple thing can *necessarily proceed.*"[84] Maimonides' argument is to be that on the theory of necessary emanation no satisfactory explanation of the actual universe is feasible. For the process of necessary emanation from a simple incorporeal cause could never give rise to a composite effect; and even granting that it could do so inasmuch as the emanated being has two thoughts, duality of thought is far removed from the manifold composition to be found in the universe.

Maimonides writes: though the hierarchy of emanated beings flowing out of the simple first cause should descend "through thousands of stages," no stage would possess a greater degree of composition than the preceding one, and therefore the "last [emanated being] . . . would be simple" exactly like the first cause. The process of necessary emanation from an absolutely simple being could, consequently, never give rise to a composite effect. But, further, even conceding that the second incorporeal being does have two objects of thought and is compound, the full complexity of the universe remains unexplained. Maimonides makes the point in several ways. He contends: (a) in necessary emanation "a correspondence always obtains between the cause and the effect" so that "a form cannot proceed necessarily from matter nor a matter from form." An incorporeal being, granting the duality of its thought, could then produce only things of the same kind, in other words, only incorporeal beings and not a corporeal celestial sphere; and corporeality in the universe remains unaccounted for. Moreover, granting for the sake of argument that an incorporeal being could emanate something corporeal, the emanation scheme of Arabic Aristotelianism is yet inadequate. For (b) a single one of the two thoughts of the supernal incorporeal beings could not emanate a full-blown celestial sphere. A celestial sphere is not unitary, but consists of four distinct factors, to wit, the matter and form of the sphere and the matter and form of the star imbedded in the sphere.[85] On the assumption of necessary emanation, the thought that is the source of the celestial sphere would have to contain four distinct aspects, to serve as the source of the four factors in the sphere.[86] Finally (c) the complexity of the sphere of the fixed stars would remain totally unaccounted for. That sphere contains stars of various types, and each type is comprised of two factors, its matter and its form. The single thought from which the sphere is assumed to emanate could not give rise to all those factors.

The actual complexity and corporeality of the universe is thus completely at odds with the principle affirming that "from a simple thing only one simple thing can necessarily proceed." The principle, as comprehended and formulated by Maimonides, appertains, however, solely to necessary emanation. An incorporeal cause acting, by contrast, not through necessity but voluntarily could produce composite as well as simple, and corporeal as well as incorporeal effects. The corporeality and the composition of the universe, which are inexplicable on the assumption that the first cause produced the universe through a process of necessary emanation, can therefore be satisfactorily explained on the contrary assumption that the first cause acted voluntarily. Since, as already seen,[87] a voluntary agent does not act eternally but only after not having acted, the world must, Maimonides concludes, be created.[88] Elsewhere Maimonides stresses that the sole conceivable kind of causation attributable to incorporeal brings is the process of emanation.[89] Here, then, he is advocating a theory of voluntary, noneternal emanation in which God initiated the process at a given moment through the exercise of His will; God switched on the emanation process, as it were, and brought the entire universe into existence.[90]

The present argument for creation,[91] unlike the previous two, endeavors to establish not merely that the first cause of the universe is possessed of free will and that the structure of the universe was created. It endeavors to establish that matter too was created; the material aspect of the universe in particular is inexplicable on the assumption that the world was emanated necessarily.

5. *Summary.* The three possible positions on the issue of creation and eternity distinguished by Maimonides represent three possible beliefs that Maimonides himself may have held. Maimonides may have believed in the eternity of the world, hence in a deity bereft of free will and bound by necessity. He may have believed in creation from a preexistent matter, hence in a deity possessed of free will and capable, in principle, of intervening in the universe and performing miracles. Or else he genuinely believed in creation *ex nihilo,* hence in a deity possessed, again, of free will and capable of intervening in the universe, with the added detail that God can perform even the supreme miracle of creating matter out of nothing.

Aid for uncovering Maimonides' esoteric beliefs is furnished solely by his statements on contradictions and by the contradictions discoverable in the *Guide.* In each pair of contradictory propositions, Maimonides writes, one proposition is to be deemed incorrect, its function being to hide his esoteric belief from the masses; the other is to be deemed correct, its function being to disclose the esoteric belief to the select few. The contradictions that are discoverable in Maimonides' discussion of creation involve two of the three possible positions on the issue: creation from a preexistent matter, and creation *ex nihilo.* According to the rule set down by Maimonides regarding contradictions, his esoteric position, if he has such a position, would have to be one of the two. And since creation *ex nihilo* is an exoteric, not an esoteric, position, if Maimonides does have an esoteric position on the issue of creation and eternity, it could only be the doctrine of creation from a preexistent matter.

The contradictions we discovered were these: Maimonides asserts that the doctrine of creation from a preexistent matter is as unacceptable as the doctrine of eternity; but later he concedes that the doctrine of creation from a preexistent matter is, from a theological standpoint, no less acceptable than creation *ex nihilo.* The contradiction would appear to indicate that Maimonides secretly countenanced the belief in creation from a preexistent matter. Then Maimonides asserts that the positions on prophecy are "like" the positions on creation; but he assigns designations to the respective positions which do not match. The logic of that contradiction would indicate that Maimonides secretly did embrace the belief in creation from a preexistent matter. In the course of presenting arguments in support of his own position, Maimonides describes his position merely as creation, despite his earlier insistence on the qualification that creation took place from nothing. The indication here would appear to be that Maimonides' position was simply creation, without the *ex nihilo* qualification. Finally, Maimonides' first two arguments in support of his position are designed to establish creation and no more despite his earlier insistence that his position is creation *ex nihilo*. The indication would once again appear to be that Maimonides' true position is creation without the *ex nihilo* qualification.

Maimonides' third argument for creation diverges, however, from the pattern. It proves not merely creation but creation *ex nihilo;* it thus does prove the doctrine Maimonides had at the outset characterized as the position of Scripture and as his own position. The temptation might be to dismiss the argument as feigned, as a stratagem in the enterprise of concealment. But the temptation is not easily justified; for whatever we may think of Maimonides' arguments for creation, he surely seems to advance all three of them in earnest. In each instance, notions that earlier thinkers had employed for other purposes are carefully reworked by him into a new argument for creation. A wily philosopher with esoteric beliefs might, as a stratagem, rehearse familiar and commonplace arguments that run counter to his secret position. We can hardly conceive, though, of a philosopher's taking pains to fashion and publish brand new arguments that undermine his position.

The evidence, to conclude, is not unambiguous and might permit either of two portraits of Maimonides. Maimonides may have secretly countenanced or embraced the doctrine of creation from a preexistent matter. If so, he believed—or countenanced the belief—that matter is eternal and that at a given moment God, through an act of will, emanated the incorporeal part of the universe; the incorporeal part of the universe would immediately organize matter into the physical part of the universe. In conflict with this interpretation—a form of the narrow estericist approach—is Maimonides' third argument for creation, which seeks to establish the creation of the entire universe, including matter. On the alternative portrait, Maimonides genuinely did believe in creation *ex nihilo*. The various contradictions we discovered in his discussion of creation would not be deliberate and intended to conceal an esoteric belief. They would be inadvertent; and Maimonides would have been less immune to error and carelessness than he and his readers through the centuries have imagined. In any event, the decision between the two interpretations does not affect Maimonides' concept of God. On both interpretations, Maimonides believed that God is possessed of free will and capable, in principle, of intervening in the universe.

As for the thesis of the thoroughgoing estericists, it is refuted by the logic of the contradictions, since none of the contradictions in Maimonides' discussion involve the doctrine of the eternity of the world.

NOTES

1. *Guide for the Perplexed,* II, 25.
2. The first four of the seven reasons relate to contradictions in Scripture and Talmudic literature. When a scriptural metaphor is taken literally, for example, it may contradict another statement in Scripture. And Talmudic statements sometimes contradict one another because they stem from different authors or from a single author who changed his mind over a period of time.

The sixth of the seven reasons for contradictions is error due to poor reasoning.

3. Cf. Aristotle, *Metaphysics* V, 1, 1013a, 2-4.

4. *Guide*, Introduction.

5. S. Munk, *Le Guide des Egarés* (Paris, 1856-1866), I, 28, note 1, finds one. Also cf. Shem Tob Falaquera, *Moreh ha-Moreh* (Pressburg, 1837), p. 10.

6. *Guide*, Introduction.

7. Examples: (a) Maimonides speaks of divine providence in language indicating that God rewards the righteous and punishes the wicked. But then he states that the providence a person enjoys depends solely upon the degree to which the person develops his intellect. It follows that only men of intellect enjoy providence; and punishment is negative, consisting in the failure to enjoy the providence that men of intellect enjoy. Cf. *Guide*, III, 17; 51. (b) Maimonides speaks of divine intervention in the universe. But then he advances the proposition that all future miracles were built into the universe at the time of creation, "pre-programmed," as it were. Cf. *Guide*, II, 29. (c) Maimonides frequently speaks of God's acting in the universe, but then makes clear that God acts only indirectly, through intermediaries. Cf. *Guide*, II, 6; 48. In each of these instances, the second of the two doctrines presumably is Maimonides' esoteric belief. It is to be noted that in all the instances, the esoteric doctrines are just superficially hidden and are easily discoverable through a careful reading of the *Guide*. In that respect, they contrast with the esoteric doctrines that thoroughgoing esotericists expect to find in Maimonides; for those esoteric doctrines, if indeed present in the *Guide*, are truly hidden.

The following circumstance is to be noted as well: the system that the thoroughgoing esotericists undertake to discover in Maimonides is identical, in its most basic lines, with the systems of al-Farabi, Avicenna, and Averroes. The three Arabic Aristotelians, as it happens, also preached esotericism; they insisted that their systems are reserved for the chosen few and accordingly should not be divulged to the majority. Yet, in reality, al-Farabi, Avicenna, and Averroes made no effort at all to conceal their systems. The thoroughgoing esotericists would therefore have us understand that Maimonides embraced a system like that of al-Farabi, Avicenna, and Averroes, while going far beyond them in his efforts to hide it. The one Arabic philosopher who undoubtedly harbored truly esoteric beliefs was a thinker on the conservative wing, to wit, Ghazali.

8. Particularly, Joseph ibn Kaspi and Shem Tob ibn Shem Tob.

9. Cf. L. Strauss, "The Literary Character of the *Guide for the Perplexed*," reprinted in his *Persecution and the Art of Writing* (Glencoe, 1952), pp. 38-94. Also cf. J. Bekker, *Sodo shel Moreh Nebukim* (Tel Aviv, 1957); J. Glicker, "Ha-Be'aya ha-Modalit ba-Pilosophia shel ha-Rambam," *'Iyyun,* X (1959), 177-191; A. Nuriel, "Hiddush ha-'Olam o Qadmuto 'al pi ha-Rambam," *Tarbiz*, XXXIII (1964), 372-387; S. Pines, "Spinoza's *Tractatus Theologico-Politicus*, Maimonides, and Kant," *Scripta Hierosolymitana*, XX (1968), 3-45.

10. See the works cited in the previous note.

11. *Guide*, II, 25; cf. II, 21.

12. Aristotle, *De Generatione et Corruptione* II, 11, 337b, 35 ff.; *Metaphysics* VI, 2, 1026b, 27.

13. *Guide*, II, 21; 25.

14. *Guide*, Introduction.

15. Strauss, "Literary Character of the Guide," pp. 68-73. Stated summarily, Strauss's rule is that the more hidden a contradictory proposition is, the more likely its being Maimonides' genuine esoteric belief.

16. *Guide*, II, 1.

17. Maimonides takes up the Platonic position before the Aristotelian position, but I have reversed the order.

18. *Guide*, II, 13 (1).

19. *Guide*, II, 13 (3).

20. *Guide*, II, 13 (2).

21. *Guide*, II, 13 (1).

22. *Guide*, II, 25.

23. *Guide*, II, 17-18.

24. Strauss, "Literary Character of the Guide," pp. 83-84. Strauss is dealing with other instances of Maimonides' use of the expression "our position," but he presumably had the present instance in mind as well.

25. Joseph ibn Kaspi, *'Amude Kesef*, ed. S. Werbluner (Frankfurt, 1848), pp. 101, 104.

26. Cf. *Guide*, II, 13 (end).

27. Ibid.

28. See Maimonides' three arguments in Section 4.

29. *Guide*, II, 25.

30. See above, at note 14.

31. *Jāhilīya* properly means "heathendom"; cf. Munk's note to his translation, *ad locum*. But I have followed the translation of Ibn Tibbon, who understands Maimonides to have used the term *jāhilīya* as the plural of *jāhil*, "ignoramus." Two considerations support Ibn Tibbon's translation: (a) In *Guide*, II, 11 (end), Maimonides contrasts the *jāhilīya* specifically with the "wise"; cf. S. Pines' note to his translation of the *Guide* (Chicago, 1963), p. 276. (b) According to the passage in *Guide*, II, 32, which we are now considering, the *jāhilīya* believe in the existence of God; thus they are not in fact heathens. Both *Guide*, II, 11, and II, 32, indicate that the *jāhilīya* are primarily Gentiles, and that Jews who have acquired the attribute have done so under Gentile influence.

32. *Guide*, II, 32.

33. Ibid.

34. See H. Davidson, "Alfarabi and Avicenna on the Active Intellect," *Viator*, III (1972), 175-177.

35. *Guide*, II, 32; 36. For Maimonides' source, see the preceding reference.

36. *Guide*, II, 32.

37. Ibid.

38. Isaac Abravanel, *Commentary on Guide*, II, 32.

39. See note 27.

40. See note 6.

41. See above at note 14.

42. See above at note 36.

43. For the scope of the concept *ignoramus*, see *Guide*, II, 11.

44. See above, end of Section 2.

45. *Guide*, II, 16; cf. I, 71.

46. Cf. Aristotle, *Posterior Analytics* I, 2; Maimonides, *Millot ha-Higgayon*, chap. 8.

47. *Guide*, II, 15; 16; 22 (end).

48. Very few quotations from Aristotle appear in the *Guide* in any other connection. Cf. Pines' translation of the *Guide*, introduction, pp. *lxi-lxii*.

49. *Guide*, II, 15; 19. Judah ha-Levi, it may be noted, also maintained that the

issue of creation and eternity is not amenable to demonstration and suggested that such had been Aristotle's view as well. Cf. *Kuzari*, I, 65-67; H. Wolfson, "The Platonic, Aristotelian and Stoic Theories of Creation in Hallevi and Maimonides," reprinted in his *Studies in the History of Philosophy and Religion* (Cambridge, 1973), p. 244.

50. *Guide*, II, 16.

51. *Guide*, II, 19.

52. See note 6.

53. See note 27.

54. Cf. H. Davidson, "Arguments from the Concept of Particularization in Arabic Philosophy," *Philosophy East and West*, XVIII (1968), 305-314.

55. Aristotle, *Metaphysics* XII, 8; Maimonides, *Guide*, II, 4; 9. In order to explain the course traveled by the planets around the earth, the planets were assumed to be imbedded in spheres that revolve along the surface of other spheres, the latter, in their turn, revolving along the surface of still other spheres.

56. Cf. note 65.

57. Maimonides observes that Aristotle attempted to draw up such a theory in *De Caelo* II.

58. Maimonides also calls it a "particularizing factor." See reference in note 54.

59. *Guide*, II, 19. Cf. also II, 24.

60. Maimonides cites a statement to the same effect in al-Farabi's commentary on the *Physics*.

61. *Guide*, II, 19.

62. Cf. note 12.

63. *Guide*, II, 19.

64. Rudolph Otto interprets God's speech in the Book of Job in the same vein; cf. Otto, *The Idea of the Holy* (Oxford, 1950), pp. 78-80.

65. *De Caelo* I, 2.

66. *Guide*, II, 19.

67. Such was Avicenna's reading of Aristotle; Averroes, by contrast, rejected the notion that the spheres contain the distinction of matter and form. See H. Wolfson, *Crescas* (Cambridge, 1929), pp. 594-598, for citations.

68. The previous argument focused on the movement of the several spheres whereas this argument focuses on the forms of the several spheres; but the movements were understood to be an expression of the forms. The present argument is not given prominence by Maimonides. It appears as a sort of footnote to the third of the three arguments for creation.

69. As cited by Simplicius, *Commentary on the Physics*, ed. H. Diels (Berlin, 1895), p. 1329. Philoponus contends that the matter of the celestial region should behave as the matter of the sublunar region does, continually shedding its forms and adopting new ones. He advances the contention in the course of a proof of creation; but his proof is completely different from Maimonides'. Cf. H. Davidson, "John Philoponus as a Source of Medieval Islamic and Jewish Proofs of Creation," *Journal of the American Oriental Society*, LXXXIX (1969), 364.

70. Ghazali, *Maqāsid al-Falāsifa* (Cairo, n.d.), p. 247. Ghazali there explains that the matter of each sphere must be unique; for otherwise the spheres would continually change their forms. Cf. next note. (I could not find the theory in Avicenna's Arabic works but did find it in his *Dānesh Nāmeh*; see *Le Livre de Science*, trans. M. Achena and H. Massé [Paris, 1955], p. 193.)

71. Maimonides apparently means that God produces each of the spheres and

stars by permanently assigning—through an act of will—a unique form to a portion of the matter common to all the spheres or all the stars. He might, however, mean that God has, through an act of will, created each sphere and each star in a matter unique to itself.

72. *Guide*, II, 22.

73. See notes 50 and 51.

74. See notes 18 and 27.

75. Averroes was the notable exception.

76. Avicenna, *Shifā': Ilāhīyāt* (Cairo, 1960), p. 405; Ghazali, *Maqāsid*, p. 218; *idem, Tahāfut al-Falāsifa*, ed. M. Bouyges (Beirut, 1927), III, §29; translation of same: *Averroes' Tahāfut al-Tahāfut*, trans. S. van den Bergh (London, 1954), I, 104. Cf. Plotinus, *Enneads*, V, 1, 6; V, 2, 1; V, 3, 15. In Avicenna and Ghazali, the term for "proceed" is *yūjad* or *yasdur*.

77. Aristotle, *Metaphysics* XII, 9. Plotinus maintained that the first cause, the One, is above thought; exactly what he meant thereby is, however, open to interpretation.

78. The emanated incorporeal beings are called "intelligences" and they are simply Aristotle's movers of the sphere with added functions.

79. In Avicenna's version, each intelligence has three objects of thought. Each intelligence, in his system, is *possibly existent by virtue of itself, necessarily existent by virtue of its cause*. Accordingly, he explained that each intelligence has the following objects of thought: itself insofar as it is a possible being; itself insofar as it is a necessary being; the first cause. Those three aspects in the intelligence give rise to the body of a sphere, the soul of a sphere, and the next intelligence in the series. See the references in note 80.

80. Al-Farabi, *Al-Madīna al-Fādila*, ed. F. Dieterici (Leiden, 1895), p. 19; translation: *Der Musterstaat*, trans. F. Dieterici (Leiden, 1900), with pages of the Arabic original indicated; Avicenna, *Shifā': Ilāhīyāt*, p. 406; Ghazali, *Maqāsid*, pp. 219-220. Cf. Davidson, "The Active Intellect in the *Cuzari* and Hallevi's Theory of Causality," *Revue des études juives* CXXXI (1972), 356-357.

81. Ghazali, *Tahāfut*, III, §§39 ff.

82. Ha-Levi, *Kuzari*, IV, 25; Davidson, "The Active Intellect in the *Cuzari*," p. 358.

83. Ghazali advances six separate objections but the two central points are the same as those to be made by Maimonides.

84. The Arabic term which I have translated as "necessarily proceed" is *lazama*.

85. Cf. notes 66 and 67.

86. As it happens, one of ha-Levi's criticisms was that each succeeding intelligence would have more objects of thought than the preceding one (since there are more entities above it) and therefore should have a larger number of emanated products. Cf. *Kuzari*, IV, 25.

87. See note 12.

88. *Guide*, II, 22.

89. *Guide*, II, 12.

90. Maimonides is presupposing his proofs of the existence of God which established that the entire universe, matter and form, have a cause.

91. It is again a nondemonstrative argument; it does not move from true and certain premises to an indisputable conclusion but rather exposes the implausibility of the doctrine of eternity and the attendant plausibility of creation *ex nihilo*.

3

Rabbinical Authority and Authorization in the Middle Ages

Jacob Katz

Judaism of the Middle Ages conceived of itself as a direct and legitimate continuation of the Judaism of ancient times. This conception prevailed in the face of the Christian church's contention that, with the appearance of Jesus the Messiah, Christianity superseded Judaism. One of the central arguments in proof of the Christian contention was the discontinuation of many Jewish religious institutions. How could Judaism maintain its validity when the Temple was in ruins, the priestly function of daily sacrifice—and thus the continuous expiation of people's sins—unfulfilled? The loss of political independence and the reduced status of Jewish juridical institutions reinforced the contention, exegetically based on Genesis 49: 10, that the diminution of power entails the revocation of divine election.[1] Jews had, as we know, their answers to the challenges of their opponents.[2] I am not concerned here, however, with how they defended their position, but rather with how they reacted internally to the dissipation of their juridical authority.

Tradition had it that in Biblical and post-Biblical times the courts functioning in Israel—if not all of them, at least the more important and central ones—were composed of authorized, ordained judges. These judges received their authority through ordination by someone who had himself been ordained—the chain of ordination going back to Joshua, who received his ordination from Moses, the fountain of authority as the recipient of the divine revelation. When this concept of the uninterrupted chain of tradition arose is unknown;[3] the problem does not at any rate concern us here. What is certain is that the ordination, the *Minnuy* or *Semikah,* was in force during Tannaitic times and well into the Talmudic period and perhaps even beyond. It remained, however, the prerogative of the Palestinian scholars or of the central Palestinian institution, the Patriarchate.[4] By virtue of ordination, the function of the judges had been invested with religious sanction, the discontinuation of which, whenever it took place, must be regarded as a major change.

In order to assess the practical consequences of that change, we have to recall what the formal prerogatives of the ordained judges were. Only an ordained person could be appointed as a member of the Sanhedrin, whether to the Great Sanhedrin composed of seventy-one and convoked for special functions or to that of twenty-three authorized to judge capital cases. The court of three handling private litigation and the like, had a more comprehensive jurisdiction if composed of ordained judges. It could administer Biblical and oral law in all its details, including what is defined by the Talmudic term *Dine Kenassot,* imposition of fines prescribed by the law beyond the restitution of damages done or obligations incurred.[5] There was also another, very important function of the court of three, of a practical ritualistic nature, and restricted to ordained judges: the administration of the Jewish calendar. There being then no fixed calendar, the length of the month had been determined from case to case on the basis of the testimony of witnesses who had observed the new moon. The investigation of the witnesses and the ensuing declaration of the beginning of the new months, as described in the Mishnah, could only be executed by a court of three ordained judges.[6] Similarly, the intercalation of a thirteenth month that became necessary in order to make up for the difference between the lunar and solar years was restricted to a court of the ordained.[7]

As far as the practical functions that depended on the ordination are concerned these were either discontinued or partly or entirely replaced by some surrogate. The Sanhedrin ceased its operations at the latest with the destruction of the Temple. As ordination was restricted to Palestine, *Dine Kenassot* in the Diaspora communities could be implemented only if a scholar ordained in Palestine happened to be present. As this was highly impractical, the courts and the communities learned how to live without the implementation of these laws, either declaring them to be inapplicable or introducing a juridic device to achieve the law's intent. Instead of directly imposing a fine, the person to be penalized was put under ban until such time as he "voluntarily" paid his debt.[8] This practice replaced the direct administration of fines in post-Talmudic times also in Palestine.[9] The administration of the calendar in the manner described became unnecessary as well as unfeasible, the latter because the fixing of the length of the months and the years was not all that was required. The decision of the court had to be conveyed from month to month and from year to year to the Diaspora communities by some system of communication—by fire signs from one mountain to the other or by sending out emissaries with the information.[10] This could be accomplished as long as the Palestinian institutions were somewhat free politically and backed by a substantial community economically. As is well known, this ceased to be the case in the fourth century with the growing influence of the Christian church in Palestine.[11] But the ad hoc fixation of the calendar was by then unnecessary, for in the interim Jewish scholars had learned the method of astronomical calculation and most probably employed such knowledge already at the time the traditional fixation was still practiced. When this traditional practice became impossible or too burdensome, the astronomic calendar was adopted as the only basis of fixation. Contemporary sources have only slight references to this not unimportant transition, but on the authority of a later tradition it is attributed to the Patriarch Hillel II (330-365).[12]

II

The solution of the practical problems deriving from the discontinuation of the *Semikah* was, however, not accepted as an equivalent substitute for it. Not only was the absence of the Sanhedrin perceived as a deficiency, but even the impossibility of implementing *Dine Kenassot* was something to be deplored, as expressed by Maimonides, for example, in his famous suggestion that the *Semikah* will possibly be restored prior to the coming of the Messiah.[13] When sixteenth-century scholars, moved by the hope of the approaching Messianic age, wished to act upon Maimonidan suggestion, they pointed to the reintroduction of *Dine Kenassot* as the most important reform to be gained as if rectifying by it a great deficiency in the life of the nation.[14] Obviously the discontinuation of any part of the ancient constitution, regardless of its practical relevance, was regarded as a sign of the spiritual exile of the Jewish nation. Thus even the introduction of the astronomic calendar, in practical terms an immense improvement, could not be acknowledged as such. It was rather taken as an expedient to be relinquished when circumstances permitted, that is, when the *Semikah* in the Messianic age or, according to Maimonides, in preparation for it, will once again be reinstituted. Indeed, Maimonides, in order to legitimate the astronomic calendar for the period of the exile, constructed an oral tradition according to which the use of the calendrical system is prescribed as long as the absence of an ordained court prevents the functioning of the ad hoc fixation of the months and the years.[15]

There is, however, one exception to this evaluation of the relative status of the two systems: the theory of Saadia Gaon, evolved, as we know, in response to the Karaites' criticism of the Rabbanites for their deviation from the tradition of old. The fixation of the calendar by observation, it was pointed out to the Karaites,[16] would lead to utter confusion in the life of the community, because there was no central institution to regulate it; but we must realize that such practical considerations could not pass as a justification for changing the tradition. No doubt the Karaite criticism carried weight with the more thoughtful among the Rabbanites, and a solution, to be effective, had to be acceptable also within the Rabbanites' frame of reference. Saadia's theory was meant to be such a solution. The Gaon contended that there was never a break in the rabbinic tradition, for the astronomically based calendar has always been the guide to the fixation of the months and years, while the observation of the moon and other natural phenomena for the intercalation of a leap year, as well as the formal announcement by the court, was never more than a formality, a ritual.[17] This theory was at such obvious odds with much of the data reported in Talmudic literature that later critics of Saadia—Hai Gaon and Maimonides—doubted that it was meant to be more than an apologetic device scarcely taken seriously by its author.[18] Such a view, however, underestimates the lengths to which rationalist exegesis would go in explaining away written sources when the justification of current practice seemed to demand it. The unbridled readiness of Saadia to follow the line of rationalist reasoning is, in addition, well attested by his attitude in general,[19] and particularly by the position he assumed in connection with the fixation of the calendar in the course of the Ben-Meir controversy.

I shall review the basic facts of this by now much belabored subject, which is still in need of clarification on at least one important count.[20] For some five hundred years, that is, from the middle of the fourth until the first decades of the tenth century, the new system of fixation, as far as we know, operated without a hitch. Then in the year 921 a controversy arose between Aaron ben Meir, the head of the Academy in Jerusalem (or, according to a recent reading, Meir the head of the Academy in Jerusalem, and his son Aaron[21]) and the Babylonian schools represented by Saadia—at that time only a newcomer from Egypt without official status. The difference concerned the fixation of the following year's calendar. The Palestinian scholar let it be known that the months Kislev and Heshvan of the year 922 would be defective, consisting in twenty-nine days, and the festivals would have to be fixed accordingly. The Babylonian calculation, however, put the two key months at thirty days, with the festivals postponed by two days. We know exactly on what the difference in calculation turned. Ben Meir and the Babylonians had different deadlines for the appearance of the new moon under certain circumstances—though both possessed the text of the *'Arbah She'arim* that contained the rules of the calendarial system—and from this the differing calculations resulted. What we do not know is how the original divergence on the deadline arose. This lack of information has opened the way for hypotheses and speculations. Some historians simply assumed that with the relative strength of the Babylonian schools the fixation of the calendar had become by then a function administered by them and that the controversy arose because Ben Meir wished to recover the authority previously held by the institutions of the Holy Land. This theory is still being repeated in popular presentations of the issue,[22] but has been rejected by most modern scholars. For to accept it means to impute to Ben Meir a tampering with authoritative traditions, implying a conscious misleading of the community for an ulterior motive on a matter of religious consequence—an accusation that was voiced by Saadia only at the end of the conflict when both parties dropped all restraint.[23] So scholars such as Epstein, Bornstein, and Cassutto tried to find the key to the divergence rather in the assumption that when the system of calculation was transmitted from Palestine to Babylonia it was not yet complete in all its details.[24] Thus two different solutions could be evolved for the special case that arose in 921. This explanation, however, is at variance with two sources pertaining to the controversy, one published by Jacob Mann in his *Jews in Egypt*,[25] the other already by Solomon Schechter in his *Saadyana*.[26] The first of the two indicates that in the year 835 the Babylonian school, although well versed in the rules of calculations, awaited the decision of the Palestinian Academy in all cases of doubt. The second source, written at the start of the Ben-Meir controversy, most probably by Saadia himself,[27] states that in former times the Babylonians used to apply to the Palestinian scholars for the fixation of the calendar, "for they were not versed in the *Seder-ha-'Ibbur* (the rules of calculation) like them." But "many years ago," the source continues, Babylonian scholars went to Eretz Israel and acquainted themselves with all the details of the calculation, and after that time were accustomed to prepare their own calendar, which, based upon the same rules, always concurred with that of the Palestinians. Now, if we take this statement about the visit of the Babylonian scholars to Palestine sometime between 835 and 921 as a historical fact,[28] it is impossible to account for the divergence of the two schools without attributing to one of them an alteration in the text of the *'Arbah She-'arim*,[29] or at least a conscious deviation from the accepted tradition. I am not at all sure, however, that we have to accept this statement at face value. Saadia fails to mention a source for his information, nor does the report contain any date, name, or place that would lend the story a semblance of historicity. The whole story is possibly no more than the result of reasoning. The author was faced with the fact of the Babylonian scholars' possession of the system of the calendar while, according to Talmudic tradition, this was originally the exclusive secret of the Palestinians. An independent development of the system in Babylonia, or a gradual transmission through informal contact between the two schools, had to be ruled out, for this would have weakened the reliability of the Babylonian version in comparison with the original Palestinian one. The only satisfactory answer was that the Babylonians received their knowledge through direct, almost official, communication with the Palestinians. Thus the story of the meeting between the Babylonian and Palestinian scholars could in this way have arisen. Such quasi-historical statements, which in fact are only the logical conclusions of their authors, are quite common in medieval literature. A critical view of them is called for by modern historiography.

It is thus not impossible to assume that as far as the rules of calculation were concerned both parties relied upon their respective traditions, and we need not suspect either of them of studied innovation. There was, however, an innovation involved in the controversy with regard to the authority of the two schools, but in this connection Saadia, and not Ben Meir, must figure as the revolutionary. The special standing of the land of Israel in matters of the calendar was, as mentioned above, a well-established principle. Though the introduction of the fixed calendar divested this principle of much of its practical significance, the principle has not been discarded, and the Palestinian scholars in announcing the dates of the calendar might have felt they were giving the fixation its sanctification. Such a conception could have found an expression or support in the ceremony that surrounded the

fixation of the calendar, proclaimed as it was on the Mount of Olives on behalf of the president and the members of the Palestinian academy.[30] We
ought to recall here that this was later exactly the theory of Maimonides,
who in his *Sefer ha-Mizvot* goes so far as to say that if there were no Jews
remaining in Eretz Israel to announce the new month, the Jewish calendar
would lose its validity and the observance of festivals would be of no
avail.[31] On the basis of this special standing of the land of Israel Ben Meir
made the claim that also in the case of conflicting views on the exact fixation
the Palestinian authority has the prerogative. Saadia, on the other hand, in
reacting to Ben Meir's claim, assailed the basic principle on which it was
based. He asserted that the Palestinian prerogative lasted only as long as the
method of observation was in use. Even then it concerned only the intercalation of the leap month, and this for practical reasons, for only in Palestine was the natural phenomenon—the coincidence of Passover with the
spring—in evidence.[32] The fixation of the month, on the other hand, depended on acquaintance with the astronomic rules, and these indeed were
formerly in the possession of the Palestinian scholars. Even then their privilege had only a practical basis. Once the knowledge reached the Babylonians—in the way which Saadia inferred logically it did—they were entitled to make use of it, as indeed was their wont as far back as anybody
could remember.[33] Saadia dismissed from the procedure of the calendar
fixation any notion of irrationality, in full accord with his stand on this
matter when defending it against the Karaites.

III

Saadia's postulation of expertise as the exclusive source of the scholars'
authority was certainly not shared by the Geonim, the ranks of whom
Saadia later joined. The authority of the Babylonian academies and their
heads, the Geonim, was sustained, or at least strongly supported by their
claim to represent an uninterrupted tradition which hailed from earliest
times. This claim was continually demonstrated by the formal authorization of the Gaon, to which the term *Semikah* has been applied. Institution-
ally this *Semikah* differed from its Palestinian counterpart. For there ordination had been granted to students as an indication of their worthiness to
assume some office, while in Babylonia the *Semikah* meant appointment to
an office invested by some authority. Still, the ordination carried with it a
transferable charisma, which in the Palestinian case depended on the chain
of transmission from person to person, in the Babylonian on the incum-
bency of the same office. That, in spite of this difference, the Babylonian
ordination has been identified with that of the Palestinian, is evident not
only by the use of the same term but also by the attempt to harmonize the
Babylonian practice with the divergent Talmudic tradition. For according
to that tradition (*Sanhedrin* 14a) "there is no ordination outside the land of
Israel." This objection is mentioned by Samuel ben Ali of Baghdad at the
end of the Geonic period and refuted by him through a typical qualification

of the Talmudic tradition: that is, the impossibility of ordination outside the land of Israel relates only to the implementation of *Dine Kenassot* but for other purposes the *Semikah* is valid.[34] Samuel ben Ali indicates that this qualification had been the accepted answer to the above mentioned objection in the Babylonian academies ever since.[35] This means that the Babylonians defended their *Semikah* by attributing to it the same dignity as the Palestinian, despite its limited practical application.

Jacob Mann assumed that Samuel ben Ali's defense of the *Semikah* is a direct reference to a letter by his rival the Exilarch of Baghdad, Daniel b. Hisdai, written thirty years earlier.[36] This letter concerned the authority of the Exilarch over the Jewish community of Egypt, which was formerly subject to the Geonim of Palestine.[37] In that letter the Talmudic sentence "no *Semikah* outside of the Land of Israel" is indeed quoted.[38] Yet, as Mann observed, this quotation is flagrantly contradicted by the Exilarch's report on his having himself ordained Netanel from Fustat, confirming him as president of the Jewish court in Egypt. Mann disposes of this contradiction by taking the term "ordain" to be a "stylistic flourish."[39] This interpretation ignores, however, the main thrust of the letter, which stresses the weight of the authority conferred upon Netanel by the Exilarch. The latter is far from contesting the validity of the act he is engaged in practising, and the phrase "no *Semikah* outside the land of Israel" appears in a casual aside correctly characterized by Mann as a mere "historical retrospect."[40] The crucial sentence in this letter concerning the problem of the *Semikah* is the statement

כי יסוד הסמיכה בנוי בהיות הנסמך חכם דורו ומנוקה מכל

רשע לפני צורו ויהיו הסומכים בעלי מנין נסמכים מפי

סומכים כי סמיכת יחיד אינה סמיכה,

that the ordination in practice depends upon the worthiness of the ordained and the authority of those who confer it, who themselves must be ordained persons. These persons can exercise their authority only as a collective; no single person, even if ordained, is entitled to arrogate this right.[41] This is a clear reference to the Exilarch's claim to possess with his court the prerogative of ordination, contrary to the counterclaim of the Gaon, who is regarded as a single person only. In conformity with this conception of the procedure of authorization the letter described the ordination of Netanel as having taken place "in the presence of our princes and worthies, the whole community joining in with amen."[42] To prove the denial of one man's right to exercise the *Semikah* the Exilarch quotes the Mishnah (*Sanhedrin* I, 1),[43] according to which "ordination needs three," to indicate that even when the original Palestinian *Semikah* was still practiced it could not be conferred by a single person. This quotation causes him to drift into his "historical retrospect," in the course of which he also cites the phrase "no *Semikah* outside the land of Israel." This phase clearly refers, as does the whole passage, to the ordination of Mishnaic times and to it alone. Accordingly he enumerates

the prerogatives of the original *Semikah*, which are *Dine Kenassot*, the fixation of the calendar, and the right to blow the shofar on Rosh ha-Shanah
even if it falls on a Sabbath.[44] These prerogatives, however, are by his time
obsolete. The date of the diminution of the authority of the *Semikah* is
equated with the disfunctioning of the Sanhedrin in its last location, which
was according to the Talmudic tradition Tiberias.[45] Diminution of authority is, however, not tantamount to its abolition. Far from contradicting the
contention of Samuel ben Ali the Exilarch takes it for granted that the contemporary *Semikah* is a restricted but still legitimate residue of the old institution. In another context the Exilarch seems to predict the disfunctioning of
the *Semikah* in his own generation. He speaks of the interruption of the
chain of ordination in Palestine in his own time through the death of the
Gaon Daniel.[46] This does not refer to the abrogation of the old *Semikah*, as
has been misunderstood by Aptowitzer and others,[47] but the canceling of
the office of the Gaonite or, rather, the denial of the authority of Daniel's
successors. The ordination of the latter is contested by the Exilarch because
of their unworthiness or because of the lack of authority of those from
whom they received it or probably because of both.[48] According to Mann's
historical reconstruction it was Samuel ben Ali from whom the contested
ordination of the successors of Daniel was derived.[49] At any rate what
emerges from the correct reading of these sources is that there was no controversy between the adversaries concerned over the validity of a restricted
kind of *Semikah* but rather that there was a conflict on the question of who
has the right to exercise it.

IV

The problem of religious authority shifted considerably when, in the
wake of political events and processes, the centers of Jewish communal life
shifted to the Mediterranean countries—North Africa, Italy, Spain, and
even France and Germany. The scholars of those countries could not base
their authority on either a chain of personal linkage or the continuity of
their institutions. The *Semikah* as the means of legitimation of authority
based on Talmudic tradition nonetheless played a certain role. Rabbi Yehuda al-Bargeloni in his *Sefer ha-Shetarot* describes the procedure of ordination.[50] His description is reminiscent of, but not identical to, the procedure of Daniel, the Exilarch of Baghdad. The ordination is here conferred by
"the elders of the community, or the elders of the Synagogue and the house
of study."[51] The purpose of the *Semikah* is not direct appointment to an office but testimony handed down in a writ that the incumbent is worthy to be
admitted to the position of judges and the "counsel of the learned" (*sodot
ha-haberim*).[52] The direct consequence of the ordination is that its incumbent thereafter bears the title of rabbi and joins the elite of the learned,
adopting their demeanor in clothing and conduct. It is a kind of initiation of
the student into the ranks of the scholars. Besides this ordination by the representatives of the community we find also the authorization of outstanding

disciples by their master. Rabbi Isaac Alfasi is said to have ordained before his death his pupil Joseph ibn Migash,[53] and the latter is said to have done the same to one otherwise unknown scholar.[54] How long each of the two types of ordination continued to be practiced in Spain we do not know. Toward the close of the fourteenth century the eminent Sephardic Talmudist, Rabbi Isaac Perfet, characterized it as an indigenous Ashkenazi custom unknown in Spain except by hearsay.[55] It stands to reason that the institutions had indeed fallen into desuetude at an early stage in the history of Sephardic Jewry, while in Ashkenaz—in France and Germany—it either never ceased to function or was instituted anew some time in the twelfth or thirteenth century.[56] By the fourteenth century it was the accepted custom in these countries that the master granted his capable disciples a *Semikah* testifying to the worthiness of the student to serve as a master and rabbi. What made ordination of students a necessity in France and Germany, either as a restored or a novel institution, was the weakness of communal organization. The community there was not accustomed to appoint salaried officers—with the possible exception of the Hazan[57]—but resorted to the services of the learned who dwelt among them. In earlier generations such services were rendered gratuitously, but later those like the administering of an oath, a divorce, *Halizah*, and the like, became a source of income for certain scholars. The rabbinate became, at least partly, professionalized. Naturally, it also became an object of competition between rivals and open to abuse.

Some kind of control to maintain standards was certainly called for. The ordination, the *Semikah*, was found to be an appropriate means to this end.[58] If this generally accepted explanation for the development in Ashkenaz is true, it contains at the same time an explanation of the converse course of events in Spain. The Sephardic communities succeeded in evolving at an early stage of their history a well-functioning organization. Their rabbis were salaried officers chosen from among the Talmudically trained by the discretion of the lay leaders. These lacked no opportunity to ascertain the qualities of the candidates; they followed their own judgment or relied upon the recommendation of established authorities in the field.[59] Under these circumstances no formal means of authorization by the rabbinical hierarchy along the lines of the Ashkenazi *Semikah* became necessary, and even the traces of the tradition that reached it from Babylonia and Palestine disappeared. It was due to the peculiar conditions in Ashkenaz that the *Semikah* attained there its unprecedented status and dissemination.

But what about the formal justification of the *Semikah*? It is interesting that for many generations we do not hear about this question, except from Sephardic authorities who had either a limited interest in the institution or none at all. Rabbi Yehuda al-Bargeloni dismissed the possible identification of the contemporary usage with that of Talmudic times on account of the dictum that there is no *Semikah* outside the land of Israel. The current *Semikah* is no more than *Zeher le-Semikah*, a mere vestige of the former institution.[60] Similar was the trend of thought of Rabbi Isaac Perfet, the Ribash, who as late as the end of the fourteenth century was the first to grant the institution more than fleeting notice. How this came about is well known. Rabbi Yohanan, the incumbent of the chief rabbinate in Paris, came into conflict with a colleague, Rabbi Yeshayah by name, a former student of his late father, Rabbi Matatyah, his predecessor in the rabbinate.[61] We are here at the last stage of the history of French Jewry, expelled in the beginning of the century and readmitted by Charles V in 1359. It was a small community of businessmen under the direct control of the king, which included even the royal appointment of the chief rabbi—a far cry from the autonomous life of the Jewish community in its classic period of the eleventh to thirteenth centuries. Still, although Yohanan was an appointee of the king, as was his father in his time, he was willingly accepted by the community as an ordained rabbi, having received *Semikah* from his father along with other capable students of the *yeshivah*. It was his colleague, the above-mentioned Yeshayah, who contested his authority. In his attempt to undermine the position of the chief rabbi, Yeshayah enlisted the assistance of an outside rabbi of eminence, Rabbi Meir of Vienna, under whom he had once studied. The famous halakist seems to have accepted the applicant's contention that the conditions in France required extraordinary measures. He granted his former student a writ, investing him with the highest religious authority, by virtue of which all the rabbis in France would owe him allegiance. Rabbi Yohanan refused to accept this strange ruling and appealed to the rabbis of Catalonia, and especially to Rabbi Isaac Perfet, to support him in his struggle. He indeed received an unqualified vindication of his case.[62] As the case in point turned formally on the validity of rabbinical authorization, Ribash started off his response with a thorough analysis of the nature of the *Semikah* practiced by the Ashkenazi French rabbis. He proceeded from the assumption—commonplace for medieval halakists—that a custom which prevailed in a large Jewish community cannot possibly be at variance with Talmudic law. But the Talmudic statement that there is no ordination outside the land of Israel clearly controverted the legitimacy of this custom. Ribash went on to state his conclusion that the Ashkenazi *Semikah* had nothing to do with the ancient institution that went by the same name. Still, in order not to disqualify the custom altogether, Ribash found that its relevance derived from the Talmudic rules governing the relations between the master and his disciple. The latter is not permitted to lay down the law in religious issues during the lifetime of his master or to teach publicly without the latter's permission.[63] The *Semikah* is, according to this interpretation, no more than the formalization of this permission on the part of the master—a concept that is far from doing justice to the real function it fulfilled in the life of the community.

Of course Ribash did not belong to the community that practiced the *Semikah* and had no motivation to fortify it. Had the institution been examined by one of the Ashkenazi worthies, it might have been vindicated along lines of thought which were evolved by some of the Geonim in dealing with their type of ordination. That the Ashkenazi *Semikah* was not always regarded as the product of local conditions, but rather as a direct continuation of the Palestinian institution is clearly reflected in a casual remark of the fifteenth-century Rabbi Moshe Mintz. Differentiating between lay judges appointed by the community and those who act on the basis of their rabbinical authority, he remarks about the latter[64] "for every Rabbi and expert has been authorized as a master from the mouth of a master up to our teacher Moses, peace be with him." No better testimony could be asked for the spontaneous evaluation of the *Semikah* by those who practiced it.

A more reflective appraisal was forthcoming a generation or two later when, after the expulsion of the Jews from Spain, Sephardic and Ashkenazic communities found an opportunity to examine their respective customs and criticize one another.[65] The Italian Rabbi Messer David Leon, of Ashkenazi origin, came into conflict with some Spanish exiles living side by side in the town of Valona in Albania. Leon's adversaries questioned his rabbinical authority in spite of the *Semikah* granted to him by famous Ashkenazi rabbis in Italy.[66] Of course the Sephardim made light of this Ashkenazi institution, which was unknown to them. Thus Leon felt called upon to defend the Ashkenazi tradition. The gist of his argument was that many other functions originally dependent on the ordained institutions in the land of Israel had been continued on the assumption that the earlier authorities tacitly or explicitly commissioned the later generations to do so. The administration of the calendar was a case in point as was the acceptance of proselytes, the continuation of which in the absence of ordained judges had been justified by the Tosafists on the basis of this argument. Why not, then, the whole institution of ordination?[67] Whether this theory stands up to halakic criticism is not relevant here. Leon did not count as a great halakic authority and his arguments were advanced in a polemical pamphlet that was not published until the nineteenth century.[68] Still, such an argument and its harmonizing tendency are certainly not uncommon in halakic reasoning.

Nor was Leon the only one who followed this trend. He was supported in his private contest by Rabbi David Kohen from Corfu, and this eminent halakist too found himself duty bound to speak up in defense of the Ashkenazi *Semikah*.[69] His argument is strongly reminiscent of Samuel ben Ali's, proposing a partial identity of the later *Semikah* to the Palestinian one, although conceding its limited validity. He applied exactly the same formula that the dictum "no Semikah outside the land of Israel" pertains only to *Dine Kenassot*.[70] On the other hand he becomes more explicit as to the functions of the ordination outside Palestine. First, ordination always included, besides the authorization to execute certain juridical acts like *Dine Kenassot*, testimony that the ordained person had attained the degree of knowledge necessary to handle the law. Though the authorization may be inapplicable the function of such testimony is continuously applied.[71] Next

Rabbi David, like Isaac Perfet before him, refers to the Talmudic prohibition of a student from making decisions even in matters of rituals without receiving explicit permission to do so by his master.[72] While Perfet regarded this Talmudic regulation as an independent enactment unconnected with the *Semikah*, the Rabbi of Corfu presented it as an integral part of it. The conferring of the title of rabbi in Palestine implied the master's permission for his student to lay down religious law for people who requested such guidance. The same purpose is served by conferring the title *morenu* on the ordained at the present time.[73] Whether Rabbi David regarded the Ashkenazi *Semikah* as a historical continuation of the Palestinian institution is not entirely clear. In view of the tendency inherent in the halakic thinking to blur the difference between historical statements and logical conclusions the question is probably altogether irrelevant. Halakically the two institutions have been identified, and thus the contemporary usage has been invested with the dignity of Talmudic law.

Neither Messer David Leon nor the Rabbi of Corfu was acquainted with the contrary opinion expressed before them by Rabbi Isaac Perfet. Once the thoroughgoing analysis of the Ribash included in his response had been published, in 1546, the way to further vindication of the *Semikah* along the line of the Ashkenazi scholars was blocked. So the official attitude toward the institution was finally fixed. Though practiced by the Ashkenazim alone, the Sephardic interpretation of its validity, granted somewhat grudgingly, became the universally accepted version.

The practical application of the *Semikah* however failed to conform to the accepted theory. For if the *Semikah* is no more than the permission of the master for his pupil to exercise the authority of a rabbi in the lifetime of the master, then if the latter passes away without having granted *Semikah* to the pupil, the pupil ought nonetheless to be entitled to assume rabbinical authority without having been ordained. This consequence of the theory, though explicitly stated by Ribash, was nowhere adopted in practice.[74] Wherever the *Semikah* was customary it became mandatory for each rabbi without exception. If the student had not received it from his main teacher (*rav muvhak*) he had to obtain it from another scholar of rank.[75] Thus theory and practice patently diverged.

Two years before the publication of Ribash's response another Sephardic comment on the *Semikah*, by Isaac Abravanel, became known. Abravanel encountered the institution in Italy where he stayed after the expulsion from Spain. He referred to it in his commentary on *Abot*, where he wondered from what source Ashkenazim might have received this custom.[76] Provoked by this remark, David Ganz, the Ashkenazi chronicler of Prague (1541-1613), traced its origin and stated that the fifteenth-century rabbis Jacob Moellin and his masters were the first to have carried the title of *Morenu* to indicate their authorization in receiving a *Semikah*.[77] Thus the comparatively recent parentage of the institution, as it were, was historically established; whether correctly so is still, however, open to doubt.

NOTES

1. The argumentation based on this verse is well summed up by Bernhard Blumenkranz, *Juifs et Chrétiens dans le Monde Occidental, 430-1096* (Paris, 1960), pp. 227-237.

2. Ibid.

3. Hanoch Albeck, *Zion* VIII (1942-43), 35 (Hebrew) assumes that the ordination in practice in the Tannaitic period has been projected back into Biblical times. Still this projection is not a simple predating of a later event, since the implied Mosaic origin of the *Semikah* lent it its basic significance.

4. On the history of the ordination during the Tannaitic period see Hugo Mantel, *Studies in the History of the Sanhedrin* (Cambridge, Mass. 1961), pp. 38-39 and the literature listed there.

5. Summed up by Maimonides, *Yad ha-Hazakah, Sanhedrin*, chap. 4.

6. Maimonides, ibid., *Kiddush ha-Hodesh*, chap. 5, 1.

7. Ibid. Theoretically some other activities of the courts—for instance, compulsory enforcement of the law and the initiation of proselytes—ought to have been restricted to ordained judges, *Gittin* 88b and *Tosafot* (ibid). How the practical inconsistencies have been rationalized, we shall see later.

8. Maimonides, *Sanhedrin*, chap. 5, 17.

9. That *Dine Kenassot* had been discontinued in Geonic times in Palestine as well has been conclusively established by A. Aptowitzer, *Mehkarim be-Sifrut ha-Geonim* (Jerusalem, 1941), pp. 95, 104-114.

10. Mishnah, *Rosh ha-Shanah*, chaps. 1 and 2.

11. Graetz, Geschichte der Juden (Leipzig, 1833), IV, 318-320, 457. J. Halevy, *Dorot ha-Rishonim* (Frankfurt a/M, 1901), II, 393-399. A. H. Fraenkel, *Encyclopaedia Hebraica*, XXI, 341-342.

12. See previous note.

13. Maimonides, *Sanhedrin*, 4, 11.

14. J. Katz, "The Controversy on the *Semikah* (Ordination) between Rabbi Jacob Be-Rav and Ralbah," *Zion*, XVI (1951), 42-43 (Hebrew).

15. Maimonides, Kiddush ha-Hodesh, chap. 5, 1-2.

16. Tobias b. Eliezer, *Lekah Tob* on Exodus 12, 1, ed. Buber, p. 54.

17. The sources that contain the direct or indirect statements of Saadia are collected by M. M. Kasher, *Torah Shelemah*, XIII, 40-50.

18. B. M. Lewin, *Ozar ha-Geonim* IV, 4. Kasher, *Torah Shelemah*, XIII, p. 25; Maimonides, *Commentary on the Mishnah, Rosh ha-Shanah* 2, 6.

19. J. Heinemann, "The Rationalism of R. Saadya Gaon" (Hebrew) in J. L. Fishman, ed., *Rav Saadia Gaon* (Jerusalem, 1943), pp. 191-240.

20. A lucid presentation of the controversy is in Saadia's biography by H. Malter, *Saadia Gaon: His Life and Works* (Philadelphia, 1921), pp. 69-88, where (pp. 409-419) the bibliographical data up to that time are listed. The problem is reexamined by Salo W. Baron, "Saadia's Communal Activities" in *Saadia Anniversary Volume*, the American Academy for Jewish Research (New York, 1943), pp. 36-47. The relevant texts are included in the article by H. J. Bornstein, "Mahaloket Rav Saadia Gaon u-Ben Meir," in *Sefer ha-Yobel N. Sokolow* (1904), pp. 19-189.

21. Moshe Gil, "Some Comments on the Geneology of the Palestinian Geonim," (Hebrew) *Tarbiz* XLIV (1974), 144-146.

22. J. L. Fishman, *Rav Saadia Gaon* (Hebrew) (Jerusalem, 1943), pp. 34-43;

Max L. Margolis and Alexander Marx, *A History of the Jewish People* (Philadelphia 1945), pp. 267-269.

23. Malter, *Saadia Gaon*, p. 85.

24. A. Epstein in *REJ*, XLIV (1902), 230-236. For Bornstein see note 20. V. Cassutto, "On What Did Saadia and Ben Meir Differ," in J. L. Fishman, ed., *Rav Saadia Gaon*, pp. 333-364.

25. Jacob Mann, *Jews in Egypt and in Palestine under the Fatrimid Caliphs*, I-II (Oxford, 1920, 1922, reprinted New York, 1970). The text referred to is in II, 41-42, and explained in I, 52-54.

26. The text first was published by Solomon Schechter in *JQR*, XIV (1901), 53-54, reprinted in his *Saadyana*, pp. 16-17, and complemented by a missing fragment by A. Guillaume in *JQR*, n.s., V (1914-15), 552-555.

27. Schechter saw "strong reason" to attribute it to Saadia (*Saadyana*, p. 15). Bornstein denied it was his (*Sefer Sokolow*, p. 87) because of an alleged stylistic discrepancy between this letter and other writings of Saadia known to us, and because the halakic opinion propounded about the fixation of the calendar contradicts the known view of Saadia. As to style the argument cannot be conclusive, and as far as the halakic opinion is concerned, Bornstein was mistaken; see below note 31. Mann (see note 25, I, 51) thinks the letter "probably" originated from the Exilarch, while Malter ascribed it to the "Babylonian authorities, including Saadia." There are cogent reasons to accept Malter's view. As Saadia was involved in the controversy from its start and conducted it on behalf of the Babylonian it is unthinkable that the letter stating the principal position and its halakic justification went out without his consent.

28. S. Eppenstein (*Monatsschrift*, LIV (1910), 317), aware only of Saadia's letter, projected the supposed meeting of the scholars of the two countries into Talmudic times after the fixation of the caldendar by Hillel II. Rejected by Bornstein for textual reasons, this explanation had to be absolutely excluded in view of the information contained in the text published by Mann. Confronting the two texts, Mann (*The Jews in Egypt* I, 51-52) narrowed down the time of the meeting between 835 and the time of the Ben Meir controversy. This dating has since then been accepted by other scholars (Baron, *A Social and Religious History of the Jews*, VIII, 195-196), no one doubting the factuality of the event.

29. There is one suggestion that seems to steer clear of the dilemma. It is that of S. Sh. Bialoblocki, *Knesset*, VIII (1943-1944), 164-165. According to his reading Ben Meir may have been in possession of a tradition of an individual or minority opinion which, though overruled, could, under certain circumstances, halakically be resorted to. In his zeal for the reestablishment of Palestinian supremacy Ben Meir did just this. This theory, however, fails to account for the rationale of this minority opinion in the first place. Then Ben Meir in his polemics is as absolute in the defense of the Palestinian version as the exclusive truth as the Babylonians are in the defense of their own. Bialoblocki's theory is a typical construction of a halakist taking a logical possibility for historical truth.

30. Mann, *The Jews in Egypt*, I, 50.

31. *Sefer ha-Mizvot*, *Mizvat 'Aseh*, 153.

32. Bornstein's argument referred to above, note 27, understands Saadia to have said that the natural signs mentioned in the Talmud would have never played any part in the fixation of the leap year. What Saadia maintained, however, was that the astronomical rules known to the Jerusalem court served as a guide or as a

means of control in fixing the calendar. Still, the court was entitled to deviate from the system for reasons of climate and the like, as mentioned in the Talmud. See H. M. Kasher, *Torah Shelemah* XIII, 40-42 (Hebrew).

33. See the text of the letter referred to in note 26.

34. S. Assaf, "Letters of R. Samuel ben Ali and his Contemporaries," *Tarbiz*, I (1930), 2.82.

35. Ibid. Mann, *Texts and Studies in Jewish History and Literature* (Cincinnati, 1931), I, 239-240, understood the reference to the "corroboration of this practice," i.e., the continuation of the ordination, but the citing of "Hai Gaon's and others' writings on this matter" in addition to the known practice evidently refers also to the theoretical justification of the practice.

36. Mann, *Texts and Studies*, I, 239-240. The respective dates are 1161 and 1191. See ibid., pp. 200, 237.

37. The letter was reconstructed and published by Assaf, *Tarbiz* I, No. 3 (1930), 68-77 and analyzed by Mann, *Texts and Studies*, I, 228-235.

38. Assaf, "Letters," p. 70.

39. Mann, *Texts and Studies*, I, p. 231, note 64.

40. Ibid., p. 232.

41. Assaf, "Letters," p. 70.

42. Ibid., p. 68.

43. Ibid., p. 70.

44. Ibid.

45. For the halakic significance of these statements see H. Z. Taubes, *Ozar ha-Geonim, Sanhedrin*, p. 129, note 20.

46. Assaf, "Letters," p. 69.

47. Aptowitzer, *Mehkarim*, pp. 120-121, Taubes, *Ozar ha-Geonim*, pp. 129-130.

48. The unworthiness of Daniel's successors is stated explicitly. Assaf, p. 69.

49. Mann, *Texts and Studies*, I, pp. 231-232.

50. Yehudah al-Bargeloni, *Sefer ha-shetarot* (Berlin, 1898), pp. 132-133.

51. Ibid.

52. Ibid.

53. Abrahm ibn Daud, *The Book of Tradition* (Sefer ha-kabbalah), ed. Gerson D. Cohen (Philadelphia, 1961), p. 85.

54. S. D. Goitein, *Jewish Education in Muslim Countries* (Jerusalem, 1962), p. 192 (Hebrew).

55. Issaac Perfet, *Responsa* (edition 1559) N 271 (p. 193a).

56. The Ashkenazi *Semikah* has been discussed by scholars and often misinterpreted. The last and adequate treatment of the subject is that of M. Breuer, *The Ashkenazi Semikha"*, *Zion* XXXIII (1968), 15-46 (Hebrew).

57. See the letter of R. Eliezer from Prague to R. Yehudah ha-Hasid, *Or Zarua* I, 113, and that of R. Moshe ben Hisday to the community of Magdeburg, ibid., 115. A revised version of both letters based on a parallel source is offered by E. E. Urbach, *The Tosafists* (Jerusalem, 1955; Hebrew) pp. 182-184, 348-349. Most recently M. Breuer (*The Rabbinate in Ashkenaz during the Middle Ages* [Hebrew], Jerusalem, 1976) collected the relevant material concerning rabbis and hazanim. In his introduction (p. 15-16) he has not drawn a clear distinction between the two.

58. See Breuer, *The Ashkenazi Semikah*, 18-25, and the sources quoted by him.

59. See Abraham A. Neuman, *The Jews in Spain* (Philadelphia, 1942) II, 86-91. Yehuda al-Bargeloni describes the document, a *ketav minnuy*, used on the occasion of appointment of the head of the academy, an elder, a judge or a patriarch. No previous ordination is required for any of these appointments. Al-Bargeloni, *Sefer ha-shetarot*, p. 131.

60. Ibid.

61. The historical circumstances are now clarified through the well-documented study of Simon Schwarzfuchs, *Etudes sur l'Origine et le Développement du Rabbinat au Moyen Age* (Paris, 1951), pp. 39-64.

62. The sources relevant to this controversy are Isaac Perfet's *Responsa*, 268-272, and no. 11 of his *New Responsa* (Jerusalem, 1860), first published in *REJ*, XXXIX, 90-94. See Schwarzfuchs, *Etudes sur l'origine du rabbinat*, pp. 39-40.

63. Perfet, *Responsa*, no. 271 (pp. 193a-194b).

64. In Mintz's *Shelosha 'Anafim*, published by Breuer, *The Rabbinate in Ashkenaz*, p. 109.

65. Breuer, *The Ashkenazi Semikah*, pp. 29-30.

66. Messer D. Leon, *Kebod Hahamim*, ed. Sh. Bernfeld (Berlin, 1899), pp. 53 ff.

67. Ibid.

68. See notes 65-66.

69. David ben Hayyim ha-Kohen from Corfu, *Responsa* (Constantinople 1637), 22, 9-11.

70. This key sentence recurs twice in connection with each of the two arguments spelled out in our presentation. See ibid. in the first paragraphs of section 9 and 11.

71. Ibid., section 9.

72. Ibid., section 11.

73. Ibid.

74. Perfet, *Responsa* no. 271 (195a-b).

75. Breuer, *The Ashkenazi Semikah*, 26 ff.

76. Isaac Abravanel, *Nahalat Abot* on the first Mishnah of chap. 6.

77. David Ganz, *Zemah David* (Prague, 1592) pt. 1, 59b-60a.

4

Some Medieval and Renaissance Hebrew Writings on the Poetry of the Bible

James L. Kugel

Biblical Parallelism

The songs and psalms of the Bible were not written in quantitative meters, as were the songs of the ancient Greeks, nor do they have regular rhyme or alliterative patterns, as do the songs of many other peoples. Rather, the basic feature of Biblical songs—and, for that matter, of most of the sayings, proverbs, laws, laments, blessings, curses, and prayers found in the Bible—is the recurrent use of a relatively short sentence-form that consists of two brief clauses:

Happy are the dwellers of your house, ever do they praise you.

Ps. 84:5

The clauses are regularly separated by a slight pause—slight because the second is (as above) a continuation of the first and not a wholly new beginning. By contrast, the second ends in a full pause. (Here and there, ternary sentences also occur, but the binary form is definitely the rule in Hebrew.)

Often, the clauses have some element in common, so that the second seems to echo, answer, or otherwise correspond to the first. The common element is sometimes a word or phrase that occurs in both halves; or the same syntactic structure; or commonly paired concepts ("By day . . . by night . . . "); or some similarity in the ideas expressed. For example, Psalm 94 begins:

God of retribution, Lord/ God of retribution, appear!//
Rise up, earth's ruler/ give the arrogant their due//
How long shall the wicked, Lord/ how long shall the wicked rejoice?//
They brag, speak brashly/ the evil-doers do act haughtily.//

The common element in the first verse is the repetition of the phrase "God of retribution." In the second, each half begins with an imperative addressed to God ("rise up . . . /give . . . //"). The third verse repeats a phrase, just as in the first. The fourth verse describes successively aspects of the evil-doers' arrogant behavior, in speech and general conduct.

Robert Lowth, an eighteenth-century British exegete, named this trait of correspondence *parallelismus membrorum*, "the parallelism of the clauses," and since his time critics have tended to see in it the organizing structure of

Hebrew songs, the Biblical "equivalent" of such Western structuring devices as meter or rhyme. But this is somewhat overstated. To begin with, parallelism, while it is unquestionably the hallmark of this style, is not quite its *sine qua non*. Actual semantic or syntactic parallelism between A and B (as the two clauses are sometimes called) can be rather muted, or even entirely absent. Moreover, the dividing line between what is and is not "poetry" in the Bible is hardly clear-cut,[1] so that the search for an equivalent "system" is somewhat ill conceived. There is no Biblical word for poetry,[2] and it is obvious that parallelistic sentences appear in the Bible in widely varying strengths: consistently, fairly consistently, intermittently, and sparsely. For this reason, the polarity of poetry-or-prose is a somewhat misleading concept in regard to the Bible: it is simply not an either/or proposition. Furthermore, this style occurs in its intensest form not only in poetic genres like songs and odes but in such unpoetic compositions as laws, genealogies, and so forth. Thus it is better to think of parallelism (to use Lowth's term for this style, but qualified by the foregoing understanding) as the mark not of "poetry" but of elevated speech in Hebrew and to leave that elevation as a matter of degree: the more intense the "seconding," the higher the stylistic effect.

For both these reasons, then, there is cause to balk at the modern assessment of Lowth as the discoverer of Biblical poetry's structure (though none can dispute his sensitivity and persuasiveness as a Biblical critic). His *parallelismus membrorum* is too narrow a concept, and one that has proven dangerously misleading to subsequent critics. Moreover, Lowth's predecessors, whose views have been somewhat neglected since his time, ought now to be reexamined and, perhaps, reassessed. They had their own ideas about this (after all) rather obvious aspect of Biblical expression: were not their views and descriptions in some ways preferable to Lowth's? And did they have any direct or indirect influence on him? On this last point one case is well known: Lowth was acquainted with the ideas of the Renaissance Hebrew writer Azariah dei Rossi, and in fact cited him in his own work. But Azariah himself had sources: his remarks were made in the context of a definite exegetical tradition, that of the Jewish Middle Ages.

Passive Awareness of Parallelism

Faced with the most striking sort of parallelistic line—"I will sing to the Lord with my life, I will make melody to my God while I live" (Ps. 104:33) —the Biblical exegete has a choice. He may either seek somehow to distinguish A from B by focusing on some real or imaginary nuance and so dispel the appearance of synonymity, or he may accept the synonymity as the *whole point* and dismiss any real differences of meaning as having been necessitated by the goal of restating a single idea in different words. In the former approach, the exegete would perhaps claim that "while I live" means something other than "with my life"—life in the world to come, for example, or spiritual versus physical existence. In the latter approach he would stress their equivalence, and this would probably lead him to discuss the parallelism itself or otherwise speculate on the purpose of such restatement.

Anyone acquainted with Talmudic exegesis will recognize the former as the attitude consistently adopted by the rabbis. It is in fact the bread-and-butter of rabbinic writing, from the earliest specimens of midrash to the end of the rabbinic period. Now while such a "nuancing" approach has its roots in the reality of Biblical style—for it is clear that *B is* often more than mere restatement—its rabbinic elaboration was often fanciful in the extreme. Whatever distinction could be found to differentiate *A* from *B* was found, and if none presented itself, there was, quite simply, nothing to say. As a result of this approach, the fact of parallelism, and the very evident workings of this "seconding" style, were overlooked. Because B always had a *raison d'être* beyond mere restatement or reinforcement, these functions were simply never invoked.

This same predisposition was passed on to medieval Jewish exegesis, and parallelism, as a consequence, tended to be neglected even when some of the underpinnings of the rabbinic approach to texts began to be challenged. Most *parshanim* continued to be ingenious in seeking nuances to distinguish *A* from *B*, and to the extent that they succeeded, they managed to remain blind to, or purposely overlook, the parallelism before their eyes. Only where "nuancing" was impossible does one find a somewhat grudging admission of the parallelistic style.

Thus Rashi (1040-1105) is, in general, scrupulous in reading *B* as a distinction over against *A*. For example, on Numbers 23:7, "Come, curse Jacob for me, come condemn Israel" he remarks: "Balak had told him to curse them using both the names of the Israelites, lest one alone not be precise enough." Similarly, on Deuteronomy 32:7 "Ask your father and he will tell you, your elders and they will say to you," he (following Sifre) adduces the verse of 2 Kings 2:12 to show that "your father" refers to the Prophets of Israel, and then explains "your elders" as a reference to the Talmudic sages. However, Rashi is occasionally forced to confront a purely rhetorical feature, such as the parallelistic use of repetition. On Exodus 15:1 he writes about the phrase *ki ga'oh ga'ah*: "The form is repeated here to show that He did what it is impossible for flesh-and-blood to do, for when a man fights with his fellow and conquers him, he throws him from his horse, but here 'horse and rider He cast in the sea . . .' And likewise you will find repetition throughout the Song: 'My strength and power . . . ' (15:2), 'The Lord is a warrior, the Lord is His name,' and so forth." Rashi feels the necessity, just as the Talmud had, to explain any form of repetition or other apparently superfluous usages—and to explain them not as a feature of rhetoric, but as *signifying* something. So, in quite Talmudic fashion, he advances the idea that repeating—not only doubled verbs, but any repetition—is peculiar to this Song to distinguish God's actions from human ones. He sticks to the same explanation in his handling of verse 6, but then adds something:

"Thy right hand, O Lord, is glorious in power"—to save Israel; and the second "thy right hand" crushes the enemy, and so it seems to me that that same right hand [that saves Israel] also crushes the enemy, which is something a man cannot accomplish, two deeds with one hand. But the simple meaning of the verse is: "Thy right hand, O Lord, which is glorious in power—what does it do? Thy right hand O Lord crushes the enemy." And there are many such verses in the Bible, such as "For behold thy enemies, O Lord, for behold thy enemies will perish" (Ps. 92:10), and the others like it.

This verse presents another instance of repetition, and Rashi offers the same explanation for it: "right hand" is repeated to emphasize the difference between human and divine deeds. But his addition about the "simple meaning" of the verse shows he was perfectly aware that the repetition in *B* was simply that, a repetition and continuation of *A*'s thought. He even cites another example of this "repetitive parallelism," Psalm 92:10.[3]

The notion was dealt with in more explicit terms by Rashi's grandson, R. Samuel b. Meir (Rashbam) in his commentary on the same passage: " 'Thy right hand . . .' etc. This passage is like 'The waters have lifted up, O Lord, the waters have lifted up their voice' (Ps. 93:3), 'For behold thy enemies, O Lord, for behold thy enemies perish" (Ps. 92:10). In all these the first half does not finish its idea until the last half comes and repeats it and then completes its idea. In the first half it [only] mentions who or what it is talking about."[4] It is clear from here that Rashbam understood the structure of the verses mentioned, that is, understood "repetitive parallelism" as a specific stylistic construction that divided the verses.

Equally perceptive are various remarks about parallelism in the commentary of Rashbam's contemporary, Abraham ibn Ezra (1089-1164). He frequently remarks on the repetition of meaning in sections identified as songs and the like. For example, about Balaam's verse in Numbers 23:7 he observes: "The idea is repeated according to the practice by which one idea is spoken twice in different words. They repeat for the sake of emphasis." He makes similar remarks about the "Song of the Well" (Num. 21:17) and the Song of the *Moshelim* (Num. 21:28); about Deuteronomy 32:7 he observes "the idea is repeated for this is a form of elegant speech (*ki ken derekh sahut*)." One of his most interesting explanations is of Genesis 49:6: "R. Moses haKohen [ibn Gikatilla] said that 'my glory' is like 'my soul,' and that there are many in the Psalms like this. It is a nice explanation, for the meaning is repeated as is the practice in prophecy: 'Ask your father . . .' (Deut. 32:7), 'How shall I curse . . .' (Num. 23:8). Similarly here 'in their company' is like 'in their group,' 'go' is like 'proceed,' 'my soul' is like 'my glory.' "

But his most interesting comment on parallelism comes on Exodus 23:10, where he attempts to understand the meaning of the word *sappir* in the expression *kema'aseh libnat hassappir* by looking at another instance in which the word is parallelistically apposed:

Sa'adya Ga'on has said that a *sappir* is white, and [his proof] is this text, *kema'aseh libnat hassappir*. But on the contrary, a *sappir* is red: this proven by the fact that it is the practice of Hebrew to repeat an idea in different words, so that where it says (Lam. 4:7) "Her princes were purer than snow, whiter than milk" the idea is being repeated. So when the verse continues, "Their bodies were ruddier than red coral, their form was a *sappir*," *sappir* ought to be compared to red corral.

Not only had ibn Ezra used parallelism of meaning as an exegetical tool, he also identified it (correctly in my view) as a "habit of the language" and *derekh sahut*, the "rhetorical" style, rather than associating it (like others) specifically with songs and poetry. This notwithstanding, it is noteworthy that in *Safah Berurah* he discusses the same question of apparently needless repetition and writes:

If someone should cite as an example the verse "and the earth and the land were unformed" (Ps. 90:2), I would answer that the first word (*'eres*) is a general name for the inhabited and uninhabited parts, while the second word (*tebel*) means specifically the inhabited part. But if one objected that there is then no need to specify the assertion for a part if that part is included in the whole, I would answer that *this is the way the divinely inspired speak* (*kakha minhag 'anshei haqqodesh ledabber*). For does it not also say, "Both the sons of Adam and the sons of men . . ." (Ps. 49:3).[5]

Here he avoids claiming the text repeats, preferring the "lesser charge" of stating a particular unnecessarily, since the general has already been held to be true.[6]

Both ibn Ezra and Rashbam use the phrase *kefel lashon* ("repetition of an expression") and the like. The origin of this phrase is apparently rabbinic: *kappel* is used in the general sense of "repeat" as well as the more common meaning of "to double," and one finds such usages as *lashon kaful* (*Song of Songs Raba* 1:66) and *nehamot kefulot* (*Lev. Raba* 10:12). There, however, actual repetition is meant. Similarly, when Rashi used this word (above) he meant actual repetition of a word or phrase. But in ibn Ezra and Rashbam, what is meant is not necessarily repetition but any form of reiteration or re-statement. Thus on Exodus 15:2 Rashbam writes: "The repetition of the verse's ending" (*kefel sof happasuq*) proves that *nw'* means to "praise"; similarly on Num. 23:7 " 'From the eastern mountains' is a repetitive expression (*kefel lashon*) for the text has already said 'From Aram.' This is to emphasize the great trouble [it took to come] from a distant land." Although this looks like rabbinic language, it embodies a considerable new insight.

Ibn Ezra and Rashbam were contemporaries, and it is certainly possible that the appearance of this expression in both is the result of direct influence (rather than a similar adaptation in both of an existing usage). But if so, who influenced whom? It is to be noted that ibn Ezra resorts to this explanation more often than Rashbam and more explicitly, "he repeated the same idea *in different words*," and so on. But perhaps they have a common ancestor among earlier commentators: ibn Ezra's evocation of Moses ha-Kohen (whose commentary is lost) is most suggestive in this regard.

Mention ought to be made as well of the commentator David Kimhi (c. 1160-c. 1235), since he has been cited along with ibn Ezra as describing parallelism *avant la lettre*.[7] On Hosea 12:5 he says "He repeated the idea for emphasis since it was a great wonder for a man to fight an angel." About Habbakuk 3:8—"He repeated the idea for emphasis." On the other hand he does not notice the parallelism in either Exodus 15 or Deuteronomy 32, nor for that matter in those other songs of the Torah, Numbers 21:17 or 21:27. He uses the same phrase, *kippel happassuq lehazzeq ha'inyan* to describe an actual repetition (Ps. 118:8-9); in his language, at least, he does not distinguish between paralleling and repeating. Furthermore, he, like ibn Ezra, speaks of "repetition" in the same way when it is individual words, rather than verse halves, that are involved; for example, on Judges 5:27: " 'Between her feet he bowed he fell': such is the habit of Hebrew to repeat things in order to reinforce the meaning, for he bowed down to the ground so as never to rise again. [Hence the justification for emphasis.] That is why it says next, 'where he bowed, there he fell stricken.' " Similarly Deborah's cry, "Arise, arise" is described as an emphatic "doubling."

Joseph ibn Kaspi (1279-1340) is another commentator who touches on the issue of parallelism. In general he is ready to admit the poetic character of parts of the Bible,[8] but for him this is a statement about the figurative quality of the language, not one with formal implications. Among his Biblical commentaries are two on Proverbs (a work in which the play of parallelism is particularly apparent). Like many of his predecessors, Kaspi interpreted in the "sharp" manner where possible, and in his first commentary even went to Lowthian lengths to catalogue the different sorts of ways in which the second half-verse relate back to the first.[9] But his concern is with the *logical* relation of the verse halves: citing Boethius, "Logic is the silver key which opens the chambers in which Philosophy lies on a golden couch," he proceeds to examine different classes of assertions via logical categories. The fact of their binariness does not interest him as such.

Lastly, allusion must be made to Tanhum Yerushalmi, a thirteenth-century commentator who lived first in Palestine, then in Egypt.[10] His surviving commentaries are remarkable for their freedom from convention and, occasionally, their striking insight. Tanhum frequently resorts to Arabic literary terminology for describing Biblical style: in his Habbakuk commentary he commonly labels expressions as "metaphor," "exaggeration" (related in Arabic rhetoric to eloquence), "simile," and so on, and at Chapter 3 compares the style of the prophet to that of Deborah in Judges 5, Isaiah 38:9, and certain Psalms for its "concision, obscurity, and use of metaphors." Now apparently in his commentary on Psalm 91:1 Tanhum had explained at some length about repetition of meaning, for he refers to it not only in the

Habbakuk commentary but (on the subject of repetition of meaning) in his commentary on Song of Songs as well. Unfortunately, the passage has not yet turned up among the existing Tanhum fragments.[11]

This brief sketch should capture some of the flavor of medieval Jewish exegesis. In all these commentaries there is some occasional movement beyond the midrashic approach to parallelism. Now to some extent, this is a reflection of the precise nature of Biblical commentary—whose task is, after all, to comment on all that is unclear, troublesome, or otherwise in need of explanation—as opposed to midrash, which has less of a commitment to completeness. Thus, as noted above, where midrashic exegesis did not have a "nuancing" reading to propose, it proposed none at all; Rashi could not allow himself the same silences. But this in turn reflects a difference in orientation. There is something more open-minded, even scientific, about the undertaking of such Biblical commentary *per se*. The commentaries seen probably represent not so much *new understanding* as a new willingness to approach the Bible's manner of expression—its style, as it were—phenomenologically. Now just as these commentators were at first handicapped by a rabbinic tradition committed theologically and temperamentally to the reading of *B* as significantly different from *A*, so they had a compensating advantage: as ibn Ezra, Rashbam, et al. evolved their increasingly phenomenological approach, they were somewhat freer than Christian exegetes from the canons of rhetorical orthodoxy. As a consequence they were, like today's Biblical form-critics, intent on deriving the Bible's rhetoric from itself: ibn Ezra's "This is the way the divinely inspired speak" is witness to this tendency.

Yet there is something quite wrong-headed in describing any of these commentators as "understanding" parallelism, for even in ibn Ezra it is a most passive act of comprehension. They embraced this seconding style only in its most obvious form and only insofar as it aided them in their main task, explaining the meaning of the words. Where it was possible to read verse halves as differentiated by nuances of meaning, they usually did so; only when the text literally repeated itself, or in an unmistakable way restated a single idea did they speak of "doubling," repetition, and so forth. And "elegant style," "the manner of prophecies," and "the habit of Hebrew" all explain what, to these commentators, ought really not to exist, mere repetition or restatement. This was an orthodoxy that remained. Repetition still ran counter to their notion of the text's perfection, and likewise violated the rules of style set even for ordinary men.

On this last point, the testimony of Moses ibn Ezra, the author of a lengthy treatise on poetry,[12] is most instructive. It is in his eighth chapter that he takes notice in general of the phenomenon of repetition and restatement in the Bible, noting "in our language, the repetition of an idea is permitted so long as the words are different; on the contrary, in the opinion of one of the masters of the study of rhetoric [Jonah ibn Jannah][13] this is a form of elegant style and rhetoric (*fasaha wabalagha*)." He then cites Isaiah 41:4,

43:7, 41:20, Deuteronomy 25:18, Genesis 25:8, Leviticus 17:5, Exodus 25:23, and so on—some of these entire verse halves, but most of them individual pairs of words. (For him, as for the other commentators seen, there was no difference. They posed the same problem, seemingly needless repetition of ideas, and they received the same solution, the label "rhetorical style.")

These examples notwithstanding, he cautions Hebrew poets against imitating Biblical practice: "In poetry, brevity is the correct thing." He cites many verses that *seem* repetitive, interpreting their repetition as adding in each case a significant nuance. (Hence Psalm 115:12 is a "general statement followed by a specification.") Then he adduces a few examples of parallelism which he reads in the "distribution" manner. Thus Leviticus 25:37 "Do not lend your money out at discount/ and your food do not give out at interest/ /" he reads "Your money and your food do not lend out at interest or discount." For parallelism he has little feeling. His comments here, like those of the commentators, have a defensive quality—he wishes to show it is *not bad style* to repeat in Hebrew, even though in the values of Arabic rhetoric, which he had embraced as his own, it is.

These efforts were "passive" and defensive because their aim was not to strike out on a mission of discovery, but only to explain away something in the text which (they were willing to admit) contradicted the midrashic assumption of the text's signifying even in its minutest details—and, in the view of Moses ibn Ezra and others, violated the canons of Arabic rhetoric as well. There is no doubt that thanks to ibn Jannah, Abraham ibn Ezra and Rashbam, the emphatic function of restatement and repetition came to be accepted as a fact of Biblical style. But that this explanation was not particularly comforting is apparent from the other explanations these same commentators adduce on occasion. Moreover, they were unable to see beyond repetition and restatement to grasp what is the *essential* of this style, B's subjunction to A (of which repetition and restatement are but a manifestation). Yet awareness of this last fact, and of its quasi-structural role in certain parts of the Bible, was not entirely lost on Jewish writers in the late Middle Ages. It owes its existence to one extremely significant development: the introduction of Arabic-style meters into Hebrew poetry, which began in Spain in the tenth century.

The Meter of Biblical Poetry

The story of medieval Hebrew poetry has been told elsewhere.[14] What is important to us here is not the poetry itself, but the effect of its existence on Jewish perceptions of the Bible. For poetry came, in a short period of time, to dominate utterly Jewish consciousness (as it already had the Arabs') in a way without analogue in modern societies. It was used for everything: praise of patrons, shaming of enemies; love-songs, wine songs, occasional verse of all kinds; religious poetry incorporated into the synagogue service; learned treatises and polemics—all these found the new poetry their natural

medium. "If you wish to make some matter well known," said Yedaya ha-
Penini, "put it in a poem. If you put it in a book, never on your life will it
spread abroad."[15] An astonishing quantity of poetry was known by heart,
for it was the medium of all memorizing:

> Since I saw verse superior to all else, and its use so highly approved,
> I have metered my treatise and set it in rhyme, so that it will aid the
>   memory[16]

Jews learned poetic compilations of *halakha* by heart, and in the detailed
course of study outlined by Joseph ibn Aqnin (contained in his "The Healing
of Souls") poetry plays a significant role. Moreover, secular and occasional
poetry was well known: a wealthy man required his own house poet at least
as a defensive weapon, to counter the withering epigrams aimed at him by
the poets in his rivals' employ—for these passed amongst the people and
spread fame and shame to every quarter. Similarly, he expected that if a
song of praise of his was well wrought, it would survive long after his death.
Poems passed from mouth to mouth; ibn Jannah recounts how he heard a
line of his master, Isaac b. Mar Shaul, misquoted many times in public,
until he finally heard the correct line from his teacher's mouth.[17] Likewise,
Moses ibn Ezra says of ibn Jannah, "his poems were recited and passed on
from one person to the next."[18]

Kalonymus b. Kalonymus's fictional poet[19] is—or at least thinks himself
—the superior of mere Talmudic scholars. Indeed, though Kalonymus's aim
is obviously satirical, it was certainly true that the poet's position was an
exalted one—admired, feared, quasi-divine in that "he builds a whole world"
in his words. No wonder his immortality seemed assured: "He thinks his
name will live on, perhaps its merits increase, 'Let his name be great in the
world created at his will.' " (This last line is the familiar refrain of the Kad-
dish, where it of course is spoken of God.) Poets were compared to prophets: even the stern Shem Tob b. Joseph Falaquera (c.1225 - 95), who had
much to criticize in poets, speaks of "the prophets of song," and poetic inspiration was sometimes identified with *ruah haqqodesh*, divine inspiration: "He whom the Creator has blessed with his own inspiration (*ruah
me'ito*) to speak his words in poetic meters is considered to be among those
who speak with the Holy Spirit."[20]

All this could not but keep the attention of Hebrew poets focused squarely
on their Biblical "homologues." Whatever of their own craft could be connected with the Bible, no matter how fancifully, was. Thus the author of
Imrei Shefer[21] claimed the number of possible meters in medieval Hebrew
was fifteen because "fifteen types of songs were sung in the Temple."[22] In a
similar vein, by juggling a single letter the exhortation of Deuteronomy
22:10 "Do not plow with an ox and an ass together" was converted into an
admonition to poets: *lo' taharoz beshor ubahamor yahdav*, that is, do not
rhyme *shor* (ox) with *hamor* (ass), for though the last vowel and consonant
are the same, the penultimate consonants differ, hence the rhyme is unfit.[23]

In the whole matter of Jewish awareness of the Bible as a *composed* and, as it were, literary text, Sa'adya Ga'on is again a figure of crucial importance. As M. Zulay argued forcefully,[24] it was Sa'adya's concern with Biblicizing Hebrew style and usage which determined the direction taken by Hebrew poetry in the Golden Age of Spain; but this concern in turn sprang from Saadia's larger view of the Bible, his careful balancing of a willingness to countenance stylistic judgments of Biblical language with a somewhat contrary tendency to assert the role of divine inspiration in the *meaning* of each verse.[25] It is clear his *'Egron* was the model for Moses ibn Ezra's stylistic reading of the Bible in *Kitab al-muhadara wal-mudhakara*,[26] but Sa'adya's overall influence was far greater—and again, it was his conception of the interplay between divine inspiration and human composition that was the key. As Abraham ibn Ezra remarked: "The Ga'on said that Isaiah's language was 'eloquent and pleasant.' [Dunash b. Labrat] said this was an error, since all the words of the Bible are the Almighty's own—but the error is that of [Dunash], for the meanings of the words are straight-forward and figurative together . . . and the prophet puts together the meanings with such power as he received from the Almighty."[27] On the precise matter of parallelism neither Sa'adya nor Moses ibn Ezra was particularly informative,[28] but this should not obscure the importance of their overall approach. They made possible later inquiries into the structure of Biblical compositions.

Now the Hebrew translation of Arabic *shi'r* (poetry) was the similar sounding (but unrelated) Hebrew word *shir* (song). Gradually but surely, *shir* came to mean *poetry* in the minds of Sephardic Jewry, and it therefore became natural to examine those parts of the Bible specifically labeled *shir* (or the variant *shirah*) to discover what was "poetic" about them. Sa'adya, it was true, had felt that the category of poetry was inappropriate in the Bible, but this hardly satisfied all parties. It became an increasingly pressing concern to explain the presence of *shir-shirah* in the incipits of Psalms and songs like Exodus 15 or Deuteronomy 32.

An obvious answer might be: some things in the Bible are called *shir* because they were sung, that is, the name refers to the manner of performance. But in the Middle Ages, singing, musical accompaniment, and the like, all implied the presence of meter—this is an important point for the modern reader to grasp[29]—and consequently Biblical references to music and song, Talmudic descriptions of the Levite choirs and their training, and midrashic discussions of the "Ten Songs,"[30] the meaning of the title "Song of Songs," and so on, all implied to Spanish Jewry a poetic art in ancient Israel which was in some basic way comparable to their own. Abraham ibn Ezra, in his commentary on Ecclesiastes 12:9, had interpreted the verb *'izzen* as meaning Koheleth (= Solomon) had composed metrical poems, presumably those spoken of in Kings 5:12.[31] Shem Tob b. Joseph Falaquera had defended poetry in his "Book of the Seeker":

For in poetry are said the praises of God
Which men have composed since Moses and the Israelites
    (i.e., Exod. 15)
And the Song of Moses (Deut. 32) which contains all the Torah's
    principles
Is written entirely in the manner of poetry
And amongst poets have been righteous and upright men
Who spoke in the Holy Spirit
The Book of Psalms is written in the Holy Spirit and it is entirely songs
And our Sages called Song of Songs the Holy of Holies.[32]

They knew their own meters and had been adapted from Arabic ones, but it seemed plausible to some that these, like the Arabic language itself, ultimately came from Hebrew. Would not an analysis of the Song of the Sea (Exod. 15) and others yield up the evidence necessary to prove Israel's precedence in every aspect of poetry and musical arts?

Other factors also pointed to a "poetic structure" in the Bible. By convention (and later, *halakha*) certain parallelistic parts of the Bible were written stichographically, that is, with some sort of break separating the verse halves. The same convention existed in most Arabic poetry and naturally led Jews to wonder if the formal resemblance did not stop there. Furthermore, the books of Psalms, Proverbs, and Job had been punctuated with special *te'amim* (Masoretic accents). From earliest times this fact had suggested that these texts had some special connection with song, and now was understood to mean that these books were, via the *shi'r-shir* connection, the "poetry" par excellence of the Bible. Even for those otherwise skeptical of the notion of a Biblical poetry, the argument of the stichography or special accents was convincing.[33] The question they were left with—indeed, the one that confronted medieval poets generally, as well as grammarians and other scholars—was: in what precisely does the poetic quality of Biblical *shirim* lie?

To this question there emerged a whole range of possible answers: they date from the earliest days of metrical poetry in Hebrew until the Renaissance scholar Azariah dei Rossi and beyond. Some writers, in searching for Biblical meters, attributed a structural role to the fairly regular binariness of Biblical songs; others, in rejecting the notion of meter, hit on another piece of the truth, the lack of exact equivalence of line length, syllables, accents, and so on, in Biblical verse halves. The theories proposed were not necessarily mutually exclusive, and later commentators therefore often maintained that *shir* consisted of two or more different subcategories of compositions, and then went on to incorporate several "answers" into their definitions. From the time of Moses ibn Tibbon on, such multiple definitions are commonplace.

Amongst the various approaches to this topic one may distinguish four basic "families" of answers:

1. *By poetry is meant figurative, indirect, or hidden forms of expression.* Arabic and Jewish commentators were acquainted with the (Aristotelian) distinction between poetic form and poetic content[34] and could account for the appelation "song" in various parts of the Bible by demonstrating that the writing was "figurative" without entering into meter or other questions of poetic structure. This was common practice in the case of Song of Songs from Talmudic times.[35] Joseph ibn Kaspi and Samuel ibn Tibbon both advance the argument that Solomon wrote three books (Ecclesiastes, Song of Songs, and Proverbs) to illustrate three different sorts of writing, respectively: the wholly literal (or "revealed"), the wholly figurative (or "hidden"), and the partially literal and partially figurative. But this tack held great dangers, for Arabs and Jews were also in possession of a pseudo-Aristotelian tradition that "the best part of poetry is its falsehood" (*metab hashir kezabo*).[36] Arguing that what constitutes the "poeticity" of Biblical songs is their content was the equivalent of saying that they were full of lies, or at best, exaggeration and overstatement.[37] Under these circumstances, a formal or structural explanation for the use of the word *shir, shirah,* and the like, was to be preferred.

Furthermore, figures and devices such as are found in poetry could be found in parts of the Bible clearly not labeled as poetry, but prophecy.[38] Moses ibn Ezra's eighth chapter contains a catalogue of poetic devices used in Arabic and Hebrew, and for many he finds Biblical precedents and examples—yet he felt the only true poetic books of the Bible were Psalms, Proverbs, and Job.[39] It is also significant about the "devices" approach to Biblical style that it tends to obscure rather than illuminate the parallelistic structure: this is as true of ibn Ezra, ibn Kaspi, and their contemporaries as it was of Augustine, Isidore of Seville, and others earlier. For in his search for different devices, the commentator mistakes for ornaments those features of surface (repetitions, restatements, chiastic balancing) which are specific manifestations of the overall seconding. Perhaps the most egregious of the Hebrew practitioners of this particular reading is the Renaissance commentator Judah b. Yehiel (Messer Leon) whose *Nofet Sufim* (written after 1454) viewed the Prophets as "masters of rhetoric" and set out to catalogue their various devices according to classical models, chiefly Cicero and Quintillian. Leon seems largely unaware of the overall parallelism of Biblical songs, though it is noteworthy that he defines *sahut* as the style in which "one idea will be said in different ways, and this sort of thing is found a great deal in Isaiah."[40]

2. *Original Hebrew meter, or meter's substitute, is now lost.* This view assumes a poetic craft perhaps going back even to the time of Abraham—an Ur-poetik, as it were—which has been forgotten by Jews during their long exile.[41] Thus, in opposing the introduction of Arabic-style meters into Hebrew, the followers of Menahem b. Saruq (tenth century) had argued that grammatical distinctions crucial to Hebrew were swallowed up in the new style, and it was therefore irreconcilable with the "rhythmic structure" of

Hebrew; perhaps Hebrew had had some sort of meter of its own, but it was now irretrievably lost:

> And if we had not been exiled from our land but on the contrary possessed the entirety of our language as in days of old when we dwelt securely in our pleasant habitations, then we would know all the details of our language and the different types of structures produced in it and we would know its meter and would keep within it. For the language of each and every people has its own rhythmic structure (*mishqolet*) and grammar, but ours was lost to us because of our many sins and hidden from us for our great transgressions ever since we were exiled; what had been of such breadth was now diminished and hidden and became lost. Indeed, had not the God who works wonders looked on his people's suffering, even the small part that remains would have been closed off and lost as well.

The poet Judah ha-Levi (c. 1075-1141) similarly believed metrical poetry was natural to every language and presumably could have existed in Biblical times. However, his position was somewhat different:

3. *"Song" in the Bible means only something sung and does not imply meter.* Ha-Levi's position[42] was that Biblical authors had purposely foregone the superficial beauties of meter for the sake of comprehension (*Kuzari* II 72), for the rhythm and choice of words imposed by strict meter might impede understanding. For this reason the system of *te'amim* was devised, so that the shades of meaning transmitted by phrasing and pitch in face-to-face conversation might also be carried in the written word: with the *te'amim* "a hundred people reading the same text will all pause and continue in exactly the same places" (*Kuzari* II 76).

What then of the appellation "song" in the Bible? Ha-Levi brilliantly perceived what has since been reforgotten, namely, "melodies do not necessarily require metrical texts" (*Kuzari* II 70). In a refrain composition such as Psalm 136, he noted, the structure implies a line like "To the worker of great wonders alone" is to be sung to exactly the same notes as "Praise the Lord greatly"—yet the latter is manifestly much shorter than the former and could not possibly be its metrical equivalent. In other words he succeeded in rejecting the idea of Biblical meters while at the same time asserting that, far from a defect, this aspect of the Bible makes it praiseworthy above the most elaborate of Arabic rhythms. Nor should one see in this an apologist's expedient: ha-Levi was apparently so persuaded by his own argument that at the end of his life he repented of ever having written in the Arabic meters of which he was such a master.[43]

Insofar as parallelism is concerned, Yehuda ha-Levi's stance eliminates the necessity of finding any structure in Hebrew songs (other than the *te'amim*, which follow the "meaning").[44] Many later commentators followed him and repeated his arguments to show there was nothing resembling a formal structure in the Bible's songs. Thus his student Solomon b. Abraham ibn Parhon writes in his *Mahberet ha'Arukh*:

If songs of rhyme and meter were good, then the sons of Korah would
have produced them, and David the King of Israel, and Solomon, who
were poets, for they made the songs and the melodies . . . In the Temple
there were outstanding poets, and why should they not have made
their songs with rhymes and metered poems like the Arabs? For if we
with our modest gifts and in our own age can make metered and
rhymed poems, could not they do likewise? But surely it was after our
exile that we saw the Arabs making rhymes and metered poems and we
began to do like them and caused our Holy Tongue to go astray and
enter into a place where it ought not to go.[45]

Among the many descendents of the *Kuzari's* arguments one of the most
influential was Samuel ibn Tibbon's (c. 1160-c. 1230) discussion of poetry in
his Ecclesiastes commentary:

The craft of poetry has requirements which are either common to all
[literatures] or specific to each nation; Aristotle listed them in his book
on poetry, and so he noted there that in the poetry of some nations no
attempt is made to make the last letters [of the line] the same, but only
to make them equal in the time of their reading. Likewise he mentions
that the poetry of some nations does not require that there be a uniform
meter based on vocalization (that is, that the long and short vowels be
of like number and placement in each line), but that whatever is lacking
be compensated for in the melody, though doubtless there was some
[general] ordering in this system, for melody cannot be used to compensate for *any* discrepency [in line-length].
    I have written this because it seems to me that at the time of David
and Solomon their songs were of this sort, for these will not be found to
contain either meter or rhyme. It might well be said that in this their
songs had an advantage over those that are brought out nowadays, for
their path was not so narrow, and they could put into poetry exactly
the idea that they wished to put in, and in its complete form. But nowadays poets have accepted upon themselves many preconditions, things
they must do or must avoid doing, and have thus greatly narrowed the
path before them, so that they have not the slightest leeway, and this
causes them to concentrate and abbreviate and leave out, or to permit
themselves to say foolish things, all of which causes them to sacrifice
the ideas, or at least to make them difficult to understand.[46]

In these lines one finds a view of Biblical poetry which is well argued and
full of insight. Ibn Tibbon flatly asserts that rhyme and meter are not to be
found in Biblical songs, but since (as his pseudo-Aristotelian *auctor* states)
neither rhyme nor meter is a universal *sine qua non* in poetry, their absence
in Hebrew is not to be wondered at—indeed, he repeats the *Kuzari* claim
that, far from being a defect, this aspect of Biblical song is to be regarded as
an advantage. That advantage consists not (as in the *Kuzari*) in the substitu-
tion of the *te'amim* for metrical arrangements, but simply in the greater
freedom allowed the poet in framing his ideas. Like the *Kuzari* he argues
that melody can make up for the lack of exact equivalence in long and short

vowels or total line length;[47] however, ibn Tibbon adds that there must be a general *seder* to the poem, for melody's compensatory powers are not limitless.

Another discussion influenced by the *Kuzari's* arguments was Isaac Abravanel's (1437-1508) treatment of Biblical songs in his commentaries on Exodus 15 and Isaiah 5. Here he presents a threefold classification of poetry;[48] his second class, Biblical songs, are called songs not because they have meter or rhyme, but because they are actually sung. This is essentially what ha-Levi had said, but Abravanel goes on to assert that the fact that they are to be sung imposes upon their authors the necessity of composing them in a certain form:[49]

> Now by "form" I mean an arrangement of formal elements which establishes both the pattern for their reading and the musical structures to which they are to be sung. This is what our Rabbis meant by "a large brick over a small brick, a small brick over a large; a small brick over a small, a large over a large."[50] What this means is that those who established [the rules of] the earlier type of song required that the number of letters [in each word] be set up in accordance with the musical structure which they had decided to accompany it with, and that the order of their rhythmical placement be the order of their syllables. Once in this rhythmical pattern they were attached to the musical structures.
>
> For there is music arranged in such a way that the first element corresponds to the third and the second to the fourth as being equal in length or brevity of the music's duration. The musical pattern of long duration they called "large brick" and that of short duration they called "small brick," which is half the size of a large brick. The rhythm arranged in such a way that the first element corresponds to the third and the second to the fourth they called "small brick over small, large brick over large," and this is the pattern of Moses' Song [Deut. 32] and the plaints of Job and Proverbs, because the arrangement of the poem's content was constructed for being read in this form.

In other words, Abravanel has attached to the practice of stichography a new significance; it indicates a musical pattern of long and short phrases. Of the second sort of these patterns, "large brick over small brick" is the Song of the Sea (Exod. 15), and Abravanel then procedes to distinguish eight "musical structures" in its pattern of phrases. The classification is complicated and (so one must conclude after repeated attempts at making it consistent) somewhat arbitrary, but it was sufficient to qualify Biblical poetry as *systematic* for Abravanel, a significant departure from ha-Levi's position. (It is also most remarkable that he does not disguise his preference for Arabic-style meters over the Biblical "system.")

Finally, one of the most interesting reincarnations of ha-Levi's arguments is found in the Renaissance Hebrew tract *'Arugat ha-Bosem* by Samuel Archivolti (1515-1611). After repeating the *Kuzari's* argument against strict meter (and adding some of his own from Talmudic sources) he notes that there are two general categories of song:

The first is melody which is built to fit the words in consideration of their content. For by melodic changes it is able to distinguish between pause and continuation, a hurrying tempo and a slow one, between joy and sadness, astonishment and fear, and so forth. And this is the most excellent type of melody in music, for not only does it consider the ear's pleasure, but also strives to give spirit and soul to the words that are sung. This type of song was used by the Levites [in the Temple], for it is the only way they could have composed their music, and it is the type fit to be written for songs in our sacred language.

The second type is the popular sort of tune in which the words are written to fit *it* [the music], and its only concern is for what the ear hears, so that a single popular melody will be applied to many songs whose subjects are from each other "as far as the west is from the east" (Ps. 103:12) [but will fit] so long as they are all written in one meter and with one rhyme scheme.[51]

Here we have a reversal which surely would have astounded Abravanel: the fact that there are a limited number of meters to which poems must conform is, far from a virtue, an indication of their inferiority. For while music in Biblical times was tailored to the words, here it is created to be sold, as it were, "off the racks" to poems of any subject and theme; their meter vouch-safes a proper fit, but of course the music will not be able to apply its resources to match the particularities of any one poem's words.

4. *Biblical songs do have meter.* In the earlier period of medieval Hebrew poetry this idea is frequently rejected quite specifically. Any kind of meter is *hokhmat ha'arabim, hokhmat hayishma'elim,* etc.[52] Even in the fifteenth century, Sa'adya ibn Danaan remarked:

We know not when our countrymen first began to busy themselves with the practice of this craft, but it seems to me that it is not the product of our own ancestors, but to its case as well as others applies the verse "and they mingled amongst the nations and learned their ways" (Ps. 106:35). I have looked and searched a great deal and have concluded that before the poems of R. Eliezer Kallir nothing at all of poetry (*haruzim*) was known to our people.[53]

However, the opposite is also maintained. The introduction of Moses ibn Tibbon to his Song of Songs commentary assimilated to the category of metrical poetry the Biblical books of Proverbs, Job, and "most of the Psalms," "because they are verses that are divided up like [Arabic-style] poetic lines, even though the units are not equal in long and short syllables. This is why they are written 'short brick over short brick, long over long,' like poetic lines."[54] This is a remarkable observation as far as parallelism is concerned, for it recognizes that the essence of Biblical "poems" as the *binariness of their lines,* the fact that a pause separates two corresponding halves. In this binariness they resemble Arabic-style poems, even though the two halves do not correspond in long and short syllables: the fact that they break into roughly equal halves is enough for ibn Tibbon to classify them in the same category as Arabic poems, namely, metrical poetry.

Some writers even went so far as to suggest the Arabic meters were themselves derived from Biblical "meters." The anonymous thirteenth-century author of "Handbook of the Grammar of the Hebrew Tongue" claimed that all the resources of poetry are "indicated" or "implied" in the Biblical text, including alphabetical verses, acrostic spellings, rhymes, notarikon, gematria, and, lastly, meter.[55] (His argument is more chauvinistic than his examples convincing, however.)

The author of *Sheqel ha-Qodesh*[56] invoked the popular argument that much, perhaps most, of the Hebrew language had been lost with the Exile[57] to argue that Arabic meter was in fact copied from Hebrew:

About this craft [of metrical poetry] we do know of a single one of our sages who discussed it and did not conclude that its roots lay among the Ishmaelites for [they say] from them did we take it, and [the proof is] they are most adept at it. But I myself believe on the contrary that everything that the Ishmaelites know of this craft they took from the sages of our nation, just as they took their somewhat confused language from the Holy Tongue. For it has happened in this matter of poetry just as it befell us in the study of grammar as a whole; [for though our language and its grammar are far older than Arabic, and were certainly understood in Biblical times, nevertheless it was forgotten and] from their language's grammar our own study of grammar has been derived.[58]

In a similar vein, Moses ibn Habib's *Darkhei No'am* (completed before 1486) records its author's being shown an ancient tombstone in Italy which was written in rhyming verse; "then I truly believed that this sort of metered poetry has existed and been with our people since the days in which our forefathers were dwelling in their own land." Unlike *Sheqel ha-Qodesh*, however, Habib's book goes on to justify the claim of Biblical meters with a (Tibbonide) threefold classification of poetry:

The first is poetry metered insofar as the number of syllables in each column[59] is concerned, save the first agrees with the second neither in any part of its various parts nor in its ending [rhyme], unless this happens by chance, without having been intended.

The second is like the first, save that sometimes the first column will not agree with the second even in the number of syllables, but they will compensate for what is lacking by means of the melody or movements of the throat or they will swallow what is extra with notes of the voice. Of these two categories are the books of Psalms and Proverbs and Job.

Examples may be found of the first type in Psalms [he cites here Ps. 119:146 and Ps. 146:9], and many others like these, in which the first half verse agrees with the second solely in the number of syllables. Similarly in Proverbs [here he cites Proverbs 1:8 and 10:5] and likewise in Job [Job 5:20] and many more in addition to these. However, the majority of the verses are rather of the second class, that is to say the number of [syllables in] the first half-verse does not agree with its fellow: and of this second type is the song of the Red Sea and the song of Moses and the Song of David and the song of Deborah:[60] for whatever is missing or extra [and so destroys the syllabic symmetry] between the half-verse and its fellow will be stretched out or swallowed through the melody as we have explained . . .

The third type is metered poetry in which lines agree in all respects, in the number of feet and the correspondence of the two columns each with his fellow in an equal rhyme. Not only that, but even in the matter of long and short syllables poets are quite careful and will put a short syllable only under a short and long only under and long; and these [are arranged] in various ways, as we shall show, with the help of the Almighty.

In this [third type] the Hebrew tongue has a degree and honor above all other nations, for among them it is impossible to meet one requirement [meter] and also another connected to it, the practice of poets bringing Biblical verses into their poems,[61] either in their literal sense or via a homonymous meaning or metaphorical sense, and there is no other language that can attain this merit.[62]

Any poem not metered in regard to its long and short syllables "shall surely be put to shame" (Song of Songs 8:7) amongst poets, and embarrassment and pain and injury will they cause to its author.

Ibn Habib views meter in the same way Renaissance poets in Europe viewed numerical symbolism: once the concept is accepted, there is no place where it cannot exist. The notion of a poem without meter is for him a contradiction in terms. However, he has borrowed the idea (from the *Kuzari*, and from Moses ibn Tibbon's introduction to Songs of Songs) that melody can equalize unequal verse halves by swallowing syllables or drawing them out in order to assert that the traditional Biblical songs are also, approximately, metrical. (His first and second classes of poetry might easily have been combined into a single class, since in either case the source is the Bible, and none of the Biblical songs will be seen to fit all of its lines into Class One; perhaps he acted as he did in order to stay within the tradition of three classes already seen in ibn Tibbon and Abravanel.)

Thus it was that the problem of Biblical "meters" led ibn Tibbon, ibn Habib and others to set down what perhaps many others had grasped without consciously formulating their ideas: that Biblical verses often divide into halves, and that this (let us call it) seconding structure can work in a way comparable to meter—it can shape the utterance and gives it a regularity, line after line. This is not all there is to be said about Biblical parallelism—it says nothing of the ways in which the correspondence of the two halves is established—but it is the proper beginning.

Azariah dei Rossi

Azariah dei Rossi (c.1511-c.1578) was a true Renaissance scholar who brought to the Jewish world knowledge of texts previously known only to Christians. In his discussion of Biblical poetry he cites the opinions of Philo, Josephus, Eusebius, and Jerome: among his Jewish authorities are Judah ha-Levi, Abravanel, and ibn Habib (though he does not cite the passage translated above). "According to these sages," Azariah writes, "our holy tongue, by its nature and by its usage from earliest times, does not exclude poems with rhythm and meter—not only by virtue of [the equalizing accomplished by] the melody to which the songs are sung, as Don Isaac [Abravanel] says above, but from the standpoint of the words themselves. Indeed, some of these songs may be found in the Bible." Azariah then relates how he arrived at his own solution to the metrical crux:

And "as my cares welled up within me" (Ps. 94:19) to find some answer from among these opinions and discover at least part of what I wanted, my heart said to me: there exist without doubt poetic measures and structures to the Biblical songs mentioned, but they are not dependent on the number of complete or incomplete syllabic feet as in the poems written nowadays—since these are, as the Kuzari says, practices of the poems of Arabic (which is but our language somewhat confused)[63]—but their structure and measures are in the number of ideas and their parts, subject and predicate and whatever is connected to them, in every sentence or clause that is written.

There are cases in which the clause will have two feet, and with the second part that is attached to it there will be four; others will have three, and with the second will have six perfect feet. For example, "Thy right hand, O Lord" which is a clause unto itself with two units, or if you will, two "feet": "wondrous in might," which is connected to it, is quite the same, and together they make four. Similarly, the second "Thy right hand, O Lord" has again two feet; "crushes the enemy" two more, making again four. In the same manner are "The enemy said," I shall pursue and get," "I shall divide and spoil," "I shall be sated," "I shall bare my sword" . . . , etc. Unlike this is the song of Deut. 32, which is three-three, making six, to wit: "Listen O heavens, and I will speak," "And hear, O earth, my words," "Let my lesson flow as rain," "and my words drop as dew."

Sometimes in a single verse (and even more so in a whole song) these two types of [arrangement] of feet will exist together, i.e., two-two and three-three, however the spirit may have rested on the prophet (and also because such variations may fit his purpose). An example of this would be "And with the breath of thy nostrils the waters were piled up," which is two-two: "They stood up like heaps of water, the billows froze in mid-sea" three-three . . .

Now in some of the verses the learned reader must recognize a few words which for one reason or another do not count in the metrical arrangement, as in Deut. 32: "And he said, 'I will hide My Face from them' " the word "And he said" is a separate entity, thus [leaving] "I will hide My Face from them," three feet, and "I will see what becomes of them," another three . . .

You must not count the metrical units [according to the Arabic system] nor yet the words themselves, but the ideas (*'inyanim*). And as regards this it often happens that a little word will be joined to whatever is next to it, so that verses from the Psalms will be seen to observe the order we have described: "Favor me, O God, with your love," "And with your abundant mercy erase my sin . . ." (Ps. 51:3)

It does not escape my attention that there are many verses which I
am unable to fit into the above systems: perhaps even the exceptions
are more numerous than those that obey the rules. For certain the
learned reader will examine my presentation with caution, and so go
forward and find out what I have been unable to find. But ought we
not in any case to believe that all the songs found in the Bible—the
Song of the Sea and of the Well, and Moses' Song, and Deborah's, and
the Song of David, and the books of Job, Proverbs and Psalms—all of
them without doubt have an arrangement and structure, this one in one
manner and this in another, or one song alone possessing different [ar-
rangements of] feet. For we sense when we read them aloud some marvelous special quality, even if we do not completely grasp their structure.[64]

Azariah's account of the genesis of his discovery is perhaps misleading in
one respect: what his "heart" told him was not terribly different from what
ibn Habib had told him (and even more so Moses ibn Tibbon, if he had read
him): that Hebrew lines divide into roughly equal halves. The nuance added
in Azariah's presentation rests on his insistence that one "must not count the
metrical feet, *nor yet the words themselves*, but the ideas." As he shows,
"little words," introductory phrases, exclamations and the like, may be eliminated from this "count," for in distinguishing the ideas from the mere
words themselves he has freed the question of the verse halves' correspondence from the tyranny of syllable and word counting (this is why he need
not invoke the Tibbon-Habib-Abravanel argument that imbalance of the
verse halves is covered over by the melody). By hinging the correspondence
on the question of meaning, he had taken a great step forward in the understanding of parellelism. It is true, of course, that Azariah still thinks in
terms of a quasi-metrical regularity and consequently fails to perceive that
the relationship of *B* to *A* was not a matter of meter, but emphasis, seconding. At least, however, he turned the search for regularity away from counting syllables or words and connected it to the meaning of the words.

Lowth, needless to say, perceived more: he saw the semantic-syntactic
parallelism of *A* and *B*. Yet the interpretation he (and more than Lowth
himself, his followers) imposed on this fact has proven more misleading
than helpful: *parallelismus membrorum* became (what it really is not) a
kind of conscious tinkering to symmetrize *A* and *B*, and this misunderstand-
ing was then exaggerated into being a metrical substitute, the "system" of
Hebrew "poetry."

The structure of Biblical songs was one of those questions whose answer
is far too simple to satisfy the questioner. The chief virtue of Azariah's
answer may thus lie in the fact that it made no grandiose claims. Like his
predecessors, he felt that verse halves should be numerical equals, for poetry
was a matter of numbers; but his "equal" was flexible enough to accept
extra syllables, constructs, and particles without disturbance. In counting
up the number of ideas he came close to bringing together two matters be-

fore and since strictly segregated, line length and meaning: but the essence of Biblical parallelism is that they are not separate.

In a spirit similar to Azariah's are later remarks on the subject of Biblical poetry, notably those of Yehuda b. Yosef Moscato[65] and Abraham b. David Portaleone.[66] Noteworthy also is the statement of Immanuel Frances (1618-1710) that the first "poem" in the Bible appears to be Lamekh's war boast (Gen. 4:23-24) *mikkefel hallashon bemillim shonot:*[67] ibn Ezra's phrase is now actively applied to equate parallelism of meaning with the presence of poetry. Frances also classifies Biblical writing as either narrative, rhetorical, or poetic, listing in the last category Exodus 15, Deuteronomy 32, Psalms, and others: "However I have not found these songs to have either rhyme or meter, save for the fact that in each and every line there is a pause (*hefseq*). Perhaps they were sung to a melody no longer known."[68] Clear thinking such as this might not have satisfied those (particularly English and German Protestants) of Frances' contemporaries bent on finding the "secret" of Hebrew poetics, but had it been accepted, Lowth's "discovery" might have been properly tempered. Amidst the confessions of ignorance or incomplete knowledge of Azariah, Portaleone, or Frances lies more wisdom than in the certainties advanced by other critics in the centuries that were to follow.

NOTES

1. Many critics have noticed this without, however, calling into question the validity of the very concept of Biblical "poetry." See, for example, W. L. Holladay, "Prototypes and Copies: A New Approach to the Prose-Poetry Problem of the Book of Jeremiah," *Journal of Biblical Literature (JBL)* 79 (1960), 351-367, and "The Recovery of Poetic Passages of Jeremiah," *JBL* 85 (1966), 401-435; Luis Alonso-Schoekel, "Poésie hébraique" in C. Cazelles et al., *Supplément au dictionnaire de la Bible*, fasc. 42 (Paris, 1967), pp. 56-57; J. S. Kselman "The Recovery of Poetic Fragments from the Pentateuchal Priestly Source," *JBL* 97 (1978), 161-173.

2. *Shir* or *shirah*, "poetry" in later Hebrew, are in the Bible but two of many genres named which feature some use of parallelism. There is no indication that these words (or any others) were used in Biblical times to describe as a whole the type of composition written in relatively elevated style, still less to mean anything like "poetry." Indeed, where lists of genres occur, as in Proverbs 1:1-6 or Ben Sirah 46:17, the absence of such grouping comes into bold relief. If an opposition was made, as in I Kings 5:12 or Ben Sirah 44:5, it was between sung and spoken (or written) genres (*shir* or *mizmor* versus *mashal*), all of them, however, parallelistic to some degree.

3. Some editions of Rashi contain other examples, but this may simply be a back-formation from his grandson's commentary: see below.

4. Cf. his remarks on Gen. 49:22, where he adduces a similar list.

5. (Fuerth, 1839), p. 9a.

6. Cf. Saadia Gaon's explanation of the same phenomenon in 2 Sam. 22:2 ff., Ps. 29:8, etc. (cited by Samuel b. Isaac ha-Sefardi in his Samuel commentary and

reprinted in J. Kafih, *Perushei R. Sa'adya Ga'on 'al ha-Torah* (Jerusalem, 1963), p. 175. Of course it is unnecessary to explain a specification of a part *followed* by the whole, since what is said second is not included in the first. Thus in solving this difficulty Saadia and ibn Ezra were separating off the only problematic usage of parallelism, but thereby failing to consider the phenomenon as a whole.

7. Kimhi was so credited in Dukes, *Zur Kenntnis der neuhebräische Poesie* (Frankfurt, 1842), p. 125; in a reply, Schmiedl adduced ibn Ezra's comment on Gen. 49:6 (see *MGWJ* [1861], p. 157).

8. On Job and Jeremiah see his *'Asarah Kelei Kesef* (Pressburg, 1904), p. 153.

9. See Ibid., pp. 27-29.

10. His work was well known among Oriental Jews but was only rediscovered in the West in the nineteenth century. See I. Goldziher, *Studien über Tanhum Jeruschalmi* (Leipzig, 1870); also B. Toledano in *Sinai* 42 (1961), p. 339 (a general review) and Hadassah Shai, "Almurshid alkafi," in *Leshonenu* 33 (1969), p. 196.

11. H. Shai, oral communication.

12. *Kitab al-Muhadara wal-mudhakara*, ed. A. S. Halkin (Jerusalem, 1975).

13. In *Kitab al-luma'* (Hebrew translation *ha-Riqma*, ed. M. Wilensky [Berlin, 1931], p. 303).

14. A brief summary is available in English in S. Spiegel's article "Medieval Hebrew Poetry" in L. Finkelstein, *The Jews* (New York, 1965), II, 82.

15. See E. Dukes, *Nahal Qedumim* (reprinted Tel Aviv, 1970), p. 22.

16. S. ibn Gabirol, in *Shirei Hol*, ed. Brody and Schirmann (Jerusalem, 1975), p. 170. Cf. Joseph ibn Kimhi's explanation of his title *Sheqel haqqodesh*: "I have written [my book] in meter so that it will be easy to grasp and to copy correctly— therefore I have entitled it *The Holy Sheqel* ('weight' but also 'meter')."

17. See B. Klar, *Mehqarim ve-'Iyyunim* (Jerusalem, 1954), p. 102.

18. Ibid.

19. In *'Eben Bohan* found in H. Schirmann, ed., *Ha-Shirah ha-'Ibrit bi-Sfarad*.

20. David b. Yom Tob Bilia (Villa?) (first half of the fourteenth century), *Derekh la'asot haruzim*, ed. N. Allony in *Kobez 'al Yad*, XVI, 234. On poets as prophets cf. D. Yellin, *Torat ha-Shirah ha-Sefaradit* (Jerusalem, 1946), p. 3 note. Joshua b. Israel Benveniste (1595-1676) in *Quntrus Pereq be-Shir* cites an "ancient" anonymous treatise in which the equation of poet and prophet leads its author to apply to poets the same strictures and requirements imposed by the Talmud on prophets.

21. Attributed by E. Carmoli to Abshalom Mizrahi; but see A. Neubauer, *Melekhet ha-Shir* (Frankfurt, 1865), p. *iv*.

22. *'Imrei Shefer* in Neubauer, *Melekhet ha-Shir*, p. 25.

23. For a discussion of this see Allony's introduction to *Ha-'Egron*, p. 114.

24. M. Zulay, *Ha'eskola happaytanit shel R. Sa'adya* (Jerusalem, 1964), pp. 19-31; see also Saadia's *Haggalui*, ed. Harkaby (St. Petersburg, 1891), pp. 155-157.

25. See especially his preface to his Psalms translation, where he refutes even the notion that the Psalter's prayers and exhortations imply words addressed *to* God and hence not given by God: "When it says (Ps. 39:13) 'Hear my prayer' [it means] 'I am [a God] who hears the prayers of my servant'; 'Keep me, God, for I rely on you' (Ps. 16:1) means 'I keep my servant because he relies on me.' " J. Kafih, ed. *Tehillim 'im targum RSG* (Jerusalem, 1966), p. 24.

26. See Allony, ed., *ha'Egron*, pp. 114 ff.

27. Cited in Harkaby's edition of *Ha-galui*, p. 98. Cf. Maimonides' view, as

articulated in his introduction to the *Guide of the Perplexed* and part 2, chaps. 43-45, as well as his *Mishneh Torah, Hilkot Yesodei Hattorah* 7:3-5: "The things that are shown to the prophet in prophetic visions are shown to him figuratively, and he immediately imprints in his heart the interpretation of the figure in the prophetic vision and he knows what it is . . . Some prophets give both a figure and its interpretation . . . and some the interpretation alone, and sometimes they say the figure alone without the interpretation." Cf. Joseph Albo, *'Ikkarim* (Philadelphia, 1930), III, 222-223.

28. Though Saadia certainly understood a great deal about parallelism, he was not driven (as others were later) to attempt to systematize his knowledge, precisely because he did not consider it a *poetic* regularity. Thus the catalogue of the forms of poetry at the end of the *'Egron* (Allony ed., pp. 387-389) is most emphatically post-Biblical. See also Allony, p. 395, note 83.

29. See on this N. Allony, *Mittorat hallashon vehashirah bimei habbeinayim* (Jerusalem, 1944), p. 5.

30. See the *Mekilta*, ed. J. Z. Lauterbach (Philadelphia, 1933), II, 2ff; also R. J. Loewe, "Apologetic Motifs in the Targums to Song of Songs" in A. Altmann, ed., *Biblical Motifs* (Cambridge, 1966), p. 169; Eric Werner, *The Sacred Bridge* (New York, 1963), p. 139.

31. See on this Moses ibn Ezra, *Kitab al-muhadara*, pp. 46-47; for Saadia and ibn Ezra on Job 12:11 see *ha'Egron*, ed. N. Allony (Jerusalem, 1968), pp. 112, 389.

32. In Schirmann, *ha-Shirah ha-'ibrit*, III, 338.

33. M. ibn Ezra identifies these three as the only poetic books of the Bible; Moses ibn Tibbon does likewise (see below); Solomon al-Harizi (1170-1235) wrote in his *Tahkemoni*: "For whilst our forefathers were still dwelling in the Holy City/ They were not acquainted with metered poetry in the Holy Tongue/ Still, the books, of Job, Proverbs and Psalms/ Have verses which are short and simple (*pesuqim qesarim wegalim*)/ And they seem like poetic lines but they have no rhyme and are not metered." (Contained in Schirmann, *Hashirah ha'ibrit*, II, 133: for al-Harizi's use of *haruz to* mean "line of poetry," cf. Abravanel's commentary in Exodus 15, also *Derekh la'asot haruzim*, p. 235, note 17.)

34. See Aristotle's *Poetics* 1447b.

35. See R. J. Loewe, "Apologetic Motifs," p. 161.

36. Cf. E. Dukes, *Nahal Qedumim*, p. 54; Schirmann, *Hashirah ha'ibrit*, I, intro. p. *xxxvii*; and D. Pagis, *Shirat ha-Hol vetorat hashir* (Jerusalem, 1970), pp. 46-50.

37. These two, via Arabic poetics were closely associated with all poetry and rhetoric. Caught in this predicament, the author of *'Imrei Shefer* notes: "Therefore, while the songs of David and Solomon, Asaph, Heman and Jeduthun are all truthful utterances, the songs of our day are completely or largely falsehood and lying" (Neubauer, *Melekhet ha-Shir*, p. 25).

38. Crucial here is the threefold division of the canon. Poetry, in the common view, was to be limited to parts of the *Ketubim*, plus those parts of the Torah and Prophets specifically labeled as "song." In his commentary on Isaiah 5:1, Abravanel specifically asserts that this "song" of Isaiah by its nature excludes divine inspiration.

39. *Kitab al-muhadara*, pp. 46-47. Early Christian exegetes, notably Augustine and Cassiodorus, pursued a similar line; note also Bede's treatise, *De Schematibus*. In Renaissance England there was a revival of this approach, and the Bible was used

in schoolboy manuals of rhetoric and good style. See I. Baroway, "The Bible and the English Renaissance," *Journal of English and German Philology*, XXXII (1933), 470.

40. *Nofet Sufim* (Vienna, 1863), p. 184.

41. An idea foreign to the modern sensitivity is that the sorts of poems one writes depends on where one is, but this notion is central to M. ibn Ezra's explanation of Arabic preeminence in poetry, and there is a hint of something like it in the *Mekilta's* notion that prophecy is only possible in certain places (J. Lauterbach, ed., *Mekilta* 1, 4-6).

42. It has been discussed at length in N. Allony, *Mi-Torat ha-Lashon veha-Shirah*, pp. 1-17.

43. See Solomon b. Abraham Parhon, *Mahberet ha'Aruk* (Pressburg, 1844), p. 5a.

44. But in fact often obscure the parallelism. For example, Balaam's opening oracle (Num. 23:7) begins with a parallelistic pair, "From Aram Balak summons me, the king of Moab [brings me] from the hills of the East"; in this verse "hills of the East" corresponds to Aram, and "Balak" to "king of Moab." However, the *te'amim* parse "Balak king of Moab" as a single phrase, obscuring the pause which should fall right in the middle of it.

45. Parhon, *Mahberet ha'Aruk*, pp. 4b-5a.

46. The only part of this commentary to have been published is the passage cited, which I have taken from Judah Moscato's commentary on the *Kuzari*, *Qol Yehuda* (Venice, 1594 and subsequently), sec. 2, 70.

47. This idea he passed on to his son, Moses ibn Tibbon (see his commentary to Song of Songs, ed. 1874, p. 7), who repeated it in the same formulation; thence it was passed on to Abravanel in his commentaries to Exod. 15 and Is. 5, to M. ibn Habib in *Darkhei No'am*, and ultimately to Azariah dei Rossi.

48. This threefold division comes as well from Moses ibn Tibbon, but see below, note 54.

49. Cf. also ibn Danaan in Neubauer, *Melekhet hashir*, p. 5, where he describes the fitting of words to "musical structures."

50. Terms to designate two different stichographic systems (see Meg. 16b and Jer. Meg. 3:7 as well as M. Breuer, *Keter 'Aram Soba*, [Jerusalem, 1976], pp. 149-189). "Large brick over small" was the interlocking system of blank spaces and groups of words found, for example, in Exod. 15. "Small brick over small" made for the two-column effect found, for example, in the scribal rendering of the Sons of Haman (Esther 9:7-10).

51. *'Arugat ha-Bosem* (Amersterdam, 1730), pp. 100a and b.

52. See, e.g., A. ibn Ezra, *Sahot* (Fuerth, 1827), p. 118.

53. In Neubauer, *Melekhet ha-Shir*, p. 6; cf. note 33 above.

54. M. ibn Tibbon, *Song of Songs*, p. 7. I do not know the ultimate source of the threefold division of the classes of poetry found in M. ibn Tibbon's commentary and in so many subsequent works. It is interesting that his comments are repeated almost word for word in the Song of Songs commentary on his near contemporary, Immanuel of Rome (see ed. of Frankfurt, 1908, p.5): he introduces this catalogue with "it is well known to every learned man that the classes of song are three in number," a phrase hardly appropriate if ibn Tibbon were the originator of this division. Note also that Falaquera's poet gives a (quite different) threefold division in *The Book of the Seeker*.

55. See *Quntrus be-Diqduq Sefat 'Eber*, ed. S. Posnanski (Berlin, 1894). No

doubt the impetus to find standard metrical patterns in *individual* Biblical lines comes from the medieval practice of *shibbus* or "interweaving" Biblical phrases into metrical poems. Usually the citation was only a brief phrase, but occasionally an entire Biblical verse was found which coincided with one of the standard medieval meters.

56. Felt by H. Yalon to be Samuel Almoli; see his edition of the book (Jerusalem, 1965) for a summary of the argument.

57. An argument already seen above in the students of Menahem b. Saruq whereafter are many restatements. See especially P. Duran, *Ma'aseh 'Efod* (Vienna, 1865), pp. 39-43. It is also treated in the Kuzari, II, 68; A. ibn Ezra, *Safah Berurah*, p. 46; S. ibn Gabirol, "Ha'Anaq" in *Shirei Hol*, p. 169; Yedaiah ha-Penini in Dukes, *Nahal Qedumim*, p. 23; Moses b. Isaac b. Hanesiah, *Sefer ha-Shoham*, ed. B. Klar (Jerusalem, 1945), p. 5. See also ibn Tibbon's preface to his translation of Bahya ibn Pakuda's *Hobot ha-Lebabot*.

58. H. Yalon ed., *Sheqel ha-Qodesh*, pp. 52-53.

59. Of verse halves; in what follows he uses *tor* to mean an individual verse half as well as an entire column of them. D. Pagis has pointed out Habib's innovation here in counting the *shewa* as a full syllable; see "Development of the Hebrew Iamb," in *ha-Sifrut*, IV, 686.

60. I.e., those four songs named in *Massekhet Soferim*.

61. On this practice, *shibbus*, see D. Yellin, *Torat ha-Shirah*, pp. 119-138.

62. This idea comes from Profiat Duran, *Ma'ase 'Efod*, p. 43. Habib was an admirer of Duran and his influence is felt elsewhere in this work.

63. Cf. ibn Danaan in Neubauer, *Melekhet ha-Shir*, p. 3.

64. D. Cassel, ed. *Me'or 'Eynayim* (1866), pp. 208-209.

65. See his commentary on *Kuzari* sections 68-72; also, *Nefusot Yehudah* (Lwow, 1859), pp. 1a-5b, a remarkable synthesis of Jewish and Christian writings on music.

66. *Shiltei ha-Giborim* (Mantua 1612), p. 3b.

67. *Meteq Sefataim*, ed. H. Brody (Cracow, 1892), p. 30.

68. Ibid., p. 30. The last idea is also stated in Abravanel's commentary on Exodus 15:1.

5

The Limitations of Human Knowledge According to Al-Farabi, ibn Bajja, and Maimonides

Shlomo Pines

One of the most perplexing problems posed by the *Guide of the Perplexed*—and to my mind a fundamental one—relates to two apparently irreconcilable positions held by, or attributed to, Maimonides. On the one hand, he sets very narrow limits to human knowledge; on the other, he affirms that man's ultimate goal and man's felicity consist in intellectual perfection, that is, in knowledge and contemplation (*theoria*).[1] It is hard to admit that a knowledge that includes neither metaphysics—the cognition of God and immaterial beings, that is, separate intellects—nor celestial physics is man's final end. I will attempt to show that an unpublished text of Ibn Bajja[2] throws light on the antecedents of this problem and thus clarifies the issue.

The text in question is one of the treatises of Ibn Bajja collected in MS Pococke 206 of the Bodleian Library. It deals with a lost but much quoted work of al-Farabi, his *Commentary on the Nicomachean Ethics*, concerning which it provides important new information. I have tried to show that, given the evidence—ibn Bajja's quotations and those of other authors—we are justified in asserting that al-Farabi's *Commentary* was a seminal work[3]: the necessity to disprove one of its theses may have shaped Averroes' thinking on the hylic intellect, and its Latin translation may have provided Marsilius of Padua with one of his most incisive formulae. It may have also given Ibn Bajja's reflections a new turn.

In this chapter I shall *inter alia* consider the possibility that the direct or indirect influence of this work of al-Farabi may account for some distinctive traits of Maimonides' thought. A translation of a small section of Ibn Bajja's text follows. (In the MS on which it is based some words are missing.)

[The following belongs also] to his [Ibn Bajja's] Discourse: As to what is believed about Abu Nasr [al-Farabi] regarding that which he says in his *Commentary* on the Book of *Ethics*, namely that after death and demise[4] there is no afterlife,[5] that there is no happiness except political happiness,[6] that there is no existence except that which is perceived by the senses and that that through which it is said another existence than the one which [has just been mentioned comes about] is nothing but an old wives' tale. [I am of the opinion that] all this [that which is believed about al-Farabi] is false, [that those are lies (used to attack) Abū Nasr [al-Farabi]. For Abū Nasr [al-Farabi] has made these remarks at his first reading [of the *Ethics*[7]]. But what he says on this subject does not resemble these statements of his that are entailed by a demonstration.

It is worth noting that in this rather involved passage Ibn Bajja does not deny al-Farabi's having made the remarks which were used to denigrate him. The point he wishes to make is that these pronouncements do not carry much weight and need not be taken seriously; unlike other statements by al-Farabi, they are not backed by a demonstration. This objection does not seem to be wholly correct. Al-Farabi based his negations on a logical argument (which Ibn Bajja apparently found unconvincing).[8]

In the passage quoted above one bit of information is new and startling: al-Farabi is reported to have affirmed that there is no happiness except political happiness.[9] This phrase, which is identical with a formula found in the *Defensor Pacis* of Marsilius of Padua, denies that happiness (*eudaimonia*) is achieved by contemplation (Greek *theoria*). In the framework of the Aristotelian system this means that intellectual perfection is not the final end of man. This view seems to be due to the fact that, according to al-Farabi, metaphysics, regarded as cognition of the immaterial entities, is a science that transcends human capacity. The other statements attributed in the passage to al-Farabi can by and large be matched by quotations from the *Commentary* on the *Ethics* found in a variety of sources. But reference to political happiness provides a clue for this interpretation. They negate traditional philosophy at least as much as they negate naive religion, which perhaps was not foremost in al-Farabi's mind when he made the observations under discussion.

The consequences of al-Farabi's position are spelled out by Ibn Bajja in a passage that occurs some lines after the one translated:

A statement (*qawl*) made by al-Farabi [in the work in question], which does not resemble other statements of his [is concerned with the opinion] attributed by him to some[10] of the Ancients; [according to al-Farabi] they [opposed] a violent negation [to the teaching concerning the separation[11] of the soul from the body]. Now this is not the doctrine (*qawl*) of one of the ancients, but that of the miscreant (*dāllīn*) Ikhwān al-Safā'. It is an evident [consequence] of this doctrine that happiness [consists] in a [human] individual being a part of the city in such a way that he serves[12] [it] in a manner appropriate to his degree so that he and the people [of the city] obtain many good things[13] perceived by the senses, [things] that pertain to civic[14] [life] and that procure pleasure in ways consonant with the interests of the community.[15] [In] serving [the latter] in a manner appropriate to his station he [helps] to bring about both for himself and for the people [of the city] the most excellent political circumstances, those that are most favorable for the permanent existence (*baqā'*) in security of the [human] species throughout the length of durable existence (*Tūl al-baqā'*).

This is a model for a state, the activities of whose inhabitants are wholly directed toward material security and welfare, a totalitarian state which is clearly an end unto itself. In imputing this conception to the Ikhwān al-

Safā', Ibn Bajja has probably had in mind their Ismā'ili leanings.[16] On the other hand, it seems evident that only his immense respect for al-Farabi prevents him from taxing the author of the *Commentary* on the *Ethics* with this conception.[17]

In our text Ibn Bajja's view of the objectives that should be pursued in civic governance (*al-tadbīr al-madanī*) seems to be more or less identical with the doctrine expounded by al-Farabi in such treatises as *Ārā' Ahl al-Madīna al-Fādila*. Ibn Bajja makes it plain that civic government, especially in the case of a virtuous city (*al-madīna al-fādila*), may be of great help in the furtherance of intellectual development, that is, in bringing about in man the existence of an intellect cognizing many intellecta.[18] Some of these intellecta are mentioned: God, His angels, His scriptures, His messengers, all His creatures. The "degree" of these cognitions, that is, their greater or lesser adequation to true intellection varies, since it depends on the degree of the cause of the cognition.[19]

This enumeration of intellecta resembles in part a similar enumeration occurring in *Arā' Ahl al-Madina al-Fādila*[20]: Al-Farabi lists in that passage the things and matters that the people of the Virtuous City know (*ma'rifa*). He does not have in mind intellection in the strict sense of the word. Thus there may exist some excuse for the conjecture[21] that in the passage cited Ibn Bajja's reference to intellecta in connection with the knowledge of God and the angels lacks semantic rigor. Or he may have been guilty of inconsistency.

In the text under discussion there is no indication that Ibn Bajja at the time of writing had renounced the philosophical politics advocated by al-Farabi,[22] that is, the obligatory participation of the philosopher qua philosopher in public affairs. Such a renunciation is a main theme of this *Tadbīr al-Mutawahhid*. This attitude could be fully explained by the political climate of his time, in which the revolutionary, partly philosophical, propaganda of the Ismā'ilīs had spent its force.[23] It would be mere speculation to imagine that his revulsion from the reduction of all human goals to the pursuit of political happiness propounded by al-Farabi in the *Commentary* on the *Ethics* may have been one of the factors which had brought about this renunciation.

In his *Commentary*, al-Farabi maintained the mortality of the soul[24] and of human intellection. In the first place I shall try to place in a historical perspective his assertion concerning the soul. One of the interesting points about this assertion is that the *Commentary* on the *Ethics* may have been the earliest work written by an Arab philosopher in which this conception was spelled out. Al-Kindi professed belief in the separate existence of the soul. Al-Farabi himself refers in other works, as is pointed out by Ibn Tufayl,[25] to the afterlife of the soul. The aggressive tone which he apparently used, in the *Commentary* on the *Ethics*, in denying this afterlife, may be due to the circumstance that no Arab philosopher had previously formulated this denial (which may be regarded as a necessary consequence of some formulae of Aristotle's *De Anima*).

After al-Farabi, the belief that the individual souls have an afterlife is criticized by Ibn Butlan, a Christian philosopher from Baghdad.[26] This critique may be derived directly or indirectly from al-Farabi's *Commentary*, whose doctrine on the point in question may have been adopted by the philosophers of Baghdad. Avicenna, on the other hand, taught that the individual souls continued to exist after death. I have suggested elsewhere[27] that this may be one of the main questions in which the two doctrines and philosophical traditions posited by Avicenna—the occidental tradition, which to a large extent is represented by the philosophers of Baghdad, and the oriental tradition, which may be assimilated to the personal opinions of Avicenna—are supposed to be in total disagreement.

As regards the Intellect, Averroes quotes in the *Long Commentary* on the *De Anima*[28] from al-Farabi's *Commentary* on the *Ethics* an argument by which the Cordovan philosopher seems to have been so impressed that, in order to be able to answer it with a show of reason, he conceived his well-known theory concerning the hylic intellect. "If it had been possible for a substance subject to generation and corruption to intellect abstract forms (*formas abstractas*), that is, forms that are totally separate from matter, it would have been likewise possible (*possibile esset*) for the nature of the contingent (*natura possibilis*) to become necessary." In other words human cognition transcends temporality. This argument clearly entails the denial, as far as men are concerned, of the highest kind of knowledge which is free of any recourse to sense data: it is the knowledge in which the knower, the known, and the act of knowing are identical. The abstract forms to which al-Farabi refers are, among other things, God and the separate intellects: man can have no knowledge either of the former or the latter.

The Arab and Jewish philosophers who had accepted al-Farabi's conception of the mortality of the individual soul, that is, by and large all the philosophers with whom Avicenna's influence was paramount,[29] tried to construct theories that might legitimate the rejection of the view of the human intellect propounded in al-Farabi's *Commentary* on the *Ethics*. An account of these theories would make up a considerable part of the history of Arab and Jewish philosophy.

I have made a brief study of Averroes' position;[30] in this chapter Ibn Bajja will be the only Arab philosopher (except for al-Farabi) with whom I shall deal in this connection. It would seem that he had no less than two[31] theories on the point at issue. One of them is set forth in the text in which he quotes and criticizes al-Farabi's *Commentary* on the *Ethics*. According to this theory, man has an intellect that grasps intellectual objects (*ma'qūlāt*) by means of insight (*basīra*), the latter being a divine faculty[32] that emanates from the active intellect but is not identical with it. This faculty relates to the percepts of the imagination in a way analogous to the relation between the senses and their percepts. It grasps, by means of something analogous to light that subsists in it, quiddities[33] of the percepts of the imagination. To speak metaphorically, it chisels these percepts into shape. For example, we grasp in this way the quiddities of the celestial motions and thus the noblest objects of cognition are actualized in us.

It is man's own essence that grasps the quiddities actualized in it, and for this it has no need of a body. Man's intellect (which exercises this activity) is perdurable, it is immortal. It belongs to the category of intellect, although it is the lowest among them.

This conception of Ibn Bajja calls for the following observations: the percepts of the imagination undergo a transmutation when they are transferred to the sphere of the intellect, are actualized in man's essence, become objects of intellection. It is true that after this transmutation they have no relation to matter and to sensual objects. There is, however, in what may be called the epistemological section of the text,[34] no reference to objects of intellection that were not prior to their transmutation percepts of the imagination (and before that percepts of the senses). The fact that the quiddities of the celestial movements are regarded as the noblest objects of intellection is in keeping with the foregoing observation.

This doctrine is similar in many respects to views expounded by al-Farabi in *R. al-'Aql wa'l-Ma'qūl*, mentioned by Ibn Bajja in the text under discussion. The main difference seems to be that the cognition of forms that have no connection with matter and never have had, is regarded as possible in this treatise by al-Farabi and is not mentioned at all in Ibn Bajja's text. It is tempting to suppose that this omission is due to the influence of al-Farabi's *Commentary* on the *Ethics*, but there is no proof.

What appears to be a different theory is set forth in other treatises by Ibn Bajja. I have profited by A. Altmann's masterly analysis of this theory,[35] but for my purposes here I shall put a somewhat different emphasis on various points. The treatise I shall refer to in this connection is Ibn Bajja's *Risālat al-Ittisāl*,[36] The *Epistle on Conjunction*. In the first lines of the treatise Ibn Bajja speaks of the "knowledge"[37] for which he had found demonstration and of the "greatness" and "remarkable characters" (*gharāba*) of the matter (p. 103). The indications he gives show that the conception expounded in the *Epistle* was influenced by nonperipatetic sources, one of which he did not recognize as such: on page 112 he quotes Alexander of Aphrodisius' *K. fi-l-Suwar al-Rūhāniyya*. In point of fact this treatise is an extract from Proclus' *Elements of Theology*. However, he also refers explicitly (pp. 114-115) to Plato's theory of ideas,[38] which he criticizes. I shall not go into the details of Ibn Bajja's doctrine, referred to both in the Kuzari and in Maimonides, concerning the unity of the human intellect, that is, the identity of the intellect which subsists in different human individuals.

The doctrine of the unity of the intellect is not mentioned in the treatise of Ibn Bajja which gives his views on the *Commentary* on the *Ethics*. A second point of disagreement between this text and the *R. al-Ittisāl* may be found in the fact that according to the former the objects of intellection that are divorced from matter and are actualized in the intellect are transmuted percepts of imagination that have been grasped by the divine faculty called insight. In the *R. al-Ittisāl* the higher objects of intellection have as their substrata not percepts of the imagination but other objects of intellection.

The following passage from this treatise goes even further (and is perhaps not quite consistent with the statement, based on other passages,[39] that has just been made concerning the doctrine of the treatise):

From what I have said it has become clear that there are three degrees: the first is the degree of the multitude (*al-jumhuriyya*); it is the natural degree (*al-martaba al-tabi'iyya*). For them the object of intellection is bound up with the material forms. They only know it through and from them, [derived] from them (*'anhā*) and with a view to them (*lahā*). All the practical crafts (*al-sanā'i' al-'amaliyya*) pertain to this (p. 112).

The second is theoretical cognition (*al-ma'rifa al-nazariyya*). It is at the summit of the natural [cognition]. [The difference is that] the multitude look first at the [material] substrata (*al-mawdū'āt*) and [only] in the second place and for the sake of the substrata, at the object of intellection. The theoreticians of the natural sciences[40] [on the other hand] look first at the object of intellection and [only] in the second place, and for the sake of the object of intellection, [to which] they liken them,[41] at the material substrata. For this [reason] the propositions employed in the sciences contain all of them a subject (*mawdū'*) and a predicate[42] which is referred to (*al-mushār ilayhi*). For this [reason] the propositions are universal (*kulliyya*). It is evident that in our statement "every man is an animal," there is a third [term] which the Arabs omit, in expressing the meaning [contained] in this statement, as they omit the particle[43] [which is known as] the copula (*al-rābita*). For our statement every man is an animal indicates that which is indicated [by the statement] "everything that is a man is an animal" and "whatever thing is described as being a man is also described as being an animal." [Statements which present] similar [modes of] expression are either tautological or they indicate aspects[44] that are concomitant and equivalent.[45] It is clear that this differs from the meaning of our statement "man is a species as an object of intellection . . . [A person who has achieved] this degree of theory[46] sees the object of intellection, but only through an intermediary, as the sun is seen[47] in water, for what is visible in water is [the sun's] image, and not [the sun] itself. The multitude sees an image of the image; this is similar to the sun's casting its image into water, and this image being reflected in a mirror and being seen in the mirror, which does not [contain the particular thing[48]] that is reflected. The third degree is that of the happy ones that see the thing [as it is] in itself (p. 113).[49]

In the treatise there are also other accounts of the three (or four) degrees; some of the variation in the terms and the imagery used are of some interest. On page 114, there is an interpretation of the myth of the cave. There are people dwelling in almost total darkness; there are people, they are the great majority, who are aware of the existence of the intellect; they are compared to the cave dwellers who do not see light as separate from colors. Then there are the men of speculation,[50] who may be compared to people who have come out of the cave, and separately see the light and all the colors. Finally there are the happy ones who might be compared to people whose sight has been transmuted to light.

On page 117 the people belonging to the second degree, the men of speculation, are referred to as the *tabī'iyyūn*, the physicists, the men studying natural sciences, who use definitions. They see the intellect, but jointly with other things.

Aristotle and other happy (men) belong to the third degree. In spite of appearances, they are "one in number,"[51] for there is no difference between them except in externals.

On page 116, people belonging to the second degree are likened to "a polished surface (*al-sath al-saqīl*), as [for instance] the surface of a mirror which makes itself seen and in which other things may be seen. He is nearer to deliverance (*takhallus*) than [the people belonging to] the first degree and yet he is in a state that is subject to corruption (*bālin*). People belonging to the third degree are most like . . . the sun itself. However [in point of fact] nothing that is a material body is like unto them . . . They are not subject to corruption and passing away."[52]

A summary of some of the main points of the theories which have been discussed would seem to be in order. But before this I shall make a brief reference to a relevant doctrine of Alexander of Aphrodisias, which may help to bring the other theories into focus.

According to Alexander,[53] a (human) intellect *in actu*, which is identical with the act of intellection, intellecting something subject to corruption is itself subject to corruption. If however the object is not subject to corruption, neither is the intellect; this being a consequence of the identity of the intellect with the object of intellection. We may surmise that in the *Commentary* on the *Ethics* al-Farabi had in mind *inter alia* the doctrine of Alexander. What the *Commentary* appears to mean[54] is that, since man is incapable of intellecting abstract forms, his intellect cannot be transmuted into a perdurable substance; nothing in man escapes death. The abstract forms that cannot be *cognized* by man certainly include the separate intellects; they may also have included forms that, according to other theories, one of the theories of Ibn Bajja for instance, the human intellect is able to abstract from sense percepts or percepts of the imagination.

Given the logic of the doctrinal system deriving from Alexander, it should have been, and apparently was, a moot question whether the cognition of such abstract forms survives the death of the body, that is, is immortal. Gersonides, who discusses this point at some length, answers the question in the affirmative and concludes that this is the only kind of immortality vouchsafed to man,[55] men being unable to cognize and achieve union with the active intellect. This may have also been in substance the conclusion of Ibn Bajja in the theory I have dealt with in the first place. However, according to Ibn Bajja's "second" theory, man can transcend this degree of cognition, intellect incorporeal entities, attain identity with the active intellect.

These preliminary observations may possibly help us find the right perspective in our inquiry concerning Maimonides' views as expressed or hinted at in the *Guide of the Perplexed*, on the limitations of human knowledge and on the final end of man. They will help us in the first place to give a narrower and perhaps clearer definition of the object of our inquiry.

With a view to this, reference will be made to Maimonides' Introduction to the *Guide* (page 7 of my translation): "We are like someone in a very dark night over whom lightning flashes time and time again. Among us there is one for whom the lightning flashes time and time again, so that he is always, as it were, in unceasing light . . . That is the degree of the great one among the prophets, to whom it was said: *But as for thee, stand thou here by Me*[56] . . . Among them there is one to whom the lightning flashes only once in the whole of his night; that is the rank of those of whom it is said: *they prophesied, but they did so no more.*[57] There are others between whose lightning flashes there are greater or shorter intervals. Thereafter comes he who does not attain a degree in which his darkness is illumined by any lightning flash. It is illumined, however, by a polished body or something of that kind, stones or something else that give light in the darkness of the night. And even this small light that shines over us is not always there, but flashes and is hidden again . . . It is in accord with these states that the degrees of the perfect vary. As for those who never even once see a light, but grope about in their night, of them it is said: *They know not, neither do they understand; they go* about in darkness.[58] The truth, in spite of the strength of its manifestation, is entirely hidden from them."

The simile of lightning flashes seems to be derived from Avicenna's *K. al-Ishārāt wa'l-Tanbīhāt*. According to this work[59] experiences of the *'ārifūn* perceiving something of the light of truth may be likened to lightning which flashes momentarily and is then extinguished. These are called moments, *awqāt*, a sufi term. If, however, a person has by dint of (spiritual) exercise attained a certain station, the lightning flash may be transformed into a permanent luminous phenomenon seen in the sky, an experience which has some resemblance with that of Moses in Maimonides' Introduction to the *Guide*. The Avicennian category *'ārifūn*,[60] "those who know," appears to include some of the sufi mystics, those who have attained spiritual degrees and also in all probability the prophets. In Maimonides' Introduction only the prophets appear to see the lightning flashes. If this image refers *inter alia* or exclusively to cognition, as seems likely, it would mean that, according to Avicenna, only the *'ārifūn* or, according to Maimonides, only the prophets are able to cognize intelligibles that are not abstractions of corporeal objects. In the case of Maimonides, the reference in the Introduction to the man whose darkness is illumined "by a polished body" may be adduced in support of this interpretation. The word "polished" (*saqīl*) calls to mind "the polished surface" (*sath saqīl*) to which people belonging to Ibn Bajja's second degree are likened. The simile is somewhat different, but it could have been inspired by *R. al-Ittisāl* or by some other treatise by Ibn Bajja. As far as I can see, it means that the people, whose degree in the hierarchy is inferior to that of the prophets, need (like the persons who belong to Ibn Bajja's second degree) for their intellection perception of corporeal objects (the polished bodies).

Maimonides' Introduction thus appears to indicate that only prophets (and not the philosophers belonging to "the third degree" of *R. al-Ittisāl*) can cognize incorporeal entities. This seems to mean that the cognition that can be achieved by the prophets is different in kind from that of all other men (including the philosophers) and may be beyond their ken. The possibility that this position of Maimonides may have been determined by theologico-political reasons need not concern us for the moment. What matters is that Maimonides did not consider himself a prophet[61] and certainly did not write with a view to being read by prophets. Everything points to his having envisaged the possibility of his being read by philosophers, and he may have thought that he was one himself. This being so, it is of great significance that, as the common run of people as well as the philosophers (but not the prophets) are concerned, Maimonides may seem to adopt in the Introduction to all intents and purposes the theory that we have designated as Ibn Bajja's "first" doctrine, according to which human intellection depends on the perception or imagination of material objects.

It is not my task in this chapter to find out to what extent various relevant texts of the *Guide* confirm or disprove this interpretation of Maimonides' epistemology. His theologico-political assessment of the superiority of Moses' faculty of intellection over that of other people will concern us only indirectly; it may throw light on the nature and limitations of the intellectual activity of men who are not Moses. Maimonides' views on the other prophets seem to be less significant in the context of this investigation.

In the first place, I shall quote two passages that at first may not seem to accord with or easily to fit into the interpretation referred to above.

This passage occurs in the course of a discussion concerning knowledge of the Name composed of forty-two letters.

It has been made clear in the books that have been composed concerning the divine science, that it is impossible to forget this science; I mean thereby the apprehension (*idrāk*) of the Active Intellect (I, 62, my translation p. 152).

Furthermore the relation of the intellect in actu existing in us, which derives from an overflow of the Active Intellect and through which we apprehend the Active Intellect, is similar to that of the intellect of every sphere that exists in the latter. (II, 4, my translation p. 258).

Does the term *idrāk* (apprehension) mean that the human intellect *in actu* cognizes the active intellect in the Aristotelian sense of the verb—in other words does it achieve identity with this intellect, which is separate from matter? An investigation of the way Maimonides employs *adraka, idrāk* shows that this interpretation is not obligatory. This may be inferred from the last chapter of the *Guide* (III, 54, pp. 636 and 638 of the translation), in which we encounter twice the expression: "the apprehension (*idrāk*) of Him, may He be exalted." On page 638 the phrase reads: "It is clear that the perfection of man that may truly be gloried in is the one acquired by him who has achieved, *in a measure corresponding to his capacity*, apprehension of Him, may He be exalted." Given this wording and Maimonides' views on the limits of man's cognition of Deity, it is evident that *idrāk* of God does not mean an intellectual act that brings about the identity of the subject and object of intellection. The meaning of the term is much weaker. It is legitimate to suppose that Maimonides, when referring to man's apprehension of active intellect, likewise gave *idrāk* this weaker meaning. As far as I can see, all the texts of the *Guide* that might seem to postulate man's capacity to cognize immaterial being or to intellect without the help of sense percepts or images are as ambiguous and indecisive as the two that have been quoted.

The reasons for assuming that the opposite thesis was regarded by Maimonides as correct are much stronger and, it seems to me, cannot be gainsaid. Two categories of texts are relevant in this connection: those which describe or characterize in some manner man's cognitive activity and those (more important in this context) which refer to the limitations of the human intellect. Some texts may be held to belong to both categories. The clearest and most detailed description of an act of human intellection found in the *Guide* is this:

> Know that before a man intellectually cognizes a thing, he is potentially the intellectually cognizing subject. Now if he has intellectually cognized a thing (it is as if you said that if a man has intellectually cognized this piece of wood to which one can point, has stripped its form from its matter, and has represented to himself the pure form—this being the action of the intellect), at that time the man would become one who has intellectual cognition *in actu*. Intellect realized *in actu* is the pure abstract form, which is in his mind, of the piece of wood. For intellect is nothing but the thing that is intellectually cognized (I, 68, pp. 163-164).

This intellectual act is described apparently in order to enable the reader to compare it with the intellection of God, discussed in the second half of the chapter, with which it has both points of similarity and differences. It is doubtless significant that the intellectual cognition of a material object, a piece of wood, is used in this context as an example of human intellection. A question which may spring to mind is whether this choice of an example is intended *inter alia* to produce the impression that all human intellection is of this type.

At this point Maimonides' views on the limitations of human knowledge should be examined. It seems to me that his so-called negative theology admits of two interpretations, which, to some extent at least, are mutually exclusive. Textual evidence may be adduced in support of either of them. To put the matter succinctly, Maimonides may have adopted the doctrine professed by Greek Neoplatonists, Christian theologians, and Muslim mystics and sectarians that the deity is unknowable *per se*, that it cannot be cognized by any conceivable intelligence, that of men or that of the separate intellects if these are assumed to exist; or he may have considered that God, like the separate intellects cannot be grasped by a human intellect,[62] whose activity is dependent on sense data and images. Many of Maimonides' statements seem to be in accord with the first interpretation,[63] but the second appears to account for the following passage (III, 9; translation, pp. 436-437): "Matter is a strong veil preventing the apprehension of that which is separate from matter as it truly is . . . Hence whenever our intellect aspires to apprehend the Deity or one of the intellects, there subsists this great veil interposed between the two." The term "intellects" means in this context the separate intellects. This passage entails at least two conclusions: man cannot cognize God because the human intellect is tied up with the body. For the same reason man cannot cognize the separate intellects.

The second conclusion is of considerable importance, as it appears to mean that man can only know material objects or objects connected with matter. The view, based on III, 9, that according to Maimonides men do not have the capacity to achieve naturally—through an exercise of their cognitive faculty—knowledge of the separate intellects[64] is indirectly confirmed by the *Guide* I, 37, and I, 38. Both chapters refer *inter alia* to God's answer to Moses's request (in Exod. 33) to see His face. In I, 37, Maimonides sets forth his interpretation of Onkelos' translation (Exod. 33:23) of this answer. According to this interpretation Onkelos wished to convey that the text signified that God informed Moses that "there are . . . great created beings whom man cannot apprehend as they really are. These are the separate intellects." The things that can be apprehended in their true reality are those "endowed with matter and form." I, 38, purports to give Maimonides' own explanation of one part of God's answer. According to this explanation Moses was granted the favor of apprehending "all the things created" by God. This clearly implies that as a result of God's response to Moses's request, the latter was given the capacity to know even such transcendent beings as the separate intellects.

Maimonides had no need to give in this context Onkelos' translation or to put on it an interpretation that runs counter to the explanation which is put forward as his own. This way of proceeding may possibly be accounted for by the supposition that he wished to hint that the natural limitations of the knowledge of a corporeal being made it probable that "Onkelos' interpretation" was correct and that Maimonides' own explanation was propounded for theological reasons,[65] a doctrine emphasizing the uniqueness of Moses being needed for the defense of religion.

It is significant that Moses is given a similar role in Maimonides' discussions of astronomy and celestial physics. According to the *Guide*[66] (III, 22 and 24, and elsewhere), no theory intended to explain the nature of the heavenly bodies and to account for their motions can, because of the human limitations, be regarded as certain. Moses is the only human being that may be assumed to have had this knowledge (III, 24, translation p. 327). In this context too the exception made in favor of Moses is in all probability connected with Maimonides' interpretation of Exod. 33:23 and may also be supposed to have been formulated for theological reasons.

It should be noted that as regards astronomy, Maimonides adopts a position that is different from that which is set forth in the text in which Ibn Baaja propounds his "first" theory. As stated above, the essence of the motions of the heavenly bodies is, according to this theory, the most sublime object that can be intellected by man. Maimonides, on the other hand, considers that man can have scientific knowledge (which involves intellection) only of the phenomena of the sublunar world.

At this point the analysis of Maimonides' views on the limitations of the human intellect can be summed up as follows: as in Ibn Bajja's "first theory" the human intellect can only cognize objects perceived by the senses and images deriving from sense data; in contradistinction to that theory, Maimonides is of the opinion that no scientific certainty can be achieved with regard to objects that are outside the sublunar world.

The first of these theses is of considerable importance; it provides, if taken seriously, a criterion which might permit us to distinguish in the philosophy of Maimonides[67] the conceptions that conform to this epistemology and can therefore be regarded as having been reached through the application of a critical method, from those that may be termed "metaphysical" (if the adjective is not given its medieval meaning, but is used, as in many modern writings, in a somewhat pejorative sense). Another possible designation of the conceptions set forth in the *Guide* which, according to Maimonides' epistemology, cannot be verified because they transcend the limits of human knowledge would be to describe them as forming a part of a philosophical theology.

Guide I, 68, is a case in point. The chapter begins (translation, p. 163): "You already know that the following dictum of the philosophers with reference to God . . . is generally admitted (*shuhrat hadhihi al-qawla allatī qālathā al-falāsifa fi'llāh*); the dictum being that He is the intellect as well as the intellectually cognizing subject and the intellectually cognized object (*innahu al-'aql wa'l-'āqil wa'l-ma'qūl*) and that those three notions form in Him one single notion in which there is no multiplicity."

It is obvious that, if Maimonides' epistemology is accepted, man cannot possibly[68] have the knowledge of God that is presupposed in the "dictum of the philosophers." In this respect the analogy that is drawn in the chapter between God's and man's intellection does not and probably is not intended to prove anything. It may be significant that Maimonides refers to the *shuhra* (rendered in the translation as "generally admitted") of the "dictum." The Arabic word has the same root as *mashhūrāt*, a term used by Maimonides to denote notions that are generally admitted without either being self-evident indubitable truths or having been proven by rigorous rea-reasoning.

It would thus seem that to Maimonides' mind the so-called Aristotelian philosophical doctrine would be divided into two strata: intellectually cognized notions whose truth is absolute, and which form a coherent system, namely terrestrial physics; a much more comprehensive and ambitious system, namely celestial physics and metaphysics which is concerned with the higher being. However the conceptions and propositions which make up this system cannot be cognized by the human intellect. They are in the best case merely probable. It is, however, possible, but there is no explicit Maimonidean warrant for this hypothesis, that they provide the philosophers with a system of beliefs, somewhat analogous, as far as the truth function is concerned, to the religious beliefs of lesser mortals. It is, however, significant that the thesis concerning the Deity set forth in *Guide* I, 68 is also propounded—as Maimonides quite correctly points out at the beginning of the chapter—in *Mishneh Torah*.[69] In both works, the thesis in question forms a part of a theological system, which may be believed, but cannot be proved to be true. In passages in which this critical (in the Kantian sense) attitude is expounded, Maimonides refers to his sources; he may also have had sources which he does not mention.

The authors whom he explicitly cites in support of his attitude are Aristotle and Alexander of Aphrodisias. Both these authors have occasionally given expression to their awareness of the fact that some of the theories they propound are not certain, but merely plausible, and Maimonides makes much of this. His overemphasis is tantamount to a misrepresentation of the views of these authors.[70] For our purpose it is particularly significant that in *Guide* II, 3, Maimonides makes use of the authority of Alexander in order to buttress his statement "that the opinions held by Aristotle regarding the cause of the motion of the spheres—from which opinions he deduced the existence of separate intellects—are simple assertions for which no demonstration has been made;" they are however "of all the opinions put forward on this subject, those that are exposed to the smallest number of doubts and those that are the most suitable for being put into a coherent order." This view clearly entails the consequence that the existence of the separate intellects is merely probable and that no way has been found to attain certainty with regard to this matter. This being so, there is no point in setting oneself the aim to intellect or achieve a conjunction with a separate intellect.

When expounding his "critical" attitudes Maimonides does not refer to Ibn Bajja, but it may be assumed with a certain degree of likelihood that he was acquainted with what we have called "the first theory" of his Spanish predecessor.

Finally there is al-Farabi's *Commentary* on the *Ethics*. There is a quota-

tion in *Guide* III, 18,[71] to this seminal work, whose impact has been mentioned above. This quotation appears to refer to the moral progress of
human individuals "who have the capacity of making their soul pass from
one moral quality to another." But Maimonides was also exposed to the
influence of other opinions set forth by al-Farabi in this work.

As has been stated, al-Farabi, in this *Commentary*, denies man's ability
to intellect incorporeal entities; apparently in connection with this denial,
he rejects the conception according to which the human intellect may survive death. He has nothing but contempt for the belief in the afterlife (of the
soul).

A second point which should be mentioned is that, according to evidence
of Ibn Tufayl,[72] al-Farabi propounds in the *Commentary* in question the
idea that the imaginative faculty, and it alone, produces prophecy—the
implication being that the intellect has no part in it—and that philosophy is
superior to prophecy. It is not a matter of indifference that Maimonides
encountered in a work written by al-Farabi, on whom he relied more than
on any other Arab philosopher, a conception which by and large seems to
have corresponded to what was Spinoza's conception of prophecy. A third
point that has already been mentioned, is that Ibn Bajja appears to indicate
that in the *Commentary* al-Farabi made it clear that political (or civil,
madanī) happiness was the only happiness that men could achieve.[73]

What was Maimonides' position with regard to the afterlife and more
especially to the philosophical conception of the survival and permanence
of the intellect?

In the *Sefer ha-Mada'* and the *Treatise on Resurrection*[74] there are explicit
references to the afterlife, which are calculated to leave no room for doubt
as to Maimonides' acceptance of the idea. If, however, one turns to the
Guide, one is struck by the meagerness of the evidence found in that work
concerning Maimonides' views on the point at issue.

As far as I can see, the only passage in the *Guide* which contains an apparently unambiguous affirmation of the survival of the intellect occurs at
the end of III, 51 (translation, p. 628). After having described the death by a
kiss of Moses, Aaron, and Miriam, Maimonides goes on:

> The other prophets and excellent men are beneath this degree; but it
> holds good for all of them that the apprehension of their intellects
> becomes stronger at the separation . . . After having reached this condi-
> tion of enduring permanence that intellect remains in one and the same
> state, the impediment that sometimes screened him off having been re-
> moved. And he will remain permanently in that state of intense plea-
> sure, which does not belong to the genus of bodily pleasures, as we
> have explained in our compilations and as others have explained be-
> fore us.

In speaking of "our compilations" (*tawālīfunā*) Maimonides refers to
Mishneh Torah, called by him in the *Guide ta'līfunā al-kabīr*, and no doubt

also to other nonphilosophical works of his. The contexts in which these writings are cited in the *Guide* should be examined. It may be a tenable hypothesis that these references are at least sometimes used by Maimonides to indicate that the passages in the *Guide* in which they occur pertain to theology or a theological philosophy which is not wary of putting forward assertions that the limited human intellect is unable to verify. This hypothesis may be *inter alia* valid for the passage quoted above, as its comparison with two other passages tends to show. One of these occurs in I, 74, *Seventh Method* (translation, pp. 220-221). In order to rebut the argument of a believer in the creation of the world in time—who makes the point that if on the one hand the world were eternal and consequently "the number of men who died in the limitless past" were infinite, and, on the other hand, the souls had, as the philosophers say, a permanent existence, there would be an infinite number of souls existing simultaneously, which because of the impossibility of an actual infinite is impossible—Maimonides remarks in the first place "that this is a wondrous method, for it makes clear a hidden matter by something even more hidden . . . It is as if he already possessed a demonstration of the permanence of the souls and as if he knew in what form they last and what thing it is that lasts."

The argument is continued as follows:

> Now you know that regarding the things separate from matter—I mean those that are neither bodies, nor forces in bodies, but intellects —there can be no thought of multiplicity of any mode whatever, except that some of them are the causes of the existence of others . . .
>
> However, what remains of Zayd is neither the cause nor the effect of what remains of 'Umar. Consequently all are one in number, as Abu Bakr Ibn al-Sa'igh (Ibn Bajja) and others who were drawn into speaking of these obscure matters have made clear. To sum up: premises by which other points are to be explained should not be taken over from such hidden matters, which the mind is incapable of representing to itself.

This passage can be interpreted in two different ways. It may be understood as expressing Maimonides' agreement with the theory of Ibn Bajja, which, according to the *Guide*, postulates the permanence and the unity after death of the human intellect; or it may be held to indicate Maimonides' view that the permanent existence of the soul or of the intellect are "hidden matters," which the mind is incapable of representing to itself. On the whole it seems to me[75] that the second interpretation is, more than the first, in line with Maimonides' argument, though as far as "philosophical theology" as defined above is concerned, he may have inclined to Ibn Bajja's opinion. The second passage with which we are concerned occurs in *Guide* I, 72, and is related to the issue of afterlife, in a circuitous way. Maimonides makes the suggestion that the relation of God to the world may be compared to that obtaining between man and the acquired intellect (*al-'aql al-mustafād*), which is separate from the organic body. He then goes on (translation,

p. 193): "However, the case of the intellects of the heavens, that of the existence of separate intellects, and that of the representation of the acquired
intellect, which is also separate, are matters open to speculation and research. The proofs with regard to them are well-hidden, though correct;[76]
many doubts arise with regard to them; the critic may well find in them objects for his criticism and the caviller objects for his cavilling."

There is no need to discuss in connection with this passage the various
theories concerning the acquired intellect. Maimonides makes it abundantly
clear that the latter has a relation to, but is separate from, the corporeal
human individual. It should be added that the philosophical doctrine concerning the afterlife is predicated on the existence of this and/or of the other
separate intellects.

Again, as in the passage quoted before this one,[77] Maimonides inclines to
accept the argumentation of the philosophers, but points out that these matters are hidden. It is, as it seems to me, on the face of it unlikely[78] that the
immortality of the intellect, which in the judgment of the Maimonides of the
Guide is an obscure and problematic matter, should be considered by him
as the goal of the human individual. With regard to another moot question,
the eternity of the world or its creation in time, Maimonides endeavors to
prove in the *Guide* at great length, that the human reason is incapable of
discovering the truth of the matter. It very clearly serves his purpose to
drive this fact home. It seems to me probable that he takes a similar agnostic
position with regard to the thesis of the permanence of the intellect, but pre-
fers not to expatiate on this matter.

The discussion whether, as Aristotle affirms, the theoretical life is superior to the practical, is in the context of medieval philosophy closely connected with the question of the goal of man. It may seem at first that in this
point Maimonides adopts in the *Guide* an attitude conforming to orthodox
Aristotelianism; however, a closer scrutiny seems to show that his position
is at least ambiguous, and this ambiguity calls for an interpretation.

In this matter, an observation on one of the roles assigned within the
frame of reference of the *Guide* to *al-'ilm al-ilāhī* "the divine science" (the
term can often be correctly rendered by "metaphysics") may serve as a starting point.

Al-'ilm al-ilāhī which appears to be a rendering of the *epistēmē theologilēē*
(used by Aristotle to designate the science of metaphysics) is variously defined by the Arab philosophers.[79] There is no general agreement as to the
scope and objects of this discipline. Thus, for instance, some texts (*inter alia*
one by al-Farabi) consider the science of being and the investigation of the
principles of the particular (*juz'ī*) sciences as forming an integral part of
al-'ilm al ilāhī. There is a general censensus on one point: the knowledge
of God and the incorporeal entities is regarded as one of the main subject
matters of this divine science. According to Avicenna's *Mantiq al-Mash-
riqiyyīn* it is its only subject matter, the other areas dealt with in Aristotle's
Metaphysics being regarded as belonging to another discipline, the general

science, *al-'ilm al-kulli*. This terminology partly corresponds to the one used
by al-Farabi in *al-Maqāla fī Aghrād al-Hakīm fī Kull Maqāla min al-Kitāb
al-Mawsūm bi'l-Hurūf*, but al-Farabi states in his treatise that *al-'ilm al ilāhlī*
forms a part of *al'ilm al kullī;* the unity of metaphysics is thus preserved.

Given these texts and others that could be adduced, there can be no doubt
that God and the immaterial beings are either the unique or one of the main
objects of *al-'ilm al-ilāhī*. On the other hand, we know that, according to
Maimonides, men other than Moses (whose status is determined by theological rather than philosophical considerations) cannot cognize the immaterial
beings or perhaps even know for certain that they exist. And no man without exception can have positive knowledge of God. He can have negative
knowledge of Him, and he can know His attributes of action, that is, he can
grasp the natural phenomena and their causes. Negative knowledge, which
is highly prized by Maimonides, is knowledge of what is not God. It is difficult, or rather impossible, to equate it with the traditional *'ilm ilāhī*. This is
also the case with regard to the knowledge of the attributes of action. This
knowledge appears to correspond at least in part to natural science.

These preliminary remarks may facilitate the understanding of the difficulty presented by a passage in *Guide* III, 51. In a parable in which God is
figured as a ruler dwelling in his palace, various classes of men are differentiated according to their ability to approach the palace or to enter it.

The highest degree, that of Moses, and the second, that of the other
prophets, need not concern us for the moment. The other higher degrees are
those of the men who engage in science and philosophical speculation.
Maimonides enumerates them in an ascending order (translation, p. 619):

> Those who have plunged into speculation concerning the fundamen-
> tal principles of religion, have entered the antechambers. People there
> indubitably have different ranks. He, however, who has achieved dem-
> onstration, to the extent that that is possible, of everything that may be
> demonstrated and who has ascertained in divine matters, to the extent
> that that is possible, everything that may be ascertained, and who has
> come close to certainty in those matters in which one can only come
> close to it has come to be with the ruler in the inner part of the habita-
> tion.
>
> Know, my son, that as long as you are engaged in studying the
> mathematical sciences and the art of logic, you are one of those who
> walk around the house searching for its gate . . . If, however, you have
> understood the natural things, you have entered the habitation and are
> walking in the antechambers. If, however, you have achieved perfec-
> tion in the natural things and have understood divine science (*al-ilā-
> hiyyāt*), you have entered in the ruler's place into the *inner court* and
> are with him in one habitation. This is the rank of the men of science;
> they, however, are of different grades of perfection.

This hierarchy of the sciences is the traditional philosophical one. It may
be added that in the traditional philosophy the place of a particular science
in the hierarchy corresponded, as it does in the passage of the *Guide* that

has been quoted, to the degree of perfection that the cognition of the subject matter of the science in question conferred upon man. This is justified as far as Alexander of Aphrodisias' doctrine and others similar to it are concerned; for they postulate man's capacity to cognize and thereby to achieve union with immaterial entities.

In Maimonides' epistemology (which may have been formed under the influence of al-Farabi's *Commentary* on the *Ethics* and of Ibn Bajja's "first theory"[80]) this kind of intellection of the immaterial entities and of the union with them consequent upon this are impossible for man. This means that *al-'ilm al-ilāhī,* the divine science, with regard to whose object matter no certainty is possible for man, compares unfavorably (if one accepts Ibn Bajja's "first theory," as Maimonides may have done by and large) with terrestrial physics, for the subject matter of the latter enables man to intellect concepts that endure. This seems to lead to the conclusion that there is a discrepancy between the hierarchy of sciences expounded in III, 51, and Maimonides' epistemology. As has already been pointed out, there exists a conflict between the latter and the traditional philosophical commonplaces.

The final good and the ways of life man should pursue are set forth in the conclusion of the *Guide for the Perplexed* (III, 54, translation p. 638): "It is clear that the perfection of man that may be gloried in is the one acquired by him who has achieved, in a measure corresponding to his capacity, apprehension of Him . . . , and who knows His providence extending over His creatures as manifested in the act of bringing them into being and in their governance . . . the way of life of such an individual, after he has achieved this apprehension, will always have in view loving kindness, righteousness and judgment, through assimilation to His actions . . . as we have explained several times in this Treatise."

Apprehension of God may, in view of the limitations of the human mind, be equated with the knowledge of God's governance. This knowledge characterizes the men who belong to the highest class, mentioned in the parable of the palace in III, 51, the people who have the rank of prophets (translation, p. 620). The last words of the passage quoted from III, 54 refer first and foremost to I, 54.[81] The latter chapter deals with God's favorable answer (Exod. 33:19) to Moses' first request; Moses is shown God's goodness. According to the interpretation of Maimonides this means that Moses learned to know the divine attributes of action, that is, the way the world is governed. The examples of this governance given by Maimonides refer to natural phenomena, some of them assuring the preservation and the permanence of the living beings, such as the production of embryos, the development of their faculties, and the care bestowed by the progenitors upon their offspring. Because of these phenomena God is called merciful, though He is not affected by compassion. In a similar way, because of destructive phenomena such as earthquakes, violent storms, and wars bringing about the extermination of a people, He may be called jealous and vengeful without His being affected by the passions which these epithets appear to refer to.

The three qualities, loving kindness (*hesed*), judgment (*mishpat*), and righteousness (*zedakah*), that according to the conclusion of the *Guide* should be initiated by certain men, are also attributes of action. They do not imply that God in His essence is righteous, just, and full of loving kindness. This applies also to men who become similar to God (I, 54, translation, p. 126): "It behooves the governor of a city, if he is a prophet, to acquire similarity to these attributes, so that these actions may proceed from him according to a determined measure, and according to the deserts of the people who are affected by them and not merely because of his following a passion." To become similar to God in respect of the attributes of action constitutes the highest perfection of man (I, 54, p. 128): "For the utmost virtue of man is to become like unto Him, may He be exalted, as far as he is able; which means that we should make our actions like unto His."

The only positive knowledge of God of which man is capable is knowledge of the attributes of action, and this leads and ought to lead to a sort of political activity which is the highest perfection of man. The practical way of life, the *bios praktikos,* is superior to the theoretical.

It would be easy to challenge this view of the position of Maimonides; there are passages in the *Guide* which appear to disprove it. In part the internal contradiction may be laid at the door of Plato, whose political philosophy had—mainly indirectly, through the intermediary of al-Farabi—deeply influenced Maimonides. This philosophy is profoundly ambiguous (and that of al-Farabi perhaps even more so[82]). The recommendation that the philosopher, considered as the highest type of man, should return to the cave or should engage in political action, must if carried out, lead to a renouncement of the life of thought, that is, to his ceasing to be a philosopher.[83]

This chapter may *inter alia* tend to show that this contradiction need not remain unresolved. If, to use the Platonic image, man, because of the nature of his cognitive faculty is unable, or able only to a limited extent, to leave the cave, as Maimonides, probably under the influence of al-Farabi and the "first theory" of Ibn Bajja, appears to hold, the superiority of the theoretical life may appear as less than evident. Both Kant and Maimonides, the first outspokenly and the second partly by implication, have tried to show that because of the limitations of his mind man is incapable of intellecting some of the main objects of the traditional metaphysics. There may be a correlation between this fact and the tendency of both philosophers and also of al-Farabi to accord primacy to the life of action.[84]

APPENDIX

The Fourth Source of Disagreement and Error according to the Guide I, 31

The following passage occurs in the *Guide* I, 31 (translation pp. 66-67):

Alexander of Aphrodisias says that there are three causes of disagreement about things. One of them is love of domination and love of strife, both of which turn man aside from the apprehension of the truth as it is. The second cause is the subtlety and the obscurity of the object of apprehension in itself and the difficulty of apprehending it. And the third cause is the ignorance of him who apprehends and his inability to grasp things that it is possible to apprehend. That is what Alexander mentioned. However, in our times there is a fourth cause that he did not mention because it did not exist among them. It is habit (*ilf*) and upbringing. For man has in his nature a love of, and an inclination for, that to which he is habituated. Thus you can see that the people of the desert—notwithstanding the disorderliness of their life, the lack of pleasures, and the scarcity of food—dislike the towns, do not hanker after their pleasures, and prefer the bad circumstances to which they are accustomed to good ones to which they are not accustomed. Their souls accordingly would find no repose in living in palaces, in wearing silk clothes, and in the enjoyment of baths, ointments, and perfumes. In a similar way, man has love for, and the wish to defend, opinions to which he is habituated, and in which he has been brought up and has a feeling of repulsion for opinions other than those. For this reason also man is blind to the apprehension of the true realities and inclines towards the things which he is habituated. This happened to the multitude with regard to the belief in His corporeality and many other metaphysical[85] subjects as we shall make clear. All this is due to people being habituated (*ilf*) to, and brought up on, texts that it is an established usage to think highly of and to regard as true and whose external meaning is indicative of the corporeality of God and of other imaginings with no truth in them, for these [texts] have been set forth as parables and riddles (*al-muthul wa 'l-alghāz*).

The definitions of causes one, two, and three are taken over by Maimonides from Alexander of Aphrodisias' treatise on *The Principles of the All*.[86] The fourth cause has apparently been added by Maimonides,[87] and it poses a problem. For it seems to indicate that Maimonides considered that "our times," that is, the times when people are brought up on, and taught to venerate, the revealed scriptures and other religious texts, are less propitious, as far as the acquisition of true knowledge and the avoidance of errors are concerned, than the pagan times in which Alexander of Aphrodisias lived. This is difficult to reconcile with Maimonides' well-known position according to which the hints given in the Scriptures, which are full of parables and riddles help those who have the capacity to become philosophers to achieve true knowledge.

In fact the reference to the fourth cause is derived from a text of Aristotle. A comparison of this text, of Averroes' *Commentary* on the text and of another passage of Averroes with this reference may throw some light on Maimonides' method of composition and perhaps also on his intention.

The text of Aristotle (*Metaphysics*, II, 3, 995a, 2-6) may be rendered as follows: "The habitual is intelligible. The strength of habit is shown by the *nomoi* in which that which is mythical and childish prevails by force of habit over our knowledge of what it is."[88]

The Arabic translation of the passage quoted by Averroes in his long

Commentary on the *Metaphysics* (ed. M. Bouyges, Beirut, 1938, I, 42-43) is on the whole accurate: "The thing which is arranged (*jarat bihi*) [in accordance] with habit, with what is familiar (*al-'āda wa'l-alfa*), and in obedience to what has been heard is more intelligible. We come to know the extent to which habits order (*jarat bihi*) things through an examination of the nomoi (*nawāmīs*). For you will find that the riddles (*al-alghāz*) and the things resembling idle tales (*al-khurāfāt*) that are in them have such a high [status] in the souls of the people that their true reality cannot be recognized."

It seems to me certain that the passage of the *Guide* quoted above derives di.ectly or indirectly from this text of Aristotle. It may be noted that in the Arabic translation of the *Metaphysics* the word *alfa* occurs, while Maimonides in *Guide* I, 31 uses in a similar sense the cognate word *ilf* (habit). In both passages the word *al-alghāz*, "riddles," is employed in similar contexts. As for the meaning, the two passages treat of the strength of habit and give as an example the uncritical acceptance by men of the riddles that occur in the *nomoi* (according to Aristotle) or in religious texts (according to Maimonides).

The text of the *Metaphysics* cannot, however, be adduced in support of Maimonides' contention that in pagan times (more accurately, the Greek pagan times) people were less apt than in the monotheistic, revealed religions to adopt, because of habit and their upbringing, false notions considered by them part of their religion.

Averroes in his *Commentary* on this text of Aristotle (pp. 43-44) does not explicitly affirm this superiority of paganism over the monotheistic religions, and it is not quite certain whether he gives a hint to this effect in the following passage.

His [Aristotle's] purpose in this passage is to call attention to the things that hinder [man] from attaining the truth in the human sciences . . . The strongest of these [hindrances] is the fact of being brought up since childhood in some opinion. It is the dominant factor[89] in causing [men of] inborn intelligence[90] to turn away from the knowledge of the true realities of things, especially of those that are dealt with in this science [metaphysics]. This is because most of the opinions dealt with in this science [pertain to the religious] nomos (*namusīyya*) and have been invented for the sake of the people (*al-nās*) in order that they should seek [to acquire] virtue (*fadīla*) and not in order to make truth known to them. Truth is referred to them in riddle (*alghāzan*). The reason for all this is that the existence of men (*al-nās*) can only become perfect in society (*ijtimā*); and society is only possible through virtue. The acquisition of virtues is therefore a necessary matter for all of them. This, however, is not the case with regard to the acquisition of knowledge concerning the true realities of things. [For] not everyone has the capacity for this. This [lack of capacity] is not found in respect of the opinions pertaining to the religious law (*al-ārā' al-shar'iyya*, nor in respect of the science with, preceding [the others] are the first to be studied by man. We may see this happened to many young men, who studied first of all, before [the other sciences] the one which is called among us the science of kalam.

The use of the adjective *shar'iyya* shows clearly that Averroes had in view the Islamic society, but he does not state in so many words that he considered that religious education was less harmful in Greek times. Indeed his words may be construed to mean that the religious upbringing whose effects he deplores is a necessary evil, as society cannot exist without it.

In another work, the *Prooemium* to the *Long Commentary* on Aristotle's *Physics*,[91] Averroes, referring to statements made by Alexander of Aphrodisias in his *Commentary* on the *Physics* with regard to the beneficial effect of the knowledge of the theoretical sciences on the moral character and conduct, remarks (pp. 451 f.) that the scholars of his own (Averroes') time do not show the good qualities mentioned by Alexander. This is due to something "unnatural" (*hus min ha-teva'*) that happened to them. The text of the Hebrew translation which treats of this "unnatural" thing is partly unintelligible. The Latin translation (see p. 470, n. 8), which does not concord with the Hebrew is somewhat clearer. The general sense seems to be in part as follows.

The philosophers hold in small esteem the ideal of perfection in which they were educated, not because of the religious law, but because of the people who corrupt the law. On the other hand, they are considered by people in general to be unworthy of playing a part in the life of the city. The consequence is that in Averroes' times most of the philosophers are swayed by worldly desires and do not in fact deserve to be regarded as part of the city. S. Harvey (p. 470) considers that the remark concerning wordly desires may contain a reflection on Ibn Bajja's conduct. It may be added that the statement concerning the philosophers not participating in the life of the city seems to refer to a theory propounded by Ibn Bajja in *Tadbīr al-Mutawahhid*. According to this theory the philosophers should consider themselves strangers in the city. In contradistinction, Averroes and Maimonides endeavored to integrate philosophy into the life of the community.

This text of Averroes appears to refer to the harm caused by the prejudices of Islamic society to the moral character of the philosophers, but it does not mention the hindrance that an upbringing in a society professing a monotheistic, revealed religion constitutes to intellectual development. In the passage in *Guide* I, 31, in which Maimonides added to three causes of disagreement enumerated by Alexander a fourth one (derived from *Metaphysics* 995a, 2-4) for which habit and upbringing are responsible, this hindrance is described at some length. Maimonides may have encountered this idea in some text that is not known to us.[92] But the available evidence does not negate the possibility that in his statement concerning the fourth cause Maimonides may not have been wholly dependent on Aristotle and some commentaries (from whom the greater part of the statement may be assumed to be derived) but may have introduced some traits of his own into the passage, in which he indicates very clearly that it was easier to attain truth in Greek pagan society than it is in Jewish society, whose members are brought up in the veneration of the Scriptures.

NOTES

1. In this context it should be noted that in the *Guide of the Perplexed* Maimonides affirms that the patriarch and Moses combined unremitting intellection and contemplation with practical activity.

2. I intend to edit the text in question.

3. In a paper read in Paris in 1976 at a colloquium on Averroes, "La Philosophie dans l'Économie du Genre Humain selon Averroès: Une Réponse à al-Fārābī." It will be published in the Acts of the Colloquium.

4. Literally, "separation." The manuscript has *al-mawt al-mufār.qa* I read *al-mawt wa'l-mafarāqua*. The reading *al mufāriq* is likewise possible.

5. *Baqā'* (the reading is not quite certain), "permanence, permanent existence."

6. Or "civic happiness," *al-sa'āda al-madaniyya*.

7. Another possible translation might be "on his first studying philosophical texts." The phrase might also be rendered "Abu Nasr has in effect made these remarks according to what one understands at the first reading."

8. On Ibn Bajja's views see below.

9. It is difficult to reconcile this report with a statement made by Averroes. According to the Latin translation of the *Grand Commentary* on the *De Anima* (ed. F. Stuart Crawford, Cambridge, Mass., 1953, p. 433), al-Farabi affirmed in his *Commentary* on the *Ethics* that man's final end was speculative perfection, *perfectio speculativa* (*kamāl nazarī*). This may mean that in the *Commentary* al-Farabi adopted on this point two contradictory positions. The text of Ibn Bajja also points to a certain lack of consistency on al-Farabi's part in the *Commentary*. On the other hand, the purport of Averroes' statement may be that man cannot achieve cognition which transcends speculative knowledge; the latter, which is based on sense data, is not the highest kind of knowledge. Ibn Bajja uses the term *nazarī* to denote the kind of knowledge possessed by the physicists.

10. Or "one."

11. *Al-mufāraqa*. The Word may simply mean death.

12. Or "is served."

13. *Al-khayrāt: bona.*

14. *Al-Madaniyya.*

15. *Al-jamī'*, "all, the generality."

16. In point of fact the *Ikhwān al-Safā'* refer time and again to the soul as being an entity that is separate from the body and to the destiny of souls after death. But their critics may not have taken such statements at face value.

17. Al-Farabi does not seem to have adopted throughout the *Commentary* an attitude which Ibn Bajja found inadmissible. The latter refers with approval to a statement made near the end of that text. He also states in a different context that al-Farabi's position regarding the notion of intellect in the *Risālat al-'Aql* is quite different from that propounded in the *Commentary*.

18. In some extant political works of al-Farabi, notably the *Tahsīl al-Sa'āda*,

the function of practical reason is occasionally made to appear as almost as important as that of theoretical reason. The total elimination of the latter in the system propounded in the *Commentary* on the *Ethics* could be regarded as an exaggeration, or an outspoken avowal, of this tendency.

19. Perhaps the degree of the intellectum is meant.

20. Ed. Dieterici, p. 69. In the same work, but in a different context, al-Farabi refers to the superior man in whom the active intellect resides (*halla*). This reference is made in the course of an exposition of the theory of prophetic revelation.

21. It is no more than this.

22. In the *Tahsīl al-Sa'āda* and other works.

23. Another explanation appears to be suggested by Averroes, see the appendix.

24. Ibn Tufayl, at any rate, interpreted a statement in the *Commentary* on the *Ethics* as an affirmation of the mortality of the soul. *Hayy ben Yaqdhān*, ed. L. Gauthier (Beirut, 1930), Arabic text, pp. 13-14.

25. Ibid. Ibn Tufayl mentions in this connection *al-Milla al-Fādila* and *al-Siyā-sāt al-Madaniyya*. An afterlife of the soul is also part of the doctrine of *Ārā' Ahl al-Madīna al-Fādila*.

26. See S. Pines, "La '*Philosophie Orientale*' d'Avicenne et sa Polémique contre les *Bagdadiens*," *Archives d'Histoire Doctrinale et Littéraire du Moyen Age*, XXVII (1953), 18 ff.

27. Ibid., esp. pp. 26-27.

28. See the Latin translation, ed. F. Stuart Crawford, p. 487.

29. And, of course, the Ishrāqī thinkers of Iran.

30. See note 3.

31. In all probability at least three. The doctrine of his *R. al-Wadā'* seems to be somewhat different from that of *R. Al-Ittisāl*.

32. Or "force," *quwwa*.

33. Māhiyyāt.

34. This in contradistinction to the theologico-political section treating of the virtuous city.

35. See A. Altmann, "Ibn Bajja on Man's Ultimate Felicity," in *Studies in Religious Philosophy and Mysticism* (London, 1969), pp. 73-106.

36. One of four treatises published in the supplement to A. F. Ahwani's edition of Averroes' *Talkhīs Kitāb al Nafs*, (Cairo 1950), pp. 103-118. A subtitle amplifies the title; the topic of the treatise is described as being *ittisāl al-'aql bi' l-insān*, the conjunction of the intellect with man.

37. Or "science," *'ilm*.

38. And to the strictures on the theory found in Aristotle's *Metaphysics*.

39. This inconsistency may possibly be accounted for by the fact that the passages do not appear to treat of the highest "degree" posited by Ibn Bajja, see below.

40. *Al-nuzzār al-tabī 'iyyūn*, literally, "the natural theoreticians."

41. The substrata.

42. Literally carried, borne (*mahmūl*).

43. Literally, "the instrument," *adāt*.

44. *Jihāt*, literally, "sides."

45. *Mutalāzima talāzum al-takāfu'*. More or less literally concomitant in a comcomitance of equivalence (or equality).

46. Literally, "this theoretical degree."

47. Literally, "appears."

48. *Al-shakhs*; more or less literally, "person," *atomon*.

49. *Al-shay' bi-nafsihi*, the *Ding an sich*.

50. Or theoreticians, *al-nazariyyūn*.

51. Being all of them pure intellect.

52. Ibn Bajja (pp. 114-115) points out that in Plato's theory the forms (*suwar*, the ideas) are called by the name of the things of which they are the form; one and the same definition applies both to the thing and to its form. This is the reason for the absurdities of this theory as set forth in Aristotle's *Metaphysics*. Ibn Bajja eliminates this weakness of Plato's theory by affirming the existence of a third term. He differentiates between the perceived things; forms; and the meanings (ma 'ānī) of the forms. For the third category he also uses the term *ma 'qūl* (intellectum, or object of intellection).

53. See Alexander, *De Anima*, ed. I. Bruns (Berlin, 1887), p. 90.

54. What follows is not spelled out in every particular in the relevant quotation.

55. The relation between the doctrine of Ibn Bajja and that of Gersonides relating to the human intellect will be discussed elsewhere. There is an essential resemblance, but Gersonides elaborated the doctrine in a way that is different from that of Ibn Bajja, if we may go by the evidence of the texts that have been studied.

56. Deut. 5:28. The reference is to Moses.

57. Num. 11:25.

58. Psalms 82:5.

59. Ed. J. Forget (Leiden, 1892), pp. 202-203.

60. *'Ārif* may in the last analysis be a rendering of term *gnōstikos*, used by early Christian theologians, for instance, Clement of Alexandria, to designate a high spiritual degree. The same Greek term is used to denote the Gnostics, but in their case the connotations are somewhat different.

61. Heschel's hypothesis according to which he might have done so is most unlikely.

62. An interesting discussion of this and related problems in Maimonides' doctrine occurs in W. Harvey, *Hasdai Crescas' Critique of the Theory of the Acquired Intellect*, Columbia University, Ph. D. dissertation, 1973 (University Microfilms, Ann Arbor, Mich., 1974) pp. 40 ff., 54 ff.

63. In an article entitled "Shī'ite Terms and Notions in the Kuzari" (forthcoming in *Jerusalem Studies in Arabic and Islam*, II), app. 6, I have attempted to show that some indications point to Maimonides' borrowing one trait of his negative theology from Ismā 'īlī theologians, who professed the doctrine of the unknowability of God *per se* in a very extreme form.

64. The following passage occurs in the *Guide* I, 1: "Man possesses as his proprium something in him that is very strange as it is not found in anything else that exists under the sphere of the moon, namely intellectual apprehension. In the exercise of this, no sense, no part of the body, none of the extremities are used, and therefore this apprehension was likened unto the apprehension of the Deity, which does not require an instrument, although in reality it is not like the latter apprehension, but only appears so to the first stirrings of opinion. It was because of this something, I mean because of the divine intellect (*al-'aql al-ilāhī*) conjoined (*al-muttasil*) with man, that it is said of the latter that he is *in the image of* God and in His likeness." The fact that Maimonides uses in I, 1, the term *al-'aql al-ilāhī* rather than *al-*

'aql al-fa''āl tends to show that in this commentary on a biblical verse he is interested in the refutation of speculations concerning the corporeality of God rather than in philosophical epistemology. *Al-'aql al-ilāhī* has no exact philosophical connotation. The meaning of the word *muttasil* in this passage may be clarified by referring to a passage of Avicenna's *De Anima* being the psychological part of *Kitāb al-Shifā'*, ed. F. Rahman (Oxford, 1959), p. 247). "While the human soul (a soul that belongs to a) common [man, *al-āmmiya* apparently a man that is not a prophet] is in a body, it is impossible for it to receive [unto itself] the Active Intellect all at once. . . . If it is said that a certain person knows intelligibles, this means that wherever he wishes, he makes their form present to the perception [*dhihn*, the word in this context is untranslatable] of his soul. The meaning of this is that whenever he wishes he can be conjoined (*yattasil*) with the active intellect in a conjunction in which he (received from the Active Intellect) a representation of the intelligible in question without this intelligible present in his perception (*dhihn*) and represented *in actu* in his intellect all the time . . . This is [different] from what was [the case] prior to his having learnt [to know the intelligible, p. 246]. When he is freed from the body and the accidents of the body, it may be possible for him to be conjoined with the Active Intellect in a complete conjunction." This passage makes it clear that in Avicennian terminology, at least, *muttasil, ittisāl*, with the active intellect need not refer to conjunction in the sense of total union. The terms may be applied to a man's intellecting one intelligible. As far as the use of the terms is concerned, it does not seem to matter whether the intelligible was or was not intellected in the first place through an act of abstraction applied to a sense datum or an image. In *Guide* I, 1, Maimonides possibly used *muttasil* in the Avicennian sense. If this is so, the passage could conform to the first theory of Ibn Bajja.

65. "Kalāmic" reasons would have been preferable if the term *Kalām* in the sense given it by al-Farabi in *Ihsā l-'Ulūm* were sufficiently known. The objective of the science of Kalam, as described by al-Farabi, is to protect religion against all forms of attack.

66. Cf. my Introduction to the translation.

67. And of other philosophical authors (Gersonides may be one of them), who by and large accept a similar thesis (even if it is not quite identical).

68. If God is not conceived as a corporeal substance, a hypothesis which would of course be in flagrant contradiction to the doctrine of Maimonides. It may however be noted that some remarks occurring in the *Guide* may engender the suspicion—which is invalidated by other passages of that work—that the God of Maimonides has an intimate connection with the cosmos, that in fact he may be conceived if we use Spinozistic terms, as an idea whose *ideatum* is the world. It is of course difficult or impossible to reconcile a conception of this sort with Maimonides' epistemology, but it could form a part of his philosophical theology as well as of the doctrines of other medieval Jewish and Arabic philosophers.

69. *Sefer ha-Mada', Yesode ha-Torah*, II, 9.

70. Maimonides references in the *Guide* to Aristotle and Alexander of Aphrodisias are dealt with at some length in my Introduction to the translation of that work, see pp. lxi-lxxiv.

71. Cf. my Introduction to the translation (pp. lxxix f.).

72. Ed. L. Gauthier, p. 14, of the Arabic text. Speaking of al-Farabi's *Commentary on the Ethic:* Ibn Tufayl refers to "That which he made clear with regard to his reprehensible belief concerning prophecy: it pertains exclusively, as (al-Farabi)

thinks, to the imaginative faculty, and he considers that philosophy is superior to it" *mā sarraha bihi min su'i mu 'taqadihi fi 'l nubuwwa wa- 'annaha li'l quwwa al-khayāliyya khāssa bi-za'mihi wa-tafdīlihi al-falsafa 'alayhā.*

73. In my introduction to the translation of the *Guide* (p. lxxx) I state that Ibn Bajja defends al-Farabi against the charge that in his *Commentary* he professes the opinion that there is no afterlife, that there is no happiness except political happiness, and so forth. This is correct as far as Ibn Bajja's wording is concerned. But it can be clearly understood from the text that Ibn Bajja's defense consists in playing down and explaining away the incriminating statements of al-Farabi. He does not deny that the statements in question occurred in the *Commentary*.

In the paper referred to in note 3, I put forward the hypothesis that al-Farabi's view according to which political happiness is the only one which men can achieve might have influenced Marsilius of Padua. A Latin translation of al-Farabi's *Commentary* on the *Ethics* is known to have existed; it was still existant at the time when in the twenties of the fourteenth century Marsilius wrote his magnum opus entitled *Defensor Pacis* (finished in 1324). The passage to which I refer occurs in this treatise in Diccio I, Cap. 1, 7 (ed. W. Kunzmann and H. Kusch. p. 24). *Possent securius studiosi principantes et subditi tranquille vivere quod est desiderabile propositum in huius operis inicio, necessarium debentibus civili felicitate frui, que in hoc seculo possibilium homini desideratorum optimum videtur et ultimum actuum humanorum.*

74. Cf. also the 13 principles of religion in Maimonides' *Commentary* on the *Mishnah*, Introduction to *Perek Helek*.

75. I held a different opinion at the time when I prepared the translation. See p. 221, n. 11.

76. Or "The proof with regard to them, even if they are correct, are well hidden."

77. But which precedes it in the *Guide*.

78. The contrary opinion is put forward by W. Harvey in the work quoted above.

79. See S. Pines, "Abstracta Islamica," 6th series, *Revue des Etudes Islamiques* (1938), pp. A51-A53. According to the *Rasā'il Ikhwān al-Safā'*, an encyclopedia which did not achieve philosophical respectability, the science of politics also pertains to *al-'ilm al-ilāhī*.

80. And also rather paradoxically under the influence of Alexander's *Principles of the All*.

81. Possibly Maimonides has deliberately seen to it that both chapters should have the number 54.

82. An exact analysis of al-Farabi's *Tahsīl al-Sa'āda* might show an internal contradiction similar to that which is encountered in the *Guide*. A conception which may point to the influence of the *Tahsīl al-Sa'āda* on the *Guide* is set forth on p. 44 (Hyderabad edition) of this treatise by al-Farabi. This philosopher asserts there that the lawgiver who is the true philosopher has a knowledge that achieves certainty of matters about which the great mass of people have only imaginings and (conceptions due to the influence of) persuasive arguments, *iqnā'* (and which thus fall short of certainty). The lawgiver invents these imaginings and conceptions and causes others to entertain them, but they have no place in his own soul. This may be compared with *Guide*, II, 36 (translation, p. 373). Maimonides speaking of Moses states there that "the imaginative faculty did not enter into his prophecy."

83. Some observations made by A. Kojève in a debate with Leo Strauss are

relevant in this connection. Cf. Leo Strauss, *On Tyranny: A Study of Xenophon's Hiero*, Alexander Kojève's critique of that study (Glencoe, 1963), pp. 159 ff. Kojève poses the problem in terms of what he calls the "Epicurean" conception of philosophy. This conception is applicable to some extent at least to Plato's and Aristotle's philosophy. Kojeve's Hegelian answers need not concern us in this context.

84. Employed by Ibn Bajja (see above). It should be stated, however, that the political activity which Maimonides considers as superior to every other way of life has very little or nothing in common with the accomplishment of the moral law which Kant regards as man's principal task. Nor does it consist in—though it may not be incompatible with—the observance of the religious commandments. It should also be noted that the text of the *Guide* gives no prima facie warrant for the view that Maimonides considered—as al-Farabi is supposed to have done—that political happiness is the only one of which man is capable.

The primacy given to the life of action contradicts Aristotle's view, but the epistemology which legitimates this position by demarcating the limits of human knowledge derives probably indirectly in the last analysis, as far as Maimonides is concerned, from certain traits of the Aristotelian doctrine. This may also be partly true in a more complicated way with regard to Kant's epistemology. The relation between the views expressed in al-Farabi's *Commentary* on the *Ethics*; and Ibn Bajja's first doctrine, both of which may be supposed to have influenced Maimonides, and the epistemology of Gersonides will be examined elsewhere. The possibility that Judah ha-Levi's and Crescas' critique of the philosophical doctrine concerning the human intellect may owe something to al-Farabi's *Commentary* on the *Ethics* will also be investigated. Ibn Khaldūn's "refutation of philosophy" found in his *al-Muqaddima*, may have also been directly or indirectly influenced by this commentary. See M. Quatremère's, edition of *al-Muqaddima*, III, 215, II. 9-12 (F. Rosenthal's translation, III, 252).

85. Or "divine," *ilāhiyya*.

86. See my translation of the *Guide*, p. 66, note 7, and the translator's introduction, pp. lxvii f.

87. See the translator's introduction.

88. The last part of the passage reads in Greek: *hoi nomoi dēlousin, en hois ta mythōdē kai peidariōdē meizon iskhyei tou ginōskein peri autōn dia to ethos.*

89. Literally, "thing."

90. Literally, "intelligent inborn dispositions."

91. A critical edition of the Hebrew translation of this *Prooemium*, an English rendering, and a reference to the Latin translation of the *Prooemium* are found in Steven Harvey's Ph.D. dissertation "Averroes on the Principles of Nature: The Middle Commentary on Aristotle's Physics, I-II" (Harvard University, 1977), appendix 6, pp. 439-471.

92. Averroes' *Commentary* on the *Metaphysics* was not the only Arabic one. Yahyā b. 'Adī's commentary on book 2 of that work is still extant. A reference to it may be found in the contribution made by S. Pines and M. Schwartz to a volume in commemoration of Baneth, which will soon be published in Jerusalem.

6

The Autobiography of Obadyah the Norman, a Convert to Judaism at the Time of the First Crusade

Joshua Prawer

Three quarters of a century passed since the name of a converted Norman, Obadyah, came to the attention of scholars. It appeared for the first time in a letter of recommendation written for the convert by a Rabbi Baruk bar Itzhak, in all probability a rabbi of Aleppo.[1] In 1919 E. Adler published a fragment of what looked like an autobiography.[2] Since then a large number of other fragments and additional material related to the same personality came to light. And although we are still far from having all the pieces of this autobiography, there is by now a compact enough body of fragments to attempt an evaluation and to try to penetrate the extraordinary personality of its writer.

Following the studies of J. Mann, A. Scheiber, and S. D. Goitein,[3] we know today the probable sequence of the different fragments, though some of it is rather conjectural. In the form in which it was proposed by A. Scheiber we have a chronological sequence of the different fragments and there is enough data in each of them to made the sequence a logical possibility.[4] Still, one has to bear in mind that it does not follow that this was the place of the different fragments in the original treatise. Moreover there is a fairly well-founded possibility that the fragments, though all of them written by Obadyah, might belong to two different versions of his autobiography.[5] Here are problems which cannot yet be satisfactorily solved but they relate rather to the literary aspects of the problems than to the reconstruction of events and the evaluation of the author.

As an instance of its literary genre, the autobiography, written some time after 1121-22 (this being the last date which can be accurately fixed), is the earliest written by any Westerner in the Middle Ages, probably contemporary with that of Guibert of Nogent.[6] Autobiographies written by Jews in the Middle Ages are even scarcer than those of their Christian contemporaries. One written slightly earlier, the "Scroll of Ebiatar," was written in the Levant and its purpose was polemic. Another that can be regarded as an autobiography, the "Scroll of Ahīma'az," was written in Byzantine Italy in the eleventh century but is more a history of a family than an autobiography in the strict sense of the term. Thus the "Scroll of Obadyah" takes its place as the first example of a literary genre.

The importance of this autobiography is that it is a unique document that allows a glimpse into the life of an individual at the turn of the eleventh century who is neither a member of royalty or of the higher aristocracy or a prelate of the church. He belongs rather to the mass of small anonymous knights, whose deeds are seldom known and never sung. Moreover, we have here a confession which contributes to the understanding of what might be called the mechanism of conversion of a Christian to Judaism at a time of persecution of Jews as well as a time of Messianic élan during the First Crusade. Finally, this problem of conversion seems to be directly related to some aspects of Jewish-Christian intellectual relations in the twelfth century.

The first fragment, mutilated at its beginning, allows us to place the future convert in space and time. The foregoing but missing part no doubt dealt with the immigration of the family from Normandy and its settlement in Italy. It must have dealt with the father of the family who migrated from the north and settled in a place whose

> name[7] was Oppido (Hebrew text, Oppidey). And he took to himself a wife by the name Maria and Maria conceived and bore to Dreux (Hebrew, Drō), her husband, two sons in one day. The first according to the manner of the women to their sons[8] and he was called Royerius, that is, Roger (Hebrew text, Roggiré). And the second . . . after the first[9] and in great sorrow his mother bore him[10] and called his name Joha(nn)es, he is Guwān[11]. And the boys grew up and Royerius became a man skilled in sword and war and Johannes a man who pursued knowledge and wisdom in books.[12]

The township of Oppido and its surroundings are described in more detail in the same fragment:[13]

> And here are the names of the cities[14] which are around Oppido, the birthplace of Johannes, the son of Drocus. From the west the city of Rome and the city of Salerno (Hebrew text, Salernus) and the city of Potenza (Hebrew text, Potenz) and the township Petrogalli (Hebrew text, Pe[t]tragali) and the township Anzo (Hebrew text, Ans). And from the East the city of Bari and the city of Montepeloso (Hebrew text, Muntplūs) and the township Genzano (Hebrew text, Genzan) and the township Benzano (Hebrew text, Banz). And from the north Acerenza (Hebrew text, Agranz) and the river Baradano (Hebrew text, Baradanū) is between Oppido and Acerenza. And from the south the city of Tolve (Tulv) and the city . . . a . . . ibarg and Oppido in the middle.[15]

The detailed description of the topographical position of Oppido, stretching far to the west to Salerno and even Rome, and to the east to Bari, was written some fifty years after the events and some twenty-five years after John left his birthplace. Although the topographical data were apparently introduced into the narrative to describe the area in which certain rumors were rife, Obadyah may have been prompted by nostalgic memories or by the wish to impress his readers in the faraway Levant with great names to enumerate cities and townships.

There are some particularities in the Hebrew transcription of names. His father is called by his Norman-French name Dreux (Dreux, Drux, or Drox) or by its Latinized form Drocus (1.24,1.25,1.35). The name of his twin brother is spelled in the Latinized form of Royerius (1.4,7) and a hybrid form Roggiré (1.4); unless the vocalization is wrong and should be read Roggier, in which case it could have a French or Italian (Ruggiero) pronounciation. Maria, his mother's name, is in all probability Greek (although it could be the Latin or Italian form of the name). The vocalization is very clear and precludes Miryam or French Marie.

His birthplace is constantly spelled Oppīdey (1.1, 25, 31, 33) and the adjective appears as Oppuda(n)im (1.37). His own name, like his twin brother's, appears in its Latin and vernacular form: Johannes (1.6,7) and Guwãn, that is Jean or Giovan. The last name is mentioned only once, whereas the form Johannes appears many times in this fragment (1.6, 7, 23, 26, 38) as well as in other fragments. The names as a rule are pronounced without their final vowel: Potenz=Potenza; Petragalli=Pietragalla; Ans= Anzi; Muntplūs=Montepeloso; Genzan=Ganzano; Banz=Banzi; Tulv= Tolve; Agranz=Acerenza. The last name, Agranz for Acerenza, may be due to its Roman classical form Acherontia.

It seems possible to reconstruct the early history of the family in Oppido, which coincides with the last episode of Norman immigration and settlement in southern Italy. The place is that of the classical Lucania, later called Basilicata, and the time was probably the 1060s. The political situation of the area was one of utter confusion. Three major forces were vying for domination of Lucania and its eastern maritime board: the Byzantines, the Lombards, and the immigrating Normans. Shortly thereafter one more element intervened, the Roman papacy striving for a stronger hold in the south against the Patriarch of Constantinople. Also involved were the Muslims of Sicily. Swiftly changing alliances between the contending parties followed by feuds and wars made the area between Bari in the east and Salerno in the west one of permanent insecurity.

Bari, destined to be of major importance in the life of Obadyah, was the mainstay of Byzantine power.[16] Its major opponents were the Lombards. Some of the places listed by Obadyah recur in contemporary chronicles. By the beginning of the eleventh century the Byzantines dominated the whole area south of Acerenza and this also included the little township of Oppido. In 1009 Montepeloso and the neighboring Cosenza witnessed Lombard revolts and even Muslim rulers, at that time allies of the Lombards.

The Norman immigration, small at the beginning of the century, became stronger in the second quarter, when Norman mercenary troops were employed by the Byzantines. Their major stronghold became Aversa, south of Naples, but we see them as Byzantine commanders in places like Melfi, which finally in 1041 became Norman. Relations between the Normans and Lombards then improved and both became anti-Byzantine. The brother of the Lombard prince of Benevent was even elected chief of the Normans. In the 1040s there were Lombard revolts against Byzantine rule in Bari, Monte-peloso, Giovenazzo, and some other areas. Effective Byzantine rule was then reduced to the southern part of the eastern coast: Brindisi, Otranto, Tarent, Trani, and Oria.

A new Byzantine offensive in 1042 was only partially successful as the growing Norman power, headed by William Bras-de-Fer in alliance with Lombard Salerno, became more and more menacing. In 1043 (treaty of Meifi) the Normans took root in Lucania. Dreux, one of the Hauteville clan, became lord of Venosa; another, Tristan, became lord of Montepeloso, and Ascletin, who came with the first wave of Normans headed by his brother Gilbert le Tonnelier in about 1017, became lord of Acerenza. Ascletin's family based in Acerenza came to play a decisive role in the area. In 1047 newcomers from Normandy, attracted by the good fortunes of their com-patriots and relatives, appeared in the south, among them Robert Guiscard and Ascletin's son Richard (later lord of Capua). At that time Genzano was a Norman fief held from Ascletin of Acerenza. Richard, who was coldly re-ceived by his uncle Rainulf at Aversa, joined forces with Sarule, lord of Genzano and vassal of Richard's father.

In the following years Lombard power was clearly in decline, though the Lombard population remained an important factor. The wars between the Byzantines, Lombards, and Normans were replaced by fratricidal feuds be-tween Norman warlords. Richard warred against Dreux, duke of Apulia and Calabria, and was taken prisoner at Montepeloso. The populace de-manded his liberty to assume the regency at Aversa after the death of Rainulf.

Meanwhile, Robert Guiscard emerged as the most important single leader of the Normans. His ambitions in Calabria and Sicily were thwarted by Byzantine politics and by revolts of his Norman allies and vassals in Apulia. A major revolt broke out in 1064 headed by the powerful Godfrey of Con-versano, a nephew of Robert Guiscard, whose domains included Polignano, Monopoli, Montepeloso, and Brindisi. By treachery Robert Guiscard be-came lord of Montepeloso, where Godfrey sought refuge, a few miles from Oppido. Godfrey was liberated by a lenient Guiscard, who wished to con-centrate on his major task, the capture of Byzantine Bari. This was accom-plished after a successful four-year siege (1068-1071). With the capture of Bari in 1071 southern Italy became Norman.

During this turbulent period Dreux, the father of Obadyah, came to Oppido. Dreux must have been a fairly common name among the Nor-mans, possibly deriving from the city of the same name in Normandy, but the father was certainly not Dreux of the Hauteville family, who died in 1048. He was probably an unimportant Norman knight, who held as fief the township of Oppido, dependent on his mighty neighbor, Ascletin of Ace-renza, or Godfrey of Conversano, lord of neighboring Montepeloso.

Oppido, a small fortified township in a grain growing area, about five miles from Acerenza, was also the highest place in the area and consequently of strategic importance. Nearest to Oppido was Tolve, the ancient Tulbium. The small monastery of St. Peter in Tolve is probably the one mentioned in Obadyah's autobiography.[17] In the subsequent Norman administration of Apulia and Calabria, the whole area was to be included in the Constabulary of Tricarico; it came to own the service of eight knights: three from Albano di Lucania (Potenza), two from Petragalla, four from Tolve, and one from the bridge crossing Baradano.[18] Later on in the recommendation of Rabbi Baruk ben Rabbi Itzhak it is written that "those who live in the land of Obadyah told us that the man is from a great family and his father was a great lord (*Sar*),"[19] but Hebrew sources are notoriously vague in feudal vocabulary, and in any case the writer of a letter of recommendation would be interested to show his protégé in the best possible light. Once in possession of Oppido, the Norman Dreux, like his compatriots, took root in the country. He married a local girl. Her name, spelled by her son as Maria, makes it plausible that she was Greek. The date of their marriage is nowhere stated, but it was probably not earlier than 1071, that is not before the capture of Bari by the Normans and the following stabilization and growing security in Lucania.

The sons of Dreux, Roger and John, were twins, but Roger was the first born and as such the heir apparent of his father. According to normal medieval custom he was therefore brought up as befitted a warrior, whereas his younger brother was destined for the church. He became, as he wrote later "a man who pursued knowledge and wisdom in books." There can be little doubt that his early education was received at the hands of the parish priest of Oppido, but he was later sent to the nearby monastery of St. Peter at Tolve. When he wrote his autobiography he remembered the local church as "the great high place[20] of the Oppidans his compatriots," whereas the abbot of Tolve appears later in his narrative in connection with the ecclesiastical preaching of the First Crusade.

John was still a child when an event shocked his region. It is told by Obadyah himself:[21]

> And it came to pass at that time and Andreas the archbishop, the High Priest in the city of Bari, God put into his heart the love of the Law of Moses. And he left his land and his priesthood and all that was his and he came to the city of Constantinople. And he circumcized the flesh of his foreskin and great and sore troubles he came to pass. And he got up and ran for his life before the non-circumcised, who sought to kill him, and Jehova, God of Israel, saved him from their hands in purity. God guards proselytes, let His name be blessed to eternity.
>
> And strangers began to follow him and saw what he did and they did what he did and they entered the Covenant of the Living God. And the man went to the Kingdom of Egypt [or city of Cairo][22] and he stayed there until the day of his death. And in those days the king of Egypt was al-Mustansir. And the name of his vizier a . . . al . . .
>
> And the rumours about Andreas the archbishop came to all the land of Lombardy (Hebrew, Langubardia) and to the Sages of Greece and

the Sages of Rome, that is the seat of the kingdom of Edom; and the Sages of Greece who heard the tidings were ashamed and the Sages of Edom confused.

And Johannes heard about it and he was still a boy in the house of Drocus his father.

This episode which obviously had a tremendous impact on the boy Johannes—or so at least he was later to describe it—drew the attention of many scholars. This is in fact the only place at which the life of Johannes is interwoven with external events in Europe, though he comes near to it in some other episodes, namely those relating to Messianic movements in the Levant. Whereas some scholars were skeptical about the story of the converted archbishop of Bari, others tried to identify him with a real archbishop of the city. A. Scheiber has pointed out that there was an archbishop of Bari named Andreas, but he did not pursue the study further.[23] B. Blumenkranz continued along that line, but he was misled like many others (myself among them) by another Hebrew text dealing with a converted Christian.[24] It now seems that a plausible solution can be proposed. There was actually an archbishop of Bari by the name of Andreas and the years of his pontificate are recorded as between 1062 and 1078. A number of studies dealing with Bari mention his pontificate. The most detailed is that of M. Garruba,[25] who based his work on that of other historians, namely Beatillo, Ughelli, and Lombardi,[26] rather than on primary sources.

Several chronicles of Bari, related and continued, deal with our period,[27] but the most relevant chronicle is that known as *Anonymi Barensis Chronicon* (855-1115).[28] In the rather dry enumeration of the prelates of Bari there are three lines dealing with Andreas, and all three are, to say the least, rather curious. Short as the entries are, they prove that his election and elevation to the See of Bari was disputed; he relates for 1062 that he was "a quibusdam" only elected. Under the year 1066 we read: "Perrexit Andreas archiepiscopus Constantinopolim,"[29] and this is the last we hear of Andreas until 1080, when we learn that a man by the name of Urso was elevated to the See. Why did Andreas leave his See during this perilous and decisive period in the history of Bari? Did he ever come back, and if not, what happened in Bari between 1066 and 1078? Moreover there is a gap of three years between the death of Andreas and the accession of Urso to the See of Bari in 1080. Whatever happened, it was certainly a far cry from Garruba's pious epilogue to the biography of Andreas: "sappiamo di aver chiuso gli occhi nella pace del Signore nell'anno 1078."

The chronological difficulties connected with the metropolitan Andreas are beyond the scope of this chapter.[30] What is relevant is the fact that archbishop Andreas of Bari did actually leave his city for Constantinople and thus the name, the act, and the place correspond to what Johannes remembered from his childhood. But neither Andreas' conversion, nor his settling in Egypt, are recorded in the contemporary chronicle. The actual events in Bari are only marginally related to this story. What counts is the memory of the events as perceived a generation later by Obadyah. The rumor that reached his native southern Italy from the east reverberated through the country. We can understand the confusion of the "Sages of Rome," and that of the "Sages of Greece," who were the Byzantine prelates in the disputed area, which ecclesiastically depended on Constantinople and the "Land of Langubardia." The latter, of course, is not Lombardy but the Byzantine "thema" of Lombardy in southern Italy, a name that will continue to exist for many centuries. "Lombard" was still the name given to the host of Frederick II on his Crusade to the Holy Land in the thirteenth century.

What happened to Andreas after 1066 and what happened in the See of Bari until the year when a new metropolitan was consecrated, a long period of fourteen years, is unknown. Moreover, an attempt to synchronize actual data is not too satisfactory. We assumed as the birth date of Johannes a time after 1071, but Andreas went to Constantinople in 1066; by 1078 when Johannes was a small child, Andreas was no longer living, but in any case a new metropolitan was officiating in Bari. There is the additional problem of correspondence of the chronology of the events with the names of the contemporary rulers of Egypt. At the end of the episode dealing with the escape of Andreas, Obadyah mentions that he settled and lived until his death in Egypt. The caliph, whom he mentions by name, is al-Mustansir, that is, al-Mustansir billāh (1036-1094). The name of the vizier should be completed as Badr al-Jamāli (which fits very well with the extant letters in the *lacuna* of the text), an Armenian convert to Islam, a commander in Syria and in Acre in Palestine before he became the omnipotent ruler of Egypt. As he became vizier about 1073 and died only a few months before his caliph (1094), Obadyah's story would better suit a period after 1073 than before that date.[31]

The authenticity of names and places and the simultaneous ambiguity of other aspects of the story may be explained by the fact that the autobiography was written some fifty years after the events. Yet this is only a partial explanation. Another part of the puzzle can be solved only by data from sources which have not yet been connected with Obadyah's autobiography. They will bring us remarkably near to disentangling the story.

The source in question is connected with the successor of archbishop Andreas in the See of Bari, Urso, former bishop of Rapolla in Apulia. Urso was befriended by the Norman conqueror Robert Guiscard.[32] It was on the latter's request that Gregory VII appointed Urso to this most important See, which after its capture from the Byzantines in 1071 became directly dependent on Rome. We have a hagiographical treatise written by John, a disciple of Urso and archdeacon of Bari,[33] so that Urso is better known than his predecessor. Moreover it was during his pontificate that sailors of Bari brought to their native city the relics of the patron saint of Bari, St. Nicholas, from Myra, and this memorable event attracted a great deal of attention. It was in 1087, according to archdeacon John, that archbishop Urso decided on a pilgrimage to the Holy Land, but he cut his preparations short to welcome the holy relics of St. Nicholas in Bari. Afterwards, as we are told: "He went to pray to Jerusalem, to the Sepulchre of the Lord and in the same year he returned to Bari, went to Canusium (Canosa di Puglia) where he was overcome by sickness, died and was buried on the 16 Kal. of March."[34] Urso must then have gone to the Holy Land in the summer of 1087, returned shortly thereafter, and died on February 14, 1088.

Besides this hagiographic source, however, there is another version of the last years of the life of Urso. This comes from an unexpected quarter, a Norman chronicle written a generation later. The manuscript of this chronicle, preserved at Monte Casino, was discovered and published by Mabillon.[35] It is one of a series of interpolated versions of the anonymous *Gesta Francorum*. It was written by a Norman from Apulia in the camp of Tancred and Bohemond, the leaders of the Italo-Normans on the First Crusade. The author continued his story down to the year 1130, that is, a generation after the end of the original *Gesta*, hence the name *Tudebodus imitatus et continuatus*, under which it was republished in the *Recueil des Historiens des Croisades*.[36] The chronicle is, then, contemporary with the autobiography of Obadyah, and was written by a man from the same region of southern Italy.

Among the interpolated episodes[37] there is the story of an Egyptian embassy which reached the Crusaders during the siege of Antioch. On behalf of the vizier al-Afdal or the Caliph al-Must'ali the Crusaders were invited to send an embassy to Cairo.[38] Their embassy, according to the author,[39] went to Cairo, where they were astonished to find five Christian bishops among many Christian prisoners. These are described as bishops of Tarent in southern Italy, Beauvais and Reims in northern France, and two others, who are not mentioned by name. With the five bishops was also a fierce monk, William the Hermit. The Crusader ambassadors brought back a marvelous story from the captives. The caliph, according to their tale, had tried to confuse them and force them to abjure their religion. Accordingly he summoned them before his court and said: "Do you believe that it is true what Christ said in the Gospel, namely: 'If ye have faith as a grain of mustard seed, ye shall say unto the mountain: Remove hence to yonder place and it shall remove; and nothing shall be impossible unto you' (Matt. 17:20)?" The Christians confessed that they did. Then the caliph told them that unless they perform the miracle of moving a mountain they must convert or die. William the Hermit asked for a three day respite and then, after expounding the *Credo*, easily moved the mountain to another place, and he did so in the presence of the Egyptian court and the assembled masses of Cairo.

These events must have taken place in 1098-1099. One wonders about the knowledge of the Gospels by the caliph, but we are told that all this happened on the instigation of no one other than Urso, Archbishop of Bari." And behold in the court of the king," we read, "there was a man by the name of Urso, who was once the Bishop of Bari. But he was taken prisoner during his pilgrimage and was brought to Egypt. Under the hardship of punishment he abjured his Christian faith. And the king [of Egypt] loved him so dearly that he did not do anything without his advice."[40] Naturally after the miracle of the mountain, Urso was smitten by remorse "and Urso who gave the advice to the king became demented and like a dead man fell to earth."[41]

As if doubts about Andreas were not troublesome enough, we now have two archbishops of Bari, Andreas and Urso, who are both possible candidates for identification with the hero of the story of Obadyah. One, Andreas, actually went to Constantinople; the other, Urso, actually converted. True, as far as our sources go, none went over to Judaism. If Obadyah referred to the disappearance of Urso, which can be fixed in 1089, the "official" date of his death, then Obadyah, still in his father's home in Oppido, was fifteen years old. Writing more than 30 years later the story became confused with the name of another disappearing bishop of Bari, Andreas.

It remains anyone's guess whether Obadyah heard a rumor (and he speaks explicitly about rumors) of actual conversion to Judaism, or whether he consciously changed the rumor of conversion to Islam into a tale of conversion to Judaism. The fact of apostasy was enough to shock Christians; whether the conversion was to Islam or to Judaism was of secondary importance. There is, in any event, little doubt that in Johannes' childhood rumors circulated from Apulia to Lucania about an archbishop of Bari who went through Constantinople to the east (this was the normal route of pilgrims going to the Holy Land) and who then abjured his religion.

An impressionable boy of fifteen or so guarded this rather dramatic memory until some seven years later, when new events influenced his life. These events seem to have been connected with the earliest stirrings of the First Crusade, which followed Urban II's appeal from Clermont in 1095, namely, the recruitment and the beginning of the popular Crusade of 1096.

Obadyah introduces this chapter by a dream or two which played a major role in his life. The time of these events can be deduced from the description of the Crusader propaganda, but also from Obdayah's introduction to the story: "And it came to pass in the first year in which Johannes was defiled, the beginning of his impurity by the Lords of Darkness in the house of his father Drocus. And it was in that year that Johannes dreamt a dream." If no correction is introduced into the text,[42] it refers then to an ordination, probably that of an exorcist, whose canonical age was fixed at eighteen, unless he meant the ordination (in the *ordines maiores*) to a subdeacon, canonically fixed as age twenty-two, but often given earlier.[43] I am inclined to favor the "exorcist," as Johannes was still living in the home of his father; there is, however, no decisive proof one way or another. It was in that year that Johannes dreamed:[44] "And behold here he is officiating at the great church[45] which was of the Oppidans his people. And here a man stands on his right against the altar[46] and says unto him: 'Johannes' " (lacuna).

Three missing lines at the opening of a new page prevent us from knowing what Johannes saw in his dream. But the result was that Johannes "was afraid of the non-circumcised." The much damaged fragment makes it still clear that this had something to do with the Crusader propaganda in which the "abbas Talbestis," the abbot of Tolve, played some role. This is followed by a page in which we find the familiar story of the Popular Crusade. The sewing of crosses on garments: "[And when they rose] to go to Jerusalem one spoke to another saying: 'Why should we go to the land of our enemies and here in our lands and cities there are settled our enemies and haters of our religion and how can we leave them with our wives.' "[47] The last line of this page has three words only: "And the Franks."

Between the story of the dream and the beginning of the Crusader propaganda there are some enigmatic words and a most curious passage of the autobiography:[48] "And in that year (lacuna) the sixth of the (lacuna) as it is written in the book of Joel in the language of the Franks and (in Latin?): *Sol convertetur in tenebras et luna in sanguinem antequam veniat dies Domini magnus et horribilis.* And in the language of Israel (or Hebrews): 'The sun shall be turned into darkness and the moon into blood before the great and terrible day of the Lord come.' "[49] Unfortunately the missing words in the opening paragraph prevent us from fixing the date of the events. The phrase reminds one of Ezekiel 8:1,[50] but there can hardly be any connection. Rather it must relate to the last digit in the date 256 of the fourth millennium in Jewish chronology, which corresponds to the year 1096 of C.E. As is known in the Jewish exegesis of a verse of Jeremiah (31:7): "Sing with gladness for Jacob," the numerical value of "sing" (*Ranu*), 256, was interpreted as pointing to the year of the coming of the Messiah, a date which became the year of Jewish massacres during the so-called Popular Crusade.

Whatever the exact meaning of this enigmatic sixth year, it was then that strange and frightening visions in heaven and earth announced unheard-of events. The description of cosmic signs which is here introduced by verses from the book of Joel is paralleled by similar descriptions of forebodings to be found in the Western chronicles of the First Crusade. But a quotation from Joel, as far as I could check, is not to be found in other chronicles. Moreover he quotes Joel in the Latin version of the Vulgate which is followed by the original Hebrew text.[51] For a man destined to priesthood there is, of course, nothing extraordinary in quoting the Vulgate, but Obadyah wrote for a Hebrew-reading public, and it is inconceivable that he just wanted to impress them by his knowledge of Latin. This quotation must have had a special meaning to Obadyah in the context of time and space. We should note that the quotation follows his first dream and the appearance of a celestial personality. A lacuna in the text prevents us from knowing what possible message he received in his dream, but the fright it caused him is clear. If the proposed reading is correct, his anxiety was the "fear of the non-circumcised" (*arelīm*). The quotation from Joel is then followed by another vision, when the "man of God," probably Moses, shows him an apocalyptic image: an unearthly host with resplendent faces (green or red—smaragd or carbuncle—as the word *nofek* was translated) appear in his dream. And then "those coming from the East were escaping to the West in full pursuit."[52] In his dream Obadyah is then hit on his head and frightened: "And Obadyah kept in his heart [what he saw and heard] and did not know its meaning, until he learned the Law of Moses the Servant of God in the letters (or language) of God [and in the language of the Hebrews] from the beginning of the Torah to its end." And again we hear about "the dreams and their meaning in the prophecy of Moses"[53] and in between an extant line mentions "the tribes of Israel."

The quoting of the Bible in Latin and then in Hebrew, the recurrent insistence on the knowledge of Hebrew for the understanding of the Bible and in this case of the prophecy of Joel, brings us to consider in some detail the pertinent problem of Biblical exegesis. Let us then turn to the quotation from Joel: *Sol convertetur in tenebras et luna in sanguinem antequam veniat dies Domini magnus et horribilis.*

This verse of Joel has to be considered in its Biblical context. The whole chapter introduced by "For the day of the Lord cometh, for it is nigh at hand" (2: 1) relates to the approaching Day of Judgment. The three verses preceding the quoted verse of Joel begin: "And it shall come afterwards that I will pour out my spirit upon all flesh and your sons and daughters shall prophecy," etc. (2: 28) But the quotation from Joel, which in itself points to cosmic upheavals and the mention of "the tribes of Israel" becomes much more meaningful if we read its continuation: "And it shall come to pass, that whosoever shall call on the name of the Lord shall be delivered. For in Mount Zion and in Jerusalem shall be deliverance, as the Lord hath said, and in the remnant whom the Lord shall call." (Joel auth. ver. 2:32.)

For the Christians, contemporaries of the First Crusade who so often identified themselves with "True Israel" or "Israel according to the Spirit," for those who called their kingdom the "Kingdom of Jerusalem" or "Kingdom of David," there was a hint of reality in the following verses: "For behold in those days and in that time, when I shall bring again the captivity of Judah and Jerusalem. I will also gather all nations and will bring them down into the valley Yehoshaphat, and will plead with them there for my people and for my heritage Israel, whom they have scattered among the nations, and parted my land."

Johannes, like all his contemporaries, witnessed the signs in heaven and on earth, and certainly was aware of their current eschatological interpretation.[54] He also knew his Latin Bible and its Christian interpretations. But at a given point this pious and assiduous priest was struck by some doubts.

If the prophecies actually related to his own time, to *whom* did they relate? The dreams and visions, the Messianic tensions whipped up by the preaching of the Crusade, brought thousands to sew the Cross on their garments and: "Those who decided to go to Jerusalem,[55] said one to another as follows: 'why should we who go to a distant land to our enemies and here in our lands and in our cities sit our enemies and haters of our religion. Why should we leave them with our womenfolk'; and a voice was heard in the hosts of the Franks."[56] This became a turning point in the life of Johannes. If the Crusade was a God-willed movement, and the celestial upheavals the fulfillment of a prophecy, then one had to look deep into the Bible to furnish a key to history.

The study of the Bible in the Middle Ages, among Christians and Jews alike, meant the reading of the Holy Scriptures through eyes of accepted and authoritative exegesis. And the different interpretations of the prophecy are what hold the key to our problem. The differences in the exposition of Joel among Jewish exegetes are minimal. With one or two very hesitant exceptions, there is a general consensus that the prophecy of Joel, quoted by Obadyah, refers to the future, the Day of Judgment and the coming of the Messiah. Even an exegete who relates it to past historical events leaves the door open for the millenary fulfillment. Strangely enough, a Palestinian Karaite of the second half of the eleventh century is often quoted by the rabbinical authorities. Yeshu'a ben Yehuda[57] simply states: "All that prophecy is for the future." This is also succinctly stated by Rashi. In this connection Moses Gikatilla raises a point of special interest. Expounding the verse: "And it shall come to pass *afterwards*, that I will pour out my spirit upon all flesh" (Hebrew orig. 3:1. Auth. vers. Joel 2:25), which introduces the prophecy: "The sun will turn," etc., he says: "So why did he say 'And afterwards,' just to indicate that this refers to what will happen at the End of Time." Ibn 'Ezra quotes R. Yeshu'a as well as Moses Gikatilla, but adds his own view: "But this prophet [Joel] was at the time of Jehoshaphat and that is the reason why he mentions the Valley or Jehoshaphat." In relation to the extraordinary behavior of the heavenly bodies he says: "These are signs of wars and they indicate that many people will die." Then expounding Joel 3:13 (Hebrew orig. 4:1) on the deliverance and the return of Judah to Jerusalem, Ibn 'Ezra says: "Because of this verse many thought that this prophecy relates to the future. Perhaps it is so." R. Eliezer of Beaugency without hesitation expounds the verses as relating to the future after the destruction of the four kingdoms[58]; the changes in heaven will take place at the time of the last judgment. But the return of Judah to Jerusalem he connects with the prophecy of Zechariah (14:2) on the gathering of all the Gentiles in Jerusalem and their destruction by God.

Maimonides stresses the possibility of a historical interpretation. In his *Guide for the Perplexed* he writes: "But what is said by Joel 'And I will show wonders' etc., what seems most probable in my opinion is that he is describing the destruction of Jerusalem by Sennacherib; but if you do not accept that, then the destruction of Jerusalem by Gog will take place at the time of the King Messiah, although he did not mention it in his chapter, but rather the proliferation of killings and the conflagration by fire and the eclipse of the two luminaries."[59] David Kimhi, finally, is the latest but also the most explicit among the exegetes. He quotes Ibn 'Ezra, Maimonides, perhaps also

Gikatilla, but adds a particular eschatological stress: "When he said *'before
the day of the Lord came,'* he should have said: *'when* the day of the Lord
will come.' But it is also possible that he meant to say that this tribulation
will come over Israel and the light will turn into darkness before the day of
the defeat of Gog and Magog, who, together with many other nations will
move against Jerusalem to battle, and half of the city shall go forth into captivity (Zechariah 14:2) and this is the darkness . . . and the fall of Gog and
Magog is the day of the Lord, the great and the terrible, as he said about the
locust 'for the day of the Lord is great and very terrible' " (Joel 2:11).

It is against this background of Jewish exegesis that we have to envisage
its Christian counterpart. The prophet Joel plays in Christian exegesis a far
more important role than in the Jewish one. The chapter of Joel we are dealing with belongs to a small number of texts from the Old Testament to be
found in the New Testament. Moreover the excerpt from Joel appears in one
of the most dramatic scenes of the New Testament, namely the gathering on
Mt. Zion and the descent of the Holy Spirit. The apostles gathered there
during Pentecost after the crucifixion and prophesied in many tongues to
the great amazement of the inhabitants of Jerusalem. It was then that St.
Peter said: "These are not drunken . . . but this is what was spoken by Joel."
This is followed by a direct quotation of the chapter from Joel (Acts. 2:14-
21). St. Peter then explained the miracle of the descent of the Holy Spirit as
the fulfillment of the prophecy of Joel. As the prophecy of Joel was related
in the New Testament to an actual event, and by the highest possible authority, one would have expected that this fixed the framework of all future
Christian exegesis.

Events took a different turn. The difficulty was inherent in the verses of
Joel, because whereas St. Peter could relate the descent of the Holy Spirit to
the verse: "I will pour out of my spirit upon all flesh and your sons and your
daughters shall prophesy," there was a difficulty with the beginning of the
verse: "And it shall come to pass in the last days" (Acts 2:17); moreover the
miracle of sun and moon was not actually mentioned.

St. Jerome already had to tackle the problem.[60] As St. Peter pointed out
that the prophecy was fulfilled, why does one get the impression that some
of the events are connected with different times? He quotes some expound-
ers of the Holy Scriptures who maintain that the promise was partially fulfilled. The apostles mention, "the first fruits of the miracles so that we can
perceive what will come in the future." Others, following Psalms 111:5
(112:5)—"He will guide his affairs with discretion"—say that they strengthen
what they said by references to other times. St. Jerome's attempt to "accom-
modate" the two parts of the confusing chapter, which he describes as a "difficult piece of work," is put into its proper setting by St. Jerome himself.[61]
As a matter of fact he has to respond to Jewish exegesis: "What the Jews
promise to themselves in the flesh at the End of Times, they [the Christians]
say that it was spiritually fulfilled with the first coming of the Lord Saviour.
The Jews, as well as we, say that the promise is fulfilled in the Messiah. We

only differ in one point, namely that the Jews say that this relates to the future, whereas we are convinced, that the things happened already."[62] He runs into obvious difficulties: "The sun turned into darkness when it did not dare to see his Lord hanging and the moon turned into blood, which we believe either happened according to history but was passed in silence by the Evangelists, because not all things done by Jesus are told by the Scriptures; or that the sun did not actually turn into darkness but introduced darkness and the moon did not turn into blood, but the Jews covered by the horrors of blasphemies and the negation of Christ were condemned to eternal blood by their testimony, according to Matthew (27:25): 'His blood be upon us and on our children.' "

It was a thorny text for St. Jerome. "All this," he says, "will happen before the Day of the Lord, which is great and terrible, and describes the future. The great and terrible Day of the Lord, we have to believe, is either the Day of Resurrection, or surely, after a long time, the Day of Judgment, which is truly a great and terrible day. But as this is followed by: 'And it *shall come* to pass, that whosoever shall call on the name of the Lord shall be delivered' and this is referred by the apostle Paul to the time of the Passion of the Lord, it is better (*magis*) to understand it as relating to the Day of Resurrection."[63] The difficulties of this chapter are not yet over, however, and St. Jerome explains the verse (2:32): "And it shall come to pass, that whosoever shall call on the name of the Lord shall be delivered; for in Mt. Zion and in Jerusalem shall be deliverance, as the Lord hath said, and in the remnant whom the Lord shall call," as follows: "This place is an extremely difficult one and can be interpreted in many ways . . . As it is impossible that the former part [of that chapter] refers to the time of the Passion, and the following one to the time of (Last) Judgment, especially as it is followed by the verse (3:1): 'For behold in those days and at that time (when I shall bring again the captivity of Juda and Jerusalem)' and this phrase which connects the foregoing with the following, says that all these events happened at one time."[64] St. Jerome then goes into a lengthy anagogical explanation. The interpretation of St. Jerome was already opposed by Rufinus (410), who related it to historical events during the Assyrian conquest, but, he argued, the prophecy was not entirely fulfilled at that time.[65]

The difficulties encountered by St. Jerome, and his ambivalent exposition of this chapter in Joel, left the door open for different interpretations. These obviously depended on the particular attitudes of the exegetes and that, in turn, on the time when they composed their commentaries. Thus in times of Messianic tension they would tend to view the prophecy of Joel, as they did similar parts of the Holy Scripture, in the light of eschatological expectations. True there was always a more ancient and authoritative exposition, that of the Fathers of the Church, but that did not always prevail when events tended to give a new meaning to the Holy Scriptures. But precisely at such times they might be interpreted in similar ways in the Jewish camp. The contention would then center around the question of who is the object of the prophecy. Is it Israel of the Scriptures, the historical Israel, or Israel "according to the Spirit"?

Such a situation was created on the eve of the First Crusade, when we witness a Messianic tension which can be traced for almost a whole generation after the capture of Jerusalem by the Crusaders. For many the Crusade was the fulfillment of prophecies,[66] for others the approaching time of the Last Judgment and preparation for the descent of Heavenly Jerusalem upon earth. It is in this connection that the Western chronicles of the First Crusade enumerate the apparition of heavenly bodies and the strange dreams which accompanied and interpreted these ominous unnatural events. Among the many sources[67] there is a special interest in the description of the Apulian chronicler, the contemporary compatriot of Obadyah (who told the story of Urso of Bari) who describes the heavenly signs at the beginning of the First Crusade: "All over the world stars were seen falling from Heaven to earth. They were so numerous and crowded, like hail or snow when falling. And again a short time later, half the skies turned into the colour of blood. So many dreams and revelations were experienced that nobody can count them."[68] Here we come quite near to the prophecy of Joel.

The feeling in the Christian camp, that the Crusade is the fulfillment of prophecies which were usually regarded as already fulfilled, met with an intellectual movement which brought the interpretation of the Bible into a new focus, and thus furnished the Christian scholars with a new perspective. One must look into the conjunction of these two events, the Crusades and the early stirrings of the Victorine school of Biblical exegesis, to understand the enigmatic use of the prophecy of Joel in the autobiography of Obadyah.

The spiritual founder of the new Christian exegesis was Hugh of St. Victor, who settled in the monastery on the left bank of the Seine, after the school had become famous under Guillaume de Champeaux. A lengthy commentary on the book of Joel, probably the longest ever written among Christians or Jews, which emanated from the school and was written either by Hugh of St. Victor or by a Victorine in his entourage,[69] stresses plainly the direct conflict between the Jewish and the Christian exegesis of the relevant chapter of Joel. But in our context the most relevant fact is the stress of the commentator of Joel on the existence of a trend in contemporary Christian thought or perhaps even a sectarian inclination to follow in this respect the Jewish and not the traditional line of Christian exegesis. This trend or sectarian way of thinking (I hesitate to speak of a sect) the author of the commentary on Joel assigns to *Judaizantes nostri*. This was an expression which might denote anything from those who are inclined to Judaism to those who follow Jewish customs or rites and, in our context, in all probability, those who accept the Jewish interpretation of the Scriptures.

Following the system practiced by Hugh of St. Victor,[70] the commentary begins with the literary or historical explanation to be followed by the allegory and tropology.[71] In his introduction, Hugh of St. Victor makes a distinction between the two parts of Joel. Whereas he accepts two possibilities—the Christian one being that the prophecy relates to the mystery of Incarnation—he stresses: "It can be understood more *correctly* however as referring to the siege and depopulation of the city . . . when the town was besieged by the Assyrians under Sennacherib."[72] This includes also the verse on the unnatural phenomena related to the moon and sun, but what follows about the "pouring of spirit upon all flesh" must refer, he says, to Paraclete, and this he regards not as an allegory but as the literal sense of the verse.

In this connection he adds, "What we explained about the coming of Christ and the mission of Paraclete ('Whosoever shall call on the name of the Lord shall be delivered'), the Jews refer to the coming of their Messiah. At that time, as they say, the cult of the law will be entirely restored, nay the erstwhile bliss will be restored. Only the Jews will receive the Messiah: they will be the only ones to call upon Him and He will hear them out. Some of the Doctors [Christians or Jews?] refer the interpretation of this prophecy to the Last Judgment . . . But we, without prejudicing the case, refer this case as well as the appearance of Christ in flesh and of the Holy Ghost in spirit, we assign to it also the 'Whosoever shall call on the name of the Lord will be delivered.' "[73]

If there is some doubt who the *Doctores* are, this becomes entirely clear when he comments *moraliter* on the refugees in Mt. Zion and Jerusalem, the gathering in the Valley Jehoshaphat, the judgment of the Gentiles and their handing over into slavery.[74] "In this place," he says, "the Jews promise to themselves or rather dream that at the End of Time they will be gathered by God and come to Jerusalem. Moreover, not satisfied with that, they argue that God will give into their hands the sons and daughters of Rome to be sold not to the Persians and Ethiopians and other neighborly nations, but to Sabaeans, a distant nation to avenge the injuries of their nation. Thus they [the Jews] and our *judaizantes* who wish to themselves the rule of a thousand years inside the frontiers of Judea and Jerusalem the Golden and the blood of sacrifices, sons and grandsons and incredible delights and gates resplendent with multifarious gems!"[75] The condemnation of Tyre and Sidon (Joel 4:3) brings to the fore again the clash of commentaries. The Jews understand it as a prophecy for the future, but as this is said after "the great and terrible day," it obviously refers to the times of Titus and Vespasian.[76]

The parallel explanation of Joel follows the same system where the "true meaning" is opposed by Jewish interpretations or what he sometimes calls fabulations or dreams.[77] I will just note that when commenting on the verse "then shall Jerusalem be holy and there shall no strangers pass through her any more" (3:17), he says, "This is referred by the Jews and our *judaizantes* to the fables of the Millennium, when they think Christ will dwell in Zion; and in Jerusalem the Golden and bejewelled, will be gathered the nations of the Saints. And so that those who are oppressed in this world by all the nations, in the other they will rule all the other nations. Thus dreams the fable of the Jews, whereas the truth gives us entirely different things. Jerusalem denotes the Church of the present day, it denotes also the faithful soul, also that soul which is (Gal. 4:26) high up free, our mother."[78]

The Jewish view as it is quoted by Hugh of Saint Victor is no novelty, though I did not find any direct sources relating to Joel which could have been used by the schoolmen. It is quite possible that he learned it through oral contacts with Jewish sages. What is new is the existence of *judaizantes* among his Christian contemporaries.[79] To what extent they were *judaizantes* cannot be gauged by this commentary on Joel. They were certainly irritating enough to the author of the commentary. As a matter of fact we know that a great luminary of the Victorines, Andrew of St. Victor, merited strong rebukes from his colleague Richard of St. Victor.[80] A remarkable marginal note on a manuscript of the same Andrew reads: "Satis violenter hunc textum exsequeris dum nimis iudaizare tu niteris"—"You punish your text with sufficient violence, while you strive too much to judaise!"[81] What is rather perplexing is the phrase of the commentary: "Haec illi et nostri judaizantes, qui mille annorum in Judaeae sibi finibus pollicentur." This makes sense as far as the Jews are concerned but it is disconcerting when he refers it to Christian *judaizantes*. Could he possibly refer to a Christian sect or a Christian group of scholars, or is it simply a slip of the pen?

One way or another we can here find a solution to the perplexities of Obadyah. Caught up in the great élan of 1095-1096 of the First Crusade and the following establishment of the Kingdom of Jerusalem, he pondered the text of Joel with its references to the unnatural signs on heaven and earth, the ingathering of the exiles, the place of the Valley of Jehoshaphat, of Mount Zion and Jerusalem. Under the cloak of Christian exegesis they became symbols and figures and moral teachings. But there was another current in the Christian camp, the *judaizantes*, who explained it differently. If the Crusade was a part of the Divine will, was it not, then, the time of the Messiah?[82] And if this was the truth, and the Christian accusation of Jewish forgeries of the Holy Scriptures baseless, should not one also accept the Jewish exegesis of the Holy Scriptures?

This brought Obadyah or rather Johannes to study assiduously or to reread the Bible in the context of the tremendous and unheard-of movement of the First Crusade. He dreamt and saw visions, as did many of his Christian contemporaries, but the celestial apparition pointed in another direction and brought him to doubt the Christian exegesis. There was a Jewish exegesis, which some time later will be called in the North the *Hebraica Veritas*. We do not know if he learned it from the Jews in the numerous communities near his native Oppido or Tolve.[83] One thing was clear, it was the language of the Hebrews which was the key to the understanding of the Scriptures. The importance of studying the Scriptures is formally attested in the letter of recommendation of R. Baruk ben Itzhak of Aleppo: "And the man (Obadyah) was deeply versed in the reading of their books and following his understanding of what he read in their mistaken books, he came back to the God of Israel."[84] A foggy memory from his childhood about the conversion of the Archbishop of Bari or at least about his leaving the Christian camp also played not an unimportant role in his decision to convert to Judaism.

This "mechanism" of conversion is not an isolated fact. We have a contemporary description of another conversion, not to be confused with our Obadyah despite some similarities, which points in the same direction. The story is told in rather poor Hebrew by a converted Christian brought up and destined to priesthood. His ecclesiastical education and the study of the Scriptures brought him to doubt the meaning of the Holy Text. Thus he began questioning its meaning and with more daring than wisdom he wrote fourteen treatises to prove the correct interpretation of the Scripture.[85]

Like many converts he was sure that once his treatises were read Christians would see the light. Instead he was imprisoned and threatened by death if he did not abjure his new religion. Miraculously he escaped from his jail because one of the guards had a dream which prompted him to help the convert to escape. It seems (the Hebrew of his story is hesitant) that he then wrote six treatises (in Hebrew?) in which he expounded his arguments against the Christian exegesis. Thus another Christian with an ecclesiastical upbringing decided to convert to Judaism, because at a given point his Biblical studies brought him to doubt the truth of the Christian interpretation of the Holy Scriptures.

Seven or eight years after the hosts of the First Crusade moved out of Europe, Johannes took the final step of conversion. By his own reckoning he converted in 1102, though we do not know if it was in Europe or in the Levant, where we find him studying Hebrew and taken care of by the Jewish communities. Perhaps he became a convert in Europe and knew some Hebrew before going to the Levant, though this was hardly sufficient for a man whose feeling of salvation depended on the right exegesis of the Hebrew Scriptures.

It is beyond the scope of this chapter to deal with the different events in the Orient described by Obadyah, but in which he was not personally involved. His wanderings are described in detail, though we do not know their sequence.[86] The last we know about him, unless new fragments of the autobiography come to light, is his appearance in Syria on the frontier of the Latin Kingdom of Jerusalem. It is here that we have our last glimpse of Obadyah. By that time he lived in Damascus on communal charity, which he calls, perhaps jokingly, "the tithe of Obadyah the convert in Damascus."[87] From Damascus he moved to Banyas on the Cruader frontier and met a Karaite Jew by the name of Solomon. Obadyah must have been by then in his late forties and it was, as he mentions on this occasion, nineteen years after his conversion.[88] Banyas, or by its Biblical name, Dan, was the southernmost outpost of Damascus, which a few years later became an Assassin fortress, before finally becoming a Crusader frontier stronghold. A Jewish community existed in the place in the eleventh century, and in all probability a Karaite community as well.[89]

In the autumn of 1121, just before the approaching Jewish New Year, Obadyah moved here from Damascus. Yet he was not alone: "And Obadyah, the convert," he tells us, "rose and went from Damascus to Dan in Eretz Israel and some people of the Sons of Israel, few in number and poor, came with him and stayed there with Obadyah the convert." Here he met a Karaite, Solomon ha-Kohen who declared, "In two and a half months God will gather his nation of Israel from all the lands to Jerusalem, the holy city." When asked about the legitimacy of this prophecy, the Karaite answered, "Because I am the man whom Israel is waiting for," that is to say, he declared himself to be the Messiah. The date which he proclaimed for the ingathering of the Exiles seems to coincide with the feast of Hanukkah, end of Kislev, two and a half months after the middle of Elul. What ensued was a short theological discussion in which Obadyah pointed out to the would-be Messiah that the Savior was expected to come from the family of David, whereas the Karaite was from the tribe of Levi. Asked about proof for his Messianic claim, the Karaite said, "I do not eat neither bread nor water. "He sustained himself by eating "Pomegranates and figs, almonds and nuts, fruits of the sycamore trees, dates and apples which come from trees, and I drink milk." Whatever the meaning of this vegetarian diet (the abstention from drinking water in this context is really puzzling, as even the ascetic "Abelei Zion" would not abstain from water), Obadyah was clearly impressed by his interlocutor.

This last fragment of the autobiography ends in a very enigmatic way. Solomon the Karaite pleaded with Obadyah: "Do not go to Jerusalem, as in two and a half months time we and all of Israel in the Diaspora will be gathered in Jerusalem." And Obadyah answered, "I will go to Egypt and I will come back with our brothers the Sons of Israel who are in Egypt to Jerusalem." How are we to understand this reaction? Did he accept Solomon as a Messiah? Was it only a mocking answer? Or did Obadyah, finally, regard himself as the Messiah? The gathering in Jerusalem at this juncture has to be envisaged in purely Messianic terms as Jerusalem was not only in Crusader hands, but was the *only* city from which the Crusaders barred the Jews in the Kingdom.[90] Thus going to Jerusalem actually meant its liberation from the rule of the Crusaders. The last fragment of the autobiography strikes an enigmatic chord ending with Obadyah's voyage to Egypt and his expectations to come to Jerusalem with the Jews of Egypt. He certainly reached Egypt, since the fragments of his autobiography found their way to the treasures of the Genizah.

At that time Obadyah might have regarded himself as a Messiah. He lived in a period of Messianic tensions. His interest in Messianic movements is evident even in the fragments of his autobiography, where three such movements are mentioned in the space of one generation. He pointed out to the Karaite that being a Kohen he could not be the Messiah,[91] but did he regard himself as a Messiah? There was a Jewish tradition that King David descended from Ruth the Moabite. Could he have found consolation in this fact? And then Obadyah was not alone. There was a small following who wandered with him, a following of poor men who stayed with him and would probably go with him to Egypt. He was definitely the leader of that small band. At this stage there is no way to explain this strange phenomenon. Perhaps one day some lucky finds in the Genizah will furnish an answer to the problem.

NOTES

1. S. A. Wertheimer, *Ginzey Yerushalaym*, II (1901), 16-17.

2. E. N. Adler, "Obadia le prosélyte," *REJ*, LXIX (1919), 129-134.

3. The letter of recommendation (above note 1) with additional fragments was published by J. Mann in *Ha-Tekufah* (Hebrew) XXIV, 337; cf. *ibid.*, 352-354; J. Mann, "Obadia, prosélyte normand converti au judaïsme et sa Megila," *REJ*, LXXXIX (1930), 245-259. Cf. *REJ*, LXXI (1920), 89-93. Newer discoveries were published by S. D. Goitein, "Obadyah, a Norman Proselyte," *JJS*, IV (1953), 74-84; A. Scheiber, "Additional Fragment from the Scroll of Obadyah the Norman Convert (Hebrew), KS, XXX (1955), 91-98. Facsimilia were published by A. Sheiber in *Acta Orientalia Hungarica*, IV (1954), 271-296, and *HUCA*, XXXIX (1968), 163-173. All extant materials were published (but without the vocalization of the original) and according to the order proposed by A. Scheiber in a dissertation of Z. Malaki, *Chapters in Mediaeval Hebrew Literature* (Hebrew; Tel-Aviv, 1971), 62-97.

4. A. Scheiber in *KS*, XXX (1955), 91-96. Bibliographies were printed by N. Golb in *Sefunot* (Hebrew), VIII (1964), 102-104, and S. D. Goitein, *A Mediterranean Society*, II (1972). A lively discussion has centered around musical annotations written down by Obadyah, cf. N. Golb, " The music of Obadia the Proselyte," *JJS.*, XVIII (1967), 43 ff. (with bibl.). The present study does not deal with the problem.

5. This was suggested by A. Scheiber based on the fact that the "Scroll" is vocalized but one fragment is not.

6. Guibert of Nogent wrote his *De Vita sua* about 1115-1121.

7. What follows is the translation of the fragment from the Kaufmann manuscript in Budapest published by A. Scheiber in *Acta Orientalia* and in *KS* (see above note 3). I recto, 1.1-8.

8. A rather awkward expression: *Kehukkat hanashim li-benayhem* reminiscent of the Book of Esther 2:12: *Kedat ha-nashim*, "according to the manner of the women."

9. A lacuna in the text, probably reminiscent of the birth of Esau and Jacob, *Genesis*, 25:23-25.

10. *Genesis* 3:10.

11. *Guwān*, probably to be pronounced Jean, if not Giovan.

12. Reminiscent of *Genesis* 24:26ss and the characteristics of Esau and Jacob.

13. See above note 7. Verso, 1.7-14.

14. Obadyah follows the customary eastern vocabulary distinguishing between Medina (city) and 'Ir (township). I give the Hebrew transliteration of the place names, as they may represent the way the names were pronounced by the Normans in southern Italy. The sound "o" is systematically represented by a *kamaz*, consequently then a *kamaz gadol*. The name *Salernus* is odd for the original Latin Salernum. It is in all probability a misreading or misprint. The city of Ans is described

by Obadyah as to the west of Oppido. In reality it is to the south. This is either Obadyah's mistake or the identification is wrong.

15. The place names were identified by A. Scheiber and a map was drawn up by H. Avenari, "Genizah Fragments of the Hebrew Hymns and Prayers Set to Music," *JJS*, XIV (1965), 87-105. Avenari's reading of the name in the last line, *a . . . ibrg*, as *nahalei Vargo* the rivulets of Varco, identified in this neighborhood, seems hardly fitting, as the text has explicitly: "the city of . . . a . . . ibarg." We have therefore to look for a city in this vicinity. There is perhaps a possibility to identify . . . *a . . . ibarg* with Baragiano to the west of Oppido or with Vaglio (also spelled Baglio) to the southwest of Tolve. Good maps of the area in Vendola, below note 17 as well as in E. Jamison, below note 18.

16. On the situation in southern Italy see F. Chalandon, "The Conquest of South Italy and Sicily by the Normans," *CMH*, V, 167-184, and *Histoire de la Domination Normande en Italie et en Sicile*, I (Paris, 1907), pp. 42-257; J. Gay, *L'Italie Meridionale et l'Empire Byzantin, 864-1071* (Paris, 1904), esp. 431 ff.

17. *LaLucania: Discorsi di Giuseppe Antonini*, II (Naples, 1717), discorso VI, pp. 79 and 84. Cf. L. Giustiniani, *Dizionario Geografico Ragionato del Regno di Napoli*, VII (Naples, 1804), 78. The monastery of St. Peter at Tolve is mentioned in the list of ecclesiastical tithes of 1310 in this area. Cf. D. Vendola, *Rationes Decimarum Italiae nei Secoli XIII e XIV: Apulia, Lucania, Calabria* (Vatican, 1939), p. 160, nos. 2025-26, 2105, 2027.

18. E. Jamison, *Catalogus Baronum: Fonti per la Storia Patria* (Rome, 1972), no. 100, pp. 19-20.

19. S. A. Wertheimer, *Ginzey Yerushalaym*, II, 17; J. Mann in *REJ*, LXXXIX (1930), 247-249.

20. The expression is taken from 1 Kings 3:4.

21. Verso, 1.8-19.

22. *Medinat Mizrayim* can be understood either way.

23. *KS*, p. 94, note 10.

24. B. Blumenkranz, "La Conversion au Judaïsme d'André Archevéque de Bari," *JJS*, XIV (1963), 33-36.

25. M. Garruba, *Serie Critica de Sacri Pastori Baresi* (Bari, 1844), pp. 122-125.

26. Ibid., p. 123.

27. *MGH. SS.*, ed. G. H. Pertz, V (1844), 52 ff.

28. *Anonymi Barensis Chronicon* in Graevius, *Thesaurus Italiae*, IX, 1 (Lugudunum Batavie, 1723), pp. 654ff.; Muratori, *Scriptores V*, pp. 147 ff.

29. Graevius, *Thesaurus Italiae*, IX, 1, col. 657.

30. The difficulties, very well known to earlier historians, were pointed out and strangely construed by F. Nitti de Vito (see below note 33). His tortuous thesis was refuted by F. Baduri, "Le Note Autobiografiche di Giovanni Archidiacono Barese e la Cronologia dell'Arcivescovato di Ursone di Bari," *Archivio Storico Pugliese*, II (1949), 134-146.

31. I am aware of the possibility that Johannes could have been born earlier in the 1050s or 1060s. Thus in 1066 when Andreas went to Constantinople he might have been six years old or so. This would make him around forty at the time of his conversion and sixty or seventy when he came to Baniyas on the Crusader-Damascene frontier. This is not impossible but highly improbable. Moreover, as said, the synchronization with the rulers of Egypt fits very well with the period after 1073.

32. As such he witnessed a charter of Robert Guiscard in 1074. F. Ughelli, *Italia Sacra*, VII, 26.

33. *Ioanni archidiaconi de Inventione Sancti Sabini episcopi*, ed. F. Ughelli, *Italia sacra*, VII, 605 ff. On Urso see the controversial study of F. Nitti de Vito, *La Ripresa Gregoriana di Bari, 1087-1105* (Trani, 1942), and *Le Questioni Giurisdizionali tra Basilica di S. Nicola e il Duomo di Bari*, I (Bari, 1933). Cf. above note 30.

34. *Italia sacra* (above note 33): *Tandem autem Hierosolymam causa orationi ad Sepulchrum profectus est Domini et in eodem anno exinde Barum rediit et aliquanto transacto tempore ivit Canusium, ibi infirmatus obiit et sepultus est, 16 kal. Martii.*

35. Mabillon, *Museum Italicum*, I, 2 (1687), pp. 130 ff., and *Anonymi Belli Sacri Historia, Museum Italicum*, I, 2 (Paris, 1724²).

36. *Historia peregrinorum euntium Jerusalem seu Tudebodus imitatus et continuatus*, cap. 100-101. *Recueil des Historiens des Croisades, Historiens Occidenteaux*, III, 213-214 (hereafter *RHC, HOcc*). On this chronicle see C. Pollock, *Questionum de quatuor primi belli sacri historiis quae sub nomine Tudebodi comprehenduntur* (Bratislava, 1872), but competently H. Hagenmayer, *Anonymi Gesta Dei per Francos* (Heidelberg, 1889) pp. 89 ff.

37. The interest of this Norman of Apulia is apparent in all the interpolations, which almost always center around Bohemond and Tancred. See list in *RHC, HOcc.*, II, 168. One of the episodes refers to the sending of the tent of Karbogha from Antioch to Saint Nicholas in Bari, ibid., c. 68, p. 206.

38. There were actually two embassies sent to Cairo. The second, to which our chronicle refers was sent at the beginning of the siege of Antioch, October 1097 and came back only a year later, as it was kept by the Egyptian authorities in Cairo. Cf. R. Röhricht, *Geschichte des ersten Kreuzzuges* (Innsbruck, 1901) pp. 89, 122, 178.

39. *Tudebodus imitatus et continuatus*, chaps. 100-101, pp. 207-209. The chronicler introduces his story as follows: *Qui videlicet legati quaedam tunc Christi magnalia, quae in Babylone [Cairo] et Jerusalem oculis suis conspexerant, fideliter recitabant, quae opusculo huic inserere dignum ducimus ad laudem Dei in perpetuum commemoranda.*

40. Ibid.: *Porro in aula regia erat vir quidam Ursus nomine, qui olim Barensium episcopus fuerat, sed captus post in peregrinationis itinere Babyloniam ductus est; sicque deinde poenis constrictus fidem Christianam negaverat. Rex enim valde eum diligebat, in tantum ut fere nihil sine ipsius consiliis ageret.*

41. Ibid.: *Verum Ursus apostata, qui regi consilium dederat, videns tanta mirabilia amens affectus est, velutque mortuus in terra aliquantulum jacuit.*

42. *KS*, XXX, 97. Verso 1.14-17. It was suggested by my colleague N. Golb that *misare layla*, the Lords of Darkness, should be corrected to *mikre layla*, the ejection of semen during the night *Sefunot*, VIII, 102. This is not very plausible and there are parallel texts for *sare layla* in the sense of lords of darkness, that is, priests. Cf. A. Scheiber, ibid., note to line 35.

43. The canonical age was officially fixed as follows: *Ordines minores:* Ostiarius 7, Lector 15, Exorcista 18. *Ordines maiores:* subdiaconus 22, diaconus 23, presbyter 25. The canonical age of a bishop not less than 30.

44. The original was published by A. Scheiber in *HUCA*, XXXIX (1968), 169-173. What follows is taken from verso, 1.17-19.

45. *Bama*, altar or church.

46. In the original: *Mizbeah.*

47. Above note 44, verso, 9-13. It was already rightly pointed out by A. Scheiber in *HUCA*, XXXIX, 170, and S. D. Goitein in *JJS*, IV, 80, that the text is related to one of the Hebrew chronicles describing the anti-Jewish pogroms of 1096.

48. Ibid., II, recto 1.7 ff.

49. Joel 3:4; *Vulgata*, 2:31. The excellent decoding of the Hebrew transcription is due to S. D. Goitein in *JJS*, IV, 81.

50. "And it came to pass in the sixth year and in the sixth month in the fifth day of the month." This may refer to the month of Elūl or Adar, that is autumn or spring of the year.

51. There is a *lacuna* in the text, which begins: "And in the language of Israel or of the Hebrews." I recto, 1.13.

52. See next note. The quoted text is reminiscent of the eschatological writings composed between the seventh and twelfth centuries, known as *Midrashe Gēulah*, but I did not find any quotation.

53. The foregoing and present quotations from verso, 1.5-15 ff. and 1.9.

54. The most relevant texts are the following: *Gesta Francorum* I, 1; Guibert of Nogent, *RHC, HOcc.*, IV, 139; Fulco Carnot., I, 6. Ekkehard, *Hierosolymita*, XXXIV, 1; Wil. Tyr., I, 16.

55. This description of Crusader propaganda is introduced by the phrase (1.15-16): "And in that year . . . sent . . . to the Abbot of Tolve." There is no doubt that this refers to a letter sent by the Pope or one of his legates to the Abbot of Tolve announcing the Crusade after the Council of Clermont in November 1095.

56. The foregoing quotation corresponds, as already pointed out by A. Scheiber, *HUCA*, XXXIX (1970), notes 51-52 to Jewish chronicles of the First Crusade. The last phrase points to the decision of the Crusaders to bring death or apostasy to those who sit in their midst, before going to fight the Infidel overseas.

57. Yeshu'a ben Yehuda or in his Arabic name Abū l'Faraj Furqān ibn Asad wrote two commentaries on the Pentateuch in addition to a number of legal treatises. See M. Schreiner, *Studien über Jeschu'a ben Jehuda* (Berlin, 1910), with detailed bibliography. See also J. Mann, *Texts and Studies*, index *s.v.* There seems to be no extant commentary on Joel, but his views are known from quotations.

58. *Perush 'al Tre-'Asar* of R. Eliezer de Beaugency (Balgensi), ed. S. Poznanski (Warsaw, 1911), p. 141.

59. *Guide of the Perplexed*, II, 29.

60. *Hieronymi Commentarius in Joelem, P.L. XXV*, col. 974-975.

61. Ibid., col. 975 C: "Laboris est maximi, quomodo quae sequuntur, his quae disserimus coaptanda sint."

62. Ibid., col. 975D-976A.

63. Ibid., col. 977 B.

64. Ibid., col. 979 A.

65. *Rufino Presbytero ascriptus in Joel commentarius, P.L. XXI*, col. 1049-1052, esp. col. 1049B and 1052A.

66. There are several studies dealing with the problem, but none of them seems to be exhaustive. P. Alphandéry et P. Dupront, *La Chretienté et l'Idée de Croisaae*, (Paris, 1954), I, 51 ff. P. Alphandéry, "Notes sur le Messianisme Médiéval Latin," *Rapport Annuel de l'École des Hautes Études* (1912), and "Les Citations Bibliques chez les Historiens de la Première Croisade," *Rev. d'hist. des religions*, XCIX (1929), 134-157. P. Rousset, "L'Idée de Croisade chez les Chroniqueurs d'Occident," *Relaz. del X Cong. internaz. di Science storiche*, III (Florence, 1955), pp. 547-562. J. Prawer, "Jerusalem in Christian and Jewish Perspective of the Early Middle Ages." *Settimane di Studio del Centro Italiano sull' Alto Medio Evo* (1979). Cf. above note 54.

67. Worthwhile noting the rain of stars in the spring of 1095 in Apulia, the birthplace of Obadyah. Lupus Protospathus, *Chronicon, MGH. SS.*, V, 51, and cf.

next note. From among the chronicles of the First Crusade the most detailed enumeration in Ekkehard, *Hierosolymita*, X, *RHC, HOcc.*, V, pp. 18-19; cf. ibid., V and p. 14, note 18. Baldricus Dolensis, *Hist. Hieros.* VII, *RHC, HOcc.*, IV, 16. Albert. Aqu., I, 5, *RHC, HOcc.*, IV, 274. Guibert of Nogent, *Gesta Dei per Francos*, *RHC, HOcc.*, IV, 139, who assigns to Urban II the exegesis of Isaiah 43:5: *Ab oriente adducam semen tuum et ab Occidente congregabo te*, and similarly II Thessal. 2:3: "The plentitude of time before the salvation of Israel," as relating to the Crusade.

68. *Tudebodus imit. et cont. RHC, HOcc.*, III, 173; *Nam stellae de coelo per totum mundum visae sunt fluere in terra, ita crebrae et spissae, uti grandines vel floci dudum ninguent. Post pauco vero tempore via ignea in coelo apparuit. Transacto namque parvo tempore, medietas coeli versa est in colorem sanguinis. Somnia et revelationes plures visae sunt, quas enumerare nemo protest.*

69. There is a lively controversy as to the authorship of this commentary. Whereas B. Hauréau, *Les Oeuvres de Hugues de Saint Victor* (Paris, 1886), pp. 18-20, assigned it to the thirteenth century, there is a consensus today to assign the commentary (together with the commentary on Obadyah and Nahum) to Hugh of St. Victor or to his disciple Richard of Saint Victor. A view which seems very plausible assigns the contents of the commentary to lectures of Hugh written by one of his disciples. This brings the *opusculum* to the first half of the twelfth century, that is, almost contemporary or written slightly later than the autobiography of Obadyah. A summary of the discussion: D. Van den Eyden, *Essai sur la Succession et la Date des Écrits de Hugues de Saint Victor* (Rome, 1960). Cf. Van den Eyden, "Les Commentaires sur Joël, Abdias et Nahum Attribués à Saint Victor," *Franciscan Studies*, XVII (1957), 366-372; R. Baron, "Richard de Saint Victor est-il l'Auteur des Commentaires de Nahum, Joël et Abdia?," *Revue benedictine*, LXVIII (1958), 118-122.

70. See the classical study of B. Smalley, *The Study of the Bible in the Middle Ages* (1970²), pp. 83 ff.

71. *Hugonis de Sancto Victore adnotationes in Joelem*, *P.L.*, CLXXV, col. 353-368.

72. Prologue (not printed in *P.L.*) and translation quoted by B. Smalley (above note 70), p. 101.

73. *Hugonis de Sancto Victore adnotationes in Joelem*, *P.L.*, CLXXV, col. 358A: *"Et erit quicunque invocaverit nomen Domini, salvus erit."* Quaecunque super adventum Christi ad missionem Paracleti interpretati sumus, Judaei ad adventum sui Messiae referunt. In quo, ut ipsi aiunt, cultus legis ad integrum reparabitur, felicitas pristina restituetur. Solus populus Judaicus Messiam recipiet; solus eum invocabit, et ipse exaudiet. Quidam vero doctorum praefatae prophetiae interpretationem ad judicium ultimum transferunt . . . Nos vero sine cujuscunque sententiae praejudicio, ad adventum Christi in carnem et Paracleti in mentem, et hoc referimus quod dicitur: "Omnis quicunque invocaverit nomen Domini, salvus erit." Unde et Hieronymus, etc.

74. Joel 4:1-8.

75. *P.L.*, CLXXV., col. 359 A-B: Judaei in hoc loco promittunt sibi, imo somniant, quod in ultimo tempore congregabantur a Domino et reducentur in Hierusalem. Nec felicitate contenti ipsum Deum suis manibus Romanorum filios et filias asserunt traditurum, ut vendant eos non Persis, et Aethiopibus, et caeteris quae vicinae sunt nationibus, sed Sabaeis, genti remotissimae, quia Dominus locutus sit, quod populi sui ulciscatur injuriam. Haec illi et nostri judaizantes: qui mille annorum regnum in Judaea sibi finibus pollicentur, et auream Hierusalem, et victimarum sanguinem; et filios, ac nepotes, et delicias incredibiles, et portas gem-

marum varietatae distinctas.

76. Ibid., col. 361C.

77. Ibid., col. 362D-363A.

78. Ibid., col. 367D-368A: *Haec Judaei et nostri judaizantes ad mille annorum fabulas referunt: quando putant Christum habitaturum Sion: et in Hierusalem auream, atque gemmatam sanctorum populos congregandos: ut qui in isto saeculo oppressi sunt ab universis gentibus, in hoc eodem cunctis imperent nationibus. Haec Judaeorum fabula somniat: dum nobis veritas longe alia ministrat. Hierusalem significat hujus temporis Ecclesiam; significat quoque fidelem animam; etiam illam, quae sursum est libera, matrem nostram!* The "mille annorum fabulae" etc., depend on St. Jerome's commentary on Isaiah, l. XVIII. *CCSL,* LXXIII, p. 741.

79. A large number of recent studies deal with the intellectual contacts between Christian and Jews at that period. A very good survey (with abundant bibliography) was published by A. Grabois, "The *Hebraica Veritas* and Jewish-Christian Intellectual Relations in the Twelfth Century," *Speculum,* L (1975), 613-635.

80. B. Smalley, *The Study of the Bible,* p. 157.

81. Quoted and translated by B. Smalley, ibid., p. 164, note. 1.

82. His interest in Messiahs who appeared at that time in the different parts of the Jewish world bears testimony to his permanent preoccupation with the problem.

83. A map of Jewish communities in the area was published by H. Avenari, see above note 15.

84. The corrected version of this letter was published by J. Mann, "Obadya, Prosélyte normand converti au Judaïsme," *REJ,* LXXXIX (1930), 247-248.

85. Text published by S. Assaf, "New Documents on Conversion and Messianic Movements" (Hebrew), *Zion,* V (1940), 118-121, reprinted in *Sources and Studies on Jewish History* I, 149. The late S. Assaf identified the man with Obadyah and a number of students, among them myself, accepted the identity. But this is certainly incorrect. The language of their biographies, as well as all the circumstances are different. This was already rightly argued by N. Golb in *Sefunot,* VIII, 102.

86. They deal with the persecution of the Jews in Baghdād, published by A. Scheiber, "A New Fragment of the Life of Obadyah the Norman Proselyte," *KS,* XXX (1955), 93, 98. J. Mann, "The Appearance of a Messianic Movement in the Vicinity of the Abbaside Capital and Obadyah's Stay in Aleppo," *REJ,* LXXIX (1930), 245-259; cf. S. D. Goitein, "A Report on Messianic Troubles in Baghdād in 1120-1121," *JQR,* XLIII (1952), 57-76.

87. This quotation and the following are taken from the fragment published by E. N. Adler in *REJ,* LXIX (1919), 129-134.

88. The date of the meeting is ascertained as 19 years after his conversion. The date of the conversion is known from the colophon of a copy of Friday prayers written by Obadyah, namely: "Obadyah the Norman convert who entered the Covenant of God of Israel in the month of Elūl in 1413 of the Seleucid era ('leshītrot') which is 4862 of the Creation [C.E. 1102]. Obadyah the convert wrote it himself."

89. "Two communities" in Dan are mentioned in a letter from Fustāt at the turn of the eleventh century. J. Mann, *The Jews in Egypt,* II, 203.

90. J. Prawer, *Histoire du Royaume Latin de Jérusalem,* II (Paris 1974²), pp. 529-530.

91. As we know now some early Jewish sects believed that the Messiah would be a Kohen.

7

The Prohibition against Jewish Printing and Publishing in Venice and the Difficulties of Leone Modena

Benjamin Ravid

I

Ever since the publication of Horatio F. Brown's standard work *The Venetian Printing Press* in 1891, it has been accepted that on December 18, 1571, the Venetian government, or more specifically the Venetian Senate, prohibited the Jews from engaging in printing or publishing books in Venice.[1] In his book Brown related that "in the year 1571, 18th December, the Senate made a general order forbidding Jews to print at all: *non possa alcun hebreo lavorar di stampa ne far stampare libri, et contrafacendo incorrino in pena di perder la robba, et pagar ducati cento. Et quelli che facessero stampar sotto nome de Christiani incorrino nell istessa pena et li libri stampati si intendano esser et siano di colui in nome de chi fussero stati stampati.*"[2] In English this passage reads: "No Jew may work at the press or publish books under penalty of confiscation of the goods and payment of one hundred ducats. And those who have published under the name of Christians shall incur the same penalty and the printed books will be considered to belong to those in whose name they have been published."[3]

Unfortunately, Brown gave neither a source nor a reason for this legislation, only prefacing the quotation with the unelaborated general statement, "The antagonism of the government towards Hebrew presses did not abate."[4] Apparently, he was unaware that previous authors of specialized multivolume histories of Venice had already written that the Jews had been prohibited from engaging in printing in Venice earlier; four authors had given the date as 1566, and one as 1558.[5] Nevertheless, that date 1571 was accepted by subsequent scholars, some of whom even advanced reasons for the prohibition.[6]

To students of the history of Venetian Jewry, the date December 18, 1571, has a special significance. It was on that day that the Venetian Senate ordered that at the end of the two-year grace period provided for in the five-year charter of 1566, which was then expiring, the Jewish moneylenders had to leave the city. However, it has not been hitherto noted that this legislation did not represent the consensus of the Venetian government. The Jewish moneylenders of Venice resided in the city on the basis of five-year charters, which contained the stipulation that if that charter were not renewed, then the Jews were to be permitted to live in the city for two more years before being compelled to leave. As the charter of 1566 had expired, the College (a government magistracy, one of whose main responsibilities was to prepare legislation for consideration by the Senate) introduced on the floor of the Senate the text of a new charter providing that the Jews could live in the city for an additional five years so that the urban poor would have a source of loans in case of need. Simultaneously, as was possible under Venetian parliamentary procedure, some members of the College introduced on the Senate floor another motion requiring that the Jews leave Venice upon the expiration of the two-year period of grace. In addition, a third motion was introduced, proposing that a decision on the course of action to be taken vis-à-vis the Jews be deferred in order to allow the College to spend the rest of the month working out provisions that would be in the best interest of the poor of the city. The three motions were then voted upon; the official motion to recharter the Jews received only twenty-one votes, the motion to require the Jews to leave at the end of the two-year grace period received one hundred and eight, while the third motion to defer a decision received only sixteen affirmative votes; additionally, nine abstentions were cast. Thus, by an overwhelming majority, the Senate legislated that the Jews had to leave the city at the end of their two-year period of grace.

To date it has been taken for granted that only the motion requiring the Jews to leave was introduced on the Senate floor, and that this constituted the official government policy. That view does not take cognizance of the differences of opinion on the Jewish question within the Venetian government, a matter of importance serving as a reminder of the often neglected fact that anti-Jewish measures did not always reflect a unanimously hostile attitude toward the Jews on the part of the authorities.[7]

Although it is open to discussion whether strictly speaking the nonrenewal of a charter valid for a given period constitutes an expulsion or whether the term expulsion should be reserved for arbitrary acts requiring a community to leave suddenly (as, for example, had been the case in England in 1290 and Spain in 1492), the nonrenewal of the charter can be termed an expulsion since its net effect was that as of a certain date the Jews had to leave Venice.

An examination of the text of this rejected charter of 1571 establishes the fact that its twenty-fourth paragraph is identical with the passage quoted by Brown. Brown probably had not seen that charter in its primary location in the *Deliberazioni* of the Senate, but rather an excerpt from it in a secondary location in the holdings of another magistracy, possibly in connection with printing, and accepted it as law, not realizing that in reality it only represented a section of legislation introduced into the Senate but not passed by that body.[8]

II

Once it has been ascertained that the legislation prohibiting the Jews from engaging in printing and publishing in Venice constitutes a clause in a proposed but rejected charter of 1571, the question obviously arises whether the provision had already been included in previous charters. An examination of the two previous charters of 1566 and 1558 establishes that it was indeed included in both in exactly the same wording.[9] Moving further back, it is unclear whether a charter was issued in 1553; so far I have not found any reference to it. Since the five-year charter of 1548 had stipulated that if neither the Jews nor the government gave notice two years in advance, that charter was to be automatically renewed for successive five-year periods (a provision that was afterwards reversed in 1566; without a specific renewal the charter was to expire), it is possible that an automatic renewal took place in 1553. However, in the present context, it is not essential to establish whether a charter was reissued in 1553, for the preceding charter of 1548 contains a passage prohibiting the Jews from engaging in printing activities. From the wording of the passage, it is obvious that this prohibition was then being instituted as a new measure. It was stipulated that henceforth the Jews were prohibited from working at the press or publishing books; however, they were to be allowed to buy and sell books, and to finish those projects which they had already commenced. Anyone disobeying this prohibition would incur the loss of the books and a fine of a hundred ducats. The same penalty was also to be imposed to those who published under the name of Christians.[10]

Establishing this earlier date, twenty-three years prior to 1571, for the enactment of the prohibition against Jewish printing activities is of significance. It shows that the prohibition was not instituted after the adoption of the new harsher papal counterreformation attitude toward the Jews, which commenced in 1555, but rather preceded it. It should be noted that this Venetian prohibition also preceded the conflict between the two Christian Venetian printers of the *Mishneh Torah* of Maimonides, which supposedly culminated in the burning of the Talmud under papal instigation in 1553. In prohibiting Jewish participation in printing, the Venetian republic, which had already adumbrated the later papal policy of 1555 by establishing the compulsory *ghetto nuovo* in 1516 and *ghetto vecchio* in 1541, again on its own initiative, without waiting for the example from Rome, embarked on a more rigorous policy toward the Jews in yet another sphere.[11]

III

At this point, the question of why the Venetian government instituted a prohibition against Jewish participation in printing activities in 1548 naturally arises. It should first be pointed out that in the 1540s the government passed several acts of legislation dealing with printing and publishing. Specifically, in 1543, the Council of Ten, complaining that many unlicensed books which were offensive to the honor of God and Christianity and also very obscene were being printed and sold in the city, ordered the Essecutori contro la Bestemmia to punish all those publishing, selling, or even possessing such books. Then, in 1547, the additional provision was made that anyone importing religiously offensive books was to forfeit them and pay a fine of at least fifty ducats, while the books were to be publicly burnt. The implementation of this legislation was again entrusted to the Essecutori contro la Bestemmia, with the assitance of the Tre Savi sopra Eresia. These measures were apparently to some extent motivated by the desire to halt the importation and printing of Protestant works in Venice.[12] No evidence has come to light to indicate that they were in any way intended against Jewish or Hebrew books. In any case, the motivation for the new clause incorporated into the charter of the Jewish moneylenders in 1548 clearly was not to control the contents of the books of the Jews, since it made no reference to the nature or contents of the books, but rather forbade Jews from engaging in specific activities. Thus, it would appear that the restrictions on the Jews enacted in 1548 are not to be linked to the legislation of the Council of Ten directed against blasphemous and obscene books.

Then, in the following year, on January 18, 1549, the Council of Ten passed legislation providing for the establishment of the guild of printers and booksellers in Venice.[13] The preamble to that legislation related that printing was one of the most important "arts" of the city, and yet was almost the only one not organized. Consequently, it often happened that when the Tre Savi sopra Eresia sought to obtain information about the authors and printers of scandalous and heretical books, they could not find any place to turn to. Similarly, many improprieties which required remedying were arising daily in connection with printing in general, and again it was difficult to clarify matters, since there was no one representing that art and everyone did what he wished, causing great disorder and confusion. Therefore, the preamble concluded, it was necessary to make suitable provision, first for the honor of God and of religion, and then for the honor of the city and for other public considerations such as providing galleots.[14] For all these reasons, the legislation stipulated that a guild should be established for all those who engaged in printing, held shops, and sold books in any manner in the city. Finally, to assure implementation, the Provveditori di Comun were charged with working out the appropriate regulations for establishing the guild and assuring its good government.

This legislation nowhere referred to the Jews. As Brown pointed out,[15] it was probably the desire of the Catholic church to suppress heresy that led to the plan to organize a guild of printers and booksellers. Additionally, it was also necessary, as stated in the preamble itself, to establish order in the general civic interests. But in view of both the legally circumscribed position of the Jews[16] and the religious nature of the guilds, it was unthinkable that the Jews should be admitted to the guild. Thus, it is likely that as the desirability of forming the guild was being recognized and the appropriate legislation for its establishment was being formulated, a clause prohibiting the Jews from engaging in printing activities was inserted into the new charter of the Jews, which was then being introduced in the Senate. This innovation could either have constituted a spontaneous action of the government, possibly still acting at the clerical urging, or a response to the specific demands of the Christian printers[17] who were faced with increasing Jewish competition.

Although many details remain to be clarified, something is known about at least three Jews who were active in printing in Venice around this time: Judah ben Isaac ha-Levi of Frankfort, called Loeb Kulpa, his partner Jehiel ben Jekutiel ha-Kohen Rapa, and Meir Parenzo. Judah ben Isaac and Jehiel ben Jekutiel worked as correctors for Christian printers in Venice, the Frari brothers in 1544, and from 1545 on, for Giustiniani. In the Hebrew colophon to their edition of the commentary of Nahmanides to the Pentateuch (Venice, 1545), they related that Giustiniani had perceived that "for several years we have been laboring on improvements to make letters and by the grace of God, we have never found any craftsman who outdid us for we paid no attention to the great labor and extensive expenses." Consequently, they continued, Giustiniani had ordered his administrator (probably Cornelius Adelkind) to print books hitherto available only in manuscript, and now this book was being printed in a new manner. Their work was described in another Hebrew colophon, probably written by Adelkind, who greatly praised it as being of unprecedentedly high quality.[18] This success, if the accounts are accurate, may have aroused the resentment of Christian competitors and led to the restriction of 1548. Also at this time, Meir Parenzo, who had worked for Bomberg in 1546, and then for both Giustiniani and Bragadini, remaining with the latter until Bragadini died, "attempted to print on his own account, probably at the Bomberg press in 1548-49 . . . during which time he is recorded as an independent printer in Cicogna's list as Mazo de Parenzo."[19]

Whatever the circumstances that motivated the legislation of 1549 providing for the organization of the guilds, that legislation did not produce any immediate results. The guild apparently was not organized for seventeen years, until in 1566 the Council of Ten again requested the Provveditori to establish it. Then the Provveditori summoned the "presidents of the trade" to a meeting, and after the necessary consultations, the desired by-laws were worked out in 1567. The opening passage of the by-laws expressed the hope that "our art may guide its actions to the praise of the Divine Majesty and to the general weal, under the protection of the glorious Virgin, Mother of our Lord Jesus Christ, and of this thrice happy and right well-established Republic." The first clause provided that a college of the members was to be established and meet in the chapel of the rosary in the Church of SS Giovanni e Paolo to hear mass said at the altar of the Virgin Mary, and then in that same place elect their officers.[20] While the invocation and the provision for the place of meeting were not specifically adopted to exclude Jews, they obviously had that result; additionally, in general, no evidence has yet come to light indicating that Jews were ever admitted to the guilds of the city of Venice.

However, although the government intended membership in the guild to be obligatory for all printers and booksellers in Venice, this requirement could not be rigidly enforced, since no machinery had been provided for compelling membership. Accordingly, in 1571 a board of five guild members was established as "proctors" to represent the guild in the courts of justice, and generally to protect its interests and to see that they were not infringed upon by printers or booksellers who were not enrolled.[21]

In the following year, in order to remedy the alleged situation whereby many persons, believing that printing was a matter that required little skill, embarked upon it with slight knowledge and lack of experience, a rashness which, it was claimed, was also manifesting itself in bookselling, causing the greatest harm and shame to the city and ruin and dishonor to the art, new steps were adopted. Henceforth, no one who was not a member of the guild might set up a print shop or open a bookstore, or exercise any of the functions of bookseller or printer unless he had first served a five-year apprenticeship in the city, then labored as a workman for three more years continuously, and finally passed an examination and paid a five-ducat fee. Anyone violating these provisions by engaging either in printing or in selling books or sheets with letters printed on them was to incur a fine of fifty ducats for each violation.[22] This measure, while again certainly not in the first place adopted to restrict the Jews, obviously added yet another official barrier to their already legally forbidden participation in the printing trade.

While the guild was probably intended only for owners of presses and print shops and not their apprentices and journeymen, apparently not all of those eligible for membership joined the guild.[23] Therefore, it failed to secure a monopoly of the trade in Venice until 1604, when the Provveditori di Comun empowered the members of the guild to seize all books printed or sold by nonmembers and to seal up their presses and shops.[24] Yet even this proved ineffective and in 1653, the Senate, concerned with the abuses and defects of the printing trade in Venice—which allegedly included low technical standards and the clandestine publication of impious, obscene, and slanderous works—issued sweeping legislation. It included the provision that no one who was not a member of the guild was to own a printing press or printing characters under penalty of a fine of a thousand ducats or print anything whatsoever of any sort, subject to a fine of two thousand ducats and other penalties including possible corporeal punishment for any actual printing undertaken.[25]

In the light of the lax enforcement of existing legislation, it is not surprising that after 1548, Jews continued to engage in officially prohibited printing activities. Legislation was one thing, and its enforcement quite another. While no attempt has yet been made to compare systematically Jewish printing activity in Venice before and after 1548 to determine the effect of the new legislation, a cursory examination of a brief printed summary of some unpublished material in the Venetian archives and also published Hebrew sources reveals that Jewish participation in printing was most certainly not eliminated.[26] Quite possibly, the Venetian Christian printers, in view of the profits derived from printing Hebrew books and selling them both at home and abroad, did not seek the enforcement of the law, since in order to obtain satisfactory texts they had to employ Jewish typesetters and proofreaders. The Venetian government, if it was aware of infringements of the law, may have closed its eyes to them in view of the fact that the Jewish participation facilitated the continued activity of the Christian print shops and led to the employment of Christian laborers involved in other aspects of the production of the Hebrew books. Additionally, customs revenues obtained from export to the Ottoman Empire, Holland, the Germanic lands, and Poland could have played a not insignificant role in inducing the government to embark upon a policy of nonenforcement.[27]

IV

One highly articulate Venetian Jew, the prolific Leone Modena (1571-1648) has left an account of Jewish involvement in printing activities which were opposed by one of the magistracies of the Venetian government. In his autobiography, Modena related that:

In Adar 5394 [January 30 to March 29, 1634; there were two months of Adar that year] I began to print my book *The House of Judah*, a supplement to *Ein Yisra'el* which I greatly desired, may God make me worthy of seeing its completion, for it is my very great wish . . . I have mentioned above the beginning of the printing of the book *The House of Judah*, a supplement to my *Ein Yisra'el*. There was never anything which I waited for and desired all the days of my life as much as to see it printed and distributed and disseminated among the dispersion of Israel, for I was certain that from it I would derive merit, honor and an everlasting name. I began its printing, as stated above, in Adar 5394, and many impediments occurred concerning it and the matter took until Heshvan 5395 [October 23 to November 21, 1634]. Previously, in Elul 5394 [August 25-September 22, 1634] some of the scoundrels of our people informed regarding the printing to the Cattaveri and the print shop was sealed and remained closed for around six months. Afterwards, it was opened and they returned to their work and to printing my above-mentioned book, which was almost completely done by my grandson, Isaac of the Levites, may God guard and preserve him, for I introduced him to this work around two years previously so that he would learn to derive benefit from his labor in a clean and easy craft and not desist from his studies. And on Wednesday 28 Iyyar 5395 [May 16, 1635] suddenly government agents came to the printing house and seized my grandson, the said Isaac, with two of his friends, and placed them in jail, in darkness, and again sealed up the printing house. And I was very troubled for despite great efforts, I was unable to conclude the matter and get him freed. And with great difficulty, at the end of fifteen days they allowed him to go out from darkness to light, but still in jail, and he remained there for sixty-six days. And every day I came with labor and effort and great expense, until God was merciful in his great graciousness, and by ruling of the Qua-

rantia Criminale he was released without penalty on Friday 28 Tammuz 5395 [July 14, 1635] . . . And at the beginning of that year (that is
5396) [New Year's Day was September 13, 1635], I completed the printing of the book *The House of Judah,* and I paid off all the expense of
the printing, which amounted to 250 ducats, all on my own without a
loan, from the profits which God gave me from proofreading other
printed books and from my income from the sale of those books in
Venice, Ferrara and some other places in Italy; I also sent some of them
to the Levant, Germany and Flanders and they are being sold there
daily.[28]

It would seem that this experience of Leone Modena served as the immediate stimulus for a request made by the Jews for a major change in the
clause of their charter which prohibited them from engaging in printing
activities. Fortunately, the procedures involved in the charter system insisted upon by the Venetian government led to the recording and preservation of that request and also the reactions of three magistracies of the government, as well as information on the actual state of Hebrew printing in
Venice and the involvement of the Jews in it.

After two years of insecurity, from 1571 to 1573, the charter of the Jewish
moneylenders had again been renewed for five years in 1573. Subsequent
renewals, always for five years, took place in 1580, 1586, 1591, 1597, 1602,
1607, 1613, 1618, 1624, and 1629. On each occasion, as the Jewish moneylenders petitioned the government for a renewal of their charter, they also
stressed their deteriorating financial situation in view of the unprofitable
nature of their moneylending (pawnbroking) business and the decline of
their second-hand goods (*strazzaria*) trade (the only two pursuits they were
legally allowed to engage in other than the presumably minor activity of
making and selling veils and coifs) and requested certain alleviatory
changes. These included the permission to charge higher interest rates on
loans to the poor, to levy a "transaction fee," to open additional loan banks
that would lend sums in excess of the three ducats maximum per transaction
in the existing banks for the poor at higher rates of interest, and finally to
engage in the Levant trade, as did the Levantine and Ponentine Jewish merchants residing in Venice on the basis of their own ten-year charters, first
granted in 1589.[29]

In addition, some of the petitions requesting the renewal of the charter
also sought relief from certain specific vexations and harassments. Thus, for
example, the petition submitted on or before November 2, 1634, seeking the
renewal of the expiring charter of 1629, requested among other things the
modification of the prohibition against printing and publishing.[30] Since
Leone Modena related that in Elul 1634 (August 25–September 22) informers
had denounced the printing of his book to the Cattaveri and as a result, the
press was closed for six months, it seems most likely that it was the experience of Leone Modena that induced the Jews of Venice to raise the issue.
Specifically, they wanted the paragraph in their charter which forbade them

from engaging in printing and publishing (still worded identically with the phrasing of 1571) interpreted (*dichiarito*) in such a manner that they could engage in printing and publishing only Hebrew books (which they were doing anyway, despite the legal prohibition[31]) and also employ the services of Christians in their print shops.[32]

Unfortunately, the Jews did not specify why they sought these two privileges. The difficulties encountered by Leone Modena and the general problem of dissatisfaction with the quality of the typesetting done by Christians[33] would explain why the Jews desired to print Hebrew books. Also there may have been considerations of an economic nature: in view of the extensive market for Hebrew books both in Venice and abroad, and the fact that authors residing in other cities and countries sent their Hebrew manuscripts to Venice to be printed, the printing of Hebrew books was doubtlessly a profitable enterprise. Since the legislation of 1548 explicitly and the guild restrictions de facto permitted printing and publishing only to Christians, the Jews were compelled to request specific permission to engage legally in printing Hebrew books. However, it is not clear why the Jews sought permission to employ Christians. Possibly, they made the request in order to assure the government and the guild that the establishment of the Jewish-operated Hebrew print shops would not displace Christian laborers, but on the contrary would employ additional Christian labor. Also, perhaps the technical skills of experienced Christian printers were desirable or even essential for certain aspects of the printing process. In any case, it should be noted that the request of the Jews was confined to Hebrew books only; apparently they accepted their exclusion from the production of books in other languages and thus were not seeking to compete in the general sector.

Whatever the reason for the request, in accordance with the usual procedure, the petition of the Jews was referred to the three magistracies of the Venetian government which were most involved with matters concerning the Jews: the Cattaveri, the Board of Trade (Cinque Savi alla Mercanzia), and the Sopraconsoli, with the instructions to submit their reactions in written reports (*risposte*) which were to serve the College as a basis for formulating legislation to be then introduced into the Senate.[34]

The first magistracy to respond was that of the Cattaveri, which usually was not favorably inclined toward the Jews. In its report of November 23, 1634, it related that the intention of the thirty-third paragraph was very clear and required no *dichiarazione*, for it very explicitly forbade the Jews to engage in printing or publishing books. It further stated that the request of the Jews to be allowed to employ Christians should under no circumstances be granted, for it was not good to allow the Jews to possess print shops nor to permit them such continual contact with Christians.[35]

The Board of Trade responded much more sympathetically on December 9. Its report is of special interest, since it contains information on the actual practice of printing Hebrew books at the time.[36] It related that the wording of the charter indeed seemed to imply that the Jews were not to engage in printing. Consequently, since there were print shops engaged in printing Hebrew books in which there were Hebrew typesetters, the Cattaveri had objected and harassed them. The Board, the report continued, had investigated the matter and discovered that there were two Christian print shops engaged in printing Hebrew books, and they had to use Jewish typesetters and proofreaders.[37] The Board pointed out that no Hebrew book could be printed unless it was first examined by the Deputies[38] and then, as other books, given the license of the Tre Inquisitori sopra gli Eresia, the Reformatori of the Studio of Padua, and the Heads of the Council of Ten, with the said license printed in Italian on each book.[39] Therefore, concluded the report, since it was necessary that the Jews have the books they used in their religious rites, and these books could not be printed easily without the employment of Jewish typesetters and proofreaders, the Board believed that the paragraph could be interpreted in such a manner that Jews employed in the Hebrew print shops on properly licensed books would not be molested. Thus the Board seemed to be partially endorsing one of the two requests of the Jews regarding printing.

Finally, on December 22, the third magistracy, the Sopraconsoli, submitted its report.[40] It stated that the request of the Jews could be granted if it would not harm the Christian guild of printers, who strongly protested that if their tax obligations continued, all Hebrew printing would pass into the hands of the Jews, depriving the Christians of their business. Presumably, since the Christian printers' guild was subject to special taxation[41] which would not be imposed on Jewish printers who were not in the guild, the guild feared that the Jews would be in a position to undercut them.

On the basis of these three reports, which also dealt with the other requests of the Jews and the general question of the renewal of the charter, the College approved on December 29, 1634, a legislative proposal which was introduced on the Senate floor on the same day. The proposal, which passed by a vote of eighty-seven in favor, seven opposed, and fourteen abstentions, provided for the renewal of the charter of the Jewish moneylenders of Venice and also dealt with their other specific requests. Regarding their request to be allowed to print Hebrew books, it was only stated that one or more of the Deputies of the Jews could proofread those books necessary for their religious rites before they were printed, on the condition that the usual regulations of the Inquisitors and of the Reformatori of Padua were followed and the license obtained from the Cattaveri. Otherwise, all previously enacted legislation was to remain in effect.[42]

This new provision, as could be expected, did not bring any immediate alleviation of the problems of Leone Modena. According to his account, the press remained closed for six months, that is, until February-March 1635, and subsequently, on May 16, his grandson and the two assistants were jailed until they were released by the Quarantia Criminale on July 14, only then presumably returning to the printing of the book in apparent violation of the letter of the law.

V

Although the legislation of December 29, 1634—which did not grant the Jews even the legalization of the status quo, let alone further rights—was maintained to the end of the Venetian republic, it did not seem to inhibit actual Jewish printing activities. The two Christian printing houses of Bragadini and Vendramin continued to print Hebrew books and to employ Jews throughout the seventeenth and eighteenth centuries. As Cecil Roth observed, "It was perfectly obvious that the two establishments existed merely as cloaks to enable the Jews who were excluded from the publishing trade to print what was desired."[43]

Thus, while Jews could not legally engage in printing or publishing in Venice, it seems that the prohibition against Jewish participation in the printing trade in the city was laxly enforced, paralleling the general disregard of other Venetian legislation on the press. Nevertheless, an investigation in the State Archives might reveal further cases of harassment such as those recorded by Leone Modena, and acknowledged by the Board of Trade in its report of December 9, 1634. However, whatever the actual state of affairs, from the formal legal point of view Jews were not allowed to engage in printing books in the major printing center of Venice for over 200 years, from 1548 to the end of the republic in 1797.[44]

NOTES

1. Horatio F. Brown, *The Venetian Printing Press* (London, 1891). For a summary of subsequent views, see note 6, below, especially the concluding paragraph.

2. Brown, *Venetian Printing Press*, p. 106; quoted with partial English translation in David W. Amram, *The Makers of Hebrew Books in Italy* (Philadelphia, 1909), p. 354.

3. I wish to thank Paul Grendler for kindly reading the typescript of this article and confirming my inclination to render in the above context *far stampare* in a wider and more inclusive sense as "publish," rather than more narrowly and technically as "print." See also notes 6 and 12, below.

4. Brown, *Venetian Printing Press*, p. 106.

5. Vettor Sandi, in his *Principii di Storia Civile della Repubblica di Venezia dalla sua Fondazione sino all'Anno di n.s. 1700*, 3 vols. (Venice, 1755-56), III, i, 445, in outlining the terms of some of the clauses of the charter granted to the Jews in 1566, included the brief notice, "Con il vigesimo quinto si vieta ad essi la stampa o far stampar libri nè pur sotto il nome de'Cristiani; gelosa cosa sempre da tutti i Governi riputata e per la Religione, e per lo Stato." The first part of this was repeated almost verbatim by Cristoforo Tentori, *Saggio sulla Storia Civile Politica Ecclesiastica e sulla Corografia e Topografia degli Stati della Repubblica di Venezia*, 11 vols. (Venice, 1785-90), II, 200-201, whose presentation was quoted by Giuseppe Cappelleti, *Storia della Repubblica di Venezia dal suo Principio sino al Giorno d'Oggi*, 13 vols. (Venice, 1850-55), IX, 148. Additionally, Giambattista Gallicciolli, *Delle Memorie Venete Antiche ed Ecclesiastiche*, 8 vols. (Venice, 1795), II, section 955, pp. 313-314, noted briefly that according to the charter of 1566 "fu a essi interdetta la stampa."

Gallicciolli and Cappelleti did not seem to have been aware that in the interim the charter of 1558 had been published in its entirety in Andre A. Viola, *Compilazione delle Leggi . . . in Materia d'Offici e Banchi del Ghetto*, 5 vols. in six (Venice, 1786), V, ii, 210-221. Its twenty-fifth and final paragraph contained the prohibition cited by Brown, with the opening words "E di più sia aggiunto alli Capitoli sopradetti, che alcun Ebreo non possa lavorar."

6. Amram, *Makers of Hebrew Books*, p. 354, linked the Senate decree of 1571 with an attempt of the Christian printer Di Gara to use Jewish compositors; see also pp. 155 and 324. It should be noted that the *Derek Emunah (Via della Fede)* of Giulio Morosini was published in 1683 and not 1563 (see p. 244); presumably Amram had in mind the *Derek Emunah* of Rabbi Meir ibn Gabbai (Padua, 1563); see Jacob A. Benjacob, *Ozar ha-Sefarim: Thesaurus Librorum Hebraicorum* (Vilna, 1880), p. 116, item 396; Chaim B. Friedberg, *Bet 'Eked Sefarim: Bibliographical Lexicon*, 2nd ed., 4 vols. (Tel Aviv, 1951), I, 246, item 1104. Also, p. 378, the year 1684 given for the death of Leone Modena is presumably a typographical error for 1648.

Cecil Roth, [*History of the Jewish Community of*] *Venice* (Philadelphia, 1930), pp. 260-261 gave a completely different reason for the prohibition, relating that in 1571 the Venetian Senate, "true to its protectionist economic policy, forbade Jews to work in the printing industry, even when the production of Hebrew books was in question. Henceforth, the type had to be set up by Christians."

Joshua Bloch, in his article "Venetian Printers of Hebrew Books," *Bulletin of the New York Public Library*, XXXVI (1932), 71-92 (now photoreproduced in *Hebrew Printing and Bibliography*, selected and with a preface by Charles Berlin [New York, 1976], pp. 63-88) often followed Roth closely; see the comment of Roth in his *Jews in the Renaissance* (Philadelphia, 1959), p. 353. Specifically, on the edict of 1571, see Bloch, p. 89.

Finally the *Encyclopaedia Judaica* (Jerusalem, 1971), XVI, 101, s.v. "Venice, Hebrew printing," also ascribed "the prohibition barring Jews from working in the printing trade" to the year 1571.

Since Brown, only two authors have given other dates. Angelo Sacerdote, in his lecture, "Simone Luzzatto," published posthumously in *In Memoria di Angelo Sacerdote* (Rome, 1936), observed that in 1566 the Jews were forbidden to have print shops (p. 105), while Brian Pullan, *Rich and Poor in Renaissance Venice* (Cambridge, Mass., 1971), p. 521, correctly noted in passing that by the terms of the charter of 1548, the Jews "were now forbidden to print or publish books, though they were still entitled to buy and sell them, and to finish those works they had already begun to produce." See also Pullan, *Rich and Poor*, p. 552, quoted in note 26, below.

7. This reconstruction, based on Archivio di Stato di Venezia (henceforth ASV), Senate, Terra, reg. 48, 180r-185v, December 18, 1571, differs from the accepted account; see e.g., Roth, *Venice*, pp. 88-89; Salo Baron, *A Social and Religious History of the Jews*, 16 vols. to date (Philadelphia, 1952-), XIV, 78 (both misdated December 14). The "expulsion" of 1571 and subsequent rechartering of the Jews in 1573 has been treated in greater length in my forthcoming article to appear in a Festschrift in honor of Ben Halpern, ed. Phyllis Albert and Frances Malino. Brief extracts from the edict of expulsion were published in Viola, *Banchi del Ghetto*, V, ii, 224, and Gallicciolli, *Delle Memorie Venete*, II, section 957, pp. 314-315 (misdated October 18); partial English translation in Pullan, *Rich and Poor*, p. 537.

8. According to Ester Pastorello, *Bibliografia Storico-Analitica dell'Arte*

della Stampa in Venezia (Venezia, 1933), p. 102, Brown had collected and tran-
scribed senatorial copyrights and related material concerning press censorship between 1527 and 1597 into three bundles, then (in 1933) preserved in the Biblioteca
Nazionale di Venezia, and still now (1977) apparently unpublished; bundle B of
Brown's three bundles, "Senatorial Copyrights down to 1597" contains the prohibition of 1571 for the Jews to print books, in the words of Pastorello, divieto a gli
ebrei di stampar libri (1571)."

9. ASV, Senate, Terra, reg. 46, 36*v*, April 2, 1566, clause 25; Gallicciolli,
Delle Memorie Venete, II, section 955, p. 314 (see note 5, above). For 1558: ASV,
Senate, Terra, reg. 41, 152*r*, November 16, 1558 (passed on November 26), clause
25; Viola, *Banchi del Ghetto*, V, ii, 221 (see note 5, above).

10. ASV, Senate, Secreta, reg. 66, 76*v*, December 19, 1548; "Et de più, sia
aggionto alli capti sopraditti, che alcun hebreo non possa lavorar de stampa, nè far
stampar libri, possendo però comprar et vender qlli, et finir qlle opere, che hano
principiato fin hora, et contrafacendo incorrino in pena de perder la robba et pagar
ducati 100 et qlli che facessero stampar sotto nome de cxani incorrino nella istessa
pena, et li libri stampati se intendano esser et siano de colui in nome de chi fossero
sta stampati." This provision was not included in the previous charter of 1538, issued by the Council of Ten, the only ten-year charter granted to the Jewish moneylenders of Venice in the sixteenth and seventeenth centuries. The opening words "et
di più sia aggionto alli capitoli sopradetti" are also found in the charter of 1558.

11. This point has been well made by Pullan, *Rich and Poor*, pp. 516-537. To
his data on the Venetian reaction prior to 1555, the date generally accepted as the
beginning of the impact of the counterreformation on the Jews, should be added the
curtailment in 1549 of the period for which the visiting Levantine Jewish merchants
were allowed to stay in Venice from two years to one year; see Benjamin Ravid,
"The First Charter of the Jewish Merchants of Venice, 1589," *AJS Review*, I (1976),
191.

12. For the legislation of 1543, see Brown, *Venetian Printing Press*, pp. 78-79,
text on pp. 210-211; for the legislation of 1547, see pp. 80, 124-125, text on pp. 211-
212.

The impact of church policy on printing in Venice has been examined in Paul F.
Grendler, "The Roman Inquisition and the Venetian Press, 1540-1605," *Journal of
Modern History*, XLVII (1975), 48-65, and more extensively in his *The Roman Inquisition and the Venetian Printing Press, 1540-1605* (Princeton, 1977). On the
establishment of the Tre Savi, see pp. 39-42, and on the legislation of 1543 and 1547,
p. 78. Attention should be paid to Grendler's comment in "The Roman Inquisition,"
p. 49, note 2, that "Rather than attempt to distinguish among publisher, printer, and
bookseller (an artificial distinction in any case, because one man or firm frequently
did all three), the general term "bookman" is preferred. In the documents, *stampatore*, *libraio*, and *bibliopola* are used interchangeably and indiscriminately"; cf. *The
Roman Inquisition*, p. 4.

13. Brown, *Venetian Printing Press*, p. 81, also pp. 126-127; text on p. 213; see
also Frederic C. Lane, *Venice: A Maritime Republic* (Baltimore, 1973), p. 320.

14. The Venetian guilds were required to provide galleots to serve in the fleet;
for recent references to this responsibility, see Pullan, *Rich and Poor*, pp. 90, 125,
140-155; Lane, *Venice*, pp. 318, 367, 414-415; and Richard T. Rapp, *Industry and
Economic Decline in Seventeenth Century Venice* (Cambridge, 1976), pp. 23, 49-57,
183. The Jews were also required to contribute toward the maintenance of the gal-

leots, as noted by Simone Luzzatto in his *Discorso circa il Stato de gl'Hebrei et in Particolar Dimoranti nell'Inclita Città di Venetia* (Venice, 1638), 30v, Hebrew translation of 1950, pp. 99-100; see Ravid, *Economics and Toleration in Seventeenth Century Venice: The Background and Context of the Discorso of Simone Luzzatto* (to appear in the monograph series of the American Academy for Jewish Research), section five, note 79.

15. Brown, *Venetian Printing Press*, pp. 81, 126-127.

16. The Jews were required to reside in a ghetto, to wear a special yellow hat and to make annual payments to the Venetian government until 1571, while allowed only to engage in moneylending (pawnbroking), the sale of second hand goods (*strazzaria*) and the making and selling of veils and coifs; for details see Pullan, *Rich and Poor*, pp. 476-578, and my forthcoming article mentioned in note 7, above.

17. For some examples of attempts on the part of local authorities on the terra ferma, presumably acting under the influence of the guilds, to restrict Jewish commercial activities, see Pullan, *Rich and Poor*, pp. 518-535 *passim*, and specifically on Padua, Daniel Carpi, *Minutes Book of the Council of the Jewish Community of Padua, 1577-1603* (Jerusalem, 1973), pp. 18-19, and the related Hebrew and Italian texts itemized in Carpi, notes 14, 15, 16, and 19.

18. This information is taken from Menahem Schmelzer, "Rashi's *Commentary on the Pentateuch and on the Five Scrolls*, Venice, Bomberg, 1538," in *Studies in Jewish Bibliography, History and Literature in Honor of I. Edward Kiev*, ed. C. Berlin (New York, 1971), p. 428. Schmelzer comments, "It is evident that the partners were for many years engaged in improving printing machinery and types and had introduced a new method in typography" and relates that "the books printed by them are listed by M. Steinschneider, R. N. Rabinowitz, and D. W. Amram" (see his notes 10, 16, 17, 18, 19).

19. Amram, *Makers of Hebrew Books*, p. 368. Cicogna's "List of Venetian printers and booksellers from 1469-1799" was published in Brown, *Venetian Printing Press*, pp. 397-420; the reference to Mazo de Parenzo is on p. 410. In the colophon to the 1547 edition of the *Kuzari* of Judah ha-Levi, Parenzo wrote, "I am the printer known as Meir of Parenzo as that is the name of the city," Amram, *Makers of Hebrew Books*, p. 367. Additionally, in 1549, he printed part of the Mishnah in the house (print shop?) of Carlo Quirino; see Moritz Steinschneider, *Catalogus librorum hebraeorum in Bibliotheca Bodleiana*, second (facsimile) edition (Berlin, 1931), nos. 1983, 9496. The typecutter Guillaume le Bé claimed to have cut various Hebrew types for Mazo da Parenza in 1547, 1548, and 1556; see Henri Omont, "Spécimens de Caractères Hébreux Gravés à Venise et à Paris par Guillaume le Bé," offprint from *Mémoires de la Société de l'Histoire de Paris et de l'Ile-de-France*, XIV (1887), 4-7, summarized in *REJ*, XVI (1888), 308-309, which contains additional details on the activities of Parenzo, and also Amram, *Makers of Hebrew Books*, pp. 370-371. See also the account in Roth, *Venice*, p. 254: "Meir Parenzo, one of Bomberg's principal collaborators, printed a few works on his own account; the only Jew, as it happens, who ever acted as an independent publisher in Venice, the city *par excellence* of the Hebrew book until the period of its decadence!" (on the "period of decadence" see below); cf. Bloch, "Venetian Printers," p. 91. For additional references to the publishing activities of Meir Parenzo, see Grendler, *The Roman Inquisition and the Venetian Press*, pp. 90, 140, 145.

20. Brown, *Venetian Printing Press*, pp. 83-87; text on pp. 243-248.

21. Brown, *Press*, p. 87.

22. Brown, *Press*, p. 88; text on pp. 253-254.

23. Brown, *Press*, p. 91.

24. Brown, *Press*, pp. 91, 181.

25. Brown, *Press*, pp. 178-182; text of legislation of 1653, pp. 227-230.

26. On the basis of the archives of the Venetian magistracy known as the Cattaveri (see below, note 34), Pullan in his *Rich and Poor*, pp. 552-553 observed that "The ban on Jews printing or publishing books, imposed in 1548, seems to have been enforced less rigorously at the close of the century, when Jews occasionally obtained copyrights for works they had printed. Jewish printers may possibly have been allowed to work only on presses owned by Christians—in Venice, the magistrates occasionally, as in 1590 and 1594, granted permission to small groups of Jews to stay out of the Ghetto beyond the normal curfew to assist in the printing and correction of works in Hebrew. In 1594, Israel, his son Elisama and Rabbi Nessim were proposing to attend for this purpose at the printing press of Missier Giovanni a Gara. There were Jewish printers called Esdra in 1593 and Israel in 1607. Bookselling had not been prohibited, and booksellers also bound books."

Accounts based on Hebrew sources support this picture of Jewish participation in printing. See Amram, *Makers of Hebrew Books*, pp. 202, 253, 346, 350, 352, 354-356, 368, 373-374; Bloch, "Venetian Printers," pp. 85, 87, 88, 90; also Grendler, *The Roman Inquisition and the Venetian Printing Press*, pp. 140, 145, 255.

Any attempt to reconstruct the actual Jewish participation in printing in Venice must also take cognizance of the names of proofreaders mentioned in Abraham Yaari, "The Complaints of Proofreaders Regarding Printing on the Sabbath by Gentiles" (Hebrew) in his *Studies in Hebrew Booklore* (Jerusalem, 1958), pp. 170-178 (expanded version of material originally published in *KS*, XIII [1936-37], 524-528, XV [1938-39], 500-501), and the wealth of information contained in Meir Benayahu, *Copyright, Authorization and Imprimatur for Hebrew Books Printed in Venice* (Hebrew; Jerusalem, 1971)., *inter alia*, pp. 29, 50, 191, note 1, 198-203, 210, 225, 236 and the general remarks on pp. 141-142.

27. On the significance of books in the Venetian export trade, see Gino Luzzatto, "La Decadenza di Venezia dopo le Scoperte Geografiche nella Tradizione e nella Realtà," *Archivio Veneto*, 5th series, LIV-LV (1954), 178-180. Also, one of the arguments employed by Paul Paruta in his partially successful attempt to dissuade the papacy from issuing a new index of prohibited books in 1593 involved the concern that it would adversely affect Venetian printing; see Brown, *Venetian Printing Press*, p. 137, William J. Bouwsma, *Venice and the Defense of Republican Liberty* (Berkeley, 1968), p. 252, and Grendler, *The Roman Inquisition and the Venetian Press*, pp. 237-252, 258-261, also 231.

On the export of Bomberg's Hebrew books, see Bloch, "Venetian Printers," p. 78, based on passing remarks in Amram, *Makers of Hebrew Books*. According to Amram, p. 364, the books of the printing house of Bragadini "went out to all corners of the earth, to the depths of Poland and Russia to the North Sea to Holland and France to the Barbary Coast and to the recesses of the land of the Crescent." See also the information related by Leone Modena in the passage from his autobiography, quoted in section IV.

28. My translation from the autobiography of Leone Modena, *The Life of Judah* (Hebrew), ed. Abraham Kahana (Kiev, 1911), pp. 52-53. A somewhat freer English translation is to be found in Amram, *Makers of Hebrew Books*, pp. 382-383, based on the Hebrew selections from the autobiography included in Abraham

Geiger, *Leon da Modena Rabbiner zu Venedig* (Breslau, 1856), 16*v*. On *The House of Judah*, see Benjacob, *Ozar ha-Sefarim*, p. 73, item 319, and p. 74, item 352; Friedberg, *Bet 'Eked Sefarim*, I, 138, item 648, and I, 142, item 758. I have converted the dates given according to the Jewish calendar in the autobiography of Modena in accordance with Eduard Mahler, *Handbuch der jüdischen Chronologie* (Leipzig, 1916). On the basis of Mahler's charts, 28 Tammuz in 1635 would be a Saturday, not a Friday. Also, from 28 Iyyar to 28 Tammuz inclusive in 1635 was not sixty-six days, but only sixty. The printed Hebrew text of the autobiography has sixty-six written out in words, but possibly an earlier manuscript read 60 in Arabic numerals, which was subsequently misread as 66. Additionally, from the context, perhaps the date Heshvan 5395 (October 23-November 21, 1634) should read Heshvan 5396 (October 13-November 10, 1635). Regarding the *realia* it should be pointed out that the Venetian penal system differentiated between dark cells (*prigione serrata alla luce* or *prigione oscura*) and those into which daylight penetrated. Finally, it should be noted that the title page of *The House of Judah* stated, in Hebrew, that the book was "printed in the name of the *commissaria* of the patrician Giovanni Vendramin."

29. For aspects of the history of the Jewish moneylenders from 1573 to 1618, see Pullan, *Rich and Poor*, pp. 538-578. On the Levantine and Ponentine Jewish merchants of Venice, see Ravid, "The First Charter," and *Economics and Toleration*, section three.

30. The Jewish moneylenders (referred to by the government as the Tedeschi Jews to differentiate them from the Levantine and Ponentine Jewish merchants) made three other requests. The first was to be allowed to engage in the Levant trade, as were the Levantine Ponentine Jews. In a forthcoming study, I plan to deal with the struggle to obtain this privilege, apparently first sought in 1613, in the context of Venetian commercial policy.

The second request dealt with the requirement contained in their charter to furnish rooms used by the government, and also those assigned to visiting rulers or guests of the government. The Jews complained that they were required to furnish not only the main rooms for visitors, but also a large number of additional places, including those intended for servants, all with items of quality which were mishandled, and therefore, they requested that the government grant them whatever relief it deemed reasonable; for further details see Ravid, *Economics and Toleration*, note 74.

Finally, they requested that the government recognize that the Levantine and Ponentine Jews were to contribute to the *gravezze* in accordance with their agreement of the previous month of October, and that the Jews of the terra ferma continue to pay as in the past.

For the decision of the Venetian Senate on these three requests, see below, note 42.

31. See above, note 26, and the report of the Board of Trade of December 9, 1634, reproduced in note 36 below.

32. ASV, Senate, Terra, filza 368, December 29, 1634: "Et perché nel capitolo 31 di essa condotta viene prohibito alli Hebrei il lavorar di stampa nè far stampar libri, la supplichiamo riverentemente dichiarir detto capto che non possi alcun Hebreo lavorar di stampa, nè far stampar libri, solo che de libri Hebraici, et nelle stamparie tener de Christiani."

33. See, e.g., the complaint of Rabbi Isaac Gerson, related in Amram, *Makers of Hebrew Books*, pp. 354-355; also p. 202, the first note, and additionally the

sources assembled in A. Yaari, "The Complaints of Proofreaders Regarding Printing on the Sabbath by Gentiles."

34. For a brief introduction to these three magistracies, see Andrea da Mosto, *L'Archivio di Stato di Venezia*, 2 vols. (Venice, 1937-40), I, 100, 101, 196-197. The petition was also referred to the magistracy of the Rason Vecchie, which, however, only addressed itself to the problem of the furnishing of the rooms.

35. ASV, Senate, Terra, filza 368, December 29, 1634: "Et in oltre addimandano dichiaracione del capto trentauno della condotta loro, il quale è chiarissimo, nè stimiamo habi bisogno de altra dechiaracione, il qual capti prohibisse con parole pienissime et chiare alli Hebrei il lavorar o far lavorar di stampa per quelle importantissime cause che mossero all'hora la Serenità Vra a tal prohibicione, pretendendo di più nelle stamparie pretese tenir Christiani, dimanda che per niun rispetto deve esser essa udita, non essendo bene, che a tal Nacione sij lecito a tenir stamparie, ne meno è lecito comercio così continuale col Christiani, come suplicano, per quel zelo di Religione con che sempre la Serenità Sua visse."

36. ASV, Senate, Terra, filza 368, December 29, 1634: "Circa alla regolatione del capto 31 della stessa loro condotta diremo, che pare, che detto capitolo determini, che non possano li Hebrei haver ingerenza in stampe, da che nè segue, che essendovi stamparie a questo destinate, dove vi sono Compositori Hebrei, pretendendo gl'Illustrissimi signori Cattaveri, che non possino havervi mano, et per ciò li travagliano; nel che havendo noi voluto certificarsi come passa questo negotio dlla stampa delle scritture Hebree, habbiamo trovato che vi sono doi stamparie de Christiani, che stampano li libri Hebraici, et sono neccessarij li Compositori et Correttori delle loro stampe li Hebrei, che pur hora s'impiegano, nè si può stampare libro o compositione alcuna Hebraica, se prima non è veduta et essaminata da Deputati, così apunto come si fa nelle stampe de gl'altri libri con le licenze ordinarie dl Tre Inquisitore, dell'Illustrissimi Refformatori dl studio di Padova, et de gl'Eccelentissime signori Capi del Eccellentissimo Consiglio di Dieci, con stampar appresso sopra cadaun libro in lingua Italiana la licenza sodetta, siche essendo neccessario, che loro habbino li libri che servono al proprio rito, et questi non potendosi facilmente stampare et perfettionare, se non con l'impiego delli detti Compositori et Correttori hebrei, crediamo, che possa esser dichiarito esso capto, affine che non siano molestati qlli Hebrei, che nelle stamparie hebree s'impiegano, et stampano libri con li requisiti et licenze ordinarie."

37. These two print shops were those of Bragadini and Vendramin; see Amram, *Makers of Hebrew Books*, pp. 363-378, 395-397; Roth, *Venice*, pp. 262-265; Bloch, "Venetian Printers," pp. 90-92 and on Bragadini, also *Encyclopaedia Judaica* (Jerusalem, 1971), IV, 1288. For some references to their activities in the seventeenth and eighteenth centuries, see note 43, below.

38. Presumably, the reference is to the Deputies of the Jewish Community; on Jewish self-censorship of books in Italy, see Louis Finkelstein, *Jewish Self-Government in the Middle Ages* (New York, 1924), pp. 92-93, 301, 304, summarized in Bloch, p. 90, note 79. On Finkelstein, pp. 313-314, for "according to the command of his highness Gambur" read "according to the command of the avogadori" (presumably the Avogadori di Commune); Benayahu, *Copyright, Authorization and Imprimatur*, p. 40, note 1, observed that the Hebrew text (p. 311) which was faulty in the 1924 edition of *Jewish Self-Government* was corrected in the 1964 second printing; however the English translation was not changed. Also, Finkelstein, p. 314, for "on the gate of the ghetto" read "in the courtyard of the ghetto"; cf. He-

brew text, p. 311. For an interpretation of the decrees of the synod of Ferrara differing from the generally accepted views, see Benayahu, pp. 80-83, 89-99.

39. On the licensing and censorship of Hebrew books in Venice, see Popper, *Censorship of Hebrew Books*, pp. 54, 56, 93-96; Amram, *Makers of Hebrew Books*, pp. 384-386; Roth, *Venice*, p. 260; Bloch, "Venetian Printers," pp. 89-90, and Benayahu, *Copyright, Authorization and Imprimatur*, pp. 155-244, 339-353.

40. ASV, Senate, Terra, filza 368, December 29, 1634: "Quanto allo stampar libri Hebraici, potrebbe concederle, se cio non pregiudicasse all'arte di stampatori, quali reclamarano forte, perché continuando gli oblighi delle stesse gravezze pubblice possino, col passar tutto il negocio delle stampe hebree nelle mani delli hebrei, rimaner essi privi del beneficio di detta stampa."

41. See above, note 14, for one example.

42. ASV, Senate, Terra, reg. 112, 131*v*, December 29, 1634, also in Senate, Terra, filza 368, December 29, 1634; the text of that charter has been published in Ravid, *Economics and Toleration*, appendix, document D. The passage on printing read: "Et quanto alle stampe, sia permesso ad uno o più Deputati da medesimi Hebrei il poter riveder liberamente quei libri che fossero neccessarij stamparsi per il rito loro, avanti che il stampatore vi metta la mano, ma però con le solite regole dell' Inquisitione, delli Rifformatori del Studio di Padova, e con precedente licenza del Magistrato al Cattaver, et nel resto con intiera osservanza di quello che viene in questa materia delle stampe decchiarito nelle passate deliberationi."

Regarding the complaint concerning the furnishing of the rooms, the legislation provided that henceforth the government was to determine on each occasion on the basis of the number and status of the visitors, the quantity of rooms that the Jews were to furnish; for further details see Ravid, *Economics and Toleration*, note 74.

Next, the legislation authorized the Board of Trade to grant to Tedeschi Jews the right to trade in the Levant as did the Levantine and Ponentine Jews, since it could only be beneficial to the customs and advantageous to the state. The statement of Attilio Milano, *Storia degli Ebrei in Italia* (Turin, 1963), p. 311, that finally in 1629 the Tedeschi Jews obtained permission to engage in trade with the Levant with the obligation, however, to restrict their exportation only to wool and silkcloth locally manufactured is erroneous; for further details, see Ravid, *Economics and Toleration*, note 34.

Third, the Senate legislation dealt with the request to engage in printing, and finally it endorsed the request regarding the payment of the *gravezze*.

43. Roth, *Venice*, p. 263. Cf. also p. 264: "A few courageous Jews continued to use the ancient patrician names to cloak their literary activity"; see also Bloch, "Hebrew Printers," pp. 90-91. For a list of seventeenth-century Jewish "correctors and factors" and of "printers, compositors, etc." at the Vendramin press, see Amram, *Makers of Hebrew Books*, p. 376, and for a "partial list of Jewish printers, compositors and correctors at Bragadini press" in the eighteenth century, Amram, p. 397. On the prominent Foa family, see Amram, pp. 396-397; also Roth, p. 264, Bloch, p. 91.

For a far more comprehensive treatment, not available to Amram, Roth or Bloch, see Yaari, "The Printers of the Foa Family" (Hebrew), in his *Studies in Hebrew Booklore*, pp. 323-419 (originally published in *KS*, XVII [1939-40], 222-237, 393-420, XVIII [1941-42], 67-104). In addition to a list of all books printed by members of the Foa family (at least eighty-four editions prior to the end of the Venetian republic in 1797; pp. 384-409), Yaari's study also contains references to the printing activities of Benjamin ben Aaron Polacco, Solomon ben Moses, David Ashkenazi, Meshullam Ashkenazi Finzi, Mordechai Civita, and an alphabetical list of thirty individuals who worked for the Foa family as "proofreaders, type-casters, typesetters, workers and supervisors" (pp. 383-384); see also p. 381 for the interesting account of the visit of Rabbi Haim Joseph David Azulai in 1776 to the printshop of Bragadini "held" by Gad ben Isaac Foa; original in R. Chajim Josef David Asulai, *Ma'gal-Tov ha-Shalem*, Aaron Freimann, ed. (Jerusalem, 1934), p. 84.

44. The eighty-second clause of the ten-year charter issued for the Jews of Venice in 1777 (in 1738, the two separate charters of the Tedeschi Jewish moneylenders and of the Levantine and Ponentine merchants were combined into one) retained the provision "Che non possano stamparsi, o farsi stampare Libri, nè sotto il proprio, nè sotto qualunque altro nome, ma per quello che fossero necessarj al loro Rito sia permesso ad uno, o più Deputati degli Ebrei rivederli, con precedente però licenza del Magistrato al Cattaver, e con le solite regole dell'inquisitor, e Riformatori dello Studio di Padova" (ASV, Senate, Terra, filza 2660, September 27, 1777). This clause was apparently not affected by the subsequent ten year renewal enacted on August 16, 1787, and shortly before its expiration, the Venetian republic capitulated to the surrounding army of Napoleon Bonaparte on May 12, 1797.

8

Bahya ibn Paquda's Attitude toward the Courtier Class

Bezalel Safran

Introduction

Bahya Ibn Paquda's *Hobot ha-Lebabot*[1] has been the most widely read book of Jewish ethics. Since its composition in Muslim Spain in the second half of the eleventh century,[2] it has influenced all subsequent works in its genre.[3] Its impact on religious trends and movements has been noted in culturally diverse settings ranging from Abraham Maimonides' thirteenth-century Egypt[4] to the Hasidic movement in eighteenth-century Poland.[5]

Historical examination of the work in the context of its own cultural setting, however, has heretofore not been undertaken. This essay therefore will attempt to view *Hobot ha-Lebabot* not as an abstract ethical treatise but as a cultural expression of Jewish life in eleventh-century Muslim Spain. Such a reading of the book in the light of its historical background reveals that Bahya is aware of Jewish courtiers and he delivers a sharp critique of various facets of their culture.[6]

An important source for reconstructing the social milieu of courtier Jews in Muslim Spain is the poetry of the period. Joseph Weiss in his article "Shirah Hazranit ve-Tarbut Hazranit"[7] pointed to the possibilities offered by Spanish Hebrew poetry for outlining aspects of Jewish courtier cultural history. He showed that the courtiers represented a distinct class in Jewish society, conscious of their unique identity and fostering specific social ideals.

Through service for their royal superiors in administrative, financial, medical, or intellectual capacities, they were able to attain power and wield influence in court and in the Jewish community. Impressed by court life, Jewish courtiers appropriated the lifestyle and some cultural values of their Muslim counterparts, which they transferred to an elitist segment of the Jewish community. Overriding goals for the courtiers—in fact, the basis of their paideia—now became a pursuit of elegant style, cultivation of courtly grace and tact, a quest for mastery of the poetic form and techniques of eloquence.

Following Muslim usage, the highest-ranking Jewish courtier would become a patron of literary creativity. Poets were encouraged to compose wine songs, garden poetry, and poems of praise and friendship, forms popular with Arab versifiers, for the amusement of courtiers. In Weiss's opinion, this literary output represents more than imitation by Hebrew poets of Arab poetic genres. It also mirrors the new social milieu of the audience, the modes of their pursuit of pleasure. The poems evoke the soirees in the magnificent garden of the courtier's palace, highlighted by witticisms and repartees, laughter and joviality, displays of eloquence and poetic virtuosity. Poetry thus becomes a "literary abbreviation" of the courtly circle and its quest for pleasure.

J. Weiss's methodological lead has been picked up by Gerson Cohen in his interpretation of Abraham ibn Daud's *Sefer ha-Kabbalah*.[8] He also shares the premise that Jewish courtiers comprise a separate class in Jewish society and draws upon Spanish Hebrew poetry in order to crystallize their self-image. The insight emerging from the two studies is invaluable in providing a backdrop for understanding Bahya's critique. Awareness of the courtiers as a distinct social class with its own self-consciousness sensitizes a reader of Bahya to the historical import of disparate courtier-related phrases, sentences, and paragraphs throughout the book.

Bahya's critique of the courtiers is not systematic. Indeed, many references to the excesses of the courtiers appear merely as one or two of several illustrations of a more general ethical or religious concern. Nevertheless, it is possible to make a case for the legitimacy of synthesizing the diverse remarks about the courtiers into a coherent, unified statement.

Other ethical works frequently do not mirror accurately the social reality they purport to judge. The ills of society are stereotyped; an audience of "sinners" is portrayed typologically.[9] Bahya's addressees, however, emerge as clearly differentiated individuals. Their goals are delineated sharply, their major concerns are recounted in great detail. The specificity of the account makes comparison and corroboration through other contemporary sources possible. Furthermore, once these details are integrated into a composite image of the courtier, other contexts, less explicit yet highly suggestive, can be related to him as well. That is to say, proof that the courtiers represent a portion of Bahya's intended audience, enables the reader to interpret even some implicit references as relevant to Bahya's view of and message to the courtier class.

Critique of Courtier Education

The ideals of a culture are mirrored in its paideia, its theory of education. The paideia of courtiers is therefore a focus of Bahya's close scrutiny. The fifth part of Chapter 5 is structured as a confrontation between man's evil passion and his noble religious sense. In the ensuing struggle, a resolute religious force counters the advance of worldly temptations and the perversion of theological error. In this context, several courtier aspirations are articulated by the evil passion, especially the courtiers' ideal of knowledge, our concern in this section.

The first curricular proposal advanced by the evil passion spells out the high points of courtiers' schooling:

Do not preoccupy your mind with any studies except those through which you can ingratiate yourself into the favor of your contemporaries and through which you can become acceptable to the great ones of your generation—the vizir, the chief of the royal police, the royal finance officer and political dignitaries. [These are studies of] the unusual features of language, the laws of prosody, the principles of grammar and poetry. [Know the] choice anecdotes, exotic parables and strange tales. Frequent the sessions of eloquent men, learn to communicate with all sorts of people. Master the science of the stars, on the basis of which the appropriate course of action for the public and for individuals can be determined (p. 254).[10]

The second, related, proposal identifies intellectual concerns which Jewish courtiers shun:

When the evil passion will discern your desire to pursue wisdom it will say to you: Does it not suffice for you [to study] that which suffices for the great ones of your generation and your elders, that is, the [condensed] knowledge of Torah? Are you not aware that study has neither an end nor a limit? Set therefore as your goal knowledge merely of the roots of religion and basic principles of Torah. Focus your attention on that with which you can adorn yourself in the eyes of people—poetry and its meter, knowledge of the unusual features of language, strange tales, traditional parables. Leave aside matters of law and the discussions of scholars regarding them. Do not turn to the mastery of the principles of logical demonstration, principles of dialectics, or the various syllogisms; [turn away from] the various kinds of proofs, the way to relate the cause to its effect, [or the allegorical method through which to relate] the exoteric to the esoteric meaning—[turn away from these studies] because of their profundity and subtlety of meaning. Lean on the masters of religious tradition even concerning those matters which you can verify independently (p. 274).

These passages serve as the core of Bahya's critique, but their value is not limited to criticism alone. They also contribute toward the identification of the content and telos of the educational program of courtiers, "the great ones of the generation, the elders." Their curriculum is limited to the study of the Arabic and Hebrew languages, grammar, poetry, Arab proverbs and anecdotes, and astrology. The focus is utilitarian; in fact, it is particularly geared to success in the royal service. While providing for the professional skill necessary for advancement in court, it also helps cultivate a social "polish": it encourages exposure to masters of eloquence, in order to perfect one's own capacity for refined and eloquent conversation. Being pragmatic in nature, the educational program rules out the rigorous academic pursuit of theoretical disciplines.

Comparison of this program with contemporary Muslim educational models suggests an identity between the former and the ideal of *adab*.[11] At its best, adab consisted of the general culture expected of any man of superior education. In contrast to *'ilm*, another educational ideal, which advocated specialization, particularly in religious learning, adab's concerns were broader and more humanistic. It encompassed history, ethics, and philosophy as well as poetry, prose, and the sciences corresponding to the latter two areas: rhetoric, grammar, lexicography, and metrics.

But adab was more than a curriculum. It also meant good upbringing, urbanity, and courtesy.[12] The adab educational ideal therefore combined intellectual requirements with social demands; it intended to mold an individual as a whole (especially one who belonged to the upper classes). To possess learning was not sufficient. The grace of adab had to be added in order to enhance both the scholar and his knowledge.[13]

Starting with the ninth century, the great literature of adab, characterized by its varied and pleasing erudition, came into being. It was prepared with close attention to form; elegance of style was considered essential. Historical and ethical material was presented as belles-lettres. Illustrative examples were drawn from poems, anecdotes, and parables to please the reader; frequent switches from one subject to another were employed to sustain his interest. Even philosophy was adapted for the adab audience. It was included in the literature, but without rigorous, methodical analysis.[14]

Already during the Abassid caliphate, the concept of adab narrowed in scope from its broad, humanistic meaning to a more restricted rhetorical sphere which included poetry, artistic prose, collection of anecdotes and proverbs.[15] Style came to be cultivated for its own sake. The substance of what the author set out to communicate was diluted by his rhetoric. Reason ceased to be a precise analytic tool of the scholar; it became *Lebensklugheit.*[16]

The great worth placed on polished style by the upper classes and by the ruling clique of Muslim societies translated itself into practical benefits for one group in particular: the litterateurs. Since official documents and state correspondence came to be judged by the elegance of their phrasing, scribes, the katibs, were constantly in demand.[17]

The form and polish that adab offered thus were professional prerequisites for civil service. Adab became so specialized as to represent the education of the courtier scribe or the courtier poet, whose roles would coincide. The requirements of the katib—theoretical and practical—his adab, came to set the standard for the concept of adab par excellence. In Ibn Qutaybah's *Adab al-Kātib* written around 847-861 in Baghdad (and repeated by ibn 'Abd-Rabbih fifty years later in Muslim Spain), knowledge in the realm of adab refers to the katib's most important intellectual capacity: the ability to handle the complicated tool of the Arabic language.[18]

The study of historical works, too, was highly recommended for princes and their prospective katibs. For the potential future ruler, the study of history was considered the best way to internalize political wisdom.[19] Knowledge of history filtered down also to officials and scholars. A secretary in government service needed a thorough knowledge of the past. His letters and documents greatly gained from the insertion of examples drawn from a large store of historical curiosities.[20] The ambitious courtier would therefore strive to master the field. The court's interest in history was coupled with interest in astrology. Often the same person would be both historian and astrologer. Current and historical developments would be explained through the positive or negative influence of stars.[21]

The general education of the katib served as a standard of adab not only in terms of its curriculum, but also in terms of its goal: usefulness. There was a notion strongly held that knowledge brings worldly success; that pragmatic benefit is a necessary consequence of wisdom. On the other hand, educational literature is replete with emphatic condemnation of "studying for the world."[22] The seeming contradiction was resolved in the following manner: worldly success is a natural result of knowledge. In order to attain knowledge, however, a person must rise above material considerations and show contempt for the ordinary goals and pleasures of this world. This resolution had theoretical import only. In reality, the incidental result was often taken to be the intended goal, and the material rewards going with knowledge were construed as its true ends. The frequent criticisms of "studying for this world" show that many scholars did just that.[23]

Adab works often contain fathers' advice to their sons to pursue knowledge as a means to wealth and political power: "If you have wealth, knowledge will be an ornament to you. If you do not have wealth, it will mean wealth to you," wrote one author. "Acquire knowledge," wrote another, "for if you are lords, you will thereby advance in power and rank. If you belong to the middle class, you will become lords. And if you are common people, it will enable you to make a living."[24]

When Bahya equates the Muslim adab ideal with the paideia of Jewish courtiers, he is faithful to the historical reality. Recent studies have demonstrated the pervasiveness of adab ethical and educational ideals in the poetry of Samuel ha-Nagid.[25] Further corroboration can be adduced from traces of adab in other literary documents of the time.

Judah ibn Tibbon's will[26] reflects important elements of the Spanish courtier's educational program. He stresses the art of penmanship, even the quality of the parchment and ink.[27] Grammatical accuracy is crucial.[28] It is the gracefulness of style, however, that is the key to the author's true worth.[29] Men of renown attained to their high station only through their proficiency in Arabic writing. To illustrate this point, Ibn Tibbon cites Samuel ha-Nagid's own assessment of his political success. The Nagid's couplets in *Ben Mishle* are indeed an ode to the power of the pen:[30] "Hold on to a pen, for through a pen a fortune will be gathered; a pen will elevate the lowly to rulership; a pen will speak in writing [the words of] the tongue of kings. O pen, I will tell of your loving kindness, because through you, my right hand became filled with fortune and honor, and [riding] on your tongue my tongue dumfounded every ruler."[31]

The underlying motive for pursuit of elegant style in particular, and study in general, emerges clearly from ibn Tibbon's will. He borrows the Nagid's formulation of the advantages of knowledge, namely, that the wise man's opinion will earn the esteem of "the great" and that his fame will exceed that of his colleagues.[32]

Bahya's account of adab in Jewish society—reflecting the focus of its curriculum and the motive for its pursuit—is thus corroborated by ibn Tibbon's will. But Bahya communicates new historical information as well, concerning the pervasiveness of the adab ideal in the Jewish community, particularly that of the katib: "Indeed you see that most people exert efforts to acquire knowledge and to disseminate it only in order to be honored by the kings" (p. 347). This passage (correlated with the one on p. 254) indicates that courtier culture served as an orienting principle. It set the educational tone for a large segment of Jewish society striving for mobility and status. In order to achieve the coveted rank in the royal hierarchy many pursued the adab program.

The resultant association in the minds of his audience between mastery of elegant style and entree into the king's court enables Bahya to employ this commonplace as a basis for religious exhortation.[33] Appealing for the investment of as much effort in interpreting the Bible as in unraveling the intricacies of a royal missive, Bahya tells: "Concerning a written document which is brought to one from the king, [one would not have delayed attempting to understand it even] if it was difficult due to the script and phraseology being unclear, the meaning recondite and subtle, the style convoluted and unusual. On the contrary, one would have exerted all intellectual efforts to understand its intention, and be most anxious until one would comprehend its meaning" (p. 336). Describing the great lengths to which one would go in expressing gratitude to a ruler, and the modes one would employ in so doing, Bahya asks that at least as much as accorded to God: "If one undertakes to thank the ruler and to praise him for his favor, or for the abundance of his goodness, whether in poetry or in rhyme, in writing or in speech, one would use all one's linguistic prowess and eloquence: metaphor and parable, truth and falsity" (pp. 341-342). These two citations imply that it would be difficult—if not impossible—to impress the king and his court or even to communicate with them, without a mastery of elegant style, or without being able to decipher their recondite messages.

Why does Bahya object to adab as an educational program? His criticism can be considered from one of two vantage points. It can be viewed as a strictly educational evaluation, analyzing the merits of adab as a curriculum. It can also be treated as a critique of the courtier personality in general, with emphasis on the role of adab in the formation of that personality. The present discussion will be restricted to the former, Bahya's critique of adab learning. His treatment of the courtier personality will be dealt with separately.

Bahya objects to the utilitarian criterion guiding adherents of adab in their training. He resents the emphasis they place on pragmatic benefits, particularly advancement in court. He shares this objection with Muslim critics who condemned adab's "studying for the world," though he arrives at it from traditional Jewish sources.

Bahya's censure emerges, we have seen, from the advice of the evil passion to the potential "climber": "And do not preoccupy your mind with any studies except for those through which you will attain grace in the eyes of your contemporaries, and through which you will become acceptable to the great ones of your generation . . . such as the principles of grammar and prosody" (p. 254). Once more echoing the voice of temptation, Bahya rhetorically suggests: "And abandon the remaining studies for the toil required [in mastering them] is great, while their usefulness is little" (p. 256). On a more straightforward note, he forbids a study of metaphysics (in which he includes the Torah) motivated by the quest for material goals:[34] "We are obliged to study metaphysics . . . but it is forbidden to study it in order to attain to worldly benefits" (p. 15). Intellectual attainment, Bahya implies, is an end in itself. Its pursuit is self-validating, requiring no extraneous justification.

Proponents of study for study's sake, oriented toward the attainment of truth only, would insist not only on purity of motive but also on specialization and rigor of method. In Islamic culture, therefore, advocates of adab education who espoused a broad knowledge in all branches of useful learning were sometimes at odds with the advocates of specialization. Scholars militated against the spread of a type of encyclopedic knowledge which consisted of superficial awareness of many subjects.[35] They exposed the shoddiness of a scholarship which sacrifices analysis and depth, and which trivializes complex intellectual problems. History, the core of adab curriculum, was relegated by some ninth- and tenth-century scholars to an inferior place among propaedeutic or practical sciences which contained, among others, reading, grammar, and poetry.[36]

Scrutinizing courtier-oriented education in the Jewish community, Bahya, too, focuses on the nonrigorous erudition of adab. When he assigns the evil passion to urge the mastery of the adab curriculum and to shun the disciplines of logic and philosophy (p. 274), Bahya means to manifest his displeasure with an intellectual climate which relegates rigorous pursuit of science and philosophy to insignificance, while elevating what he considers the trivial curriculum of adab. He denigrates a culture which neglects proved modes of logical analysis, and ignores the methods of philosophical demonstration in favor of a popularized historical and ethical literature whose only virtue is stylistic elegance.

Turning specifically to poetry, it would seem that Bahya's criticism is that it has no serious intellectual value. Bahya assumes what by this time has become a conventional philosophical stance toward poetry: condescension. All medieval Arab philosophers adopted Aristotle's classification of poetics as a branch of logic in which context it figures as the inferior "fifth syllogism" (below the demonstrative, dialectical, rhetorical, and sophistic syllogisms).[37] Implicit in this classification of poetry as logic is the notion that poetry qua aesthetics has no worth. Since the poetic "syllogism" does not yield cognitive results, since it does not contribute to knowledge—it is superfluous.

When Bahya the philosopher, therefore, juxtaposes poetry and logic (p. 274), the results are predictable: poetry and the entire rhetorical adab program are the target of mockery. In evaluating poetry from the philosophical perspective, Bahya anticipates similar critiques of poetry by Maimonides,[38] Falaquera,[39] and Kalonymus.[40] The latter conceives of poetic attainment as a "trivial acquisition" and considers poetic creativity as "neither wisdom nor a craft."[41]

Bahya himself was practiced in poetic form.[42] His *Bakkasha* (pp. 434-441) and *Tokaha* (pp. 432-434) are written in verse. Religious poetry, he believes, can arouse men to piety (p. 424). Not only did Bahya utilize poetic form, he even incorporated adab content—proverbs and stories—into his work.[43]

These excursions into adab and poetic form are not aberrations and do not render Bahya's position inconsistent.[44] His critique concerns itself not with poetry and adab per se, but with the disproportionate emphasis placed on their cultivation. Adab literature has its place in a total, integrated educational program, but cannot transcend it. Poetry is useful; it can inspire ethical ideals (for example, the Tokaha, p. 432) or arouse religious fervor, but the intrinsic intellectual worth even of such poems is minimal.[45]

In the passage under consideration, Bahya does more than criticize the exclusive emphasis on adab. He goes on to show how this excessive stress has adversely affected the quality and standards of the study of Judaism in two areas: Jewish philosophy and Jewish law. Disregard for the rigorous methods of philosophic demonstration renders it impossible to achieve what is the ideal for Bahya: intellectualized faith.

Following in Saadia's footsteps, Bahya contends that only an intellectualized faith is a legitimate faith. In treating the issues of God's existence, unity, and incorporeality, he not only asserts the possibility of their rational intelligibility, he proceeds to prove them in rigorous, meticulous detail. These efforts at rationalizing traditional beliefs are designed to serve as a stimulus to everyone who is intellectually capable of doing the same (p. 80).[46] One who fails to do so is remiss not only intellectually, but religiously as well, for intellectualizing belief is a primary "duty of the heart." Biology and physics, psychology and astronomy are disciplines wherein Bahya finds "traces of [God's] wisdom" (pp. 104-124). Meditation on the insights they yield reveals the order God has established in the cosmos and points to His power and goodness. Uniformity of natural law, remarkable aspects of zoology and botany, the intricacies of human anatomy, the faculties of human psychology—these are phenomena whose cognition induces in man a feeling of reverence, a sense of wonder. Man's forgetfulness of God and His goodness, Bahya maintains, stems from routinized living which disposes him to take for granted wondrous natural phenomena simply because of their regularity (p. 366). When man, however, through intellectual cognition confronts nature—both in the physical world and in man, the microcosm[47]—he is shocked out of his routine, and overwhelmed with a profound feeling of reverence.

Without mastering the methods of logical reasoning and philosophical analysis—areas which Bahya feels adab scholars neglect—it is impossible to rationalize religious tradition and it becomes necessary to merely assent to "roots of religion and basic principles of the Torah" and to "lean on the masters of religious tradition even concerning those matters which one can verify independently" (p. 274).

Lack of intellectual rigor and discipline takes its toll also in the approach to the study of Jewish law. The Jewish adab scholar, interested only in "[condensed] knowledge of Torah" shuns, "matters of law and the discussion of scholars regarding them" (p. 274). Such a study of Jewish law, powered by discussion among scholars, is for Bahya the intellectually superior form of Talmudic scholarship. It is scholarship which is not content with an unreflective, uncritical reading of the legal opinions in the Talmud (the seventh level) (p. 149). Rather, it seeks to come to grips with the Talmudic text: understanding its deliberations, resolving contradictions, elucidating complexities (the eighth level) (p. 150). Bahya is critical of this level of study on ethical grounds: the motive of study is the quest for self-aggrandizement. Intellectually, however, this approach is superior to the preceding one.

Bahya thus finds Torah study in his time to be superficial,[48] a casualty of the shoddy approach fostered by the courtiers' adab program. Knowledge of Jewish theology and Jewish law is concerned only with the end products of the learning process, not with the process itself, with its method. Theological dogmas are affirmed with no awareness of the rational demonstrations which underlie them. Talmudic material is recited and memorized without comprehension of its logical structure, its problematics, its profundity.[49]

The discussion thus far focused on Bahya's criticism of the adab curriculum in its totality. Poetry, grammar, language, and adab historical literature are treated by Bahya as a unit, and his evaluation of these areas is not particularized. Just one aspect of adab education is singled out for specific criticism: astrology. "Master . . . the science of the stars, on the basis of which the appropriate course of action for the public and for individuals can be determined" (p. 254).

The pervasiveness of astrology in Jewish intellectual circles, both before and after Bahya, has been amply documented by scholars.[50] Jews in the Muslim orbit, as far back as the eighth and ninth centuries, were masters of astrology.

Bahya's suggestion that the interest in astrology is linked to the ambition of courtiers[51] has a historical basis. Jewish astronomers in the service of courts were "obliged to adapt themselves to the fashion of the time," and to the commands of rulers who considered the practical object of astronomy to consist in prognostication and drawing of horoscopes.[52]

The Talmudist Isaac ben Baruch Albalia (1035-1094), a contemporary of Bahya, was a court astrologer. In 1069 he was appointed by al-Mu'tamid, king of Seville, as rabbi and nasi. Ibn Daud ascribes this appointment to Albalia's position as court astrologer: "He . . . was appointed as rabbi and nasi in 4829. [This he attained] when the Muslim king known as al-Mu-'tamid appointed him an official in his residence and palace, where he consulted him in the science of astrology in which R. Isaac was learned."[53]

Most medieval Jewish scholars, predecessors and near contemporaries of Bahya, gave currency to astrology. Through them, it was endowed with legitimacy and worth. Against a background of wide diffusion of astrological notions and profound conviction of their truth, Bahya emerges as the first medieval Jewish writer to offer a critique of astrology. In that role, he antedates Maimonides' *Letter on Astrology* by over a century.[54]

While Bahya preceded Maimonides in attacking astrology, it would not be accurate to speak of influence. Their opposition flows from fundamentally different sources. Maimonides predicates his case on the "foolishness" of astrology. He undermines its cogency by demonstrating its baselessness, its nonscientific character. The only sources of knowledge are reason, sense perception, and religious tradition, but astrology derives from none of these.[55]

The rational thrust of Maimonides' objections to astrology is briefly, but poignantly, formulated in a passage of *Mishneh Torah*: "Whoever believes in these [astrology] and similar things and in his heart holds them to be true and scientific and only forbidden by the Torah , is nothing but a fool, deficient in understanding. Sensible people, however, who possess sound mental faculties, know by clear proofs that all these practices which the Torah prohibited have no scientific basis but are chimerical and inane."[56]

Bahya, however, assumes a different stance. He censures astrology on two theological grounds (pp. 254-255). His first objection rests on the exegetical premise that divination and astrology are as abominable as the pagan cult of child sacrifice. In interpreting the Torah's injunction against astrology in this way, Bahya appeals not to reason, but to an emotional revulsion against pagan barbarities.

The second objection consists in the loss of faith which results from the practice of astrology. A person who believes that the stars determine the fate of nations and individuals, compromises - indeed, negates - his belief in monotheism and trust in God's providence: "Attributing the determination of fortune and misfortune to astrology, divination and the like, undoubtedly constitutes polytheism, and will lead to lack of belief in God, and to complete denial of Him" (p. 255).

Once more, a comparison with Maimonides on these points is illuminating. Maimonides, too, treats of the pagan antecedents and determinist consequences of astrology,[57] but with different conclusions. The pagan origin of idolatry is relevant only historically, not normatively. Rejection of astrology is not rooted in a sense of recoil from pagan abominations, as it is for Bahya, but in a rational conviction that astrology is baseless foolishness.

The deterministic outlook engendered by astrology is viewed in terms of its psychological impact, not its theological consequences. Preoccupation with astrology, Maimonides contends, was the root cause for the destruction of the Temple and loss of Jewish political sovereignty. Military efforts at self-defense against the Roman onslaught were not even considered, much less undertaken, because of the helplessness and passivity caused by astrological determinism.[58]

Why does Bahya, a most articulate exponent for the rational understanding of Jewish tradition, offer what is basically a nonrational critique of astrology? If he was aware of Avicenna's critique of astrology, the question becomes more poignant. Avicenna, too, rejects astrology on rational grounds, pointing to its nonempirical, nonscientific basis.[59]

To account for the different ways in which Bahya and Maimonides repudiate astrology, it may be helpful to consider the different audiences for whom they wrote. Maimonides' correspondents were Talmudic scholars in southern France. They appear from their letter to Maimonides not to have been adepts of astrology.[60] They have heard much about it and read some astrological writings from which they quote, but they are not convinced of its truth. On the contrary, it is they who suggest to Maimonides reasons for the irreconcilability of astrology and faith in God. The religious mind, they contend, rebels against astrological determinism because it renders prayer futile. By their admission, there *are* Jews in their midst who subscribe to popular astrological beliefs, but they too are deeply troubled by the inevitability of the often ominous future adumbrated by astrological signs.

Judging from the tone of their letter it seems fair to say that nothing would relieve the Lunel scholars' agitation more effectively than an outright condemnation of astrology. Maimonides' correspondents are thus poised to embrace his response. He therefore proceeds to dispel the confusion by offering a popularized intellectual critique of astrology.[61] There is no need to invoke religious injunctions, for the French rabbis and their communities are already persuaded of the theological difficulties connected with astrology.[62] What they need, and request, is a clear, intelligible statement exposing the nonscientific basis of this belief.

Such is not the case for the Spanish courtiers to whom Bahya addresses himself. Their belief in fatalism was apparently viewed as somehow compatible with the strictures of religious philosophy. Courtiers apparently found it possible to live on two existential levels. They maintained an intellectual commitment to the religious doctrines of providence, free will, reward and punishment; but simultaneously gave poetic expression to their experience of a capricious fate, and an apathetic nature.[63]

In much Spanish Hebrew poetry of the Muslim period, from Samuel ha-Nagid to Moses ibn Ezra, "time" and "cosmos" are portrayed anthropomorphically as intrinsically malicious; their aim is purported to be the subversion of human welfare and happiness. They seem to act as blind forces transcending mercy and justice and therefore create a mood of passivity and pessimism.[64]

The pervasiveness of these subversive ideas in the poetry has been documented.[65] The implications of the diffusion of this theme for the intellectual and social life of the period was indicated by Joseph Weiss, who took the poetry to be not mere imitation of Arab poetic genres but a genuine reflection of the state of mind of the courtier.[66] Bahya, too, is aware of the widespread belief in determinism: he is cognizant of confusion among Jews concerning free will, and the adverse effect of this confusion on religious action. He finds it to be a most serious religious problem in the Jewish community.[67]

It seems to be Bahya's assessment, however, that determinism and its corollary, astrology, cannot be rebutted on intellectual grounds.[68] After all, the poetry of Samuel ha-Nagid, a towering intellect of the age, manifests divergent, logically contradictory strands in his poetry—astrological determinism on the one hand, faith in a purposeful God on the other. Bahya therefore proceeds to offer not a rational critique of astrology, but a theological one. In this way, especially through his analogy to pagan abomination, he hopes to effectively impress upon his audience the glaring contradiction inherent in their religious thought and to shock them with its destructive implications for religious faith and practice.

Critique of the Courtiers' Social Ethic

In the preceding section Bahya's evaluation of courtier society was considered from the perspective of ideals of knowledge. Such an account, however, while helpful, is not exhaustive. Focusing criticism on the curriculum of the courtier exclusively, without relating it to a broader life orientation, necessarily fragmentizes perception of the problem. Particular educational goals are a mirror of a unique personality type and his specific lifestyle. Bahya understood this and his book therefore offers a basic critique not only of adab curriculum but also of the Jewish courtier's culture as a whole.

The confrontation between Bahya and the courtiers will be reconstructed with material culled from courtier poetry—especially the Nagid's, who is a predecessor of Bahya (d. 1055)—and from statements of Bahya which are directed toward the courtier's cultural values, either explicitly or by implication.

Hobot ha-Lebabot consists of ten chapters, each of which is concerned with a different ethical or philosophical duty: for example, a rationalized belief in the existence of God; meditation upon manifestations of God in the world; trust, self-reckoning, service of God, love of God. Bahya defines all these areas precisely, so that, at least theoretically, there is no overlapping.

Yet there is one issue which defies the confines of its own chapter (on humility), and surfaces in almost every one: pride, or the quest for fame and publicity. It figures even in the chapter on God's existence. A person whose action—religious or mundane—is motivated exclusively by a desire to win the praise of other people or calculated to cater to their caprices is guilty of "secret polytheism" (p. 91).

Perhaps more telling than the frequency of the condemnation of pride is a problem of classification: the incongruity of the chapter on humility vis-à-vis the other chapters in the book. The other chapters treat of philosophical concerns—God's existence, traces of His wisdom, or theological goals—service of God, love of God. The scope of the problems constituting the nine chapter headings is broad and comprehensive. They deal not with specific details, such as a particular ethical disposition or injunction, but with orienting religious principles (trust or self-reckoning) or general theological perspectives (love or service of God). Devoting a whole chapter exclusively to the treatment of pride and humility seems out of context. After all, these traits are aspects of a larger issue—ethical perfection—which Bahya had not considered under a general rubric. Ibn Gabirol in his *Improvement of the Moral Qualities* analyzed the moral traits of pride and humility in separate chapters, but he does the same for anger, jealousy, and so on. Maimonides (in his "Laws of Ethical Dispositions") and many subsequent writers too treat various moral qualities but do not direct special attention to a particular one.

Bahya's emphasis on pride can easily be accounted for. His audience, it will be seen, consists of individuals for whom pride and the quest for honor and fame are more than qualities of their personality; they are a consuming passion, a life orientation. Ibn Gabirol already notes this fact decades earlier. Explaining why his own ethical work begins with a chapter on pride, he says: "For I have seen many of the elect exercise this quality unnecessarily and give it preference over their other qualities, so much so that the masses take it unto themselves."[69]

In shifting perspective from Bahya's work to courtier poetry in order to perceive the nature of the courtier quest, our concern will be with the quest for fame as a motive force in courtier culture. The most remarkable representative of the courtier ideal is the Nagid. In a poem written at the age of twenty, "On Leaving Cordova," he sang of faith in his destiny and vowed to strive ceaselessly until he attains to the summit of greatness and fame:

> Can one restrain himself whose soul is pure,
> and who, like the moon, aspires to rise? . . .
> Until he and his accomplishments are renowned,
> and he surpasses his reputation like the sea . . .
> I will roam until I ascend and reach the peak,
> which will as a result be known forever."[70]

Underlying these lines is the desire to have feats "heard" and widely acknowledged.

A desire for acclaim is also the motivation for courtier study. As was mentioned previously, ibn Tibbon quotes the Nagid, urging his son to strive for intellectual accomplishment, for it will bring him honor among the great, and enhance his reputation. Bad grammar should be avoided, ibn Tibbon advises, because it will result in disrepute; for elegant style, on the other hand, the praise of the writer will travel far.

Philanthropy especially is viewed as a sure means of glory and power. The Nagid advises in *Ben Mishle:* "Charity may diminish your fortune, but will increase your glory."[71] Through contributing generously to a worthy cause one minimizes his faults in the eyes of others, while maximizing his praise.[72] Philanthropy is viewed as a deprivation which will, however, be compensated by power and wide acclaim.[73]

These admonitions by the Nagid serve perhaps as the most revealing introduction to the institution of the courtier patron.[74] Responsibility for sponsoring courtier literary productivity was assumed by the highest rank-ing courtier. He would set the cultural tone by providing financial impetus for the creation of suitable literary expressions for his class. If we are guided by the Nagid's poetry, the quest for glory and fame was a motive for the patron's sponsorship of literary and scholarly pursuits. One of the most common genres of courtier poetry, the poems of praise written for the patron, bespeak this drive. Within the context of a courtier culture these songs of praise—exaggerated and fawning though they may seem to us— filled a social need in providing the patron with a vehicle of fame.[75] Since poetry was widely circulated, it served as a propagandistic device. Songs of praise—panegyrics and eulogies—presented the patron in the most favor-able light and publicized his supposed virtues and accomplishments. Satire lent support to this effort by tarnishing the "image" of his foes and rivals.

Bahya's censure of "pride" and advocacy of humility should be read against this background of the courtiers' quest for advancement and fame. This is quite evident from Bahya's formulation of the problem. He rarely considers pride in abstract ethical terms. The term "pride" is seldom men-tioned in isolation. Bahya speaks concretely of the specific cultural manifes-tation of pride:

> Contemptible traits are many, but their roots are two: first, the love of physical pleasures . . . the second is the love of [political] authority and honor, arrogance and pride, haughtiness and vulgarity . . . The forces [reinforcing these] are . . . love of praise and honor . . . scorn for others and remembering their vices . . . (p. 159).
>
> Humility drives away pride and haughtiness, pomposity and vulgar-ity, self-praise and self-exaltation, domination over others and self-aggrandizement, lording it over the weak, and lusting for what is be-yond . . . (p. 278).
>
> Beware . . . of the temptations of your passion leading you to pride and arrogance, haughtiness and vulgarity, pursuit of [political] author-ity and greatness, the desire to command and to forbid, and to become famous among men (p. 303).
>
> The passion will try to cause you to stumble through your pride, haughtiness and lack of humility, saying, you have already reached the

highest degree of His righteous ones . . . you are unique in your generation and distinctive among your contemporaries; therefore it is fit for
you to accentuate your superiority to them by . . . telling of their shortcomings, and publicizing the wickedness of their heart (p. 270).

One of Bahya's arguments against pride is rooted in the principle that
every human act must have a religious focus exclusively. Only an act which
is God-centered, "directed toward God," has worth. The criterion by which
to determine the religious meaningfulness of a deed is to consider its motive:
"Is it rooted in a desire to please God, or is it calculated to please men?" (p.
267).

It follows for Bahya that a religious act prompted by ulterior motives is
reprehensible. But more importantly, *any* act spurred by self-seeking or
self-aggrandizement, that is, man-centered acts, constitutes "secret polytheism" (p. 91). Bahya has deepened the concept of monotheism. In his
writing, it represents not only philosophical truth and theological dogma,
but a practical norm as well. Any action geared to enhance the honor of
others or of one's self, instead of God's honor, is polytheistic. Honor for
man is inconceivable to Bahya. The most elemental religious feeling—
according to Bahya, reflected in the petitionary benedictions of the service
(p. 344)—is man's absolute dependence upon God. What justification exists
then for honor or pride?

There are other factors which militate against pride and reinforce humility: awareness of man's lowly origins and his looming end (p. 286); cognizance of the inconstancy of political power, "the speed with which kingdoms and governments are being dismantled," coupled with a sense of the
insecurity of human existence in general (p. 289); meditation on the majesty
of God as against the inadequacy of man's religious service (pp. 287-288).

Notwithstanding Bahya's criticism, courtiers did not necessarily consider
their pursuit of fame and glory as an end in itself. It was coupled with,
indeed, it propelled, a keen sense of pragmatism, a persistent quest for
achievement in worldly affairs.[76] The Nagid's poem "On Leaving Cordova"
pulsates with an intense desire for action and practical accomplishment.[77] In
Ben Mishle,[78] The Nagid considers study which cannot be put to practical
use or which does not motivate action as sterile and worthless. Success is
the fruit of action, and a person's claim to honor increases with his effort
and practical initiatives.[79]

Little effort, nonexertion or passivity are the choice of the foolish idler,[80]
whereas the alert, practical person will not spare any effort, as strenuous as
it may be, to make his fortune. He knows that one must search for wealth,
even if it involves travel to faraway places.[81] The Nagid considers the strenuous effort linked with long business trips and arduous voyages as indispensable to successful achievement.[82]

In constrast to the pragmatism of *Ben Mishle* is Bahya's espousal of total
reliance on God. Bahya devotes an entire chapter to *bittahon*.[83] The call to

bittahon is a summons to place one's trust in God only, since all that happens in one's life is under the direct control of God's will. Man is therefore absolutely dependent on Him. It follows then that human activism—practical exertion or effort— is theoretically irrelevant. God has assured everyone of his basic sustenance and practical means can neither increase one's sustenance nor detract from it. God's decree is the exclusive determinant (p. 192). If God had ordained for a person more than his basic sustenance, it will come to him with no hardship as long as he trusts in God. Man should exert the necessary effort, but not rely on it in his heart. If God had not ordained for a person more than his basic sustenance, "even if the inhabitants, both of heaven and earth wished to increase his portion, they could not do so under any circumstances, by any means" (p. 214).

Practical efforts and initiative are still desirable, but not because they bring about the sought-after results. They serve, rather, two extraneous functions. First, man cannot exercise his freedom to obey or disobey God in a vacuum. Religious imperatives can be realized, or violated, only through practical activity in human affairs, not through inaction or passivity. Second, idleness leads to sin and betrayal of God (pp. 202-203).

Active economic pursuits should therefore not be shunned if they suit one's abilities, temperament, religious outlook,[84] and status (p. 192). But reliance should not be placed on these secondary causes, for they directly depend on the decree of God. It follows that "one should not suppose that his sustenance is contingent on a certain [necessary] cause, that if the cause were lacking, he would not be able to get it by any other means. He should rather trust in God exclusively concerning his sustenance, and know that all secondary causes are equal before Him, that He can sustain him through whichever means He wishes, from wherever He wishes" (p. 208).

The advantages of trust which Bahya enumerates at the beginning of the chapter are several. Aside from living a genuinely religious life, free to pursue spiritual goals, the trusting person is spared the anxieties of "traveling to distant places" in pursuit of economic gain, he is relieved from undertaking hard work and laborious vocations which "make the bodies weary" (p. 192). Those strenuous efforts and exhausting travels, which to the Nagid's audience held out the promise of achievement and success, represent to Bahya a burden to be rid of.

Bittahon serves as the ultimate standard for evaluating courtiers' professional activity and social responsibility. Abuses and excesses in these areas are shown to stem from courtiers' lack of absolute reliance on God, from their denial that everything comes from Him, and that it comes from Him for a purpose. Bahya views courtiers as an economic instrument of providence. Royal appointees are entrusted with the material well-being of the many members of their court. Most people have limited economic responsibility, but: "sometimes God arranges for the sustenance of many people to be provided for by one person . . . such as the king who sustains his army and his servants; or the vizirs,[85] government officers and royal appointees under whose aegis many subsist—members of their household, their servants, officials, slaves, children and relatives. [To provide] for them, they [the courtiers] resort to [various] means in order to acquire wealth, [and choose] between the permissible methods and the forbidden ones" (p. 214). Bahya considers the courtiers' economic sphere of influence to be not a privilege, but an obligation, not a gift, but a trial. God invests the courtier with authority in order to test his trust in Him. The "fools" among them fail their test on three counts (p. 215), and in enumerating these, Bahya zeroes in on the failings of contemporary courtiers. First, courtiers acquire their possessions through illegitimate, dishonest methods. They do not realize that if they had employed legitimate means, they would have achieved the same results, for God ordained their wealth for them in any case. Second, the courtier is guilty of insatiable greed. He assumes that all his affluence (even beyond his own immediate needs) is his to consume and to hoard. He forgets that God channels wealth through him for the benefit of his extended household, and presumably also for the community as a whole.[86] Third, in dispensing livelihoods for others, the courtier deludes himself into believing that it is he who supports his beneficiaries, that his role is indispensable. He ignores the fact that it is God who provides the sustenance and that he, the courtier, is simply an agent of providence. When in return for his generosity he demands gratitude, panegyrics, and submission, he arrogates to himself that which is really due to God. When achievement generates pride and a sense of his own importance, he actually usurps God's honor. (Courtier pride is here invalidated from an additional perspective, that of bittahon. Not only is pride theologically unpardonable as "secret polytheism," aiming as it does at the aggrandizement of man rather than the glorification of God. It is also immoral, for the courtier claims credit for an achievement which is God's, not his.)

The social reality of the courtiers reflects itself not only in their economic position, but also, and perhaps more characteristically, in their modes of diversion, in the way they spend their leisure. Once more, the source for reconstructing this reality is courtier poetry—wine and garden songs—for the Nagid and other poets who composed these poems actually experienced many of the scenes to which they gave verbal expression.[87]

These poems seem to reflect a particular mentality. Beyond the light and playful moments captured by the poet, there is a sense of the satisfaction he, and his intended listeners, take in sensuous delights, of the joy of living in this world, of the pursuit of pleasure for pleasure's sake. While there are no orgiastic or licentious portrayals as in some of the Arabic counterparts,[88] there is also no trace of asceticism.

In fact, in one of his wine poems the Nagid turns to those who hesitate to share in the wine party because of religious reasons, and urges them to give unto God what is God's, and unto themselves what is rightfully theirs:[89]

> Do not spend the entirety of your days in His service,
> Rather make time for God, and periods of time for yourselves,
> Give him half the day, and the other half [set] for your own activities,
> And during your nights, give no respite to wine [drinking].[90]

Others he advises not to set a time limit on the enjoyment of wine, but to let it become a constant companion:[91]

> When you are awake, let your right hand stretch to a
>   winecup which is like a candle in the darkness,
> And refrain from making a day of respite from the glass,
>   at night too let your sleep be little
> For your lifetime is short, and in the grave there will
>   be plenty of slumber.[92]

Wine parties are localized in the palace garden, which emerges from the poetry in full splendor: fragrant flowers, blooming trees, sparkling pools, illuminated brightly during long nights of merrymaking. The party provides the setting for fun-loving guests, the background for a lover inspired to extol the beauty of his beloved, or to bemoan her remoteness. Socializing and music and laughter complement the highlights of the evening: recitation and singing of poetry, recounting of riddles and anecdotes, light philosophical causerie, and for the gifted, playful improvisation on wine and garden themes. For poetry serves as the courtiers' chief form of amusement. It is the adornment of their social gathering, objectifying as it does their happy-mindedness and optimism.[93]

Filtered through the eyes of Bahya, the party scene evokes a different response. Bahya knows the mystical[94] bliss that an experience of closeness to God can bring (p. 348) and urges his readers to live in a way which will make that closeness possible. A person "intoxicated by the wine of this-worldliness succumbing to his animalistic lusts" (p. 38) is diverted from Godliness, and cannot achieve the ethical and religious goals prerequisite to spiritual fulfillment.

Bahya defines his position as "moderate" asceticism.[95] Extreme asceticism as a way of life which renounces worldliness absolutely, which advocates self-abnegation, a reclusive existence, total dedication to the service of God, he recommends only for a select group (p. 385). This religious elite personifies a standard, sets a tone for the spiritual life of society as a whole. Society, however, while inspired by the ideal, could not imitate it. It should strive for a "moderate" asceticism, a way of life characterized by restraint in the indulgence of the passions, by moderation in the pursuit of materialistic objectives: "Wholehearted commitment to God's unity cannot be achieved in the soul of the believer if his heart is intoxicated with the wine of the love of the world, and if he is devoted to his animalistic desires. Only when he decides to divest his heart and empty his mind of the superfluities of the world by abstaining from its pleasures, will total commitment to God's unity be made possible" (p. 38).

In advocating a "moderate" asceticism, Bahya is motivated not only by the opportunity for religious bliss in the temporal world. He is even more acutely aware of the contingency of the ultimate reward—existence in the hereafter (p. 355)—upon a life devoted to the crucial religious elements: intellectualized knowledge of God, absolute trust in Him, and doing everything for His sake. A person cannot take these elements seriously, indeed, he gives them the lie, if he zealously pursues comforts and luxury, or if he indulges in pleasure for pleasure's sake. A moderate asceticism—restraint and moderation—holds a promise for reducing the dualism of spirit and flesh, and provides spirit with the opportunity to prevail. This program of moderate asceticism will furnish the provisions necessary for the inevitable journey to the hereafter (p. 391).

In propounding his own religious ideal, Bahya denounces those who subvert it in word and deed. It would obviously be simplistic to identify the target of Bahya's censure with one specific group; in any society many, if not most, of the members are oriented to this world. Still, it is noteworthy that part of Bahya's critique in this regard is focused on the courtiers.

Pinpointing the methods which the "evil passion" will employ in tempting individuals, in diverting them from Godliness, Bahya mentions physical lusts. Then, he continues: It will endear to us pleasures and the refinements [of luxury], envy of kings, rulers and men in their service, in order [that we] emulate them, adopt their practices, and follow their ways in quest of pleasures" (p. 253). The courtiers of Arab society emerge here as the "pace setters" for a class in Jewish society. They determine not only the Jewish adab curriculum but even prescribe to Jewish courtiers a mode of diversion, ways for the pursuit of pleasure and amusement.[96]

Bahya spells out his concerns about these diversions. He warns against overindulgence in the drinking of wine, in wine parties. Wine is useful for medicinal reasons, or for assuaging anxiety. But "beware of the excessive drinking of wine, of quaffing, of drinking in company, for these are most serious ills for religion and the world" (p. 400). Wine parties are here discouraged presumably because they may disintegrate into drunken brawls and orgies. Bahya is more specific in a different passage: "Let him avoid parties of eating, drinking and diversion. Let him beware, if he does mingle, of all that may lead to defiance of God, to violating the rules of modesty, the regulations of morality." The frivolity of a wine party may lead to breaches of decency, to violation of conventional as well as religious restraints. Bahya therefore cautions his readers to shun the different kinds of song and music and hilarity, which divert man from his religious obligations (p. 399). From Bahya's perspective, there is no positive value to pleasure for its own sake (p. 396). If it is not channeled toward religious service or necessary for essential physical needs (for example, permissible uses of wine) it is superfluous. Bahya goes on to show that it may even be harmful, socially as well as religiously.

Nor does Bahya see positive merits in friendship for its own sake or in the pleasantries of social intercourse, elements which pervaded both the poetry and the reality of the courtiers. A gathering of people is almost invariably associated by Bahya with malicious intent or conspiracy to sin: "In summation, most sins are committed only between two . . . all sins committed verbally are conceivable only in company where people mingle" (p. 358). Company inevitably diminishes—nay, eliminates—reverence for God. Social gatherings have the effect of "numbing" reason and arousing the passions, presumably because of the sensual stimulation associated with parties. Other evils stemming from mingling with people are "distortion of thinking, a diminution of logical discernment, and the raising of passions" (p. 358).

Socializing entails idle talk which inevitably leads to gossip, slander and calumny. When a person longs for the pleasure of company, Bahya says, he should recall these disadvantages, and his desire to mingle will dissipate. Seclusion and isolation are the most effective means to avoid the pitfalls of sin and to insure religious and ethical perfection, unless one can associate exclusively with the pious or the wise (pp. 358-359).

It is clear that Bahya's ethical ideal is not outer-directed. His concern is not with social ethics, but with the individual's attainment of his perfection. Man's obligation to society is realized through exhortation and protest when need be. One's own perfection, however, is achieved outside society, not within it.

Critique of the Courtiers' Claim to Leadership

A critique as basic as Bahya's, hitting at such sensitive targets as the paideia and social ethic of the courtiers, might strike even deeper than seems at first. Displeasure with courtier culture could conceivably be translated into an outright rejection of the courtiers' claim to leadership of the Jewish community. Bahya questions the courtier leaders' authority to judge others and even to ensure religious conformity.[97] He apparently doubts the sincerity of the leaders' behavior, suspecting that they are interested more in displaying their own virtue and flaunting their power than in reforming their community.

The pride of the courtiers—"the unique ones in their generation"—results in the arrogant display of their authority: "And then the evil passion will say: you are unique in your generation and distinctive among your contempoaries; therefore, it is fit for you to accentuate your superiority to them by denigrating them, scorning them, telling of their shortcomings, and publicizing the wickedness of their heart, humiliating them and reproving them, until they are ashamed and repent" (p. 270).

But Bahya goes even further. He believes that castigating others or even reproaching them is, in principle, absurd. Any act, ostensibly good or ostensibly bad, is rooted in a motive, which determines its true moral or religious value. Since the motive necessarily eludes the judge or the moral critic, being a matter of conscience, any judgmental or moralizing gesture is meaningless: "How can I denigrate and humiliate a person whose heart and inner sentiments concerning God I do not fathom?" Only God who penetrates man's inner being, Bahya goes on to say, can unravel hidden motives. Only He, therefore, can reprimand and censure wrongdoers through His prophets (p. 270-271).

While Bahya's last point logically follows from his stress on inwardness and his valuation of motive, it is, however, in sharp contrast with several other statements in the book which encourage religious protests and castigation of the wrongdoer. Castigation, Bahya says, can take the form of corporal punishment, verbal censure, or a mental attitude of antipathy: "We have to admonish others against doing evil, using three methods: first, by striking with the hand . . . secondly, by protesting in words . . . thirdly, by protesting in thought" (p. 257). The individuals or groups in society which are antagonistic to religion must be reproached and castigated, ruthlessly if necessary, and finally suppressed: "A man should take revenge upon those who rebel against God. Let not his forbearance in matters which concern himself result in forbearance concerning [violations of] religious matters or in apathy toward those who rail against God's prophets, His messengers, His chosen ones, His elite, . . . when people wrong one another, he should not be apathetic as he might be concerning his own affairs, but should save the oppressed and help judge the oppressor . . . he must not be humble, nor forbearing in such circumstances" (p. 293).

It is not clear whether Bahya's words here are related to any one group in particular.[98] What does emerge clearly is that Bahya can conceive of a situation when judgment, castigation, or suppression would not only be justifiable in principle, but necessary as well—after all, Bahya himself was probably a communal judge.[99] Bahya's position that reproach or castigation of sinners is in principle unjustifiable should therefore be qualified by its particular context: a section dealing primarily with courtier deficiencies in education and excesses in their social deportment. It is the courtiers to whom Bahya denies the authority to judge. The theoretical basis for this denial, namely, that human judgment cannot fathom the *Innerlichkeit* of the offender, is conditioned by a practical consideration: that courtier judges have a long way to go in improving themselves before they can sit in judgment on others' faults: "If I preoccupy myself with criticism of people's shortcomings and focus on their sins, I would be prevented from observing my own shortcomings and becoming aware of my own deficiencies, which is really what I am obliged to do" (p. 271).

Perhaps the most notorious recorded case of a courtier's capricious judgment is ibn Shaprut's expulsion of Menahem ibn Saruq from his home on the Sabbath. The details of the case might even fit Bahya's characterization: "It is fit for you . . . to denigrate them, tell of their shortcomings, and to publicize the wickedness of their heart, humiliating them and reproving them, until they are ashamed and repent" (p. 279). As S. D. Luzzatto reconstructed the case,[100] ibn Shaprut suspected Menahem of Karaite leanings, and his public disgrace served as punishment. In his response to Menahem's

bitter complaint, ibn Shaprut retorts: "If you sinned, I have already castigated you." The next line of ibn Shaprut's response poignantly reveals the
courtier's presumption: "If you are innocent, I have enabled you to share in
the world to come."[101]

Menahem rejects ibn Shaprut's claim in principle. No human judge can
usurp the prerogative of God to unravel the workings of his inner being:

> Should you say: "If you sinned [I have already castigated
>   you], and if not [I have enabled you to share in
>   the next world],"
> Is it correct to judge on the basis of "if,"
>   would it be pleasing in God's eyes?
> And if you followed your heart, and judged me on the
>   basis of your deliberation,
> It is not proper to do so.
> Did you stand in the council of God,
>   are you in God's stead?
> Have you penetrated the hidden recesses of man,
>   do you discern the secrets of his inner being?
> Were the secrets of hearts revealed to you,
>   did you search into thoughts?
> Did you seek the inner parts of man,
>   did you examine his musings?
> Which is He, who is He?
> He is indeed One, to whom these [capacities] appertain.
> He is everywhere, and nothing eludes Him.[102]

Bahya's insistence that one "cannot denigrate and humiliate a person
whose heart and inner sentiments concerning God one does not fathom,"
that only God can censure sinners (through His prophets), expresses essentially the same idea as Menahem's. It might have been borrowed from the
circumstances which surrounded this case of a courtier's arrogant judgment.
In any case, courtier leaders' excesses of this sort motivate Bahya to deny
authority to the courtiers' judgment and decry their methods of enforcement.

Bahya adds another detail to his censure of courtier rule. He clearly indicates that courtiers lord it over their subordinates and exploit them. In his
discussion of trust Bahya points to the practical advantages of total reliance
on God: it becomes unnecessary to pursue certain wearying and demoraliz-
ing professions. Among these professions is tax collecting, a widespread
courtier occupation.[103] A person who trusts in God "avoids the royal service of [collecting] kings' taxes and oppressing the inhabitants" (p. 192).

"Oppression of the inhabitants," disregard of the masses' economic well-
being on the part of the courtiers, is a concern of Bahya elsewhere. In a passage already cited, Bahya censures the "forbidden" methods, the "worst and
most detestable means," which courtiers employ to gain their wealth (p.
215). He goes on to expose their insatiable greed which deprives their extended household and other potential beneficiaries of possessions that God

intended them to have through the agency of the royal appointee. Rather than hoard wealth and property which is in any case expropriated by the courtier's murderer (p. 215), the courtier, Bahya seems to imply, might have dispensed it for his constituents' benefit, during his lifetime.[104]

A fuller critique of the courtiers' exploitation of the poor classes in Christian Spain appears in Shlomo Alami's *Iggeret Mussar* (1415).[105] During this period too, however, there are echoes of such exploitation,[106] and Bahya here registers his protest.[107]

Resentment of courtier leadership was provoked not only by the arrogant flaunting of its authority, nor solely by its exploitation of the poor (which Bahya as a judge probably observed at first hand). It might also have been triggered by a barrier resulting from the masses' lack of the linguistic virtuosity which enabled the courtier to reach his position of power. Several statements were cited earlier to prove Bahya's awareness of the fact that only through the cultivation of elegant speech could one attain to royal service. These skills, however, were not acquired by the broader masses.[108] Works written in recondite poetic style precluded a readership of the Jews who had not mastered it. From that point of view, the lack of cultivated language deprived certain Jews not only of economic advantages, but of culture as well.

Bahya may be addressing himself to this problem when he insists on writing *Hobot ha-Lebabot* in a clear, understandable language. He will employ, so he states in his introduction to the book, language which is simple, intelligible and current, in order to facilitate comprehension. He will avoid abstruse formulations and unusual expressions (p. 35). Bahya contrasts his own clear formulations to the use of "unusual expressions." The latter is associated by Bahya with poetic skills in other contexts of the book.[109] In saying this, Bahya seems to add another detail to his criticism of poetry. Poetry is taken to task not only for its minute intellectual worth but also for its elitism. The recondite poetic style, a pivot of courtier culture, denies many Jews access into Jewish literature. Bahya shows that he is concerned with this problem and trying to deal with it, by emphasizing that he is writing the book in a nonpoetic style.

When Bahya does summarize his ideas in verse form at the end of the book (pp. 432-441), he explains that he is really writing a religious *piyut*, designed to arouse people to God's service (p. 424). It consists of paraphrases from the Bible, in free verse, without a set meter or a consistent rhyme scheme.[110] Bahya's language is direct, often repetitious,[111] avoiding the intricate prosody, abstruse vocabulary and hidden allusions that were customary in formal Arabic and Hebrew versifying of the time. Bahya wanted to be accessible to a wide segment of the Jewish population, not only to its highly cultivated elite.[112]

Bahya's polemic against the leadership claim of the courtier class centered not only on lack of courtiers' qualifications but also on their conception of recent Jewish history, a conception which lent support to their authority, legitimacy to their rule. Courtiers maintained that the Geonic period had come to an end in Sura and Pembeditha, and was being superseded on Spanish soil by a new center. In the course of time this sense became crystallized in ibn Daud's "Story of the Four Captives." The arrival of Rabbi Moses in Spain,[113] in particular, spells the end of Babylonia's hegemony, and ushers in a new period, the Rabbanite period, around the year 1000.[114]

Ibn Daud reflects the attitude of the leadership of Spanish Jewry that they need not turn to the Babylonian academies for religious and Halakic guidance. A plan to make Spanish Jewry religiously and culturally independent was executed by the courtier Hisdai ibn Shaprut.[115] Though he did not break openly with the Jews of Babylon—he continued, for example, to contribute to the Babylonian institutions—he did begin to establish the Jews of Cordova and all of Spain as an autonomous unit. How deep the rift with Babylonia was may be inferred from the report that under ibn Shaprut the Jews of Spain began to regulate the calendar without recourse to the academies of Babylonia.[116]

Rabbi Hanok, son of R. Moses, also maintained a distance from the Babylonian authorities. The tension betwen him and R. Hai Gaon is echoed in *Sefer ha-Kabbalah:* "[Ibn Shatnash was under the impression] that Rabbenu Hai . . . was an enemy of R. Hanok."[117] Around the time of R. Hanok's death in 1051, R. Samuel ibn Nagrela, the Nagid, published a commentary on certain Talmudic themes, containing a thorough critique of R. Hai's Talmudic commentaries on several tractates. The critique was intended as a challenge to the Geonic claim of exclusive authority over Talmudic interpretation. It demonstrated that the Spanish scholars no longer needed to rely on Geonic traditions, that they could hold their own.[118]

The seriousness of R. Samuel's challenge to R. Hai, a Gaon of Pumbeditha, evoked a strong defense by R. Dosa, Gaon of Sura. R. Dosa attempted to prove that R. Hai's comments are correct beyond the shadow of a doubt: "Rabbenu Hai's words are of consummate perfection . . . no objection can be raised against them."[119]

In Spain, the response to Samuel's work was split. A circle represented by ibn Gabirol hailed Samuel's triumph in a panegyric to the Nagid: "Considered in relation to Samuel, it is as if Rabbenu Hai never existed; Rabbenu Hai is too insignificant to respond to Samuel [in words]."[120]

Others in Spain accused Samuel of arrogance towards the Geonate. This second response can be reconstructed from an apology by the Nagid thirty-four years later:[121] "I know that a community [misled by] deficient opinions will speak of me haughtily and arrogantly; they will become presumptuous and shake their heads . . . and they will say, who dared state that there is an error in the mouth of a Gaon, [an error] in the words of a man of authority." The apology probably reflects Samuel's regret only for this specific critique of the venerable R. Hai, but his broad aim—liberating Spanish Jewry from the authority of the Geonim—was not relinquished. In the poetic preface to his work *Hilketa Gabrata* the Nagid outlines the history of the oral tradition. After lauding the achievements of Tanaim and Amoraim, his account interjects criticism of the Geonim. He suggests that many Geonic judgments are at variance with Talmudic law, that the Halakic codes of the Geonim contain misleading errors "which gave strength to heretics": "And many [Geonim] conveyed to people instructions which nullify the Talmud. Erroneous statements were quoted in the name of worthy and mighty [Geonim]. Responsa attributed to them are current which lead many astray from the right path: therefore, heretics strengthened their hand, religion was weakened, and the stringent laws were made light of."[122]

These factors and others constitute the Nagid's justification for writing a new Halakic code. In contrast to the previous Geonic codes (*Halakot Gedolot, Halakot Pesukot, Sheiltot*) which often simply reproduced selected Talmudic material verbatim, the Nagid placed stress on an orderly arrangement and on clarity of expression. *Hilketa Gabrata* aimed for a broad scope: "all earlier and later sources," a thorough, updated presentation of all Geonic material relevant to a given theme in practical Halaka—but it also allowed for a critical analysis of that material.[123] Once more, the Nagid's desire to outdo the Geonim, and thereby undermine their leadership, emerges clearly.

Samuel ha-Nagid considered his Talmudic attainments as the source of his renown. His eulogy, he says, should emphasize above all his uniqueness as a Torah scholar:[124] "And when I die at the end of [my] days, in every city you will hear [people say], 'come mourn the unique one in his generation, in wisdom and in Torah.' " Often he stresses that he is on par with leading Torah scholars in Babylon or North Africa. In a poem he expresses open resentment of the fact that the Babylonian center is still popularly acknowledged as the exclusive center. Authority, he maintains, is not rooted in a locale; it flows from a scholar of stature. Once scholars leave the locale, its authority ceases. The association with Babylon is made quite explicitly.[125]

In anticipation of shifting the center of learning to Spain he solicits Halakic problems from abroad, for which he promises most satisfying answers. He doubts, however, that his summons will be heeded—not because he is not worthy, but because he happens to be in the "west," whereas people assume the seat of wisdom to be in the "east": "Turn to me regarding any knotty problem, any arrested secret, and I will free it of its shackles; and do not hold a man in disdain because his country is in the west, and [do not scorn] all who rush to the gates [of his academy]."[126]

The Nagid's campaign to shift the center of learning from east to west did not elicit the universal support of Spanish Jews. The Nagid himself suggests in his poem of apology to R. Hai that his challenge of the Geonate did not generate unanimous support. There is evidence that the Geonim resisted Spain's challenge and probably were able to retain the loyalty of some Spanish Jews.[127]

On the whole, however, the Spanish courtiers' (ibn Shaprut, Nagid) disparagement of the Geonate enhanced their own worth and made possible their claim to leadership. The sun of the Geonate had set in Babylon in the days of R. Hai Gaon: the new dawn of the rabbinate had broken in Spain with the advent of R. Moses and R. Hanok, and burst into bright daylight in the days of the Nagid. Ibn Daud reinforces this point using both subtle and obvious literary devices: he does not even shrink from contending that the Babylonian academies closed down completely after the days of Hezekiah the Exilarch, though he knew this was not true.[128]

In questioning the legitimacy of the courtiers' authority, Bahya should attempt to expose not only their practical deficiencies, but more important, to undermine the theoretical basis of their claim: their rejection of the Geonate. An assessment of the Geonim in *Hobot ha-Lebabot* therefore assumes significance once the current controversial status of the Geonim in Spain is taken into account. Bahya's attitude to the Geonim is one of unqualified veneration. In a remarkable passage he portrays ideal Jews. This ideal represents the ninth level of religious and scholarly perfection, surpassed in achievement only by the direct recipients of tradition: members of the Great Assembly and Tanaim. This lofty ninth category consists of scholars

> who have exerted themselves to know the duties of the heart and the duties of the limbs, and those factors which inhibit [worthy] actions; they understood the exoteric sense of the Scriptures and their esoteric meaning as well; they corroborated the truth of tradition on the basis [both] of Scripture and the use of reason; they have arranged the laws into an orderly system, classified the practical duties on the basis of the needs of various times, and of differences in the practice at various places, [this done] after they assembled the fundamental [theological[129]] principles of the Torah, preoccupied themselves with them, and admonished concerning them [mindful of the need for] conformity of reason with the exoteric and esoteric senses. They were following the truth in whichever direction it happens to point. They were the Talmudic teachers and the Geonim who continued in their predecessors' ways (p. 150).

The most striking aspect of this passage is Bahya's coupling of Amoraim and Geonim. No other writer, previous or subsequent, ever did this. All authors of histories of tradition perceived a clear line of demarcation between the Talmudic period and the Geonic, between Amoraim and Geonim.

It does not appear likely that Bahya had a substantially different perception of the history of Halaka from the aforementioned writers. It is implausible that he rejected the conventional interpretation of the Talmudic statement: Rab Ashi and Rabbina concluded [Amoraic] teaching [B. Talmud *Baba Mezia* 86a). What does emerge as probable is that Bahya sought a persuasive literary device through which to reaffirm the continuing legitimacy of the Geonate, currently under fire in Spain. At stake, he seems to be saying, is the preservation of an ongoing Talmudic-Geonic tradition, a tradition borne by extraordinary individuals who reached the peak of scholarly and religious accomplishment.

That Bahya invokes the authority of Amoraim only to bolster that of the Geonim becomes obvious upon close examination of the passage under consideration. While the ninth level is purportedly concerned with the religious attainments of both Geonim and Amoraim, it is in fact focused exclusively on Geonic achievements. Bahya alludes to high points of Geonic intellectual history, in particular to the contributions associated with Saadiah Gaon[130] toward the rationalization of Judaism in the preceding century: "They corroborated the truth of tradition on the basis [both] of Scripture and the use of reason." It was Saadia Gaon who ushered in medieval Jewish philosophy by insisting on the corroboration of the tradition by reason as well as by Scripture. He explains his philosophic program in the *Book of Doctrines and Beliefs*: "We speculate and search in order that we may make our own what our Lord has taught us by way of instruction."[131]

"They understood the exoteric sense of Scriptures and their esoteric meaning as well." In the realm of Biblical exegesis, it was Saadiah Gaon who was first to justify the use of allegory when Scripture appeared to defy reason. His allegorical exegetical method, *ta'wil*,[132] is clearly what Bahya has in mind.[133] "They have exerted themselves to know the duties of the heart and the duties of the limbs, and those factors which inhibit [worthy] actions." Once more, it was Saadiah who authored a systematic formulation of Jewish ethics (the tenth chapter of his *Book of Doctrines and Beliefs*), the first of its kind.[134] "They were following the truth in whichever direction it happens to lead." In general, it was a Gaon who posited rationality as the exclusive criterion for Biblical exegesis, even if that entailed rejection of a traditional interpretation.[135] It was a Gaon who warned against reading one's own preconceptions as the meaning of a text.[136]

"They have arranged the laws into an orderly system, classified the practical duties on the basis of the needs of various times, and of differences in the practice at various places, [this done] after they assembled the fundamental [theological] principles of the Torah, preoccupied themselves with them, and admonished concerning them [mindful of the need for] conformity of reason with the exoteric and esoteric senses." Bahya here points to a Geonic achievement in the realm of halaka: codification of the law. His reference, considered as a unit, appears to be a specific one: Hefez ben Yazliah's *Sefer Mitzvot*, the only halakic work prior to Bahya's time exhibiting these traits.[137] Hefez's literary influence on Bahya had been noted (Bahya drew from Hefez's proofs for the existence and unity of God),[138] and it is not surprising that Bahya singles out this particular Geonic code. Hefez ben Yazliah meets with Bahya's enthusiastic approval probably because, unlike most halakists, he concerned himself not only with practical duties of the limbs, but with philosophical duties of the heart as well, in fact, giving the latter precedence in his arrangement.

The core of the Geonic achievement is thus its religious philosophical orientation which, in Bahya's view, immunized Judaism not only against stultification from within but also against onslaught from without.[139] This recognition in itself would make the Geonim deserving of veneration and continuing loyalty. Rather than abet heretics, as the Nagid charged, Geonim succeeded in achieving the contrary: fortifying faith by stressing philosophical and ethical duties of the heart.

The Nagid's contention to the contrary, Bahya lauds the Geonic codes for their "arrangement of the laws into an orderly system." Indeed, reviewing halakic literature at the beginning of his work, (pp. 17-18) Bahya cites *only* Geonic codes: *Halakot Gedolot*, *Halakot Pesukot*, Hefez ben Yazliah's *Sefer Mitzvot*, and others. He omits mention of the Nagid's *Hilketa Gabrata*, allegedly an improvement over the Geonic works. If Bahya knew of the Nagid's halakic work, not an unlikely assumption given its wide circulation even outside Spain,[140] his conspicuous omission of *Hilketa Gabrata* is suggestive and would indicate that Bahya belonged to the circle, referred to by the Nagid, who resented the attack on the Geonate.

Beyond the rebuttal in this passage of specific points made by the Nagid or his circle, beyond emphasizing the Geonim's ethical stature and intellectual integrity, Bahya seems to set a mood. In hyphenating the Talmudic and Geonic traditions, Bahya is really saying to his readers: If you acquiesce to the courtiers' rejection of the latter, you ipso facto reject the former. Just as you would not deign to refute the former, do not dare to reject the latter.

Bahya's appeal is thus rooted in the subtle suggestion that the Talmudic-Geonic continuum would be ruptured if Spanish scholars prevailed in their usurpation of the Geonic claim. He might have been attempting to arouse the same suspicions on the part of his readers that ibn Daud decades later tried to allay. When Ibn Daud in the beginning of his story ascribes the emergence of the "four captives" to divine fiat, he may be addressing himself to prevalent criticism of the Spanish "Rabbanites" for assuming their posts without receiving authorization from the preceding link in the chain of tradition. Those four scholars are the only ones mentioned in *Sefer ha-Kabbalah* who had not received authorization from a recognized predecessor.[141] In arguing for loyalty to the academies of Sura and Pumbeditha, symbols of Geonic rootedness in the Talmudic past, Bahya gives rise to doubts and misgivings which must have gnawed in the minds of many Spanish Jews about the legitimacy of the new order.

If this assessment of Bahya's relationship to the struggle between Geonim and courtier scholars is correct, certain statements drawn from Bahya's criticisms of proud scholars assume added significance. Pride in acquisition of spiritual values is blameworthy, says Bahya, when one becomes complacent with his attainments, his reputation and the high esteem in which he is held by people. It drives him to degrade and disparage others, to humiliate the wise men of his generation, and to aggrandize himself by pointing out the shortcomings of his fellows and their lack of knowledge (p. 299).

This passage echoes similar criticism by Bahya of the courtiers. Conceivably, however, there is a new element here, in light of our awareness of Samuel's controversy with the Geonim. Bahya might here be criticizing past courtier scholars but specifically the Nagid, for treating the Geonim—"the wise men of his generation"—as inferior and for enhancing his own prestige by mocking them (for example, the Nagid's criticism of R. Hai's Talmudic commentaries).

Similarly, Bahya criticizes the proud scholar for considering it below his dignity to study from another. Such a person will never attain clear understanding: "[The proud man] cannot attain genuine learning, nor reach the goal of true knowledge, for he is too proud to seek those who know God and His Law" (p. 302). Sensitized as the reader now is to the issue at hand, an association is made with the Nagid's dismissal of Geonic scholars, and his solicitation of Halakic questions for his own academy.

Finally, when Bahya articulates the advice given by the "evil passion" to the courtier (in what is unquestionably a courtier context)—"You are unique in your generation and distinctive among your contemporaries; therefore it is fit for you to accentuate your superiority to them by . . . telling of their shortcomings, and publicizing the wickedness of their heart, and humiliating them" (p. 270)—Samuel ha-Nagid's self-image as "unique in his generation" is recalled.

Bahya's opposition to the courtiers—his rejection of their claim to leadership, his censure of their paideia, his condemnation of their quest for power and pragmatic reality—raises a basic question.

Was Bahya oblivious to the political realities of his day? Did he not realize that courtiers ensured the vital interests of Jewish communities in Muslim Spain? Ibn Shaprut, the Nagid, Isaac b. Baruch ibn Albalia, were in a position to promote Jewish interests, to effect improvements in the situation of the Jews, only because of their position in court. Ibn Daud reflects general awareness of this fact when he says of various courtiers: "They accomplished great good for Israel."[142]

Even in Christian Spain centuries later, when courtiers' ostentation, religious laxity, or exploitation of the poor was censured, there was never a rejection of the courtier class per se. Its function of lobbying with the king on behalf of the community is viewed as indispensable.[143] Shlomo Alami in his *Iggeret Mussar* of 1415 therefore urges courtiers to reform their conduct, so that they may continue to serve their people.[144] Approbation of the courtiers flowing from recognition of their crucial function continued even in the days following the expulsion of 1492.[145] Why then is Bahya's criticism directed not only at courtiers' deficiencies but ostensibly at the courtier institution as such? He certainly is not unmindful of the Jews' favorable position in Muslim Spain.

Muslim Spain in the second half of the eleventh century continues to be a tolerant society where Jews can go about their business with no interference:[146] "Let one ponder . . . our situation among the Gentiles since the beginning of the exile[147] and the way our affairs are managed among them though we differ with them, secretly and openly, and they know it" (p. 121). Jews enjoy the same economic opportunities as their Muslim or Christian neighbors:[148] "Our situation . . . as far as our subsistence is concerned is the same as theirs." Jews need to exert themselves much less in making a living: "The masses and villagers [among the Gentiles] toil much more than the middle and poor classes among us."[149] Probably reflecting the unparallelled privileged treatment which Jews, especially courtiers, received from both Muslim rulers and Christian kings in the war-ridden second half of the twelfth century,[150] Bahya notes: "Our situation . . . is even better than [the Gentiles'] in times of war and conflict." (All citations in this paragraph are from one passage on page 121.)

Bahya is thus aware of the Jews' advantageous social and political situation, but this awareness does not evoke on his part an ode to the courtiers,[151] the group which is not only the beneficiary of the situation, but in many ways responsible for its continuance. Bahya explicitly attributes the Jews' fortunate position in his time to God's miraculous intervention: "If one of our contemporaries looks for miracles nowadays, [similar to the "alteration of nature" which occurred at the time of the Exodus], let him ponder and rightly assess our situation among the Gentiles since the beginning of the exile" (p. 121). This consciousness of God's miraculous presence in Jewish history reinforces Bahya's trust in God, who has not loathed his people even when they are in exile.

Indeed, it is probably Bahya's profound trust in God which is at the core of his critique. It may be true, he would say, that the courtiers functioned as "secondary causes" to accomplish great good in Israel. But if they became a permanent institution within the structure of Jewish society, Jews would place their reliance in them and forget God. Concerning bittahon, Bahya writes: "When a man's sustenance will be achieved through any one of the causes with which he busies himself, it is fit that he should not habituate himself to that cause, nor become enthusiastic over it, nor should he continue to hold on to it—for then his trust in God will be weakened and he will incline to the cause, rather" (p. 212). In fact, Jewish dependence on the courtiers' political influence would actually backfire, for one who relies on secondary causes is abandoned by God (p. 185). It is through God's decree that the secondary causes are energized; in themselves they have no efficacy. Even a powerless agent could be activated by God to bring about salvation, if trust is placed in Him. Bahya stresses that if one petitions another for help, it should be irrelevant whether the person approached is weak or strong. The desired end may be achieved even through the weak one, if trust is placed in God (p. 221).

Pursuing his theory of bittahon, Bahya would say that a causal relation between courtiers' efforts on behalf of the community and the achieved results is merely an illusion. God promised to preserve His people in the

Diaspora, and He implements the promise in His own way. Even if the courtiers were not on the scene, the Jews' good fortune would flow from elsewhere. The king, says Bahya (p. 328), is an instrument of God, to be manipulated in God's good time, and no human effort, in support or in defiance, would make a difference.

What was the courtier circle's reaction to Bahya's frontal attack? At first the answer seems elusive. There is no recorded mention of any response. Perhaps, however, the response of the courtiers can be reconstructed precisely from this silence, a silence which has rendered even Bahya's dates a matter of speculation.[152] Ibn Daud, the apologist for courtier culture, chose to ignore Bahya completely in his historical survey of Jewish writers in Spain. If anyone who questions the courtier circle's claim to leadership is condemned as a "villain" in *Sefer ha-Kabbalah*,[153] ibn Daud's obliviousness of Bahya's book is to be expected. Bahya's attitude to the courtiers did not qualify him as a member of the "select circle." In a work which told contemporaries and posterity of the fabulous courtier ideal and its realization, there was no room for an individual who simply was not impressed.

NOTES

1. Page references in the body of this essay are to Joseph Kapah's edition of *Torat Hobot ha-Lebabot* (Jerusalem, 1973).

2. On the problem of Bahya's dates see P. Kokowzoff, "The Date of Life of Bahya ibn Paquda," in *S. Poznanski Memorial Volume* (Warsaw, 1927), pp. 13-21. Kokowzoff's dating, based on M. ibn Ezra's mention of Bahya in *Arugat ha-Bosem* as belonging to the previous generation, places Bahya sometime between 1050 and 1090. See also I. Tishbi and J. Dan, *Mibhar Sifrut ha-Mussar* (Jerusalem, 1970), pp. 109-110. For an internal indication which militates against dating the book in the early twelfth century see note 146. For a summary of suggestions on where Bahya lived, see D. Kaufmann, "Torat ha-Elokut shel Bahya ibn Paquda," *Ha-Sifrut ha-Ibrit bi-Yemei ha-Beinaim* (Jerusalem, 1962), p. 11, note 5. (The article originally appeared in German in 1874.) L. Zunz's choice of Saragossa has been confirmed on the basis of a manuscript of 1340. See C. Ramos Gil, "La Patria de Bahya Ibn Paquda," *Sefarad*, XI (1951), 103-105.

3. I. Tishbi, *Mibhar*, p. 109.

4. Concerning Bahya's influence on Abraham Maimonides see G. Cohen, "The Soteriology of R. Abraham Maimuni," *Proceedings of the American Academy of Jewish Research*, XXXV (1967), 87, note 34.

5. I. Tishbi and J. Dan, "Hasidut," in *Ha-Enziklopedia ha-Ibrit*, XVII, 770. See also the observation of M. Piekarz, *Bi-Yemei Zemihat ha-Hasidut* (Jerusalem, 1978), p. 7.

6. This perspective does not, however, exhaust the book's significance. There are other addressees as well, most obviously those Talmudists who are insensitive to ethics and spirituality. See I. Twersky, "Religion and Law," in *Religion in a Religious Age*, S. D. Goitein, ed., Association for Jewish Studies (Cambridge, Mass., 1974), esp. pp. 71-72.

7. Joseph Weiss, "Shira Hazranit ve-Tarbut Hazranit," *World Congress for Jewish Studies* (Jerusalem, 1952), pp. 396-403.

8. Gerson Cohen's edition of *Sefer ha-Qabbalah* (Philadelphia, 1967), esp. p. 284 and note 124.

9. Scholars have noted the opportunities but also cautioned about the methodological pitfalls to be avoided in reconstructing a historical period from works of ethics and homiletics. See B. Z. Dinur, "Reshitah shel ha-Hasidut," *Be-Mifneh ha-Dorot* (Jerusalem, 1955), pp. 97-100, esp. p. 97 (originally printed in *Zion*, VIII, 1943, 121-125); J. Katz, "Al Halacha u-Drush ke-Makor Histori," *Tarbiz*, XXX (1960), 62-68; G. Cohen in *Jewish Social Studies*, XXIX (1967), 184.

10. This passage is appropriated by Bahya from a poem by al-Mutanabbi, the noted Arab poet of the tenth century. See A. S. Yahuda's edition, *Al-Hidaja 'Ila Fara'id Al-Qulub* (Leiden, 1912), pp. 112-113. While the "great ones" enumerated in this particular passage are neither Jewish nor Spanish (Mutanabbi wrote in Aleppo), Bahya quotes the passage because he perceives an identical situation in Spain. The role of the "great ones" as the model for prospective courtiers hailing from Jewish society emerges clearly from the full context (pp. 253-254).

11. The subjects listed by Bahya (p. 254) are classified as adab in Menahem Mansoor's translation, *The Book of Direction to the Duties of the Heart* (London, 1973), p. 282, note 5, but the connection to the courtier class is not noted.

12. Bahya uses the term in this sense. See Kapah's edition, pp. 171, 395, and A. Altmann's translation of adab (in the passage on p. 171) as good manners. A. Altmann, "The Religion of the Philosophers: Free Will and Predestination in Saadia, Bahya and Maimonides," in *Religion in a Religious Age*, p. 34.

13. G. E. von Grunebaum, *Medieval Islam: A Study in Cultural Orientation* (Chicago, 1953), p. 252.

14. Ibid., p. 251.

15. F. Gabrielli, "Adab," in *Encyclopedia of Islam*, new ed. (Leiden, 1960), I, 176.

16. Grunebaum, *Islam*, p. 252.

17. Ibid., pp. 252-253.

18. Franz Rosenthal, *Knowledge Triumphant: The Concept of Knowledge in Medieval Islam* (Leiden, 1970), pp. 264-265.

19. Franz Rosenthal, *A History of Muslim Historiography* (Leiden, 1968), p. 49.

20. Ibid., p. 52.

21. Ibid., pp. 110-113.

22. Rosenthal, *Knowledge Triumphant*, p. 317.

23. Ibid., pp. 317-318.

24. Ibid., p. 327.

25. Y. Ratzaby, "Pitgamei Adab be-Sifrut Yemei ha-Beinaim," *Ozar Yehudei Sefarad*, IV (Jerusalem, 1961), pp. 114-122; N. Bar-On, "Le-Heker ha-Mekorot shel Ben Mishle le-Rabbi Shmuel ha-Nagid," in *World Congress of Jewish Studies* I, 279-284; Y. Ratzaby, "Li-Mekorot Ben Mishle u-Ben Kohelet," in *Tarbiz*, XXV, 301-302; I. Levin, "Le-Heker Ben Mishle shel Rabbi Shemuel ha-Nagid," *Tarbiz* XXIX, 146ff.

26. The "father of translators" was born in Granada c. 1120 and died in Lunel c. 1190. Judah Ibn Tibbon, "Mussar Ab," in Israel Abrahams, ed., *Hebrew Ethical Wills* (Philadelphia, 1926), pp. 54-92. The document is pervaded with the Nagid's ethical and educational legacy.

27. *Ibid.*, p. 69. Samuel ha-Nagid, too, addressed poetic messages to his young son, Yehosef, stressing the importance not only of elegant style, but also of a beautiful handwriting, straight margins, and perfumed parchment. E. Schirman, *Ha-Shira ha-Ibrit bi-Sefarad ube-Provence*, bk. 1, pt. 1 (Jerusalem, 1959), p. 119.

28. Judah Ibn Tibbon, "Mussar Ab," p. 68.

29. Ibid., p. 91.

30. Samuel ha-Nagid, *Ben Mishle*, S. Abramson, ed. (Tel Aviv, 1948), pp. 271-272, nos. 953, 954. These are here cited in full. Ibn Tibbon cites only the beginning of no. 954. Another relevant couplet from *Ben Mishle* is no. 1196.

31. Ibn Daud, probably reflecting the general view, also attributes the Nagid's rise to the pen. See G. Cohen, *Sefer ha-Qabbalah*, p. 72. Concerning other figures in Bahya's period exemplifying the relationship between elegant Arabic style and high position in the royal court, see E. Ashtor, *Korot ha-Yehudim bi-Sefarad ha-Muslemit* II (Jerusalem, 1966), 162, on Joseph ibn Hasday; p. 320 on Abu-l-Fahdl Hasday Ibn Hasday. See also B. Klar, "Ha-shirah veha-hayim," *Mehkarim ve-Iyunim* (Tel Aviv, 1954), p. 95.

32. Ibn Tibbon, "Mussar Ab," p. 67.

33. On the association between vizir and katib in general as a basis for religious exhortation, see *Hobot ha-Lebabot*, pp. 177-178.

34. The propaedeutic sciences and physics, however, in contrast to metaphysics, may be put to pragmatic use. See *Hobot ha-Lebabot*, pp. 14-15.

35. Franz Rosenthal, *Technique and Approach of Muslim Scholarship* (Rome, 1947), p. 61.

36. Rosenthal, *Historiography*, p. 34.

37. See the first chapter of M. ibn Ezra's *Sefer ha-Iyunim veha-Diyunim*, where rhetoric is classified among the branches of logic (lower than dialectic). In Maimonides' *Treatise on Logic* poetry is treated in chapter 8.

38. See, for example, Maimonides' comment on *Sanhedrin*, chapter 10, Mishna 1, "Sefarim Hitzonim," where he refers to poetry as possessing neither *hokmah* nor *to'elet*.

39. Shemtob Falaquera, *Sefer ha-Mebakesh*. Relevant section is quoted in Schirman, *Ha-Shira ha-Ibrit*, vol. II, pt. 1, pp. 334-342.

40. Kalonymus b. Kalonymus, *Eben Bohan*, quoted in ibid., pp. 514-517.

41. Ibid., p. 517.

42. Bahya's merits as a poet are acknowledged by Moshe ibn Ezra who includes him as one of the important poets of the preceding generation. See his *Sefer ha-Iyunim veha-Diyunim*, A. Halkin, ed. (Jerusalem, 1975), p. 77, and note. On the possibility that some twenty more piyutim may actually be Bahya's, see E. Schirman, *Shirim Hadashim min ha-Genizah* (Jerusalem, 1965), pp. 203-204.

43. A. S. Yahuda, *Hidaya*, pp. 110-113.

44. Ibn Hazm, the noted Spanish Muslim theologian of the eleventh century, provides a parallel to Bahya's position. He, too, denied intellectual merit to poetry but employed his great skill to write religious verse. Cited in Raymond Scheindlin, "Rabbi Moshe Ibn Ezra and the Legitimacy of Poetry," in *Medievalia et Humanistica*, n.s. VII, Paul M. Clogan, ed. (Cambridge, 1976), pp. 107-108.

45. Maimonides too examines poetry under two aspects: pragmatic, the use to which poetry is put (see, for example, his Commentary on Abot, chap. 1, Mishna 16), and axiological, the value of poetry in the intellectual hierarchy (see note 38). Ethical poetry may thus be deemed useful, but lack intrinsic intellectual worth.

46. Theoretically there is a discrepancy between pursuit of knowledge for its own sake and predication of the standard of its religious usefulness. For Bahya, however, there is no conflict. The disciplines considered worthwhile by the religious usefulness criterion also happen to be those which have intrinsic intellectual merit. Considerations of religious utility impose no restrictions on the depth with which these disciplines are investigated. On the contrary, for Bahya, the more rigorous the scientific investigation ("the examination of created things"), the more profound the religious awareness. On Bahya's requirement of rigorous philosophical method see Julius Guttmann, *Ha-Pilosofia shel ha-Yahadut* (Jerusalem, 1953), pp. 101-102.

47. For the relevance of Bahya's account to the recurrent theme of man as a microcosm pointing to God, see A. Altmann, "The Delphic Maxim in Medieval Islam and Judaism," in his *Studies in Religion, Philosophy and Mysticism* (London, 1969), p. 24.

48. Bahya's assessment is borne out by a recent study. See I. Ta-Shma, "Shiput Ibri u-Mishpat Ibri . . . bi-Sefarad," *Shnaton ha-Mishpat ha-Ibri*, I (1974), esp. 353-354, 369-371.

49. On this method of Talmud study see S. D. Goitein, *Sidrei Hinuch bi-Yemei ha-Geonim u-Bet ha-Rambam* (Jerusalem, 1962), pp. 160-161.

50. See "Astrology," *Encyclopedia Judaica*, III (Jerusalem, 1971), 790-795, and the bibliography on p. 795.

51. This can be inferred from its inclusion and treatment in a courtier-related context (pp. 253-254).

52. Moritz Steinschneider, *Jewish Literature* (London, 1857), p. 191.

53. G. Cohen, *Sefer ha-Qabbalah*, pp. 80-81.

54. None of the secondary literature surveying medieval attitudes to astrology notes this fact. It should be noted in this connection that the passage in *Hobot ha-Lebabot* expressing Bahya's opposition to astrology was not included in Judah ibn Tibbon's translation. It re-emerges in print in A. S. Yahuda's Arabic edition (1912) p. 237, note 2, and was subsequently included by A. Zifroni in his Hebrew edition (Jerusalem, 1927), pp. 160-161, and note 5 on p. 160. See also Kapah's note 1, p. 254, of his edition.

55. Maimonides' "Letter on Astrology," in A. Marx, "The Correspondence between the Rabbis of Southern France and Maimonides about Astrology," *Hebrew Union College Annual* III (1926), 350.

56. *Mishneh Torah, Abodah Zarah* 11:15. Citation is from Moses Hyamson's translation of the *Mishneh Torah*, bk. 1 (New York, 1962).

57. *Guide for the Perplexed*, III, 29.

58. "Letter on Astrology," in Marx, "Correspondence," p. 350.

59. A. F. Mehren, "Vues d'Avicenne sur L'Astrologie et sur le Rapport de la Responsabilité Humaine avec le Destin," *Museon*, III (Louvain, 1884), pp. 383-403. Concerning Bahya's awareness of Avicenna's works see the conflicting conclusions of D. Kaufmann, "Torat ha-Elokut," pp. 16-19, and H. Malter, "Yahuda's Edition of Bahya's 'Duties of the Heart,' " *JQR*, n.s. VII, 389.

60. Marx, "Correspondence," pp. 315, 317. For the text of their letter, ibid., pp. 343-349.

61. See the end of Isadore Twersky's introductory comments to "Letter on Astrology," *Maimonides Reader* (New York, 1972), p. 463.

62. See Asher b. Meshullam's formulation of the problem, recorded by Judah ibn Tibbon following the latter's translation of *Hobot ha-Lebabot*, Chapter 4.

63. There are always contrary attitudes formulated even in the poetry, as Pagis shows p. 241 ff. See note 66. The methodological difficulty in reconstructing the poet's own viewpoint on these issues has generated different scholarly approaches.

64. I. Levin, "Zeman ve-Tebel ba-Shira ha-Ibrit bi-Sefarad," *Ozar Yehudei Sefarad*, V (Jerusalem, 1962), 68; D. Pagis, Shirat ha-Hol, p. 238.

65. Levin, "Zeman ve-Tebel," pp. 68-79; D. Pagis, *Shirat ha-Hol*, pp. 225-245. See ibid., p. 238, note 34, and p. 239 for poems by the Nagid and Moshe ibn Ezra reflecting astrological determinism; on fatalistic expressions in some of the Nagid's poetry, see ibid., p. 234 and note 21.

66. Weiss, "Shira Hazranit," p. 401, and Pagis, *Shirat ha-Hol*, p. 241, modifying Weiss's thesis. Whether philosophic views implicit in the Nagid's poetry (e.g., *Ben Mishle, Ben Kohelet*) should be taken to reflect his own attitude has been a matter of contention among scholars. N. Bar-On and Y. Ratzaby argue that the Nagid simply adapted existing adab material without committing himself to their content. I. Levin maintains that the Nagid's adaptation is also an act of appropriation. (For a summary of the views and the references see Pagis, *Shirat ha-Hol*, p. 230.)

Even if we accept Ratzaby's assessment of the Nagid's literary intention, there can be no doubt that many readers did view the poems as philosophical statements. Whatever the poet's intention, the poetic themes of "Cosmos" and "Time" were read as deliberate expressions of fatalism. This can be gathered from Maimonides (Guide III, 12, the S. Pines translation, University of Chicago Press, 1963). "Often it occurs to the imagination of the multitude that there are more evils in the world than there are good things. As a consequence, this thought is contained in many sermons and poems of all the religious communities, which say that it is surprising if good exists in the temporal, whereas the evils of the temporal are numerous and constant. This error is not found only among the multitude, but also among those who deem that they know something." (See also Judah ha-Levi's statement in *Kusari*, IV, 23.)

67. Bahya deals with the problem in III, 8 and V, 5. See A. Altmann's discussion of Bahya's approach in "Free Will," pp. 34-35.

68. In III, 8, Bahya offers a pragmatic, not a philosophically rigorous solution to the problem. Ibid., pp. 34-35. The justification for the courtiers' attitude may be related to that articulated by Abraham bar Hiyya, summarized in "Correspondence," pp. 312-314, and in B. Z. Benedict, "Mezone be-Mazala Talya," *Torah she-b'al Peh*, XIX (Jerusalem, 1977), 228.

69. Ibn Gabirol, *The Improvement of the Moral Qualities*, trans. Stephen Wise (New York, 1902), p. 55. This account of Bahya's emphasis on humility in social historical terms is intended to supplement rather than supersede the literary account suggested by G. Vajda in *Encyclopedia Judaica* IV, top of p. 107.

70. Schirman, *Ha-Shira ha-Ibrit*, I, 1, p. 83. The translation is based in part on that in *Jewish Prince in Moslem Spain: Select Poems of Samuel Ibn Nagrela*, trans. Leon Weinberger (Alabama, 1973), pp. 19-20.

71. Samuel ha-Nagid, *Ben Mishle*, p. 162.

72. Ibid., p. 161.

73. Ibid., p. 21.

74. This motive displaced the traditional rationale for the financial support of learning, epitomized in the symbiotic relationship of Yissachar and Zebulun. Under this scheme, both entrepreneur and scholar share in the rewards of study, acknowledged by both to be higher than financial reward: the entrepreneur by subsidizing the scholar, the scholar by cultivating scholarship for the benefit, practical and

"metaphysical," of the community. See Weiss, "Shira Hazranit," p. 398.

The theme of courtier pride is treated from a different perspective and for a different end by G. Cohen, *Sefer ha-Qabbalah*, pp. 276-289.

75. E. Schirman, "The Function of the Hebrew Poet in Medieval Spain," *Jewish Social Studies*, XVI (1954); B. Lewis, "The Qasida of Abu Ishak," *S. Baron Jubilee Volume* (Jerusalem, 1974), pp. 663-664.

76. In ibn Gabirol's ethical treatise pragmatism is treated as a moral quality in its own right. A chapter is devoted to analyzing the virtue of diligence. Ibn Gabirol's *Tikkun Midot ha-Nefesh* (Lyck, 1859), pp. 32-33.

77. Schirman, *Ha-Shira ha-Ibrit* I, pt. 1, p. 83.

78. *Ben Mishle*, ed. Abramson, p. 66.

79. Ibid., p. 70.

80. Ibid., p. 214.

81. Ibid., p. 15.

82. Ibid. There are also aphorisms in *Ben Mishle* which are antithetical to this approach. See Abramson's comments in his edition, p. xxv-xxvi. On the methodological problems in reconstructing coherent views from *Ben Mishle* see note 66. The aphorisms cited in the article, however, are compatible with the "pragmatic" spirit of poems from the Nagid's other collections. See, e.g., the poem covered by note 70.

83. On the theme of trust in Bahya and its relation to the Muslim concept of *tawakkul*, see G. Vajda, *La Théologie Ascétique de Bahya Ibn Paquda* (Paris, 1947, pp. 60-86; on Bahya's concept as it relates to the intellectual history of the term, see R. J. Zwi Werblowsky, "Faith, Hope and Trust: A Study in the Concept of Bittahon." *Papers of the Institute of Jewish Studies*, London, I, ed. J. S. Weiss (Jerusalem, 1964), pp. 118-139; on the relation of trust to free will, see A. Altmann, "Free Will," pp. 33-35.

84. Discussing (p. 192) the courtier activities of tax collecting and the "laborious work which makes the bodies weary," Bahya shows that *bittahon* will make these particular pursuits unnecessary. In selecting an occupation, says he, a person should be guided by the four criteria enumerated in the text. The criterion of religious outlook, "[the occupation] should not hinder him from fulfilling the obligations of the Law," considered in the courtier context, suggests a recurrent criticism of courtiers in subsequent periods: their violation of Jewish law. To cite just one critic, see Maimonides' comment on Abot 1:10, and his letter in *Iggerot ha-Rambam*, ed. Baneth, (Jerusalem, 1946), p. 63.

85. By Bahya's period, the political significance of the title vizir is eroded. It is an honorific title only, but still reflects a closeness with the royal circle. See E. Lévi-Provencal, *L'Espagne Musulmane au Dixième Siècle* (Paris, 1932), p. 67. Bahya, however, seems to use it in a sense connoting very high authority. See *Hobot ha-Lebabot*, pp. 177-178, 328. The most famous Jewish vizirs are Samuel ha-Nagid and his son Jehoseph. For another example see Ashtor, *Korot ha-Yehudim*, II, 291. A question addressed to Rabbi Isaac Alfasi refers to a Jewish vizir in the royal court of Seville. *See She'elot u-Teshuvot Rabbenu Yizhak ben Yaakov Alfasi*, ed. D. Rotstein (New York, 1977), p. 30 and note.

86. The presumption is based on Bahya's distinction between the two kinds of wealth the courtiers possess: that which finds practical use in the sustenance of the courtier and his extended household and that in excess of those requirements (p. 215). Bahya mocks the courtier who craves for and hoards excessive wealth, since in time it would be passed on or expropriated. The inference is that if the courtier is

endowed by God with affluence, Bahya would have him share it with the poor. See also *Hobot ha-Lebabot*, p. 256 and note 25.

87. Y. Ratzaby, "Shirat ha-Yayin le-Rabbi Shemuel ha-Nagid," in *Bar Ilan-Sefer ha-Shanah* X, Sefer Shapira I (Ramat Gan, 1972), 439.

88. Ibid., p. 438.

89. Schirman, *Ha-Shira ha-Ibrit*, vol. I, pt. 1, pp. 161-162.

90. The blend of incongruous features in the Nagid's intellectual portrait—a first-rate Talmudic scholar and revered halakic authority, a creator of much-acclaimed sensual poetry, a proud and assertive warrior, man of the world—has been and remains a source of fascination and provocation.

Y. N. Simhoni, reacting to one of the Nagid's wine poems in *Iyim*, I (London, 1928), pt. 3, p. 110, comments that the views expressed therein are contrary to the spirit of Jewish tradition. How remarkable are these words, he says, coming from Samuel ha-Nagid, a rabbi and member of a Talmudical academy!

G. Cohen, however, believes that the sense of incongruity one gets about the Nagid stems from an unhistorical assessment: "Why should we judge the courtiers of Andalus by the standards of Troyes, Mainz and Cracow? Perhaps it would be fairer and more productive historically to understand each age and each form of expression in its own terms." (G. Cohen, *Sefer ha-Qabbalah*, pp. 286-287).

Dan Pagis addresses the problem in his article "U-shte b'leb tob ye-neha," *Studies in Literature Presented to Simon Halkin*, ed. Ezra Fleischer (Jerusalem, 1973), pp. 131-151. He examines three wine poems of the Nagid, including the one partially cited here.

His close textual analysis yields the conclusion that in these poems the Nagid balances the competing claims of hedonism and asceticism, of *carpe diem* and *memento mori*. He concedes the premise of asceticism that the hereafter is real, but not its conclusion that life in the here and now must therefore be viewed exclusively as a "corridor for the next." He accepts the conclusion of hedonism to "eat, drink and be merry" but not its premise that there is no afterlife.

Basing himself on Ecclesiastes 2:10 and 9:7-10, the Nagid affirms the value of pleasures, enjoyment, and conviviality, which are for him in fact a religious obligation. Renunciation of pleasures is sinful because it means rejecting a gift of God. One would be penalized in the next world for depriving one's self of pleasure in this one.

The Nagid, in those poems, does not deny the traditional religious ethics, nor does he ignore it. Rather, Pagis suggests, he offers his own unique synthesis.

91. The Nagid's religiously provocative wine poems apparently drew the protest of Yitzhak ben Khalfoun. See Ratzaby, "Shirat Ha-Yayin," pp. 438-439.

92. Samuel ha-Nagid, *Ben Tehilim*, ed. Dov Yarden (Tel Aviv, 1966), p. 135.

93. Weiss, "Shira Hazranit," p. 399.

94. On the mystical character of the passage on p. 348, see D. Kaufmann, "Torat ha-Elokut," pp. 76-77, and Joseph Dan, *Sifrut he-Musar veha-Drush* (Jerusalem, 1975), pp. 55-57.

95. On the sources for asceticism in Bahya's thought, see Allan Lazaroff, "Bahya's Asceticism against its Rabbinic and Islamic Background," *Journal of Jewish Studies* XXI (1970), 11-38.

96. Wine parties were regulated by their own adab. They were guided by rules of etiquette and fixed modes of conduct, e.g., the social background of the guests, the desirable number of guests. See Ratzaby, "Shirat ha-Yayin," p. 425.

It is possible that Bahya intended to advance a "moral" critique of courtier poetry.

When he cautions against "ornamenting" (*zayyana*) the following: falsity (p. 186), overindulgence in food and drink referred to in context of the pleasures of kings and courtiers (p. 253), and socializing (p. 358), he may have intended to include poetry among various other means of "ornamenting" and glorifying courtier culture. The references would then relate to poems of praise, wine songs and poems of friendship, respectively. Judah ibn Tibbon who translates *zayyana* as *yippuy* may have so understood Bahya's meaning. On *yippuy* as connoting poetry, see Maimonides' *Millot ha-Higgayon*, trans. Moshe ibn Tibbon in *Proceedings of the American Academy for Jewish Research*, VIII (New York, 1938), 41.

97. Ashtor, *Korot ha-Yehudim*, II, 236, discusses the courtier as judge.

98. The statements, if they have historical addressees, may be directed to Karaites in Spain during this period. See *Hobot ha-Lebabot*, pp. 251-252 and notes, pp. 258-259 and notes. On treatment of Karaites in Spain prior to and during Bahya's times, see G. Cohen, Sefer ha-Qabbalah, pp. *xlvi-l*.

99. D. Kaufmann, "Torat ha-Elokut," p. 11, notes 5 and 6; C. Ramos Gil, "La Patria," p. 104.

100. S. D. Luzzatto, *Beit ha-Ozar* I (Lwow, 1881), 30-65; N. Eloni, "Hashkafot Karayiot be-Mahberet Menahem," *Ozar Yehudei Sefarad*, V (Jerusalem, 1962), 21-54.

101. Schirman, *Ha-Shira ha-Ibrit*, vol. I, pt. 1, p. 15.

102. Ibid., p. 16. More on the same theme: ibid., pp. 17-18.

103. Ashtor, *Korot ha-Yehudim*, II, 139-141, 234-235, 298.

104. Bahya's implied social criticism in this passage directly concerned with courtiers may have been written after Jehoseph ibn Nagrela's murder during the 1066 massacre in Granada, and is possibly aimed against this courtier leader, the son and successor of Samuel ha-Nagid. Jehoseph's fabulous wealth, specifically his magnificent palace, the Alhambra, had been described by contemporaries, both friend (Ibn Gabirol) and foe (Abu Ishaq). (See F. Bargebuhr, *Alhambra*, pp. 89-104.) If this conjecture is correct, Bahya feels that Jehoseph had overindulged himself when he might have supported the poor and disadvantaged. Even if one does not accept Bargebuhr's equation of Jehoseph's palace with the Alhambra, the monumental character of the edifice Jehoseph built is in any case attested to by contemporaries: "The ape of theirs [Jehoseph] has his mansion lined with stones, and makes the purest spring flow thither" (ibid., p. 93). 'Abd Allah reports that a member of the royal council, aiming to cast Jehoseph in an unfavorable light, tells the king that Jehoseph's edifice is "better than your own castle" (p. 90).

105. Y. Baer, *A History of the Jews in Christian Spain* II (Philadelphia, 1971), 241-242.

106. H. H. ben Sasson, *Toledot Am Yisrael bi-Yemei ha-Beinaim*, II (1969), 75; Ashtor, *Korot ha-Yehudim*, II, 161, 302.

107. Bahya's censure of the courtiers as it is reflected in this citation (p. 192) concerns his opposition to government service on the grounds that it is linked with oppression and corruption. This attitude is compatible with the Muslim views discussed by S. D. Goitein, "Ha-Yahas el ha-Shilton be-Islam uva-Yahadut," *Tarbiz*, XIX, 157-158, and F. Rosenthal, *Knowledge Triumphant*, p. 330. For the general background against which Bahya's attitude can be viewed, see S. Baron, "Some Medieval Jewish Attitudes to the Muslim State," in *Ancient and Medieval Jewish History*, ed. Leon Feldman (New Brunswick, 1972), pp. 82-84.

Bahya's highly laudatory description of the king (pp. 121-122) is not inconsistent with his attitude to government service and the courtier class. This royal portrait is obviously an idealized one, and bears no resemblance to the historical reality. The empirical proof for God's providence which Bahya finds in this context has to do less with the king's virtues than with the consensus to choose him in an otherwise contentious society. For a discussion of an analogous discrepancy between the ideal king and the real sultan in Muslim sources, see Gustave E. von Grunebaum, *Medieval Islam*, pp. 249-250.

A more authentic representation of Bahya's attitude to kings is found in II, 5. Describing the benefits of occasional lapses in memory, Bahya is grateful for the opportunity to forget the "yoke of royal authority" (p. 113), probably meaning a burden of excessive taxation. Still, conscientious obedience to the king is taken for granted. In fact, when Bahya urges obedience to God, he cites obedience to the king and his laws as a model (pp. 371, 375).

Francisco Elias de Tejada's article "Las Doctrinas Politicas de Bahya ben Yosef Ibn Paquda," (*Sefarad* VIII, 1948, pp. 23-47), must be read cautiously. The article is an example of the errors to which an uncritical use of ethical and homiletical texts (for reconstructing historical and philosophical themes) lends itself. The author often selects phrases from *Hobot ha-Lebabot* out of context in order to prove his assertions. See, for example (p. 40), his citation of Proverbs 24:21 (in Kapah's edition, p. 371), as Bahya's source for the obligation to comply with the law of the prince. The author is completely oblivious to the meaning of the passage as a whole, which brooks no such inference.

In general, the article is a rather impressionistic treatment of the subject (pp. 39-47). Its contentions, though true, that God's will is the exclusive determinant of the king's decisions and that for Bahya, political philosophy is secondary to ethical philosophy, is often supported by ill-chosen references purported to have a significance never assigned to them by Bahya (e.g., the texts covered by his notes 55, 64). Also, there is no attempt in the article to relate the abstract generalizations to the concrete reality of eleventh century Spain.

108. G. Cohen, *Sefer ha-Qabbalah*, p. 284, note 124.

109. The Arabic phrase here (p. 35) is *al-lafz al-gharib*. Compare with *'ilm gharib al-lugha* (p. 254 and p. 274) which is included as one of the ingredients of the rhetorical adab curriculum. The Hebrew term relevant here is *zarut*. On *zarut* see D. Pagis, *Shirat ha-Hol*, p. 55.

110. Schirman, *Ha-Shira ha-Ibrit,* etc., vol. I, pt. 2, p. 344.

111. M. Sister, "Bachja-Studien," in *Fünfzigster Bericht der Lehranstalt fur die Wissenschaft des Judentums in Berlin* (Berlin, 1936). See "Ergebnis der Untersuchung" on p. 75 where Sister concludes that Bahya is much more redundant than ibn Tibbon's translation would lead us to believe.

112. Compare with B. Lewis, "Qasida," pp. 664-665.

113. G. Cohen, *Sefer ha-Qabbalah*, p. 66.

114. Ibid., pp. 70-71.

115. G. Cohen, "The Story of the Four Captives," *Proceedings of the American Academy of Jewish Research*, XXIX (New York, 1961), 115.

116. Ibid., p. 116.

117. G. Cohen, *Sefer ha-Qabbalah*, p. 68.

118. M. Margoliot, *Hilkot ha-Nagid* (Jerusalem, 1962), p. 34.

119. Ibid.

120. Ibn Gabirol's *Shirei Kodesh*, ed. L. Dukes (Hannover, 1858), p. 71. Cited by Margaliot, *Hilkot ha-Nagid*, p. 35.

121. Ibid.

122. Ibid., p. 16.

123. Ibid., pp. 17-18.

124. Ibid., p. 54.

125. Ibid., p. 65.

126. Ibid., pp. 65-66.

127. J. Mann, *Texts and Studies in Jewish History and Literature* I (New York, 1972), 87, 111.

128. G. Cohen, "Story of Four Captives," p. 94.

129. *Asl* (translated as *shoresh, yesod;* fundamental principle) is used by Bahya in the sense of a theological principle (p. 44), but also in the sense of a halakic one (p. 28). In our context (pp. 148-150), the word *asl* is used twice: for the fifth level and for the ninth. In both levels, the reference is to principles of Torah. These principles of Torah are probably not halakic, for in the ninth level, Bahya characterizes the principles in question as being compatible with reason both in the exoteric and esoteric sense. Such a requirement seems irrelevant to practical halakic duties, where esoteric meaning cannot affect the legal sense. When Bahya speaks of the esoteric meaning of laws, he means the duties of the heart. In the fifth level, the "principles" are a new contribution, relative to lexical and grammatical achievements of the previous levels. They could not be principles of halaka, since the fifth level is not bound by Rabbinic tradition. Scholarly and religious accomplishments in the various levels are viewed positively in themselves and are seen wanting only compared to the higher levels. Karaite halakic principles, however, could not be viewed by Bahya as positive in themselves (pp. 251-252). Theological principles would be.

130. Bahya's explicit acknowledgment of Saadiah Gaon's achievements is indicated not only when he briefly reviews Jewish medieval literature and notes Saadiah's works in philosophy and Bible exegesis (pp. 17-18), but in other contexts as well. See pp. 15, 42, 78. Saadiah's influence on Bahya's religious poetry has been noted by H. Malter in *Saadiah Gaon: His Life and Works* (Philadelphia, 1921), p. 154 and note 344, and analyzed by Y. Ratzaby, "Bakashat Rabbenu Bahya ve-Hashpaot Rasag ve-Rashbag Ale'ah," *Sinai* 75 (1974), pp. 97-103.

131. Saadiah Gaon, *Book of Doctrines and Beliefs*, trans A. Altmann, in *Three Jewish Philosophers* (New York, 1972), p. 45.

132. On *ta'wil* in Saadiah see S. Rawidowitz, "B'ayat ha-Hagshamah be-Rasag ube-Rambam," in *Iyunim be-Mahshevet Yisrael*, I (Jerusalem, 1969), 187-189; M. Zucker, "Mi-Perusho shel Rasag la-Torah," *Sura*, II, 318-320; Zucker, *Al Targum Rasag* (New York, 1959), pp. 229, 234.

133. S. Rawidowicz, "B'ayat ha-Hagshamah," p. 189, and references in note 47.

134. There was certainly a consciousness of the duties of the heart in Amoraic sources, and Bahya is the first to acknowledge it (in his introduction, p. 21). In the quoted passage, however, Bahya seems to refer to a full exposition of ethical problems, since he mentions a specific practical point: the factors inhibiting moral action. This Saadiah does in his tenth chapter, indicating how the extreme pursuit of certain inclinations or ways of life lead to negative practical results.

The allusion to Saadiah notwithstanding, Bahya may still maintain in his introduction that prior to his own ethical treatise there was no work of this kind in Jewish literature. For Bahya, Saadiah's attempt is only a formal model, not a substantive one. Saadiah's ethical system is pragmatic and utilitarian. It is rooted in and serves as an "orienting ideology" for the "middle class" in Saadiah's period. It is really the adab of the Jewish "bourgeois." See B. Z. Dinur's programmatic comment in *Yisrael ba-Golah*, vol. I, bk. 2 (Tel Aviv, 1961), p. 468, note 96, and I. Tishbi and J. Dan, *Mibhar Sifrut ha-Mussar* (Jerusalem, 1970), p. 11.

One example may serve to illustrate the difference between Saadiah's ethical ideal and Bahya's. In arguing against pride, Saadiah shows that the proud man's disdain for other people's opinions and his contentiousness will lead him into trouble. For Bahya, pride is "secret polytheism." Thus, Saadiah's ethics are man-centered, Bahya's God-centered.

135. See Samuel b. Hofni's statement quoted by David Kimhi in his comment on Samuel I, 29:24.

136. See R. Hai Gaon's responsum quoted by B. Z. Dinur, *Yisrael ba-Golah*, vol. I, bk. 3, pp. 48-49.

137. On Hefetz b. Yazliah's method of classifying laws, see S. Assef, *Tekufat Ha-Geonim Ve-Sifrutah* (Jerusalem, 1967), p. 206. On his use of philosophy and treatment of "philosophical" mitzvot see B. Z. Halper, ed., *Hefez b. Yazliah's Book of Precepts* (Philadelphia, 1915), pp. 28-45.

138. See David Kaufmann's note in Judah ben Barzillai al-Bargeloni's *Perush al Sefer Yezira*, ed. S.Z.H. Halberstam (Berlin, 1885), p. 335.

139. Philosophy, Bahya says, provides the arguments against those who dispute us (p. 18).

140. Margaliot, *Hilkot ha-Nagid*, pp. 37-51.

141. G. Cohen, "Story of Four Captives," p. 93. The meager information available on the Geonate during Bahya's period is assessed by Mann, *Texts* I, 202-208.

142. G. Cohen, *Sefer ha-Qabbalah*, pp. 81, 86. See also E. Ashtor, *Korot ha-Yehudim* p. 299 and note, for other expressions of this idea. On the courtiers' own self-consciousness as protectors of the Jewish community see Y. Baer, *A History of the Jews in Christian Spain* I (Philadelphia, 1971), 30 (Ibn Shaprut), 35 (Samuel ha-Nagid).

143. H. H. Ben Sasson, "Dor Golei Sefarad al Azmo", *Zion* XXVI (1961), 28-34. The author documents a consistently positive attitude on the part of Jews to the courtiers because of their usefulness to the Jewish community. See p. 34 for a passage reflecting a lenient attitude toward courtiers even in a matter of Jewish law (imitating Gentile ways), in consideration of the courtiers' need to associate with non-Jews in the interests of the Jewish community. In contrast to Bahya, who resents adab because it aims for royal service, Joseph Jabez (see p. 32) allows courtiers to pursue secular studies *only* because it gives them entree to the king's court, hence an opportunity to plead for their people.

For an account of the courtiers' role in converting the traditional alliance between Jews and the royal authority in Christian Spain from a pragmatic necessity into a central ideology, see Yosef H. Yerushalmi, *The Lisbon Massacre of 1506 and the Royal Image in the Shebet Yehudah*, Hebrew Union College Annual Supplement I (Cincinnati, 1976), pp. 35-66, esp. p. 38.

144. See note 105 of this essay and S. Alami, *Iggeret Mussar* (Vienna, 1872), p. 27. "God did not wish to forgive [the courtiers] because they did not repent of their evil deeds." The "evil deeds" Alami enumerates concern a corruption of the courtier ideal. The ideal itself of Jews "with access to the king, to promote His people's welfare and intervene on its behalf," he would like to preserve.

145. Ben Sasson, "Dor," pp. 31-34. Expressions of profound disillusionment with the courtier institution emerged three generations after the Expulsion. See J.

Hacker, "Yisrael ba-Goyim be-te'uro shel Rabbi Shlomo laBet ha-Levi mi-Saloniki," *Zion* XXXIV, 73 and note 178.

146. In Muslim Spain Jews were part of a heterogeneous society where Jews, Christians, and Muslims were living side by side. In contrast to their situation in the rest of Europe, Jews were not the only minority in an otherwise Christian society. On the roots of tolerance in Muslim Spain, both pragmatic and ideational, see Americo Castro, *The Structure of Spanish History*, trans. Edmund King (Princeton, 1954), 222-223.

The situation changed for the worse with the invasion of the Almoravides in 1090 and the Almohades in 1148. The disillusionment of the generation following Bahya, represented by Moshe ibn Ezra and Judah ha-Levi, is caused by events following 1090 and the shattering of the Jewish sense of security in Spain. The tragedy and its aftermath contributed to a sober assessment of Jewish suffering, and irrelevance, in the Christian-Muslim struggle. On Ibn Ezra's and ha-Levi's reaction to the political situation in their time see Baer, *History* I, 59-77 and his article in *Zion* I and I. Levin, "Ha-Sebel be-Mashber ha-Reconquista be-Shirato shel Yehuda ha-Levi," *Ozar Yehudei Sefarad* VII (Jerusalem, 1964), 49-64. Bahya did not experience the events of 1090 and the resultant pessimism, and his evaluation of the Jewish status hence exudes contentment.

Herein lies one difference between the two critiques of the Jewish courtier culture of Muslim Spain—ha-Levi's and Bahya's. Ha-Levi's critique is colored by and re-' sponds to the deteriorating political situation of the Jews at the end of the eleventh century and the beginning of the twelfth, of which Bahya, writing before 1090, is yet innocent. Ha-Levi's critique is thus offered at a time of crisis and reassessment for courtiers. Bahya's is offered during the heyday of courtier political achievement (their "true golden age", see note 150, below) and this fact points up his critical independence. (The other difference between the two critiques lies in their attitude to the philosophical pursuits of courtier culture. For ha-Levi, "the grandeur of Islam, the glory of Greece are vanity beside the Urim and the Tummim" [quoted in G. Cohen's *Sefer ha-Qabbalah*, pp. 298-299]. Bahya, on the other hand, views the courtier paideia as not being rigorous enough in its pursuit of philosophy.)

147. Though Bahya purports to generalize about the Jews' political and social situation since the beginning of the exile, it is clear that his characterization reflects the situation in Muslim Spain.

148. On the Jews' diversified economic position during this period in the context of their overall social position, see Ashtor, *Korot ha-Yehudim*, II, 259-260.

149. Bahya's assessment of the relative economic position of the Jewish middle and lower classes vis-à-vis their Gentile counterparts is a new datum concerning the Jewish economic history of the period. (There is no material in Ashtor's economic review of the period against which this statement may be checked). The sad economic plight of the non-Jewish lower classes during this period is documented by Ashtor, *Korot ha-Yehudim* II, 306, 321-322. The difficult situation of the Jewish lower classes is described in ibid., p. 323.

150. Bahya's is a period (the second half of the eleventh century, see note 2) in which Muslim kingdoms in the south are coming under increasing pressure (both military and economic) from the Christian north as well as from rival Muslim kingdoms in the south. They therefore rely more than ever before on Jewish courtiers' experience in economic and diplomatic affairs, the Jews harboring no loyalty to

other Muslim rulers or Christian kings.

Ashtor, *Korot ha-Yehudin*, pp. 296-301, sees this period as the "true golden age" for Jewish courtiers. Until this time the political fortunes of courtiers like ibn Shaprut and the Nagrellas were exceptional. In the last third of the eleventh century, however, Spanish Jews were "accustomed to the sight of Jewish statesmen negotiating with kings and princes—in Granada and Seville, Toledo and Saragossa." Jewish courtiers saw themselves as part and parcel of the political and economic, social and cultural life of Spain.

The same was true of the attitude to Jews in Christian states to the north. King Alfonso VI of Castile (reigned 1065-1109), initiating the Christian reconquest of the Muslim south on a large scale, extended special privileges to Jews. This was done in order to attract Jewish settlers to newly conquered territories, now desolate as a result of prolonged warfare. From Alfonso's perspective, Jews would be able to provide the manpower he needed, as well as skilled financial and political administration (ibid., pp. 310-317). Benefiting from the Christian attitude were not only Jewish courtiers but also the Jewish burgher class (ibid., p. 304). In general, on the more favorable standing of Jews vis-à-vis Christians in Muslim kingdoms see ibid., pp. 161, 233, 239.

151. One such poetic expression is in Yitzhak ibn Giat's elegy for Jehosef ha-Nagid (in E. Schirman, *Shirim Hadashim min ha-Genizah*, p. 191).

152. The fact that Moshe ibn Ezra does mention Bahya favorably in two works —*Sefer ha-Iyunim veha-Diyunim* and *Arugat ha-Bosem*—does not militate against this argument. Moshe ibn Ezra's own attitude to poetry was ambivalent. See R. Scheindlin's analysis, "Rabbi Moshe ibn Ezra," pp. 104-107, 114. Ibn Ezra's attitude to the social ethic of the courtier circle turned from approbation to censure. See G. Cohen, *Sefer ha-Qabbalah*, p. 297; *Sefer ha-Iyunim veha-Diyunim*, p. xiii.

153. G. Cohen, *Sefer ha-Qabbalah*, pp. 289-293. On *Sefer ha-Kabbalah* as an apology for the courtier class see ibid., pp. 293-302.

This essay was originally presented as a seminar paper at Harvard University to Professors Isadore Twersky and Yosef Yerushalmi. I wish to thank my teachers for their invaluable counsel, criticism, and encouragement. My gratitude is also extended to Professor Jacob Katz of the Hebrew University who was kind enough to read the essay and to offer very helpful comments.

9

Piety and Power
in Thirteenth-Century Catalonia

Bernard Septimus

רדי אשכח זכו   באוריתה מלכו

לאחסנא מלכו   תשלטן יתירא

(פתיחת רמב"ן לס' מלחמות ה')

An Obscure Anti-Aristocratic Rebellion

Early in the thirteenth century, the poet, Judah al-Harizi, described Barcelona as "the city of princes (nesi'im)."[1] Al-Harizi's "city" was the Jewish
community and its "princes," an aristocracy adorned with culture and
wealth. "Nasi" was more than a flattering title conferred by literary clients
upon patrons who affected noble lineage and high station. The nesi'im possessed well-defined political powers and social prerogatives. In the Jewish
community of Barcelona, aristocracy ruled.

A document setting forth the privileges and powers of the aristocracy had
been drawn up by the great nasi, R. Sheshet b. Isaac Benveniste.[2] In a "city
of princes," Sheshet was "the prince of all princes." Al-Harizi even styles
him "the pillar of the world."[3] Another prominent contemporary refers to
him as "the singular [member] of our generation."[4] It was no idle compli-
ment. Sheshet had wealth, power, learning, and good deeds. He served as
finance minister, diplomat, and personal physician to two kings of Aragon.
He was expert in Arabic literature and philosophy. And scattered sources
attest to his communal leadership, philanthropy, literary patronage, poetic
skills, and medical prowess.[5] R. Sheshet was likely the mainstay of the aristocratic regime. For within three or four years of his death (about 1209) that
regime was threatened by open rebellion from within the community.

The nature and course of this rebellion are obscure. The documentation is
incomplete and, at times, baffling. Following is an attempt to reconstruct
what the sources allow of this murky chapter in the history of the Barcelona
Jewish community.[6]

Little is known of the nesi'im who survived Sheshet Benveniste. Their
leader, R. Makir b. Sheshet (probably not a son of Sheshet Benveniste), was
praised by Al-Harizi for his princely character and largess.[7] Makir was in
the service of the Aragonese court.[8] His political position and the extent of

his power are unclear, but whatever political influence he could muster, he certainly needed. In the face of strong internal challenge, royal power was the ultimate prop of the aristocratic regime of the *nesi'im*.

The *nesi'im* had obtained a royal charter affirming their powers and privileges,[9] but royal grants are subject to revocation. The opponents of the *nesi'im* were economically strong,[10] not without political influence of their own, and were attempting an appeal to the king.[11] And so the embattled *nesi'im* sought allies outside Barcelona.

An exchange of letters between the *nasi*, R. Makir b. Sheshet, and three Provencal communities has somehow found its way into a collection of documents about a completely different controversy that took place a century later.[12] Thus preserved from oblivion, these letters provide our only source of information about the course, even the very existence, of the Barcelona revolt.

There was a religious, as well as a political side to the revolt—that much is clear from Makir's correspondence. What it was about is harder to pin down. Little direct testimony survives on the religious style of the *nesi'im*. But it is not difficult to characterize the religious posture of their late leader, Sheshet Benveniste. He was the first public defender of Maimonidean rationalism in the European arena.[13] In defending Maimonides' views on resurrection, Sheshet presses his position with an aggressive and forthright vigor unmatched by later, more circumspect, rationalist polemicists. Although a patron of halakists as well as poets,[14] Sheshet thought many a Spanish talmudist arrogant and self-serving.[15] As both patron and scholar, he was committed to a cultural ideal that stressed the cultivation of literary style, broad general knowledge, and serious philosophical study. A fair preliminary guess is that the other *nesi'im*, though lesser men, moved in a similar religio-cultural ambit.

The opposition is harder to characterize, for we are fully dependent upon a hostile and less than limpid prosecutor's brief—the letter of R. Makir b. Sheshet to the community of Lunel.[16] Makir's first two charges are directed against the leader of the anti-aristocratic revolt, one Samuel b. Benvenist. Nothing is known about him from other sources. But a chance remark of Makir reveals a significant piece of information: that Samuel b. Benvenist "fancied himself a teacher of (*marbiz*) Torah."[17]

Makir's letter opens with the charge that Samuel b. Benvenist spoke blasphemously of Rashi. What precisely Samuel said about Rashi, Makir does not say; "for Heaven forbid that we . . . utter outright what was heard from his mouth."[18] We are left wondering why anyone who considers himself a *marbiz Torah* should be moved to "blaspheme" Rashi. In any case, Samuel had his own, more innocent, version of what he had said. "He proclaimed in *his* congregation (*kahal*) that, under pain of *herem*, any who had heard him speak blasphemously of Rashi come, within three days, and testify before three men whom he had chosen."[19] Makir goes on to explain why "we and the members of *our* congregation paid no heed to his *herem.*" We learn, in passing, that Samuel's party had organized as a separate *kahal.*

The second charge leveled by Makir against this *marbiz Torah* is even stranger than the first: "Showing himself worse than any *epiqoros* and heretic," he taught that the prophet Samuel was superior to Moses.[20] It is easy enough to see how this teaching could be considered heretical.[21] But it is well nigh impossible to imagine why any reasonably learned Jew in early thirteenth-century Barcelona should want to teach it in the first place. It would be a view unparalleled in all medieval Jewish thought and completely out of place in the context of any contemporary religious tendency.[22] The problem is best left in temporary abeyance.

Makir's next group of charges brings us closer to the political side of the rebellion. The circle of culprits is now widened to include the "party" of Samuel b. Benvenist. Makir says nothing explicitly about attempts to seize communal power. Formally, most of his charges deal with breach of synagogue etiquette. The rebels, for example, sinned against the late *nasi,* Todros b. Kalonymos by calling to the Torah before him "a foolish, evil, base man named She'altiel b. Reuben" and arrogating for the latter "an honorable place to which his fathers and fathers' fathers had not attained."[23] As if that were not enough, "the above mentioned fool and his friend Samuel b. Isaac—known as ben Maimon—b. Haim rose up and, when the *nasi* [Todros] wished to leave the synagogue together with the princes in the prescribed manner, the former two, with arrogance and levity, went ahead of them."[24] Apparently, synagogue ceremonial which had, in the past, served to confirm the communal status and authority of the *nesi'im* was now being used as a medium through which to challenge that status and authority. Makir's letter enumerates several other incidents in which princely prerogative had been violated and concludes that the time has come to persecute "the arrogant and evildoers . . . to avenge the deeds of the blasphemer who despises the word of the Lord and violates his commandment."[25]

All told, we remain in the dark about Samuel and his party. A man who considers himself a teacher of Torah is accused of cursing Rashi and teaching the superiority of the prophet Samuel to Moses! Likely enough he was not a participant in the "court culture" of the *nesi'im.* But what religio-cultural tendency *do* he and his party represent? To this question, Makir's letter provides no clear answer.

That the *nesi'im* sought support north of the Pyrenees rather than in Spain is indicative of the very close political and cultural ties between Catalonia and Provence at the turn of the thirteenth century.[26] In fact, Makir's letter was not the first that the communities of Provence had heard of the Barcelona revolt. The party led by Samuel b. Benvenist had already been condemned "by agreement of all the holy communities [of Provence] in a document of rebuke, uprightly written words of truth." But meanwhile,

Samuel had succeeded in convincing the queen of Aragon, Maria of Montpellier (d. 1213) "that the men of Provence had perverted justice in his case."
He was planning to escape the wrath of the *nesi'im* by fleeing to Montpellier
"and requested that she ask the elders of Montpellier to remove their yoke
from him and—should they decline—that she command her appointee, the
governor of Montpellier, to force them to release him from the ban (*nidduy*)." It was this development which led to that further correspondence
between Makir and the communities of Provence which survives as our sole
source of information on the anti-aristocratic revolt of Samuel b. Benvenist.[27]

Makir's letter is formally addressed to the community of Lunel. The response consists of a long lead letter from Lunel to which are attached brief
confirmatory communications from Beziers and Montpellier. The Lunel
leaders do not respond like distant, detached arbitrators. They are inti-
mately acquainted with the events in Barcelona and passionately partisan:
"Impudent, unbridled men . . . have risen up in Barcelona, a most venerable city and mother in Israel . . . to desecrate the covenant of its mighty
founders . . . They have denied God and their king, the exalted prince, the
honored *nasi*, R. Makir . . . before whom peoples tremble, a prince and a
commander of nations who has many times saved them in his love and
mercifulness."[28]

Among the Provencal allies of the Barcelona aristocracy were Levi b.
Moshe, one of the Kalonymide *nesi'im*, Meshullam b. Moshe, an important
representative of the Provencal talmudic tradition and the celebrated grammarian and exegete, David Kimhi.[29] Their aim is to ". . . restore the rule of
authority to its rightful place . . . that all countenances not be equal."[30]
Upon what, one wonders, is this alliance based? It is difficult to say for sure.
At the turn of the century, with Aragonese power in Provence at its peak, it
is likely that Provencal communal leaders were in close touch with Jewish
aristocrats at court in Barcelona and had perhaps incurred debts of gratitude to some of the latter. The late Sheshet Benveniste, we know, had been
on intimate terms with the Provencal *nesi'im* and was deeply involved in
Provencal communal affairs.[31] Moreover there is some indication that the
Barcelona and Provencal aristocracies may have been linked by family
ties.[32]

In any case, the leaders of Lunel pronounce a severe *herem* against any
who would violate the inherited rights of the Barcelona *nesi'im* or seek to
void any of those rights by litigation before the royal court. For the various
sins enumerated by Makir, punishments of exile, flogging, and *nidduy* are
prescribed. And finally, a provision with teeth: should the seven chief culprits (Heaven forbid!) remain rebellious and refuse to accept their sentences,
the Lunel elders *command* Makir to fine them a total of one thousand
maravedis, payable to the royal treasury.[33] This punishment, perhaps aimed
at breaking the back of the rebellion economically, was doubtless designed
with an eye toward encouraging royal enforcement.

A brief but vigorous letter from Beziers confirms the sentences handed down by the community of Lunel.[34] Finally, the communal elders of Montpellier, in a letter which shows no signs of wavering in the face of political pressure, reaffirm their solidarity with the Barcelona *nesi'im* and proclaim their readiness to accept and enforce all measures that have been or will be directed against the rebels. And here, with the outcome still very much in doubt, our documentation stops short.[35]

Communal Upheaval and the Maimonidean Controversy

A quarter of a century later, the rule of the Barcelona aristocracy was under attack again.[36] This time, the leaders of the revolt were not obscure men, forgotten by history. They include two of the outstanding figures of the thirteenth century: the towering Talmudist, mystic, and Biblical exegete —Nahmanides, and his almost equally famous cousin, the pietist, preacher, and Talmudic scholar—R. Jonah b. Abraham Gerondi.[37] Again, political and spiritual conflict are intertwined. This time the religious side of the conflict is less elusive. It is, in fact, connected with one of the major struggles of the century: the great Maimonidean Controversy of the 1230s.[38]

At the turn of the century, the traditional talmudic-midrashic culture of Provence was undergoing rapid reorientation in the direction of Spanish philosophical culture.[39] By 1230, the Provencal Jewish "establishment" seems firmly committed to an interpretation of Judaism and its educational ideal informed by Maimonidean rationalism. This development was not without its opponents. The leading critics of the new Provencal rationalism were R. Solomon b. Abraham of Montpellier and his students, R. David b. Saul and R. Jonah b. Abraham Gerondi. Controversy somehow moved beyond the plane of polite or even impolite scholarly discussion and erupted into a bitter battle engulfing communities throughout France and Spain. The Provencal rationalists engaged in a vigorous campaign to isolate and excommunicate R. Solomon and his pupils. They sought ratifications of their *herem* throughout Spain "in order that those wicked men be unable to find their hands and feet [find sanctuary] in all the boundaries of Israel."[40]

Fear that the Montpellier anti-rationalists might escape punishment by fleeing south was apparently justified; for that is precisely what happened. At some point in the 1230s R. Jonah and perhaps other members of R. Solomon's party moved to Barcelona. R. Jonah was simply retreating, under fire, to his native Catalonia. True, the Barcelona *nesi'im* were staunch allies of the Provencal rationalists. But the opponents of the *nesi'im* included close friends and kinsmen who had vigorously opposed the Provencal *herem*. That R. Jonah found refuge in Barcelona indicates that the anti-aristocratic party was holding its own. Before long, R. Jonah had joined the leadership of the revolt against the aristocratic regime of the Barcelona *nesi'im*.[41]

A partially preserved propaganda letter dating from the late 1230s or early 1240s takes up the cause of the *nesi'im* with a bitterness and abandon that suggest desperation.[42] Channeling its venom into ornate and heavily allusive rhymed prose the letter denounces "slaves" who have "revolted against their kings and rebelled against their masters," the *nesi'im* of Barcelona.[43] Its language, throughout, suggests an aristocratic ideology that sees revolt against the inherited authority of the highborn as repulsive and sinful. The leaders of the revolt are attacked in virulent, though (to us) somewhat opaque terms. Here, the confluence of political and religious conflict is much in evidence.

One of the leaders of the revolt "joined with . . . the men of Zarfat [northern France] . . . and they spoke against God, Moses and his books; he led them astray and they let themsleves be led."[44] "Moses" is, of course, Moses Maimonides, his authority allusively compared to that of the Biblical Moses.[45] Speaking against him and his books is tantamount to speaking against God. The complicity of the men of northern France in this defamation of Maimonides points to the unique circumstances of the Maimonidean Controversy of the 1230s. The leader attacked as the instigator of the fickle French is likely R. Jonah Gerondi.[46]

Another leader of the revolt against the *nesi'im* is described as a "faithless teacher" who worships, "in fear and in awe," a mixed bag of angels and pagan dieties![47] This representation makes sense only if taken to burlesque the beliefs of a kabbalist. Kabbalistic teaching was, during this period, beginning to break the bonds of strict esotericism. It was also, perhaps not coincidentally, beginning to provoke opposition. At about the time of the Maimonidean Controversy, the Provencal Talmudist, R. Meshullam b. Moshe, whom we earlier met as an ally of the Barcelona *nesi'im*, was conducting an anti-kabbalistic campaign. At R. Meshullam's direction, his nephew, R. Meir b. Simeon of Narbonne, circulated a letter, attacking Catalonian as well as Provencal kabbalah, among the communal leaders of Provence. It charges that the kabbalistic practice of directing prayer toward the particular *sefirot* deemed appropriate to the circumstances is tantamount to polytheism.[48] Our polemic, it would seem, is leveling a similar charge in somewhat more extravagant and figurative language. The most prominent of contemporary Catalonian kabbalists, Nahmanides, was a leader of the revolt against the *nesi'im*. He may well be the "faithless teacher" denounced in our polemic.

In one of his ethical works, R. Jonah argues the remarkable proposition that shaming one's fellow publicly is, like murder, a sin to be avoided even if martyrdom be the price; "for the pain of shame is more bitter than death."[49] The Maimonidean Controversy may have provided painful personal proof. In the heat of that controversy some of R. Jonah's most bitter Provencal enemies even went so far as to charge that his family was of impure descent.[50]

R. Jonah was united by family ties to several leaders of the anti-aristocratic party, including Nahmanides. Not content to denounce these usurpers of aristocratic privilege as lowborn, our pro-aristocratic propaganda letter, using oblique Biblical and Talmudic allusion, repeats the charge of their family's impure descent.[51]

The sinfulness of slander and "the evil tongue" are among the central themes of R. Jonah's ethical works. Often, perhaps not coincidentally, the particularly pernicious sin of casting aspersions on family purity is singled out in this context.[52] One such passage begins by explaining why slander is likened to "a warrior's sharpened arrows" (by Psalm 120:4):

> For one who draws a sword, if he be moved by the pleas of his victim, resheathes his sword. Not so the archer; the arrow is beyond his power to recall. And similarly the slanderer, once the word has gone forth from his mouth, the [damage] is beyond his power to repair. Moreover he sometimes casts aspersions on a family causing injury to all its future generations. No pardon can reach him for this. For this reason our rabbis said that one who casts aspersions on a family has no atonement, ever. Moreover, one who sets his tongue loose will speak even against "the saints that are upon the earth"; for upon whom has not come his unceasing evil? And our rabbis have already said that the *epiqoros* has no share in the World to Come.[53]

Autobiographical echoes are almost unmistakably audible.

The slanderous shafts let fly in the Barcelona struggle of the 1230s were apparently still aloft a century and a half later. Writing in defense of his family, an anonymous descendant of Nahmanides describes the circumstances under which "noble families in the kingdom of Barcelona and Gerona" were first maligned. These families boasted great scholars—Nahmanides, R. Jonah b. Abraham, R. Jonah b. Joseph and R. Isaac Kastion—who "grew exceedingly zealous for the sake of God that violent and sinful men were called by the name 'nasi' and so they deposed them in accordance with the law." The deposed *nesi'im* retaliated with slander.[54]

This anonymous descendant has preserved precious excerpts from Nahmanides' otherwise lost account of his struggle with the *nesi'im* and the ensuing attack on his family. It is, ironically, Nahmanides whose style reveals "aristocratic" sensibilities. Men of refinement, Nahmanides anticipates, may deem him in poor form for taking pained public notice of desperate, viperous slander. Still, it allows him the opportunity to acknowledge divine justice: He is deserving of his suffering. For, Nahmanides confesses, he was guilty of protracted delay in joining battle against the *nesi'im*. He long allowed himself to address the aristocrats with their titles, *nasi* and *nadib*. He would misguidedly speak in their defense. He feared the consequences of open confrontation. And even after the battle had begun, says Nahmanides:

> I made of myself
> A mute, who speaks not
> A deaf man, who hears not
> Till my friends judged me
> A fool who understands not.[55]

But the opinion of Nahmanides' friends finally prevailed. Perhaps it was R. Jonah who was instrumental in ultimately securing the engagement of his reluctant cousin.

Nahmanides makes the case against his aristocratic opponents in rather strong terms. They are *ame ha-arez* and of scandalous religious behavior. They don't pray, are suspected of sexual immorality, and privately desecrate the Sabbath. Their houses are filled with deceit and great hatred. The likes of them are unworthy of bearing noble title and holding sway over the community.[56] We, Nahmanides asserts, and for that matter anyone with an understanding of Talmud, have numerous proofs, clear as the noontime sun, that communal position is not to be passed on as an inheritance from father to son unless the son be worthy. Moreover, a ruling to this effect has already been issued by the lions of the academy. And immemorial custom confirms it. Nahmanides is, of course, responding here to the aristocratic claim to inherited authority.[57]

The real power base of the *nesi'im* was, according to Nahmanides, "their [possession of the] office of bailiff and their moving in the courts of kings and their palaces."[58] Use of the plural here ("kings") tactfully downplays the relationship of the *nesi'im* to the one king that counted, "our lord the king, his glory be elevated and his majesty exalted," James I of Aragon.[59] It was he who ultimately decided the outcome of the conflict. A solemn judicial proceeding was conducted before the royal court. Nahmanides describes the scene. Holding a Torah scroll in his hands, James I himself adjured Nahmanides in the name of the God of Israel to give truthful testimony. The subject of Nahmanides' testimony was "the meanings of '*nasi*' and '*nadib*' among us [that is, according to Jewish law and custom]."[60] The upshot of the trial was that the Barcelona aristocracy "were made subject to the rule of law" and permission was granted Nahmanides' party "to break the bars of [their] yoke."[61]

The defeated defendants may have lost more than their authority over the Jewish community. The defamation of his lineage, Nahmanides reports, was an act of reckless retaliation perpetrated by the deposed aristocrats "when evil had been determined against them by the king." Nahmanides is at pains to make clear that he had no part in suggesting sentence or even arguing their guilt.[62]

The royal decision in favor of the anti-aristocratic party as well as the new regime's efforts to combat its slanderers are reflected in a privilege granted the Jewish community of Barcelona by James I of Aragon in December of 1241. It empowers two or three *probi homines* elected by the community to fine or even expel from the city those guilty of defaming the *probi homines* and to adjudicate civil cases among the Jews.[63] By the end of 1241, then, the Jewish community has been empowered to establish a rudimentary elected government. The civil jurisdiction of this government is mentioned almost as a postscript to what appears to be the primary concern of the charter: power to punish slanderers. Viewed out of context, the charter seems strangely unbalanced. But against the background of personal attack that characterizes the propaganda of the ousted aristocratic regime, its preoccupation with punishment of slanderers is readily understandable.

Our sources allow for some informed speculation on the reasons for the decline and fall of the Barcelona aristocracy. The ideology of the *nesi'im* may have stressed noble lineage and rightful succession as the bases of their venerable regime. But, in the face of internal challenge, their power was in fact dependent upon present influence at the royal court. As such, it was possessed of that inherent instability which attaches to all things dependent upon the affairs of kings and their whims. Moreover, in the thirteenth century, the influence of Jewish officials at court in Barcelona was in decline. The relative strength of merchants in a still booming Reconquista economy probably increased accordingly. The opponents of the *nesi'im* apparently included such men of means.[64] Indeed, aristocratic propaganda scornfully reports that the usurpers seek to substitute money for lineage as their claim to leadership.[65] Understandably, the *nesi'im* fail to mention a further factor: the spiritual leadership and religious ideology of their opponents.

The issue raised by the anti-aristocratic opposition is one which recurs frequently in subsequent Spanish Jewish history: the scandal of communal power wielded by hedonistic, haughty, high-handed courtiers. In denouncing the regime of the *nesi'im*, the opposition asserts, instead, the ideal of communal leadership by men of scholarship and piety.[66] And it possessed not only the economic strength and political ability but also the spiritual authority to sustain its claim. R. Jonah's arrival in Barcelona and his assumption of a leadership role in the revolt were likely of crucial importance in this connection. The deciding factor in the struggle may have been Nahmanides' decision to join his colleagues and kinsmen in revolt. For the *nesi'im* were then faced with a brilliant opponent of immense spiritual stature who had the royal ear, to boot.[67] His leadership and influence may have tipped the balance.

The victory of the party led by Nahmanides and R. Jonah marks a major transition in the history of the Jewish community of Barcelona. The form of its government is no longer an aristocratic regime dominated by courtiers but rather an elected government dominated by scholars and merchants. The spiritual world of the dominant group is now informed less by literary "court culture" and philosophical rationalism than by profound study of Talmud and kabbalah. This new order has long been familiar to us from sources on Barcelona in the second half of the thirteenth century. Its unquestioned political and spiritual leader was R. Solomon ibn Adret, the outstanding disciple of R. Jonah and Nahmanides.[68] It would seem that ibn Adret's regime was built upon ground won and foundations laid by his great masters.

Lines of Continuity

I have attempted reconstruction of two revolts, a quarter century apart, against the *nesi'im* of Barcelona. The first, though of uncertain conclusion, could hardly have been a smashing success: the aristocracy was still there to be overthrown by the second. The aristocracy that succumbed to the second revolt was presumably the same that survived the first. But what about its opponents? Was the abortive revolt led by the obscure Samuel b. Benvenist in any way linked to the victorious struggle led some twenty-five years later by the illustrious R. Jonah and Nahmanides? In fact, it was. But before we can take testimony to that effect, some preliminary effort must be expended on establishing the authorship of the letter that serves as our witness.

Among the documents that stem from the Maimonidean Controversy of the 1230s, one group, emanating from Nahmanides' circle, stands together as a unit.[69] Each document in this collection is introduced by a brief editorial note. The editor was himself involved in the events of the controversy. He was the author and the recipient of some of the letters included in his collection and, in the editorial notes, describes his role in the first person. The bulk of the correspondence is devoted to the defense of R. Jonah Gerondi against his Provencal slanderers. But a somewhat earlier exchange with R. Solomon b. Abraham of Montpellier, chief of the Provencal anti-rationalists, begins the collection. R. Solomon's letter attempts to set straight the record of his involvement in the Maimonidean Controversy. He describes his efforts to combat dangerous and destructive rationalistic ideas, blames on the scholars of Beziers the escalating conflict that ensued and explains how an appeal for moral support from northern France evoked an unexpectedly strong denunciation of the *Guide* and its students. R. Solomon denies ever denouncing Maimonides and warns against giving credence to the inflammatory propaganda of David Kimhi, the leader of his Provencal antagonists.[70]

R. Solomon's addressee was "the great scholar," R. Samuel b. Isaac—long identified by students of the Maimonidean Controversy as the Barcelona civil-law codifier, R. Samuel b. Isaac ha-Sardi.[71] R. Samuel ha-Sardi was indeed a great scholar. He was in full control of the Spanish, Provencal, and Franco-German talmudic traditions, resembling, in this respect, his younger colleague, Nahmanides, with whom he enjoyed close scholarly contact and intimate friendship.[72] R. Samuel's *Sefer ha-Terumot* had a major impact on the development of Jewish civil law.[73] His was not the poor man's wisdom. Contemporary documents, in fact, indicate that R. Samuel was extraordinarily wealthy.[74] It is not hard to see why R. Solomon sought him as an ally. Besides, R. Samuel was apparently an old friend. For R. Solomon could "recall the days past when we delighted in your love and gloried in your distinction."[75]

Students have long puzzled over the editor's note preceding R. Solomon's letter. It reads: "Text of the letter which the great scholar R. Solomon b.

Abraham sent and his student R. David b. Saul copied (?) [*he'etiq*] to Nahmanides . . . ."[76] This seems to contradict the text of the letter which quite
explicitly addresses R. Samuel b. Isaac, not Nahmanides. It is syntactically
strange, since it interposes a clause between the verb "sent" and its indirect
object, "Nahmanides." The clause, moreover, seems irrelevant: who cares
who copied the letter? Besides, David b. Saul was more than a mere copyist:
his signature appears on the letter after that of his teacher, R. Solomon.[77]

The problem is readily solved if we accept the following hypothesis: our
editor is none other than Solomon's addressee, R. Samuel ha-Sardi. "*He-
'etiq*" should be translated "transmitted." The editorial note may now be
rendered as follows: "Text of the letter which the great scholar R. Solomon
sent [to me, the addressee named in the letter] and [which] his student, R.
David b. Saul transmitted to Nahmanides."

The unsigned text of a reply to R. Solomon's letter is prefaced by the editorial note: "And this was his reply."[78] The antecedent of "his" would seem
to be the name that appears at the end of the note immediately preceding:
"Nahmanides."

Our hypothesis thus yields the following reconstruction. The editor of the
collection is R. Samuel ha-Sardi. It was to this powerful and scholarly
friend that R. Solomon wrote in search of support. His letter may have been
carried to Barcelona by David b. Saul. R. Samuel, as was his wont when
faced with difficult problems, sought the collaboration of his close friend,
Nahmanides.[79] Preferring to leave to Nahmanides the delicate task of composing a reply to R. Solomon, he had David forward the letter to Nahmanides in Gerona.

In his statesmanlike response, Nahmanides gently questions Solomon's
alarming appraisal of his rationalist opponents, counsels conciliation, attempts to "reinforce" Solomon's stated respect for Maimonides and yet assures him of sympathy and support. R. Samuel's confidence in his colleague's diplomatic skills was clearly not misplaced.[80]

This hypothetical identification of the editor proves quite consistent
when tested against the remaining documents and notes of his collection.
Introducing the first of these letters, the editor notes that "some ten of the
scholars of Beziers joined in writing false accusations against the faithful
scholar, R. Jonah; then the great scholar Nahmanides wrote to me . . . ."[81]
Gone is the tone of almost detached diplomacy that had characterized Nahmanides' letter to Solomon of Montpellier. Nahmanides urgently enlists the
editor's aid in mounting a determined battle against the slanderers of his
cousin, R. Jonah. The letters that follow represent measures taken by Nahmanides and the editor toward that end: an open letter of protest by
Nahmanides to the communities of Provence and two letters of protest—
one by Nahmanides and one by the editor—to R. Meshullam b. Moshe, the
leading scholar of Beziers. These documents provide independent information about the editor. Especially important is the letter to him from Nahmanides.

Nahmanides addresses his correspondent as a scholar of the first rank. (The latter's stature is evident too in the remarkable assurance with which he is later able to rebuke the formidable R. Meshullam b. Moshe.) Nahmanides was on the closest terms with his correspondent, as is evident from the language in which he couches his request. ("I implore you, invoke the merit of my fathers and our intimate closeness, and so on.")[82] This scholarly friend must have been a particularly powerful person, for Nahmanides requests that he "excommunicate all the signatories of that perjurious document [slandering R. Jonah]. And should anyone perchance protest, excommunicate [those] sinners. For you can do everything; and everything is in your hands; and you are all . . . yours is a mighty arm . . ."[83] Where did this influential intimate of Nahmanides live? Neither—the letter makes clear—in France, southern or northern, nor in Nahmanides' home town of Gerona. It was, however, a town in which Nahmanides had close friends and allies; for he requests that his correspondent "gather together our elders, all our beloved, faithful friends" to excommunicate R. Jonah's slanders.[84] Elsewhere, in his angry letter to R. Meshullam, Nahmanides indicates that his most trusted allies are "our close brothers, the scholars of Barcelona."[85] Barcelona thus seems the likely address of Nahmanides' letter. Among all the scholars of Barcelona, there were none so distinguished, powerful, and close to Nahmanides as R. Samuel b. Isaac ha-Sardi.[86] He seems the likely addressee of Nahmanides' letter. The hypothetical identification of the editor with Samuel ha-Sardi is thus confirmed. It may be said, in sum, with some plausibility, that the collection consists of letters representing the joint activity of Nahmanides and R. Samuel ha-Sardi during the course of the Maimonidean Controversy, edited by the latter.[87]

Our somewhat digressive detour returns to the main road with what we now take to be a letter of R. Samuel ha-Sardi. "When I saw," writes the editor, "that they [the Beziers opponents of R. Jonah] had wronged them [R. Jonah and his kin], I composed these verses and this letter and sent it all to the scholar, R. Meshullam b. Moshe, to Beziers."[88] In poetry and prose, R. Samuel protests the defamation of distinguished scholarly families, hinting to R. Meshullam that "even those who hear [slander] are obligated to protest."[89] "And if [the slanderers] have said: 'behold, our hand is high, who will question our decision . . . ' Do they not know, have they not heard that even the great is to be confuted if we see him persecuting the innocent, in order to save the oppressed from his oppressor?" But beyond salvation of the oppressed, R. Samuel feels a personal stake in the matter: "There is a time to be silent and a time to speak and to intervene in wrath on behalf of one's kinsman. For when they stand apart from one another, the cord can be snapped; whereas the threefold cord is not quickly broken." Apparently, R. Samuel too had family ties to R. Jonah.

The issue of Provencal persecution of R. Samuel's kin seems now to recall an old grievance: "And who can remain silent at this time; and who can restrain himself in the face of a multitude of vexations; and who can hold back his words? For yesteryear, they persecuted our friends—and some of them were our brothers, our kinsmen—confounding them and destroying them, expropriating their money, wealth, possessions and might. And they released it to the gentiles, up to a thousand gold shekels, to the government which cries 'give, give.' "[90]

The persecution of which R. Samuel complains sounds unmistakably familiar. It was surely no everyday occurrence for Jewish circles in Provence to release exactly one thousand gold pieces belonging to a Barcelonan Jewish party to the latter's government. Yet this, we recall, was precisely the punishment decreed by the Provencal communities against the party of Samuel b. Benvenist. It is therefore reasonable to assume that this very decree—which had apparently been carried out—is the subject of R. Samuel's bitter complaint. The expropriation must have been a severe blow: two decades later the wounds still rankled. The structure of R. Samuel's complaint seems to be: "You've wronged us egregiously before and now you're doing it again." This assumes a certain continuity not only among the persecuted but also among the persecutors. And indeed, we recall that the signature of R. Samuel's addressee, R. Meshullam b. Moshe, appears on the Beziers decree against the party of Samuel b. Benvenist.

The letter of R. Samuel ha-Sardi demonstrates a direct link between the obscure anti-aristocratic rebels defeated about 1210 and the circle that finally succeeded in overthrowing the Barcelona aristocracy about 1240. For R. Samuel, a kinsman and staunch ally of Nahmanides and R. Jonah, was also "friend, brother and kinsman" to members of the party led by Samuel b. Benvenist. Closely knit and bound by family ties, this party apparently survived the setbacks handed it by the *nesi'im* early in the century and provided a nucleus for the successful revolt of the 1230s. Though the evidence to this effect must remain circumstantial, it can be safely assumed that R. Samuel ha-Sardi was a prominent leader of that revolt, alongside R. Jonah and Nahmanides. The victory achieved under their leadership marks the conclusion of an old struggle.[91]

Now that we know what eventually came of Samuel b. Benvenist's party, a second look at the sources on that mysterious figure seems in order. Samuel's reported conception of himself as a *marbiz Torah* seems quite consistent with what one would expect of a member of R. Samuel ha-Sardi's circle. What, though, is one to make of the charge that Samuel "blasphemed" Rashi? Perhaps Samuel b. Benvenist, in the heat of an agitated Talmudic disputation, had directed some disparaging remarks at a particular position of Rashi.[92] His enemies might then have seized upon these remarks in order to add the sin of "blaspheming" Rashi to the more obviously political counts on his indictment.

But what of the even stranger charge that Samuel b. Benvenist taught the superiority of the prophet Samuel to Moses? An intriguing, though admittedly conjectural, interpretation suggests itself. Twenty years later, men associated with Samuel's party would be accused, by the *nesi'im*, of dishonoring Maimonides. Can Samuel himself have been subject to this same accusation? It is tempting to interpret the charge against him figuratively. Using the standard Moses-Maimonides motif, it could be taken to mean that he, Samuel, had claimed himself superior to Maimonides. Such a charge would by no means be anachronistic about 1210. Already at the turn of the century, certain Spanish Talmudists are reported to have claimed themselves just as good as Maimonides. They were—consistently enough—roundly condemned by Sheshet Benveniste, the greatest of the Barcelona *nesi'im*.[93]

It may even be possible, carrying conjecture a step further, to locate within the original circle of Samuel b. Benvenist the man who later, during the Maimonidean Controversy of the 1230s, became known as the archcritic of Maimonides: R. Solomon b. Abraham of Montpellier. As is implied by his name, R. Solomon was a resident of Montpellier. Yet Nahmanides refers to him as "R. Solomon of Barcelona."[94] Barcelona would therefore seem to have been his place of origin. Writing to his Barcelonan friend, R. Samuel ha-Sardi, R. Solomon recalls "the days past when we delighted in your love and gloried in your distinction." Apparently, then, R. Solomon not only lived in Barcelona, but belonged to the circle of friends of R. Samuel ha-Sardi.[95] That circle, we recall, included the party of Samuel b. Benvenist. And so when we find among the seven members of Samuel b. Benvenist's party explicitly condemned by the Provencal communities one "R. Solomon b. Abraham,"[96] it seems reasonable to conjecture that he is none other than the future R. Solomon of Montpellier. It is even possible to speculate on the circumstances of R. Solomon's removal from Barcelona to Montpellier. For, we recall, that when last heard from, Samuel b. Benvenist was preparing to escape the wrath of the Barcelona *nesi'im* by fleeing to Montpellier. Perhaps some allies escaped with him; and it was thus that "R. Solomon of Barcelona" became "R. Solomon of Montpellier."

This reconstruction allows us to make some sense of a strange statement made toward the end of the thirteenth century by Hillel of Verona. Theological disagreement, Hillel claims, was not the real cause of the Maimonidean Controversy. It was rather because of enmity that had grown up between some of the scholars of Catalonia and Provence, that one group charged the other with heresy.[97] Hillel's reporting on the Maimonidean Controversy has, of late, come under suspicion of tendentiousness and inaccuracy.[98] And one hesitates, in any case, to entertain so reductionist a reading of an ostensibly religious controversy. Yet if our reconstruction is correct, there may be a "kernel of truth," or perhaps even more, to Hillel's claim. For it stands to reason that a background of bitter personal and social conflict between R. Solomon and members of the Provencal establishment would tend to exacerbate any religious controversy into which they entered. Such a background of conflict would help explain the uncommonly harsh tone in which R. Solomon's party is denounced by the Provencal communal fathers and the bitter relentlessness with which they were bent on securing its punishment.[99] R. Solomon's most prominent and determined antagonist during the Maimonidean Controversy was the famous grammarian-exegete, R. David Kimhi. It is perhaps not insignificant that Kimhi had, some two decades earlier, been among the first to sign the Provencal condemnation of the party of Samuel b. Benvenist.

In the midst of his Spanish crusade against R. Solomon's party (about 1232), Kimhi reported success in securing the support of all the Catalonian communities for the Provencal *herem*.[100] He doubtless had in mind the Catalonian communal leadership that *he* considered legitimate—that of the *nesi'im*. Like Sheshet Benveniste, thirty years earlier, the Barcelona *nesi'im* had little sympathy for critics of Maimonides—certainly not for critics of Maimonides led by an old enemy.

Kimhi was an old friend of one of the Barcelona *nesi'im*, the translator and poet, Abraham ibn Hisdai.[101] A circular addressed by Abraham and his brother, Judah, to the Jewish communities of Aragon and Castile has been preserved among the documents of the Maimonidean Controversy. It is, in some ways, typical of rationalist polemic in that controversy, rehearsing the sins of the Montpellier anti-rationalists, decrying the desecration of Maimonides' honor and demanding that it be avenged.[102] But the Ibn Hisdai brothers' letter seems later than the other documents of the controversy. The culprits, despite all their sins, are reported to be unrepentant "to this day."[103] Though outwardly whistling a different tune, they are wicked as ever. The *nesi'im* have "borne their reviling, behaving toward them like those who are insulted and insult not, hear and make no response."[104] It sounds as if they are suffering this insolence close at hand. And well they might. For although the *nesi'im* shared the determination of their Provencal allies that R. Solomon and his pupils find no refuge "in all the boundaries of Israel," at least some of them did find sanctuary—and in the very heart of Barcelona. Not surprisingly, they joined the opposition to the *nesi'im*. In a sense, they were merely rejoining an old struggle. And this time they emerged victorious.

The New Order and the Old

Triumph is rarely total. The resounding victory of the anti-aristocratic party concealed a quiet defeat. Though nowhere mourned or even mentioned it may be elicited from the sources. The letter of R. Samuel ha-Sardi to R. Meshullam b. Moshe was written at the height of the Maimonidean Controversy, before the final defeat of the *nesi'im*. R. Samuel, we recall, complains bitterly of the punitive expropriation, some twenty years earlier, of large sums of money from the party of Samuel b. Benvenist to the royal Aragonese treasury. His letter goes on to buttress complaint with legal argument. Although our text of the letter breaks off in the middle, the gist of R. Samuel's argument seems fairly clear:

> Yesteryear they persecuted our friends . . . confounding them . . . expropriating their wealth . . . And they released it to the gentiles . . . to the government . . . Now if they had expropriated it for children of the

exile of Ariel [i.e., Jews] as was the custom past in Israel, we could have justified them a bit. But [acting] in this manner, our rabbis have forbidden . . . and they prohibited it to Mar 'Uqba. And in truth it is clear and evident to all that the king whom they cause to ride over their head, should their property not suffice him . . . will hunt their very lives.[105]

The penalty imposed on the party of Samuel b. Benvenist is claimed to have been illegal despite the fact that it was decreed by recognized communal bodies, acting (in their opinion) to preserve justice. R. Samuel ha-Sardi bases his argument on the Talmudic case of the exilarch, Mar 'Uqba. The latter was forbidden to "hand over to the [Persian] government" for punishment, men who were persecuting him.[106] The conclusion drawn from this case in the Spanish halakic tradition is that "even in the face of affliction, it is forbidden to hand over a son of Israel to a gentile government—neither his person nor his property."[107] The inclusion of property in this prohibition was probably justified by an argument like that given by R. Samuel ha-Sardi: once the gentile government is given power over property, loss of life may ensue.[108]

The letter's last surviving sentence puts the issue in slightly different perspective: "Shall an expropriation of this sort be considered justice, which interposes strangers between us, though the Sages disapprove of [such behavior]?"[109] The appeal here is to the ideal of Jewish autonomy. Disputes within the community should be settled internally without inviting the intervention of "strangers," that is, non-Jewish governments.

Less than a decade later, R. Samuel's party achieved victory over the *nesi'im* by successfully appealing to the court of James I of Aragon. Though not without its irony, this ought not be viewed as a betrayal of principle. It was, after all, the regime of the *nesi'im* which maintained its power through the continued intervention of royal "strangers." R. Samuel's party sought only the king's "permission to break the bars of [their] yoke."

But once that permission was granted, royal involvement did not cease. The charter of 1241 gives the Barcelona community the right to levy fines *payable to the king's bailiff*. It thus institutionalizes much the kind of intervention of "strangers" which R. Samuel had found so distasteful. The imposition of this sort of price for the exercise of communal authority was part of an increasing royal involvement in the communal affairs of Spanish Jewry. R. Samuel ha-Sardi and his colleagues would probably have preferred it otherwise. They are not suspected of willingly abandoning "the custom past in Israel." In accepting communal autonomy on the only terms upon which it was available, they were bowing to reality; presumably with regret.[110]

But it is possible that R. Jonah Gerondi, at least, had become convinced that royal involvement need not necessarily lead to grievous injustice. In his occasional remarks on kings, he is surprisingly sanguine about their devotion to justice and truth. This conviction even justifies a forced interpretation of the famous Mishnaic warning (*Abot* 2:3) to beware of the [imperial] powers, who use men but know no loyalty: "The simple sense of this *mish-nah* would [seem to] speak to the discredit of kings. But Heaven forbid, Heaven forbid, this thing cannot be nor can it stand! For it is through them that the whole world is preserved. They execute judgment and justice. And there is no man on earth who can be as truthful as they. For being unafraid, they need not fawn upon people. And nothing prevents them from following a straight path."[111] This remarkable enthusiasm may stem, in part, from R. Jonah's own reassuring experince with royal justice.

The shift in power that took place in the Catalonian Jewish community during the first half of the thirteenth century corresponds to a shift in spiritual authority and cultural creativity. The newly dominant political group represented a newly ascendant religio-cultural trend. It may be in order to make some brief and very tentative comments on the relationship of the two rival "cultures."

They seem, on the surface, to be a study in contrasts. The *nesi'im* represent continuity with the political and cultural style of Muslim Spain, but no longer its glory. Their opponents are ablaze with creativity but of a sort that represents a turning away from the tradition of Muslim Spain. The *nesi'im* are aristocrats, courtiers, literate and rationalistic, worldly and perhaps not untouched by decadence. Their opponents are "new men," merchants, talmudists, and mystics, striving for spirituality and full of fresh energy.

But these antitheses require qualification. For one thing, the relationship of the new Catalonian leaders to the literary-philosophical heritage of Muslim Spain is not so simple. Nahmanides, their greatest representative, is a good example. Like many a prominent figure of the Muslim period, he supported himself as a physician.[112] Though no longer in touch with Arabic sources, Nahmanides' style reveals the cultivation of a Spanish gentleman. He was able to build upon the Spanish tradition of Biblical exegesis and advance it significantly.[113] Even his relationship to Spanish rationalism is complex. Nahmanides would hardly have gone as far as his older colleague, R. Azriel of Gerona, who could assert that, on an important point of kabbalah, "the words of the Torah and the words of the philosophers . . . are one . . . "[114] But the impact of the philosophical tradition is much in evidence in his work. And even when sharply critical of its solutions, he often shares its problems.[115] Nor was poetry, that most typical expression of Andalusian court culture beyond his ken. In fact, Nahmanides' circle included perhaps the most interesting Spanish poet of the post-Muslim period, Meshullam da Piera. Da Piera, standing in the old Andalusian tradition of the poet as public relations man, propagandizes brilliantly for the new Catalonian cultural ideal.[116]

It is, of course, the profound influence of Franco-German talmudic culture and Provencal kabbalah that set Nahmanides and his circle on a cultural course so different from that of the *nesi'im*. But it is the confluence of these northern traditions with the powerful and often divergent tradition of

Muslim Spain that helped maintain so remarkable a level of creative tension among the new leaders of Catalonian Jewry and determined the character of their cultural ideal.[117]

Medieval writers often attach the title *hasid* to the name of R. Jonah Gerondi.[118] This title might seem indicative of those new qualities of piety and spirituality, most foreign to the culture of the *nesi'im*, most indebted to northern influence. Interesting then that Al-Harizi should refer to the great *nasi*, Sheshet Benveniste, as "the foundation of all the saints" (*hasidim*).[119] Sheshet's "sainthood" was not purchased. His letter in defense of (what he considered) Maimonides' denial of physical resurrection combines uncompromising rationalism with an expression of deep spirituality. It is, in some ways, quite close to a spiritualistic mysticism.[120] Abraham ibn Hisdai, the only other *nasi* whose works survive, shows a similar bent.[121] Some of the *nesi'im* clearly shared their opponents' interest in the spiritual, contemplative life. This suggests a view of the philosophy of the former and the mysticism of the latter as different expressions of a common quest for spirituality. But it would seem that this spiritual impulse had been seriously corrupted among some or even most of the *nesi'im*.

It is hazardous to speculate on the causes of corruption. But the *nesi'im* were courtiers; and the courtier's career does seem less conducive than most to the spiritual life. Certainly this proved the case for many Jews at the courts of Christian Spain. R. Jonah Gerondi, despite his positive evaluation both of working and of kings, would discourage working for kings.[122] His warnings moreover have an immediacy that points to royal service as a ready option—and not only for aristocratic opponents. Even the devoted student of Torah is in need of providential protection from royal designs upon his talents and time.[123] In the political sphere, no less than the religious, the picture of diametric opposition between the *nesi'im* and their opponents needs to be qualified. That royal service was not restricted to the families of the *nesi'im* is evident in the court career of Nahmanides' son and some of the early activities of R. Solomon ibn Adret.[124] Nahmanides himself might have been a fine courtier. It was spiritual vocation rather than any cultural barrier that kept him and his talented colleagues from closer contact with the royal court. Suggestive, in this connection, is Nahmanides' comment on Genesis 45:10, in which Joseph, upon sending for his father to come to Egypt, informs him that he is to live in the nearby "land" of Goshen: "Joseph knew that his father would not want to stay in the land [here, in the sense of district] of Egypt which contains the royal capital and so he immediately sent to him that he would settle him in the land of Goshen."[125] The conception of Jacob is interesting. He wants to avoid the royal court, yet senses that he may be unable to resist its pull should he but reside in the capital district. Nahmanides lived in the small town of Gerona, about a day and a half north of the capital city of Barcelona. Did he think of Gerona as his Goshen?

The Barcelona *nesi'im* have, throughout this study, been referred to as an aristocracy and their opponents as an anti-aristocratic party. This terminology is accurate enough in a political-legal sense, at least as long as the *nesi'im* retained power. But its broader social and cultural connotations can be misleading. The "anti-aristocratic" party may have numbered some new men and been broader based than that of the *nesi'im*. But in terms of style, its leaders, men like R. Samuel ha-Sardi and R. Jonah Gerondi hardly seem plebeian. And Nahmanides is thoroughly courtly. Nor is he indifferent to lineage.[126] In fact, the regime led during the second half of the thirteenth century by R. Solomon ibn Adret, which we now know was founded by our "anti-aristocratic" party, has been characterized as "aristocratic!"[127] In some ways, our anti-aristocratic revolt seems more like a struggle between rival elite groups.

Both groups seem united by strong family ties. The cultural differences between them suggest the possibility that the families of the *nesi'im* originated in Muslim Spain while their opponents were of native Catalonian stock.[128] But there is really no evidence for this. There are, to the contrary, indications of extremely close ties between the *nesi'im* and the leading families of Provence. A prosopographical study of the parties to the struggle might be helpful.[129] Meanwhile, the precise nature of the family bonds that seem to have been so significant in defining the political and cultural alignments of the Jewish community in early thirteenth-century Catalonia must remain an unsettled question.

Preaching, Politics, and Power

To a degree rare among major medieval halakists, R. Jonah Gerondi displays a deep interest in the art and vocation of preaching. The term in his language, roughly equivalent to "preacher" is *"moki'ah"* (lit., reprover). According to R. Jonah, the extent of a man's love for the reproof of the *moki'ah* is the touchstone of his quality. "Whosoever's deeds exceed his wisdom, his wisdom will endure" (*Abot* 3:9); but how, asks R. Jonah, can deeds possibly exceed wisdom when knowledge is a prerequisite for right action? They can, he answers, if a man determines to follow faithfully the instruction of the *mokihim*. From that moment on he becomes transformed; and though instruction and actual observance are yet to come, it is as though he carried out every one of the commandments! But hatred of the preacher's *tokahah* doubles a man's sin and seals his doom.[130]

R. Jonah proposed the appointment of *mokihim* on a neighborhood basis in all Jewish communities.[131] Explaining in concrete terms how "wisdom cries aloud in the street" (Prov. 1:20), he even suggests that "the *mokihim* should speak in the streets of the city and the marketplace and in all places where people gather in order to make their words heard by the public."[132] R. Jonah's surviving ethical works can be seen as an extension, in written form, of his own oral work as a *moki'ah*.

R. Jonah apparently thought it the duty of a scholar to cultivate the preacher's art: " 'The tongue of the wise makes knowledge good (Prov.

15:2) . . . ' It does not suffice the wise that they make known the way of knowledge by saying: 'this is the way of knowledge; walk therein!' Their tongues [speech] rather beautify knowledge [by] uncovering great reasons and using glorious eloquence so that the knowledge will be acceptable to their listeners and the subject will be sweet on account of its uprightness."[133] Even in the course of a lecture on Talmud, R. Jonah could find occasion to comment on the importance of preaching with proper timing and a sense of the appropriate.[134]

What it was like to listen to one of R. Jonah's sermons, we cannot know. But there is evidence, scattered throughout his written work, that he was not without the rhetorical skill which he so valued: a neatly turned phrase, a stylistic flourish, a pithy proverb, a parable borrowed from the world of chivalry, a touch of humor; and, of course, there are R. Jonah's homiletical interpretations of the Bible.[135] These manage to edify and sparkle without being textually outlandish, reflecting the delicate skills of a preacher who seeks to exhort and expound without offending the well-honed philological sensibilities of an educated Spanish audience.

R. Jonah's preaching figured prominently in the conflict with the Barcelona nesi'im. A now lost letter to northern France, signed by twenty-one distinguished members of the anti-aristocratic party told "of the deed of those wicked men and their arrow sharp tongues who wrote an accusation against that great man, our master the rabbi, R. Jonah [claiming] that he was preaching reproachful sermons. Yet all the congregation of Israel knows . . . that he was preaching on the principles of repentance, fear and humility, the gates of purity and sanctity . . . "[136]

What could the nesi'im have found so reproachful about sermons on such seemingly unexceptionable topics? It is conceivable that their objection was theological, a kind of continuation of the Maimonidean Controversy: R. Jonah might have earned the reproach of the nesi'im by preaching anti-rationalism and aggadic literalism. But R. Jonah's written tokahah provides scant support for this explanation. Anti-rationalism is hardly its central preoccupation.[137] Nor is his preaching style of the sort calculated to offend rationalistic sensibilities. R. Jonah's homiletical sins were more likely political than theological. For in the midst of his writings on repentance, fear, humility, purity, and sanctity are ideas that could easily have served as an ideology of the anti-aristocratic revolt in Barcelona. R. Jonah's homiletical skills, then, were probably a potent weapon in the battle against the nesi'im.

Some rousing sermons could have been constructed from the material in R. Jonah's Gates of Repentance on the subject of zaddiqim (the righteous) and resha'im (the wicked). R. Jonah knew full well that these two groups are not always so clearly defined, so easily distinguishable from the merely middling.[138] And yet he generally writes of the zaddiqim and resha'im as if they are readily identifiable. R. Jonah's reader needs guidance on the proper relationship to zaddiquim and resha'im; but it is presumably clear who belongs to each of these groups. This sort of binary opposition, where one would ordinarily expect complexity and blur, often points to a polarized situation in which the opposing sides are clearly defined.

The *zaddiqim*, in R. Jonah's works, are usually locked in struggle for power and influence with the *resha'im*. Praise of the *resha'im* is a serious offense, for a man shows, thereby, his true colors. " 'The crucible is for silver and the furnace for gold, but a man is tested by his praise' (Prov. 27:21). *This means that a man's worth is in accordance with what he praises.* If he praises good deeds, scholars and the *zaddiqim*, know that he is a good man . . . And though he may have hidden sins, still he is among the lovers of righteousness . . . But one who praises improper deeds or lauds *resha'im*, is himself a complete *rasha'* and one who desecrates God's worship."[139] R. Jonah includes under the sin of flattery (*hanufah*) anything less than total commitment to the battle against the *resha'im*. Neutrality, passivity, fence sitting, even prudent restraint are condemned as a kind of complicity.[140]

Pious scruple ought not cripple the *zaddiq* tactically in his struggle against the *resha'im*. Exhort though R. Jonah may against anger, "the evil tongue," separating oneself from the community, and contention, these vices become virtues in the battle against the *resha'im*, a battle in whose cause R. Jonah does not shrink from demanding the ultimate sacrifice:

Our rabbis of blessed memory said: "Whoever persists in contention violates a negative commandment; for it is said: 'And let him not be like Korah and his company (Num. 16:40)' " . . . [But] he who fails to persist in contention against . . . sinners is himself punished for all their sins; and *he* violates a negative commandment; for it is said: "And you shall not bear sin because of him (Lev. 19:17)" . . . And it is said: "You shall not be afraid of the face of any man (Deut. 1:17)." Anyone who belongs to God, will offer his life for the sanctification of the Name; for it is said: "Who is the Lord's? Let him come to me (Exod. 32:26)." And it is said: "When Pinehas saw . . . he took a spear in his hand (Num. 25:7)." It is the obligation of every fearer and certainly [every] lover [of God] of pure heart to rouse up his jealousy when he sees the hand of princes and nobles at transgression; for it is written: "And the hand of the princes and the nobles were foremost in this transgression (Ezra 9:12)."[141]

The concluding emphasis of these lines reflects the real context of R. Jonah's preaching: the *"resha'im"* with whom he had to contend were "princes and nobles." The prooftext from the Book of Ezra alludes to what, for Spanish moralists, would become one of the chief crimes of the Jewish courtier: consorting with gentile women. The example of Pinehas was particularly powerful in this context: his zealous sword avenged precisely this sin by piercing the belly of an offending *nasi*.[142] No wonder R. Jonah's sermons were unpopular among the Barcelona aristocracy.

The struggle of the *zaddiqim* against the *resha'im* is, R. Jonah makes clear, at least in part, a political one. He denounces the arrogant and power-hungry *resha'im* who lord it over the community.[143] Instead of seeking to set fear of God in their hearts, they seek to cast fear of themselves upon God's people. "The ruler of men [ought rather to be] a *zaddiq* who rules in fear of God" (II Sam. 33:3).[144] R. Jonah counts among the "enemies of God" "men who begrudge the honor of scholars who are upright and righteous (*zaddiqim*) and hate the crown of their glory, or whose hearts grieve should they achieve rulership over the generation. And so it is written: 'for it is not you whom they have despised, it is rather me that they have despised from reigning over them' (I Sam. 8:7). How much more so if they seek to shame and lower their honor and if they love the honor of the *resha'im* and their dominion over the earth. For these are indeed enemies of God."[145] Peaceful sharing of power between *zaddiqim* and *resha'im* is, for R. Jonah, impossible. "The honor of the *zaddiqim* can prosper only after the honor of [the *resha'im*] is brought low."[146] It is probably in this light that R. Jonah viewed and projected the conflict in Barcelona. For him, the revolt against the *nesi'im* was no less than a sacred struggle to overthrow the rule of *resha'im* and to secure for the *zaddiqim* "rulership over the generation."

It is one thing for pietists to dream of power. Actually attaining it is an entirely different matter. The most remarkable thing about R. Jonah's vision is that it seems, at least in part, to have triumphed. R. Jonah's writing provides a glimpse not only of the spiritual force and rhetorical skills with which he waged his successful struggle. It reveals also the ideal of a *zaddiq* whom piety has not disarmed of the more mundane weapons of political combat.

Although R. Jonah's primary concern as a *moki'ah* is the cultivation of observance and spirituality, his human ideal is far from a passionless, unworldly ascetic. R. Jonah recognizes the positive function of pleasure.[147] Wasting even a penny and weakening the body, he considers sinful.[148] Careful planning and good counsel should precede placing one's trust in Providence.[149] People err, R. Jonah claims, in thinking the righteous innocent of the ways of the *resha'im*. They confuse righteousness with simplicity. In fact the *zaddiq* is most sophisticated in the wiles and worldly ways of the wicked.[150] Though arrogance is despicable, maintaining one's dignity (*silsul*) is, according to R. Jonah, a proper and acceptable way.[151] The prohibition against bearing a grudge does not apply to the target of "arrogant, contemptuous speech and maliciousness."[152] Anger is important when one has been wronged: "Don't be too sweet or they'll eat you up."[153] And, of course, humility and piety are not to stand in the way of the struggle against evil. One may serve God with his evil inclination by pressing it into battle against the *resha'im*.[154]

The pragmatic streak in R. Jonah's ethical preaching is especially pronounced in the economic sphere. R. Jonah often argues the virtues of hard honest work. The *zaddiq* and the slothful, he points out, are juxtaposed as opposites in Proverbs 21:25-26.[155] And although R. Jonah can hardly be accused of urging a single-minded pursuit of riches and luxury, he can, at times, speak quite positively about wealth and its acquisition: " 'He who is slack in his work is a brother to him who destroys (Prov. 18:9).' [This verse] comes to reprove the lazy man who is slack in his work, that he not say that there is punishment only for being slack in others' work, but if he is slack in his own work there is no sin therein. It, therefore, says concerning this: 'he is a brother to one who destroys.' For one who destroys his own money is considered a sinner . . . And one who is slack in his work and loses [potential] profits, and brings about the loss of much good is a brother to him who destroys . . ."[156] R. Jonah can even surprise us with sound advice on the profitable management of business affairs: " 'The thoughts of the diligent lead surely to profit (Prov. 21:5).' Quickness is not part of the rule of diligence and industry. Rather the *thoughts* of the diligent—that one put thought and deliberation before action—*this* is of the essence of diligence. And even though one has lost some of his hours on planning, he will always find profit in this method."[157]

No one more than the scholar would need R. Jonah's advice on how to increase efficiency through intelligent planning. For the scholar, according to R. Jonah, while devoting the lion's share of his time to Torah, ought still to seek dignified sustenance from some secular occupation. This noble but tricky ideal, he enthusiastically adopted from Maimonides.[158] R. Jonah frequently urges upon his scholarly reader the importance of economic self-sufficiency as insurance both of his personal spirituality and of his independence.[159] He was particularly sensitive to the latter: "Destitution and poverty are a disgrace to a man; for they bring him to speak entreaties and to lower himself before men and to flatter them. And fear of men and fawning are a defect of the soul; dependence upon men is a disgrace."[160] Not that wealth is without moral pitfalls. But the righteous will seek wealth for the sake of Heaven and use it to noble purpose.[161]

But doesn't full devotion to scholarship preclude meaningful economic activity? Apparently not, according to R. Jonah. Far from impeding economic activity, the pursuit of wisdom can itself contribute to the acquisition of wealth:

> "By wisdom a house is built (Prov. 24:3)." Because [the author of Proverbs] has [just] warned [in the previous two verses] that one ought not be jealous of the wealth of the *resha'im* and their tranquility nor crave their association in order to make money, he now says that if one occupies himself with wisdom, understanding and knowledge he will achieve, *from them*, tranquility and wealth, besides the future and the hope that the soul achieves through them . . . "By knowledge the chambers are filled with all precious and pleasant riches (Prov. 24:4)." For knowledge includes the ways of men's thoughts . . . Therefore the man of knowledge will perceive the methods of [earning] profits and the path of prosperity and will gain in many matters. And his chambers will be filled with all precious and pleasant riches, silver and gold, perfume and spices, coral and crystal and a multitude of rubies.[162]

This picture of the prosperous merchant-scholar was no figment of an overwrought imagination. It could easily have been modeled on some of R.

Jonah's own wealthy companions in the Barcelona struggle. It might even have been autobiographical.

We have no facts and figures on R. Jonah's economic situation—nothing comparable, say, to the documents concerning the very substantial estate left by his colleague, R. Samuel ha-Sardi.[163] But a poem written in R. Jonah's honor, by Meshullam da Piera, is, in its own way, even more informative. For in the course of its verses of praise, R. Jonah's wealth is not only attested, it is defended:

> There's a grace to property. And the man without wealth, though he be wise, won't be thought clever.
> But should the sage have its grace, he'll not be called "fool," so long as his sun rise and shine.
> Captious critics pervert the truth [in attacking you for pursuit of wealth] . . .
> Don't respond to [their] contention. Set a fixed time for your work and watch over your [business] affairs
> Without sloth, and [then] await God's mercies, and your path will prosper.
> Fools say: "So they say: 'a sated soul and a halting heart.' "
> [But] how, O my lord, could you be satisfied with little, when yours is a hand that yearns always to open?

R. Jonah's picture of the scholar whose pursuit of wisdom produces good business sense as a by-product was apparently also something of a self-portrait. For Da Piera declares in passing, "On business affairs, your advice is always sought." [164]

It would seem, then, that R. Jonah practiced what he preached in the economic sphere, and successfully so—to the point that certain critics found such worldly occupation and wealth unseemly. Were these critics purists, who thought R. Jonah's spirituality compromised? Or were they perhaps opponents who preferred their pietists powerless?

R. Jonah and his colleagues would not likely have defeated the *nesi'im* had they been religious functionaries salaried by the aristocratic regime or scholarly clients patronized by its leaders. Independent economic power played an important role in their victory. And it seems likely that R. Jonah realized this full well. He had a healthy understanding of the fact that wealth serves as an instrument of influence and power and a conviction that it would be for the best if scholars could keep that instrument firmly in grasp: "Wealth is the crown of the wise. For 'the poor man's wisdom is despised and his words are not heard (Ecc. 9:16).' But the wise, when they prosper in wealth and honor, their arms become mighty to show love to the *zaddiqim* and to arouse fear and worship of God in the world and to lower the *resha'im* and [their] flatterers and to raise up the head of Truth."[165]

But it would be caricature to portray R. Jonah as an economic determinist. He believed that a man should work rationally and realistically toward the realization of his goals and then put his trust in the mercies of Heaven.

Providence has the final say.[166] Though probably aware of the economic factors that contributed to his party's victory in its battle against the *nesi'im*, R. Jonah doubtless viewed the outcome of that long and difficult struggle as a triumph, not of wealth or power, but of virtue: " 'Like a muddied fountain, a dirtied spring is the *zaddiq* who falls before a *rasha'* (Prov. 25:26)' . . . For just as when a man muddies a spring with his feet it turns turbid temporarily and afterwards the waters settle and are clear as before, so the *zaddiq*, when he falls before a *rasha'*, is not lowered thereby. And though he be troubled temporarily, 'seven times the *zaddiq* falls and yet will rise up again (Prov. 24:16)' and return to his power and glory."[167]

NOTES

1. *Tahkemoni*, ed. Y. Toporofsky (Tel Aviv, 1952), p. 346. For another glimpse of the Barcelona aristocracy (toward the end of the twelfth century), see Joseph ibn Zabarah, *Sefer Sha'ashu'im*, ed. I. Davidson (Berlin, 1925), pp. 7, 15 f., 35, 145 f.

2. See A. Neubauer, ed., "Ergänzungen und Verbesserungen zu Abba Maris Minhat Qena'ot," *Israelietische Letterbode*, IV (1878-79), 165. The nature and significance of these documents is discussed below.

3. *Tahkemoni*, p. 346.

4. "Shirim u-Miktabim mi-Rabbi Meir ha-Levi Abulafia," ed. H. Brody, *Yedi'ot ha-Makon le-Heqer ha-Shirah ha-'Ibrit*, II (1936), 63. The appraisal is particularly interesting in that its author, Meir ha-Levi Abulafia, did not see eye to eye with Sheshet on matters theological. See, e.g., Y. Baer, *A History of the Jews in Christian Spain* (Philadelphia, 1961), I, 100. I hope to discuss this matter in full in a forthcoming monograph on Abulafia.

5. See H. Graetz, *Dibre Yeme Yisrael* (Warsaw, 1897), IV, 408 f.; F. Baer, *Die Juden im christlichen Spanien* (Berlin, 1929), I, 34 f.; Y. Baer, *History*, I, 100.

6. For the only treatment of this rebellion to date, see Baer, *History*, I, 94 f., 398, note 43. Note that Ibn Zabarah's *Sefer Sha'ashu'im*, dedicated to Sheshet Benveniste, contains a satiric attack on an unidentified person—presumably no friend of Sheshet; see Davidson's introduction, pp. 12-14, 16-20. But he was apparently not a resident of Barcelona. It seems doubtful therefore that he can be connected with the anti-aristocratic revolt that broke out after Sheshet's death.

7. *Tahkemoni*, pp. 346-439. Most of the literary sources on Sheshet Benveniste were collected by Graetz (above, note 5). M. Steinschneider took exception to the claim that all these sources refer to the same Sheshet; see *Hebraeische Bibliographie*, XIII (1873), 106-110. On the basis of archival material, Baer (*Christlichen Spanien*, I, 34 f.) showed Graetz correct. Yet it would seem that there *was* another, less famous contemporary Spanish *nasi* Sheshet: the father of Makir; see *IL*, IV, 168. Al-Harizi mentions Makir and Sheshet Benveniste in the same breath without hinting at any relationship between them, whereas Sheshet's nephew, R. Isaac Benveniste, is identified as such. Moreover, it would seem that Sheshet Benveniste lost his last son about 1195; see D. Kaufmann, "Lettres de Scheschet b. Isaac de Saragosse aux Princes de Narbonne," *REJ*, XXXIX (1899), 224 f. See too, D. Baneth, "R. Yehudah Alharizi ve-Shalshelet ha-Targumim shel Ma'amar Tehiyyat ha-Metim,"

Tarbiz, XI (1939), 269. One wonders about the absence from our sources on the rebellion of any mention of Sheshet's powerful nephew, R. Isaac Benveniste; see on him, S. Grayzel, *The Church and the Jews in the Thirteenth Century* (New York, 1966), pp. 63-65; *Tahkemoni*, p. 346.

8. See *IL*, IV, 165.

9. Ibid.

10. See, e.g., the respectable real-estate transactions of R. Samuel b. Isaac b. Hayyim (see on him, below) in J. Millàs i Vallicrosa, *Documents Hebraics de Jueus Catalans* (Barcelona, 1927), nos. 10-11.

11. See below and *IL*, IV, 165.

12. *IL*, IV, 162-168. The later collection, *Minhat Qen'ot*, ed. by R. Abba Mari of Lunel, deals with the controversy over rationalism in Provence in the first years of the fourteenth century; see Baer, *History*, I, 289 ff.

13. See Baer, *History*, I, 100; Sheshet's letter was published by Marx, *JQR*, XXV (1935), 414-428.

14. See Isaac b. Abba Mari, *Sefer ha-'Ittur*, ed. Meir Yonah (Jerusalem, 1970), I, 3.

15. See *JQR*, XXV, 426 f.

16. *IL*, IV, 162-164.

17. Ibid., 162. "Benvenist" was the given name of Samuel's father and should not be confused with the surname, "Benvenist(e)," of the *nasi*, Sheshet (b. Isaac). It is quite unlikely that the two were related. Sheshet's nephew, whose father's given name happened also to be Benvenist, signs his name, to avoid confusion: Isaac bar Benvenist ben Benvenist. See "Shirim u-Miktabim mi-Rabbi Meir ha-Levi Abulafia," no. 23, p. 49.

18. *IL*, IV, 162; *halilah lanu la'asot perush le-perusho ulehagid et shenishma' mipiv beferush*. See *Baba Batra*, 52a and *Sanhedrin*, 7:5. The latter allusion picks up the charge of "blasphemy."

It may be noted, in passing, that Makir's letter is perhaps the earliest Spanish document to reflect the image of Rashi as a towering figure "without whom Torah would have been forgotten from Israel." Cf. Abraham ibn Daud, *Sefer ha-Qab-balah*, ed. G. Cohen (Philadelphia, 1967), pp. 88 f. In his brief note on French scholarship, Ibn Daud doesn't even mention Rashi, though he has heard of his grandson, R. Tam. The omission is made good in an early gloss to *Sefer ha-Qabbalah*; see A. Neubauer, ed., *Medieval Jewish Chronicles* (Oxford, 1887), I, 82-84. But this gloss is more likely Provencal than Spanish.

19. *IL*, IV, 163. For this practice, see *Bet Yosef, Hoshen Mishpat*, 28:1.

20. *IL*, IV, 162.

21. It violates the seventh of Maimonides' thirteen principles; see *Mishnah 'im Payrush R. Moshe b. Maimon*, ed. Y. Qapah (Jerusalem, 1965), IV, 212 f., 217.

22. Makir alludes to the midrashic observation that, in Psalm 99:6, "Samuel . . . is balanced against Moses and Aaron (*Nu. Rabba*, 18:8)"; cf. the sources collected by L. Ginzberg, *Legends of the Jews* (Philadelphia, 1956), VI, 228 f. But drawing doctrinal conclusions from this source would have been exceedingly strange in the thirteenth century. Baer in his *Toledot ha-Yehudim be-Sefarad ha-Nozrit* (Tel Aviv, 1959), p. 483, note 43, suggests the possibility of Christian influence but does not explain. The suggestion is omitted in the English version (*History*, I, 398, note 43).

23. *IL*, IV, 162. Todros may have been an uncle of Makir; see Millàs i Valli-

crosa, *Documents*, no. 13. For precedure in being called to the Torah, see *Gittin*, 60a. It is not entirely clear whether the last expression, *v-lebazbez lo makom nikbad lo zakv lo abotav ve-abot abotav*, represents a new charge or merely explains the significance of the first. But use of the term *le-bazbez* here, suggests the latter; see Tosefta *Megillah*, 3:21 (Lieberman ed., p. 359) quoted by Alfasi, *Megillah*, 14a (no. 1136).

24. *IL*, IV, 163; cf. *Megillah*, 28a; *lo za'adti lifne mi shegadol mimeni*.

25. *IL*, IV, 163. Among the other misdeeds of the rebels: attempting structural changes in the synagogue without permission; disrespectful behavior during the burial and mourning period of the late *nasi*, R. Todros—including perhaps the earliest reference to *"'ikkub tefillah"* in Spain; (for another instance, in Barcelona, about a half century later, see S. Assaf, *Sifran shel Rishonim* [Jerusalem, 1935], p. 53). The rebels also declared unfit a *Sefer Torah* donated by the late *nasi*, R. She'altiel (*IL*, IV, 165).

26. See, e.g., J. O'Callaghan, *A History of Medieval Spain* (Ithaca, 1975), pp. 195, 218, 249-253.

27. *IL*, IV, 163.

28. Ibid., pp. 164 f.

29. Ibid., p. 167. See: on Levi b. Moshe, H. Gross, *Gallia Judaica* (Paris, 1897), p. 407; on Meshullam b. Moshe, I. Ta-Shema, "Meshullam b. Moses," *Encyclopaedia Judaica* (Jerusalem, 1972), XI, 1402 f.; on Kimhi, F. Talmage, *David Kimhi: The Man and the Commentaries* (Cambridge, Mass., 1975). Their role in this controversy has gone unnoted with the exception of Kimhi whose participation is mentioned by Baer, *History*, I, 398, note 43. "The scholar R. David b. Joseph" who heard a partial confession from Samuel b. Benvenist, together with "the scholar R. Isaac b. Solomon" (*IL*, IV, 64), is probably not Kimhi but a member of the Barcelona *bet din*; see Millàs i Vallicrosa, *Documents*, no. 10, where he appears together with his colleague, R. Isaac b. Solomon and Nahmanides' teacher, R. Judah b. Yakar. His signature appears on other Barcelona documents as early as 1181; see, e.g., ibid., nos. 9, 13; J. Miret y Sans and M. Schwab, "Documents sur les Juifs catalans," *REJ*, LXVIII (1914), 78. For reasons unknown, there was no separate communication from the major Provencal community of Narbonne on the Samuel Benvenist affair. Levi b. Moses and Kimhi, both of Narbonne, sign at the head of the elders of Lunel.

30. For this expression, see *Yerushalmi Sanhedrin*, 28c; *Pesiqta de-Rav Kahana*, ed. B. Mandelbaum (New York, 1962), II, 365; *Lam. Rabba, petihta 9*. But here its sense is clearly an assertion of aristocratic inequality.

31. See Kaufmann, "Lettres de Scheschet," pp. 62-75, 217-225.

32. Several facts point to this possibility. In a document from Barcelona dated 1200, Bonadona, now the wife of the Narbonne *nasi*, Levi b. Moshe, sells property in Barcelona acquired from the estate of her late husband, the *nadib*, R. Solomon b. Isaac; see Millàs i Vallicrosa, *Documents*, no. 5; cf. too nos. 4, 8. "Nadib" was a standard title for members of the Barcelona aristocracy, apparently second in rank to *nasi*. See below, note 55. The same two titles are used by the Provencal aristocracy; see, e.g., Kaufmann, "Lettres de Scheschet," p. 71, where Sheshet Benveniste diplomatically attempts to get the Narbonne *nasi*, R. Kalonymos b. Todros, to accept the apology of a man who forced the *hazan* to call him up to the Torah with the title *"nadib"* against Kalonymos' wishes. Sheshet, at least formally, seems to accept the authority of the Narbonne *nesi'im*. It is interesting that the names of some of the Barcelona *nesi'im*—Makir, Todros, Kalonymos—recur often among the

Provencal *nesi'im*; see Gross, *Gallia Judaica*, pp. 406-408. Kaufmann even suggested that Sheshet Benveniste was originally from Narbonne; see "Lettres de Scheshet," p. 63. Baer disagrees; see *Christlichen Spanien*, I, 35. But the possibility that Sheshet's family was at one time in Narbonne is far from disproved.

33. *IL*, IV, 165 f. Cf. Baer, *Christlichen Spanien*, I, 37 f.

34. *IL*, IV, 167.

35. Ibid., pp. 167 f. Baer writes that Samuel b. Benvenist made a successful escape to Provence (*History*, I, 398, note 43). The sources, however, attest only to his plans, not their success.

36. See the author's "Communal Struggle in Barcelona during the Maimonidean Controversy" (Hebrew), *Tarbiz*, XLII (1973), 389-400, upon which this section draws. (In the concluding line of that study, p. 397, the words *bittuy b* should be deleted.)

37. See on them: A. Shrock, *R. Jonah ben Abraham of Gerona* (London, 1948); C. Chavel, *R. Moshe b. Nahman* (Jerusalem, 1967). Independent evidence places R. Jonah in Barcelona during this period; see *Tarbiz*, XLII, 390 f. Nahmanides, as far as we know, was living in Gerona. It is quite possible, however, that the authority of the Barcelona *nesi'im* extended to surrounding communities. Nahmanides certainly speaks as if he had been under their rule; see below and *Tarbiz*, XLII, 389.

R. Jonah died in Toledo in 1263. The date of his transfer from Barcelona to Toledo is unclear; but it would seem that his Barcelona career was a long one; see Shrock, *R. Jonah ben Abraham*, pp. 49f., 63ff. R. Solomon ibn Adret considered R. Jonah rather than Nahmanides his principal teacher (ibid., pp. 43 f.) probably because he studied with the latter only during occasional trips from Barcelona to Gerona. Another student of R. Jonah, R. Solomon b. 'Eli of Soria, occasionally mentions Nahmanides as his teacher; see Chavel, *R. Moshe b. Nahman*, pp. 69 f. Thus he too probably studied with R. Jonah in Barcelona. Likewise, R. Aaron b. Joseph ha-Levi (see Shrock, *R. Jonah ben Abraham*, p. 46) probably studied with R. Jonah in Barcelona. Nahmanides' famous responsum to R. Jonah on concubinage was, according to Baer (*History*, I, 436, note 14), sent to Toledo. But its concluding lines include the wish: *u-kebodeka yigdal me'al ligebul 'arzenu* (*Teshubot ha-Ramban*, ed. C. Chavel [Jerusalem, 1975], p. 163). "*Arzenu*" would seem to refer to Catalonia; see B. Dinur, *Yisrael ba-Golah*, vol. II, bk. 3 (Tel Aviv, 1968), p. 258. Cf., e.g., Isaac Israeli, *Yesod 'Olam* (Berlin, 1845), 4:18, p. 35: *ba me'ir Barcelona le-Toledo . . . ve-shav le-arzo*. It is likely therefore that Nahmanides' responsum was sent from Gerona to Barcelona.

38. For a good up-to-date study of the Maimonidean Controversy, see A. Schochat, "Berurim be-Farashat ha-Pulmus ha-Rishon 'al Sifre ha-Rambam," *Zion*, XXXVI (1971), 27-60.

39. See B. Benedict, "Le-Toledotav shel Merkaz ha-Torah be-Provence," *Tarbiz*, XXII (1951), 85-109; I. Twersky, "Aspects of the Social and Cultural History of Provencal Jewry," *Journal of World History*, XI (1968), 185-207.

40. See J. Schatzmiller, "Le-Temunat ha-Mahloqet ha-Rishonah 'al Kitve ha-Rambam," *Zion*, XXXIV (1969), 140.

41. See *Tarbiz*, XLII, 389-397.

42. Published ibid., pp. 397-400.

43. Ibid., p. 398.

44. Ibid., p. 399.

45. For this motif, see the poems collected by M. Steinschneider, "Moreh Meqom ha-Moreh," *Qobez 'al Yad*, I (1885), 1-32.

46. R. Jonah was apparently the emissary who brought the Provencal anti-rationalist case before the French; see Shochat, "Berurim," pp. 30 f. The object of this attack could conceivably be R. Solomon of Montpellier himself; but there is no independent evidence placing him in Barcelona after the Maimonidean Controversy.

47. *Tarbiz*, XLII, 399.

48. See G. Scholem, *Ursprung und Anfänge der Kabbala* (Berlin, 1962), pp. 349-358. This becomes a standard complaint against kabbalists; see, e.g., Isaac b. Sheshet, *She'elot u-Teshubot*, no. 157. For the centrality of *kavvanah* to the correct *sefirah* in Nahmanides' circle, see "Shire Meshullam da Piera," ed. H. Brody, *Yedi'ot ha-Makon le-Heqer ha-Shirah ha-'Ibrit*, IV (1938), 109, line 30.

49. R. Jonah Gerondi, *Sha'are Teshubah* (New York, 1949), 3:139; see too *Perushe R. Yonah 'al Maseket Abot*, ed. M. Kasher and Y. Blochrovitz (Jerusalem, 1966), p. 46.

50. See *Tarbiz*, XLII, 390-392.

51. See ibid., pp. 390-392, 399 f.

52. See, e.g., *Perush Abot*, p. 94; *Sha'are Teshubah*, 3:112; *Perush 'al Mishle*, ed. A. Lowenthal (Berlin, 1910), 12:8.

53. *Sha'are Teshubah*, 3:208. The concluding allusion to Mishnah, *Sanhedrin*, 10:1, presumes an interpretation of *"epiqoros"* as "one who dishonors scholars"; see *Sanhedrin*, 99b.

54. S. Z. Halberstam, ed., "Milhemet ha-Dat," *Jeschurun*, VIII (1872-75), 120f. "The poet, R. Isaac Kastion" is unknown from other sources. On R. Jonah b. Joseph, see Chavel, *R. Moshe b. Nahman*, pp. 66 f.

55. *Jeschurun*, VIII, 121, 123 f. On the titles *"nasi"* and *"nadib,"* see above, note 32. See too Ibn Zabarah, *Sefer Sha'ashu'im*, p. 15, line 14.

56. *Jeschurun*, VIII, 122 f.

57. Ibid., p. 122. See Maimonides, *Mishneh Torah, Melakim*, 1:7. Another somewhat more colorful response to the claims of the *nesi'im* may be preserved in the following couplet:

> If after his fathers every fool
> Is called prince and first in command,
>
> Then prince I'll be calling my mule
> Since Hamor his father was prince of the land.

(Translated with small liberties from Steinschneider, ed., "Moreh Meqom ha-Moreh," pp. 1, 23); see Genesis 34:2. The target of this poem is generally taken to be Judah Alfakar; see ibid. It is more likely directed at the claims to legitimate succession made by the Barcelona *nesi'im*. Its author, R. Isaac b. Zerahiah, is probably the Gerona *payyetan* of that name who was also referred to by Meshullam da Piera as his teacher; see H. Schirmann, *Ha-Shirah ha-'Ibrit be-Sefarad uve-Provence* (Jerusalem, 1961), II, 281; "Shire Meshullam da Piera," ed. Brody, pp. 5, 15. The poet is possibly hurling back at the *nesi'im* the "mule symbolism" of their own propaganda; see *Tarbiz*, XLII, 391-394.

58. *Jeschurun*, VIII, 123f. Cf. R. Jonah, *Perush Abot*, p. 47, on how to behave toward the king's bailif (*gizbar*).

59. *Jeschurun*, VIII, 121.

60. Ibid. Nahmanides may have requested that he be adjured "in the name of the God of Israel"; see Mishnah, *Sanhedrin*, 7:6. On the titles *"nasi"* and *"nadib,"* see above, note 32.

61. *Jeschurun*, VIII, 124.

62. Ibid., pp. 121 f.

63. Baer, *Christlichen Spanien*, I, 96 f.

64. For consciousness of prosperity among this group, see Nahmanides, *Commentary on the Torah* to Deut. 28:42. Nahmanides' remarks may have been influenced by Bahya ibn Paquda; see *Hobot ha-Lebabot*, ed. Y. Kapah (Jerusalem, 1973), 2:5, p. 121. But they no doubt reflect Nahmanides' own appraisal of contemporary economic realities. See too R. Jonah's *Iggeret ha-Teshubah* (Bene Braq, 1968), p. 70, where it is assumed, as a matter of course, that the reader's wife has a Muslim servant at her disposal; see further, below.

65. *Tarbiz*, XLII, 398.

66. See below.

67. See *Jeschurun*, VIII, 121.

68. See Baer, *History*, I, 281 ff.

69. *Jeschurun*, VIII, 98-120. Cf. Baer, *History*, I, 399, note 48.

70. *Jeschurun*, VIII, 98-101.

71. See *Tarbiz*, XLII, 394, note 34.

72. See Chavel, *R. Moshe b. Nahman*, pp. 51 f.

73. Via R. Jacob b. Asher's *Tur Hoshen Mishpat*.

74. See S. Assaf, *Sifran shel Rishonim* (Jerusalem, 1935), pp. 53-55.

75. *Jeschurun*, VIII, 99.

76. Ibid., 98: *Tofes ha-ketab asher shalah ha-hakam ha-gadol R. Shlomo bar Abraham z"l ve-he'etiq talmido R. David bar Sha'ul z"l leha-Ramban 'al ha-mahloqet asher benam u-ben hakme Bedershi.* "z"l" here is quite possibly the work of the copyist; cf. ibid., p. 103, where it follows the name of Nahmanides but not R. Jonah although the latter died earlier.

77. Ibid., p. 101. See Schochat, "Berurim," pp. 38 f.

78. *Jeschurun*, VIII, 102.

79. See Chavel, *R. Moshe b. Nahman*, pp. 51 f.

80. *Jeschurun*, VIII, 102 f. I retract, on the basis of this reconstruction, my assertion (*Tarbiz*, XLII, 395, note 34) that R. Solomon's respondent could easily be R. Samuel ha-Sardi.

81. *Jeschurun*, VIII, 103.

82. *Jeschurun*, VIII, 105.

83. Ibid.

84. Ibid.

85. Ibid., p. 119.

86. R. Jonah, it would seem from Nahmanides' letter, had not yet returned to Catalonia.

87. This reconstruction is not new; it was briefly suggested by S. Z. Halberstam in *Jeschurun*, VIII, 104, note 4. But because it is important for our conclusions and has not been generally adopted, it has been argued here at some length.

88. Ibid., p. 113.

89. Ibid., p. 114. R. Meshullam was not, himself, one of R. Jonah's slanderers; see *Tarbiz*, XLII, 392, note 21.

90. *Jeschurun*, VIII, 115. For the last expression, see *Abodah Zarah*, 17a, and Rashi, *ad. loc.*

91. J. Schatzmiller (*Mehkarim le-Zeker Zvi Avineri* [Tel Aviv, 1970], p. 130, note 5), who conjectured, in passing, that the pro-aristocratic propaganda letter discussed earlier pertains to the revolt of Samuel b. Benvenist, was, thus, much closer to the truth than I was able to acknowledge in *Tarbiz*, XLII, 389.

92. See, e.g., Nahmanides, *Commentary on the Torah*, Genesis 6:3; Leviticus, 19:16. Less temperate members of this circle, not committing their remarks to writing, could, no doubt, be much sharper.

93. *JQR*, XXV, 426 f. See *IL*, IV, 162, for the full text of Makir's charge against Samuel. According to the interpretation proposed here, the (in this context) enigmatic clause having Samuel as its subject, *kam leh be-derabah mineh*, should be translated: "he rose up against one greater than himself." In claiming that this offense shows Samuel "worse than any *epiqoros* or *min*," Makir may have had in mind the definition of *epiqoros* as one who is irreverent to a scholar; see note 53. Still, Makir's reference to *Nu. Rabba*, 18:8 and Jeremiah 15:1 as Samuel's sources is hard to understand if the charge is not to be taken literally. See too Nahmanides, *Commentary on the Torah*, *Num.* 12:16, who warns that one should not take the aggadic balancing of Samuel against Moses literally. Could he have been aware of someone who did? In any case Sameul b. Benvenist was accused of teaching not the equality but the superiority of Samuel to Moses. Note that this charge of Makir is the only one not mentioned in the response from Lunel. Perhaps they too were not quite sure what it meant.

94. *Qovez Teshubot ha-Rambam ve-'Iggerotav*, ed. A. Lichtenberg (Leipzig, 1859), III, 10d; see Schochat, "Berurim," p. 39.

95. *Jeschurun*, VIII, 99; Schochat, "Berurim," p. 39. Nahmanides too refers to R. Solomon as *haveri*; see *Qovez*, III, 10d.

96. *IL*, IV, 166.

97. *Qovez*, III, 14a.

98. See Baer, *History*, I, 401 f.

99. Cf. Schochat, "Berurim," p. 55. In Hillel's pro-rationalist version it is only the anti-rationalists who act unreasonably.

100. *Qovez*, III, 1c.

101. Talmage, *David Kimhi*, p. 31.

102. *Jeschurun*, VIII, 48-56. Reflecting their still strong Provencal connections, the *nesi'im* also rebuke their Spanish brethren for insufficient concern at the plight of the communities of Provence "who have . . . now, for many days, been given over to violent peoples" (ibid., pp. 52 f.). The allusion is probably to the Albigensian Crusade and its impact on Provencal Jewry. Why this complaint is relevant to the main topic of the Ibn Hisdai brothers' letter is unclear. Apparently they felt that Spanish failure to support the *herem* against R. Solomon's party was a betrayal of the Provencal communal leadership and continue, by association, to rebuke a second injustice to the communities of Provence; see too their reference to "our fathers, the elders of Provence" (ibid., p. 49). Interesting, that in fragments of an allegorical *maqamah* into which Ibn Hisdai introduces the figure of Maimonides, the latter is given the title "*nasi*"; see Schirmann, *Ha-Shirah ha-'Ibrit*, II, 238.

103. Ibid., p. 51.

104. Ibid., p. 54.

105. Ibid., p. 115.

106. *Gittin*, 7a.

107. Alfasi, *Baba Qamma*, 43b (no. 222); see too *Mishneh Torah, Hobel u-Mazziq*, 8:9.

108. See *Baba Qamma*, 117a; Elijah of Vilna, *Hoshen Mishpat*, 388, gloss 58.

109. *Jeschurun*, VIII, 115.

110. Cf. H. H. Ben-Sasson, *Peraqim be-Toledot ha-Yehudim bi-me ha-Benay-yim* (Tel Aviv, 1969), p. 123, contrasting Spanish and Ashkenazic practice on the question of involving non-Jewish governments in communal affairs.

111. *Perush Abot*, p. 22; see too *Perush Mishle*, 16:10, 19:2; *Sha'are Teshubah*, 3:167. Cf. Y. H. Yerushalmi, *The Lisbon Massacre of 1506 and the Royal Image in the Shebet Yehudah* (Cincinnati, 1976).

112. Chavel, *R. Moshe b. Nahman*, p. 36.

113. See, e.g., M. Segal, *Parshanut ha-Miqra* (Jerusalem, 1952), pp. 96-102.

114. *Perush ha-Aggadot*, ed. I. Tishby (Jerusalem, 1945), p. 83.

115. A study of this topic is an important *desideratum*; see for the present S. Krauss, "Ha-Yihus ha-Madda'i ben ha-Ramban veha-Rambam," *Ha-Goren*, V (1905), 78-114.

116. See H. Schirmann, *Ha-Shirah ha-'Ibrit be-Sefarad uve-Provence*, II, 295 ff., 319 ff.

117. An integrated cultural history of thirteenth-century Catalonian Jewry seems, unfortunately, far off. In fact, the remarkable burst of achievement in Nahmanides' circle has, *as an overall phenomenon*, scarcely been noticed. On the question of R. Jonah's relationship to kabbalah, see Scholem, *Ursprung und Anfänge*, p. 347. See too *Perush Mishle*, 2:5: "*veyitbonen . . . be-ma'aseh merkabah*." Since R. Jonah clearly didn't consider philosophy *ma'aseh merkabah*, kabbalah is the sole remaining candidate. Cf. too *Perush Mishle*, 15:11: "*ki ha-nefesh ne'ezelet min ha-kabod*." The philosophers' *kabod nibra* is not, to my knowledge, described as a source of the soul. *Kabod* is probably used here as *shekina* in the kabbalistic sense. But see *Perush Abot*, p. 50, for what seem to be serious reservations about the attainability of *debekut* and proposal of an alternative ideal: *lo lehitrahek ve-lo lehit-kareb ve-hakol lefi rov ha-ma'aseh*; cf. too the apparently incomplete discussion in *Perush Mishle*, 2:5. The entire question requires separate treatment.

118. See Chavel, *R. Moshe b. Nahman*, p. 57; B. Dinur, *Yisrael ba-Golah*, vol. II, bk. 3, pp. 251 f.

119. *Tahkemoni*, 346. See too Ibn Zabarah, *Sefer Sha'ashu'im*, pp. 145 ff.

120. See Scholem, *Ursprung und Anfänge der Kabbala*, p. 358.

121. See S. M. Stern, "Ibn Hasday's Neoplatonist," *Oriens*, XIII (1961), 58-120; cf. too Ibn Hisdai's introduction to his translation of the pesudo-Aristotelian *Sefer ha-Tappuah* (published with Ibn Gabirol's *Tiqqun Middot ha-Nefesh* [Jerusalem, 1967]), p. 1. It is possible that Ibn Hisdai's translation of Maimonides' *Sefer ha-Miz-vot* was the occasion for Nahmanides' composition of his *Hassagot*; see M. Stein-schneider, *Die hebraeischen Uebersetzungen des Mittelalters* (Berlin, 1893), II, 927; cf. however Ch. Heller, ed., *Sefer ha-Mizvot* (Jerusalem, 1946), pp. 7 f. On the possible relationship of Ibn Hisdai and Meshullam da Piera see Brody, "Shire Meshul-lam da Piera," p. 4.

122. See below and *Perush Abot*, p. 12.

123. Ibid., pp. 41 f.

124. See C. Chavel, ed., *Kitve R. Moshe b. Nahman* (Jerusalem, 1963), I, 369-371; Baer, *History*, I, 439 f. Nahmanides' letter to his son at the Castilian court shows him concerned lest his son fall into precisely those sins for which he had condemned the *nesi'im*. Obviously neither group had a monopoly on vice or virtue. Cf. too Baer, *History*, I, 102 f. Baer suggests that one of Nahmanides' poems may be

taken as a "personal confession" of youthful pursuit of the enjoyments typical of contemporary southern European urban society. (The conjecture of the original Hebrew [*Toledot*, p. 60] has become an assertion in the English translation.) This poem (*Kitve ha-Ramban*, I, 397-402), written in honor of R. Jonah, does make some strikingly strong statements about the temptations of youth. But one must exercise caution in drawing far-reaching biographical conclusions from general poetic pronouncements. There is, in any case, no question here of a conversion (on the style of St. Francis). The volume, brilliance, and maturity of what Nahmanides had written by his late twenties indicates that youthful flings were at most quite occasional and probably quite prudent. See Assaf, *Sifran shel Rishonim*, pp. 54 f.; Chavel, *R. Moshe b. Nahman*, pp. 30 ff., 102 f.

125. *Commentary on the Torah*, Genesis, 45:10.

126. See *Jeschurun*, VIII, 103-124, *passim*. Baer (*History*, I, 102) describes Nahmanides as "the scion of an aristocratic family of Gerona"; on his family, see Chavel, *R. Moshe b. Nahman*, pp. 27-30.

127. And not without some justice. See Baer, *History*, I, 281-283. But talk about the artistocracy as if it were a single coherent class, when no such coherence exists, can be misleading. See, e.g., H. H. Ben-Sasson, *A History of the Jewish People* (Cambridge, 1976), pp. 498f.; Baer, *History*, I, 225.

128. See Baer, *History*, I, 90ff.

129. Such a study might also shed light on the important question of what eventually happened to the families of the *nesi'im:* were they kept completely from communal authority? Or did they eventually integrate themselves into the new power structure? See, e.g., the reference to R. Aaron La-Levi, Ibn Adret's colleague and critic, as being "*mi-zera' nesi'im*" in Isaac, *Yesod 'Olam*, 4:18, p. 35. After this paper went to press I discovered (from Bodleian ms. 2237.7, 253a and passim) that Solomon ibn Adret married into the family that was at the forefront of the struggle against the *nesi'im*.

130. *Sha'are Teshubah*, 2:10-11; *Perush Abot*, pp. 44f.; cf. too *Perush Mishle*, 12:1, 15:17. My colleague, Sid Leiman, calls attention to a usage of moki'ah similar to that of R. Jonah in *Mishneh Torah, Teshubah*, 4:2. See too Al-Harizi, *Tahkemoni*, p. 37.

131. *Sha'are Teshubah*, 3:73. But here, R. Jonah may have had in mind individual reproof more than public preaching; cf. Baer, *History*, I, 251f.

132. *Perush Mishle*, 1:20.

133. *Perush Mishle*, 15:12.

134. See *Talmide R. Yonah* to Alfasi, *Berakot*, 21b, *s.v. ha-qore pasuq*.

135. For some samples of R. Jonah's rhetoric, see, e.g., *Perush Abot*, pp. 4 (*s.v. ve-'al ha-'abodah*), 26 (*s.v. marbeh nekasim*), 77 (5:3), 88 (top); *Sha'are Teshubah*, 3:71 and below.

136. See *Tarbiz*, XLIII, 391, note 19.

137. See Shrock, *R. Jonah of Gerona*, pp. 57f. The oft-quoted warning against *hokmot hizoniot* in *Perush Mishle*, 1:8, is atypical. The entire question requires separate treatment.

138. See, e.g., *Sha'are Teshubah*, 2:9. Suggestions on how to recognize a *rasha'* were contained in a now lost section of R. Jonah's work; see ibid., 3:190.

139. Ibid., 3:148.

140. See ibid., 3:187-199.

141. Ibid., 3:58-59; see too 3:219; *Perush Abot*, p. 23; *Perush Mishle*, 24:28. On

the demand that one risk his life in battle against the *resha'im*, see too *Sha'are Teshubah*, 3:188; but cf. 3:199.

142. See Num. 25:14.

143. *Sha'are Teshubah*, 3:162-167.

144. Ibid., 3:164.

145. Ibid., 3:160.

146. Ibid., 3:152. But the downfall of the *resha'im* ought not to be the occasion for rejoicing; see *Perush Abot*, pp. 70f.; cf. too ibid., p. 51.

147. *Perush Mishle*, 19:10.

148. *Sha'are Teshubah*, 3:82.

149. *Perush Mishle*, 16:20.

150. Ibid., 21:12; *Perush Abot*, p. 9.

151. *Perush Mishle*, 12:9.

152. *Sha'are Teshubah*, 3:38.

153. *Perush Abot*, p. 88, quoting Ibn Gabirol's *Mibhar ha-Peninim*.

154. *Talmide R. Jonah, Alfasi Berakot*, 44b (*s.v. be-kol*).

155. *Perush Mishle*, 21:25.

156. *Perush Mishle*, 18:9; see too ibid., 12:9; *Perush Abot*, pp. 11f.

157. *Perush Mishle*, 21:5.

158. *Perush ha-Mishnayot, Abot*, 4:5; *Mishneh Torah, Talmud Torah*, 3:10-11. I hope, in a forthcoming study, to trace the history of this ideal in medieval Spain.

159. *Perush Abot*, pp. 20f., 41f., 62f.

160. *Perush Mishle*, 18:23.

161. Ibid., 10:5.

162. Ibid., 24:3.

163. Millàs i Vallicrosa, *Documents*, nos. 17-22.

164. "Shire Meshullam da Piera," pp. 24f.

165. *Perush Mishle*, 14:24 and 11:11.

166. Ibid., 16:20; cf. this and the previous passage to the lines quoted above from Meshullam da Piera.

167. *Sha'are Teshubah*, 3:149. The centrality, for R. Jonah, of the struggle between *zaddiqim* and *resha'im*, may explain his consistent use of the term "*zaddiq*" rather than "*hasid*;" see Y. Tishby, *Mishnat ha-Zohar*, II (Jerusalem, 1961), 657, note 12.

10

Joseph ibn Kaspi
Portrait of a Medieval Jewish Intellectual

Isadore Twersky

The Study of ibn Kaspi

This paper might well be entitled Joseph ibn Kaspi *redivivus*—resurrected and revisited—for throughout modern times this prolific Provencal writer (1280-1340) was a relatively obscure figure.[1] His name was mentioned in standard works and histories accompanied by encyclopedia-like blurbs, bibliographical summations, or stereotype characterizations—varying in length from a few lines to a few pages.[2] His reputation—fame or notoriety —was nurtured by direct knowledge only of his ethical will, published in 1844 (ed. E. Ashkenazi), an indisputably important document of intellectual history, and his twin commentaries on the *Moreh Nebukim*, published in 1848 (ed. S. Werbluner and D. Kircheim), very significant chapters in the story of Maimonidean exegesis and the dissemination of philosophic views and values.[3] His own descriptive bibliography, *Kebuzat Kesef*, listing about 30 works, was also published by I. Benjacob in 1844 and the existence of many of these works in manuscript was noted. Passivity, however, reigned supreme and no serious attempt was made to push back the frontiers of Kaspi study. It was primarily the achievement of a dedicated English paleo-grapher, Isaac Last, who at the fin de siècle began to publish many of these manuscripts, that made the study of Kaspi possible once again. Yet, the scholarly yield is still meager and Kaspi's works, recently reprinted, are still to a great extent forlorn, unexamined and unmonographed, while many are still unpublished. One thinks of two pioneering articles by W. Bacher (1912),[4] a noteworthy little German dissertation (1930),[5] a penetrating He-brew essay by S. Pines.[6] He thus remains a fetching figure, with a deter-mination still to be made as to how original, influential, or interesting; even if careful analysis shall sustain the impression of mediocrity, he may still re-main historically important and instructive, for, as has been noted else-where, articulate, aggressive mediocrities may surpass great "classical" thinkers in their significance for intellectual history and their writings may be more protean and influential.[7] We have here incidentally a paradigm for the slow process of scholarly absorption of new material into the main-stream of monographic analysis and textbook synthesis.[8]

Let me add immediately that, in referring to the fact of Kaspi's relative obscurity, I purposely emphasized "in modern times" in order to dissipate the notion of censorship, of any conspiracy of silence or premeditated concealment of his works. It would appear that for several centuries at least he was known and studied—quoted, criticized, or supported. He elicited strong feelings of approval or censure, never an attitude of indifference or nonchalance. On the crucial issue of Talmud study, for example, he is mercilessly indicted by R. Joseph Jabez, the forceful sixteenth-century antagonist of philosophic culture in the *Or ha-Hayyim*, and enthusiastically commended by that colorful Renaissance figure Leo de Modena in the *Behinat ha-Kabbalah*.[9] This vertical relationship is, in itself, of obvious historical significance. It tells us not only about Kaspi's *Nachleben* and the representative, typological value of his works; the search for pedigree by later (in this case, sixteenth-century) writers reveals much about the self-consciousness of a period vis-à-vis the phenomenon of continuity and change and the concomitant justification or repudiation of change or the attempt to root apparently novel attitudes in certain precedents.[10] In any event, only in premodern and modern times do his writings, along with those of many Provencal contemporaries like R. Menahem ha-Me'iri, Yedaya ha-Penini, Moses Narboni, Kalonymos b. Kalonymos and Gersonides, fall into oblivion and the manuscripts are left to collect dust in libraries.

From a formal-material point of view, that is, the approach used by a cataloguer or bibliographer, Kaspi should be characterized and classified as an exegete, with a special yen for logical-philological interpretation, for his works are primarily exegetical. There is some "pure" philosophy, for example, an epitome of Samuel ben Judah of Marseilles' Hebrew translation of Averroes' *Middle Commentary*,[11] but the center of gravity is Biblical exegesis. Moreover, self-consciousness as an exegete suffuses his literary creativity and, while an author's self-evaluation may not be precise and need not be normative for the historian, it is always significant per se. Kaspi never tired (his readers may become weary) of underscoring the ardor of his aspirations and the originality of his achievements in exegesis; he was totally obsessed with the importance of his method and its value as a precision instrument that would enable sensitive students to interpret Scripture correctly, that would accelerate the progress of speculative thought and rational understanding. He insisted that he would not repeat or summarize, would not write postscripts or hackneyed ideas but would regularly aim to focus on novel insights; it is almost as if he were responding to the charge-challenge of his contemporary R. Yedaya ha-Penini, who asserted that only poets are creative and truly original while thinkers are only able to collect and repeat old, classical ideas. The eclectic, repetitive philosopher is contrasted with the innovative, inspired poet.[12] In any event, this simple bibliographical fact has compounded the difficulties of scholarly analysis, for exegetical writings are particularly knotty, frequently recalcitrant, sometimes repetitious, sometimes inconsistent (ranging from apparent or outright contradiction to subtle divergences of emphasis), and the attempt to systematize non-systematic writings, to extrapolate rigorously structured concepts from soft, pliable molds, is problematic. Kaspi may be said to dramatize the scope and intensity of rational exegesis and to illustrate the attendant difficulties of systematization and conceptualization on the part of students. Even his *Sefer ha-Sod*, an avowedly systematic classification of the principles of exegesis, that is, a brief methodological prologue to his exegetical oeuvre, which especially stressed the freedom of interpretation given to an exegete, is rife with problems of this kind.[13]

However, from a substantive-typological point of view, he should be characterized as a "Maimonidean," as an energetic zealous intellectual, a broker of rationalistic ideas and ideals rather than as a Bible commentator or grammarian: exegesis was the vehicle for his philosophic activity. Joseph ibn Kaspi belonged to that group I have described elsewhere as "sensitive, remarkably industrious, versatile, deeply committed writers eager to disseminate and vindicate philosophy, to prove that it was not an upstart discipline alien to religious concerns. They defended the cause of philosophy with elegance and persuasiveness, sometimes with a touch of lyricism, always with passion."[14] Specifically, he saw himself as a protagonist of Aristotelian rationalism, as a continuator of the school of R. Abraham ibn Ezra and Maimonides, the two great original influential authors of Spanish Jewry that were linked together, either for praise or criticism, by many fourteenth-century writers (for example, Ritba, R. Shem Tob, Joseph ibn Wakar). It is not only that he wrote supercommentaries on the *Perush* of ibn Ezra and the *Moreh* of Maimonides, but their writings are the pivots of his entire enterprise. Their influence is pervasive, their stimulus profound. Even when he departs from their specific views—and he deliberately underscores his freedom—his indebtedness to them is regularly and meaningfully acknowledged; moreover, the indebtedness is discernible even when not openly admitted. Kaspi is thus a major contributor to the so-called "fourteenth-century ibn Ezra Renaissance,"[15] in which the writings of ibn Ezra were carefully studied and commentaries and supercommentaries composed; he is also a sturdy prop in the spread of Maimonideanism. In short, Kaspi, together with other post-Maimonidean philosophers or devotees of philosophy (Samuel and Moses ibn Tibbon, Jacob Anatoli, Zerahiah b. Shealtiel Hen, Hillel of Verona, Moses Salerno, Yedaya ha-Penini of the thirteenth or early fourteenth century come to mind as do Joseph b. Shem Tob or Abraham Bibago of the fifteenth century), accepts the philosophic (Maimonidean) interpretation of Judaism, its ethos and its logos, as an Archimedean point; Maimonidean positions may be criticized, modified, or extended but they are axial, and essentially paradigmatic.

Seen from this vantage point, the study of Kaspi is, in my opinion, most appropriately located in the discipline of history of ideas rather than history of philosophy (or, for that matter, even history of exegesis). It is not only that he is not in the class of his predecessor, who serves as a paradigm for him, R. Moses Maimonides, or his contemporary, whom he apparently did not know, R. Levi Gersonides, but the real value of his works is to be found in the attitudes he formulates and postures he adopts. We must understand what intellectual-spiritual problems concern him and what positions typify him, what influences molded him and what aspirations propelled him, what was the nature of the intellectual revolution he wanted to strengthen and perpetuate. It is, of course, possible to add Kaspi footnotes to the history of philosophy concerning most of the major problems and themes that preoccupied medieval Jewish philosophers: faith and reason, prophecy, creation of the world, causality and natural law, miracles, free will, providence, ethical theory, rationalization of the halakah, and similar problems or details thereof. The results would most likely be a pale florilegium of views.[16]

What seems to be most worthwhile and enlightening is a reconstruction and appraisal of his attitude toward central, abiding issues in Jewish cultural life and intellectual history, issues concerning which there was room for considerable latitude, variation or selective identification with prototypal patterns. He may be seen, in other words, as a typical intellectual—and thus analysis of his works may help us construct a phenomenology of medieval Jewish intellectualism—without necessarily blurring his individual inclinations or emphases. Use of a historical phenomenology must be clear and flexible, so as to identify standard typological features as well as individual divergences and whims—accentuation or attenuation of recurrent tendencies. This flexibility bridges the gap between intellectual history, which might become ensnared in Zeitgeist theories and exaggerated sociologizing, presumptions of excessive homogeneity or uniqueness of periods, and history of ideas, which uncovers continuity, identity, or similarity of basic attitudes and intellectual postures in various periods. The vertical and horizontal dimensions of historical analysis need to be balanced. The following topics are illustrative examples, not an exhaustive enumeration, and each one could be analyzed at length, put in historic context and its ramifications outlined: (1) attitude to Talmud study, examination of its presumed centrality, and the whole complex of the relation of Talmud study to other areas as formal curricular subjects (Bible, grammar, philosophy, kabbalah, history); (2) approach to aggadah, that is, continuation of the quest for an exegetical methodology which, by disciplined allegorical interpretation, would present aggadah as a treasure trove of philosophic ideas and, at the very least, eliminate difficulties or embarrassments; (3) the literal and unliteral in Scriptural interpretation; (4) the role of language study, the nature of grammar and the proper methods for its study (involving criticism, sometimes quite strident, of ibn Janah and R. David Kimhi and marked differences with Rashi) and the whole issue of language and logic; (5) the (declining) role and status of poetry; (6) relationship of the beliefs of intellectuals and those of the masses—the whole crucial issue of elitism, esotericism together with the progressive enlightenment of the philosophically naive and untutored; (7) the quest for spirituality and the dangers of antinomism and a double-barreled polemic (contra Christian indictments as well as material for internal debate) concerning Judaism as a religion of spirituality; (8) the question of originality and innovation in medieval writing, particularly the insistence upon freedom of interpretation; (9) rabbinic leadership of the community and its socio-intellectual critics, with special emphasis upon criticism for intellectual-spiritual shortcomings; (10) the sporadic intensification of historical thought in medieval Jewish writing and its various uses and applications (for example, for purposes of causal explanation, specifically the recognition of intermediate causes in the historical process) concern with a philosophy of history, and the role of messianism; (11) openness to non-Jewish culture, particularly Judeo-Arabic philosophy and Christian scholasticism with particular attention to the quantitative aspect (how much use and influence) as well as the axiological (what were its repercussions, if any, with regard to attitudes, tolerance, relativism or skepticism); (12) anti-Christian polemics, particularly the significant shift from formal disputations to literary (historical-theological) attacks on the foundations of Christianity. Full analysis of these issues would help provide a "character study" (to use the phrase of A. R. Hall, *The Scientific Revolution*) of the intellectual revolution which Kaspi and his colleagues supported —not a scholastic analysis of philosophic problems and not even an intellectual profile of one significant protagonist but a sensitive, repercussive study in the history of ideas and their origin and impact.

Literary Oeuvre and Ideology

A few observations about his milieu and some generalizations about his literary achievement will provide a suitable background against which to present a brief exposition of two of the issues listed above: his exegetical methods, particularly a special kind of literalism, historicism and naturalism in Bible study; his attitude to Talmud study. Kaspi was the child of a dedicated philosophic movement, tested through many turbulent years, with a record of advance and regression, influence and frustration. The prolonged and heated controversy concerning the legitimacy of philosophy, culminating in the 1305 promulgation of the ban against its study and a counter-proclamation denouncing the advocates of this ban, was fresh in his memory. He may have been one of the anonymous, zealous, not too influential supporters of the philosophic party. We know that some of his townsmen, scholars of Argentière, took part in the controversy and aligned themselves with the anti-philosophic camp of Rashba.[17] The turbulence was apparently a stimulant for Kaspi, not an irritant or a deterrent. Kaspi's commitment and his determination to advance the cause of philosophy were most likely deepened, not diminished. His confidence in rationalism was pure and simple, his enthusiasm for the application of logic and philosophy to religious tradition was unabated; his goal was to prove that the victory of the Maimonidean antagonists was pyrrhic, because, like Maimonides, he considered an unphilosophical religion illegitimate, a historical and phenomenological aberration. He displayed an intransigent attitude to unphilosophical culture, insisting that there was no alternative, no room for compromise. One uses and pursues reason not as an expression of hubris, in the sense of "aggrandisement of man against God," but as a fulfillment of a religious commandment, as an attempt to ally human reason with divine norm, to bring man closer to God via knowledge. Inasmuch as philosophy was an indispensable component of Judaism, he would rather risk being accused of imprudence and impudence in elaborating philosophic insights than of insincerity or inconsistency in concealing them.[18]

Furthermore, the usual evolutionary view, which we sometimes use unreflectively, almost dogmatically, and which, therefore, can be quite arbitrary, is clearly not applicable here. Kaspi wrote intensely and intensively over the course of a few decades; his writings are steady and consistent, with salient, easily identifiable leitmotifs, characterized by uniformity of goal and immutability of method.[19] His life is characterized by intellectual restlessness but ideological steadfastness, a variety of media but consistency of vision.

This leads one to emphasize the paradox, at first glance rather strange but really quite natural, which surrounds the activity of Kaspi (and many of his contemporaries). He is an intellectual, acutely aware of the gap, sometimes widening into a complete breach, between the insights and rationalizations of philosophers vis-à-vis beliefs and assumptions of the masses (often described as foolish, dormant, unfortunate, poor in knowledge), but nevertheless he seeks relentlessly, if not to bridge the gap, at least to win adherents, to spread philosophic enlightenment and raise the level of philosophic sophistication, and this with the zeal and verve of a proselytizer. There is, needless to say, an inevitable residuum of esotericism and tension consisting, on one hand, of ritualistic assertions that not everything may be told, that there are interpretations which must not be disseminated, that in fact he does "not wish to reveal all the secrets," and on the other, that, inasmuch as full congruence between the philosophers and the masses will not be forthcoming, one should not be deterred from the truth by mass criticism or disagreement, but basically the movement is from shyness and restraint and elitism to articulateness and boldness and democratization.[20] This dialectic is, of course, not limited to philosophy; it is also typical of kabbalah, which emerges from the shadows of a tight, almost impenetrable, esotericism to the center stage of an energetic movement attempting to popularize and proselytize. Any religious-intellectual movement which possesses special insight must eventually propagate it and become public or else it faces the serious charge of egotism; if one does not make it possible for others to benefit from his achievement, he is guilty of withholding the good from him to whom it is due and of destroying important, hard-won knowledge. As Maimonides put it in the introduction to part 3 (another apology for publicizing his philosophical positions) of the *Moreh Nebukim*: "If I had omitted setting down something of that which has appeared to me as clear, so that that knowledge would perish when I perish, as is inevitable, I should have considered that conduct as extremely cowardly with regard to you and everyone who is perplexed. It would have been, as it were, robbing one who deserves the truth of the truth, or begrudging an heir his inheritance."[21] It is not for the philosopher to sit in solitary dissatisfaction, lamenting the lowly state of true learning and the prevalence of error. He must skillfully share his insights, gradually dispel error and elevate the state of philosophic knowledge. In any event, this exoteric thrust, nurtured by a medley of motives, in turn exposes the protagonists to the charge of breaching a necessary, consensual esotericism, of indiscriminate dissemination of secret teachings. In the case of Kaspi, we find this at the core of Kalonymos b. Kalonymos' indictment of him: even if everything Kaspi taught was true and unimpeachable—and Kalonymos clearly does not think that this is the case—he should still be faulted for lack of discretion, because philosophic popularization, which substitutes provocative interpretations for bland restatements of comfortable propositions, could loosen the fabric of traditional beliefs and erode the institutions of the religious community.[22] Nevertheless, the intellectual, in various degrees, has the temerity to attack features of popular religion and hence blur objects on which the popular religious consciousness focuses. He risks the danger that the unsophisticated may miss the import and impact of his philosophic interpretations and fall into total confusion, but an inner compulsion drives him onward.[23] In sum, the antithetical tendencies cannot really be united nor can the pressures be eased.

Almost a corollary of this situation is the high degree of self-consciousness in his writing, not merely with regard to exegesis, the frequency of first person references, confessional obiter dicta concerning method, motive and goal, and direct address to the reader. His ethical will is, in essence, a kind of spiritual-intellectual autobiography, a genuine *apologia pro vita sua* belonging, *mutatis mutandis*, to the genre of Plato's Seventh Letter, Avicenna's *Autobiography*, or Peter Abelard's *Historia*. It emerges as a vigorous summary of his approach to law, religion and philosophy, alerting us (through his son) not to succumb to the pressures and distortions of the opposition. Maimonides' immunity to *genut he-hamon* (the contempt which the masses feel toward the elite) reverberates, while the desire to benefit every reader in accord with his capacity is also a driving force. In many respects, it resembles, and, I would suggest, was greatly influenced by Maimonides' *Ma'amar Tehiyyat ha-Metim*, which is concerned with the central, expansive issues of religious phenomenology and axiology rather than the clearly circumscribed problem of corporeal resurrection and is thus a defense of his life's work. It is a vigorous restatement and defense of his standard, life-long approach to issues of law, religion, and metaphysics, alerting the reader to the fact that the opposition to his view in this case is not an isolated matter but is symptomatic of divergent, perhaps irreconcilable, religious conceptions. Kaspi's will, which gives us a clear vignette of a fighting intellectual, is similarly a distillation of his views and a vindication of his life's work, reflecting intellectual skirmishes with adversaries or efforts at protecting philosophic positions which must never be abandoned, for they are the bastions of traditional, rationalistic Judaism. A prominent component of this apologia is the emphasis upon his own consistency as well as originality. The heavy, obvious self-consciousness of the will is characteristic of his entire corpus.[24] We may picture him, in sum, as a crusty, probably intractable, self-confident and self-conscious, indefatigable author.

Bible Exegesis: Literalism and Historicism

Perhaps the most salient feature in Kaspi's approach to Bible interpretation is the far-reaching, relentless quest for literalism. To be sure, no exegete is ever a complete literalist and least of all a philosophically oriented exegete for whom the use of allegory is axiomatic and compelling. Yet there is dialectical divergence in both the quantitative as well as qualitative relationship between philosophic literalism and philosophic nonliteralism. Most assume that a measure of nonliteralism is mandatory; the differentiation concerns the extent and reasons for its use, and the differences may be quite substantive. While Kaspi's exegesis has its share of allegory, what is novel and striking is the way he is uniformly and stressfully critical of nonliteral interpretations. He goes so far as to suggest that, in the absence of clear hermeneutical canons or tight textual-philological restraints, they lead to anarchy, to intellectual laissez-faire. Interpretation which is not guided by context and grammar, by *higgayon*, must inevitably be wobbly; interpretation which fails to project the Biblical text against its linguistic, geographic, and sociohistorical background, thereby according primacy to natural or grammatical explanations, must fall wide of the mark.[25] These are the parameters of literalism within which the exegete should move. We may add briefly that this literalism, in addition to the emphasis on some exegetical relativism, also contains a measure of "exegetical agnosticism": certain things may not be known because we have no analogies, no similar experience, no corroborating evidence. Inasmuch as the exegete is committed to rigid canons of literalist interpretation, he must be careful not to foist unintended meanings upon the text. Kaspi shows extraordinary sensitivity to the exegesis-eisegesis syndrome and this results in restraint or readiness to withdraw and be silent.

We must be more specific and note that his extensive literalism is really a two-tiered construction. The use of grammar and logic, which adds some precision and rigor, of philology in the broadest sense of the term, all of which has precedents and sequels,[26] is only the first phase; this in turn culminates in a novel, intriguing exegetical dimension, highly suggestive and very repercussive, which deserves careful description and evaluation. Kaspi frequently operates with the following exegetical premise: not every Scriptural statement is true in the absolute sense. A statement may be purposely erroneous, reflecting an erroneous view of the masses. We are not dealing merely with an unsophisticated or unrationalized view, but an intention-ally, patently false view espoused by the masses and enshrined in Scripture. The view or statement need not be allegorized, merely recognized for what it is. Where did such a radical hermeneutic originate? How could Kaspi vali-date such an unusual methodological construct?

The key factor is Kaspi's use of the well-known rabbinic dictum: *dibrah Torah bileshon bene adam*, "The Torah speaks in the language of men," famous for its medieval use in the realm of anthropomorphism. Actually, in its original context, this statement, a cardinal rule of the school of R. Ish-mael, applies to a wide range of grammatical-lexical-interpretive issues but never to anthropomorphism.[27] Maimonides, foreshadowed by R. Judah ibn Koreish, R. Nissim Gaon, R. Abraham ibn Ezra,[28] is responsible for con-verting this dictum into the basis and rallying point for all anti-anthropo-morphic interpretations.

> You know their dictum that refers in inclusive fashion to all the kinds of interpretation connected with this subject, namely their saying: "The Torah speaks in the language of the sons of man." The meaning of this is that everything that all men are capable of understanding and repre-senting to themselves at first thought has been ascribed to Him as nec-essarily belonging to God, may He be exalted. Hence attributes indicat-ing corporeality have been predicated to Him in order to indicate that He, may He be exalted, exists, inasmuch as the multitude cannot at first conceive of any existence save that of a body alone . . . In a similar way one has ascribed to Him . . . everything that in our opinion is a perfec-tion in order to indicate that He is perfect in every manner of perfection and that no deficiency whatever mars Him. Thus none of the things apprehended by the multitude as a deficiency or a privation are pre-dicated of Him.[29]

As Maimonides continues to establish the foundations for his theory of attributes, he parenthetically defines *leshon bene adam*: "However, in accordance with the language of the sons of man, *I mean the imagination of the multitude*." In its Maimonidean adaptation, the rabbinic dictum may then be paraphrased as follows: "The Torah speaks in conformity with the imagination (and frequently crude perception) of the multitude" and there-fore uses anthropomorphic imagery when speaking of divine attributes.

Now, Kaspi rather boldly takes a third step and more or less systemati-cally extends the parameters of this philological principle to include issues and problems totally unrelated to anthropomorphism. In so doing, he con-verts it from a pedagogic principle which provides a license for allegorical interpretation to an hermeneutical principle which provides a lesson in what we would call historicism. Many scriptural statements, covered by this plastic rubric, are seen as errors, superstitions, popular conceptions, local mores, folk beliefs, and customs (*minhag bene 'adam*), statements which re-flect the assumptions or projections or behavioral patterns of the people in-volved rather than an abstract truth. In its Kaspian adaptation, the rabbinic dictum may then be paraphrased as follows: "The Torah expressed things as they were believed or perceived or practiced by the multitude and not as they were in actuality." *Leshon bene adam* is not just a carefully calculated concession to certain shortcomings of the masses, that is, their inability to think abstractly, but a wholesale adoption of mass views and local customs. With regard to the latter, Kaspi is almost adumbrating—and I am wary of modernization or precursorism—the *Sitz-im-Leben* approach. There is here in embryo a general historicistic position.

We may find snippets of historicism, occasional forays into historical explanation, in the writings of some predecessors (R. Abraham ibn Ezra, R. Samuel b. Meir),[30] but the influence seems to be Maimonides' use of the principle of *leshon bene adam*. Indeed, the impetus provided by Maimonides (ibn Ezra is also a recognized force here) is fully acknowledged by Kaspi, who repeatedly emphasizes the significance of Maimonides' interpretation but also, quite confidently, sees his extension of the principle from anthropomorphism into other areas where the Torah reflects the imagination of the multitude as perfectly natural and indisputable.[31]

There are, however, converging influences and precedents, also Maimonidean in the first instance, which most likely contributed to the full crystallization of Kaspi's method. The following example will concretize the method, elaborate its implications and repercussions, and clearly illustrate the Maimonidean impetus and inspiration.

The Torah prohibits us from cursing: "You shall not curse the deaf" (Levit. 19:14). In the *Sefer ha-Mizvot*, Maimonides explains, at some length, the nature of the act and the reasons for its prohibition.

> When a person is moved by a desire to revenge himself on one who has wronged him by inflicting upon him an injury of the kind which he believes he has suffered, he will not be content until he has requited the wrong in that fashion; and only when he has had his revenge will his feelings be relieved, and his mind cease to dwell on the idea. Sometimes a man's desire for revenge will be satisfied by merely cursing and reviling, because he knows how much hurt and shame this will cause his enemy. But sometimes the matter will be more serious, and he will not be content until he has completely ruined the other, whereupon he will be satisfied by the thought of the pain caused to his enemy by the loss of his property. In yet other cases the matter will be more serious still, and he will not be satisfied until he has thrashed his enemy or inflicted bodily injury upon him. Or it may be even more serious, and his desire for revenge will not be satisfied except by the extreme measure of taking his enemy's life and destroying his very existence. Sometimes, on the other hand, because of the lightness of the offense, the desire for vengeance will not be strong, so that he will find relief in uttering angry imprecations and curses, even though the other would not listen to them if he were present. It is well known that hot-tempered and choleric persons find relief in this way from the (annoyance caused by)

trivial offenses, though the offender is not aware of their wrath and does not hear their fulminations.

Now we might suppose that the Torah, in forbidding us to curse an Israelite, (was moved by) the shame and the pain that the curse would cause him when he heard it, but that there is no sin in cursing the deaf, who cannot hear and therefore cannot feel hurt. For this reason He tells us that cursing is forbidden by prohibiting it in the case of the deaf, since the Torah is concerned not only with the one who is cursed, but also with the curser, who is told not to be vindictive and hot-tempered.[32]

The upshot of this ethical-psychological explanation, which emphasizes the desire for revenge and the ethical shortcoming of the one who curses, is to deny the efficacy of the act: cursing is not really effective in the sense that it produces malevolent results.[33] It is prohibited because it reflects moral weakness of the one who utters the curse.

In the *Moreh Nebukim*, in the context of his discussion of criminology and penology, Maimonides again has occasion to discuss the nature of the act of cursing. Having stated that severity of punishment according to the *halakah* is commensurate with the severity, frequency, and enormity of the culpable act, Maimonides notes that transgressions in which there is no action are not even punishable by flogging for they "can only result in little harm . . . and it is also impossible to take care not to commit them for they consist in words only." Why then is cursing one's fellow man one of the three exceptions to this rule? Maimonides answers parenthetically, almost nonchalantly, that the Torah dealt stringently with cursing "for *in the opinion of the multitude* the injury resulting from curses is greater than that which may befall the body." The popular view, "the opinion (and imagination) of the multitude," erroneous and without foundation in truth or reality, is sufficient reason for the law. In a word, the Torah takes into account psychological tendencies, fears, and beliefs, and popular perceptions which, even though philosophically unfounded, exert influence and, therefore, have their own "reality."[34]

Kaspi picks up this parenthetic explanation, elaborating it and extending its applicability. In essence, he has converted this new historical awareness into a vehicle for philosophical enlightenment. If one recognizes superstition and popular error, one is in a position to neutralize or eliminate them. The Torah did not endorse or validate these views; it merely recorded them and a proper philosophic sensibility will recognize them. As a matter of fact, in certain matters—for example, the efficacy of blessing and cursing or the harmful consequences of counting the members of the community— Kaspi claims that one may readily discern a continuum of folk belief from Biblical to contemporary times.[35] This claim provides a dash of "empiricism" for the apriori philosophic sensibility which determines the direction of the interpretation.

There is thus no limit to the kinds of difficulties that may be resolved by this interpretive mechanism, which is based on a new form of historical awareness and a concomitant critical philology. It should be emphasized that this philological method did not entail text criticism or emendation, as was the case with the emergent humanist method of Petrarch and Valla. The issue was not the authoritativeness, accuracy, or sanctity of the text but its literal understanding; the method was primarily, almost exclusively, philosophical insight and application of *higgayon*, that special blend of logic and grammar, and not actual historical research or anthropological observation, which of course, could on occasion be utilized quite effectively. *Leshon bene adam*, which insists that the text be interpreted in accord with all rules of language as well as all realia, including folk beliefs, enables the exegete to sustain a literalist-contextual approach, thus obviating the need for excessive allegory and yet not doing violence to philosophic conviction. Kaspi declares that *zeh ha-ma'amar . . . matir rob ha-sefekot*; various kinds of textual and conceptual problems, apparently intractable, may thus be solved.[36] Furthermore, they may be solved without various forms of philological-textual criticism. Kaspi was critical of his predecessors because they in effect tampered with the text; a by-product of this criticism is his assertion that his explanations are more profound, sophisticated, and unassailable than those of his famous predecessors.[37] He proposes an alternate exegetic procedure, simple yet far-reaching, which will yield a literal understanding of the text without adding or emending or shuffling. This procedure combines exegetical naturalism—trying to understand everything in context of ordinary experiences—and historicism—noting cultural realities, differences in manners, habits, geography, expression.

This approach is clearly provocative. Kaspi, acutely aware of this, frequently appeals for God's forgiveness if he has erred or claims to rely on God's scrutinization of his pure, constructive intentions,[38] but there is no indication that Kaspi intended it to be latitudinarian or corrosive, to desacralize or humanize Biblical history or to secularize the understanding of the whole of Jewish history. His vision of Jewish history is indeed dynamic; he assigns a role to intermediate causes (in a way that adumbrates Vico) and emphasizes the contingencies of the historic process, but it would be incorrect to equate a measure of naturalism and human secondary causations with secularism or repudiation of providential patterns. It was a sharp tool for a philosopher, helping dispel intellectual fogginess. It also could be used to vanquish Christian claims and Christian attacks on Jewish spirituality.[39] These are, in fact, the twin axes around which Kaspi's entire literary corpus revolves: an inner-directed program of spreading rationalism and an outer-directed polemic for silencing Christian criticisms. Bible interpretation, congruent with logical rules and philosophic assumptions, is the key to both the inner- as well as outer-directed concerns and is thus his major preoccupation.

Talmud and Philosophy

This logical-philological approach to Scripture, particularly its philo-sophical-spiritualist implications, as well as the very pronounced emphasis on the special importance of this study for understanding God's word and thereby attaining intellectual-religious perfection, helps focus also on the novelty of what we shall see to be his pejorative attitude to Talmud study. The setting in which this novel attitude is to be assessed is clear.

Judaism is halakocentric.[40] One corollary of this insistence upon norms and normative behavior is the centrality, often the exclusivity, of Talmud study; for study is the handmaiden of practice and Talmudic lore is the pre-requisite for and source of halakic practice. Now, periodically, the legiti-macy and justification of this intellectual-curricular pattern (almost an axiom) are disputed, as devotees of other disciplines vigorously contend that study of Talmud is not completely self-sufficient; it must be supple-mented, and each one, needless to say, focuses on the worth and impor-tance of his own expertise as the most important supplement. For example, R. Jonah ibn Janah argues passionately for the indispensability of grammar and language study, complaining that Talmudists with very skimpy philo-logical knowledge condescendingly belittle the field.[41] Some will raise their voices and pens against that excessive preoccupation with Talmud which results in neglect of Scripture.[42] The most persistent and passionate claims come from the philosophers and the kabbalists and the various interming-lings thereof, from those protagonists who aim to construct or sustain a spiritual, meta-halakic framework for halakah. In this context, we see Mai-monides insisting unqualifiedly upon the necessity of moving from halakah to meta-halakah; actually he advocated the complementarity and recipro-city of halakah and philosophy, affirming that the religious commandment of Talmud Torah includes metaphysics as an integral, indispensable com-ponent.[43] The same is true for the religious conceptions elaborated by kab-balists, pietists, and the like, each with their own meta-halakic goals and definitions, pressures and projections.[44] These various programs—criti-cisms, challenges, curricular constructions or reconstructions—all recog-nize the centrality and universality of Talmud study but insist that it be reg-ularly related to and supplemented by meta-halakic disciplines in order to guarantee its spirituality. There is agreement concerning the indispensabil-ity of purely legal study on one hand and its theological spinelessness on the other. Extending the parameters of study should not be viewed as optional or supererogatory but as the mandatory fulfillment of a religious obliga-tion, the continuous pursuit of religious perfection. Philosophers and kab-balists agree completely concerning the principle, differing only with regard to the content of the meta-halakah. They agree, moreover, that this meta-halakah is not only the indispensable complement but constitutes the pin-nacle of religious cognition and experience.

Against this background and from this perspective, Kaspi's approach and intellectual demands are quite revolutionary. While acknowledging the centrality of halakah—antinomism is not an issue here at all[45]—he denies the correlative centrality of Talmud study. He not only wants to supplement it but he would have philosophy supersede it. Others point out deficiencies in the study of Talmud which can be remedied with spiritual exertion and intellectual determination, but he is ready to relinquish the Talmud's academic-scholarly centrality and distinction. All others, while assigning axiological primacy to the meta-halakic disciplines, underscored that one should first of all be a Talmudist and only then proceed to complement and elevate this achievement by the cultivation of philosophy (or kabbalah or hasidism).[46] Kaspi in effect proclaimed that proficiency in Talmud was not imperative, was not even an ideal, for everyone. His argument actually results in total inversion of the traditional scale of values: the truly universal subjects of study now become physics and metaphysics, the subject matter of the first four commandments. "Now, the knowledge of God is the primary precept of all our 613 laws, as may be seen from the texts enforcing this knowledge. It is the basis of the four precepts enumerated by Maimonides at the beginning of his Code. He specifically terms them the Foundations of the Torah. These four precepts are (1) to know that there is a First Cause, (2) to recognize that He is One, (3) to love Him, and (4) to fear Him. They are designated the Foundations of the Torah, for they are at once the purpose and the root of all the commandments, the observance of which is the whole end of man."[47] These are absolutely indispensable for individual perfection and cannot be achieved vicariously or collectively; they should be known "by way of demonstration" (*derek mofet*) not "by way of tradition" (*derek kabbalah*). Talmudic knowledge, on the other hand, may be professionalized; one's knowledge of law need be neither direct nor comprehensive. Expertise in Talmud is seen simply and starkly as one "area of concentration," a field of specialization similar to any other field in which one acquires special skills.

But "if there arise a matter too hard for thee in judgment," as regards any of these practical laws, follow the ordinance of Scripture, "Arise and get thee up into the place which the Lord thy God shall choose." Note the selection of terms. "Thou shalt come unto the priests the Levites and unto the judge," "and thou shalt *do* according to the tenor of the sentence which they shall declare unto thee." It is written, "thou shalt *do*," and not, "thou shalt *know*." The Scripture had previously defined the kind of law to which this rule—(of seeking expert advice) was to apply. It starts with a very wide category, "between blood and blood," and further adds "between plea and plea," another general category, and then qualifies by the phrase, "even matters of controversy within the gates." The implication is that we are not all bound to know every detail of the law of the "four bailees," of "claimant and respondent," of "loan and deposit." Acquaintance with such matters is commendable, yet is it enough for us if there be available in our age a judge or judges familiar with the law, who "shall judge the people at all times." That is to say, if I am able to pass my whole life without litigation, then ignorance of the law as to disputes is no defect in my soul. And if, God forbid, contention should arise between me and another and I go before one of the Rabbis expert in these affairs, again it is no defect at all in my soul.[48]

Kaspi shows no appreciation of pure Talmud study, utilizing *Nezikin* as the obvious example of dispensable halakic subjects. "As the Sage Ibn Ezra remarks: 'If all men are righteous, there would be no need for the tractate concerning Torts.' Yet it would certainly be a defect in my soul if, when occasion arose for applying the law, I transgressed it."[49] This, to be sure, is somewhat of a topos in medieval writing but its significance is not lost. His candid confession concerning the limitations of his own study and his aggressive conclusion concerning the relative merit of law versus philosophy are quite striking.

> I will confess to thee, my son! that though in my youth I learned a great portion of the Talmud, I did not acquire (for my sins!) a knowledge of all the posekim. Now that I am old and grey, I have often to consult rabbis younger than myself. Why should I be ashamed of this? Can one man be skilled in every craft? If, for instance, I want a gold cup, I go to the goldsmith, and I feel no shame; and so with other products, I turn, in case of need, to those whom God has gifted with the requisite skill.
>
> Once I made a great feast at which all kinds of delicacies were served. I had the table prepared, I invited my friends to eat and drink with me, for it was a family party. Then the luckless handmaid put a milk spoon into the meat pot. I did not know the ritual law, how one ought to estimate the lawfully permissible proportion of intermixture. Perturbed in mind, as well as famished in body, I went to one of the rabbis held high in popular repute. He was (for my sins!) at table with his wife and family, eating, and drinking wine. I waited at his door until the shades of evening fell, and my soul was near to leave me. He then told me the law, and I returned home where my guests and the poor were awaiting me. I related all that had happened, for I was not ashamed to admit myself unskilled in that particular craft. In this I lack skill, but I have skill in another craft. Is not the faculty of expounding the existence and unity of God as important as familiarity with the rule concerning a small milk spoon?[50]

It follows naturally that he will endorse the reliance on codes, particularly the *Mishneh Torah*, inasmuch as the textual-conceptual underpinning of study is completely superfluous; the fullness and richness of the method and substance of halakah—the interpretive process, the dialectical flow, the use of analogy and inference, the entire experience of "surfing" on the refreshing, often turbulent, waters of the "sea of the Talmud"—are remorselessly forfeited in favor of the stark normative conclusion. He even chides those contemporary scholars who seek proofs and explanations for the commandments rather than being content with the apodeictic, codified traditions of the *Mishneh Torah*.[51] There is, in sum, a definite *odium Talmudicum*, which was detected and detested by R. Joseph Jabez in his *Or ha-Hayyim*.[52]

Now, I would suggest that R. Joseph Jabez not only perceptively characterized and passionately condemned Kaspi's position (the ridicule of Talmudism) but he devised an ideological strategy for the defense and exaltation of Talmudism. When he dismisses philosophy's claim to axiological primacy by asserting that, whereas science studies the work of God, Torah studies the very essence of God, it appears quite certain that this is part of his confrontation with and refutation of Kaspi. It is as if he were discussing the philosophic question of the nobility of sciences and he concludes unequivocally that Torah is the noblest. The fact that the Talmud is so difficult proves its cardinal importance; for if indeed the noblest and most edifying subject of study were metaphysics, we would have been given a simple bare-bones listing of commandments, free of controversy, dialectic and argumentative development. It is, therefore, foolish to straitjacket Torah study into a narrow frame of relevance and functionality; debate and its complexities, dialectical unfolding of laws—all the accepted insignia of rabbinic discourse—are intrinsically significant.[53]

This confrontation continues when we find the Maharal of Prague vehemently denouncing those who ridicule the study of *Nezikin* while revering the study of physics; he repeatedly exposes the fallacy of such argumentation. If we were to look ahead, we could see the Maharal's position as a historical fulcrum: on one hand reacting against the position established by Kaspi and on the other setting the stage for that position usually attributed to the two great contemporaries and antagonists of the beginning of the nineteenth century: R. Hayyim of Volohzin and R. Shneur Zalman of Ladi, the two great ideologues of pure Talmud study which is, in the final analysis, to be perceived as study of God's essence. All Talmud study is useful and perennially relevant; expending time and energy in order to understand even the discarded opinion in a debate or the wrong view in a controversy is unquestionably meritorious, for it is study of the word of God, it is thinking God's thoughts. Study per se is practical and need not seek to anchor itself in an external, self-transcending relevance. All Talmud study is self-validating and its universality should be the ideal for all. This, of course, is the absolute antithesis of Kaspi's restrictive attitude which would make Talmudic knowledge a purely professional concern nurtured by pragmatic or utilitarian criteria.[54]

In summary, this attempt to present in compressed form a bifocal view of Joseph ibn Kaspi—as a typical Jewish intellectual sharing certain common concerns and commitments with others of this rationalist persuasion and as one who carried certain attitudes or projections to new, atypical extremes—could actually be restructured around three specific criticisms leveled at Kaspi by contemporaries and followers: Kalonymos' charge of a breach of

esotericism; Abravanel's indictment for misinterpreting the Bible and radicalizing Maimonides' *Guide*; Jabez' condemnation for ridiculing and demeaning Talmud study.

Of the two themes which were investigated, it may be said that the impact of his exegesis, a blend of literalism, naturalism, historicism, and selec-
tivity, was not too great but his attitude to Talmud study provoked considerable discussion, direct and indirect, in the medieval as well as modern
periods.

NOTES

1. See, most recently, the information made available by Richard Emery,
"Documents Concerning Some Jewish Scholars in Perpignan in the Fourteenth and
Early Fifteenth Centuries," *Michael* (Diaspora Research Institute), IV (1976), 27-49.
A condensed version of the first part of this article appeared in *Juifs et Judaisme de
Languedoc*, ed. M. Vicaire and B. Blumenkranz (Toulouse, 1977), pp. 185-205.

2. See, e.g., H. Graetz, *Dibre Yeme Yisrael* (Warsaw, 1897), V, 290-294; H.
Gross, *Gallia Judaica*, (Paris, 1897), pp. 67-69; H. Hirschfeld, *Literary History of
Hebrew Grammarians and Lexicographers* (London, 1926), p. 94; A. Neubauer and
E. Renan, *Les Ecrivains Juifs Français* (Paris, 1893), pp. 131 ff.; *Jewish Encyclopedia*,
III, 600-601; Y. Zinberg, *Toledot Sifrut Yisrael* (Tel Aviv, 1956), II, 107-144; M.
Steinschneider, *Gesammelte Schriften* (Berlin, 1925), I, 89 ff.

3. His commentaries boldly undertake to elucidate and interpret the esoteric
parts of the *Moreh Nebukim*. In his own commentary on the *Moreh* (e.g., I, 7, 8, 14
and *passim*), R. Isaac Abravanel wrathfully indicts Kaspi for radicalizing Maimonides. (My student Lawrence Kaplan had occasion to illustrate this in his dissertation
on R. Mordecai Jaffe (Cambridge, 1976), which dealt, *inter alia*, with problems in
the history of Maimonidean exegesis. In *Mif'alot Elokim*, (reprinted, London, 1961),
II, 1, Abravanel also damns Kaspi, together with Narboni and Albalag, for belonging to that "cursed sect" which apparently believed in the eternity of the world. See
also G. Vajda, *Isaac Albalag* (Paris, 1960), pp. 273-274. Moshe Edel in his dissertation on R. Abraham Abulafia (Jerusalem, 1975), 12, has observed that Kaspi was
apparently the first to quote Abulafia's commentary (*Sitre Torah*) on the *Moreh*, a
radicalization of a different kind.

4. W. Bacher, "Joseph ibn Kaspi als Bibelerklärer," *Judaica: Festschrift zu
Hermann Cohen* (Berlin, 1912), pp. 119-135; *Monatsschrift für Geschichte und Wissenschaft des Judentums*, LVI (1912), 199 ff. See also H. Stourdze, "Les Deux Commentaires d'Ibn Caspi sur les Proverbes," *REJ*, LII (1906), 71-76.

5. B. Finkelscherer, *Die Sprachwissenschaft des Joseph ibn Kaspi* (Breslau,
1930).

6. S. Pines, "Histabrut ha-Tekumah Me-Hadash shel Medinah Yehudit lefi
Joseph ibn Kaspi u-lefi Spinoza," *'Iyyun*, XIV (1964), 289-317; and see J. Schlanger,
REJ, CXXIV (1965), 450-452. See also S. Pines, "La Conception de la Conscience de
Soi chez Avicenne," *Archives d'Histoire Doctrinale et Littéraire du Moyen Age*, XXI
(1954), 23, note 4. See also the compressed, impressionistic review by H. R. Rabino-
vitz, *Bet ha-Mikra*, XV (1970), 352-359. When I wrote this chapter I had not yet seen
the recently published (Leiden, 1976) dissertation of B. Mesch. S. Rosenberg's disser-

tation on "Logic and Ontology in Fourteenth Century Jewish Philosophy" (Jerusalem, 1974) devotes considerable attention, and analysis, to Kaspi. In connection
with Professor Pines' argument, I would submit that the recognition of natural historical forces does not automatically presuppose a non-sacral attitude or a non-pro-
vidential view of history. The quest for secondary causes does not negate ultimate
divine causation. The link between Kaspi and Spinoza is thus quite flimsy.

7. See my article cited below, note 14; on the importance of "minor" writers,
see, in a different context, A. Lovejoy, *The Great Chain of Being* (Cambridge,
Mass.. 1936), pp. 19-20.

8. Cf. *Jewish Encyclopedia*, III, 600-601, with *Encyclopedia Judiaca*, X, 809-
811. Emery's article (note 1 above) shows that even biographical information is still
forthcoming. The same is true for the bibliographical record; see, e.g., A. M. Haberman, "Shene Hibburim shel Hokmah u-Musar," *Minhah li-Yehudah* (Jerusalem,
1950), p. 179. His commentary on *Song of Songs* was edited by I. Akrish, *Sheloshah
Perushim* (Constantinople, 1567). See now the brief treatments, and bibliographic
entries, in the following Keter surveys: C. Sirat, *Hagut Pilosofit* (Jerusalem, 1975),
pp. 325 ff.; J. Dan, *Sifrut ha-Mussar veha-Derush* (Jerusalem, 1975), pp. 98 ff. (concerning his will). Additional writings of Kaspi, some of which I have examined at the
Hebrew University Institute for Manuscripts, still await publication.

9. J. Jabez, *Or ha-Hayyim* (Lublin, 1912), chap. 9 (p. 88); L. de Modena,
Behinat ha-Kabbalah, pp. 34-35. See also Moses Rieti, *Mikdash Me'at* (Vienna,
1851), whose judgments are indeed strange; he puts ibn Kaspi in paradise together
with the Tibbonides and R. Eleazar ha-Rokeah. Caution is, of course, called for in
making claims concerning the extent of later acquaintance with Kaspi's exegetical
oeuvre, for the *Will* and *Moreh* commentaries are clearly the most prominent and
the most frequently cited.

10. Of related interest is the polemical tract (*Minhat Kena'ot*) of R. Jehiel of
Pisa, ed. D. Kaufmann (Berlin, 1898) against the *Iggeret ha-Hitnazlut* of R. Yedaya
ha-Penini or the critical attitude of R. Joseph Ashkenazi (see the selections published
by G. Scholem, *Tarbiz*, XXVII [1959], 59 ff.), toward ha-Penini. At the same time,
R. Moses Isserles cites the *Iggeret* approvingly; see *Teshubot*, ed. A. Ziv (Jerusalem,
1971), 7 (p. 29). Concerning the intellectual stance of R. Jehiel of Pisa, see the new
material published by A. Rosenthal, *Kobez 'al-Yad*, VIII (1976).

11. See L. Berman, "Greek into Hebrew: Samuel ben Judah of Marseilles,
Fourteenth Century Philosopher and Translator," *Jewish Medieval and Renaissance
Studies*, ed. A. Altmann (Cambridge, 1967), p. 297.

12. See, e.g., *Sharshot Kesef*, p. 6; *'Asarah Kle Kesef*, I, 8, 65, 183; II, 31, 46,
214; *'Adne Kesef* I, 137, and passim; note how in *Menorat Kesef* (*'Asarah Kle Kesef*,
II, 77) this emphasis on originality serves paradoxically (and perhaps tongue in
cheek) to justify his open treatment of esoteric themes, for it is possible that he is not
really revealing anything inasmuch as everything he writes is his own.

בי אולי אין אני אנני מגלה דבר ממה שהוא על אמתו כי לא באה

לי קבלה כלל לא מפי סופרים ולא מפי ספרים.   גם...אין

אני זוכר כי מעולם שאלתי לאיש על זה.

This dialectical interlacing of original interpretation and exoteric presentation is
noteworthy. See the significant observation (*'Asarah*, I, 184 on Ecclesiastes) that
exegesis is after all not subject to absolute demonstrations; also *Mishneh Kesef*, I, 6

(beginning of *Sefer ha-Sod*). This "exegetical relativism" is tempered only by the persuasiveness of the interpretation and the degree of natural harmoniousness with the underlying text; cf. *'Asarah Kle Kesef*, p. 28 (on possibility of intrinsic plurality of meanings). Cf. R. David Kimhi, *Joshua*, intro. (and see F. Talmage, *David Kimhi* [Cambridge, Mass., 1975], p. 215). For Y. ha-Penini, see his *Sefer ha-Pardes*, in *Ozar ha-Sifrut*, III (1889-90), chap. 8. This should be correlated with attitudes in Talmud study; note especially Nahmanides, *Milhamot*, intro.

To what extent this emphasis on *hiddush* and originality should be correlated with the growing general contemporary emphasis on modernity and "subtlety of the moderns" (*subtilitas modernorum*) needs to be investigated. See the general work of E. Gössmann, *Antiqui und Moderni im Mittelalter* (Munich, 1974), and the special study of M. T. Clanchy, "Moderni in Education and Government in England," *Speculum*, II (1975), 671ff. The theme of intellectual progress, of cognitive advance, conceptual breakthrough, and interpretive innovation (see Gersonides, *Milhamot ha-Shem*, intro.) is also relevant here. See also *Mishneh Kesef*, I, 65, 86, 90; *'Asarah Kle Kesef*, I, 127 (*lo kidmani 'adam*); *Tam ha-Kesef*, p. 8.

13. The *Sefer ha-Sod* (on the secrets [*sodot*] of the Torah) gives a good picture of rationalist exegesis; the first part contains general propositions and the second deals with select Biblical themes and topoi. Its major concern is Biblical narrative (as distinct from halakah), which, like rabbinic aggadah, has often been ignored or dismissed nonchalantly.

One of his arguments for freedom of interpretation is the fact that it is illustrated by distinguished predecessors, e.g., ibn Ezra and Maimonides. This becomes a prominent theme of Hebrew literature; see, e.g., Azulai, *Ba'ale Brit Abram* (Vilna, 1874), intro., p. 1. R. Menahem Tamar (fifteenth-century Spain) makes a similar point at the beginning of his interesting, as yet unpublished, work ("Tanhumot 'El") by referring to Rabad's strictures against Maimonides' *Mishneh Torah*. Obviously, the defense of freedom of interpretation and the possibility of intellectual progress are interwoven. Note the theory developed by R. Zerahyah ha-Levi in the introduction to the *Sefer ha-Ma'or*.

14. I. Twersky, "Aspects of the Social and Cultural History of Provencal Jewry," *Journal of World History*, XI (1968), 203; see also *A Maimonides Reader* (New York, 1972), p. 23. John Noonan's comment about scholastic authors is equally applicable to this case: "The scholastic field, in which the authors work within a common tradition and constantly refer to each other's work, is a particularly easy one in which to determine which authors were representative, influential, original, or astute." J. Noonan, *The Scholastic Analysis of Usury* (Cambridge, 1957).

15. See, e.g., A. Altmann, *Studies*, pp. 196-197. Such a fourteenth-century commentary as *Mekor Hayyim* of R. Samuel Sarsa is also representative. Note also Ritba, *Sefer ha-Zikkaron* (Jerusalem, 1955), p. 69. Kaspi's relationship to ibn Ezra, whose influence on his exegesis was formative, warrants careful study; significant correlations may be established between parenthetic remarks of ibn Ezra and more elaborate emphases of Kaspi. See generally his Commentary on "Sodot ha-Torah le-ben Ezra," *'Asarah Kle Kesef*, II, 147 and *passim*. Note, however, such a comment as *Mishneh Kesef*, I, 98, where he laments that "the sage ibn Ezra" failed to use logic.

16. See, e.g., G. Vajda, *L'Amour de Dieu dans la Théologie Juive du Moyen Age* (Paris, 1957), p. 252, note 2.

17. *Minhat Kena'ot*, p. 101. See most recently Ch. Touati, "La Controverse de

1203-06," *REJ*, CXXVII (1968), 21 ff. also idem., "Les Deux Conflits autour de Maimonide et des Etudes Philosophiques," *Juifs et Judaisme de Languedoc*, pp. 173-185. On his acute awareness of controversy, see *Mishneh Kesef*, II, 43,

עדיין בני פלג אנחנו, כלנו בני ריב ומדון ומחלוקת, והיא
שהחריבה את ביתנו, ועדיין במקומה עומדת.

Also *Mishneh Kesef*, I, 72 (following *Moreh Nebukim*, III, 29, which he does not cite). This is a leitmotif in his writing.

18. See I. Abrahams, *Hebrew Ethical Wills* (Philadelphia, 1926), I, 131 ff. The definition of hubris is found in W. Jaeger, *Paideia*, I (New York, 1965), 168, a sharp antithesis to Maimonides, *Hilkot Teshubah*, X, 6, or *Moreh*, III, 51 and 54, and Kaspi, *passim*.

19. In a very helpful seminar which I conducted on ibn Kaspi, students were able to demonstrate, by independently analyzing different parts of the extensive literary oeuvre, that almost any commentary (on Genesis, Ezekiel, or Ruth) is a real microcosm of all his methods and goals. The unformity of style, interpretation, criticism, and emphasis is striking. Indeed he suggests that he is developing a coherent, unified system, based on clear logical criteria, historical-philological guidelines, and general methodological principles which may be transferred from one work to another;) e.g., *Mishneh Kesef* II, 49. For reservations concerning the usefulness of the evolutionary view in general—e.g., Werner Jaeger's assumption that conflicting statements and conceptual problems in Aristotle should be seen as consequences of a slow evolution (in the case of Aristotle, from idealism to realism)—see N. F. Grayeff, *Aristotle and His School* (London, 1974), p. 10, and before that, M. Greene, *A Portrait of Aristotle* (London, 1963), pp. 15 ff.

20. E.g., *Mishneh Kesef*, p. 2; *Menorat Kesef*, intro. See, however, such a statement (*'Adne Kesef*, II, 44) as

והטעם לכלל האומה כי ליחידים יש אותות אחרים הכרחיים כפי
תנאי האותות והראיות והמופתים לפי ההגיון.

Note also his sardonic introduction to the commentaries on the Scrolls:

וגם ראיתי המוניני צועקים בחג השבועות מגלת רות כמו שקבעו
להם חובה לצעוק כלם בקול רם מגלת איכה בליל צום אך לאבל
ומגילת אסתר בליל יום הפורים לשמחה, אשר זה דבר טוב וראוי
בלי ספק, אך כי יבינו תחלה הענין בדבור הפנימי עד שישמיעו
לאזנם מה שירציאו בפיהם.

'Asarah Kle Kesef, II, 3. In his interpretation of Job (*'Asarah Kle Kesef* I, 176) we find an interesting typology of religious people together with a suggestive statement about tolerance of various types and about the fact and desirability of mobility from a lower to a higher stage. Nevertheless, he frequently notes that he chooses to remain esoteric, e.g., *Mishneh Kesef*, I, 2, 65, 67. His genuine contempt for the masses comes to full expression in the anecdote reported in *Asarah Kle Kesef*, I, 37-38. The entire section combines ridicule with prudent comments on how to talk to and deal with the ignorant.

21. This Maimonidean statement is referred to in a very clever way by Kaspi, *Menorat Kesef*, intro. (*'Asarah Kle Kesef*, II, 77). The idea is a pivot of his thinking and writing; see also the beginning of the commentary on ibn Ezra, *'Asarah Kle Kesef*, II, 147. Note, of course, *Sanhedrin*, 91b.

22. Kalonymos b. Kalonymos, *Teshubah (Sendschreiben)*, ed. J. Perles (Munich, 1879).

23. *Mishneh Kesef*, pp. 9, 10, and *passim*; *Tam ha-Kesef*, pp. 19, 23. Leo Strauss' evaluation of Kaspi as "a competent reader of the *Guide* who wrote an eso-teric commentary on it" is one-sided, undoubtedly reflecting Strauss' own desidera-tum of "an esoteric interpretation of an esoteric interpretation of an esoteric teach-ing." See L. Strauss, *Persecution and the Art of Writing* (Chicago, 1952), p. 56.

24. For Maimonides' *Ma'amar Tehiyyat ha-Metim* as an apology for his life, see my forthcoming *Introduction to the Mishneh Torah* (New Haven, 1979), chap. VI. On *genut he-hamon*, see *Moreh*, intro., end, *Kobez Teshubot ha-Rambam*, II, 16b; Kaspi, *'Asarah Kle Kesef*, II, 187; *Mishneh Kesef*, I, 8; I. Abrahams, *Wills*, I, 152 and note; A. J. Arberry, *Aspects of Islamic Civilization* (London, 1964), pp. 120 ff., 136 ff. Sometimes the difference between the masses (*hamon*) and those who understand—in this case understanding based on grammar and logic—is so great as to affect accepted customs; see *'Asarah Kle Kesef*, II, 28, where his explanation of the last verse of *Lamentations* eliminates its stinging, condemnatory tone thereby making the public repetition of the penultimate verse, which is of a petitionary-consolatory nature, unnecessary.

והנה לפי זה יהיה זה הסיום נחמה ואין צרך למנהגינו, לחזור השיבנו, ואם הוא טוב בעבור הַהמון.

Also *Mishneh Kesef* I, 16:

כי תועלתו להמון יותר רב מתועלתו להיחידים הַשׂרידים.

25. E.g., *Mishneh Kesef*, I, 19; II, 254, 286; *Tam ha-Kesef*, pp. 5, 7, 20 and *passim*; *'Adne Kesef*, I, 137. In *Mishneh Kesef*, I, 79 he describes allegory, nonliter-alism, as an extreme measure; it is like strong medicine which should be taken only on very rare occasions. See also *Mishneh Kesef*, II, 254, where in arguing for the absolute supremacy and indispensability of literalism, he does not spare even the Talmudic sages or the authoritative Aramaic translation of Onkelos. Non-literalism is always fraught with grave dangers.

His philological approach differs sharply from that of the Spanish grammarians. While they tamper with the text—emending, changing the order of letters or words, in the name of and under the banner of grammar—he proposes a different principle of interpretation, simple yet far-reaching: by recognizing the plurality of meanings, it is possible to understand a text without changing its syntax or sequence. Every ap-parently awkward or wayward construction is, in the final analysis, grammatically defensible. See *'Asarah Kle Kesef*, II, 11 and cf. "Sefer ha-'Emunah veha-Bittahon," *Kitbe Ramban*, ed. C. Chavel (Jerusalem, 1964), II, p. 379. His grammar is logical and analytical; see S. Rosenberg, *Logic*, p. 15. In this context, note how he insists that the rabbinic statement *mine'u benekem min ha-higgayon* cannot possibly refer to logic. A similar, very sharp statement is made by his Italian contemporary (1275-1355) Shemarya ha-Ikriti in characterizing his Bible commentary: *Ozar Nehmad*, II (1857), 91.

בכל אלה הספרים אסרתי עלי באיסור כרת ונשמרתי בנפשי לאמר
שיש במאמר אחד מכל כתבי הקדש אות אחת יתרה או חסרה, קי"ו
תיבה..כי המדבר כאלה הוא כופר בכל המכתב הקדוש, אמנם לא
בכונה מאתו, כי כל מי שיפרש מאמר אחד מן המקרא ויסף ויגרע
אות אחד מן הכתוב מושכל ראשון הוא שפירושו שקר וכזב, ולא
הוא כונת הכתוב.   ואיך יסכל לב אדם לאמר על נותני התורה
והמדברים ברוח הקדש שטעו בדבריהם ולא ידעו לדבר כראוי,
ואיך יסכים הלב להאמין להם אם גם לדבר לא ידעו.

He in turn emphasizes the literalism of
his own commentary and notes particularly that it contains absolutely no aggadah,
which he explicated in his Talmud commentary (his major works, available in
manuscript, are *Sefer Amaziah*, *'Elef ha-Magen* and *Sefer ha-Mora*). This rigid com-
partmentalization is noteworthy. Later, an original exegete such as R. Eliezer Ashkenazi (*Ma'aseh ha-Shem*) explains his exclusion of aggadic materials from his commentary as a consequence of the invention of printing: inasmuch as aggadic texts
are now readily available, there is no longer any need, or justification, for incorpor-
ating them into Bible commentaries.

For Kaspi's "exegetical agnosticism" see, e.g., *Mishneh Kesef*, I, 1, 63.

In addition, for logical as well as methodological reasons, his exegesis is general,
not specific; he repeatedly explains why detail may be omitted, why certain words
should be seen as ornamental and rhetorical and therefore not subject to microscopic
interpretation, and that his task is to give the essence, the conceptual framework and
message (see, e.g., repeated emphasis concerning the Five Scrolls—*'Asarah Kle
Kesef*, II). In other words, proper exegesis is characterized by restraint and selectiv-
ity—not all details need to be explained. This principle, rooted in the nature of language and contingencies of communication, helps the exegete get to the point. We
may recall in this context Maimonides' observations (*Moreh*, intro.) concerning the
metaphorical interpretation of prophetic parables and, mutatis mutandis, his approach (*Moreh*, III, 26) to the rationalization of the commandments which dwells on
the general import and omits details. Contingency must be recognized.

Furthermore, his socio-historical approach has certain sharp emphases which are
noteworthy: (1) There is the need to predicate interpretation upon naturalism, i.e.,
understanding scriptural passages in light of ordinary, rather than unusual, experiences. This ipso facto rules out excessive allegorizing. (2) The exegete assumes a continuity of practices and mores, learning from fourteenth-century Egypt about Egypt
in the time of Moses and the Pharoahs. In other words, not only does the exegete
endorse and utilize the historical approach, but he assumes that the contemporary
cultural and anthropological differences he observes or learns about existed also in
antiquity and thus provide insight into the text. Kalonymos b. Kalonymos is quick
to challenge and, indeed, to demolish this assumption; even granted the historical
approach, there is clearly change over the centuries. (See J. H. Brumfitt, *Voltaire
Historian* [Oxford, 1958], p. 101, who describes Voltaire as being guided by the
assumption that human nature does not change and hence the historian should use
his observation of contemporaries to understand the past.) Note the following ex-

amples of historical explanation: *Mishneh Kesef* II, 162, 182, 183; *Mazref le-Kesef*, pp. 19, 27. Note in this context Nahmanides, *Deut.* 16:22 (*vegam ha-yom 'osin ken*). As for Hebrew, Kaspi suggests that it is the holy tongue because it is grammatically correct; *'Asarah Kle Kesef* II, 17 and II, 78; cf., of course, Maimonides, *Moreh*, III, 8, and the multiple explanation of R. Judah b. Solomon (*Midrash ha-Hokmah*) cited by B. Dinur, *Yisrael ba-Golah*, II, V. 6, 19; also Profiat Duran, *Ma'aseh 'Efod* (Vienna, 1868), pp. 177-178. On the inadequacy of all translations from Hebrew, see *Mishneh Kesef*, II, 4. Preservation of the integrity of the scriptural text is thus the motive for his contextual-syntactical-historical approach and his criticism of the Spanish grammarians.

26. Particularly noteworthy is the introduction of Jacob Anatoli (author of the provocative *Malmad ha-Talmidim*) to his Hebrew translation of Averroes' Middle Commentary on the *Isagoge* of Porphyry:

וידוע שאין כֹח באדם ממנו לעמוד כנגד הפקחים משאר האומות

החולקים עלינו, אם לא ילמד החכמה הזאת. ומפני שראיתי

כי רבו הֹהוללים הרעים המתפארים עלינו בדרך המחלוקת והֹניצוח

קנאתי בהם... והתעורר תשוקתי להעתיק החכמה הזאת כפי אשר

תשיג ידי.

27. *Berakot*, 31b; *Yebamot* 71a, and parallels.

28. E.g., S. Abramson, *R. Nissim Gaon* (Jerusalem, 1965), p. 281; R. Judah ibn Koreish, *'Iggeret*, ed. M. Katz (Tel Aviv, 1952), p. 58; *Ozar Nehmad*, II (1857), 213; R. Abraham ibn Ezra, *Perush*, Gen. 6:6 (and see Exod. 32:14). *Ozar ha-Geonim*, *Berakot*, I, 131; II, 92; *Hagigah*, 30. For a partial history, see S. Abramson, "Ma' amar Hazal u-Perusho," *Molad*, 421 ff.

29. *Moreh Nebukim*, I, 26 (and see I, 33, 46, 59); *Ma'amar Tehiyyat ha-Me-tim*, ed. J. Finkel (New York, 1939), p. 8; *Mishneh Torah, Yesode ha-Torah*, I, 9, 12. See R. Bahya ibn Pakuda, *Hobot ha-Lebabot*, I, 10; Judah ha-Levi, *Kuzari*, V, 27; Abraham ibn Daud, *Emunah Ramah* (repr. Jerusalem, 1961), intro., p. 2a.

30. A. ibn Ezra, *Perush*, Exod. 12:8, where he quotes and rejects such a view in the name of one of the scholars of Spain; 20:3 (*keneged mahshebot*); 23:9 (*da'ki minhag ha-Torah ledaber 'al ha-hoveh*). On Exod. 19:23 he quotes the "Gaon" in such a context. And note the application of this by R. Isaac Arama, *'Akedat Yizhak*, chap. (*sha'ar*), 44, pt. 2. R. Samuel ben Meir, *Perush*, Gen. 25:33 (*keminhag bene 'adam*), 45:19; also Exod. 17:9; Levit. 11:34; 13:2, and others; Nahmanides, Exod. 28:2. See Maimonides, *Perush ha-Mishnah, Nedarim*, VII, 6; *Moreh* III, 39 (about the animals selected for sacrifices); *Mishneh Torah, Ma'akalot 'Asurot*, XVI, 9; *'Ishut*, XXV, 2.

31. *'Ammude Kesef* on *Moreh*, I, 26.

...ראה פירוש נכבד שעשה המורה לאמרם...ז"ל דברה תורה...

והנה זאת ההקדמה רצוני האומרת ד"ת כלשון בני אדם, בפי'

המורה הוא דבר יותר כולל מן הפחותיֹם, בענין ציור הא-ל, כי

גם זה נמצא בכל המקרא אע"פ שאינו נוגע בֹשֹם או מלאך, רק

בדברים השפלים מאד. ‎ וזה מה שכתוב יהושע (ב:ז) והאנשים
רדפו אחרהם, ואמר כפי מחשבות הרודפים, כמו שבאר א"ע ובכלל
כל המקרא מליאה מזה המין, רצוני שידבר הכתוב כפי מחשבת
רבים או יחידים או יחיד...וזה ענין נכבד מאד, והנני מעיר
על זה במקומות רבים מיתר ספרי.

The example of Joshua 2:7 is found in ibn
Ezra, Exod. 4:14 and the second example from Jeremiah 28:10 (which is omitted here
from the Hebrew quotation) is briefly alluded to by ibn Ezra, Exod. 20:3. The significance of this is self-evident but it should be noted that ibn Ezra does not invoke
the principle of *dibrah Torah*. See also, e.g., *Tam ha-Kesef*, pp. 21, 24; *Mishneh
Kesef*, I, 19, 42, 46, 49 (where he says that this solves all problems); 149; 162; II, 162;
'Asarah Kle Kesef, I, 139. In at least one place, *'Asarah Kle Kesef*, II, 27 where his
own use is conventional, i.e., related to anthropomorphism, he explicitly attributes
this first extension to ibn Ezra, and reserves credit for the second extension for himself (va'ani zerafti 'inyan shelishi le-'elah . . . vehu yakär me'od). This sharply underscores the complex nature of the relation of his system to ibn Ezra's sporadic comments.

32. *Sefer ha-Mizvot*, 317; cf. *Mishneh Torah, Sanhedrin*, XXVI, 1-2; *Teshubah*, IV, 3.

33. Cf. *Sefer ha-Hinnuk*, 23. See, Rashba, *Teshubot*, 408; R. Nissim, *Shnem
'asar Derushim* (Jerusalem, 1959), p. 85.

34. *Moreh Nebukim*, III, 41.

35. E.g., *Mishneh Kesef*, I, 43; *Tam ha-Kesef*, pp. 26, 32.

36. E.g., *Tam ha-Kesef*, p. 24; *Mishneh Kesef*, I, 49.

37. *Mishneh Kesef*, I, 1; II, 190; *Sharshot Kesef*, p. 6.

38. E.g., *Tam ha-Kesef*, pp. 18, 24, 34. The notion that the Torah writes *ad
captum vulgi* really has no connection with the principle of *dibrah Torah*, for the
assumptions, intentions, and conclusions differ radically; see, e.g., Y. Yovel, "Bik-
koret ha-Dat u-Perush ha-Mikra: Ben Spinoza le-Kant," *'Iyyun*, XVII (1966), 259,
note 49.

39. E.g., *Mishneh Kesef*, II, 254ff.; *Tam ha-Kesef*, pp. 1, 41. Indeed, the eight
theses (*derushim*) which constitute the *Tam ha-Kesef* may be seen as an attempt to
revolutionize the basis of polemic; a major goal is the reaffirmation of the eternity of
the Covenant and the spirituality of Judaism. See also *Adne Kesef*, II, 45.

40. See my formulation in "Religion and Law," *Religion in a Religious Society*,
ed. S. Goitein (Cambridge, Mass., 1975), pp. 70 ff.

41. *Sefer ha-Rikmah*, ed. M. Wilensky (Berlin, 1910), p. 19. See also J. Kimhi,
Sefer ha-Galuy, ed. H. J. Mathews (reprinted, Jerusalem, 1967), p. 3.

42. E.g., the references to R. Isaac ibn Latif in my article (note 40 above).
Kaspi himself is a forceful spokesman for this view; e.g., *'Adne Kesef*, II, 6. For earlier neglect of Bible study, see also S. Lieberman, *Midreshe Teman*, pp. 27-31.

43. E.g., *Mishneh Torah, Yesode ha-Torah*, IV, 13; *Talmud Torah*, I, 11, 12;
Teshubah, X, 6; *Moreh*, III, 51. I dealt with this at length in chapter 6 of my *Introduction to the Mishneh Torah of Maimonides* (New Haven, 1979).

44. On the *Haside Ashkenaz* see H. Soloveitchik, "Three Themes in the Sefer
Hasidim," *Association for Jewish Studies Review*, I (1976), 311 ff.; I. Ta-Shema,

"Mizvat Talmud Torah . . . be-Sefer Hasidim," *Bar Ilan Annual*, XIV-XV (1977), 98 ff.

45. Cf. I. Abrahams, *Hebrew Ethical Wills*, 128-129. Various statements about the unimpeachability and absolute indispensability of halakah are strewn throughout his writings, in addition to the unequivocal passages in the Will; e.g., *'Asarah Kle Kesef*, I, 18, 150, 175; III, 164; *Mishneh Kesef*, I, 6-7, 159, and many others.

46. See, e.g., an additional statement to this effect by R. Shem Tob ibn Gaon, cited by D. S. Löwinger, *Sefunot*, VII (1963), 23.

47. *Hebrew Ethical Wills*, p. 132. Note that he regularly uses *mizvot libiyot* (i.e., *sikliyot*) for rational commandments. See *'Asarah Kle Kesef*, I, 11, 17, 171.

(המקיים כל המצוות המעשיות, ואע'פ שעם זה ידע הלביות דרך
קבלה, אין מעלתו כמעלת המקיים כל המצוות המעשיות, ועם זה
ידע הלביות מה שנקרא ידיעה על דרך האמת רצוני במופת)

Moses is lauded (I, 176) for punctilious observance of all commandments, first via tradition (*kabbalah*) and then via demonstration (*mofet*). In I, 184, they are designated as *ikkar ha-Torah*. The introduction to the fourteenth-century abridgement of R. Bahya ibn Pakuda's *Hobot ha-Lebabot* echoes this mood and emphasis; see B. Dinur, *Yisrael ba-Golah*, II, 6, 52.

48. *Wills*, pp. 138-139. See *Mishneh Kesef*, I, 10. A striking parallel both to the supremacy of meta-halakic studies as well as to the idea of professionalization or specialization in Talmud studies is found in the recently published letters of R. Asher of Lemlein (fourteenth-century Germany) where knowledge of the commandments is deemed relevant for all; otherwise, Talmud is a subject for specialists, just like any other profession. See E. Kupfer, *Kobez 'al Yad*, VIII (1975), 403-406, 416. The language is extremely sharp.

49. See *Yesod Mora* (Prague, 1833), chap. 1 (p. 15b). R. Abraham ibn Daud, *'Emunah Ramah*, II, intro. (p. 45) that if all men were honest and did not wrong each other the legal profession would be superfluous; J. Ezobi, *Ka'arat Kesef*, (Berlin, 1860), p. 29; R. Isaac Polkar, *'Ezer ha-Dat* (reprint, Jerusalem, 1970), p. 5; Kalonymos b. Kalonymos, *'Eben Bohan*, ed. A. M. Haberman (Tel Aviv, 1936), p. 56.

50. *Wills*, p. 151 (and see above, note 47). A similar confession is made by Netanel ha-Rofe, translator of part (*Seder Kodashim*) of Maimonides' *Mishnah Commentary* into Hebrew.

ואני לא למדתי בעורנותי גמרא אלא מעט מהרבה...רק גדלתי
במלאכת הרפואה ועמדתי על מקצת ספרי חכמות.

Other contemporaries complain about the difficulties of Talmud study; e.g., R. Aaron ha-Levi, *Pekudat ha-Leviyim*, intro. I would suggest that when dealing with Kaspi, as well as other "intellectuals" who are quite critical of Talmudism, it is useful and enlightening to construct a "Talmudic profile" in order to determine their Talmudic education, their literary output, if any, in the realm of rabbinics, and their ability to use Talmudic ideas, or even idioms, creatively and compellingly. For Kaspi, see his Biblical commentary *Mishneh Kesef* I, 141, where he states that he will not deal with *Mishpatim* and refers the reader to *Nezikin*. He obviously is not competent in this area. His comments (*'Asarah Kle Kesef*, I, 51) on the *'ir ha-nidahat* are noteworthy, as is his apt use of the halakic maxim (*mesirat maf-*

teah koneh) in *'Asarah* II, 75. His various declarations of intention and motivation, or statements of achievement all revolve around Bible study, (*ba-Torah uva-mikra' kulah*) e.g., *Kebuzat Kesef*, at the beginning of *'Asarah Kle Kesef*, I, XX; and see above note 42. Although he dissociates himself from the quest for reasons of the laws, asserting that Maimonides' system is definitive, he does nevertheless suggest explanations for those Temple laws concerning which Maimonides suspended judgment, e.g., *Mishneh Kesef*, I, 5 (and *Moreh Nebukim*, III, 46). He was preceded in this by Samuel ibn Tibbon (unpublished ms., on select *ta'ame mizvot*). See also notes 20, 52.

51. See my "Beginnings of *Mishneh Torah* Criticism," *Biblical and Other Studies*, ed. A. Altmann (Cambridge, Mass., 1963), p. 172.

52. *Or ha-Hayyim* (Lublin, 1912), p. 144b. A careful reading of Kaspi's oeuvre reveals a frequently flippant and sardonic tone concerning excessive Talmud study or even the groundlessness of certain customs; see, e.g., *Mishneh Kesef*, I, 90, 159; *'Asarah Kle Kesef*, II, 1, 28; certain characterizations, like that in the Will, combine ad hominem and ad rem criticism or disdain; see *'Asarah Kle Kesef* I, 17; II, 87 (a cynical description of the long-bearded elder who uses a mantle of piety to camouflage his ignorance or insensitivity, which is reminiscent of Samuel ha-Nagid's famous beratement of such a type; see *Diwan*, ed. D. Yarden (Jerusalem, 1966), p. 228. His treatment of the famous passage in *Pesahim*, 94b, presenting an astronomical issue concerning which the opinion of the Gentile sages prevailed against that of the Jewish sages, is a barometer of his attitude. The passage has a long history of interpretation, reflecting various moods: embarrassment, perplexity, satisfaction, with some attempts at harmonization or reinterpretation or restricting the significance of the report. Kaspi seems to be very pleased, finding here support for his universalist-rationalist position. The non-Jewish sages of the world have something to teach us. The following references illustrate the range of approaches, thereby providing perspective for Kaspi. *Moreh*, II, 8; referred to by R. Moses ibn Tibbon, *Sefer ha-Pe'ah* (and see R. Samuel ibn Tibbon, *Yikkavu ha-Mayyim* [Pressburg, 1837], p. 16); R. Abraham Maimonides, "Ma'amar 'al Derashot," *Milhamot*, ed. R. Margaliyot (Jerusalem, 1953), pp. 86 ff., esp. p. 88, note 31; R. Shemarya ha-Ikriti, *Sefer ha-Mora*, p. 4; R. Menahem b. Zerah, *Zedah la-Derek*, I, chap. 22, p. 33; R. Moses Alashkar, *Teshubot*, 96; R. Elijah Mizrahi, *Teshubot*, 57; R. Moses Isserles, *Torat ha-'Olah*, III, chap. 38; R. David Ganz, *Nehmad ve-Na'im*; R. Joseph Ashkenazi, in *Tarbiz*, XXVIII (1959), 219, note 50. For the astronomical background, see G. Zarfati, *Tarbiz*, XXXII (1963), 140 ff. Note the kabbalistic approach of R. Todros Abulafia in the fragment edited by L. Feldman, *S. Baron Jubilee Volume* (Jerusalem, 1975), p. 310.

53. *Or ha-Hayyim*, pp. 21a, 33b, 42a; on the difficulty of Talmud study, see R. Menahem b. Zerah, *Zedah la-Derek*, p. 8; R. Joseph Albo, *'Ikkarim*, III, chap. 28 (p. 262). Ha-Me'iri, *Bet ha-Behirah*, intro., deals with this in a different context; also Profiat Duran, *Ma'aseh 'Efod*, p. 5. On the nobility of sciences, see H. A. Wolfson, *Philo*, I, 157. Note also Jabez' rebuttal of the philosophic position that knowledge of God (metaphysics) is indispensable for religious perfection for the following reason: this would mean that Aristotle is more important than Moses. What would then be the fate of all those who lived before Aristotle? And he quickly adds (15a) that this is like the Christian view that those who lived before Jesus were denied salvation.

54. See *Tiferet Yisrael*, chap. 10

אנשים שואלים על למוד התורה במצותיה ובדקדוקיה ובנזק השור
והבור וכירצא בזה שהיה נראה בדעתם כי יותר יצליח כאשר
ישיג בעניך היסודות ובמהות הגלגלים ובשכלים הנפרדים. לכך
דעתם כי הצלחת האדם בהשגת הדברים האלו ודעתם בהשארת הנפש
שנשאר השכל אשר קנה האדם בחייו וזהו שנשאר אחר המות...
כפירה גמורה.

This should be compared with the more restrained yet unequivocal formulation in
Netibot 'Olam, Netib ha-Torah.

כי מי שחשב כי עקר הלימוד לאדם בחכמה שישיג בנמצאים
ובגלגלים ובמלאכים ולא נתנה מדרגה זאת לתורה, לנזיקין,
ולטמאה ולטהרה, דבר זה הוא מכשלה גדולה מאד.

It is noteworthy that Maharal belonged to that school which opposed
primary reliance on codes (*Mishneh Torah* or *Tur*); he based his halakic study directly on the Talmud.

Chapter 11 of *Tiferet Yisrael* goes a step further in the reaction against the Kaspi-
type position and the vindication of pure Talmud study.

יותר ראוי שתהי ההצלחה על ידי התורה ממה שתהי בזולת זה
ואל יחשוב כאשר קונה הידיעה בארבעה אבות נזיקין שהוא קונה
הידיעה בשור ובבור...כי כאשר יקנה האדם הידיעה בהזיק ד'
אבות נזיקין וכירצא בו ממשפטי התורה נחשב זה שקנה הידיעה
בגזרת השם ית'.

In the history of ideas, this may be seen as setting the stage for R. Hayyim of
Volohzin, *Nefesh ha-Hayyim, sha'ar,* IV, chaps. 6, 10.

Let me note here that Profiat Duran (Efodi) justified his work on astronomy by
asserting that it combines two noble, actually the noblest, studies, both of which
deal with God's work—nature and Torah. I describe this work (*Hesheb ha-'Efod*) in
my forthcoming monograph on Duran.

Notes and Documents

An Unpublished Sermon of
R. Joshua ibn Shu'eib

Carmi Y. Horowitz

Ms. Huntington 232 at the Bodleian Library at Oxford, a copy of which contains the *Derashot al ha-Torah* of the great fourteenth-century preacher, Rabbi Joshua ibn Shu'eib, contains a second sermon to *Parashat Tezaveh* (pp. 12v-13v) which is not included in either of the printed versions of the *Derashot*. Ms. R91 of the Library of the Jewish Theological Seminary of America also contains fragments of the same *derashah*.[1] This derashah, which is reproduced below, differs slightly from other derashot in that its scope is somewhat more narrow than most of the derashot found in the printed versions.[2] Wide scope and richness of themes and material are characteristic features of ibn Shu'eib's derashot.

It is possible that the derashah below is fragmentary, since two formal aspects of ibn Shu'eib's derashot are missing. Almost all the derashot open with a Biblical verse, often from Psalms or Proverbs, sometimes from the Torah; infrequently they may begin with a citation from *Pirke Abot*. The exposition of the verse proceeds until it reaches some theme common to the weekly Torah portion, at which point there is usually a transition to the themes of the portion. In this derashah, ibn Shu'eib opens with a Talmudic passage connected with the portion, that is, a discussion of the priestly garments, and stays with the theme throughout the entire derashah. The usual messianic conclusion of most of the derashot is also missing.

There is, however, no reason to doubt the authenticity of the derashah. First, it is included in two independent manuscripts. Second, there are two explicit cross-references to the printed *Derashot*, on lines 9 and 24, and much parallel material as well.[3] Finally, just as in the printed *Derashot*, there are a substantial number of parallels to the *Be'ur Sodot ha-Ramban*, attributed to ibn Shu'eib's student, Rabbi Meir ibn Sahula, but which might be ibn Shu'eib's own work.[4]

The derashah to *Tezaveh* illustrates some of the principal characteristics of ibn Shu'eib as a preacher. He had an encyclopedic knowledge of Talmudic and Midrashic literature, and as a result the *Derashot* are particularly rich in aggadic traditions. Many aggadot have been preserved only in the *Derashot*, a fact not lost on Louis Ginzberg, who integrated and dealt with many of these aggadot in his *Legends of the Jews*.[5] One must use caution in utilizing the Talmudic and midrashic passages in the *Derashot*, for as a *dar-*

shan ibn Shu'eib exercised considerable freedom in the manner in which he quoted his sources. Understandably he often expanded, interpreted, cut short, or rearranged the Talmudic and midrashic sources. In the derashah below, his use of the passage from *'Arakin* demonstrates this flexibility in the artful manner in which he deployed the Talmudic sources—ever conscious of both the didactic and aesthetic elements of the derashah.

His encyclopedic scope expressed itself in his mastery of post-Talmudic literature as well. Philosophy, kabbalah, Biblical exegesis, stories, wisdom literature, all find their way into the *Derashot*. Although this derashah is somewhat limited in scope, a glance at the notes will point to sources in *Pirke Hekalot*, Maimonides, Radak, R. Azriel, Ramban, R. Jonah Gerondi, *Sefer Toldot Yeshu*, and more.[6]

There is only one practical halakic matter touched on in this derashah (line 12), but other derashot contain frequent practical halakic guidance in areas such as prayer and synagogue ritual, laws of the holidays, and menstrual laws. Many *minhagim* are preserved in the *Derashot* as well as unique explanations and rationales for these *minhagim*.

Perhaps the most significant aspect of the *Derashot* of ibn Shu'eib, however, is their kabbalistic content. Despite the rapid output of kabbalistic works in the thirteenth century, and the widening of the circles of its initiates, we have no way of judging the extent to which knowledge of kabbalah penetrated into wider circles. In ibn Shu'eib we find, for the first time, kabbalah in derashot intended for a popular audience.[7] Although at times the kabbalistic references are incidental to the main theme, it is not unusual for a kabbalistic idea to be integrally woven into at least part of the derashah.

There are times when he was obviously addressing kabbalistic initiates in his audience. But while some of the kabbalistic discussions require technical knowledge of kabbalistic symbolism, he was consciously acquainting the rest of his listeners with fundamental concepts of kabbalah and its world outlook.

The use of kabbalah in this derashah is extensive. The development of the theme of the earthly and the heavenly Tabernacle and its relationship to the *Shekinah*; the careful use of verses laden with kabbalistic key words such as *razon, kabod, tiferet,* and *hokmah*; and special status of the priestly garments; the frequent allusion to certain *Sefirot*, all combine to produce a *derashah* that skillfully weaves together aggadic and moralistic interpretation with kabbalistic underpinnings.

Ibn Shu'eib's use of aggadah deserves special attention. The use and interpretation of aggadah generally provides a useful mirror of Jewish intellectual history; philosophers, kabbalists, rabbinic scholars and literalists all interpreted the aggadah in manners consistent with their own world outlook. Ibn Shu'eib's eclecticism manifests itself in the many different types of explanation he offers for aggadic passages.[8] Here Ibn Shu'eib's treatment of the passage from *'Arakin* is dialectical. He accepts literally the Talmudic statement that the priestly garments actually atone for certain sins; but he resorts to the kabbalistic significance of the garments in order to explain why they have these special properties.

In striking contrast, for example, is R. Yizhak 'Arama's interpretation of the very same aggadah in his *'Akedat Yizhak*. The *'Akedah* asks sharply: "What relevance do the priestly clothes have to sacrifices concerning their atoning qualities? Sacrifices are brought to atone for sins, the Priestly clothes for honor and glory?" His answer is that the priestly garments do not atone directly, but rather by studying their laws and understanding their symbolic value they aid in bringing about atonement. The rationalization of the aggadah is apparent in such an interpretation.[9]

A significant passage missing from the Bodleian text but present in the JTSA manuscript is a passage from *Toldot Yeshu*. Although extensively known in the Middle Ages[10] that work led somewhat of an underground existence, as is evident from the following introduction to one of the texts: "This pamphlet passed down from person to person may only be written but not printed . . . heaven forbid it being read publicly or before young girls and simpletons."[11] Its use by ibn Shu'eib in the derashah is unusual; perhaps it was part of his eagerness to neutralize the effects of the Christian missionary sermons which Jews were forced to hear in their own synagogues.[12]

R. Joshua ibn Shu'eib flourished during the first third of the fourteenth century and was one of the outstanding pupils of Rabbi Solomon b. Abraham ibn Adret (Rashba), the acknowledged leader of Spanish Jewry during the last half of the thirteenth century. Rashba was a towering halakic authority who produced classic *hiddushim* to the Talmud, halakic codes, and thousands of responsa. He dealt extensively with nonhalakic matters too, and his aggadic commentaries and responsa contain important material for the history of philosophy, kabbalah, and religious polemics.[13]

Rivaling his literary influence was his personal impact upon a large circle of students who continued to pursue the multifaceted interests of their teacher, particularly in halakah and Kabbalah. Of great significance is the attention Rashba's students paid to "popular literature," which was an important conduit for the flow of Torah instruction and ideological stances from the intellectual elite to a less educated audience.[14] Works of biblical exegesis have always served this important function in Jewish history, and Rabbenu Bahya b. Asher, ibn Shu'eib's colleague, is a good example of this type of popularization. The success of his works in serving as a channel for the ideas which emanated from the school of the Rashba is evident by the wide distribution and frequent reprinting of Bahya's commentary to the Torah.

As a master of the classical derashah R. Joshua surpassed his contemporary. Although much of R. Bahya's literary works probably originated in sermons, he worked the oral sermons—just as many before him had reworked their sermons—into works of biblical exegesis and speculative or moralistic essays. R. Joshua, on the other hand, perceived the uniqueness of the derashah and tried to preserve it in literary garb as well.[15]

Ibn Shu'eib's encyclopedic grasp of Talmudic and post-Talmudic literature, his acquaintance with non Jewish sources and his knowledge of languages provided him with the tools to become an outstanding preacher and talented teacher. His book of *Derashot* has, therefore, a double importance: it is a distinguished link in the history of derashah literature; and is a significant cultural yardstick for assessing fourteeenth-century Spanish Jewry.

The text of the derashah below is a transcription of the entire Bodleian version of the derashah without change. The punctuation is mine, the abbreviations stand as in the manuscript. I filled in some obvious missing letters or words but I placed them in parentheses. In addition I added words or in one case a whole sentence from the JTSA manuscript, placing them in brackets. I did this only when the JTSA manuscript had additional material; when there was an alternate reading I relegated it to a footnote. I did not note insignificant variations. The original manuscript pages are noted in the margin and by a solidus in the text. All references to the printed *Derashot* are to the Cracow 1573 edition as photographically reproduced by Makor (Jerusalem, 1969).

I wish to express my appreciation to the curators of the Bodleian Library, Oxford, for their permission to print the manuscript. My thanks also to the library of the JTSA for their help, and to the Institute for Microfilmed Manuscripts at the Hebrew University where I first viewed the manuscript on film number 22459.

NOTES

1. The Bodleian manuscript is complete and contains all the derashot. The JTSA manuscript which contains only the derashot from *Tezaveh* to the end of Exodus is missing several lines at the top of each page.

2. The *Derashot* were printed twice, in Constantinople 1523 and in Cracow 1573. The Cracow edition was photographically reproduced in 1969 by Makor, with a rich and learned introduction by S. Abramson who dealt extensively with ibn Shu'eib's sources, influence, and with some of the textual problems of the *Derashot*. There are many manuscripts of the *Derashot* which include a number of other unpublished derashot. I hope to publish them separately.

3. See, e.g., lines 12, 100, 138, 194, 230, 233, and my notes there.

4. See lines 38, 58, 156. Concerning the authorship of the *Be'ur Sodot ha-Ramban*, see G. Scholem, *Perakim le-Toldot Sifrut ha-Kabbalah* (Jerusalem, 1928-*Kiryat Sefer*, V, 265), p. 46; G. Scholem, *Tarbiz*, XXIV, 294, note 13; G. Scholem, *Encyclopedia Judaica EJ*, XI, 536; E. Gottlieb, *ha-Kabbalah be-Kitve Rabbenu Bahya b. Asher* (Jerusalem, 1970), p. 214, note 7.

5. See the index volume, *s.v.* Shu'aib. Others who have dealt with the Talmudic and midrashic traditions in the *Derashot* are S. Lieberman (see, e.g., *Tosefta Ki-Feshutah*, III, 468) and S. Abramson (see his introduction to the *Derashot* and *Molad*, IV (1971), 424).

6. See S. Abramson, intro., *passim*.

7. G. Scholem already noted this. See *Encyclopedia Judaica*, XI, 536. In Rabbenu Bahya's *Kad ha-Kemah* there are kabbalistic references but, as E. Gottlieb has pointed out (*Rabbenu Bahya*, pp. 25-27), there is a distinct tendency there to omit kabbalistic themes. R. Bahya was a slightly older (?) contemporary of ibn Shu'eib.

8. See, e.g., *Derashot*, p. 24B.

9. *'Akedat Yizhak* (Jerusalem, 1961) II, 163b.

10. See S. Kraus, *Das Leben Jesu nach judischen Quellen* (Berlin, 1902), intro., pp. 1-23.

11. Ibid., p. 10.

12. See Y. Baer, *Toledot ha-Yehudim be-Sefarad ha-Nozrit*, pp. 91,100. Ibn Shu'eib was very aware of the Christian polemic, as is particularly evident in a sharp passage from a manuscript of the *Derashot*. (Paris ms. 238 and Paris ms. 237, pp. 84-85).

13. See, e.g., his *Commentaries to the Aggadot*, ed. Sh. Weinberger (Jerusalem, 1966), and the additional texts published by Leon Feldman in *Sinai* (Shevat 5729), pp. 243-247, *Sefer Bar Ilan*, VII-VIII, 138-153 and in *Hagut 'Ibrit ba-Amerika* (Tel Aviv, 1972), pp. 421-425. See the comments of I. Twersky in the *Journal of World History*, XI (1968), 203. That Rashba was a kabbalist seems certain, despite his reticence in discussing kabbalistic matters. See, e.g., his *Responsa* I, no. 94. The aggadic commentaries contain a number of kabbalistic discussions, and most of the aggadot that Rashba selects for commentary, with the exception of those that involve religious polemic, are the same aggadot selected by R. Azriel in his kabbalistic commentary to the aggadot. The testimony of his students, who attribute kabbalistic traditions to him is decisive. Concerning his activities in religious polemics, see J. Perles, *R. Salomo b. Abraham b. Adereth* (Breslau, 1863).

14. See J. Barzun, "Cultural History as a Synthesis," in *Varieties of History*, ed. F. Stern (New York, 1972), p. 396.

15. See J. Dan, *Sifrut ha-Mussar ve-ha-Derush* (Jerusalem, 1975), pp. 35-37, concerning the relationship between the oral and written derashah.

לע"נ מר"ז

ר'אברהם שלמה בר'יוסף זאב הכהן סולומון ז"ל

ליטא- ניו-יורק- ירושלים

תלמיד חכם, משכיל, הסיד

כ"ד אייר תשכו

פרשת ואתה תצוה

גרסי' במס' עדכין א"ר עינני בר ששון פרש' בגדי   12r

כהונה למה נסמכה לפרש' קרבנות לומר לך מה

קרבנות מכפרין אף בגדי כהונה מכפרין. כתנת

מכפרת על שפיכות דמים, מכנסים מכפרי' על גלוי

5 עריות בשוגג, מצנפת מכפרת על גסות הרוח, יבא
דבר שבגובה ויכפר על מעשה גובה, אבנט מכפר על
הרהור הלב, אפוד מכפר על שגגת ע'ז, מעיל מכפר
על לשון הרע, אמ' הב'ה יבא דבר שבקול ויכפר על
מעשה קול, ציץ מכפר על עזי פנים.   כבר הוזכר

10 בדר' ויקחו לי, עילוי עבודת המשכן ובית עולמים
שהיו רמוזים ודמיון למדורות עולם העליון
ותכונותיו ושלכך נתחלק לג' חלקים עזרה והיכל
וקדש הקדשים כנגד ג' עולמות עולם השפל   ועולם
הגלגלים ועולם המלאכים שכך חלק דוד המלך

15 המציאות לג' חלקים. וכנגדן אמ' "ברכו יי'
מלאכיו" כנגד עולם העליון שהוא עולם המלאכים,
"ברכו יי' כל צבאיו משרתיו עושי רצונו" כנגד
עולם הגלגלים שקראוהו משרתי עליון ועובדים
תמיד ברצון, "ברכו יי' כל מעשיו" כנגד עולם

20 השפל. וכנגדן נתחלק המשכן לג' קדושות כמו
שהזכר(נו) למעלה, וכל הדברים הנתונים בכל חלק
וחלק דוגמת העולמות עצמן, וכל זה להורות כי
המשכן ציור לו, ולכן נקרא משכן שהוא משכונט
של ישראל. וכבר אמרנו כי עיקר המשכן היה לשרות

25 שם שכינה להיות כסא השי"ת בתחתונים בבית המקדש
שלמט(ה) כאשר היה במרום בבית המקדש של מעלה,
והכהנים והלוים העובדים שם במעשה הקרבנות
דוגמת המלאכים הקדושים שמשמשין לפניו במרום
במזבח של מעלה. ומאמרם במס' מנחות רזאת לפנים

30 בישראל זה מזבח בשמים וגבריאל מקריב עליו
קרבן. ורמז למזבח ההוא אמ' הכתו' "יעלו על
רצון מזבחי ובית תפארתי אפאר", רזהו שאמרו
בתפלה בברכת עבודה ואשי ישראל ותפלתן. וכן
בגדי כהונה היו מסודדים כעין המלבוש של מעלה

כמוזכר בפירקי היכלות וכמו שאמר הכתוב "והנה 35
איש בתוכם לבוש בדים", כעין הכתו' שנ' "כתונת
בד קדש ילבש" ועל כן נאמר "כהניך ילבשו צדק".
ואז"ל במס' תמיד אלכסנדרוס מוקדון שראה לשמעון
הצדיק לבוש בגדי כהונה וקם מפניו ואמרו לו

עבדיו מלך שכמותך ישתחוה ליהודי זה ואמר להם 40
דמות דיוקנו של זה אני רואה ונרצח, כי לזכותו
של שמעון הצדיק היה המלך מחבבו יותר מדאי היה
נראה לו דמות מלאך במלחמה מלובש בבגדיו וער'
כי הוא היה חכם גדול והכיר ממה שידע במרכבה

התחתונה גודל הציוריין שבבגדים אלו כי המרכבה 45
התחתונה היא דוגמא [למרכבה] לעליונה. לכן מחמת
גודל עלוי קדושת בגדים אלו באו חז"ל לעוררנו
במס' ערכין במימרא שהתחלנו בה הקדושה הגדולה
שהיה בבגדי כהונה, כי לבד מה שהיה הכשר לכפרת

קרבנות שאין הקרבנות עולין לרצון זולתה, כי 50
עיקר כהונת הכהנים היה תלוי בבגדיהם כאמרם ז"ל
בזמן שבגדיהם עליהם כהונתם עליהם וכהן ששימש
בלא בגדי כהונה עבודתו פסולה דהוה ליה זר, היה
עוד בגייניין כפרה לישראל לעונות חמורין מאד.

וכבר הורה הכתו' על גודל עליוי באומרו בפר' 55
היום, "ואתה תצוה", "ואתה תדבר אל כל חכמי לב
וגו'" שימלאם השי"ת רוח וחכמה עד שיהא להם ברוח
חכמה להבין מה שאמ' להם משה מן הכוונה הצריכה
בבגדים ההם בשעת עשייתם כדי שתתפשט בהם הקדושה

הצריכה בהם, וזה מורה כי זה הענין הוא מעניין 60
מעשה/ מרכבה המור עד שאין ראוי למוסרו אלא
לחכמי לב בצנעה כאומרו "ואתה תדבר" בצנעה.
ואמ' "חכמי לב" "ומלאתיו רוח חכמה" עד שיהיה
בהם עוד רוח חכמה מן סתרי שהוא למעלה מן השכל.

ואז יעשו את הבגדים האלו מפיר והוא עומד   65
עליהם. והדבר השני אמ' "ועשו את בגדי אהרן
לקדשו"   כי בבגדים האלו היה קדוש וזולתם לא
יהיה קדוש ואע'פ שהוא קדש אלהים ונביא
במדותיו השלמות שבו שיקרא בהם מלאך הש' צבאות
כדברי מלאכי הנביא. ואמ' "לכהנו לי" שיהיה לו   70
לכהן השירות של מטה כדרך הכיהון והשירות של
מעלה בשש קצוות - ולכהן וא"ו, להכהנו לי,
שנבראים כמיותרת. והזכיר ע"ו הכתוב דקדושת
הבגדים האלו ופעולתם "ועשית בגדי קדש לאהרן
אחיך לכבוד ולתפארת' והדבר ידוע שאין הכוונה   75
כדי שיתכבד בהם ויתפאר בהן אהרן כי הם בגדי
קדש, וכבר ארז"ל כי בגדי כהונה לא ניתנו
ליהנות בהן כי אם משעת עבודה, אבל הכוונה
שיהיה להדאות כבוד השם ותפארתו בישראל כעניין
שנ' "ישראל אשר בך אתפאר" - כאשר הוא עושה   80
אותם במקדשו כעין בגדי קדש, שהוא כשירות של
מעלה, כדי שיהא הכבוד שהשכין ביניהם ותפארת
עוזו שורה בהם כאשר שורה במקדש של מעלה. ואמ'
"לאהרן אחיך" לומר שלא יצטער על שניטלה כהונה
ממנו וניתנה לאחר בהיותו הוא אדון כל הנביאים,   85
מאחר שניתנה לאחיו שהוא נביאו, כי מעלת התלמיד
מעלה היא לרב וחולקין כבוד לתלמיד במקום דרב
כאשר דרב פליג ליה יקרא. והנה ראינו משה
בענותנותו חלק לו כבוד לאהרן כמה מקומות
שמקדימו עליו, ולא עוד אלא שדי לך כתר תורה   90
שנקרא על שמך וכתר מלכות הנה כתר כהונה לאחיך.
וכבר אמרו כי זכה אהרן לזה בשביל מה שיצא
לקראתו בשמחתו ולא הפציר אהרן בשליחותו כאשר
עשה משה ובאמרו "הלא אהרן אחיך וגו'". אבל
העיקר כי הכהונה הזאת היתה ראויה לאהרן לפי   95

אלהים אשר המסר ואחד משם אלהים הידוע אשם כי
בדברים האלו יכופר העון והוא זכה בה מכה מדתו
של אברהם בעל החסד שנתנה לו שנ' "אתה כהן
לעולם" פי' וכי תמיד שמש אברהם אלא שיעמוד

100 אהרן שהוא ממדתו ויזכה בכהונתו מיד(ו) . והנה שם
אברהם עולה רמ"ח ושם אהרן עולה רנ"ו כשנכתב
חסר ואו והוא מנין ח' יותר על רמ"ח לרמוז שהוא
מוסיף עליו שמנת בגדי כהונה שנתחדשו במשכן
שאהרן מכהן בם שכן בגדי כהן גדול היו שמונה,

105 ארבעה שמשמש בם כהן הדיוט והם של בוץ כדכתי'
"וכתונת בד ילבש ומכנסי בד יהיו על בשרו
ובאבנט בד יחגור ובמצנפת בד יצנף", וד' שהוא
מוסיף על כהן הדיוט, חשן ואפוד ומעיל וציץ.
ושני מיני בגדים אלו חלוקין מאד בקדושתן כי

115 שירות ד' בגדי בוץ היה כעין שירות של מעלה
במרכבה התחתונה שראה יחזקאל וכאמרם ז"ל כשירות
של מעלה כך שירות של מטה "כתנת בד קדש ילבש",
ואז"ל בד בבד שנעשה אצל שירות של ארבעה בגדי
כהן גדול היה כעין שירות של מרכבה העליונה שלא

120 היה כח בשום נברא בעולם להסתכל כי אם במשה
רבי' שא"ל הב"ה "הנה מקום אתי ונצבת וגו'"
ואמר שם "וראית את אחורי". ולרוב קדושת הבגדים
לא ניתן רשות ליכנס בהם לפני ולפנים כי אם

13r   בזוץ / שלא להטיל קנאה יתירה בינו ובין

125 המלאכים וגם להרחיק המחשבה מן המקדש מראית כל
תמונה, ולרוב פנימיות הד' בגדים ההם היה בהם
ענין גדול ונכבד כי חשן המשפט שם משפט בני
ישראל, המלך המשפט הכלול מחכמה עליונה של
הב"ה, ולכן היו שם שמות האורים והתומים משם

130 המפורש מכתב אלהים שלא נעשה על ידי מלאך אומן
כשאר דברים . ולכן לא הוזכרה בהם עשיית אדם

לרמוז על תחלת עשייתן במחשבה,פי' שישראל עלו
במחשבת ית' קודם הבריאה בלבו של הב"ה ובל"ב
נתיבות [חכמה]-ולכן היו על לב אהרן ואמ' "ונשא

135 אהרן את משפט בני ישראל". והיו שם האבות ושמות
השבטים ובו ארבעה טורי אבנים - הארבעה טורים
רמז לבית אהרן ולבית הלוי יראי יי' ולבית
ישראל, וי"ב אבנים כנגד י"ב שבטים וי"ב גבולי
אלכסונין, והאפוד על שתי כתפות לזכרון להזכיר

140 זכות אברהם יצחק ויעקב זרועות עולם. והמעיל
להזכיר זכות "הקול קול יעקב" להכנס פרקליט
ולכן נאמ' "ונשמע קולו בבואו אל הקדש" וכתי'
"מעיל צדקה יעטני" מדתו של הב"ה יעקב וכתי'
"הקול קול יעקב" ובו פעמוניה ורמונים על שולי

145 המעיל להגין על הדיקנים שבישראל שהם שולי העם
ומלאים מצות כרמון. רציץ נזר הקדש העשוי על
ידי משה לבדו כאמרו "ועשית ציץ" "על מצחו"
לרמוז על שם הש' ית' הנקרא עליהם וכח נבואת
הנביאים שנתן בהם וכסאו הב---ן בהם וכי שם יציץ

150 נזר מלכות בית דוד; ולכן היה כמין נזם של זהב
רדומה לקתדרא, ומפני כח הקדושה הגדולה שהיה
בבגדים אלו והההידור הגדול שיש להם מחמת
צורותיהם ועשייתם במדותיו של הב"ה עד כי
להורות על גדולת מעשיהם שהיא למעלה ממעשה

155 בראשית הותר בהם שעטנז שש משזר תכלת וארגמן.
והיו כרובים להזכירם שלא יקצצו בנטיעות, היו
ראוים לכפר על עבירות החמורות כמו הקרבן עצמו,
ולכן נסמכו לפרשת הקורבנות כמו שאמ' החוכם הזה.
והזכיר החכם החוא מפרטם הראוי להזכיר, ואמר

160 כתונת מכפרת על שפיכות דמים כדכתי' "ויטבלו את
הכתנת בדם" והוא שפיכות דמים מן העבירות

החמורות עד שהיו ביהרג ואל יעבור-וכפרה זו על
החוטא בכך בשוגג בדברים שאין בהם גלות. ומכנסי
בד מכפרים' על גלוי עריות בשוגג כדכתי' "ועשה

165 להם מכנסי בד לכסות בשר ערוה", וזה ג'כ מן
החמורות שביהרג ואל יעבור. מצנפת מכפרת על
גסות הרוח, יבא דבר שבגבוה ויכמר על מעשה גובה,
וזו המור(ה) ושנואה לפני הב'ה ומביאה לכפור
בעיקר כדאמ' "ורם לבבך ושכחת את יי' אלהיך",

170 וכל שהוא כן אינו רואה פני שכינה כי הוא הפך
מדכיו של הב'ה ולכן לא יכון לנגד עיניו. ולכן
הוא אחד מן הדברים שהנגעים באין עליהם להרחיק
מבני אדם לשבת בדד וכל שכן להרחיקו מפני
שכינה. אבנט מכפר על הרהו(רי) עבירה קשים

175 ותשובתם קשה. ואז'ל הרהורי עבירה קשים מעבירה
והוא מטנף מחשבת הלב הטהורז שנתן הב'ה לאדם
יותר מבעלי חיים לחשוב בה בידיעת הב'ה וידיעת
דרכיו. ועבירה זו מביאה לאדם לכפור בלבו ממש על
שאמ' אין אלהים רואה וזהו שאמ' איוב "אולי

180 חטאו בני וברכו אלהים בלבבם." אפוד מכפרת על
שגגת ע'ז שבכללה האמונות הרעות בהשגחה ובחדוש
ובעונש ובשכר / ועקרי האמונה. חשן מכפר על
הדינין. מעיל מכפר על לשון הרע, אמ' הב'ה יבא
דבר שבקול ויכפר על מעשה קול. וכבר נאמ' במס'

185 שבת פרק במה מדליקין על לשון הרע [ה]חמור מאד
מג' עבירות החמורות כדכתי' "לשון מדברת
גדולות" וכי הוא ככופר בעיקר וכמו שנ' "אשר
אמרו ללשוננו נגביר שפתינו אתנו מי אדון לנו",
ומרחיק בני אדם זה מזה ואשה מבעלה ולכן בנגעים

190 באין עליו מדה כנגד מדה. ציץ מכפר על עזי פנים
כדכתי' "על מצח אהרן" וכתי' "ומצח אשה זונה

13v

היה לך", ועבירה זו חמורה מאד וכל שיש בו עזות
פנים לא עמדו אבתיו בהר סיני, והוא מאותם שנ'
עליהם "אשר קומטו בלא עת נהר יוצק יסודם" והוא
195 נהר דינור שאוכלם שאפי' גהינם אינו רוצה
לקולטם אלא בקושי כדאמרי' במס' חגיגה, ואם
ימורתו בעזותם יהיו דראון עולם והוא שאמ' ר'
עקיבא עז פנים לגהינם כדאיתא במסכ' עדיות כי
אפי' היו בו תורה ומצות סופו יורש גהינם, ולכן
200 ארז"ל כי זו המדה הרעה חובה על האב לייסר את
בניו [ביסורין] קשים בילדותם להרחיקם שלא
יקרבו לאנשים עזי פנים [עזי נפש]. אמרו, יקרב
לעובדי ע'ז ולא לעזי פנים כי עובדי ע'ז בושים
ונכלמים ממעשיהם וחוזרין בתשובה ואלו אינן
205 חוזרין [צא ולמד מישו הנוצרים (כך!) אשר מרוב
חציפותו (גלה ראשו) ועבר מלפני חכמים בקומה
זקופה עד שאמרו עליו שהיה ממזר ובן הנדה עד
שבדקו ומצאו שהדבר כן, ועליהם נאמר סוד יי
ליראיו.] ולכן תקנו בברכות השבח שיצילנו מעזי
210 פנים ומעזות פנים ולכן עכשו בעונותינו שאין
לנו הקרבנות ולא כהנים ולא בגדי כהונה לכפר יש
לנו לעשות תמורתן. תזת כתונת המכפרת על שפיכות
דמים ללבוש בגדי הכנעה ושפלות וללכת במקום
שאין מכירין אותו וילבש שחורים ויתכסה שחורים
215 ויתאדמו פניו מכלימה בדם בשמעו שפיכות דמים.
ותחת [ה]מכנסים המכפרים על העדוה לסגף הגוף
בתענית ולשבור הלב הזונה והעינים שהם סרסורי
החטא ולהורידם דמעות בכל יום ושיקבל על עצמו
שלא להרים פניו לראות שום בריה אלא שילך כפוף
220 עינים מאד וישמור עצמו מכל דבר רע יותר מכל
אדם. ותחת אבנט המכפר על הרהורי הלב יקבל עליו

שלא יעמוד לעולם בטל או מתלמוד תורה או ממלאכה
ויפנה כל מחשבתו לחשוב איך יוכל להזדמן לו
שיעשה שום מצוה וכשיהיה נעור בלילה יתלונן

225 וישתונן על עונותיו ויאמר אוי לי כי טמאתי לבי
והכעסתי בוראי ויחשוב עוד כי העולם וקיומו
והיותו והעמדתו בו הכל הבל ורעות רוח זולתי
עבודת הש'. ויתפלל לש' ית' בכל תפלותיו שימול
את לבו ויכיר ממנו כל הרהורים רעים, ותחת

230 המצנפת המכפרת על גסות הרוח יעטה מעיל ענוה
ויכנע מעצמו וישפיל רוחו לכל אדם וישמח
במקללים ומבזים אותו וירגיל [עצמו] בכך עד
שיורגל טבעו שלא להוש על בזיון שיעשו לו וכדרך
החכם שהשתינו עליו בספינה ולא חשש ושמח וידון

235 בעצמו שהוא הנבזה שבכל מין האדם. ותהות המעיל
הנשמע המכפר על לשון הרע יקבל עליו שתיקה עד
מאד ולא ידבר שיחה בטלה ויתרחק מאד מן השחים
אותה. ואפי' דיבור בצרכי חיותו כי אם המעט
שיוכל, וכשהוא בטל יעסוק בתורה מקרא ומשנה כפי

240 שכלו או ילך למקום שקורין בתורה ויעסוק בתפלות
ושירות דוד המלך ע'ה ולא יתלוה ללצים ולכל
הכתות הרעות אלא כמו שאמ' דוד "כי אם בתורת ה'
חפצו ובתורתו יהגה יומם ולילה והיה כעץ שתול
על פלגי מים וגו'".

הערות

<u>פרשת ואתה</u>/ הכותרת בכתב יד. הפיסוק משלי, הקיצורים
השארתי כמו שהם. המלים בסוגריים השלמתי ע"פ השערה.
המלים בסוגריים מרובעות הכנסתי ע"פ כת"י JTSA
שסימנתי כת"י ב.

1   <u>במס' ערכין</u>/ דף טז ע"ב וזבחים פח ע"ב. א"ש מקצר
ומשנה כדרכו לצורך הדרשה. השוה ירושלמי יומא פ"ז
ה"ג; ויק"ר י/ו,; שהש"ר ד/ד; תורה שלמה לפרשת תצוה
דף 157 ודף 196 ובהערותיו של הרב כשר. דרשתו של ר'
עיננ' בר ששון חביבה על דרשנים. עיין למשל ר' בחיי
בן אשר לשמות כח/ד (שמדרך השתמשותו נראה שאין תלות
הדדית בינו לבין א"ש בענין זה); עקדת יצחק דר' יצחק
עראמה פרשת תצוה; ר' משה אלשיך לפרשת תצוה; תולדות
יצחק לר' יצחק קארו, תצוה.

9-10   <u>הוזכר בדר'</u>/ בדרשתו לפרשת תרומה.

12   <u>ושלכך נתחלק</u>/ עיין שם (דף כט ע"ד) "כנגד שלשה עולמות
עולם העליון והאמצעי ועולנ השפל וכמו שחלק אותם דוד
עליו השלום דכתיב ברכו ה' כל מלאכיו ברכו ה' כל
צנאיו ברכו ה' כל מעשיו".

13   <u>כנגד ג' עולמות</u>/ על הקבלה בין בהמ"ק לעולם עיין א.
אפטוביצר "בית המקדש של מעלה על פי האגדה", <u>תרביץ</u> שנה
ב' 137-153, 257-285, ו י. תשבי, <u>משנת הזוהר</u> כרך שני
קפג - קצד.

15   <u>וכנגדן אמ' ברכו ה'</u>/ תהילים קג/כ. פירושו מיזוג של
פירושיהם של הרד"ק והמאירי לפסוקים אלו.

23-24 <u>משכונם של ישראל</u>/בשער' אורה (מהד' בן-שלמה I עמ'
69) וכאילו השכינה משכנו ומשכונו של הקב"ה יתברך ביד
ישראל וכשהשטאו ישראל לפניו ונחרב הבית הרי זה המשכון
שלו   ממשכנו ביד ישראל ומוליכו עמהם בגלות.

24   <u>וכבר אמרנו</u>/ דרשות ד"ק דף ל ע"א, "ודבר מקובל הוא כי

עיקר הכרונה לשכון בבית עולמים שהוא כסא הכבוד".

26-25 להיות כסא... בבית המקדש של מעלה/ אולי כורנתו
שהמשכן של מעלה הוא השכינה עצמה. עיין י. תשבי משנת
הזוהר ח"ב עמ' קפו - ז.

29 במס' מנחות/ קי ע"א בשינוים. "לעולם זאת על ישראל
א"ר גידל אמר רב זה מזבה בנוי ומיכאל שר הגדול עומד
ומקריב עליו קרבן". בספרות האגדית והקבלית מיכאל
משמש למעלה ככהן גדול; עיין אפטוביצר (למעלה בהע' 13)
דף 265, זוהר ח"ב דף רמז ע"א, והשוה ר. מרגליות
מלאכי עליון דף פט, וקיד ואילך. אבל עיין אפטוביצר
שם הערה 4 שמציין "ריש שיטה באגדה שגבריאל הוא הכהן
הגדול בבית המקדש של מעלה". מתוך השתמשותו בפסוק
מיחזקאל (למטה שורה 35) שלפי הגמ' בשבת נה ע"א מדובר
ביחזקאל מסתבר גרסתו שגבריאל הוא כה"ג. עיין גם יומא
עז ע"א ורש"י שם ד"ה לבוש הבדים. בכת"י ב' "ומיכאל
כהן גדול מקריב".

31 יעלו/ ישעיה ס/ז. עיין פירוש אגדות לרבי עזריאל מהד'
י. תשבי (ירושלים תש"ה) דף 58 שורה 25 "יעלו על רצון
מזבחי מלמד שהמזבח נקרא רצון"; ברמב"ן עה"ת, ויקרא
א/ט (מהד' שעוועל דף יד); ורב'ביאור לפירוש הרמבן ז"ל
על התורה" לר' מאיר ן' סהולא (דפוס ווארשא תרל"ה
צלום ירושלים תשל"ג) יט ע"ג.

33 בברכת עבודה/ עיין מנחות שם תוד"ה ומיכאל.

35 בפירקי היכלות/ אולי כורנתו לסדר רבה דבראשית, ב'.
ורמהימר, בתי מדרשות ח"א עמ' מא, "ומיכאל שר הגדול
עומד בראשם הכהן הגדול ילבוש בגדי כהונה גדולה
ומקריב קרבן של אש." על מדרש זה כ"פרקי היכלות" עיין
הקדמתו של ורמהימר עמ' טז. נמצאות צימטות מפרקי
היכלות בעניני בגדי כהונה בספרי ר' מנחם ריקאנאטי
ומנחם ציוני בפירושיהם לפרשת תצוה. על הרעיון של

"מלבושים" או "בגדים" בספרות ההיכלות עיין ג. שלום
Jewish Gnosticism, Merkabah Mysticism and Talmudic
Tradition (New York, 1960) פ"ה; א.אלטמן "A Note on
the Rabbinic Doctrine of Creation," *Journal of*
Jewish Studies XVI, 202.

35   וכמו שאמר הכתוב/ הוא ממזג יהזקאל ט/ב רט/יא.

36   כתרנבת/ ריקרא טז/ד.

37   כהניך/ תהילים קלב/ט.

37- 36   השורה שמות רבה, לג/ד, ועיין להלן שורה 117 והעדתה.

38   במס' תמיד/ כז ע"ב. בדפוסים שלנו הושמט. עיין יומא
סט ע"א. א"ש מקצר, משנה, ומוסיף לצרכו. גרסתו של א"ש
הוא כעין הלשון במגילת תענית (מהד' לוריא, ירושלים
תשכ"ד, דף 264). ברמב"ן שמות כח/ב (שערוועל עמ' תעב)
"וכבר אמרו דמות דיוקנו מנצח לפני בבית מלחמתי". ן'
סהולא מוסיף "כי הרגיש כי כל זה רמז לעליונים והוא
היה רואה תמיד בבית מלחמותיו מלאך לבוש בדים כדמות
שמעון הצדיק ובאותן מלבושים כי עניינו היה בעזר אלהי.
וכשראה זה נזכר מה שהיה רואה תמיד וחזר לדדכר ולא
דרע להם. ראה כי ענין אלו הבגדים רומז לעליונים..."

51   כאמרם ז"ל/ סנהדרין פג ע"ב.

52   כהונתם עליהם/ בכת" ב' ממשיך "אין בגדיהם עליהם אין
כהונתם עליהם".

58   מן הכרונה הצריכה/ רמב"ן שמות כח/ב (שערוועל - תעב)
"והיו הבגדין צריכין עשייה לשמן ייתכן שיהיו צריכין
כוונה". ן' סהולא ממשיך "לרמוז כל דבר לעניינו ולכן
היו צריכין שיהיו חכמי לב העושים אותם".

62   שמות כח/ג.

66   שם. השורה מדרש הגדול לפסוק זה.

70   מלאכי/ ב/ז.

70   שמות שם.

71-72   והשירות של מעלה וגו'/ עיין ר' בחיי בן אשר
בפירושו לתורה שמות כ״ח/ב "וזהו שאמר לכהנו לי בתוספת
רא״ו לרמוז על המדה הששית. ומלת "לי" כמו לה' והוא
הכבוד". השוה ריקנאטי ועיין שערי אורה לר' יוסף
ג'יקטיליה (מהד' י. בן שלמה, מוסד ביאליק תשל"א)
ח״א עמ' 251-252 שמסביר שאות ר' משם הויה היא תפארת
ר״ דע כי לכך נקרא תפארת לפי שהוא ית' מתלבש בכל מיני
שמות הקדש...כמו שהכהן מתלבש בבגדי כהונה לשעה
ידועה."
השורה גם פירושו של ר' עזרא לשה"ש (כתבי רמב"ן מהד'
שעוועל ח"ב) עמוד תקיא; ס' יצירה ד/ב; ובפירוש שם
המיוחס לראב"ד.

73   כמיותרת/ היינו "ר'" של לכהנו והמלה "לי".

74   שמות כ״ח/ב.

77   וכבר ארז״ל/ לא מצאתי מאמר חז"ל כזה. ביומא סט ע"א
"ת"ש בגדי כהונה היוצא בהן למדינה אסור ובמקדש בין
בשעת עבודה בין שלא בשעת עבודה מותר מפני שבגדי
כהונה ניתנו ליהנות בהן ש"מ." וכן להלכה, עיין משנה
תורה לרמב"ם הל' כלי המקדש פ"ה הל' יא. אבל השוה
תוס' שם ד"ה בגדי כהונה; מס' תמיד דף כז ע"א,
ובמיוחד פ' הר"ש לכלים פ"א מ"ט שאומר "אבל בגדי
כהונה אסורין בלבישה שלא בשעת עבודה...דלא ניתנו
ליהנות בהן כדאמרינן בפרק בא לו (דף סט.)" רעק"א
ביומא מראה מקום לר"ש בלי תמיהה. אם היה לא"ש איזה
סברה למדינית בגמ' יומא (אולי סובר כר"ש שהיתר ההנאה
נוצר ע"י העבודה בבהמ"ק שהיא המתירה לבישת בגדי
כהונה ובלי היתר זו הנאת הבגדים אסורה) או שדורש את
הגמ' כמין חומר לצרכי הדרשה, קשה להכריעה.
השוה גם הריטב"א ליומא ודיון רחב בכל השאלה בהעמק
שאלה לנצי"ב, שאילתא קכו אות ב'.

80   ישעיה מט/ג.

84   <u>שלא יצטער</u>/ עיין תנחומא-באבער פ' שמיני יב ע"ב.

87   <u>וחולקין כבוד</u>/ ב"ב קיט ע"ב.

91   <u>הנח כתר כהונה</u>/ ע"פ קדושין סו ע"א.

92   <u>וכבר אמרו</u>/ שבת קלט ע"א "ראו מלאי בשכר וראה
ושמח בלבו זכה לחשן המשפט על לבו" השוה תנחומא באבער
שמות סעיף כד (עמ' ח ע"א).

94   שמות ד/יד.

96   <u>ואהב שלום</u>/ אבות א/יב.

98   <u>אברהם בעל החסד</u>/ עיין דרשות ה ע"ב.

98   תהילים קי/ה. עיין ב"ר מו/ה.

100-101   <u>והנה שם אברהם וכו'</u>/ וכן בדרשות המודפסות לד
ע"ב.

106   ויקרא טז/ד.

116   <u>וכאמרם ז"ל</u>/ ויק"ר כא/יא (מהד' מרגליות עמ' תצא);
ירושלמי יומא פ"ז סוף הלכה ב'. עיין זוהר ח"א ריז
ע"א; ר' בחיי ויקרא טז/ד; ריקנאטי ויקרא שם; ציוני
שם. כדאי להציע כאן את המקורות.
<u>ויק"ר</u>: ..."ואין לי אלא אבות אמהות מנין ת"ל לומר בד
בבד בד בד (או: בר בד בד בד). ר' ברכיה ור' ירמיה
בש' ר' חייא בר אבא כשירות שלמעלן כך שירות שלמטן,
מה שירות שלמעלן איש אחד בתוכם לבוש בדים (יח' ט,ב)
כך שירות של מטן כתנת בד קודש ילבש (ויק' טז,ד)."
<u>ירושלמי</u>: "ולמה בבגדי לבן א"ר חייא בר בא כשירות של
מעלן כך שירות של מטן מה למעלן ואיש אחד בתוכם לבוש
בדים אף למטן כתנת בד קדש ילבש."
<u>זוהר</u>: "ועשית בגדי קדש כגוונא דלעילא דתניא כה"ג
לעילא כה"ג לתתא לבושין דיקר לעילא לבושין דיקר
לתתא...לכבוד ולתפארת דבאינון לבושין דמי לגוונא
דלעילא."

ריקנאטי: "אמרו בויק"ר...א"כ סרדם הוא כמו לבוש
הבדים ולכך הודיע כי בגדי קדש הם כי היותם בד רמז
לחוט של חסד המשוך עליו."

121   שמות לג/כא.

122   שם/כב.

129-130   משם המפורש/ עיין רמב"ן שמות כח/ל (עמ' תעד);
זוהר ח"ב רלד ע"ב.

130   שלא בעשה.../ רמב"ן שם.

134-135   ונשא אהרן/ שמות כח/ ל, ומסיים "על לבו לפני ה'
תמיד".

137-138   ולבית...ישראל/ כת"י ב' מוסיף "כמו רמזם דוד".

138-139   ורי"ב גבולי אלכסונין/ עיין דרשות דף טו ע"ג,
ועיין ס' יצירה פ"ה מ"ב; בספר הבהיר (מהד' ר'
מרגליות) אות צה "ואילן יש לו להקב"ה ובו שנים עשר
גבולי אלכסונין...והם זרועות עולם."
חשוה רמב"ן לדברים לג/ו, ודרוש להתונה (כתבי הרמב"ן
ח"א עמ' קלה).

139-140   והאפוד...זרועות/ ריקנטי פ' תצוה (מהד' ירושלים
תשכ"א עם פ' הלבוש) דף נא ע"א "ואחרי שהחשן רמז
לתפארת ישראל דין הוא דיהו עליו שתי טבעות זהב
רומזים לזרועות עולם דוגמת הכרובים על הכפורת."

141   בראשית כז/כב.

141   להכנס פרקליט/ ריקנטי שם "יסוד הפעמונים...הוא כעין
נטילת רשות להכנס." בכתי' ב' "להכניס."

142   שמות כח/כב.

143   ישעיה סא/י.

146   ומלאים מצות כרמון/ ע"פ ברכות נז.

147   שמות כח/ לו, לח.

149-150   יציץ נזר/ ע"פ תהילים קלב/יח.

156   והיו כרובים/ ב-ן' סהולא לפ' תצוה "ולזה תמצא בבגדים

כרובים מעשה חושב לרמוז לכבוד ולתפארת. והוצרכו
הכהנים לזה בעבור כי המקדש והמשכן רומזים לשם הנכבד
והיו נותנים אש על המזבה תמיד לא תכבה לרמוז לזה.
ואולי יקצצו בנטיעות היתה הכונה בזה שיהיה בהם צורות
כרובים לכבוד ולתפארת". והשוה ריקנטי למעלה בהע'
לשורה 139.

160   בראשית לז/לא.

164   שמות כח/מב.

169   דברים ח/יד.

172   שהנגעים/ תנחומא פ' מצורע דף כד (במהד' באבער מצורע
אות ב'); סוטה ה ע"א, לפי גרסת הר"ח שם. השוה ה.ד.
שערועל בהדרום טז (תשכג) עמ' 47 והע' 19 שם.

175   הרהורי/ יומא כט ע"א.

176   מחשבת הלב הטהורה/ לשון דומה בכד הקמח לר' בחיי עד'
טהרת הלב (מהד' שערועל עמ' קצא) "ומעתה יתעורר האדם
החוטא כשהוא מטמא בהרהוריו הרעים המחשבה הטהורה
הזאת".

179   איוב א/ה.

184-185   במס' שבת/ לא נמצא שם. עיין ערכין טו ע"ב. מראה
מקום זה לא נמצא בכת' ב'.

186   תהילים יב/ד,ה.

187   ככופר בעיקר/ ערכין שם.

189   ולכן נגעים/ שם.

191   ירמיהו ג/ג.

194   איוב כב/טז.

194   בלא/ כך. במטכסתים שלנו "ולא." גירסת הר"ח חגיגה יד
ע"א כמו באו"ש וכן בדרשתו לפ' נצבים, פח' א', עיי"ש כל
הענין ועיין קיטל.

196   במס' חגיגה/ יג ע"ב - יד ע"א.

197   בעזותה/ בכת' בכת"י ב' "בעונם".

198 <u>במס' עדיות</u>/ צ"ל אבות (פ"ה מ"כ); באבות המאמר הזה
מובא בשם ר' יהודה בן תימא. יש מאמר של ר"ע על עזי
פנים במס' כלה רבתי פ"ב. ר"י אברבנאל מעיר בנחלת
אבות פ"ה (מהד' ניו יורק תשי"ג עמ' שסח) שהיו ספרים
שבהם הכניסו לתוך מס' אבות את הברייתא מכלה רבתי.
אולי כך היה לפני א"ש.

199-200   ולכן ארז"ל/ בכתי' ב' "כמו שאר ז"ל".

200-201   לייסר את בניו/ השוה מנורת המאור של ר"י
אלנקאורה, מהד' ענעלאו, כרך ג' דף 117.

202 <u>אמרו</u>/ לא מצאתי היכן. בכת"' ב' "ארז"ל יתקרב אדם
לעובדי ע"ז ולא יתקרב לעזי פנים עזי נפש.

205 <u>צא ולמד</u>/ עיין קרוס (לעיל בהקדמה הערה 10)
עמ' 39 "ועבר אותו רשע בפני רבותינו בקומה זקופה
וראשה גלה" או, "ועבר אותו רשע לפניהם בקומה זקופה
וראשו מגולה". הסיפור הזה מבוסס על הברייתא בכלה רבתי
המצורטט לעיל.

209 <u>בברכות השבח</u>/ א"ש משקף כאן מנהגם של בני ספרד שלפי
עדותו של ר' אהרון מלוניל (ארהות היים הל' מאה ברכות
סע' ה) "אמנם פשט המנהג בכל הארצות האלו לאומרן
(היינו ברכות השחר) על הסדר וכן המנהג בכל ארץ
ספרד...(ו) אע"פ שלא עשה מעשה. שלא על עצמו בלבד הוא
מברך אלא על כל העולם הוא מברך על כל הטובות והחסדים
שעושה תמיד עם הכל." לפי זה ברכות השחר הם ברכות
השבח כשיטת הרמב"ן (פסחים ז ע"ב) והר"ן (שם). שיטת
הרמב"ם שברכות השחר הם ברכות הנאה (הל' תפלה מ"ז הל'
ז, ט) כנראה לא התפשטה בספרד, אבל השוה רא"ש, ברכות
פ"ט סס"ע' כג; טור או"ח סם' מו; דעת הראב"ד המובא
בארהות חיים (שם). הרא"ה כבראה נוטה לדעת הרמב"ם
והראב"ד (ברכות ס ע"ב) וכן תלמידו של הרשב"א ר' חיים
ב"ר שמואל, בעל <u>צרור החיים</u> (ירושלים תשכו) דף ג'.

על חלוקת הברכות לסוגיך עיין דרשתו לנשוא דף סב ע"ב.

ברם בכת"י ב' "בברכות השבה וההודאה".

212   <u>תמורתן</u>/ כת"י ב' "תשובה".

215   <u>בדם</u>/ כת"י ב' "כדנו."

215   <u>שפיכות דמים</u>/ השווה ספר חסידים הוצאת ר' מרגליות

סמ' נד.

217   <u>בתענית</u>/ כת"י ב' "בצרונ."

219-220   <u>כפרף ענינ</u>/ וכן במאירי <u>חבור התשובה</u> מאמר א' פרק

יב (מהד' א. סופר תש"י עמ' 217) שמביא דעה זו בשם חז"ל.

221   <u>על הרהורי הלב</u>/ השווה <u>שערי תשובה</u> לר' יונה שער רביעי

סע' ח' וי'.

222   <u>או מתלמוד תורה</u>/ כת"י ב' מוסיף או מכתיבה.

227   <u>והיותר</u>/ כת"י ב' "והוריתו."

229   <u>ויכיר</u>/ כת"י ב' "ויסיר."

230   <u>מעיל ענוה</u>/ על מדת הענוה עיי' דרשתו לפרשת נשא סא ב'

שיש בה כמה הקבלות לנדון כאן.

233-234   <u>וכדרך החכם</u>/ בפהמ"ש לרמב"ם אבות פ"ד מ"ד

240   <u>אז ילך</u>/ עיי' דרשתו לפרש' נצבים פח,ב' שבה הקבלות לכל

הקטע האחרון.

תהילים א/ב,ג.

12

The Earliest Commentary
on the *Midrash Rabbah*

Marc Saperstein

The following pages contain five annotated selections from ms. 5028 of the Jewish Theological Seminary Library. This manuscript was identified by Alexander Marx as Yedaiah ha-Penini's *Commentary on the Midrashim.*[1] Comparison with the manuscripts of Yedaiah's commentary, however, reveals that the JTS manuscript is actually a totally independent work. Its hundred folios contain comments on the beginning and end of *Leviticus Rabbah*, and on *Numbers Rabbah* to the beginning of Chapter 13. It is obviously incomplete and part of a much larger work, for the author refers to his comments on various chapters of *Genesis Rabbah*, none of which appears in this manuscript. If the entire *Midrash Rabbah* was discussed as extensively as the first twelve chapters of *Numbers Rabbah*, the original work may have been ten times the length of the surviving portion, or a full thousand folios.

Elsewhere, I have discussed in detail the evidence pertaining to the authorship of this commentary.[2] My conclusions are as follows. The author is identical with the author of the *Commentary on Abot and the Aggadot of the Talmud*, Escorial Hebrew ms. G.IV.3, itself part of a larger work to which our manuscript refers dozens of times. The Escorial manuscript was erroneously identified as the work of Yedaiah ha-Penini by Adolph Neubauer, who was followed by all subsequent scholars.[3] The true author is R. Isaac b. Yedaiah, whose commentary on the *'aggadah* is cited several times by R. Jacob ibn Habib in *'Ein Ya'aqob*.[4] These quotations are strikingly similar in content and style to the material that survives in Escorial ms. G.IV.3 and in JTS ms. 5028. However, ibn Habib's guess that R. Isaac may have been the son of Yedaiah ha-Penini is not confirmed by analysis of the manuscripts. While R. Isaac also lived in southern France, he undoubtedly preceded Yedaiah, writing probably in the third quarter of the thirteenth century. This would make the JTS manuscript part of the earliest known commentary on the *Midrash Rabbah*.[5]

The first passage is of historical interest, expressing the author's attitude toward the use of the title *nasi* in the contemporary Jewish community. Commenting on the midrash, "Whoever takes precedence in inheritance takes precedence in the receiving of honors, provided that he acts in the way of his fathers" (*Numbers Rabbah* 1.26), R. Isaac establishes a dichotomy between Gentile and Jewish practice. The Gentiles follow the principle of primogeniture exclusively, so that the first-born inherits both wealth and position no matter what his personal qualifications may be; the Jewish custom is to allow the first-born to succeed the father only if he is worthy of the position. This leads the commentator to an excoriation of those who use the title *nasi* for men unworthy of honor or responsibility, whose only claim is that their father or grandfather bore the title before them. To call such men to the Torah by this title during public worship in the synagogue is blasphemous.

During the thirteenth century, in both Christian Spain and southern France, the position of the *nesi'im* was a matter of considerable controversy. At one point, a distinguished group of Provencal rabbis, including David Kimhi, issued a solemn ban against a group of "rebels" who challenged the established authority of the *nesi'im* in Barcelona.[6] Our passage attacks the entrenched leadership structure of many Jewish communities through a reasoned critique of the hereditary transfer of official positions, and particularly the title *nasi*, all presented as explication of a rabbinic statement. It is not unlikely that this comment reflects the outlook of a different type of Jewish leader, the "courtier" whose position in the royal administration was based not on his lineage but solely on his personal competence and integrity.[7]

The second passage is also polemical, this time an attack upon a prevalent Jewish practice associated with worship. Its point of departure is the assertion that the children of Kehat always faced the ark and never turned away from it, even though this meant walking backward (*Numbers Rabbah* 5.8). After alluding to the Biblical use of the "back" of God as a metaphor for the realm of creation, R. Isaac interprets the "walking backward" of these Levites to mean that the ark inspired them to purify their intellect by investigating the universe, and thereby attaining knowledge of God. This is then applied, *obiter dictu*, to the Talmudic statement, "He who prays should take three steps backward and then pronounce 'peace' " (*Yoma* 53b). Summarizing his explanation in the commentary on *Yoma*, which is no longer extant, the author maintains that the three steps refer not to the body but to the mind; they represent philosophical investigation of the three realms of being, from which the mind gains knowledge of the Creator. Those who observe this statement literally, taking three physical steps backward after finishing their prayer, are ridiculed and scorned for acting in a ludicrous manner that God does not desire.

The potentially explosive nature of this approach should be apparent. An unbroken chain of halakic authorities beginning from the amoraic period, in Babylonia, North Africa, Spain, and southern France, as well as the scholars of northern Europe, had held that it was a religious obligation to take three physical steps backward in accordance with the simple meaning of the gemara.[8] No one seems even to have considered the possibility that the three steps are nothing more than an allegorical representation of a purely internal process. R. Isaac's critique seems to have emerged full-blown from his own head, and he is quite proud of this fact, emphasizing the originality of his interpretation. Such an approach to the *halakah* has far-reaching implications, and this passage may serve as a fine example of what many thirteenth-century Jewish leaders found so deeply disturbing in the philosophical exposition of Judaism.

The third passage deals more with the theory than with the practice of *halakah*. The problem is the exclusion of certain categories of women from eligibility for the ordeal of the *sotah*, the wife suspected of adultery. " 'The priest shall make her stand': this teaches that a lame woman does not drink [the waters required for the ordeal]; 'and place it on her arms': this teaches that a stump-armed woman does not drink" (*Numbers Rabbah* 9.33). The midrash derives the *halakah* by analysis of Biblical diction. The only reason the ordeal should not apply to these particular women is the language of the Torah. R. Isaac is not content with this explanation. All laws in the Torah were given to promote the welfare of those human beings who observe them, and the rabbinic *halakah* must also serve such a rational purpose. By endeavoring to explain the purpose of rabbinic laws that appear to be arbitrary or capricious, R. Isaac makes an important contribution to the literature of *ta'amei halakot*.

In this case, he argues that if the lame and stump-armed women were excluded from the ordeal of the *sotah*, it is not that the rabbis arbitrarily gave them permission to commit adultery with impunity. They were excluded because their situation makes it inherently unlikely that they would be guilty of adultery even if secluded with a strange man:

> Even if they brazenly seek out lovers, they will not find any with which to fornicate, because of their deformed appearance. When they feel passion and desire for another man, they commit lewdness with each other, or they stimulate themselves with phallic forms, each hidden in her own house. But no man has carnal knowledge of her except her husband, for she cannot find a paramour at home or abroad. Thus, against her will, she remains sinless, and she becomes angry and bitter because of her inability to find a lover.

The fourth passage explains the statement, "Were they [the Jews] not circumcised, they would not have been able to gaze upon the *shekinah*, but would have fallen down" (*Numbers Rabbah* 12.8). The comment purports to elucidate the causal relationship between circumcision and the ability to "behold the *shekinah*," which R. Isaac understands to mean philosophical apprehension of God. In graphic detail, he compares the sexual performance of the uncircumcised and the circumcised lover, arguing that the presence of the foreskin enables a man to delay his ejaculation long enough to bring the woman to an orgasm. Because the woman derives intense pleasure from this relationship, she makes such demands upon her partner that he becomes exhausted and incapable of concentrating upon the cultivation of his intellect. In contrast, the circumcised man ejaculates quickly and fails to satisfy his partner, whether his wife or another woman. The woman therefore quickly loses interest in him, and he is freed from such demeaning diversions to concentrate on more important goals.

It is not only the explicit nature of this passage that is so striking. A rather impressive knowledge of female sexuality is applied to the midrash by an author absolutely indifferent both to the woman's sexual fulfilment and to her spiritual destiny. Woman is presented here as nothing more than a seductive threat to man's ultimate well-being; she must therefore remain unsatisfied so that the man will not be distracted from the pursuit of philosophical enlightenment.[9] Also significant are the contrasting stereotypes: the potent, virile Christian lover, highly in demand by all women, and the ineffectual Jewish male, incapable of satisfying even his own wife because of his chronic premature ejaculation. While these stereotypes are set in an ideological framework which presents sexual prowess as a liability, they nevertheless add an interesting psychological dimension to the Jewish perception of Christians in medieval times. Whether this was a prevalent notion or merely the author's idiosyncratic outlook is difficult to determine. Contemporary sources do not confirm his conclusion that Jewish men would never be chosen as sexual partners by Christian women.[10]

The final passage has been chosen as an example of allegorical interpretation of the *'aggadah*, in which expositions of several statements are woven around a central message. The midrash associates the six wagons brought by the Israelite princes at the dedication of the tabernacle (Num. 7.3) with six steps leading up to the royal throne, and six commandments pertaining to the king (*Numbers Rabbah* 12:17). The six steps are in turn linked by R. Isaac with the ladder of Jacob's dream; both allude to the mind's ascent from discipline to discipline until it reaches the fullest possible knowledge of God.[11] After a detailed description of this process and its application to the Israelite king, the commentator turns to the Biblical assertion that each prince brought his own ox as an offering. The choice of this animal was significant, for the ox represents the intellectual speculation inspired by the tabernacle. Each prince had to bring his own ox, for he had to exercise his intellect individually, without relying on tradition received from another.

The Biblical ox leads to a Talmudic statement, usually translated "The ox which Adam sacrificed had one horn on its forehead." The allegorical interpretation of this statement totally abandons the original syntax: it is not the ox that Adam sacrificed, but the intellectual speculation which brought Adam near to God (*shur she-hiqrib 'adam*), and the *qeren*, representing purity in the physical component of a human being, is on the forehead not of the ox but of the man. This "horn" in turn brings the discussion to the Biblical description of Moses' descent from the mountain and to the Talmudic passage describing Rab's remark to *Qarna* (*Shabbat* 108a), explained not as a curse but as a blessing. Finally, the comment returns to the verses about the offerings of the princes. The associative technique, leading through Bible, Talmud, and midrash, and the intricate structure of the entire passage make it seem closer to homiletics than to exegesis.

NOTES

1. "A New Collection of Manuscripts," *Proceedings of the American Academy for Jewish Research*, IV (1933), 145.

2. See my article, "R. Isaac b. Yeda'ya: A Forgotten Commentator on the *'Aggada*," *REJ* (1979).

3. A. Neubauer, "Yedaya de Beziers," *REJ*, XX (1890), 245-248.

4. See *'Ein Ya'aqob* (New York, 1955), I, 86b, 108b, 109a.

5. See M. Benayahu, "*Rabbi Shemu'el Yaffeh Ashkenazi: Miqtzat Debarim 'alav ve'al Mefarshim Aherim shel ha-Rabbot*," *Tarbiz*, XLII (1973), app. 4, 457-460. Benayahu did not know of the present manuscript, and he speaks of Yedaiah ha-Penini's work as the earliest commentary on the full *Midrash Rabbah*.

6. A. Neubauer, "*Ergänzungen und Verbesserungen zu Abba Maris Minhat Qena'ot*," *IL*, IV (1878-79), 162-168. The discussion by Baer in *A History of the Jews in Christian Spain*, I, 94-95, does not begin to do justice to the wealth of historical information in these documents. (See above pp. 197 ff.)

7. Such a courtier, who served in the royal administration of Beziers and was apparently related by marriage to the author, is described in the *Commentary on Abot and the Aggadot of the Talmud*, f. 7b-8a. The text has been published as part of *Perushe Rishonim le-Maseket 'Abot*, ed. M. Kasher and Y. Blacherovitz (Jerusalem, 1973), pp. 53-55, where it is attributed to Yedaiah ha-Penini. Unfortunately, the transcription by the editors is so sloppy as to make even phrases based on Biblical verses all but unrecognizable and to distort in places the meaning of the passage.

8. As representatives of this tradition, we might mention, among others, the geonim Amram, Saadia, Sherira and Hai, the North Africans R. Nissim b. Jacob and Alfasi, the Spaniards R. Isaac ibn Giat, Maimonides, Rashba, R. Asher b. Yehiel and R. Jacob b. Asher, and the southern French authorities R. Abraham b. Isaac Ab-Bet-Din, R. Aaron ha-Kohen of Lunel, R. Abraham of Montpellier and R. Menahem ha-Me'iri.

9. This passage, as well as the other material on women in these commentaries, beautifully exemplifies the generalization of Joan Ferrante based on Christian sources: "Thirteenth-century literature shows the strong influence of two-anti-feminist views: the Aristotelian—of woman as a defective male, a creature lacking in reason, useful only to bear children; and the moralist—of woman as a threat to man's salvation." See *Woman as Image in Medieval Literature* (New York, 1975), p. 3.

10. Discussions of the problems caused by intimate relations between Jewish men and Christian women of various types are legion in Jewish sources. See, for example, R. Moses of Coucy, *Sefer Mitzvot Gadol*, Negative Commandment 112; Nahmanides in *Kitbe Rabbenu Mosheh ben Nahman*, ed. Chavel, I, 370; *Zohar* II, 3a-b; R. Joshua ibn Shu'eib, *Derashot*, end of Pinhas; R. Judah b. Asher, *Zikron Yehudah*, Responsa 63 and 17. Christian sources dealing with this same issue are the *Siete Partidas* of Alfonso el Sabio, VII, 24, *ix*, and the papal complaints about the abominations committed by Jewish men with the Christian nurses and servant women in their homes (S. Grayzel, *The Church and the Jews in the XIIIth Century*, pp. 107, 199).

11. Cf. A. Altmann, "The Ladder of Ascension," *Studies in Mysticism and Religion* (Jerusalem, 1967), esp. pp. 12-21.

מדרש רבה 29א-ב

1   "ובנים לא היו להם ויהן אלעזר ואיתמר,"[1] שכל הקודם
בנחלה קודם לכבוד ובלבד שיהא נוהג כמנהג אבותיו
(במדבר רבה א.כו).   מוסכם בתוך כל אומה עם ועם
כלשונו[2] לתת כבוד לבנו הבכור אביהו ואמו יולדיו,[3]
וביום הנחילו את בניו[4] העשיר בעשרו[5] יתן לבכורו עשר
ידות[6] ולשאר הבנים בניו יתן מתנות לפי עשרו ברב או
במעט.[7]   והמלכים[8] יתנו המלוכה לבן הבכור, ואף אם
יהיה בוטרא סכלא[9] לא ביונת אדם לו[10] להנהיג ולעצור[11]
בעמו לא ימנע האב רטוב[12] ממנו, ושאל לו מן השרים אף
10 המלוכה,[13] בבכורו ייסדנה[14] וירכיבוהו על הסוס[15] מטעם
המלך[16] עודנו הי[17] להורות לעמו כי הוא ימלוך אחריו[18]
כי גוע אביו ואם[19] אינו ראוי לכך, כי זה הבכור דין
אבא למלכא[20] ויקם נציבים[21] עיר ועיר אנשי אמת ושפטו
את העם[22] ולא יעבטון ארחותם.[23]
ובאה הנה לתת לפתאים ערמה[24] על הבן הבכור שירש במקום
האב המת בחיי אביו הזקן[25] וירש חלק האב בנכסי זקנו[26]
לפני אחי אביו ולא יוכל לירשו דודו או בן דודו.
ראף[27] במקום מעלה מן האב לאבן נוסעת [כך][28] שהיה
אביו כהן לאל עליון[29] או נשיא שבט רודה בעמו ומת האב
20 בעוצם תומו,[30] הבן יהיה במקום האב לכל דבר שבקדושה[31]
לכהן תחת אביו, אך בזאת[31] שימלא מקום האב במעלה
וגדולה ויחכם מכל אחיו אביר[32] ויודע דעת עליון. ואם
דוד נכבד הוא בעיני אלהים ויחכם עוד[33] עליו הוא קודם
לו[34] ללבוש את הבגדים חמודות[35] בגדי כהנה, והבן
הבכור לאיש המת ישוב בתוך עמיו[36] כאחד העם וראשו
יהיה פרוע[37] לא ישים עליו כתר כהנה או כתר מלכות[38]
אשר בקש להלמה[39] לפני אחי אביו ולא יכהן לפניהם
פאר[40] כי מנער מכבוד אלוה[41] ממעל על אשר לא מלא מקום
האב.

30 ותהי להפך כונה זו על פי התורה משאר כל אומה הנותנים
כבוד על כל בניו לבן הבכור ואם הוא בן כסיל[42] פתיות
בל ידעו מה,[43] כי לא נבזור לאלהים הכסיל בחשך הולך[44]
לעשות יקר.[45] לא כדעת החכמים בעיניהם[46] בני עמנו
הנמשכים אחר התורה בלתי הכנה והשתכלות[47] להבין ממנה
קושט דברי אמת,[48] וילכו בזקות הגרים[49] להיות להם בני
הובראים והנשיאים הביאו במקום האבות אשר כן עשו[50]
ונקרא בהם שמם[51] שם נשיא ואף אם היות הבן שואף רוח[52]
מבקר עד לערב ולא ראה לבו בעוד ירומם חכמה ודעת[53]
ויקומו לצחק בקוביא[54] לילה ללילה[55] ואל ישעו בדברי
40 הבל[56] ושחוק כל הדברים יגעים[57] ויקרא שמו בתוך עמיו
נשיא על היות האב נשיא אלהים[58] על חכמתו ומעלתו אשר
תעוז לו[59] לקראו נשיא ועל היותו האב גדול ורב[60] נגיד
היה עליהם.[61] ועל הבן אשר קם אחריו (ב29) וארח
לחברה עם אנשי[62] בלי לב שם[63] ילמדו לשונם עליו לשון
שקר[64] לקראו נשיא, כי שם נשיא מורה גדולה ומעלה
יתרה[65] בודעת בו, ואם אין מעלה בודעת בו איך יקרא
נשיא? לא באה לכסיל כבוד.[66] עוד זאת עושין[67] שיזללו
עליו[68] את יום השבת וספר התורה: כי יקום בו ביום[69]
לקרא בתורה וזה שמו אשר יקראו[70] חזן בית הכנסת לעיני
50 כל העם[71] נשיא ליום[72] וברכו אלהים[73] ויהתלו בו כהתל
באנוש[74] לכבד עם ספרו את אשר שנא[75] על אשר לא מלא
מקום הוריו.

ומשה פקח על זה כל עין עורת[76] בעמיו באמרו על נחס
כי קנא לאלהיו ועל כבוד קונו הס, אמ' פנחס בן אלעזר
בן אהרן הכהן.[77] שנה ושלש בשבחו והזכיר אבותיו
לטובה עליו שהולידו בדומה להם ויחסו אליהם כי מלא
אחרי יי[78] ובחרו לעבד לו לכהן ונחת אבותיו[79] בהיכל
מלך.[80] והורה לעם מפי עליון על פי הדברים על בן
הכהן או בן נביא שיקרא בשם האב אם הולך בתום[87] לפני

60 אל, ילך לפני אל צדקו למלוך תחת אביהו כי לו יאתה.
ומכלל הן אתה שומע לאו[82] ובין תבין[83] מדברי התורה
המחכימת פתי[84] אשר הבן הילוד לכהן ונביא איננו ראוי
לכך לא יבא אל מקדשו[85] אין המלך חפץ ביקרו,[86] כי לא
נבחר הכהן המשיח על גבה קומתו ולרוב יפיו אם לא על
חכמתו אם עמדה לו ומתקיימת בידו, והוא יהיה ירא
אלהים מנעוריו וסר מרע.[87]   והאיש שרגה או פתי[88] ישנא
אלוה ממעל תכלית שנאה.   רצוה למשה בחירו כתוב זאת
זכרון לאלף דור בספר[89] וימצא כתוב לדורות עולם
שיכבדו מכבדי,[90] ונקלה אחיך לעיניך[91] אם בזה דבר
70 המלך ודתו,[92] בוז יברזו לו.[93]

1 . . . . ועוד בדברים אחרים היו מעולים[1] משאר הלוים:
כשהיו טוענים בכלי המשכן היו הולכין כדרכן ופניהם
לארון שלא ליתן אחור לארון (במדבר רבה ה.ח).

(47ב) . . . . ואמרו עוד שהיו מהלכין לאחוריהן.   כבר
מצאת שהמשילו הנביאים[2] המציאות בכללו לאחורינו לאלהים
חי לספר כבודו כי יש גבוה על המציאות ומצוי ראשון
נורא[3] וכלם טפלים לו, כמו האחורים על דרך משל טפלים
לפנים הנכבדים לאדם לאחוריו, כי בפנים עיניו בראשו[4]
לראות להם למרחוק והולך מהרה נכון[5] במסלה יעלה[6] ולא
10 יכשל בדרך הולך כי ישמור את רגלו מדחי[7] למראה
עיניו.[8]   ואם ילך לאחוריו את רגלים[9] ימצא אבן נגף[10]
ויכשל בה ואם רוכב הסוס תמוט רגלו[11] ויפול רוכבו
אחור.[12]   ויורהו יי למשה בחירו והשיב לו על השאלה
אשר שאל[13] ממנו להדאותו את כבודו ואמתת מציאותו ואמ׳
ראית את אחורי ופני לא יראו.[14]   הורה אך במשה שהקשה
לשאול לו באלהותו להראותו אמתת מציאותו ללבב עודנו חי

חיי החומר כי החומר מבדיל בינו לבין אלהיו.[15] אך
המציאות אשר ממנו ימצא[16] למבקשים אותו מצד הפעולות
הבאות מאתו במציאות בכונת המכוין וסדר מסדר, וזה קרא
20   אחוריו המציאות בכללו להורות עליו כי הם טפלים לו
ואין להם דבקות בו.[17] ובדרך זו היו הלוים הולכים
לאחוריהם בנסעם לשאת את הארון[18] שיהיו מזככים שכלם
בארון[19] ויזהירו בו[20] לחקור על האלהים בשמים למצאו
במציאות הנקרא אחוריו וילכו אחורנית על דרך משל[21]
עד באם לסבה ראשונה לנמצאות עליונות אב לכלם ונגיד
עליהם.[22]   וזה נמשך למה שאמרו הבבליים המתפלל צריך
שיפסיע שלש פסיעות לאחוריו ואחר כך יתן שלום.[23]
והשלש פסיעות אלו שהייבו המתפלל שיפסיע שיפסיע לאחוריו המה
היו עקבות לבו[24] שיכוין אותו למצוא את אלהיו מן
30   השלשה עולמות[25] העומדים לאחוריו, ומן השלשה הכי
נכבד[26] כי ימצאנו[27] יושב ראשונה במלכות[28] וכל אשר
המה עושי' מטעם המלך,[29] כמו שבארנו במסכת יומא
בחבור התלמוד בבלי[30] פרוש אמתי ומתקבל לאוזן שומעת
לא קדמני אדם בו[31] המפרש דבריהם בעלמים כירצא באלו
וירצא בשיירה[32] לבאר הדברים עתיקים[33] ברב עם[34]
בחכמה ובמנין[35] להשכיל לבותם לדבר הזה, לא ראיתיו
עד הנה כתוב במגלת ספר[36] בכל כתבי הקדש, לא מצאו
חזון[37] בדבר הזה כי מה עין שכלם מראות[38] ולהבין
קושט עומק הדבריה האלה.   וחשבו תועה[39] על פי
40   הדברים כי הם כפשטן, וילכו אחורניהן[40] שלש (48א)
פסיעות אחר שסיימו תפלתן הזכה בעיניהם,[41] כאלו היה
מכוין מן שמים ללכת באלה אחור ולא לפני'.   וילכו
הגוי כלו שובב אחורנית פעמים שלש יום ויום בדרך לבו
הערל[42] בקרבו, לב בשר סגור וכבד להשיג האמתות
באלהים חי.   וישנו עם עור[43] האנשים האלה סרו מהר
מני הדרך[44] דרך אמת, כי איך יעלה אל אביר כל עושה

אלה ויתרצה זה אל אדניו[45] בלכתו אחורנית זה שלש
רגלים אחר התפללו לאלהיו? הלא הוא אמר לו והזהירו
על עיניו עיני בשר או עיני שכלו[46] לנוכח יביטו[47]

50   בכל דבר לטוב לו, כי סרסורי דחטאה אינון[48] אם יביטו
בקצות למרחוק[49] ולא ימשל באבן בגף מבית ומחוץ[50] כי
יראה ללבב[51] להסיר המכשולות ולא יבחר ללכת דרך עיר
בכה[52] וכל מעגל נלוז[53] ירחיק נדוד ממנו[54] ולא ירט
הקדש דרך הקדש[55] דרך עץ החיים[56] לא יסור ממנו[57] לא
ימוט לעולם[58].

<u>מדרש רבה, 66ב-67ב</u>

1   "והעמיד אותה הכהן"[1] מלמד שאם היתה חגרת אינה שותה.
"ונוון על כפיה" מלמד שאם היתה גדמת אינה שותה
(במדבר רבה ט.לג). כל אשה חגרת (67) רצולעת על ירך[3]
מום בה ואם נסתרה עם איש אחד אשר יתאו אליה והיא לא
ידעה כי זה חושק בה, לא תוכל האשה ההיא להנצל מן
האיש אם רוצה לאנסה, וכשל כחה[4] לברוח מידו כי חלה.
וכן הגדמת לא תוכל להעזר בידה הימנית אם שכב איש
אותה[5] בעל כרחה.   ולא יוכלו הבעלים להשקותן זו וזו
אם קנאה בהם[6] כמו המקנאים לנשיהם בריאות וטובות,[7] כי
לא תוכלו אלו מלט[8] מיד האיש המדבר על לבבהן, ואולי[9]
10   נאנסו אם ישכבו עמהם משכבי אשה.[10]
או נלך לדרך אחרת:[11] אם נסתתרו הנשים אלו עם איש זר
אולי לא נתכונו לדבר עברה, כי לכל אזות כלי זנניה
עליה[12] שלא יתאו לאחת מאלה, ומומה יגן לה, ואם יתיחד
עם האחת לא יעלה על רוחו לשכב עמה ולא יביט למראיהן[13]
להיות אצלה לענין רע.   כי כן חייב הטבע הכם'[14] על
עיני האדם שלא יתאוו לאשת בעלת מום[15] אם היא חגרת

הולכת על גחון[16] ולא הגדמת בכף רגלה כף אחת; לא
תתרצה לעיני כל רואיה[17] אם לא באשה יפת מראה[18] הולכת

20 קוממיות וידיה לא אסורות[19] לעשות בהמה כל מלאכה
נקיה, ואף הנשים מאירות אותן[20] ומבזות לשתיהן והלא
כל דכן הוא על הילדים רכים[21] בחורי חמד[22] שלא יחמדו
בנשים אם לא האשה יפת תואר[23] ואם חולת אהבה היא[24].
ובין דין לדין[25] לא יוכלו הבעלים להשקות הגדמת
והחגרת.

כי כל דבריהם[26] על השוטה[27] הם נסכמים עם השכל, ולא
עלה על רוחם[28] כי כן היתה גזרת הכתר' על שתי נשים
אלו בלתי טעם מאשר אמר במרחלט "והעמיד אותה הכהן"
וזאת האשה אשר לא תוכל עמוד על רגליה הותרה לזנות על

30 פי המצוה זו ולא תוכל[29] בעלה להשקותה אם קנא בה ולא
נאסרה[30] לו בקנוי. וכן הגדמת אם תזנה תחת אישה לא
נאסרה לו כי כן גזרת הכתר' על שתיהן. חלילה להם
שיזנו על זה ויתברו[31] מקום לנשים להטוא. כי כל דברי
הספר הסתום[32] באו לתועלת המחזיקים בו,[33] וכל מי אשר
חנן אלהינו דעה והשכל[34] בין יבין קרשט אמרי אמת[35]
מכל הדברים וכל צפון בהם וכל רז לא אנס ליה.[36]
ובגזרת עירין[37] שהורו הנה[38] כבר נסכמה עם השכל, כי
לא באו מן שמים גזרות לעם ולא נכתב בספר לחת לעם
תורה ומצות בלתי תועלת במצא לעושיה אחת לאחת.[39]

40 חלילה לאל אל אמת כל דבריו דברי טעם, ודבריהם[40]
נאהבים ונעימים[41] למבינים שכלם נתנו להאיר לעם
ההולכים בחשך[42] לראות בטוב יי.[43]

ובאו דברי תורה על השוטה לעם ליסר הנשים[44] כי תזנינה
תחת הבעל וישב ממזר באהלים[45] ותולות בבעליהן,[46] ולא
יודע זולתי לנואף ולנואפת. ודברה תורה בנשים בריאות
וטובות בגופן אשר יתאו להן כל רואיהן. ובאו בה כל
הדברים האלה בספר וירחקו[47] לערבב השטן[48] ולא יקטרג

בין איש לאשתו ולא יפריד בינותן, ויראו האנשים[49]
מדבר אם כל אדם זולתי הבעל, כי[50] כל דברי איש נטרי
50   שידבר עם אשה הם דברים יגעים דברי (67ב) חשק שידבר
על לבה דברי אהבים והיא שומעת מדעתה קלה העזה פניה
ותאמר לו[51] "פתה וגם תוכל!"[52] וגזרה חכמת אלהים
שיוכל בעלה לקנא באשה הפרוצה וישקנה סף רעל, וייסרו
שאר הנשים[53] בצאת נפשה כי מתה[54] בחטא וייראו לנפשם
אחרי זאת כל אשה חכמת לב[55] שלא ימצא בה בעלה ערות
דבר[56] וישקנה רוש,[57] ויתנו יקר לבעליהן[58] עוד כל
הימים ולא תבגוד בבעל נעוריה[59] כי יראה פן תמות גם
היא במי המרים ואין ירא בועט[60] ולא תמצא אחרי זאת
קדשה בנשים.   ודבק באשתו[61] הגוי כלו ולא באשת חברו
60   וילדו להם בנים מהורגנים ותמלא הארץ רוח דעת ויראת
יי.[62]

ולא דברה התורה בדרך זרות[63] על האשה המנאפת חגרת
וגדמת, לא כלל אותן עם שאר הנשים בריאות בגופן ואף
אם המה חמורת[64] לטבען, כי הם לא תזנינה לא תמצא לאדת
מאלה ואם העזה ובקשתם לא תמצא[65] מאהבים לזנות, כי
חלרות הנה ומראיהן רע.[66]   וכי יזמנה[67] ויתארו לאיש
זר, מסוללות זו בזו[68] או משמשרת בצלמי זכר[69] בבתיהן
צפרנות אחת הנה ואחת הנה, ואיש לא ידעה מבלעדי אישה
כי לא תמצאנו בבית ובשדה.[70]   ותעמוד על כרחה בלא חטא
70   והטוב חרה לו[71] כי לא מצאתו והיא מרת נפש.[72]

<u>מדרש רבה 90א-91א</u>

1   "בנות ציון."[1] בנים המצוינים במילה, שאלו לא היו
נימולין לא היו יכולין להביט לשכינה אלא נופלים, כשם
שהיה נופל אברהם, שנ' ויפול אברהם על פניו וידבר אתו

אלהים,[2] וכן בבלעם הוא אומ' נופל וגלוי עינים[3]
(במדבר רבה יב, ח).

הערל לפני אל ערל בשר מגואל הוא ורע בעיניו, כי זה
יהיה באחריתו עצל לב בהכרח, ואי אפשר בלעדי זה.[4] כי
זה נמנע בחזק למשול ברוחו[5] לערבב (90ב) את השטן,[6] לא
יוכל להנצל מיד חזק ממנו[7] אם לא יבא לו בדרך זרות[8]

10 שיהיה זה קר בטבעו מן הבטן ולא יוכל לשטנו, ולא
תמצאנו אחד מאלף. ולא דברו בדרך זרות לאנשים האלה,
בטלו כי מעטו.[9] כי זה כל האדם ערל בשר תאוה נפשו
לשכב האשה יפת מראה,[10] אמריה החליקה[11] למשכו אחריה,
ויטריד שכלו להיות אצלה ירט וירם וילאה למצוא[12] את
שאהבה נפשו[13] עמה על עסקי תשמיש.

15 והיא גם היא תסובב גבר[14] ערל בשר ושכבה בחיקו[15] באות
נפשה,[16] יען וביען כי הוא טוחן בה זמן רב לסבת הערלה
אשר היא מחיצה לבלתי נתן זרע[17] בשכיבה, והיא נהנית
ומזרעת תחלה.[18] וכי ישכב אותה הערל ויואל האיש לשוב
לביתו, היא העזה פניה[19] ותתפשהו[20] והחזיקה במבושיו[21]

20 ותאמר לאיש, "שוב, שכב!"[22] להנאת עצמה אשר היא תמצא
בשכבה עמו, בזידי פחדין[23] גיד ברזל[24] ובזרמת הסוס
זרמתו[25] אשר יורה כחץ[26] בבטנה. ויתלכדו בזה ולא
יתפצלו,[27] ויבעול וישנה וישלש בלילה אחד והנפש לא
תמלא.[28] וכן ינהג לילה לילה, ותשמיש המטה מכחש

25 כחיש ליה משמן בשרו[29] ועוכר שארו[30] וימרק מוחו בנשים
מרוק רע,[31] וימת לבו בקרבו[32] בין רגליה טרע נפל[33]
ולא יוכל לראות באור פני מלך[34] כי טח בנשים עיני
שכלו[35] ועתה לא ראו אור.[36]

30 והנמול כי יתאו ליופי הנשים ודבק באשתו[37] או באשה
אחרת אשת יפת תואר,[38] הוא ימצא את עצמו איש מהיר
במלאכתו,[39] ונתן זרע בהכנסת עטרה,[40] וכי שכב עמה פעם
אחת שבע ילין[41] ולא יסף עוד לדעתה[42] לימים עוד

שבעה.[43]   וכן ינהג הנמול כפעם בפעם עם האשה אשר אהב:
הוא מזריע תחלה, לא עצר כח,[44] כי שכב אותה מיד נקרה,
ואינה נהנית בו במשכבה ובקומה.[45]   וטוב ממנה אם הוא
לא ידעה ולא קרב אליה,[46] כי חמם אותה ולא יועיל,
ונשארה שוקקה תחת אישה עוד הזרע במגורה[47] בושה

40 וחפרה,[48] ואינה מזרעת אחת בשנה אם לא לעתים רחוקות
היא מזרעת תחלה לרוב החום והאש תוקד בה.[49]   וזה יאמר
ליי אני,[50] כי הוא לא ימרק מחרו עם שוכבת חיקו ולא
באשת חברו, וימצא חן ושכל טוב[51] ואמיץ לבו[52] לדרוש
אלהים ולא יירא מהביט אל עבר[53] וכי ידבר עמו לא יפנה
עורף.

ובדרך זו נהנית האשה מן הערל יותר מן הנימול והיא
תמיתנו לרוב חשקה בו ותריץ את גלגלתו[54] ולא במעל
ומידו היתה זאת[55] גברא דבשי קטליה.[56]   כמו שהורו
בבראשית רבה באמרם הנבעלת מן הערל קשה לפרוש,[57] ושם
בארנו על דינה ועל כירצא בה האשה ישראלית הנאה

50 שתמצא כי שכב אותה האיש הערל יהודי או ארמאי יותר מן
הנימול, כי כן חייב הטבע חכם ליהנות זה בזה לזכר
ולנקבה.[58]   ואף האיש הנקי בערלים ובר לבב[59] ירא
אלהים וסר מרע[60] יצרו תקפו[61] יונם ויום ונלחם בו כל
הלילות לסבת העולה, לא יתן דמי לו[62] ומטריד שכלו כל
ימי צבאו[63] להנצל מפח טמן לו[64] ולא ימצא שכלו (91א)
נכון עמו לבא אל שער המלך[65] כי ימצא אויבים בשער[66]
ולא יתראה לערל אלוה ממעל[67] כי ירא האיש מגשת אליו[68]
מפני חמת המציק[69] לו שם בבית, כמו שיתראה לאיש
הנימול העומד שם באהל שוקט ובוטח[70] ולא ימצא ארב

60 לו, והוא יזכך שכלו לכשירצה ותמונת יי יביט.[71]
ובדרך זו היה בלעם נופל ארצה[72] כל עת ידבר אלהיו
עמו, לא יוכל לראות מלך ביופיו[73] בכהו, ומדבר אתו
ממול ערפו.[74]   כי הערלה אוטמת אזנו משמוע[75] מה דבר

יי וסוגרת דלתי בטנו[76] ועיניו תכהינה מראות[77] אלהיו
פנים בפנים[78] לחוזק המראה, וכי ידבר עמו בלט סתר
פנים ישים[79] או יפול הנופל[80] והולך על גחון[81] אין
מאז להרים ראש. וכן תמצא לאברהם[82] שהיה נופל על
אפיו כי ידבר אלהיו עמו כל עת עדלתו בו, כי העדלה
היתה מבדלת בינו לבין אלהיו[83] ולא מכשכר (כך) ליה,[84]

70 ואם היה ירא לו מנעוריו וחרד אל דברו. והעת הסיר
ערלת הבשר הסיר עמה כל שאר ערלה מבית ומחוץ,[85] מאה
עדלות פלשתים[86] משרתיו רשעים[87] יצוריו הדבים, ריגע
לבבו[88] והסיר את מוראתו[89] עד מצאו חלל בקרבו[90] ורכך
האזן ערלה[91] והנה שבה אזן שומעת[92] וכל יצור עקש שב
רך וטוב[93] כבשר הנער[94] כי רר בשרו.[95] וכל ישראל
מצויניין במילה[96] לפני אל אשר יעשה טוב ורב אחרי המולו
ולא יחטא,[97] וכי ידבר עמו יסיר המסוה[98] מעל עין
ימינו[99] ויאר פניו לו[100] ויעננו בקול על שאלתו קול
יי בהדר.[101]

מדרש רבה 96ב-97ב

1 שש עגלות צב[1] כנגד שש מצות המלך מצוה עליהם בכל
יום.[2] שש כנגד שש מעלות לכסא.[3] כיצד? המלך עולה על
מעלה ראשונה הכרוז יוצא אומר לו "לא ירבה לו נשים."[4]
עלה על מעלה שניה הכרוז יוצא ואומר לו "לא ירבה לו
סוסים."[5] עלה על מעלה שלישית הכרוז יוצא ואומר לו
"כסף וזהב לא ירבה לו."[6] עלה על מעלה רביעית הכרוז
יוצא ואומר "לא תטה משפט."[7] עלה על מעלה חמישית
הכרוז אומר "לא תכיר פנים."[8] עלה על מעלה ששית
הכרוז אומר לו "לא תקח שחד."[9] בא לישב על כסאו אומר

10 לו "זכר נא לפני מי אתה יושב.[10]"   (במדבר רבה יב.
    יז)

כל הבא אל הבית אשר שם האלהים[11] יעלה בתחלה שש מעלות
הצריכות לו לעלות בהמה כפעם בפעם כי דרש ידרשנו[12]
במסלה יעלה[13] במעלות האלה עד באו בהיכל מלך[14] וידבר
אליו ולא ידלג כאיל[15] שתי מעלות בפעם אחת כי יפול
הנופל[16] ותגלה ערותו[17] וישוב לביתו דך ונכלה.[18]   כמו
שרמז יעקב בסלם[19] אשר עלה במעלות ממטה למעלה מדרגה
אחר מדרגה פעם אחרי פעם והזכירם על הסדר שעלה.
והורה תחלה על רגלי הסלם כי הם נצבים על הארץ,[20] ומן

20 הרגלים אלו בסלם את רגלים ריך[21] להכיר את בוראו מהם
להכיר מצד הפעלות הבאות מאתו מלמטה לארץ בכונה מכון
וסדר מסדר[22] לחיות ברעב[23] כל העם הנמצא בה.[24]
ואחר עלה עוד במעלה השניה לדעת מי הוא זה מלך[25] על
כל צבא המרום[26] והכיר בהם על פי המחקר[27] כי יש גבוה
עליהם המניעם מבלי הפסק ומנוחה,[28] אין כח בהם לעשות
דבר אם לא במלאכות עליון נורא מושל בכל,[29] כי הם
עבדיו וחילו הגדול וצבאו ופקודיו[30] אין מספר
לגדודיו[31] אשר יאמר להם יעשו.   ואחר עלה עוד יעקב גם
עלה במעלה השלישית ויפגע במקום[32] מלאכי אלהים

30 העומדים סביב לו מימינו ומשמאלו לשרתו[33] יום ויום
איש בשם אלהיו[34] וירא אליו אחד מן השרפים[35] ויצא
לקראתו אחד מן השרים הראשונים[36] בא ויאמר כי הם עלות
ועולים[37] ויש קץ למספר[38] הסבה ראשונה ואין עוד אחר
אחרי יי ויראהו באצבע[39] זה אלי ואנוהו.[40]
ואחר עלה עוד במעלה רביעית והכיר במלאך[41] הנראה אליו
כי הוא יקר בעיני אלהים[42] על כל שאר הנמצאות במדרגה
ומעלה, וממנו תצא תורה למין האנושי[43] ואורה ושמחה[44]
לנפשו אחריו בטוב תלין.[45]   ואחר עלה עוד והכיר כי
הוא יזכר לבן אדם[46] מלאכיו יצוה לו אלוה ממעל[47]

40   לְהֵרָאוֹתוֹ בֵּית בְּכֹחֹה[48] וְכָל טוּב אֲדֹנָיו[49] עַד כִּי יָבֹא בְּהֵיכַל

קָדְשׁוֹ[50] וַיֵּרָאֵהוּ יְיָ לַלֵּבָב[51] בַּמַּעֲלָה הַשְּׁבִיעִית רִאשׁוֹנָה

בַּמַּלְכוּת[52] הִנֵּה אֱלֹהֵינוּ זֶה[53] וּבָא הָאִישׁ הַמְדַבֵּר אֵלָיו וְקוֹרֵא

לוֹ מִנֶּגֶד אֵלִי אֵלִי יְיָ שָׁלוֹם[54] יְחִי הַמֶּלֶךְ לְעוֹלָם.[55] וְאֵלּוּ

הֵן שֵׁשׁ הַמַּעֲלוֹת שֶׁעוֹלָה בָּהֵמָּה כָּל מְבַקֵּשׁ יְיָ[56] עַד מָצְאוּ יוֹשֵׁב

רֹאשׁ עַל (97א) כָּל הַמַּעֲשֶׂה שָׁם.[57]

וּכְנֶגְדָן בָּאוּ שֵׁשׁ מַעֲלוֹת בַּמֶּלֶךְ[58] בָּשָׂר שֶׁעוֹלֶה בָּהֵמָּה אֶל מָקוֹם

הַשֶּׁבֶת[59] כְּעֵין מַלְכוּתָא דִרְקִיעָא[60] כְּשֶׁיַּשְׂכִּיל לִבּוֹ עַל אֱלֹהָיו

מִתּוֹךְ עֲלוֹתוֹ אַחַת לְאַחַת.[61] כִּי כֵן יְסַד הַמֶּלֶךְ[62] אֵלָיו לִקְרֹא

לְפָנָיו עַל כָּל מַעֲלָה שֶׁלֹּא יִמְשֹׁךְ אַחַר גְּרוֹן[63] וְאַל יִתְאָו

50   לְמַטְעַמּוֹתָיו[64] לַעֲנַג בְּשָׂרוֹ, כִּי תַעֲבוֹג זֶה הוּא יַפְסֵד

בְּאַחֲרִיתוֹ בַּחֲצִי יָמָיו יַעַזְבֶנּוּ.[65] וְאִם יַשְׂכִּיל לֵב הַמֶּלֶךְ עַל

אֱלֹהָיו בְּכָל מַעֲלָה הוּא עוֹלֶה תִּדְבַּק נַפְשׁוֹ בַּדֶּרֶךְ הוֹלֵךְ אֶת

שֶׁאָהֵבָה[66] וְרָוְתָה דָשֵׁן[67] בַּתַּעֲנוּג רֹחַבְנִי עַל שֻׁלְחַן הַמֶּלֶךְ[68]

וְתִשְׂבַּע וְתוֹתַר.[69] כְּמוֹ שֶׁתִּמָּצֵא עַל פִּי הַתּוֹרָה בְּהִשָּׁמַע דְּבַר

הַמֶּלֶךְ וְדָתוֹ[70] מִפִּי עֶלְיוֹן וַיְצַו עָלָיו שֶׁלֹּא יַרְבֶּה לּוֹ נָשִׁים[71]

שָׁם בְּבֵית הַמַּלְכוּת וְאַל יִתְאָו לְיוֹפְיִין[72] פֶּן יִמְרַק עַצְמוֹ

בְּנָשִׁים[73] אֲשֶׁר יִשְׁרוּ בְּעֵינָיו וְיֶחְסַר מֹחוֹ בְּהַכְּרָה וְיִלְאֶה

שִׂכְלוֹ וְהוּא עָיֵף לַמָּצָא[74] אֱלֹהִים חַי וְיַהֲרֹס לִרְאוֹת בּוֹ[75]

הַנִּמְנָע בַּחֵקֶר וַהֲלֹא גְּנַאי הוּא לוֹ.[76] וְעַל כָּל מַעֲלָה וּמַעֲלָה

60   מַזְכִּיר לוֹ מִצְוַת אֵלּוּ אֶת הַחֲמִשָּׁה[77] אַחַת לְאַחַת שִׁיתָן אֶל לִבּוֹ

מִקּוֹל הַקּוֹרֵא שֶׁיִּנְהַג עִם אֶחָיו[78] עַל סֵדֶר יָשָׁר לְהַעֲמִיד אֶרֶץ

בְּתוֹךְ עַמּוֹ[79] וְיַחְכְּם עוֹד[80] וּבֵין יָבִין וְיָשִׁיב אֶל לִבּוֹ[81]

כִּי הַגּוֹי כֻּלּוֹ בְּנֵי אִישׁ אֶחָד[82] אֲשֶׁר בָּרָא אֱלֹהִים בַּתְּחִלָּה בַּדֶּרֶךְ

פֶּלֶא בִּלְתִּי זָכָר וּנְקֵבָה[83] וּמִמֶּנּוּ נִפְרְצוּ לְיָמִים עוֹד שִׁבְעָה[84]

וְשִׁבְעָה מִשְׁפָּחוֹת כִּי הֵחֵל הָאָדָם לָרֹב.[85] וְהַמַּשְׂכִּיל[86] יָבִין כִּי

לֹא בְכֹחַ[87] לִהְיוֹת לַמֶּלֶךְ עַל כְּבוֹד עָשְׁרוֹ כִּי גָלָה מִמֶּנּוּ[88]

בְּאַחֲרִיתוֹ וְלֹא יֵרֵד אַחֲרָיו[89] וְאִם גָּבַהּ לִבּוֹ אֱלֹהִים עֲזָבוֹ וְסָר

מֵעָלָיו[90] וְכָל מֹרְאוֹ[91] יֵצֶר לוֹ וְלֹא תִכּוֹן מַלְכוּתוֹ[92]

יִשְׁפִּילֶנָּה יַשְׁפִּילָה.[93] וּבַמַּעֲלָה עֲלִירֻנָה אֲשֶׁם[94] שָׁם חֶמֶד

70 לשבתו[95] על כסא כבוד למלך הוכן[96] לשבת בו כי ידון
רוחו בעצמו,[97] שם קורא לו שישכיל ללבב לפני מי
ירושב[98] על המשפט אשר השליטו העושר והכבוד[99] והוא בחר
בו לתת לעמו צדקה ומשפט[100] משפט צדק[101] וישב ומלך על
כסא יי.[102] והנשיאים הביאו איש על דגלו בכור שורו[103]
מיוחד לכל נשיא בלתי הצטרף אליו על השור[104]הוא ושכנו
אחד נפש משאר הנשיאים ההונים עליו. ובא השור לכל
נשיא בהם על שבי פנים לרמוז[105] לו על העיון השכלי
הצריך לכל אחד לעין במלאכה מלאכת המשכן חד הראות[106]
במשכיות החמדה[107] עד נראה אליו אלוה ממעל לרגל

80 המלאכה,[108] ולרמוז להם על העיון הלז לא נבחרה הפרה
לשאת המשכן אם לא בכור שורו חדר לו.[109]
שהשאילו הבבליים השור על העיון דק ושכלי כאלו הוא
נקוד בשורוק שנופל על הבטה והראיה לענין,[10] ואמרו
שור שהקריב אדם הראשון קרן אחת היתה לו במצחו,[111]
הורו על העיון שכלי שהיה באדם על אלהיו בהבראו שהיה
אז עליוני ושכלי דמי לבר אלהין.[112] והעיון ההוא
הקריבו[113] לאלהים קרבות מעלה כי אמרם שהקריב אדם שב
אל השור[114] הקודם זכרו, כי העיון (97ב) כי הקריבו לאלהיו
לדעת אותו ולדבקה בו.   והסבה להקרבה לאלהיו היא

90 הקרן הירוצאת לו במצחו כי מן המצח ירצא הזכרנות
לאדם[115] לרוב בהירות וזכות החומר לאדם הראשון נזדכך
שכלו אז יותר ונגה עליו אור[116] פני מלך[117] שראה ביופיו
ולא יירא מהביט[118] חרזק המראה ויזכור יום ליום אשר
כבר עשהו על פי הראיה ללבב ולא שכחו מלב.
ובא הקרן לאמת הבהירות וזכות החומר באדם כי כן נופל
במקומות ואמ' כי קרן עור פני משה,[119] וכן אמרו
הבבליים גם כן מה שמך? קרנא.   יהא רעוא דתיפוק ליה
קרנא בעיניה.[120] לא קללו חברו קללת חנם[121] חלילה אך
ברכו ברכות טוב[122] שיאורו עיניו להבין דברי חפץ ולא

100 נתעלמה ממנו הלכה.[123] כמו שבארנו בחבור התלמוד בבלי

במסכת חולין בפרק אלו טרפות[124] על שור שהקריב אדם

הראשון על מה בשתנה משאר השורים להיות לו קרן במצחו

יותר מהם ועל מה קרניו קודמים לפרסותיו[125] הוסתר

בדברים אלו מה הוא, כי הוא לא היה בן הבקר הולך על

ארבע.[126] ולא קדמני אדם בו לא מלאו לבו לגלות הוסתר

ארזן אבשים[127] למצוא פשר דבר[128] נאה מתקבל באזן שומעת

לא ידע אבוש[129] עד עתה.

מצורף אל זה שבא לנשיאים שור לאחד, ועט זרים אל

יתעדבו[130] בו בשור, להורות לפניו שעמד יהידי בבית

110 וישב בדד[131] כי יעיין במרכבה[132] בעיונו השכלי להשיג מן

המרכבה הדרוכב עליה[133] יעמד יהידי איש באהלו[134] וזר

לא יקרב.[135] כמו שהורו הבבלייה ואמרו מעשה מרכבה

ביהידי[136] כמו שבארנו בחבור התלמוד בבלי במסכת חגיגה

בפרק אין דורשין.

CMR 29a-b: Annotation

1. Num. 3:4.   2. Esth. 1:22.   3. Zech. 13:3.   4. Deut. 21:16.   5. Cf. Jer. 9:22.   6. II Sam. 19:44.   7. I Sam. 14:6.   8. Moving from the general theme of inheritance to the theme of royal succession.   9. Cf. *Baba Batra* 126b. 10. Cf. Prov. 30:2.   11. The meaning is probably based on II Chron. 22:9. 12. Probably should read *ha-tov*; cf. Jer. 5:25, Prov. 3:27.   13. Cf. I Kings 2:22; the king asks the nobles for kingship on behalf of his son.   14. Josh. 6:26, used here in a totally different sense.   15. The subject is the *sarim*, or indefinite; apparently the royal steed is meant.   16. Jon. 3:7.   17. While the old king is still alive. For the technique of choosing a son as successor and providing him with the trappings of kingship in order to secure his position while the father lives, cf. Abravanel's analysis of Absalom's rebellion in *Nebi'im Rishonim*, pp. 360 ff.   18. Cf. I Kings 1:13.   19. "*Even* if the first-born is not worthy of being king."   20. I have not found the source of this expression.   21. The king will appoint local governors.   22. Cf. Exod. 18:21-22.   23. Joel 2:7.   24. Prov. 1:4.   25. As the verse (Num. 3:4) asserts that Eleazar and Itamar ministered as priests in the presence of Aaron their father.   26. The first born will inherit his father's portion of his grandfather's property.   27. Again the transition is made from inheritance of property to succession in office.   28. The meaning of this phrase in this context is unclear to me. Perhaps the reading should be *leben* with *nosa'at* referring back to *ma'alah*.   29. Gen. 14:18.   30. Cf. Job 21:23.   31. Cf. *Berakot* 21b.   31. "Provided, on condition that."   32. Cf. I Kings 5:11. The reading should probably be *'ahe 'abiv*. The restriction that the first born son succeeds his father pro-

vided that he is wiser than any of his uncles begins to undermine the entire principle of hereditary succession.   33. Cf. Prov. 9:9.   34. If the uncle is wiser than the son, he has priority over the son to succeed the father.   35. Cf. Lev. 21:10 and Gen. 27:15.   36. Cf. Ezek. 18:18.   37. Lev. 13:45: a sign of mourning.   38. Cf. Esth. 2:17 and *'Abot* 4:13.   39. Cf. *'Abodah Zarah* 44a on 1 Kings 1:5.   40. Cf. Isa. 61:10.   41. Cf. Num. 24:11.   42. Prov. 17:25.   43. Cf. Prov. 9:13.   44. Eccles. 2:14.   45. Esth. 6:6.   46. Cf. Isa. 5:21.   47. Rational insight.   48. Cf. Prov. 22:21, used by the author to refer to the philosophical content of the Torah.   49. Cf. Lev. 20:23.   50. Cf. Eccles. 8:10; the sons are accepted in the position of the fathers who acted rightly.   51. Cf. Gen. 48:16; the name or title of the father is used for the son.   52. Cf. Jer. 2:24, 14:6, meaning "panting" (Radak).   53. Cf. Eccles. 1:16 and Jer. 15:9, here referring to the previous assertion that the son pursued vain things all day long.   54. Cf. Exod. 32:6 and M. *Sanh.* 3:3.   55. Ps. 19:3.   56. Cf. Exod. 5:9, here an editorial comment that these men should *not* be doing what they are doing?   57. Eccles. 1:8.   58. Gen. 23:6.   59. Cf. Eccles. 7:19.   60. Deut. 2:10, here apparently a play on the title *rav*.   61. I Chron. 9:20.   62. Cf. Job 34:8.   63. A composite of Num. 16:2 and Job 30:8.   64. Cf. Jer. 9:4.   65. In accordance with the meaning of the root *ns'*.   66. Cf. Prov. 26:1.   67. The Jews in his time.   68. On account of the *nasi*, the Shabbat and the Torah scroll are profaned.   69. "When the *nasi* rises on the Shabbat."   70. Jer. 23:6, a reference to the use of the title *nasi* by the *hazzan* in calling to the Torah?   71. Exod. 19:11.   72. Cf. Num. 7:11.   73. Job 1:5; here, as there, the verb is used as a euphemism for blaspheming God.   74. Cf. Job 13:9.   75. By honoring in association with the Torah him whom God hates.   76. Cf. Isa. 42:7. The *'al zeh* refers to the idea that a son may succeed to the position of his father only if he is worthy of this position.   77. Num. 25:11. The turning to the first verse of the *parashah* gives the entire passage something of the structure and feeling of a *derashah*.   78. Cf. I Kings 11:6.   79. Cf. Lev. 16:32.   80. Ps. 45:12.   81. Prov. 10:9.   82. Cf. *Nedarim* 11a.   83. Prov. 23:1.   84. Cf. Ps. 19:8.   85. Cf. Ezek. 44:9.   86. Cf. Esth. 6:6.   87. Job 1:1.   88. Cf. Ezek. 45:20.   89. Exod. 17:14.   90. Cf. I Sam. 2:20.   91. Deut. 25:3.   92. Cf. Esth. 2:8 and Num. 15:13.   93. Song 8:7.

CMR 47a–48a: Annotation

1. Referring to the children of Kehat.   2. The analogy used by the prophets is that the universe is to God as the back is to the front or face of a person; therefore they spoke of the back when referring to the realm of creation. Cf. *Hil. Yesode ha-Torah* 1.10 and *Guide* I, 21 on Exod. 33:23.   3. Ps. 47:3; note the juxtaposition with the purely philosophical phrase *matzuy rishon*.   4. Eccles. 2:14.   5. Cf. Isa. 57:2.   6. Cf. Num. 20:19.   7. Cf. Ps. 116:8.   8. Cf. Ezra 23:16.   9. Apparently the object of *yimtzah*.   10. Is 8:14; here the subject of *yimtzah*.   11. Cf. Ps. 121:3.   12. Gen. 49:17.   13. In Exod. 33:18.   14. Exod. 33:23; cf. Maimonides, above note 2.   15. Cf. Isa. 59:2.   16. I.e., the realm of Creation, called God's "back."   17. I.e., the world is not *part* of the Godhead, as it might seem in a pantheistic theology, or perhaps in one which viewed the entire world as emanated from the Diety.   18. Exod. 37:5.   19. Through the Torah, contained in the ark, the intellect is purified of false notions.   20. By means of the ark (or the intellect, as either could be the referent).   21. I.e., the Levites do not actually walk backward; the phrase in the midrash means merely that through the Torah,

they learn about God from His actions in the realm of creation.   22. Cf. Mal.
2:10 and I Chron. 9:20.   23. *Yoma* 53b.   24. And *not* actual footsteps.   25.
The sublunar realm, the realm of heavenly bodies, and the realm of the immaterial
intelligences.   26. Cf. II Sam. 23:19.   27. I.e., *God* will be found.   28. Cf.
Esth. 1:14.   29. Jon. 3:7.   30. A reference to the author's commentary on the
aggadot of the Talmud.   31. The claim of absolute originality is made by R. Isaac
several times in the Midrash Commentary. Here it is apparently justified by universal acceptance of the literal meaning of three steps by other authorities.   32. Cf.
M. *Gittin* 6:5; here a long line of commentators.   33. I Chron. 4:22.   34. Prov.
14:28; here: publicly, by writing the commentary.   35. M. *'Eduyot* 1:5: an interesting statement of the author's concept of the purpose of his work.   36. Cf. Ps.
40:8.   37. Lam. 2:9.   38. Cf. Isa. 44:18.   39. The second word is probably
a noun, as in Isa. 32:6.   40. Cf. Gen. 9:23; here the actual contemporary practice
of Jews, of which the author is mockingly critical.   41. I.e., in *their* sight, but not
in God's.   42. Cf. Isa. 57:17 and Lev. 26:41.   43. Isa. 43:8.   44. Cf. Exod.
32:8.   45. Cf. I Sam. 29:4.   46. I.e., the verse can be understood either literally or metaphorically.   47. Prov. 4:25.   48. Y. *Berakot* I, 3c.   49. Cf. Job
39:39.   50. Used by the author to indicate the internal or the external causes of
sin.   51. I Sam. 16:7; here "he should look at his own heart."   52. Based on
'emeq ha-bakah (Ps. 84:7) or *'ir nebokah* (cf. Esth. 3: 5)?   53. Cf. Prov. 2:15.
54. Cf. Ps. 55:8.   55. The first *ha-qodesh* probably does not belong; cf. Num.
22:33 and Isa. 35:8.   56. Gen. 3:24.   57. II Sam. 7:15.   58. Ps. 15:5.

CMR 66b–67b: Annotation

1. Num. 5:18; should read: *ve-he'emid ha-kohen et ha-'isha.*   2. Num. 5:18.
3. Cf. Gen. 32:32.   4. Cf. Neh. 4:4.   5. Cf. Num. 5:19.   6. Should be *'im
qin'u.*   7. Cf. Gen. 41:5.   8. Cf. Isa. 46:2.   9. Cf. Isa. 40:2 and Nah. 2:8.
10. Lev. 18:22, 20:13.   11. I.e., an alternate explanation of why these women are
excluded from the category of *sotah* subject to the ordeal of the bitter waters.   12.
Should be *kele zayne* (A.Z. 25b, Yeb. 115a); i.e., her physical blemish is her weapon,
protecting her from the sin of adultery.   13. Cf. I Sam. 16:7.   14. A characteristic phrase for the natural order of things.   15. Cf. I Sam. 28:7.   16. Cf. Lev.
11:42.   17. Cf. Esth. 2:15.   18. Gen. 12:11.   19. Cf. II Sam. 3:34.   20.
Even women curse and despise other women with physical blemishes.   21. Gen.
33:13.   22. Ezra 23:6.   23. Cf. Deut. 21:11.   24. Cf. Song 2:5.   25.
"Whichever of the above two explanations is true."   26. Of the sages.   27.
Spelling based on Num. 5:12.   28. The rabbis never entertained the notion that
the scriptural verse excluded these categories of women arbitrarily, without reason.
29. Should be *velo' yukal.*   30. Still part of the hypothetical conclusion which the
commentator repudiates. The sages did *not* mean that the stump-armed woman who
commits adultery is free to return to her husband.   31. The subject seems to be
"the sages," the first verb apparently meaning "act immoderately" by giving permission for sinful behavior.   32. The Torah.   33. Cf. Prov. 3:18.   34. Based
on the fourth benediction of the *Tefillah.*   35. Cf. Prov. 23:1 and Prov. 22:21.
36. Cf. Dan. 4:6.   37. Cf. Dan. 4:14.   38. The teaching of the sages in this
midrash.   39. Cf. Isa. 27:12.   40. Of the sages.   41. II Sam. 1:23.   42.
Isa. 9:1.   43. Ps. 27:13.   44. Cf. Ezek. 23:48.   45. Cf. Zech. 9:6 and Jer.
35:10.   46. The adulteress claims that the father is her husband.   47. Job
19:23.   48. *R.H.* 16b.   49. From the context, it should be *ha-nashim.*   50.

There is a presumption that a strange man talking to a woman will be attempting to seduce her, and that she will respond to his words of love.   51. Prov. 7:13. 52. Cf. I. Kings 22:22.   53. Cf. Exek. 23:48; perhaps should be *veyivvaseru*. Note the function of the ritual not merely to determine guilt and punish sin but to frighten other women so that they will remain faithful to their husbands.   54. Gen. 35:18. 55. Exod. 35:25.   56. Cf. Deut. 24:1.   57. Cf. Jer. 8:14.   58. Cf. Esth. 1:20. 59. Cf. Mal. 2:15.   60. One who is afraid is not quick to rebel.   61. Gen. 2:24. 62. Isa. 11:2.   63. I.e., in terms of unusual cases. Cf. *Guide* III, 34.   64. Even if the women with deformities are naturally hot-blooded.   65. Hos. 2:9.   66. Gen. 41:21.   67. Gen. 30:38; here "when they have passionate desire for another man."   68. *Yeb.* 76a.   69. Cf. Ezek. 16:17. This entire chapter in Ezekiel uses sexual imagery as a metaphor for idolatry. However, as commentators such as Radak point out, the metaphor here is based on an actual practice of lewd women. 70. Gen. 39:5.   71. Cf. Jon. 4:4; here "she is very angry about it."   72. I Sam. 1:10.

CMR 90a-91a: Annotation

1. Song 3:11.   2. Gen. 17:3.   3. Num. 24:16.   4. Note that it is not the lack of physical circumcision *as such* which makes the uncircumcised evil in God's sight, but that this almost inevitably results in an "uncircumcised heart," meaning a heart devoid of knowledge of God, in a manner which will be explained.   5. Cf. Prov. 16:32.   6. *R.H.* 16b.   7. Jer. 31:11, referring here to the impulse to sin.   8. I.e., in an extraordinary case, of one with virtually no natural inclination toward sexual desire.   9. Cf. Eccles, 7:28.   9. Cf. Eccles. 12:3. Here the commentator is expressing an assumption about *'aggadah*: the rabbis do not, in their general statements, include unusual cases, which are so rare as to be for all practical purposes nonexistent. Cf. *Guide* III, 34, where Maimonides applies this principle to the law of the Torah.   10. Gen. 12:11.   11. Cf. Prov. 2:16, 7:5.   12. Cf. Gen. 19:11. 13. Cf. Song 3:4. Here the meaning seems to be, from the continuation, that because of frequent intercourse with her, he will be unable to find that which his *soul* loves, i.e., the knowledge of God which will bestow immortality.   14. Jer. 31:22. 15. Cf. I Kings 1:2.   16. Cf. Jer. 2:24.   17. Gen. 38:9.   18. Cf. *Berakot* 60a. Here the meaning seems clearly to be "has an orgasm."   19. Prov. 7:13.   20. Gen. 39:12, recalling Potiphar's wife.   21. Deut. 25:11.   22. I Sam. 3:5, 6 (there in a totally different sense).   23. Job 40:17; meaning, "testicles," in accordance with Targum, Rashi, Ibn Ezra, Ralbag, and others.   24. Isa. 48:4. Maimonides (*Guide* III, 8) points out that *gid* is the Hebrew term for penis.   25. Cf. Ezek. 23:20.   26. *Hagigah* 15a.   27. Job 41:9.   28. Eccles. 6:7.   29. *Berakot* 57b and Ps. 109:24.   30. Cf. Prov. 11:17.   31. "He devotes his brain entirely to women, an evil thing"; cf. Rashi's comment on *Shabbat* 33a beginning *hamemareq 'atzmo.*   32. I Sam. 25:37.   33. Jud. 5:27.   34. Cf. Prov. 16:15. 35. Cf. Isa. 44:18.   36. Job 37:21.   37. Gen. 2:24.   38. Deut. 21:4.   39. Prov. 22:29, meaning here, according to context, reaching a climax quickly.   40. Cf. *Yebamot* 55b.   41. Prov. 19:23.   42. Gen. 38:26.   43. Gen. 7:4.   44. Cf. II Chron. 13:20.   45. Cf. Deut. 6:7.   46. Cf. Gen. 20:4.   47. Cf. Hag. 2:19; a good example of a rather startling use of a Biblical phrase in a totally different sense from its original meaning.   48. Jer. 15:9.   49. Cf. Lev. 6:5.   50. Isa. 44:5.   51. Prov. 3:4.   52. Amos 2:16.   53. Cf. Exod. 3:6.   54. Judg. 9:53.   55. Cf. Isa. 50:11.   56. Cf. *B.M.* 97a.   57. *Genesis Rabbah* 80:11.

58. Lev. 15:33.   59. Cf. Ps. 24:4.   60. Job. 1:8, 2:3.   61. *A.Z.* 23a.   62. Cf. Isa. 62:7.   63. Cf. Job 14:14.   64. Cf. Ps. 142:4.   65. Cf. Esth. 4:2, here referring to the "presence" of God.   66. Cf. Ps. 127:5.   67. Cf. Job. 3:3.   68. Cf. Exod. 34:30.   69. Isa. 51:13.   70. Judg. 18:7.   71. Num. 12:8.   72. See verse quoted in midrash.   73. Cf. Isa. 33:17.   74. Lev. 5:8.   75. Isa. 33:15.   76. Cf. Job 3:10.   77. Cf. Gen. 27:1.   78. Deut. 54:1.   79. Job 24:15.   80. Deut. 22:8.   81. Cf. Lev. 11:42.   82. See verse quoted in midrash.   83. Cf. Isa. 59:2.   84. This should undoubtedly read *mebasqar* (*'Erubin* 19a); here, God does not "recognize" the uncircumcised man.   85. Cf. Gen. 6:14; used by R. Isaac to mean internal and external faculties of the human being.   86. I Sam. 18:25, referring here to all impulses antagonistic to intellectual development.   87. Prov. 29:12.   88. Isa. 7:2.   89. Lev. 1:16.   90. Cf. Ps. 109:22.   91. Cf. Isa. 6:10.   92. Prov. 15:31.   93. Gen. 18:7.   94. Cf. II Kings 5:14.   95. Lev. 15:3.   96. Language of the midrash.   97. Eccles. 7:20.   98. Exod. 34:34.   99. Zech. 11:17.   100. Cf. Num. 6:25.   101. Ps. 29:5.

CMR 96b-97b: Annotation

1. Num. 7:3.   2. Our text of the midrash continues and specifies the six commandments. This may well be a later gloss, as the commandments are repeated in the following material, so that their specification is unnecessary here.   3. II Chron. 9:18.   4. Deut. 17:17.   5. Deut. 17:16.   6. Deut. 17:17.   7. Deut. 16:19.   8. Ibid.   9. Ibid.   10. Our text of the midrash does not contain this admonition. Cf. *Berakot* 28b.   11. From the context of the midrash, it seems as if this should refer to the tabernacle or Temple, but it becomes clear that the author is speaking metaphorically about intellectual apprehension of God.   12. Deut. 23:22.   13. Cf. Num. 20:19.   14. Cf. Ps. 45:16 and *Guide* III, 51.   15. Cf. Isa. 35:6.   16. Deut. 22:8.   17. Cf. Exod. 20:23.   18. Cf. Ps. 74:21.   19. Gen. 28:12ff, interpreting the dream of Jacob as a metaphorical expression of the ascent on the ladder of the sciences reaching the pinnacle: metaphysical knowledge of God.   20. Cf. Gen. 28:12, representing the natural sciences which deal with the terrestrial realm.   21. Cf. Jer. 12:15.   22. From the purposefulness and order in the terrestrial world, one can learn about the Creator.   23. Cf. Ps. 33:19.   24. Deut. 20:11.   25. Ps. 24:10.   26. Cf. Isa. 24:21.   27. Through the study of astronomy and physics.   28. Cf. *Hil. Yesode ha-Torah* 1.5.   29. Ps. 47:3 & I Chron. 29:12.   30. Num. 2:6.   31. Cf. Job 25:3.   32. Gen. 28:11.   33. Cf. I Kings 22:19 and II Chron. 29:11.   34. Mic. 4:5.   35. Cf. Judg. 6:12 and Isa. 6:6.   36. Cf. Dan. 10:13.   37. The angels (separate intellects) are both causes (of change in the spheres and thus in the terrestrial realm) and effects (of the First Cause).   38. I.e., the number of causes is not infinite.   39. Cf. *Ta'anit* 31a.   40. Exod. 15:2.   41. The highest angel, who appears to man on behalf of God.   42. Ps. 116:15.   43. A characteristic phrase describing this angel.   44. Esther 8:16, referring here to the perpetual life of the soul.   45. Cf. Ps. 25:13.   46. God is mindful of man, cf. Ps. 8:5.   47. Cf. Ps. 91:11 and Job. 3:3.   48. Cf. II Kings 20:13.   49. Gen. 24:10. The fifth and sixth levels are not clearly defined.   50. See above, note 14.   51. Cf. I Sam. 16:7 and Deut. 34:1. The verb form is *hiph'il*, as in Deuteronomy, although the sense requires *niph'al*, as in I Samuel.   52. Esther 1:14.   53. Isa. 25:9.   54. Cf. Judg. 6:24.   55. Cf. I Kings 1:31. These lines contain strongly visual language for a purely intellectual apprehension of

God which is the philosopher's ideal.   56. Exod. 33:7, generalized from Jacob's dream to everyone who seeks knowledge of God.   57. Cf. Eccles. 3:17.   58. I.e., the six steps to the royal throne correspond to the six levels of intellectual ascent to the apprehension of God.   59. I Kings 10:19.   60. *Berakot* 58a.   61. The king, ascending his throne, must also attain knowledge of God by the same process described above.   62. Esther 1:8, referring here to God's command relating to the king.   63. " . . . will not be drawn after his inner corporeal impulses."   64. Cf. Prov. 23:3.   65. Jer. 17:11; the pleasures of the flesh do not last into old age.   66. Cf. Gen. 34:3, Song 3:1-4: his soul cleaves to the way leading to that which it loves (?)   67. Cf. Jer. 31:14(13).   68. II Sam. 9:13.   69. Ruth 2:14.   70. Esther 2:8.   71. See above, note 4.   72. Cf. Ps. 45:12.   73. Cf. *Shabbat* 33a and Rashi *ad loc.*   74. "His intellect will not have sufficient vigor to reach intellectual apprehension of God by mastering metaphysics."   75. "Will come to erroneous conclusions, believing things impossible in God."   76. *Berakot* 33b.   77. The number five is puzzling here, as six are mentioned.   78. His fellow Jews.   79. Ezek. 18:18.   80. Prov. 9:9.   81. Cf. Prov. 23:1. and Isa. 44:19.   82. That all have the same ancestor; cf. M. *Sanh.* 4.5.   83. Meaning probably, not distinctly male or female; cf. *Berakot* 61a.   84. Gen. 7:4.   85. Gen. 6:1.   86. The enlightened king.   87. The sense seems to require something like *lo' nibhar.*   88. Cf. Esther 5:11 and Hos. 10:5.   89. Ps. 49:18.   90. Cf. Ps. 71:11 and I Sam. 28:15.   91. Whoever encounters him.   92. Cf. I Kings 2:12.   93. Isa. 26:5.   94. Should be *'asher.*   95. Cf. Ps. 68:17.   96. Isa. 30:33.   97. Cf. Gen. 6:3; the meaning seems to be that indicated by ibn Ezra—"remains"—while still alive in the flesh.   98. As in midrash; cf. Isa. 28:6.   99. Cf. Eccles. 5:18 and I Chron. 29:12.   100. Cf. Prov. 21:3.   101. Deut. 16:18.   102. Cf. I Chron. 29:23.   103. Num 7:2-3; Num. 1:52, 2:2.   104. Without sharing in an ox, as they did with the wagons.   105. "On two levels, the manifest that they actually brought oxen, and the esoteric to allude . . . "   106. Beholding sharply and clearly.   107. Cf. Isa. 2:16.   108. "Because of the handiwork, he will attain intellectual apprehension of God."   109. Deut. 33:17.   110. I.e., the verb *shur*, meaning "to see" (physically or intellectually).   111. *Hullin* 60a.   112. Cf. Dan. 3:25.   113. "Brought him close."   114. The *subject* of *hikribo* is *shor/shur.*   115. On the physical location of the internal senses, including memory, cf. "Kimhi's Allegorical Commentary on Genesis" in *The Commentary of David Kimhi on Isaiah*, ed. L. Finkelstein (New York, 1926), pp. *lv-lvi.*   116. Cf. Isa. 9:1.   117. Referring to the intellectual vision of God.   118. Cf. Exod. 3:6.   119. Exod. 34:29.   120. *Shabbat* 108a; cf. *B.B.* 89a.   121. Prov. 26:2.   122. Prov. 21:4.   123. Cf. *Pesahim* 66a.   124. A reference to the author's commentary on the *'aggadot* of the Talmud.   125. Also a statement in *Hullin* 60a.   126. Contrast above, note 105; here the *peshat* of the statement is explicitly repudiated: Adam did *not* sacrifice an ox.   127. Cf. Job 33:16.   128. Eccles. 8:1.   129. Job. 28:13.   130. Cf. Prov. 24:21 and 14:10; here *zarim* refers to anyone other than the individual prince who might share in the *shor/shur.*   131. Intellectual apprehension can be achieved only by each individual, not vicariously through another.   132. "Let him seek philosophical knowledge of the higher realms."   133. I.e., to apprehend God through study of the higher realms.   134. Cf. Jer. 37:10.   135. Num. 18:4.   136. *Hagigah* 11b.

13

Jews "Separated from the Communion of the Faithful in Christ" in the Middle Ages

Joseph Shatzmiller

The Problem

Several documents of the Middle Ages, from different regions in Europe, present us with the apparent paradox of ecclesiastical authorities placing Jews under excommunication. In some of these documents it is simply stated that these Jews are excommunicates; in others, they are declared to be "separated from the communion of the faithful in Christ," an expression, as is well known, denoting the essential feature of the ecclesiastical excommunication. One should note immediately that the documents deal with particular Jews whose names, places, and time are clearly stated and not with Jews in general or in any abstract category. Nor do they refer to converts: the individuals are all designated as *judei* in the documents. The Jews, of course, had their own process of excommunication—the *herem*. Strangely, however, a Christian bishop is, in these cases, imposing a Christian sanction, that is, "separation" on Jews who presumably would not fall under his jurisdiction.

Could such an excommunication have had any religious, legal, or social meaning? Willy Cohn who, in an article published in 1930 presented a document of this sort about an Avignon Jew of the thirteenth century, suggested that his case must pertain to a convert who continued to be called *judeus* in the documents, "otherwise the excommunication sentence would not make real sense."[1] I would like to suggest another explanation, relying, for the most part, on already published documents. Remarkably, none of the scholars who published them knew about any of the others and none of them made this issue a special subject of inquiry. By ordering the data into one series, however, we are confronted with a phenomenon whose chronology is at least 150 years (from the thirteenth to the fifteenth century) and whose geographical range covers many parts of western Europe.

The Evidence

The oldest documents come from England. F. Donald Logan brought attention to their existence in the Public Record Office in London in an article published in 1972.[2] These are three short documents: two from the chancery of the bishop Richard Gravesent of Lincoln, March 12, 1265, and November 10, 1265, and the third from the chancery of the bishop William de

Breuse, bishop of Llandaff, January 19, 1268. These are official applications
or "significations" to King Henry III asking for his assistance in dealing with
individuals who are under excommunication "40 days and more," but who
still refuse to yield to the discipline of the church. In such cases, after the
church had done whatever it could to bend these obdurate excommunicates, it was the custom to ask for the cooperation of the "secular arm," a
practice going back to the time of William the Conqueror.[3] In England such
disobedient persons would be sent to jail. The three documents in question
pertain to this procedure of "signifying" excommunicates for secular deten-
tion. They are of standard bureaucratic character and are identical, almost
to the last detail, in their content, formula, and terminology. Nothing is
said in them regarding the specific reasons for the excommunication of any
of these individuals. But, as was the case generally in ecclesiastical excommunication, it is clear that they were first declared to be *contumaces* and
were subsequently stricken with the excommunication, *propter eius multiplicatam contumaciam pariteret offensam manifestam*, the standard
formula in such signification letters.

What makes these documents unique among other hundreds of the same
period, all preserved in the Public Record Office, is the fact that the excommunicates are undoubtedly Jews. The letters of the bishop of Lincoln refer
to *Manserus judeus de Oxonia* and to *Floria de Northamptonia vidua judea*,
whom we meet, by the way, in the plea rolls of the exchequer of the Jews.
The letter of the bishop of Llandaff deals with *Petrus le franceys de Strigvilla judeus*. One should point out that the name Peter was used by English,
German and French Jews of the period.[4]

The document to which Willy Cohn referred belongs to the same procedure of signification of excommunicates. But this time it occurs in Provence.
Published by Alain de Bouard in the collection of documents of Charles I of
Sicily, Prince of Provence,[5] the document resembles its English equivalents
in its content, as well as in the procedure which it invokes. Yet it belongs to
the next stage of the process: the signification having been received, the
Prince of Provence sends on June 21, 1273 a writ to his *sénéchal* to coerce
the disobedient. We learn the following details: the Jew Astrugus de Mas-
silia, inhabitant of Avignon, was stricken with excommunication by Hugo
de Porta Aqueria, the rector of one of the churches in the diocese of Cavail-
lon. The Jew did not react and continued to live under excommunication (*in
excommunicatione ipsa*), unimpressed, one would say, for more than a
year. "A year and more" was the term usually required in France before
which one could expect the intervention of the secular arm, the equivalent
of "40 days and more" in England. Charles I points out in this letter to the
sénéchal that the coercion exercised, again typically to France, by confiscation of goods or "in any other way."

The Jewishness of these excommunicates does not, by the way, explain
their disregard for this ecclesiastical censure. Rather, they seem to follow a
general pattern in this respect. "At the present time excommunications are
so lightly regarded," testifies Joinville in his *Life of Saint-Louis*, "that people

think nothing of dying without seeking absolution, and refuse to make their peace with the Church."[6] It would seem, therefore, that as far as disobedience goes, they were indistinguishable from hundreds, indeed thousands, of Christians. The church and the state dealt also with the former, by the same routine, bureaucracy, and indeed terminology that it used for the latter: Our documents regard the Jewishness of excommunicates as a fact that does not require any further comment or explanation. They refer to *dictam Floriam excommunicatam*, to Menasche of Oxford who was *excommunicationis sententia meruit innodari*, or to Astruc of Marseille who is *excommunicationis sententia innodatus*. That it is surprising to us is evidence of a gap in our knowledge of the legal status of medieval Jews.

To these four documents, one may add an equal number of cases relating to excommunication in England and elsewhere. Thus, for example, in Bristol, in 1275, the local bishop Giffard issued a decree to excommunicate several Jews "because the Jews were guilty of iniquitous insults, blasphemies, and injuries and of an assault upon a chaplain of St. Peter's who had administered the holy Eucharist to a sick person in the Jewry."[7] In Spain (June 25, 1275), Jews excommunicated by the church had been compelled as a consequence to abandon their place of domicile. We know this because in a special "privilege" accorded by King James I of Aragon to Jews belonging to the "collecta" of communities around Perpignan, it is mentioned in the following phrase:[8] *per excommunicationem seu interdictum ecclesie expellimini de villis et locis in quibus habitatis, propter quod plurime dampna et missiones vos oportet diversi modo sustinere*, and it is promised that in the future they will not be coerced again. A privilege of the same nature was accorded the same year (July 19, 1275) to a group of Jews whose names are specified in the Comtat Venaissin.[9] The papal judge-delegate (*judex unicus a sede apostolica delegatus*) by the agency of an intermediary *subdelegatus* orders all papal judges in the region to stop bothering and persecuting this group of Jews. The persecution is mostly through judicial procedures, the striking with excommunication being one of them. He thus forbids the practice among judges who do not receive proper authorization. In his language: *imo si predictos judeos modo aliquo citastis interdihistis vel etiam excommunicastis vel a participatione fidelium removistis una cum participantibus, visis presentibus, cessistis paenitus . . .* Michael Adler, obviously perplexed while presenting the Bristol case of 1275, remarked: "It would be interesting to learn if there are similar examples of excommunication being pronounced against Jews, seeing that this form of ecclesiastical punishment applied only to Christians." We can answer now in the affirmative. Indeed there are other examples. Clearly, this episcopal censure did not apply only to Christians.

Procedure and Significance

The phenomenon was not limited to the thirteenth century as one might suppose from the data presented thus far. The series of documents which will now be presented transports us to Provence of the second half of the fifteenth century. They are mandates and decrees issued by the *officialis* of the archbishops of Aix and Marseille[10] and are preserved in formulary books which were prepared for the use of the chanceries of these bishops. There is no doubt, as Roger Aubenas, their editor, remarks, that the authors of the formulary used genuine documents; they simply deleted names and other historical details from them so that they might serve as general examples. These formulary books of Aix-Marseille contain five documents attesting to the excommunication of Jews by bishops; Aubenas published three of them, almost *in extenso*, and provided summaries of the two others. They contribute much more than an extension of the chronological range; they show us how and when the issuing of the actual excommunication was done, and, what is more, what might have been the significance of such a "separation from the communion of the faithful in Christ" to a Jew.

The background for the first case is one of indebtedness.[11] A Jew did not pay his debt in time and was warned by the *officialis—sub separationis a participatione christi fidelium pena*. He overlooked this warning and his disobedience is now evident. The creditor then turned to the authorities and demanded that this disobedience be declared (*eundem contumacem reputari*). The official who accepted the claim took the following necessary steps and declared the Jew to be excommunicated: He approached the local ecclesiastical authorities and ordered them to take the following measure: *Volumus et vobis . . . precipiendo mandamus quatinus . . . dictum . . . judeum . . . a participatione christi fidelium in hiis scriptis presentibus separamus et per presentes separatum pronunciamus et etiam declaramus, in vestris ecclesiis publice, infra missarum solemnia, populo ibidem ad divina congregato audiente . . . a participatione christi fidelium ex nostri parte separatum nuncietis atque nunciari faciatis et mandatis . . .* And what is no less interesting is that the excommunication was to be pronounced not only in the churches at mass but concurrently in the synagogues of the city. There too he would be declared a *participatione christi fidelium separatus*. As the document stated, *necnon et in synagoga sive scola judeorum presentis civitatis per baylonos sive rectores atque scobalenos dicte scole, etiam judeis in eorum sermoniis ibidem congregatis . . . nuncietis*.

A dispute over the payment of a debt is also the reason for the next case.[12] A Jew did not pay back his debt although he had pledged himself, as the custom required, by a notarial deed and by an oath sworn according to the Mosaic law. At the creditor's demand, the *officialis* warned him with a *separatio*, but to no avail. Hence he was excommunicated and all the parishes were warned to cease communicating with him. What is important in this case is the details given about the significance and meaning of such an excommunication: *vobis tenore presentium precipiendo mandamus quatinus ex nostri parte moneatis semel secundo et tertio canonice et perhemtorie conciliarios seu sindicos dicte civitatis . . . et ceteros parrochianos vestros . . . ne deinceps cum dicto sic excommunicato aliquo participationis genere participare presumant comedendo, bibendo, loquendo, stando, redeundo,*

mercando, molendo, quoquendo victualia ministrando aut quovis alio par-
ticipationis genere conversando, nisi in causibus a jure permissis . . . The
major characteristic of the "separation" is therefore its secular and civic
dimensions: not to eat, or drink, or grind, or cook, or trade, or talk, and so
on. There is no religious or spiritual dimension to it. Excommunication in
the sense of depriving the believer from the sacraments (to use a Christian
formula) still is an exclusively Jewish affair. But an ecclesiastical excommunication of Jews, on the other hand, seems to have meaning mostly on a
social level: its effect will be felt mainly in the daily life of commercial intercourse.

Yet this ecclesiastical excommunication of Jews might mean more than
mere social segregation. About its legal ramifications one can learn much
from a short document presented to the court of Montpellier, Languedoc, in
1293.[13] A Jew by the name of Moses of Beziers sued a certain Jean Tauros.
The representative of Jean Tauros presented the court with a document
arguing three points (*tituli*) of defense which he would probably try to sustain through the cross-examination of witnesses. Each *titulus* opens, as
usual, with the expression *intendit probare quod*. What renders the document of special interest to us is the content of its claim: it concentrates on
the observation that Moses of Beziers has been excommunicated. His first
point was that *predictus judeus publice publicatur per ecclesias Montispes-*
sulani esse separatus a communione fidelium mandato prioris de Launa,
judicem unicum a sede apostolica delegatum; second, he demonstrated that
the Jew was a *contumax* and was declared as such; and third, he proved that
predictus dominus judex predictum judeum racione predicte contumacie et
ob eius contumaciam a communione fidelium separavit. If Moses de Beziers
is indeed excommunicated, he is then precluded from pleading in court,
according to a well-established principle *excommunicatus non habet per-*
sonam standi in judicio.[14] Jews excommunicated by bishops, like their
Christian peers, suffered a vulnerable and defective legal status. Their business prospects, to take but one example, were severely damaged.

Such "separation" was neither permanent nor irrevocable. Quite the contrary. As with Christians, the "separation" was not so much a punishment,
but a "therapy," an incentive to follow the law. Consequently, officials
foresaw an eventual revocation of the decree. Indeed, the first of these
documents ends with the phrase: *tamdiu donec doctorum christi fidelium*
participatione . . . meruit restitui et aliud a nobis habueritis in mandatis.
The way such Jewish obdurate excommunicates are brought back to the
"communion of the faithful in Christ" is revealed in another document of
this formulary,[15] which is interesting, incidentally, from another point of
view: the "separation" of these Jews was exacted this time at the request of
another Jew. These Jews were also excommunicated for unpaid debts. *Ipsi*
pro certis debitis sunt excommunicati a . . . participatione fidelium chris-
tianorum segregati ad instantiam talis judei talis loci. The deterioration of
their situation continued as they fell more and more into debt, so much so

that a prison punishment was pending, or so it was recorded. They do not see any other way out of it but to declare bankruptcy. Therefore they presented the court with a list of all their assets (*cessio bonorum*) and invited their creditors to appear in the court in order to get at least part of their money back. Concurrently these Jews petitioned the authorities to be brought back to the society of the "faithful in Christ," and creditors were requested to give evidence, if any, of why these Jews should not be allowed back, *dicendi causam quam . . . participationis fidelium recipi et admitti non debeant.* They themselves declared that in this way they would find it easier *ad participationem fidelium christianorum redire.* Their proctor asked the court on their behalf: *petiit . . . se dicte participationi dictorum christianorum per nos restitui.* One may assume that by following such a procedure they finally regained their lost status.

Let us come back by way of conclusion, to the historical period and geographical range of the evidence. It covers a period from the mid-thirteenth century to the end of the fifteenth century and an area from England to northern Spain, and Languedoc, and Provence. Jews from Southampton, Oxford, and Bristol were stricken by episcopal excommunication exactly as their brethren of Perpignan, Montpellier, Orange, or Marseille. This was clearly one of the elements that concretely shaped the destiny of the Jews in the latter Middle Ages. Still some vital questions remain unanswered. When, first of all, did this practice begin and when did it come to an end? It is well known that the fourth Lateran council of 1215, wishing to "protect" Christians against Jewish usurers, threatened the latter with the following censure: *ab universis christi fidelibus eis omnino communio denegetur.* This decision was repeated, word for word, by the council of Lyon in 1245 as we are reminded by F. Donald Logan.[16] Is this really the beginning of the practice? Is the end of the fifteenth century, by which time most of the West European countries were without Jews, the period when the practice faded away?

APPENDIX

Three "significations" by the bishops of Lincoln (Nos. 1-2) and Llandaff (No. 3) regarding obdurant excommunicates, all Jews, who should be coerced by the secular arm, as is the custom of the Realm. (*Sources*: Public Record Office, London C85/98/34 [No. 1]; C85/98/39 [No. 2]; C85/167/139 [No. 3].)

1. Excellentissimo domino suo Henrico dei gratia illustri regi Anglie domino Hibernie et duci Aquitannie, devotus suus Ricardus eiusdem miseratione Lincolniensis ecclesie minister humilis salutem, et tam debitam quam devotam cum omni honore reverentiam. Dominationi vestre notum facimus quod Floria de Northamptonia, vidua, judea, propter eius multi-

plicatam contumaciam pariter et offensam manifestam sententia excommunicationis meruit innodari, in qua per quadraginta dies et amplius perina-
citer perseverans, adhuc incorrigibilis existit, claves ecclesie contempnendo.
Quo circa dominationis vestre serenitati supplicamus humiliter et devote
quatinus dictam Floriam excommunicatam ad satisfaciendum deo et ecclesie
regia potestate, iuxta regni nostri consuetudinem, dignemini cohercere.
Valeat excellentia vestra in domino per tempora longiora. Datum apud
Northamptoniam III idus marcii anno domini M.C.C. sexagesimo quarto.

2. Excellentissimo domino suo Henrico dei gratia illustri regi Anglie
domino Hibernie et duci Aquitannie, Ricardus eiusdem miseratione Lincolniensis episcopus salutem et tam devotam quam debitam reverentiam cum
honore. Dominationi vestre notum facimus quod Manserus judeus de
Oxonia, ob ipsius multiplicatam contumaciam pariter et offensam manifestam excommunicationis sententia meruit innodari, in qua per quadraginta
dies et amplius pertinaciter perseverans adhuc incorrigibilis existit, claves
ecclesie contempnendo. Hoc autem celsitudine vestre intimamus ut dictum
excommunicatum ad satisfaciendum deo et ecclesie regia potestate, iuxta
regni nostri consuetudinem, dignemini cohercere. Valeat dominationis
vestre celsitudo in domino pertempora longiora. Datum Londonia IIII idus
novembris anno gratie M.CC.LX quinto.

3. Excellentissimo domino suo domino Henrico dei gratia regi Anglie
illustri, Willelmus permissione divina ecclesie Landavensis minister humilis
(. . . 3 words . . .) (. . . gibi) dat salutem. Excellentie vestre notum facimus
per presentes quod Petrus Le Franceys de Strigvilla judeus, parochianus
noster, propter suam multiplicatam contumaciam pariter et offensam vin-
culo excommunicationis auctoritate nostra existit innodatus, in qua excommunicationis sententia per quadraginta dies et amplius pertinaciter perseverans incorrigibilis existit. Quocirca excellentie vestre supplicamus quatinus ipsius pertinatiam, iuxta regni consuetudinem, dignemini cohercere.
Valeat et vigeat excellentia vestra pertempora diuturna. Datum Londonia
XIIII kalendas febroarii anno gratie M.CC.LXX septimo.

NOTES

1. Willy Cohn, "Die judenpolitik König Karls I von Sizilien in Anjou und in
der Provence," *Monatschrift fur Geschichte und Wissenschaft des Judentums,*
LXXIV (1930), 429-437, esp. p. 434, note 1. "Ob es nicht in diesem Falle um einen
getauften Juden gehandelt haben muss, der nash mittelalterlicher Sitte weiter als,
'Judaeus' bezeichnet wird? Sonst hatte die 'sententia excommunicationis' keinen
rechten Sinn." See also note 5 below.

2. F. Donald Logan, "Thirteen London Jews and Conversion to Christianity:
Problems of Apostasy in the 1280's," *Bulletin of Institute of Historical Research,*
XLV (1972), 214-229, esp. pp. 224-225 and note 2 on page 225 where references are
given to the ms. in the Public Record Office. These documents are in the appendix to
this chapter.

3. F. Donald Logan, *Excommunication and the Secular Arm in Medieval England* (Toronto, 1968). I am indebted to this book for most of the information concerning excommunication and its procedure in England as well as in France. For France, see Maurice Morel, *L'Excommunication et le Pouvoir Civil en France du-Droit Canonique Classique au Commencement du xive Siècle* (Paris, 1926).

4. Herbert Loewe, *Starrs and Jewish Charters Preserved in the British Museum* (London, 1932), III, 21-22, note 72a-b.; E. E. Urbach, *Ba ale ha-Tosafot* (Hebrew; Jerusalem, 1955), pp. 191-193 et passim (-Rabbi Peter ben Joseph, a student of Rabbi Jacob Tam).

5. A. de Bouard, *Actes et Lettres de Charles 1er, Roi de Sicile, concernant la France* (Paris, 1926), p. 190, no. 689. See also note 1 above.

6. As translated by M.R.B. Shaw in: *Joinville & Villehardouin; Chronicles of the Crusades* (Penguin Books, Harmondsworth, Middlesex, 1963), p. 177-178.

7. Michael Adler, *Jews of Medieval England* (London, 1939), p. 226; Cecil Roth, *A History of the Jews in England* (Oxford, 1964), p. 77.

8. D. Francisco de Bofarull y Sans, *Los judios en el territorio de Barcelona* (Barcelona, 1910), pp. 122-123, no. 158.

9. Bibliothèque Nationale, Paris. Collection Doat, t. 173 folios 200ro-202vo. The document is described briefly by Ulysse Robert, "Catalogue d'Actes Relatifs aux Juifs pendant le Moyen-Age," *REJ*, (1881), 211-224, esp. p. 217, no. 48. The Jews designated as *homines domini Papae et habitatores terrae seu comitatus Venaysini*. At their head is mentioned Leon de Castrogilos and all seven of them seem to be related to him, and to each other.

10. Roger Aubenas, *Recueil de Lettres des Officialités de Marseille et d'Aix*, vols. I-II (Paris, 1937-38). The documents referred to below are all from volume II of this book. The two documents merely summarized by Aubenas are: p. 37, no. 151, and p. 72, no. 237. As one may state after having examined these two documents, they do not supplement any information found in the other three documents. cf. Archives de Provence, Marseille, 5G823 fol. 74vo, 130ro.

11. Aubenas, pp. 71-72, no. 236.

12. Aubenas, pp. 133-134, no. 9.

13. Solomon Kahn, "Documents inédits sur les Juifs de Montpellier au Moyen-Age," *REJ*, XXII (1891), 267; XXIII (1891), 272, no. 16. Solomon Kahn, like Willy Cohn asks himself: "s'agirait-il d'un Juif converti? C'est probable."

14. Logan, *Excommunication and the Secular Arm*, pp. 14, 118; Gerard J. Campbell, "The Attitude of the Monarchy toward the Use of Ecclesiastical Censures in the Reign of Saint Louis," in *Speculum* XXXV (1960), 551.

15. Aubenas, pp. 40-44, 159.

16. Logan, "Thirteen London Jews," p. 225.

14

An Excerpt from the *Abot* Commentary of R. Mattathias ha-Yizhari

Michael A. Shmidman

R. Mattathias ha-Yizhari b. Moses b. Mattathias ha-Yizhari was a Spanish scholar of the late fourteenth and early fifteenth centuries.[1] His literary activity includes a commentary on tractate *Abot*, a homiletical commentary on the Pentateuch (referred to frequently in the work on *Abot*), and a commentary on Psalm 119.[2] Relevant references in the *Abot* commentary support the assertion that R. Mattathias was a disciple of R. Hasdai Crescas. It also is most probable that he is to be identified with the R. Mattathias of Saragossa who participated in the Disputation of Tortosa. Some additional details concerning R. Mattathias' family history and personal biography are contained in the introductory paragraph of the *Abot* commentary;[3] other aspects of his life and activity remain obscure or confused.

R. Mattathias' commentary on *Abot* is extant in two manuscripts.[4] I intend to publish a critical edition of the commentary in the near future in connection with my study of medieval *Abot* commentaries over the period from Rashi through Abravanel. The major commentaries of this period include those of: Rashi, R. Ephraim, Maimonides, R. Joseph b. Judah ibn Aknin, R. David b. Abraham ha-Nagid, R. Jonah b. Abraham Gerondi, R. Bahya b. Asher, R. Menahem b. Solomon ha-Me'iri, R. Isaac b. Yedaya, R. Joseph ibn Shoshan, R. Joseph ibn Nahmias, R. Isaac b. Solomon of Toledo, R. Simon b. Zemah Duran, R. Joseph b. Abraham Hayyun, R. Shem Tob b. Shem Tob, and R. Isaac Abravanel.[5] These works comprise a literary genre and body of exegesis which deserves and demands independent study. The work of R. Mattathias should constitute a significant and valuable link in this tradition of *Abot* commentary.

The following selection (from pp. 32a-39a of the Houghton manuscript) is intended to illustrate certain standard characteristics of R. Mattathias' commentary: the systematic, thorough if sometimes verbose, explanation of the text, classification of the major themes of each sage's statements, biographical information concerning these sages, attention to context, grammar, etymology and variant readings, Talmudic erudition and philosophic knowledge, and citations from Rashi, Maimonides, R. Jonah Gerondi, R. Nissim Gerondi, and R. Hasdai Crescas. R. Mattathias respects the work of Maimonides—including the *Guide of the Perplexed*, which he terms an excellent work (p. 33b)—but freely dissents from some of his interpretations and

Michael A. Shmidman

views (e.g., pp. 33b, 38a). Novel interpretations, ranging from the explanation of *hokmah* in *Abot* 3:13 (p. 33a) to the suggested derivation of the
name R. Elazar Hisma (p. 39a) are also evident in this excerpt. In addition,
the selection includes a relatively expansive discussion of the question of
astrological influences versus free will (pp. 34a-36a).

Publication of the entire commentary should help illuminate a number of
important areas and problems of Jewish intellectual history, for example:
the degree of study and knowledge of philosophy in late fourteenth- and
early fifteenth-century Spain, the teachings and attitudes of the schools of
R. Nissim and R. Hasdai Crescas, attitudes to Maimonides and especially to
the *Guide of the Perplexed*, modes of *Abot* exegesis, and the history of
interpretation of aggadic statements. The commentary also contains some
suggestive remarks regarding contemporary political and social conditions
in Spain.

R. Mattathias' work is cited often in Samuel b. Isaac Uceda's *Midrash
Shmuel*, and is referred to also in other commentaries (Hayyun's *Mille de-
Abot*, Almosnino's *Pirke Moshe* and Abravanel's *Nahalat Abot*). Abravanel classifies the commentary, approvingly, within the mode exemplified
by R. Jonah Gerondi and R. Isaac b. Solomon of Toledo.[6] In addition, parts
of pages 32a-33a of this selection are quoted or paraphrased by Abravanel,
in the name of "the commentators," as the clearest interpretation of *Abot*
3:13 prior to his own.[7]

The selection which follows forms R. Mattathias' commentary on chapter
3:13-18 of *Abot*.[8]

NOTES

1. On R. Mattathias, see Abraham b. Solomon of Torrutiel, *Supplement to
Sefer ha-Kabbalah*, in *Medieval Jewish Chronicles*, ed. A. Neubauer (Oxford, 1887)
I, 107; Abraham b. Samuel Zacuto, *Sefer Yuhasin ha-Shalem*, ed. H. Filipowski
(Frankfort, 1924), p. 225; Gedaliah ibn Yahya, *Shalshelet ha-Kabbalah* (Lemberg,
1866), p. 40b; David Conforte, *Kore ha-Dorot*, ed. D. Cassel (Berlin, 1846), p. 26a;
Midrash Tehillim, ed. S. Buber (Vilna, 1891), pp. 108-109 of introduction; H.
Graetz, *Geschichte der Juden* (Leipzig, 1864), VIII, 417; H. Gross, *Gallia Judaica*
(Paris, 1897), pp. 255-257; I. Loeb, *REJ*, VII (1883), 153-155; A. Neubauer, *REJ*, IX
(1884), 116-119; E. Renan, *Les Ecrivains Juifs Français* (in *L'Histoire Littéraire de la
France*, XXXI [1893], 778-779).

2. See Buber, pp. 108-109.

3. Published by Loeb in *REJ*, VII, 154-155.

4. (a) Ms. HEB 61 of Houghton Library, Harvard University; (b) ms. 700 of
the Sassoon collection. I wish to thank Mr. Rodney G. Dennis, Curator of Manuscripts at Houghton Library, and Rabbi S. D. Sassoon of Jerusalem, for their kind
permission to utilize and publish these manuscripts of the commentary.

5. Most of these works are listed in J. J. Cohen's bibliographic survey, "The
'Sayings of the Fathers,' Its Commentaries and Translations," *KS*, XL (1964-65), 104-
117, 277-283.

6. Abravanel, *Nahalat Abot* (New York, 1953), p. 32.

7. Abravanel occasionally utilizes parts of this selection throughout his commentary on *Abot* 3:13-18.

8. A number of emendations of the following text, based upon comparison with ms. Sassoon 700, are included in the notes.

ר' עקיבא אומר שחוק וקלות ראש וכו'.   הוא היה אומר
וכו'.   חביבין וכו'.   והכל מתוקן וכו'.   זה השלם היה
מגדולי חכמי ישראל ועשה כ"ד אלף תלמידים והיה מגדולי
תלמידי ר' אליעזר ור' יהשע וסתם תוספתא וברייתא כולהו
אליבא דר' עקיבא   כי כלם היו תלמידיו.   וא"כ הקבלה
האמיתית באה אליו וממנו באה אלי[נ]ו.   ואמר ג'
מאמרים ראויים לחכם גדול כמוהו גדולי האיכות ומעטי
הכמות.   א' הודיע ההכנות המישרות להשיג המדות
והדעות.   ב' הודיע שעשה השי"ת חסד עם המין האנושי
ובפרט לישראל בהישירם אל השלמות והודיע דרכי דינו
שיש להסתפק בענין הגמול והעונש.   ג' הודיע דרכי
העונש והאריך בהתיר הספק.   אמנם בראשון לפי שאמר ר'
ישמעאל[1] הוי קל לראש הזהיר שלא תטעה בהיתר הרצועה
בהרגילנו בענין קלות ראש כי הוא הכנה לאיסורי
העריות.   ורז"ל ערוה מלשון ערו ערו כי כל שראוי להיות
מכוסה ונתגלה נקרא ערוה ולזה נתיחד למקום היותר
מגונה של איש ואשה.   וכל בזוי שהיה רוצה האדם שיהיה
מכוסה ונתגלה נקרא ערוה.   אמר במפלת בבל[2] תגל ערותך
גם תראה חרפתך אמר כי מי שנמשך אחר השחוק יורגל
לערוה.   אז"ל פ"ק דיומא[3] יקירי ירושלים לא היו ישנים
ליל יום הכפורים כדי שישמע כהן גדול קול הברה ולא
יישן ובגבולין לא היו עושין כן עד שאמר אליהו לרב
יהודה כי נבעלו בנהרדעה ביום הכפורים כמה בתולות.

32b   וכ"ש אם / השחוק הוא מתוך אכילה ושתייה כי היין ישמח
לבב אנוש תרתי בלבי וכו'.   לשחוק עושים לחם ויין
וכו'.[4]   ואז"ל[5] למה נסמכה פ' נזיר לפ' סוטה שכל

הרואה סוטה יזיר עצמו מן היין . ומי שהוא קל התנועה
אין ספק שיביאהו לעשות דבר בלתי נאות כמו שאמרו[6] אין
ברגלים חוטא חזית איש אץ וכו׳ . ר"ל שהוא קל התנועה
בעניניו אע"פ שיש לו שכל טוב א"א שלא יחטא והכסיל
איפשר שלפעמים יתישב בהשגת דרושו בדרך נאות או ישמע
לקול מלחש וזה לא כן כי ישען על בינתו . לפיכך הזהיר
בב׳ אלה כדי שלא ינגדוהו בדעות ובמדות . ואז"ל[7] אל
יפסיע אדם פסיעה גסה ושלא יהלך בקומה זקופה כי אם
עושה כן דוחק רגלי השכינה ושלא ילך בגלוי ראש . ואמר
שלמה ע"ה[8] וגם בדרך שהסכל הולך לבו חסר ואומר לכל
סכל הוא . ואחר שהזהיר על ב׳ עניני אלו בהנהגות
האדם המכינות אותו אל החסרון הודיע ד׳ כללים בהישרתו
אל השלמות . א׳ בעיון להיותו לו בקנין והשגת האמת
והוא המסורת . וזה לפי שהענינים התוריים א"א שישיגו
בחקירת השכל האנושי בעניין[9] וברצון ודיעתו ית׳ בפרטים
מצד מה שהם פרטים וההשגחה להם וגמול ועונש ותחית
המתים והדומה להם גם בהרבה מצות התוריות כמו הקרבנות
ואיסור חמץ ובשר בחלב וכלאים וחלוקי המיתות בביאות
האסורות והם הנקראים חקים ולזה יחוייב לקבלם מרבו
ורבו מרבו עד מרע"ה . ולזה אמז"ל[10] לגרוס איניש והדר
ליסבר ואז"ל[11] חייב אדם בלשון רבו ואמרו[12] אין הלכה
כתלמיד במקום הרב ובסוף סוטה[13] משרבו תלמידי הלל
ושמאי נעשית תורה כשתי תורות . ב׳ בהיות לו די צרכו
ההכרחי והוא שקרא עושר ר"ל ההסתפקות שיהא זריז לתת
המעשרות . ואז"ל[14] עשר בשביל שתתעשר ואמרו[15] מלח
ממון חסד ר"ל הרוצה להקים ממונו יעשה מהם חסדים כ"א
לפי ממונו . וכבר האריכו בפ׳ מציאות האשה[16] בצניעות
הצדקה שלא לבייש את העני ולהלוות למי שאינו רוצה
לקבל ואמרו[17] שמעתא בעיא צלותא כיומא דסיתוה וכו׳ .
ואם אין לו מה יאכל לא יתיישב בעיונו ולזה אמרו[18]

אם אין קמח אין תורה והיתה מחכמתו של ר' עקיבא
שהזהיר בב' ענינים אלה מתהפכים ואמר סייג שהוא
המחיצה שעושין סביב השדה לשמרו / כן מגן העירן 33a
ושמירתו הוא הקבלה ושרש וקיום העושר הוא הנדיבות.
ג"כ ההכרחי בקיום העירן והעושר הוא שיזהר מהתאוה
המותרית והגבילו באמרו נדרים סייג לפרישות ומתאוה
מותריות.   והגבילו באמרו סייג לחכמה שתיקה ושני אלו
אמר אליהו לרב יהודה אחוה דרב סלא לא תרתח ולא תחטא
לא תרוי ולא תחטא[19] ר"ל לא יכעוס שהוא ענף הגאוה ולא
יחטא לא ישתכר שהוא ענף התאוה הגופיית ולא יחטא כי
התאוה והגאוה הוא שרש כל העבירות כי בשני אלה יוכללו
כל מעשה בני אדם בהנהגתם בעצמם ובהנהגתם בזולתם.
אמנם בג' אז"ל[20] מנין שנשבעים לקיים את המצוה שנ'
נשבעתי ואקיימה וכו'.   ואמרו[21] גבי בועז דכתיב חי ד'
שכבי וכו'.   שהיה יצה"ר מקטרגו אתה פנוי והיא פנויה
ובכלל זה להתקדש עצמו במותר לו.   וכתב הר"י[22] שלפיכך
אמר   נדרים ולא שבועות לפי שכירן שנשבע נאסר ואין זה
סייג אבל נדר הוא סייג שיאמר אם אעשה דבר פלוני אהיה
אסור בדבר פלוני.   אמנם כל החכמה שבכאן ר"ל המדינית
כי שם חכמה יאמר עליו כמ"ש הר"ם בסוף ספרו[23] וכתיב[24]
דרך איש ישר בעיניו ושומע וכו'.   כלומר יש בו מעלות
המדות.   וכן[25] חכמות נשים וכו'.   ר"ל הטפשיות שאינה
יודעת הנהגות ההכרחיות לבית דירה תהרסנו.   לפיכך אמר
שהחומה המוקפת לו לאדם בהנהגתו עם זולתו ומצילו
מהאויבים ומהכשל בעסקיו הוא השתיקה כאז"ל[26] שומעין
חרפתם ואינם משיבין עליו הכתוב אומר ואוהביו וכו'.
ומיחסורתא דבבל שתיקותא[27] ובכלל זה שיהיה משאו ומתנו
בנחת רוח עם הבריות ובדבריו ערבים ושקולים לא בדרך
גוזמות וערמות ומרמות ולא בדבר עתק וגאוה כי ממה
שירחיק האדם מלשאת ולתת עמו ובהנהגה הקודמת יעדב

לבני אדם וימצא חן בעיניהם.

אמנם מאמרו השני שהוא להודיע חסדי השי"ת עם
המין האנושי בחלק לד' חלקים. הא' בכלל המין. ב'
באומה ישראלית בפרט מצד עצמה. שלישי / באומה
ישראלית מצד הישרתה מחוץ. ד' יניח ד' שרשים בענין
השכר והעונש: אמנם בא' אמר חביב אדם וכו'. כבר
נודע מדברי הר"ם בספרו המעולה[28] פ"א ח"א שאמרו בצלם
אלקים יורה ויורה חסד השי"ת על האדם שנתן בו כח נאצל
מכח וממקור המלאכי בו ישיג להבין ולהשכיל בפעולת
השי"ת מהבריה היותר שפלה עד הנמצא העליון ובו ישקול
הנהגותיו ומעשיו ודיבורו לבחור הנאות מהמגונה
ומועיל מהבלתי מועיל ודומה לאלה השלומיות. וזה
כשזיכך חמרו בענין שהיה ראוי לקבל זה הכח הנכבד.
וזה נ"ל באמרו[29] וייצר ד' אלקים את האדם עפר מן
האדמה ולא אמר כשאר הביא מן האדמה לבד כלומר שיצר
ותקן מזג העפר והיותר משובה ומנוקה מן כלל האדמה
ויפח באפיו וכו'.[30] הוא הכח השכלי. ואמר זה ר'
עקיבא להודיע שמצד זה הכח הוא מוכן אל כל המוסריים
והשלמיות הנז' ואמרו חבה יתירה וכו'. הר"ם פי'[31]
לפי' שהורדעה זאת לא השיגו אותה כי האומה ישראלית
בקבלת התורה לפיכך נ"ל שאמר זה הלשון יעורר שכלנו
לומר שהוא מהפלאים שעשה השי"ת במציאות. ואני אפרש
לשון חבה יורה על הדבר הנאהב שמוקף ונסתר ונחבא מכל
צדדיו ברעיון האוהב לא יפרד ממנו בשום צד כי הוא
נחבא בתוכו. ומזה יש לי ראיות אז"ל[32] כי ידעתיו
לשון חבה ויקרא אל משה לשון חבה. מבואר אצלי במקום
אחר. ואומר כי הנמצא השפל נאהב כיון שהמציאו ית'
אבל לחסרונו נפרד מאהבתו ופושט צורה ולובש צורה אחרת
אבל מין האדם לא יפרד ולזה לא יפשוט צורתו כי הענין
השכלי המשיג לעולם קיים כי אין החומר עיקר במציאותו

רק כדמות הכנה קלה ונבזית ולזה נקרא חביב ובאמת כי
הנה זו יתירה היא שנודעת לו וזה שהוא דבר פלא אצל
השכל כי חמרו שהוא מורכב מאיברים מתחלפים המזג
מוכנים לחלאים רבים ומלחות הפכיות מוכנים מצד זה
לתכונות מתחלפות בתכלית המרחק עד שנמצא איש יתן את
אביו מאכל כלבו כמו שהעיד ר' עקיבא ואיש אשר ישחוט

34a / בנו כמו שהעידה התורה ואיש מתעלף בשחיטת עוף וברזה
מהעכבר שחמר כזה יקבל שכל מקיף בחכמות כלם וישאר
נצחי כא' המלאכים ולא יוכל להשיג זה השלמות כי אם
באמצעות החומר א"כ חבה יתירה נודעת לו ז"ש הכתוב[33]
כי בצלם אלקים עשה את האדם והביא פסוק בני נח שהזמיר
הכתוב ברציחת אדם ונתן הסבה לפי שהוא מוכן אל שלמות
גדול כי בצלם וכו'.

אמנם בשני הוא אומת ישראל בפרט שנקראו בנים
והיא חבה יתירה כי זה פלא עצום ומקום עיון איך
איפשר שיקראו ישראל בשם בנים כי כל הנמצא בערכו ית'
ראוי להקרא עבד כי הם משרתים לו. אבל בן נגזר מבנין
וזה באות לאנשים שאינן קיימים כאיש וצריכים להיות
קיימים במין וזה לא יתכן בשי"ת וי"ל שיצירת האדם
המין בכללו הוא בענין שאומת ישראל יהיו מונהגים
מהשי"ת בעצמו. להיותם כא' מהעליונים שהם נצחיים
בעבודתו ית' יותר מהאומות כמ"ש[34] ברוך עמי מצרים
ומעשה ידי אשור ונחלתי ישראל. כלומר אף כי ז'אומות
יכנעו לעבודתו עכ"ז אינם קובעים העבודה כמו ישראל
שהם כמו הנחלה. וראיתי בפירקי ר' אליעזר פ' כ"ד
רמז לזה בדור הפלגה. ר"ש אומר קרא הב"ה לע' מלאכים
המסובבים את כסא כבודו אמר להם בואו ונרד ונבלבל
לשונם ליע' אומות ולע' גריים והפילו גורלות ונפל
גורלו של הב"ה באברהם רהם שאר האומות. שיורה טבע
היצירה כן חייב להיות אומת ישראל מיוחדת להיות מוכנת

יותר משאר האומות לעבודתו ית' ולהבין הבנה אמתית
אלקית ההנהגתם בו ית' ולזה נקראו בנים כמו שהנהגת הבן
אין אדם מוסרה לזולתו והוא היודע סודותיו והוא חזייב
בכבודו והוא יורשו וקם תחתיו כן הנהגת ישראל בו ית'
כמ"ש[35] רפן תשא עיניך השמימה וכו'.　ואתכם לקח ד'
וכו'。　והשיגו מעלת הנבואה יותר משאר האומות כמ"ש[36]
ונפלינו והם קבלו התורה ולזה כל ישראל יש להם חלק
לעה"ב.

אמנם בג' אמר חביבין ישראל שמלבד הכנת יצרתם
המעולה על שאר האומות כמ"ש / נתן להם הישרה חיצונית   34b
והיא התורה שבה נבראת העולם והיא חבה יתרה.　ר"ל דרך
פלא להיות האדם משיג רוח נבואיי שבו ישיג מה שהחקירה
השכלית אינה יכולה להשיג והיות האדם מורכב מהחומר
יקבל שפע אלקי יתפשט מהעניבנים הדרגשיים ויתלבש מרוח
הקדש אם בחלום אם בהקיץ כמ"ש[37] השמע עם קול אלקים
וכו'.　ואומר[38] כי ראיתי אלקים פנים אל פנים ותנצל
נפשי.　ואולם אמרו שבו נברא העולם ב"ל שזה נמשך
למאמר בד' תנאים התנה הב"ה עם הים שיקרע.　וכן עם
האש לחנניה ועם האריות וכו'.[39]　רזה שאמר[נ]תנו
האמתית הוא שהשי"ת חדש הנמצאות לא מיש כרצונו
וכונתו היתה שכל הנמצאים יעבדוהו וישבחוהו והם ג
מלאך גלגל אדם והעניבנים הטבעיים הוכרחו לשרות האדם.
ואם במרוצתם הטבעית יזיקו לו באופן שלא יוכל לעבוד
השי"ת כחפצר ומאויו בראם ית' בעבנין ישתנו לפי שעה
כפי הצורך בקיום התורה והמצות כענין כל הנסים שאירעו
לר' פינחס ולחביריו.[40]　ומלת בר נברא ר"ל איבר בי"ת
כלי אלא בי"ת האיכות כמו בעצבון תאכלנה[41] כלומר
בריאת העולם נמשך באיכות התורה ומקיימי מצותיה.
ואמר כי לקח טוב וכו'.　הנה כל הנמצאות טוב בכלל
כמ"ש[42] והנה טוב מאד.　אבל איפשר כי בפרט ולכם לא

יהיה טוב תמיד לקח טוב נתתי לכם והיא תורתי לכן אל
תעזוב זה כי טבע הנמצאות כלם ימשך לפי קיום התורה
ומצוותיה.   ורנ"ל ע"ד זה יתפרש מחלקת ר' חנינא ור'
יוחנן בסוף שבת[43] כי ראיתי המפרשים נבוכים לפ'
הסוגיא.   כתב הר"ן ז"ל בדרשת שמעו[44] לפי שעצם הנפש
רוחני מושפע מהשכלים נבדלים חומר העולם התחתון
משועבד לו וכל נפש תפעל בגוף שלה לפי השתנות
מחשבותיו והפעלותיו הנפשיים והוא מין עין הרע והוא
מדת הקנאה והוא אז"ל[45] האי מאן דאיתיליד במאדים יהא
גבר אשיד דמא.   ואמרו שם מר נמי עניש וקטיל וא"ת כפי
מזלו יהיה האדם צדיק או רשע כי שם אמרו מאן דאיתיליד

35a באדק יהא גבר צדקן וא"כ אין / ראוי לעונש ושכר.
רי"ל שאין המזל מכריח בעניין מצוה ועבירה אלא מכיון
הנולד באדק להיות צדקן וכן כולם כי מזל פועל בגוף
לעשות רשם במזגו ואינו פועל בנפש שהיא למעלה ממנו.
והמצוה והעבירה לפי שאינו פועל טבעי ימשך כפי ההנהגה
והיא תנהיג נולד במאדים לקרר דמו ולהשקיט רתיחתו אם
לגמרי אם שתשנהו לפעולת מצוה טבח או מהולא₀   ולזה
במלאך הממונה על הדריון צדיק ורשע לא קאמר.[46]   ור'
חנינא שאמר[47] יש מזל לישראל אין כורנתו בעניין המצוה
והעבירה אלא כרבא שאמר[48] במזלא תליא מילתא בעניינים
גופיים כבני חיי ומזוני₀   וא"ת עוד א"כ בבני חיי
ומזוני אין תפלה מועיל לשנותן א"כ בטלת ייעודי התורה
לר' חנינא ורבא.   רי"ל איפשר להנצל מפגע חיוב המזל
בעניין חיצוני אם שלא יהיה במקום שירשום בו המזל או
שיכין עצמו בעניין לא יפעל בו.   ד"מ אם יחייב המזל
בבבל ביום פלוני או יברח משם קודם בואו או יסרך גופו
מסלמנדרא ובזה יודה ר' חנינא שבזכות מצוה ותפלה ינצל
וכן דעה הא"ע.[49]   אבל להחליש המזל שלא יפעל בו אמר
ר' חנינא שלא ירעיל בזה זכות מצוה.   ור' יוחנן וכל

הנז' בסוגיא חולקים ואומרים שירעיל זכות ותפלה אפי'

בעניינים גופיים ע"כ תורף דברי הרב ז"ל. ולפי ששמעתי

להרבה חכמי המשפט היות המזל מחייב פרטי הדברים כגון

במשל הנזכר ויהייב המזל שלא יברח ושלא ימצא סלמנדרא

א"כ א"א שיתמידו הייעודים לחסידי ישראל כ"ש להמון

הכללי. לפי' נ"ל לעניות דעתי מתתרצים עזה"ד אמרינן

בסוף שבת[50] ר' חנינא אמר מזל מחכים ומזל מעשיר ויש

מזל לישראל. וכבר קדם לר' חנינא האי מאן דבצדק גבר

צדקן במצות הוי ור' יוחנן אמר אין מזל לישראל שנ'

כי יחתו הגויים וכו'. ורב...ויראצא אותו החורצה וכו'.

א"ל הב"ה צא מאצטגנינות שלך וכן[51] שמואל שהעיד על

איש שאמר לו איצטגנין שישכבו נחש וניצל בצדקה וכן ר'

עקיבא שהעיד / כן על בתו. ומדר' נחמן בר יצחק ג"כ

אין מזל לישראל דאמרו כלדאי לאמיה דהוי גנבא ולא

שבקתיה לגלויי רישיה והויא אמרה ליה כסי רישיך.

רבעא רחמי ולא הוה ידע מאי קא אמרה. יומא חד הוה

גריס תותי דיקלא נפל כיסוי רישיה דלי לעיניה חזייה

לדיקלא אלמיה ליצריה כלומר והכיסורי והתפלה היו

מגינים בשאר פעמים. ונ"ל כי ר' חנינא ור' יוחנן לא

יחולקו על מה שהוסכם בחכמי התכונה הר"א בן עזרא

והרלב"ג שהבחירה מושלת על מה שישפע מהגרמיים

השמימיים אפי' לאומות שא"כ לא היה ראוי שיענש הגוי

כשאיננו מתגייר. ואמרו[52] בפ' החולץ מפני מה גרים

מעונים מפני ששהו עצמן מלהתגייר. גם לא יחלקו

שכשאין ישראל עושין רצונו של מקום שהם נמסרים למזל

והוא סוד והסתרתי ואמרו[53] בסוף מועד קטן על חסיד

ושלם כרבה דחיי בני ומזוני חסירי דמלמד דלאו בזכותא

תליא מילתא ומהסוגיא כבר ביארנו שגם בצדיק ורשע מכין

המזל ומ"ש במקום אחר[54] במלאך הממונה על ההריון וכו'.

ונוטל הטפה ומביאה לפניו ית' ואלו צדיק ורשע לא קאמר

35b

משום דהכל בידי שמים חוץ מיראת שמים ר"ל שהבחירה
בצדק וברשע היא בעניין שמנצחת מזגו שפע המערכת עליו
כשישנהו לגמרי כרב[55] שכיסה ראשו או ישנהו לטוב כמו
הנולד במאדים דהוי מוהל ואין סגולת הבחירה כ"כ חזקה
בחיי בני ומזוני וחכמה ורומיהם ואע'פ שממעטת מאד שפעי
המערכת מצד בחירתו ועמלו והרגלם בהפכם גם זכותו
ודבקותו בשי"ת יועיל בזה בדרך נס. ופי' לאו בזכותא
וכו'.   נ"ל לפי מרוצת הטבע והוא אמת והנס לא יעשה
אלא לשלם מאד יותר מרבה ואע'פ מגדולי חסידי ישראל
אבל מחלוקתם הוא שר' חנינא סובר שהכנת המערכת לטפשות
ולעוני ולשאר יסורין בעת ההריון לגוי ולישראל אם היה
שנולדו ונוצרו בעת א' ברגע א' כי לא ינצל ברשתו
הישראל אם לא בשלמות עצום כפי רבוי התנגדותם עד
שיהיה ראוי שבדרך נס ישנה השפעים ההם או יבטלם

36a / כאשר לא ינצל ממנו הגוי אם לא בדרך זה.   ור' יוחנן
ראה שלפי שזאת האומה מתחלת יצירתה לא נמסרה להנהגת
כוכב מה אלא להנהגתו ית' אין שפע הכבבים כ"כ חזק
עליהם שממעט שלמות או מעט דבקות יספיק לבטלו ולזה
מספיק אמרו[56] דרך הגויים אל תלמודו.   לא אמר עבדוני
או דרשוני אלא כאומר לא תהיו רשעים כמו הגויים אע'פ
שלא תהיו שלמים לגמרי מאותות השמים אל תיחתו.   ורב[57]
הורה מהתנגדות העצום שהיה לאברהם דקאי צדק במעדב.
ואם קרה זה לא' מהאומות והיה בגבול השלמות שהיה
אברהם אז לא יספיק להחזירו במעדב אם לא מצד טבע
האומה שהיה הוא ראשם ולזה א"י ל[58] כה יהיה זרעך כלומר
זה הוא כח אומתך.   וראיתי בויקרא רבה פ' בחקתי[59] כה
אמר ד' אשר פדה את אברהם וכו'.   יצא דינו לישרף
מלפני נמרוד רצפה הב"ה שעתיד יעקב לצאת ממנו והצילו
בזכות יעקב גם רב נח' שנראה שלא היה[60] כ"כ תפלתו
ותחבולת כסוי ראשו הועילה ולזה הקדים ר' עקיבא לומר

חביבין ישראל שנקראו בנים למקום ואהכ"א שנתן להם כלי

חמדה שמצותיה מספיקות לבטל טבע המערכת והמזג כי כן

הושם בו בתחלת יצירתם.   ור' חנינא ורבא יורו כי הושם

כן בתחלת היצירה אבל סוברים שלא יהא זה השינוי רק

לפרוש וחסיד בקצה האחרון.

ואח"כ הניח ד' שרשים בענין הגמול והעונש.   הכל

צפוי: ר"ל אין דבר בעולם לא עצם ולא מקרה ולא דבור

ולא מחשבה מה שהיה מה שיהיה מה שעתיד שלא יהא מושגח

ובמאמר הכל צפוי ביארתי חמר הצפייה וצורתה ותכליתה

ומי הוא הצופה ולמה יחס הכלל לצפוי ולא אמר הכל השי"ת

צופה.   ב' והרשות נתונה שהאדם יש לו בחירה לעשות כל

מה שירצה ואין לו אונס לא מצד המערכת לא מצד המזג לא

מצד ידיעתו ית' שאינה מכרחת טבע האיפשר.   וכבר האריך

הר"ם ז"ל בהלכות תשובה[61] שרש הפנה הזאת וכירן שהשי"ת

יודע כל מעשה האדם ותחבולותיו והוא כבר צוהו ראוי

להיות נידון.   ג' עורר זה החכם ספק גדול והיה ראוי

שנאמ' שכל העולט / ראוי להיות כלה ואובד כי כירן   **36b**

שהשי"ת יודע המרד שימרדו בני אדם והוא בראם בצלמו

היה ראוי שיהיה העונש בב"ת כי הם מרדו לשי"ת שהוא

בב"ת.   אמר כי זה מרד כי חסדיו ובטוב העולם נידון

כלומר שאין ירורד דבר רע יורד מלמעלה על הכרונה הראשונה

אלא כדי להמשיך הטוב והשלמות והנשארים ישמעו ויראו

ונוסרו כל הנשים ולא תעשינה כזמתכנה.   ובעדת הרע

מקרבך[62] לומר שזה הוא התכלית ולזה לעולם העונש למטה

מהמערכה.[63]   אז"ל בתנחומא[64] וידעת עם לבבך כי כאשר

ייסר איש וכו'.   אתה יודע מעשים מה שעשית ויסוריך

שהבאתי עליך כי לא הבאתים כמו המעשים שעשית וכו'.

ועזרא הסופר אמר[65] כי אתה אלקינו חשכת למטה מעוננינו

וכבר ביארתי אני כן ולך ד' חסד[66] נ"ל כשאתה משלם

לאיש כדרכיו בדרך חסד אתה מתנהג וזו נקראת מדת רחמים

וזה נראה לעין כי ההפסד הבא מצד תגבורת יסוד אל יסוד

או מצד סבוב הגלגל כלקיות ודומיהן הוא אם לשמירת

כלל ההויות ולהתמידן אם ליסר האנשים כמ"ש[67] והאלקים

עשה שייראו מלפניו וכו'. והכל לפי רוב המעשה זה

נמשך אחר מאמר בסוף קידושין[68] כל העולם נידון אחר

רובו וכן היחיד אם שיתמידם הוא בעצמו אם שיהיה סבה

שיתמידו אחרים ולזה היה גדול[69] מי שיש בידו למחות.

והיא חמורה עבירה קלה או דבר בלתי מתוקן שיצא מתחת

יד גדול שילמדו אחרים ממנו יותר מאלף עבירות של

ההמון. הר"ם גריס[70] אבל לא ע"פ המעשה. ופי' עד"מ

שני אנשים כא' יתנו אלף זוז לצדקה זה בפעם א' וזה

בפעמים רבים זה האחרון לו הנדיבות בקנין מפני התמדת

המתן. וג"כ נראה לעין כי פעולות האנשים פועלות בטבע

הנמצאות. ולחוש נשיג כי מצד התמדת השקר באנשים

במשאם ומתנם נראה שקר בענינים הטבעיים. ונשיאי'

ורוח וגשם אין[71] לפעמים ולפעמים ריבוי גשמים להשחית

חום מופלג קור מופלג וכדומה לפי' האירה התורה עינינו

בהגבלת פעולותינו והתמדתן.

אמנם במאמרו הג' הניח משל נכבד אמיתי מכניע

הלבבות בהנהגת השי"ת עם האנשים בהיותו ארך אפים

ואינו מוותר כאז"ל[72] האומר הב"ה ותרן וכו'. והאריך

37a בענין הבחירה / הנתונה לאדם ותכלית כל זה הוא לתועלת

הנפש והם ה' כללים הא' הכל נתון בערבון הניח בזה

חסרון האדם כמי שעבר עבירה ונתפש עליה ד"מ שלא יוכל

לצאת מהמלכות כי יש עליו שומרים והחסרון הוא שהוא

מורכב מיסודות הפכיים ולפעמים יגבר הא' ומורכב מלחות

ותגבר הא' ומורכב מהרבה איברים ההכרחיים לו. והם

ג"כ מתחלפי המזג וצריכים לקשרים רבים וסוד הנחתן

חכמה נפלאה שאם יהיה שם שינוי יהיה שם הפסד עצום.

ועוד חסרון אחר שבאלו הענינים רפיון עצום בהתחלתו עד

שמתקשה בהדרגה ומשיזקין ישוב לרפיונו עד שנתפש
במצודה והיא המות.   וזה מלבד חסרון ידיעתו ומוסריו
ההכרחיים לו אם לשלמות נפשו אם לשלמות גופו ולהיותו
ניצל מהמקרים שהוא מוכן להם.   ב׳ והחנות פתוחה.
להמשיך המשל אע״פ שהוא נתון בערבון על מה שלוה עכ״ז
מתחסדין עמו אמר להכין לו לנחת[73] סחורה או מעות לעשות
בהם מה שירצה.   ורצה לומר שהשי״ת נתן לו כח בחיריי
לבחור איזה דרך שירצה ובכל דרך הכנות בא ליטהר
מסייעין   אותו וכו׳.[74]   ג׳ הפינקס פתוחה וכו׳.   כלומר
שלא ישכח דבר ממה שיקח בחנות ואמרו פתוחה שלא יצטרך
עליו רבים ושמא ישכח בזה וזה רמז כי במדע א׳ יקיף
השי״ת ידועים בב״ת בלי עמל כמ״ש הר״ט בספרו.[75]   הר״יי
חדש בזה[76] למה הפינקס פתוחה וכו׳.   שאע״פ שישוב
בתשובה שלימה אינו דומה למי שלא חטא כלל ומ״ש[77]
במקומו שבעלי תשובה וכו׳.   ר״ל באותן הסייגים שהבעל
תשובה יתקדש במותר לו.   ולמ״ד אין צורך בזה שמחלוקת
הוא פ׳ אין עומדין[78] שיש לומר שגדול שכרו לרוב צערו
כיון שטעם טעם חטא. ד׳.   והגבאין מחזירין תמיד כלומר
שאינו כשאר דיני ממונות שאז״ל[79] לא תבא אל ביתו
לעבוט עבוטו בשליח ב״ד הכתוב מדבר ר״ל שאינו יכול
למשכנו רק מדעתו.   ויש להם על מה שיסמוכו והדין דין
אמת.   כלומר יש מי שסומך ידי הגבאים שנפרעים שלא
מדעת הלוה ולא בדרך אלמות אלא הדין דין אמת שנראה
שכך התנה עמו / והכורנה היא אז״ל[80] אין לך יום שאין
בו קללה אין לך אדם שאין לו איזה צער או יגון אם
באיבריו או בבניו או בחלאים וכדומה בהנהגתו באויבו
במשרתו וכו׳.   אז״ל[81] אפי׳ אפי׳ בהפך לו חלוקו.   אפי׳
הושיט ידו להרציא ג׳ ועלו ב׳ אז״ל[82] אין אדם נוקף
אצבעו מלמטה אלא א״כ מכריזין עליו מלמעלה.   וא״כ אין
ספק שהגבאים גובים תמיד והודיע בזה תכלית ההשגחה

37b

רשלא יאמר מקרה הוא אלא יחשוב שהוא עונש מאתו ית'
ויצדיק עליו את הדין. ואמרו שלא מדעתו כי פעמים
יבואו היסורין פתאום לא ידע בהם סבה טבעית או
באותית. ה' והכל מתוקן לסעודה. נ"ל פי' שאם יש בזה
לכאורה מעט עול שיגבר מא' יותר מדאי ומא' לא יגבו
כדי חובו והוא קושית צדיק ורע לו רשע וטוב לו כ"ז
מתוקן ומתוריץ לדבר שהוא מסעד והוא השארות הנפש כי
הצדיק יתענג והרשע יענש בגיהנם. וכן פי' ז"ל במ'
תעניות[83] א-ל אמונה ואין עול צדיקים ורשעים יורד
עמהם עד תהום רבה וכן פי' מה"ר חסדאי משפטי ד' אמת
צדקו יחדיו[84] ר"ל כשיצדקו יחד עובשי העה"ז עם ענשי
העה"ב וכו'. ואמר לסעודה ולא בסעודה לרמוז כי כל
זה הוא הכנה והנפש הוא התכלית זהו משז"ל[85] בדברי
זה השלם בתכלית הקוצר: ר' אלעזר בן עזריה אומר אם
אין תורה וכו'. עד ולא ימיש מעשות פרי. זה השלם
היה חבר לר' עקיבא ושמוהו נשיא על מחלוקת ר"ג ור'
יהשע ואמר ב' מאמרים. בא' הודיע ד' זוגות בשלמות
שכל זוג הכרחי קצתו אל קצתו בהשגת השלמות בקנין.
בשני הודיע יתרון המעשה אל הידיעה ונתן בזה
סבה סכלית. אמנם בא' זוג אחד אם אין תורה אין דרך
ארץ וכו'. כבר קדם לי[86] ששני הנהגות הכרחיות בכל
מקובץ הא' מה שיכינו למקום. הב' מה שיכינו לזולתו.
הודיע לנו סוד זה שזה משלים את זה וזה את זה שההכנע
אל השי"ת והאמות הפנות התוריות יישריהו אל שיתנהג עם
הבריות בשובה ונחת ויפתח בתועלת היישוב ויקבלם בסבר
פנים יפות לרצונו בעבודתו ית' ולהדבק בדרכיו. ואם
אינו שלם בעירן א"א להיותו שלם בענינים מוסריים
והההכנע אל תועלת היישוב והתנהג עמו / באהבה טבע
ההנהגה הזאת יישריהו אל שיבין הפנות התורניות לפי
שיהיו לו מיישרים רבים ויסורו ממנו כל מעיקים

ומטרידים ואם אינו בעל מוסר יורה על רוע מזגו וא"א
להיותו שלם בעיון . זוג ב' אם אין חכמה אין יראה
וכו' .   חכמה ר"ל בקיאות מה שאז"ל[87] אוקומי גרסא ור"ל
שיזכור כל מה שלמד בפרטי החכמים הוא ההישרה אל שיראה
לנפשר ניהא[88] ויתרחק מהתאוות הגופיים כי החכמה
תודיעהו התכלית הטוב שיהיה למי שימשך אחר העיון
ויתרחק מן העניינים החמריים . ויכלכל כל דבריו במשפטי
התורה האלקית ולש"ש כי הוא הירא חטא באמת כמ"ש פ"ב[89]
והחסרון בידיעה לא   ידע הדברים שראוי לירא מהם
וחסרון היראה יורה להתלהבות יצרו ויתבלבל שכלו בעיון
וישכח מה שלמד .   זוג ג' אם אין דעת אין בינה וכו' .
שני שלמיות הם במעלה השכלית הכרחיים לחכמה .   הא'
להמציא משכלו דברים אמיתיים וזהו נקרא דעת כלומר
שהוא נטוע בו לא קנאו מזולתו ונקרא מעין המתגבר .
ויש דעת שר"ל ברירת הצודק .   וב' אלו הם באדם בקנין .
הב' הוא ידיעתו מה שלמד בסבותיהן וישיג מהותן והבדלן
העצמי וזה נקרא בינה נגזר מן בין ובכלל זה שיבין דבר
מתוך דבר כי החכמה הוא הבקיאות שלמדו זולתו .   הכח
הראשון יישיר אל הב' והב' אל הראשון .   ונ"ל שלפי זה
אנו אומרים אתה חונן לאדם דעת לפי שהוא מעצמו .
ומלמד לאנוש בינה לפי שזה ממה שלמד מזולתו ואנו
מתפללין שיחננו בשני כחות אלה דעה ובינה ואמר והשכל
ר"ל שנסכים בב' אלה אל האמת.   והר"ם ז"ל פי'[90]
ויתפלפל לבאר כי הדעת הוא השכל והבינה הוא המושכל
והוא הוא.   זוג ד' אם אין קמח אין תורה זה אמת
שהמזורנות הכרחיים כשהם מצויין יוכל להתיישב בעיונו
וזכות התורה והעיון יישיר אל שיהיה לאדם די צרכו
כאז"ל בפ' הפועלים[91] היתה כאניות סוחר והוא פי' כי
בצל החכמה וכו' .[92] ר"ל בצל החכמה יתלונן מי שיושג
בצל הכסף וכן בהפך ויתרון דעת החכמה תחיה את בעליה.

38b ומי שיש לו יתרון דעת / החכמה החכמה שלו תחייהו והוא
פי׳ טובה חכמה עם נחלה ויותר וכו׳.[93]   כלומר ואותה
חכמה היא שיש לה יתרון לאנשים שהם תחת השמש ומביטים
אליו יען הוא מנהיגם כי חכמת המסכן בזויה היא יען לא
יוכל להתישב בה לעניו.   ואם אין לו תורה יאבד עשרו
בענין רע.   ויש גורסין יש תורה יש קמח.   במאמרו השני
הודיע שמי שחכמתו מרובה ממעשיו דומה לענפים מרובים
ושרשים מעטים שבנקלה נעקר.   והביא פסוק כערער שר״ל
אילן מגולה מגז׳ ערו ערו רז״ש ולא יראה כי יבא טוב.
ול״ב שאין זה צורך להביא לו ראיה אבל לפי שפסוק זה
נאמר על מי שבוטח באדם שהוא כאילן שאין לו שרש כלל
הודיענו כי הוא כן מי שאיננו עובד לשי״ת בכל נפשו
וסומך על חכמתו לבד שאיננה לו בקנין ובמעט צרה יכפור
בשי״ת ובתורתו.   אבל מי שמעשיו מרובין מחכמתו שרשיו
מרובין מענפיו ודומה למי שבוטח בשם בעת צרה ומסר שמו
על קדושת שמו.   זה ידמה לעץ שתול על מים וגם התפשטות
שרשיו הם על פלגי מים ולזה תמיד הוא רענן כן הענין
בשרה מי שבוטח בשי״ת והוא פי׳ פסוק[94] רבים מכאובים
לרשע וכו׳.   ר״ל במחשבותיו כי יחשוב במקרים עצומים
שהאדם מוכן להם ואיך ינצל מהם ולא ידע כי גבהו ממנו
אבל הבוטח בשי״ת יסובבנהו נסים ונפלאות בדרך חסד
להצילו.   ובמוסרי הפילוסופים פי׳ שהבטחון הוא המסר
ורצות גזירותיו ית׳ ר״ל שיחשוב בעצמו ידעתי השם לא
בראני לנקמה ממני הן יקטלני לו איחל[95] ואתן כל אשר
לי בעבור עבודתו אשר כזה חכמתו בקייה וטהורה בלי סיג
ותתקיים בידו והשגחתו ית׳ דבקה בו ויתעלה למעלה
גדולה.   וזהו שחידש ר׳ אלעזר על ר׳ חנינא[96] כוונת ר׳
חנינא היא עצה טובה להכניע איבריו לעמוד כנגד מזגו
המנגדו.   וכונת ר׳ אלעזר שיכוין לעבודתו ית׳ בכל
עניניו ויבטח בו לא בזולתו ולזה הביא פסוקים האמורים

גבי בטחון ואיפשר שר' חנינא הודיע שלא תהיה לו
הידיעה בקנין כמו ר' יעקב ור' דוסתאי הסמוכים לו[97]

39a   ור' / אלעזר הודיע הצלחתו בקנינו והשארות הנפש: ר'
אלעזר חסמא אומר קנים וכו'.   זה השלם נמצא בויקרא
רבה[98] והיה חכם גדול ולא היה יודע ברכת חתנים ואבלים
ולפרוש על שמע ונתבייש במקום עמי הארץ ואח"כ למדו ר'
עקיבא ועל זה קראו אותו חסמא שהיה חסום מתחלתו
ולמדנו שכן ת"ח צריך ללמוד כל זה ודרך אחר עקבות
הראשונים ר' חנינא ור' אלעזר.   ועשה שני חלקות בעניין
הידיעה ונמצאו בספרי הפילוסופים.   הא' הידיעה התלויה
במעשה והיא פי' המצות והם ב' חלקים.   הא' מה שיש בו
עבודת השם והוא אמרו קנים שהוא חלק מהקרבנות ונכלל
בזה כל חלק המצות התלויות בעבודת השי"ת שלא נתפרסם
בזה תועלת לאדם.   הב' והוא פתחי נדה ויוכלל בזה
איסורי ביאות ומאכלות אסורות שכשנעיין השגנו שהם
מועילים לאדם מאד אם בבריאותו אם בהכנעת עיונו.
ויוכלל בשני אלה ההנהגות המדותיות והמדיניות החקים
והמשפטים.   השלישית[99] הידיעה שאינה תלויה במעשה והיא
חשבון תקופות ומזלות שהיא מצוה גדולה כמשז"ל[100] על
פסוק כי היא חכמתכם.   ופרש"י[101] שרמז בזה בהוראת
משפטי הככבים.   והוסיף בזה גיאמטריאות שר"ל ידיעת
המספר שיש בו סגולות נפלאות וכמו שרמז הראב"ע פ'
שמות ובמקומות מספריו.[102]   ואמרו מספר הנאהב והרבה
דברים ישיגו בעלי המספר מצד המספר באיש ואשה ונוצח
ומנרצח ודומיהם ואע"פ שבתקופות תלויין במעשה
שנא',[103] שמור את חדש האביב אין המצוה של חשבון מצד
המעשה רק מצד הידיעה וכאמרו[104] כי היא חכמתכם לעיני
העמים.   ונתן יתרון לידיעה שתכליתה המעשה משתכליתה
הידיעה לבד כיתרון הפת על הפרפרא שהוא הלפתן שהוא
טפלה לו ולרמוז שהדבקות בו ית' יושג באמצעות המעשה
כמו שקדם.

הערות

1. אבות ג, יב.

2. ישעיה מז, ג.

3. יומא יט, ע'ב.   צ'ל אַף בגבולין היו עושין כן.

4. תהלים קד, טו; קהלת ב, ג; שם י, יט.

5. סוטה ב, ע'א.

6. משלי יט, ב; כט, כ.

7. ברכות מג, ע'ב; קידושין לא, ע'א.

8. קהלת י, ג.

9. צ'ל בענין חדוש ברצון.

10. שבת סג, ע'א.

11. ברכות מז, ע'א.

12. כלל זה נמצא אצל גאונים וראשונים, ועיין רשימת המקורות באנציקלופדיה תלמודית, ערך "אין הלכה כתלמיד במקום הרב".

13. סוטה מז, ע'ב.

14. תענית ט, ע'א.

15. כתובות סו, ע'ב.

16. שם סו, ע'ב - סח, ע'א.

17. מגילה כח, ע'ב.   צ'ל כיומא דאסתנא.

18. אבות ג, יז.

19. ברכות כט, ע'ב.

20. נדרים ח, ע'א.

21. במדבר רבה טו, יב.

22. פירוש רבינו יונה לאבות ג, יג.

23. ראה מורה נבוכים ג, נד.

24. משלי יב, טו.   צ'ל דרך אויל.

25. שם יד, א.

26. שבת פח, ע'ב.

27. קידושין עא, ע'א, ע'ב.

28. מורה נבוכים א, א.

29. בראשית ב, ז.

30. שם.

31. כאן חסר רצ"ל (ע"פ כ"י ששון): הר"ם פי' שהנותן מתנה
לזולתו ומודיעו היא הטבה אחרת זולת המתנה ומי שאינו
מודיע יורה היותר נבזה בעיניו. יקשה זה הפי' אצלי
לפי שהודעת זו לא [השיגו] אותה רק אומת ישראל בלבד
בקבלת התורה לפי' נ"ל וכו'.

32. ראה בראשית יז, יט, ורש"י שם; ויקרא א, א, ורש"י שם;
תו"כ ויקרא.

33. בראשית ט, ו.

34. ישעיה יט, כה.

35. דברים ד, יט - כ.

36. שמות לג, טז.

37. דברים ד, לג.

38. בראשית לב, לא.

39. בראשית רבה ה, ד.

40. חולין ז, ע"א.

41. בראשית ג, יז.

42. שם א, לא.

43. שבת קנו, ע"א.

44. ראה דרשות הר"ן, מהדורת א.ל. פלדמן (ירושלים, תשל"ד)
עמוד קלה ואילך.

45. שבת שם.

46. נדה טז, ע"ב.

47. שבת שם.

48. מועד קטן כח, ע"א.

49. שמות לג, כא ועיין הערותיו של פלדמן, דרשות הר"ן,
עמוד קלח.

50. שבת שם.

51. שם, עמוד ב.
52. יבמות מח, ע"ב.
53. מועד קטן כח, ע"א.
54. נדה טז, ע"ב.
55. צ"ל כרב נחמן.
56. ירמיה י, ב.
57. שבת קנו, ע"א – ע"ב.
58. בראשית טו, ה.
59. ויקרא רבה לו, ד.
60. צ"ל שלא היה כזה שלם כ"כ וכו'.
61. רמב"ם הלכות תשובה, פרק ה.
62. דברים יז, יג; יחזקאל כג, מח; דברים יג, ו.
63. צ"ל מן העבירה.
64. תנחומא יתרו, טז.
65. עזרא ט, יג.
66. תהלים סב, יג.
67. קהלת ג, יד.
68. קידושין מ, ע"ב.
69. צ"ל גדול חטא מי שיש וכו'.
70. פירוש הרמב"ם לאבות ג, טו.
71. משלי כה, יד.
72. בבא קמא נ, ע"א.
73. צ"ל לקחת.
74. שבת קד, ע"א.
75. מורה נבוכים ג, כ-כא.
76. פירוש רבינו יונה לאבות ג, טז.
77. ברכות לד, ע"ב.
78. שם.
79. בבא מציעא קי"ג, ע"ב.
80. סוטה מח, ע"א; בראשית רבה צב, א.

81. ערכין טז, ע'ב.

82. חולין ז, ע'ב.

83. תענית יא, ע'א.

84. תהלים יט, י.

85. צ'ל משנ''ל.

86. עיין פירושו לפרק א, ד-טז.

87. מגילה ו, ע'ב.

88. צ'ל מחטוא.

89. עיין פירושו לפרק ב, ח-ט.

90. פירוש הרמב''ם לאבות ג, יז.

91. בבא מציעא פד, ע'ב.

92. קהלת ז, יב.

93. שם ז, יא.

94. תהלים לב, י.

95. איוב יג, טו.

96. אבות ג, ט.

97. שם ג, ז-ח.

98. ויקרא רבה, כג, ד.

99. צ'ל הב'.

100. שבת עה, ע'א.

101. רש ''י שם.

102. עיין, למשל, פירושו לשמות לג, כא.

103. דברים טז, א.

104. שם ד, ו.

15

The Francesc de Sant Jordi-Solomon Bonafed Letters

Frank Talmage

The travails which afflicted the hapless Spanish Jews of the early fifteenth century did not stifle their poetic expression. During and beyond the traumatic years of the Tortosa debate, the redoubtable Solomon ben Reuben Bonafed (d. after 1445)[1] continued the tradition of his "precursor," Solomon ibn Gabirol, so that the cadences of the tongue of Eber might yet be heard on the banks of the Ebro. Bonafed was the last of the "professional" Spanish poets;[2] his poetry has been adjudged "almost entirely secular," bearing "hardly a trace of sanctity."[3] Yet this impassioned soul, who sang of his successes and failures in love and life, was not without religious sentiment, as his surviving liturgical compositions indicate. The longing for the restoration of Zion is expressed with charm and elegance in his compositions,[4] and indeed one occasionally catches a glimpse of a soul whose mournful plaint recalls the words of other Spaniards who "died because they did not die."

> My soul is penned within me in dismay.
> "Who brought me here?," she asks each passing day.
> She longs for God to bring about that end
> When to the Source she thirsts for she'll surrend.[5]

Bonafed's own self-characterization was that of a Solomon ibn Gabirol redivivus. To many, this parallel is somewhat forced,[6] but it is not entirely without foundation, even if we concede that its truth lies more in the likeness of their life histories than in that of their aesthetic attainments. Ibn Gabirol and Bonafed were both Saragossans, sons of that community which allegedly dealt so treacherously with successive generations of Hebrew poets. As with ibn Gabirol and Judah ibn Shabbethai,[7] the relations between Bonafed and the members of the aljama of the Aragonese capital were such that the poet was forced to take refuge in the town of Belchite. The apparent precipitating cause of the rift was the rise to prominence of a Sicilian rabbi, Joseph Jeshuah. To Bonafed, Joseph was a boor and a fraud, especially pernicious because he had seduced the community into believing he was a true sage. But then again, he was all they deserved. The disorienting events of 1412-15 had brought this herd of gruff and base tradesmen and entrepreneurs to power and, not being natural aristocrats, they did not know how to handle their new role with grace. To be sure, Bonafed's view

of Rabbi Joseph or the members of the community may not have been entirely just,[8] but then he was not given to dispassionate assessments. During
his exile in Belchite, he raged against his nemeses in a powerful satirical out-
burst in which he described the *takkanot* (ordinances) of a community
which might have put Sodom and Gomorrah to shame.[9] In this diatribe,
Bonafed included his remarkable *tour de force*, "Litmon be-hubbi 'amali,"
an imitation, in meter and rhyme, of ibn Gabirol's "Nihar be-kor'i geroni,"
in which the latter expressed his despair over his tragic relationship with the
Saragossan community. In this poem, Bonafed, in the depths of depression
and longing for the few friends he had left behind, describes how the spirit
of ibn Gabirol had appeared one night to commiserate with him and give
him heart.

> And as I was speaking—behold
> Ben Gabirol before me!
> As dread as an angel and bold
> Appeared in my sanctuary.
> The coruscant sword in his hand
> Flashed in my tent all along;
> His voice was full thund'rous and grand—
> His righteous words made me wax strong.
> "Son of Reubén, to you all hail!
> My truly beloved so dear:
> I've come now to be of avail
> So tremble not nor must you fear.
> Have the villains of my village
> Been vile to you as they were to me?
> Stalking and plotting a pillage
> Of every true heart they could see?"

The root of the problem was that as ibn Gabirol's reincarnation Bonafed
was persona non grata in the Aragonese capital. The oneiric visitor thus
explains:

> Like their venomous forebears they'd try
> To blot me from all memory.
> They believed that indeed you were I
> And hated you thinking you me.
> They saw then that you were my peer,
> My equal in skill and in fame—
> So alike are we that indeed we're
> Bearers of the same name.
> They thought that I rose from the grave;
> from the earth I had come into view.
> One moment, dear friend, and these knaves
> Will receive from me all that's their due.
>
>   . . . . .
>
> How can a pearl float in slime?
> A lily among the rude thorns?

> Can one expect the sublime
> On the wings of the base to be borne?
> . . . . .
> Sons of Seir they all are,
> Riffraff devoid of all worth—
> Sons of Moab and Hagar,
> Though they'd claim to be Israel by birth.
> If those wanton sots with no brain
> My reputation deride
> Against them I can yet maintain
> My intellect which is my pride.[10]

My intellect which is my pride! For Bonafed, despite the failure of contemporary rationalism to stem the tide of apostasy and despite the awareness that it may indeed have been a contributing factor, the intellect remains the one source of solace. This is so whether one is smarting from the wounds inflicted by the Saragossan curmudgeons, the onslaughts of Christianity, or even a thwarted love affair:

> The day that my hind did depart
> And her comèly grace evanesced
> A new lumen shone in my heart
> The glow of the intellect.[11]

Bonafed's conclusion of "Litmon," with an apparently disarming Maimonidean-like profession of faith,[12] in fact aptly parallels, given the transition from twelfth-century Neoplatonic mysticism to fifteenth-century scholasticism, the elegiac conclusion of "Nihar":

> I loathe this my life and abhor
> This body in which I abide
> The "joys" of this world are a bore
> My true joy would be that I'd died.
> I struggle to fathom and know
> As my vigor and strength are abated
> For relief my grief will yet follow
> And from famine I shall yet be sated.
> As long as I live I'll be prone
> To search as Sol'mon did command
> Perhaps He who reveals the unknown
> Will cause me to understand—
> For this is my lot—this alone
> All I possess, all I own.[13]

As noted, Bonafed's exaltation of the intellect was tempered by the realization that excessive indulgence in philosophical speculation led many into skepticism—a way-station on the road to conversion to Christianity. In a letter to En Shealtiel Gracian, he noted:

When I see how the hand of faith has been weakened and how the feet of many of our dispersed brethren falter for lack of hope; and how they that promote alien wisdom in order to extirpate the roots of religion; and now that our pious men believe that philosophical contemplation is more important than the performance of the commandments, so that their ignorance has led them to believe that the Torah is essential only to the welfare of the masses, who are raised in the lap of faith and tradition, whereas theory . . . is knowledge of the books of nature and of Aristotelian metaphysics, which view they have hung upon a mighty tree, that of Maimonides, may he rest in peace, etc.[14]

The mass defection to Christianity in the wake of the Tortosa confrontation in the "year of apostasies" (1414) tormented Bonafed. Present at the disputation, he watched one after another of the leaders of Aragonese Jewry fall by the wayside and despair of adhering to a covenant in whose reality they no longer believed. Our poet's role at Tortosa has been documented by Y. F. Baer.[15] He apparently was not a direct participant in the debates but functioned actively behind the scenes. His activity emerges as intensely personal as we see him plead directly with those who were on the brink of conversion or even with those whose apostasy was a fait accompli. Most of the time, Bonafed expresses himself in poetry or at least in rhymed prose. Even at the times of gravest crisis, the proper forms of expression were to be maintained. After all, mass apostasy and the progressive deterioration of peninsular Judaism was no prosaic matter. Remarkably enough, it was poetry, Hebrew poetry, that continued to bind together many of the figures in this drama—conversos and professing Jews—for years to come.

Bonafed's most specific critique of Christianity appeared in a rhymed prose epistle sent to Francesc de Sant Jordi, formerly Astruc Rimoch the Jew.[16] The events surrounding the writing of this epistle are well known and have been recounted by Baer.[17] Briefly, Francesc had sought to persuade his former comrade, En Shealtiel Bonafos, to join him in his acceptance of the Christian faith. Bonafos had been on the verge of doing so but then repented of his decision. He set forth his reasons in writing and sent them to Master Francesc. This reply has not been preserved but when the correspondence came to Bonafed's[18] hands, he clearly found Bonafos's statement wanting. He consequently took it upon himself to write his own unsolicited reply.

In terms of its structure and style, the epistle distinctly echoes the "Be Not Like Unto Thy Fathers" of Profiat Duran (Efodi). As Ibn Gabirol was Bonafed's model in poetry, so did he attempt to adopt Duran's style in polemic. Duran figures in Bonafed's poetry as did ibn Gabirol. His poem addressed to Duran during the Tortosa debates[19] is a striking document which reveals his sense of desperation at the helplessness and impotence of the Jewish participants. Our poet could think of only two individuals who might have avoided the debacle—Hasdai Crescas, who was no longer alive, and Duran, who was absent. In a flight of poetic fantasy, he appeals "Approach, Efod" and "raise the banner of those true writings which would make those enemies and rebels against the Lord flee in fear."[20] Many expressions and turns of phrase in Bonafed's works recall these writings, especially the "Be Not Like Unto Thy Fathers."[21] This is nowhere more evident than in the epistle to Master Francesc. In his opening, he attempts to achieve the sense of irony created by Duran by showering apparent praise on his correspondent but in fact damning him, although he does not attain the same level of subtlety.

Bonafed	*Duran*
I've seen a writ (*megillat sefer*)	I've seen a flying scroll (*megillah 'afah*)
Whose words are fit	Revealing the redemption;
But dull of wit.	Its words are fitly told
Its wings are of a dove	But defy full comprehension.
But its form is of a raven.	In excellence it towers,
It seems to speak of love	Its mysteries are sublime.
But hides a bear so craven.	Its brilliance overpowers
	This humble brain of mine.[22]

Bonafed's arguments essentially follow those of the "Fathers." He inveighs against the concept of vicarious atonement, asking if a king ever punishes himself for the crime of his servant, stating that there is no scriptural evidence for such an allegation. Further, one is responsible for one's own sins, not Adam's. If the world has been redeemed, where is the visible evidence? Man still works the ground and woman still brings forth in pain. All die. The doctrine of incarnation is impugned with the assertion that God is debased by clothing him in human garb and that the Jews are not to be faulted if they did not recognize one who claimed to be divine but did not appear in a manner appropriate to the majesty of divinity. The doctrines of transubstantiation and the Trinity are treated much in the same manner in which Duran and others had approached them.

Telescoping Duran's strictures, Bonafed makes light of Francesc's consciousness of having been redeemed.

> As you wish, you have done well not to wait for the Lord or His Anointed. Ah, He's right around the corner—the new Jerusalem, just six steps beyond the door! God is deep within you[23] for no savior who is remote can redeem you. That is the fate of Israel—the poor and the wretched. Rejoice in your God. Be sated in His name and in His blood. When you seek aught of Him, call upon His mother and all the saints at the time of anguish.

Despite Bonafed's jibes, his words do not suggest a posture of security and confidence. He frankly reveals his own failure to provide an adequate answer to the one Christian contention which became ever so much harder to refute after the events of 1391 and 1412-1415.

> One thing notwithstanding will I confess to you, for it is like a sword in my bowels and like an upright flame among my ribs, ... to the

length and breadth of our dispersion there is no answer; nor is there
any reply to our scattered brethren who do not return. We are the two
tails of the smoking firebrands, the light of our Torah is [hidden] in pil-
lars of smoke, and every day new reverses are borne in upon us. In the
eyes of the Gentiles we seem despicable—one righteous man as against
the traitors.[24]

Although Bonafed was at a loss to interpret this Jewish "mystery" in other
than conventional terms, he refused to yield and even appealed to his correspondent to return to the ranks of Israel.[25] In this, he displayed that tenacity which the Christians termed obduracy and the Jews faithfulness—a
tenacity long become proverbial:

> Era dueña en todo e de dueñas señora
> non podia estar solo con ella una ora
> mucho de omne se guardan ally do ella mora
> mas mucho que non guardan los jodios la tora.[26]

The letters published here were first printed in Isaac Akrish's *'Iggeret
'ogeret* (Constantinople, 1570-78) and reprinted from Akrish with variants
by A. Geiger in his *Kovez vikkuhim* (Breslau, 1844). A. Posnanski prepared
a manuscript edition of the letters now in the possession of the Jewish Na-
tional and University Library in Jerusalem. I have prepared a new edition
following in the main Bodleian ms. Mich. 155 (fols. 12v-15r [fol. 13 is out of
order and should precede fol. 12]). The text of this manuscript which houses
Bonafed's *divan* and is the major source of his poetry has been collated with
three (probably) sixteenth-century manuscripts: (Vav) Vienna ms. Heb. 95,
fols. 50r-53r, which does not contain Francesc's letter; (Lamed) Leiden ms.
Warner 64 (Or. 4802), fols. 27r-30r; and (Mem) Munich ms. Heb. 312, fols.
15r-18r. The Bodleian text has been indicated by 'Aleph.

NOTES

NOTE: Research for this paper was performed as a part of a larger project
supported by the Canada Council.

1. For bibliography on Bonafed, see H. Schirmann, "Ha-Pulmos shel Shelomoh Bonafed be-Nikbede Saragosa," *Kovez 'al yad*, n.s., IV (1946), 10, note 1, and
Ha-Shirah ha-'Ivrit bi-Sefarad u-vi-Perovans (Tel Aviv, 1956), II, 697. See also Y. F.
Baer, *A History of the Jews in Christian Spain*, 2 vols. (Philadelphia, 1966), index
s.v. "Solomon Bonafed."

2. Schirmann, *Ha-Shirah*, II, 620.

3. Jószef Patai, "Shirei Hol shel Shelomoh Bonafed," in *Mi-Sefunei ha-Shirah*
(Jerusalem, n.d.), pp. 68, 75.

4. See especially the *reshuyot* published by Schirmann, *Ha-Shirah*, II, 641-
643.

5. Schirmann, *Ha-Shirah*, II, 640.

6. "Gabirol, who longs to penetrate the mysteries of activity and existence

and who was persecuted for his opinions, is not to be likened to the sober Bonafed, who gripes about the deprivation of his livelihood" (Schirmann, *Ha-Shirah*, II, 623). See also Patai, *Mi-Sefunei*, p. 34, who criticizes Graetz for acquiescing to Bonafed's self-evaluation.

7. Along with ibn Gabirol and Bonafed, ibn Shabbethai bore an abiding hatred for the Saragossans whom he mercilessly satirized. See Israel Davidson, *Parody in Jewish Literature* (New York, 1907), pp. 8-14, and "Divrei ha-'Alah ve-ha-Nidduy," *Ha-'Eshkol* I (1909), 165-175; Naphtali Wieder, "Sifro ha-Nisraf shel Yehudah ibn Shabbetai," *Mezudah*, II (1943), 122-131.

8. See Baer, *History*, II, 248-249: "In general, it may be doubted whether all the estimable artisans who still headed the communities were only ignoramuses and malefactors, as Bonafed portrayed them. It would seem that in his old age, this satirical poet forgot that it was thanks to just these simple men and not to the notables of the community that the flame of Jewish faith was not quenched."

9. The *takkanot* were published by Schirmann, "Ha-Pulmos shel Shelomoh Bonafed be-Nikbede Saragosa," *Kovez 'al Yad*, n.s., IV (1946), 8-64.

10. Schirmann, "Ha-Pulmos," pp. 32-33.

11. Schirmann, *Ha-Shirah*, II, 626.

12. Schirmann, "Ha-Pulmos," p. 33.

13. Heinrich Brody and H. Schirmann, *Shelomoh ibn Gevirol: Shirei ha-Hol* (Jerusalem, 1974), p. 69.

14. Baer, *History*, II, 223.

15. Ibid., II, 210-224.

16. See ibid., index s.v. "Astruc Rimoch."

17. Ibid., II, 218-223.

18. The friendship of Bonafed and Bonafos is documented in a get-well poem sent the latter by the former. See Jószef Patai, "Shirei ha-Heshek shel Shelomoh Bonafed," *Ha-Zofeh le-Hokmat Yisra'el*, I (1925), 222; Aaron Kaminka in *Mi-Mizrah u-mi-Ma'arav*, vol. I, pt. 2 (1895), p. 114.

19. Published by Kaminka in *Ha-Zofeh le-Hokmat Yisra'el*, XII (1928), 38-40.

20. Ibid., p. 39. There appears to be no evidence for the often repeated assertion that Duran was present at the debate. If we accept the fact of his forced baptism —something he consistently laments in his writings—then it is hardly conceivable that he would have been allowed to dispute Christianity publicly. On the other hand R. W. Emery's conclusion that he lived openly as a Christian (while serving as tutor in the household of Hasdai Crescas) is in itself problematic and requires further study. See Emery's "New Light on Profayt Duran 'the Efodi,' " *JQR, LVIII (1967-68)*, 328-337.

21. Duran is mentioned by name in the epistle sent to En Shealtiel Gracian (*Ha-Zofeh le-Hokmat Yisra'el*, XII [1928], 40) to bolster Bonafed's point that excessive philosophizing to the exclusion of the observance of the commandments is harmful. Plays on the "Fathers" are found not only in the poem to Duran (ibid., p. 38, line 9) but in his polemic against the Saragossans in which Joseph is accused of being as ignorant of philosophy as the Christians were of ignoring it. See Schirmann, "Ha-Pulmos," p. 20, lines 117-118, 120-121, 125; p. 21, lines 129, 133-136. At greater length, Bonafed attacks his antagonist's alleged ignorance of physics, astronomy, and poetics (ibid., pp. 37-46) in the manner in which Duran had denigrated, albeit briefly, the learning of Paul of Burgos at the end of the "Fathers."

It is worth noting that ironically one statement in Francesc's letter is reminiscent of the "Fathers." Francesc complains that the Jews had dissuaded Bonafos from conversion at the last minute just as Duran points out that the same thing had been said of him. The theme of "bad company" either promoting or preventing conversion is not uncommon. Years before, Francesc, then Astruc Rimoch, blamed the apostasy of a Jew in Fraga on his association "with men devoid of honor" (Baer, *History*, II, 131).

22. The "Fathers" has been reprinted several times. See Judah Rosenthal, "Sifrut ha-Vikkuah ha-'Anti-Nozerit 'ad ha-Me'ah ha-Shemoneh-'Esreh," *'Areshet* II (1959-60), 146, no. 57. The manuscript edition of Adolf Posnanski was published in facsimile by the Department of Jewish History at the Hebrew University, Jerusalem, 1970. An English translation may be found in Franz Kobler, *Letter of Jews through the Ages from Biblical Times to the Middle of the Eighteenth Century* (London, 1953), I, 276-282.

23. Here Bonafed echoes Duran's ironic "tokal ve-tisba' u-moshi'aka be-kirbeka; 'et ha-'el ta'ariz ve-takdish, et kedosh yisra'el be-kirbeka" (ed. Posnanski, p. 86). "Your Savior is in your midst" mocks the ingestion of the eucharist.

24. Baer, *History*, II, 222-223.

25. Bonafed repeatedly calls on the wayward to return. See, for example, the letter to a forced convert published by Kaminka in *Ha-Zofeh* XII (1928), 35. Astruc Rimoch had himself lamented the apostasy of acquaintances in 1391. See Baer, *History*, II, 131-132.

26. Juan Ruiz, Archpriest of Hita, *Libro de buen amor*, ed. Manuel Criado del Val and Eric W. Naylor (Madrid, 1972), p. 29, stanza 78. In English: "She was a lady so grand like so few/I could only be with her a second or two/For in her home she is kept from men's view/Even more than the Torah is kept by a Jew."

אגרת פרנסישק די שינט יורדי

[עמ׳ 13 א] ¹טורפס כתב החכם מאישטרי אשטרוק רימוך והיה לו
שם אחר מאישטרי פרנסישק די שינט יורדי עורר חנית כתבו
בשנת ההמרות לנבון אנשלתיאל בונפוש על עניני האמונה
החדשה ודבר על כל היהודים קשה.¹

בפשי אויתיך מאז וזיתה לגוי ²מכל בשר מכל החי²·מזהב
ומפז רב הנחמדים³·שש אנכי על אמרתך בהקיץ תמונתך תמונה
לנגד עיני כימינ אשר נחו בהם היהודים⁴·בתגרומות עלי משכב
רוח יי דבר בי והנה עתי עת דודים⁵·אעירה⁶ שחר ואיקץ⁷
והנה חלום·וילך והלום⁸·קטורנתי מכל החסדים·כי זכור אני
ואתה רוכבים⁹ צמדים¹⁰·שנים¹¹ שלשה ימים והיו¹² בעיני
לאותות ולמועדים·ואולת¹³ כי נטשת¹⁴ עמך בית יעקב בלב אנוש
ועקוב יבש היה נקודים¹⁵·ובאו בביתך ¹⁶ונאספו שמה¹⁶ אנשים
רקינ ופוחזים ובאו ¹⁷ האובדים היהודים·האמללים רועי רוח

ורודפי קדים·ילדים אשר[18] בהם כל מום[19]·אוהבי לנום[20]·
ורבים מעמי הארץ מתיהדים[21]·גם מתמול גם משלשום העוה[22]
נלאו[23]·וקדש ישראל התרו[24]·וזבחו לשדים·ותשכח אל מחוללך
אדם היה כאחד ממנו ימים אחדים·חרף נפשו למות להעביר רעת
אביך הראשון חטא[25] ואנחנו ואדמתנו עבדים·ולו שם בשלשה[26]·
כתמר מקשה[27]·ולא[28] יתפרדו[29] ואעידה לו עדים·ולמען[30] ענותו
תקשיה לבך מיראתו[31] ועד השלשה לא בא[31] אם גנבים באו לך
אם שודדים·משה אמרם מפי הגבורה[32]·הגדול הגבור והנורא·מפר
אותות בדים[33]·תשכח עניו ולחצר לעת מצוא[34]עזר כנגדו[34]
וכזכי איש גדודים[35]·מהגדות והיידות בדויות[36] אשר גבלו
הראשונים[37] והיו לכם לצדיום[38]·תבחר מחנק נפשך ורוח נדיבה
יי נתן לה[39] לשרן למודינו·להאכילה תרדין[40][41] ולחם
נקודים[41]·גבר חכם הגם להבוש את המלכה[42] הענוגה והרכה
לחמשה לחזקה[43] ולשאת[44] מעליה הנטיפות והשירות והרדידים·
והלבש אותה[45] מחלצות וגנזי ברומים[46] ובגדי חפש לרכבה
בצבים ובפרדים·הן אמת[47] לולי פחד יצחק היה לי הלא הוא
אביך קנך אשר היה בנוקדים[48]·כי עתה גם אותכה[49] הרגתי[50]
ואותה החייתי[51] לתת לה מהלכים בין העומדים[52]·המה הגבורים
שעלו[53] מן הרחצה ממעיני הישועה על אדני פז מיוסדים·כלם
אנשים בחצריהם ובטירותם שנהבים וקופים [עמ' 13ב]
ותוכיים[54] וגמדים[55]·והסירו את שמלת שבים מעליהם הבגדים
הצואים וכבגד עדים·ולבשו בגדי ישע כתונת ומעיל[56]
עקודים נקודים וברודים[57]·וגם הנגשים אל יי שרי קדש ושרי
האלפים[58] לחם אלהיהם הם מקריבים ויין משתיהם בגביעים
משוקדים[59]·וכי תאמר בלבבך לא אירא מרבבות עם יצאוני
ואינם עברו תורות חלפו חק כעננים ולודים[60]·ובתוך עם טמא
שפתים אנכי יושב[61] וכשוכב[62] בראש חבל[63] ועמק השדים[64]·
ואמלטה רק אני לבדי ונהפך לשדי כעצמות וגידים[65]·אוחילה
לאלהי ישעי עדי ואדודי ואראלי[66] כראובן ושמעון יהיו לי
להיות בית יי פקידים[67]·[68]סרח וזרנפר ושועל[68] יעלו אל על

על יי[69] הנועדים·בנים אשר[70] יולדו מאחריהם[71] מניהו
מלכי מניהו אפרכי[72] להיות היהודים עתידים[73]·אמרי[74] נראש
המה[75] כבדו מזוקן לדור ודור אמונתך רבים חללים הפילה
בשחיתותיהם[76] רבים נלכדים·ויכלו באפס תקוה ובכלי גולה
שבעו נדודים·דברי ריבות וענף עץ עבות להורֹת ריב ולהשמיע
לאזנינו[77] קול פחדים את הקולות ואת הלפידים[78]·התחזיינה
העצמות[79] היבשות ברזל עשות[80] כארז בלבנון ישגא[81] ויצץ
ציץ ויגמול שקדים·הירֹרצון בסלע[82] פסח וחולה וכצבאים[83] על
הֹרים למֹדֹר עוליהֹ ויורדים·וסורה שבה פה דמה לך דודי
המשלשים קדושה[84] תורה צוה לנו משה מורשה מרציא אסירים
בכושרות מושיב ביתה יחידים[85]·ונפשך יבשה בעבודה[86] קשה
רוֹזֹץ וטהֹר בל יעֹשֹקֹרֹך זדים[87]·כֹמֹשֹפֹט לאוֹהֹבי שֹמֹך רבים
ונכבדים·ואחרי הודיעי אותך את כל זֹאת מי יתן והיית מן
השוגגים ולא מן המזידים[88]·כי רע עֹלי המעשה כל עֹדֹת[89]
ישראל[90] ישגר ואין צדיק בארץ ירֹציא מֹצֹרֹה נֹפֹשֹר ובנה עליה
מֹצֹרֹדים·ואתה באלהיך תֹשֹוֹב[91] אל אלהים[91] יי[92] שלשה המה[93]
נפלאֹו ממני[94] והיו לאחֹדים[95]·כֹנֹפֹש נֹאמנֹך לֹפֹנֹים בישראל לא
ידע אל[96] פֹרֹנֹסֹיֹשֹקֹ די שֹיֹנֹט יֹורדי[96].

הערות

1-1. ל   כתב שֹשֹלֹח החכם מאישֹטֹרֹי אֹשֹטֹרֹוק רמוך לפנים בישראל
לנכבד אנשלתיל בונפרש כֹמתחל על התֹחֹזֹק במעֹוֹזֹו ולא עבר
בין הגזרים   מ   כתב שֹשֹלֹח מאישֹטֹרֹי אֹשֹטֹרֹוק רֹימוך לפנים
בישראל שֹמֹו לנכבד אנשֹלֹתיאל בֹונֹפֹוֹס המתחל על התחזקו
במעוזו ולא עבר בין הגזרים ועם היות כי לא היה ראוי
להעלות על ספֹר דברי זֹה המשֹומד כי כלם דברי מינות הם
האמנם כדי שֹמֹתֹוֹכֹם נֹוֹכֹל לֹעמֹוד על יופֹי ומֹתֹיֹקֹות התֹשֹוֹבֹה
שֹהֹשֹיֹב החכם החסיד הנזכר בקֹנֹאֹו לאלהֹיֹו שֹֹפֹר קדמי
להעתיקו כי החכם הנזכר אנֹשֹלֹתיאל הֹשֹיֹבֹו בֹדֹבֹרֹים אך לא
על פי מֹדֹוֹתֹיו אֹוֹלֹי מֹפֹֹחֹדֹו אֹלֹיֹו או לֹאֹֹיֹזֹו סבֹה וֹזֹה נֹוֹסֹח
כֹתֹב הֹמֹיֹן.

2-2. למ מכל החי מכל בשר.

3. א ח׳.

4. אסתר ט:22.

5. יחזקאל טז:8.

6. א ח׳.

7. ל ואקיץ.

8. ל הלום; שמואל א ד:16.

9. א עומדים.

10. מ במדים; מלכים ב ט:25.

11. ל או שלשה מ ושלשה.

12. מ ויהיו.

13. ל ואולי.

14. ל + את.

15. יהושע ט:5.

16-16. ל ח׳.

17. ל ויבואו.

18. מ + אין.

19. דניאל א:4.

20. ישעיה בו:10.

21. אסתר ח:14.

22. גייגר גורס: העוו.

23. ירמיה ט:4.

24. תהלים עה:41.

25. ישעיה מז:27.

26. ל שלשה; שמואל ב כג:18.

27. ירמיה י:5.

28. מ לא.

29. איוב מא:9.

30. ל למען.

31-31. ל ח׳; דברי הימים א יא:21.

32. מגילה לא ע'ב.

33. ישעיה מד:25.

34-34. מ ח'.

35. הושע ו:9.

36. מ בדיות.

37. דברים יד:14.

38. שופטים ב:3.

39. ל ח'.

40. מ תרדים.

41-41. מ ח'; שופטים ט:12.

42. אסתר ז:8.

43. מ ולחזקה.

44. מ (שוליים) להסיר.

45. מ אותך.

46. יחזקאל כז:24.

47. מ אמרת.

48. עמוס א:1.

49. מ אותך.

50. מ הרגת.

51. מ החיית.

52. זכריה ג:4.

53. ל העולים.

54. מלכים א י:22.

55. מ ובגדים.

56. ל מעיל מ המעיל.

57. בראשית לא:10.

58. ל אלהים.

59. שמות כה:33.

60. בראשית י:13.

61. ישעיה ו:5.

62. אם ומשוכך.

63. משלי כג:34.

64. בראשית יד:3.

65. איוב י:11.

66. בראשית מו:16.

67. ירמיה כט:26.

68-68. א חוח ושרנפר ושועל ל חוח והשנפר ושועל מ
סוח וחרנפר; דברי הימים א ז:36. השורה דברי בונפיד,
קבץ על יד, סדרה חדשה ד (תש"ו), עמ' כ, שורה 112.

69-69. ל ח'.

70. ל + לא.

71. ל ח'.

72. שבועות ו ע'ב.

73. אסתר ח:13.

74. ל אמרו.

75. איוב ו:26.

76. ל בשחיתותיה מ בשחיתותם.

77. למ באזננו.

78. שמות כ:18.

79. יחזקאל לד:3.

80. יחזקאל כד:19.

81. תהלים צב:13.

82. עמוס ו:12.

83. ל כצבאים.

84. ל ח'.

85. תהלים סה:7.

86. מ מעבודה.

87. תהלים קיט:122.

88. ביצה ל ע'א.

89. ל דעת.

90. ל ח'; ויקרא ד:13.

91-91. ל לאלהים.

92. ל ח' + אלה.

93. ל ח'.

94. משלי ל:18.

95. יחזקאל לד:14.

96-96. ל פרנסישקו ד' ס' גורני מ פרנציסקו דסי' יורדינו.

אגרת ר' שלמה בונפיד

[עמ' 12א] [1] והנשיא אנשלתיאל השיבו בדברים רכים נדברים לא מובנים ולא עצבו ואני קנאתי לשם מגן לזוסים בו והשיבותיו על פי חרזיו ונתיבו ונדרשתי ללא שאלני להשיבו:[1]

ראיתי מגלת ספר·אמרי שפר·ועניניה משל אפר· יורצע לרבים ונכבדים[2]·משלי[3] העם[4] הרודים·כנפיה כנפי יונה ורגליתה כעורב[5]·שלום בפיה ובקרבה דוב אורב·חשדת[6] בלבך[7] למשוך בלוית חן דבריה·לב[8] האוהבים והידידים·ותוסף תת בלב יודעיך[9] אנחה[10] גם היא נאנחה תשיב אמריה·אל תראוני שאני שהרחורת[11]·אל תפצר אל דברי[12] פורשי מכמורת·נפשות מצודדים· דמיתי[13] לבתולה[14] לא תאר לה ולמען נחש ילבישוה אדרת תפארת ועל ידיה צמידין·וכל עוד תעדה[15] נזמה וחליתה דמעתה על להיה ועדי עדיה[16] על שדים סופדים[17]·ואני ברב חסדך והדר[18] כבוד הודך[18] מעשי[19] ידים מגידים·דברתי על לב מגלתך ביחומים·גליתי אזניה על רעיוניך[20] הנאהבים הנעימים[22]·ואנה פניך מועדים·כי כונתך[23] אמנם להעיר[24] בצחות עניניך[25] ולשמח[26] בכנף רגניך אנחנו המשוררים בניך לך[27] נולדים·ומדאגה מדבר כי לא השיב[28] [29] שולחך דבר[29] כפי חכמתו[30] הרחבה ושלח אגרת מאהבה מסותרת והשנית[31] כי פיך

המדבר הלא גם בנו דבר[32]•רחש לבי לעגות חלקי[33] בוטח
באהבתך תרציאני ממסגר•האשמה והתלונה[34] כצאת העבדים[35]
והדודים[36]•נדרשתי ללא שאלני[37] [38] ערכתי שלחן שאלותי
נגדך[39]•לאכול מפרי פיך[40] המדבר הגדול והנורא•ולי אני[41]
עבדך לא קרא[38]•באתי[42] אחריך מלקט פליטי חרזיך קורא
לשרידים[43]•[44]כי ידעתיך אמיץ כח לפקוח עינים עורות עיני[45]
הכמים טוב וישר ועשית הישר קו מעוקב והזוגות נפרדים•איש
נבון וחכם[44] פליאה דעת ממני גם בעיניך יפלא כי[46] שופט כל
הארץ יעשה משפט[47] מעצמו[48] וכפר אדמתו עמו וחטא אחד
יגרום חטאו[49] שבת אחים גם יחד אלהים ואנשים[50] בצמדים•תחת
היות עונותיר בינר לבין אלהיו מבדילים ומפרידים•אי[51]
שמים [עמ' 12ב] תחת עבד כי נתחייב[52] ראשו למלך יבא המלך
לשתות כוס חמתו ואידו•לכפר בעד עבדו•ואשר[53] בידו•ועמו
הסליחה להקדים•ואם חטא כתולע יאדים•הן האדם אכל מתנובות
שדי•ופריו מתוק לחכו חמר[54] שדי[55]•המבלעדי יי אין איש
בארץ[56] יהיה כדאי[56]•לסמוך עליו עונר ועונשו•ונתנו[57] איש
כופר נפשו•בחיר כל הצדיקים והחסידים[58]•אלהינו[59] כי ירבה
לסלוח•בארץ יגוע וילך שחוח[60]•לאסורים[61] פקח קוה•ובזולת
זה בידו כח•[62]בעד לכפר[62] [63]הפושעים והמורדים[63]•[64]דומה
דודי זה הסוד הנבדל•לבונה עיר[65] ומגדל[66]•וממחט ברזל דק
ודל יעשה[67] את העמודים[67]•הן קצרה יד כל נביא[68]כל חוזה[68]
לכתוב באר היטב כי יעשה לנו אלהים[69] את כל הכבוד הזה
וידי משה כבדים[70]•והפלא מעושה[71] פלא•להוציא מבית כלא•
אשדודים[72] ולודים[73] וחיל הכשדים[74]•יקחהו[75] אפל•ויאמר[76]
לשבן בערפל•הלל בן שחר[77]•החלק[78] הנבחר•שבו נאמר כי לי
בני ישראל עבדים•מי שלח ידו במשיח יי ונקה•ואיך לא גזרה
הכמתו העמוקה•דרך אחר[79] ולא תהיה זאת[80] לפוקה•ליעקב חבל
נחלתו•אחת[81] דתו להמית[82] צור ישועתו•מה יפה מאד גאלתו[83]•
לגאול חטאת עם[84] רב ועצום ממנו[84] חטאת ומרי עם מרדים•ומה
בצע[85] בדמו•ומה פשע בעמו•[86]לא עלינו תלונותיכם כי על

יי.[86] אם לפי דבריך.אביך קנך[87].עוטה אור[88] כשלמה.בא אחיך
במרמה[89].ויכסוהו בבגדים[90].יי הוא[91] בורא[92].ומהר לגבעה
אורח.כצפרים עפות[93] נודדים.מושיע ורב והתלמידים[94].ויתנכר
עליהם והם לא הכירוהו.ממרורות השביעוהו[95].כי לא ידעו
מה הוא[96].ויאריכו הבדים.והנה בהגלות[97] בסיני אל חי
עושה גדולות ארץ רעשה אף שחקים.מבהיקים ברקים במרקים.
ולפידים מעידים.לקול תתו הרכסים נסים והבקעים נעים
ונדים.ועתה בעלטה כארח נטה ללון.הקולות יחדלון.והלפידים
בתוך הכדים.

האמנם ישב אלהים על הארץ והרבה עמו פדות לחטא[98]
האדם ומשובתו.וזה כל פרי הסיר[99] חטאתו.מדוע לא בזה שקטה
כל הארץ הזעומה.ויחל נח איש האדמה[100].מעצבו ורוגזו[100]
ועודנו[101] האדמה עובדים.[102] וגם הנה הרה תחיל תזעק בחבליה
ומדוע אם נפשנו יצא מן הטאים הבשר עודנו בין שניהם[102]
עוד היום כלנו מתים היים ונפסדים.

לא[103] כאלה חלק יעקב[103] אבל אשמים אנחנו מודים[104].
כי[105] חטא אבינו הראשון מלוך ימלוך בנו ועדיין לא סר.כי
אחינו בשרנו הוא אך בשר.בנפשו דמו ואנחנו בנפשנו נקיים
ובצרור החיים[106] צרורים ונפקדים[107].כי לא יצדק אזי עבר
על נפשנו[108] מרי[109].האדם ועבשר.ונפשנו [14א] קשורה בנפשו.
כי אין יחס[110] והקשר[111] בין הנפשינו[112] ולא[113] קרב זה אל
זה[113] איש איש במספר[114] דמו בראשו כל העובר על הפקודים.

לא[115] דרככם[116] דרכינו[115] אבל אנחנו מעלים בקודש
ולא מורידים[117].לא איש אל בעדת אל קהל ישראל המיחדים
אלהים[118].ואדם מי מלל לאברהם היו[119] יהיה לגוי אשר[120]
לו[121] אלהים קרובים על דלתותיו שוקדים.הידוע נדע בארץ
דרכו[122] רצעדו.והנה לדעת איה[123] מקום כבודו[123].מבוהלים
ודחופים שרפים עומדים.האיש אשר המלך חפץ ביקרו[124] ואשר[125]
לדברו[125] חרדים.יביאו לבוש מלכות לייי אלהינו הגדולה
והרוממות לא ידעו איש לבוש הבדים[126].

סוף דבר¹²⁷ כל עוד נשמתי¹²⁸ בתורתי¹²⁹ תהגה באהבתה
תמיד¹³⁰ תשגה¹³¹ ¹³²כי ראיתי את הלהֹץ אשֵ¹³³ לוחצים
אותם¹³⁴ באמונתב·והקל מעליהם עול המצות בגֵרֵיתם¹³⁵ אמנם
אלה החקים ותורותב·הֵמה בצדקתב מעידים·ריהי להיפך¹³² כי
הרחיב השֵ לנו את הנפש הזאת באמונה¹³⁶·והיה שכל אזור
מתניה וטוב אמנה¹³⁷·וישימנה בחֵמֵר¹³⁸ בכל¹³⁹ עבודה בשדה
נעבדים·וזאת תורת האדם¹⁴⁰.

אולם¹⁴¹ התערב נא¹⁴² וכל¹⁴³ סורֵרֵי¹⁴⁴ אמרֵנתך
בשתים¹⁴⁵ אכסה¹⁴⁶·והסר מעלי רק את המות הזה·ואשֵר נלאיתי
הנבֵהֵם על הלחם אשֵר עם המאמרות החֵן¹⁴⁷·אל ישיב הכהֵן·
ונכֵה¹⁴⁸ רוח ישפיל גבוהים אלהים עולים ויֵרֵדֵין¹⁴⁹·יהֵ¹⁵⁰
לך אשר לך היטבה לראות לבלתי הוחיל עוד ליי ולמֵשיֵחֵו·הנה
הוא עומד אחר כתלך תחנה נכהו·ירֵושֵלֵים הבנויה אחר הדלת
והמזרזה שֵשֵה¹⁵¹ צעדים¹⁵²·בקֵרֵב קרֵבֵיֵך קרֵוב יֵי¹⁵³ ומה
ירֵשֵיעֵך מושיע מרחוק כי חֵק ליֵשֵרֵאל הוֵא¹⁵⁴ העֵנֵיים והֵמֵרֵודֵים·
ראתה באלהיך תגיל ותֵשֵבע בֵשֵמֵו בֵרֵאֵשֵו¹⁵⁵ ודֵמֵו¹⁵⁶·וֵכֵי תֵדֵרֵש
דבֵר מֵעֵמֵו·תֵזֵכֵור¹⁵⁷ נֵא לֵעֵת צֵרֵה¹⁵⁸ אֵמֵר¹⁵⁹,¹⁶⁰·וֵכֵל קֵדֵשֵים
עֵמֵר¹⁶⁰·כֵי אֵז תֵצֵלֵיֵח אֵת דֵרֵכֵיֵך וֵאֵז תֵשֵכֵיֵל כֵכֵל¹⁶¹ עֵמֵר·עֵם
בֵרֵשֵע·לֵא יֵחֵשֵב לֵהֵם עֵרֵן פֵשֵע·יֵעֵן הֵם מֵתֵורֵדֵים·אֵל תֵתֵן אֵל¹⁶²
לֵבֵך אֵם יֵש לֵהֵם פֵרֵטֵים וֵיֵחֵידֵים·לֵא יֵרֵעֵר וֵלֵא יֵשֵחֵיֵתֵו כֵי אֵם
גֵנֵוב וֵנֵאֵוף וֵרֵצֵוֵח¹⁶³·הֵבֵא הֵאֵנֵשֵים הֵבֵיֵתֵה וֵטֵבֵוֵח¹⁶⁴·כֵפֵרֵים
וֵעֵתֵודֵים·אֵתֵה וֵרֵעֵיֵך הֵיֵרֵצֵאֵים מֵתֵוֵך הֵהֵפֵכֵה וֵבֵרֵוֵח פֵיֵ¹⁶⁵ הֵזֵמֵן
לֵב חֵדֵש חֵדֵש·וֵיֵאֵמֵר שֵלֵשֵר וֵיֵשֵלֵשֵר¹⁶⁶·בֵטֵרֵם תֵחֵיֵל אֵרֵץ¹⁶⁷ יֵלֵדֵו
וֵבֵקֵשֵו מֵנֵוֵח·וֵיֵלֵכֵו בֵלֵא כֵח·¹⁶⁸אֵשֵר כֵה¹⁶⁸ בֵהֵם לֵעֵמֵוֵד עֵל
הֵדֵבֵר¹⁶⁹ מֵעֵיֵדֵים¹⁷⁰·רֵב לֵכֵם יֵרֵשֵבֵי חֵשֵך אֵוֵר נֵגֵה עֵלֵיֵהֵם¹⁷¹ כֵי
תֵשֵמֵאֵיֵלֵו וֵכֵי תֵיֵמֵיֵנֵו¹⁷²·יֵעֵן¹⁷³ הֵאֵמֵיֵנֵו¹⁷⁴·מֵלֵכֵי אֵרֵץ אֵתֵם¹⁷⁵
וֵשֵכֵבֵתֵו וֵאֵיֵן¹⁷⁶ מֵחֵרֵיֵדֵים·אֵמֵוֵנֵתֵכֵם הֵיֵא חֵכֵמֵתֵכֵם וֵבֵיֵנֵתֵכֵם
תֵרֵשֵיֵבֵכֵם בֵיֵן נֵגֵיֵדֵים·חֵדֵשֵים מֵקֵרֵוֵב¹⁷⁷ בֵאֵו¹⁷⁸ יֵקֵרֵיֵבֵו¹⁷⁹
פֵסֵוֵקֵים¹⁸⁰ רֵהֵוֵקֵיֵטֵ¹⁸¹ [14ב] עֵל שֵלֵשֵה וֵאֵלֵו תֵהֵיֵה עֵמֵכֵם רֵוֵח
אֵהֵרֵת חֵדֵשֵה יֵמֵצֵאֵו¹⁸² עֵל שֵלֵשֵים וֵעֵל רֵבֵעֵים¹⁸³ פֵסֵוֵקֵים¹⁸⁴

מוסדים[185]·ומה לעשות באיש החפץ בסבכי נבכי[186] ים

הנבואות[187] להתרפק·והנה להסיר מלבנו[188] כל ספק·בפסוק

אחד[190] נכתב ונזהם אחד חם וימצאו שלשתם בדברים אחדים[191].

ואולם הפעם אודך על אחת היא אבחת חרב[192] היא הנצבת

כשלהבת בקרב מעי יקודים[192]·על גלותנו לארכה ולרחבה·אין

תשובה·ועל נדחינו לבלתי השיב·אין לנו פה להשיב·[193]אנחנו

שני[193] זנבות האודים[194]·[195]העשנים בתמרות להב תורתנו[195]

[196] וכל יום ילדי יום על ברכינו ילודים[197].[196]בעין כל

גוי[198] נפליגו ודמינו אחד מעיר עשרת מעיר ברוגדים·זה השער·

בשלמי הצער[199].[200]איש אחד לא ימצאהו חלום אחד הוא הלא

לאלהים פתרונים[200]·והנגלות לנו ולבנינו כי [201]אין

יסורים בלא זדונים·ואנחנו יודעים כי[201] [202]אבותינו היו

כאלף שנים·רעים וחטאים[202] ומורדים[203]·ואין חמס[204].[205]אם

הייינו למס·וכליינו[205] שניינו בלא[206] טובה·פי שנים[207] כשני

חטאת[207] כתובה·ואלף[208] יניסו רבבה·אבל בחמלת השם כי רבה·

עוד[209] מעט ירחף על בנים מקנם [210]נודדים·ועתה אתה[210]

כמלאך אלהים[211]·יגער יי בך השטן[212] והסיר ממך כל [213]פגע

וכל[213] מעיק באמונתך[214] אשר בחרת[215] ואם ידעת ויש בה[215]

דברים[216] מתנגדים[217]·לו תבקש כעקש טעם ודעת אשר לא כדת

אפילו[218] יאמרו לך על שמאל שהוא[219] ימין[220]·גם מתמול[221]

גם משלשום[222] הנה ימים באים האמין[223].·כי[224] ישדים

חוקי[225] האמונה[226] והפקודים[227]·תיקר נא נפשי בעיניך[228]

והלה[229] פני אל·וריהננה[230] דעה והשכל לכלכל תעלומות

חכמות[231] האל[232].·או[233] יתן[234] לפינו מחסום·ועיני שכלנו

ואזני בחיננתנו יעצורם·מראות[235] והיות[236] באלהים[237] יודעי

טוב ורע[235] ובבלי[238] השכל וידוע ושמוע בלמודים[239]·ואל

יהשוב לבך[240] לב חדש כי דעתי לחדש[241] נעורים·לטענות אלה

נגדם כי ידעתי[242] דברי אלה[242] לנבונים[243] ישנים חדשים[243]

לבקריט·רבה אמונתך בספקות[244] ולו תחפוץ תוסיף[244] משכלך

[245]כהם וכהם[245] ותדבר נגידים·

נאם המדבר מעלה מעלות תהלות‎246 ‎247חכמתך על צוארו

רבידים·לעבוד עבודתך עם רב חולשתו נאזר בגבורה יחד עשיר

ואביון‎247 ויצוריו כלם‎248 מול הרי מעלתך‎248 סרגדים·תבחנם

ותנסט‎249 בפקדת פקודיך ויפקד המלך פקידים·יעלה ויבא

‎250זכרון יתרון‎250 חכמתך רגע באפו כפרים עם נרדים·[15א]

אך יצא ברוח מן המליצה אשר רבדת‎251 ערשה ששנים

‎252בין הזוהים‎253 ומרבדים‎252·זה שמר‎254 לעולם ישב·ש"ב‎255.

הערות

1-1. ר ח' ל והנשא אנשאלתיאל השיבו בדברים ולא עצבו
רגם הוא לא ישרו בעיניו ולא לבו והנשא אנשלמה
בונפיד קנא לאלהיו מגן לחוסים בו והשיבו על דרך
חרזיו ונתיבו וזה תורף דבריו.

2. ל העושים.

3. ר ומושלי ל במלוכת.

4. ל ח'.

5. דניאל י‎6:.

6. ום אמרת ל דמית.

7. ל ח' מ בלבבך.

8. ל ח'.

9. ל יודעיה.

10. ל הנחה.

11. שיר השירים א‎6:.

12. ום + אלה לובשי חן ל + לובשי חן.

13. ל ח' מ דמיתיה.

14. ל אנכי כבתולה.

15. ל + עדיה.

16. ולם עדים.

17. ישעיה לב:12.

18-18. ל כבודך.

19. רל מעשה.

20. ל רעיונך.

21. ל ח׳.

22. ר והנעימים.

23. רם עמקי מחשבותיך.

24. רם להכיר.

25. ר ענייניה.

26. ל ולשמוח.

27. ארם לך.

28. ל אשיב.

29-29. מ למגלתך החכם אנשלתיאל.

30. ל חכמתך.

31. מ והדאגה השבית.

32. מ + על כן.

33. ל + לאלהי צדקי.

34. ל ח׳.

35. ל + וכאשר ידעתיך אמיץ לפקוח עינים עורות ולעור דברי חכמים טוב וישר ועשית הישר קו מעוקב והזוגות נפרדים ערכתי שולחן שאלותי נגדך.

36. ל ח׳.

37. ר שאלוני.

38-38. ל ח׳.

39. רם לפניך.

40. רם חכך.

41. מ ח׳.

42. ל ואני אבא.

43. יואל ג:5.

44-44. ל ח׳.

45. ל   דברי.

46. ל   ח'.

47. ל + מות.

48. מ   בעצמו   רמ + ושפך את דמו.

49. ל   חטא.

50. מ   ואדם.

51. ל + שומו.

52. ולמ   יתחייב.

53. ולמ   אשר.

54. ר   היימר.

55. ר   ות א:20.

56-56. רמ   ח'.

57. מ   ונותנו.

58. ל + למה תאמר יעקב.

59. ל   אלהים.

60. ר   בראשיון א:17.

61. ר   לאסירים.

62-62. רמ   לכפר בעד ל   בעד ח'.

63-63. מ   הפשעים והמרדים.

64-64. ל   ח'.

65. מ + מלה מטושטשת.

66. מ   מגדל.

67. רמ   עשה.

68-68. ולמ   וזוזה.

69. ל   ח'.

70. שמות יז:2; ל + דומה דודי זה סוד הנבדל לבונה עיר
ומגדל וממחט ברזל דק עשו לך העמודים.

71. ולמ   מהאל עושה.

72. נחמיה ד:1.

73. בראשית ו:13.

74. ירמיה לד:21.

75. ר ויקחהו.

76. ומ ואמר.

77. א ח'.

78. ר וחלק.

79. ומ אחרת.

80. ל זו.

81. ר ואחרת.

82. ל להמיר.

83. ר המלה מטורשטשת למ גדולתו.

84-84. אל ח' א + חטאת ל + רב.

85. ר ח'.

86-86. ל ח'.

87. ומ + הישבי בשמים.

88. ל אורה.

89. בראשית כד:35.

90. מלכים א א:10.

91. ל + והוא.

92. ר הבורח.

93. ל עופות.

94. ל ותלמידים.

95. איוב ט:18.

96-96. ל מהו.

97. ר בהגלותו.

98. ל לחטה.

99. ומ הסר ל ח'.

100-100. ל ח'.

101. מ ועוד אנחנו.

102-102. ול ח'.

103-103. ל דרככם דרכנו.

104. מ   ומודים.
105. ל + עונש.
106. א   חיים.
107. ל   נפקדים.
108. א   נפשי.
109. ל   מה.
110. ול   ח׳.
111. ולמ   הקשר.
112. מ   הנפשות.
113-113. מ   קרבה זו אל זו.
114. ל   כמספר.
115-115. ל   כאלה חלק יעקב.
116. ומ   דרכיכמ.
117. ר   מורידין.
118. ל   אלהיו.
119. ול   היו.
120. ר + הביא אלוה בידו   מ + הביא ה׳ בידו.
121. ר   ולא.
122. ל   דרך ה׳.
123-123. ל   מקומו וכבודו.
124. אסתר ו:6.
125. מ   ח׳.
126. דניאל יב:6.
127. ל + כי.
128. ל + בי.
129. ל   בתורתו.
130. מ   ח׳.
131. משלי ה:19.
132-132. ול   ח׳.
133. ומ   ח׳.

134.   ‎רם   נפשותם; שמות ג:9.

135.   נחום ג:3.

136.   ‎ר   באמוניה.

137.   ‎ל   באמונה.

138.   ‎מ   כחמר.

139.   ‎ל   כל.

140.   ‎ל   + גם ראיתי את הלחץ אשר מצרים לוחצים אותם
באמונתם והקל עליהם עול המצות בגויתם אמרתי אלה הזקים
ותורותם המה בצדקתם מעידים תיקר נא נפשי בעיניך.

141.   ‎ולמ ח'   רם   + ואתה האיש המתערב בגוים והבא בסודם.

142.   ‎ל   ח'.

143.   ‎מ   עם.

144.   ‎ר   סותרים.

145.   ‎מ   ובשתים.

146.   ישעיה ר:2.

147.   ‎רם   הזה.

148.   ‎ר   ודכה ושפל   ל   ושפל   מ   ודכא ושפל.

149.   ‎ל   + אחי.

150.   ‎ל   יהיה.

151.   ‎ל   שש.

152.   שמואל ב ו:13.

153.   ‎ל   + ולנשברי לב.

154.   ‎ל   ח'.

155.   ‎למ   ובראשר.

156.   ‎מ   ובדמו.

157.   ‎ל   תדרוש.

158.   ‎ר   צרת.

159.   ‎מ   "אמר" מחוקה   + עצמו (בין השיטין).

160-160.   ‎אל ח'   ל   + וכל קדושיו עמו סעד לתומר.

161.   ‎ל   בכל.

162. ומ ח'.

163-163. ר גנוב ורצוחו ל נאוף ורצוח וגנוב.

164. ר וטבח ל + טבח.

165. ל כי.

166. מלכים א יח:34.

167. ל הארץ.

168-168. ל חז' מ בהם כח.

169. ל דבר החוקים.

170. אם מעידיט; עזרא י:9.

171. ומ עליכם.

172. מ תיימאנו.

173. ל ח'.

174. מ תאמינו.

175. מ אתכם.

176. מ בלתי.

177. ל חז'.

178. ולמ ח'.

179. ל תקריבו.

180. ל + רק.

181. תהלים בו:1.

182. ל תמצאו.

183. מ + ועל המושים.

184. ל דברים.

185. ל מיוסדים מ מיועדים.

186. ל ח'.

187. ל הנבוכות.

188. ל ממנו.

189. מ + שמע ישראל.

190. מ ח'.

191. מ + יי אלהינו יי אחד.

192-192. א בתוך מעי היא הנצבת כשלהבת בקרב מעי ויקודים

ל בקרב מעי הלא היא ברכת [?] הספקות הדולקות בין

צלעי כאש היקודים   מ הנצבת כשלהבת בקרב מעי כאש

יקודים.

193-193. מ מפני.

194. ישעיה ז:14.

195-195. ול ח' מ העשנים כתמרות עשן.

196-196. ול ח'.

197. בראשית ב:23.

198. ר גוים מ + ואמה.

199. יונה א:12.

200-200. ל ח' + הנח לה' הנה [?] הטוב בעיניו יעשה אין

לחרחר אחר דבר קדשו ועל גמולו ועשו רב בין רב למעט.

201-201. ל ח'.

202-202. ל + אבותינו חטאו וחיו חטאים כאלף שנה.

203. א מורדים.

204. ומ + ואין עול.

205-205. ל כי כלינו.

206. ומ בלי.

207-207. מ כחטאת.

208. ר אלף.

209. ל ועוד.

210-210. ל בדודים ואתה אדוני מ אתה ח'.

211. ל ח' מ + אתה.

212. זכריה ג:2.

213-213. ל ח'.

214. מ + החדשה.

215-215. ל ח'.

216. ל ובדברים ומ + אל המופת.

217. ל המתנגדים.

218. ר   אבל אם   מ + אם.

219. ול   ח׳.

220. מ + ועל ימין שהוא שמאל; ספרי דברים קנד.

221. מ   משלשום.

222. מ   מתמול.

223. ל   והזמן + אשרי הגבר שתום העין [במדבר כד:4] על הלחם לבדו יחיה האדם וטובים דודיך מיין ומה לך לספר חקים צדיקים מחוקקים מצוקים ופקודים עין אבות על בנים פוקדים אחת שאלתי מאת כבודך   מ   תאמין.

224. ל   כי.

225. ום   החוקים.

226. ום   ח׳.

227. מ + ועתה.

228. ל   ח׳.

229. ל   חלה בא.

230. למ   ויחננו.

231. ול   החכמות.

232. מ + והיות כאלהים יודעי טוב ורע.

233. ום   אז.

234. ל   לתת.

235-235. מ   ח׳.

236. ר   וביותר.

237. ל   האלהים.

238. ל   ובלי.

239. ישעיה ב:4.

240. ל + הגבוה [?].

241. מ + דברי (בשוליים).

242-242. ל   אלה דברי.

243-243. ום   חדשים ישנים.

244-244. מ   והלואי ותחפוץ להוסיף.

245-245. ל כהמה וכהמה.

246 . ל תהלתך.

247-247 . ל ח'.

248-248 . ר מפליאה.

249 . ל תנחם.

250-250 . ל יודון זכרון.

251 . ר דברתי ל עדשת מ רבדתי.

252-252 . ל ומגדים.

253 . מ הרחים.

254 . ל שמי.

255 . ר ר' שלמה בונפידו ל שלמה בונפיד מ וכו'.

Index

Contributors

Alexander Altmann
  Professor of Jewish Philosophy Emeritus, Brandeis University;
  Honorary Research Associate in Jewish Studies, Harvard University

Herbert Davidson
  Professor of Hebrew, University of California, Los Angeles

Carmi Y. Horowitz
  Lecturer in Jewish Thought, Ben-Gurion University of the Negev

Jacob Katz
  Professor of Jewish Social History Emeritus, Hebrew University

James L. Kugel
  Assistant Professor of Religious Studies, Yale University

Shlomo Pines
  Professor of Jewish and General Philosophy Emeritus, Hebrew University

Joshua Prawer
  Professor of Medieval History, Hebrew University

Benjamin Ravid
  Associate Professor of Jewish History, Brandeis University

Bezalel Safran
  Instructor in Hebrew, Harvard University

Marc Saperstein
  Lecturer in Hebrew Literature, Harvard University

Bernard Septimus
  Assistant Professor of Religion, Yale University

Joseph Shatzmiller
  Professor of Jewish History, University of Toronto

Michael A. Schmidman
  Assistant Professor of Judaic Studies, University of Cincinnati

Frank Talmage
  Professor of Near Eastern Studies, University of Toronto

Isadore Twersky
  Nathan Littauer Professor of Hebrew Literature and Philosophy;
  Director, Center for Jewish Studies, Harvard University